The Politics Presidents Make

THE
POLITICS
PRESIDENTS
MAKE

Leadership from John Adams
to Bill Clinton

◆

Stephen Skowronek

THE BELKNAP PRESS OF
HARVARD UNIVERSITY PRESS
Cambridge, Massachusetts
London, England

Second printing, 1998

Library of Congress Cataloging-in-Publication Data
Skowronek, Stephen.
The politics presidents make : leadership from John Adams to
Bill Clinton / Stephen Skowronek.
p. cm.
Originally published : Cambridge, Mass. : Belknap Press, 1993.
Includes bibliographical references and index.
ISBN 0-674-68937-2
1. Presidents—United States—History. 2. Political leadership—United States—History.
I. Title.
JK511.S55 1997
352.23'6'0973—dc21   97-7818

To Susan

Acknowledgments

A BOUT a decade ago, when the Reagan Revolution was afoot, I decided to undertake a general study of presidents as agents of political change. Faith in the transformative capacities of the presidency seemed to be giving rise to ever greater expectations and ever more profound frustrations, but so far as I could tell no one had attempted to analyze those capacities in a systematic way. Such an assessment must deal with a vast and varied record, and that, no doubt, is one reason why thoughts about this matter have tended to remain impressionistic. Yet, anyone inclined to look back through presidential history will discover that a substantial amount of guidance and insight is readily accessible. Each piece of the puzzle is illuminated by many fine biographies, period studies, and administration chronicles. I have made extensive use of these works, and while I have entered the debates that surround individual incumbents with my own more general purposes in view, the story that I tell is in large part a reflection on the great themes that I found running through this literature.

I set to work in earnest on this project as a fellow at the Woodrow Wilson International Center for Scholars, and I benefited enormously from the lively forum for interdisciplinary exchange created there by Michael Lacey, the Director of the Division of United States Studies. My opportunity for research in Washington was extended through the courtesy of Paul Peterson and the Brookings Institution.

Whatever merit there is to this book is a credit widely shared. Karen Orren and I began a discussion about American political development when we were colleagues together at UCLA, and the history of the presidents has figured prominently in our conversations ever since. From my first thoughts about this project through the final revision of the manuscript, Karen has sharpened my thinking with keen insights of her own and responded to my efforts with the disarming candor of a stalwart friend.

Acknowledgments

I was fortunate to join the Yale Political Science Department at a moment when its interest in historical work was blossoming. My colleagues have read and reread these chapters, offering patient support as well as careful criticism. Bruce Ackerman, David Cameron, Robert Dahl, James Fesler, Victoria Hattam, David Mayhew, David Plotke, Susan Rose-Ackerman, George Shulman, Ian Shapiro, Rogers Smith, Steven Smith, and Alex Wendt all offered valuable counsel.

Several leading scholars in presidential studies took the time to look at this manuscript in whole or in part and to give me the benefit of their seasoned perspectives and intimate knowledge of the field. Michael Nelson was an early promoter of the project and an astute critic of the results. I also received careful readings from George C. Edwards III, Sidney Milkis, Bruce Miroff, Richard Pious, Jeffrey Tulis, Aaron Wildavsky, and the late J. David Greenstone. Comments from two scholars outside the sphere of presidential studies—Ira Katznelson and Brian Balogh—were especially helpful in probing the broader issues raised by the concept and design of the study.

Aida Donald and Susan Wallace managed the publication of the book with alacrity and consummate professionalism. Mary Whitney provided able office support at Yale. I have had excellent research assistance all along; Mark Harmon, Corey Robin, Adam Sheingate, and Keith Whittington were especially helpful in the final phases. My wife, Susan Jacobs, has hastened this book to completion in every possible way, devoting long evenings to it after a full day at her own work and spending too many weekends alone with our children. For my boys, Michael and Sam, it's pay-back time.

Significant portions of previously published essays related to this project have been incorporated into these chapters. These include: "Notes on the Presidency in the Political Order," *Studies in American Political Development*, Vol. 1 (New Haven: Yale University Press, 1986), pp. 286–302; "Presidential Leadership in Political Time," in *The Presidency and the Political System*, ed. Michael Nelson (Washington, D.C.: Congressional Quarterly Press, 1988), pp. 115–159; "Franklin Roosevelt and the Modern Presidency," *Studies in American Political Development*, Vol. 6, no. 2 (New York: Cambridge University Press, 1992), pp. 322–358; and with Karen Orren, "Beyond the Iconography of Order: Notes for a New Institutionalism," *The Dynamics of American Politics: Approaches and Interpretations*, ed. Larry C. Dodd and Calvin Jillson (Boulder: Westview, 1993).

New Haven, April 1993

Contents

Preface, 1997

THE PUBLICATION of a new edition of *The Politics Presidents Make* affords me the opportunity to reflect on some of the issues that have been raised in response to the book and to update the text with some thoughts about the Clinton presidency. Like most authors, I read my own text with a keen sense of how I might have made it better. But as nothing in the course of American politics over the past four years causes me to want to modify the book's basic analytic claims or substantive arguments, I have resisted the temptation to alter the original presentation and, beyond a few minor corrections, have limited my additions to this Preface and the Afterword.

Attention has focused on the challenge the book presents to the notion that the modern presidents are a separate and coherent group of incumbents who have little in common with earlier presidents and on its claim that these pre-modern presidents still have much to tell us about how the office is working today. This is altogether appropriate. The book crosses the modern/pre-modern divide with an eye to recurrent patterns in the politics of leadership, patterns that stretch across the whole of presidential history and link the modern presidents back to counterparts acting in earlier periods at parallel moments in "political time."

I hasten to add, however, that my main objective in this book was neither to debunk the "modern presidency" thesis nor to replace it with a "cycle theory." It was, rather, to assess presidents as agents of political change. I was interested in the different premises which presidents bring to the challenge of orchestrating political change, in the capacity of the American presidency to deliver on these different premises, and in the systemic political effects of presidential efforts to do so. The recurrent patterns on which the analysis builds may be striking—they certainly stood out for me as I began thinking about presidential leadership—but I urge readers not to stop with what became a point of departure.

The "cycles" of presidential history are irregular. Jackson's reconstruction of American politics came 28 years after Jefferson's; Franklin Roosevelt's reconstruction came 72 years after Lincoln's. The length of time between political reconstructions did not concern me. What called for attention were the different types of leadership to be found within the periods bounded by these reconstructions. Each of these seemed to have distinctive political dynamics which played out in similar ways in very different historical settings. Specifying how leadership efforts within periods differ from one another, and figuring out why leadership efforts in different periods have similar political effects, would, I thought, go a long way toward accounting for the history observed, cyclic tendencies and irregularities alike.

The book rests on a set of claims about how the president's constitutional position organizes the problem of political action. Its central claim is that assuming the presidential office and exercising its powers has an inherently disruptive political effect, and that presidential leadership is a struggle to resolve that effect in the reproduction of a legitimate political order. The struggle is engaged by all incumbents, and the constitutional dynamic underlying it informs all the different pieces of my analysis. The tendency for politics to cycle over broad spans of time is, as I see it, but one of the likely consequences of this dynamic as it gets played out in different ways by successive incumbents coming to power in new situations. Another, more important, consequence is that leadership outcomes turn less directly on the powers or institutional resources of the presidency than on the incumbent's contingent political authority or warrants for changing things.

The theory of presidential action built on this central claim identifies the typical contextual configurations of the leadership problem. It relates each of these contexts to a characteristic premise or warrant for national leadership, and it links action on each of these premises to a characteristic political contest and systemic political effect. The theory explains why a handful of incumbents has been remarkably effective in orchestrating political change, and it sorts through the political consequences of the difficulties encountered by others. I believe that this is a theory of wide application, not one limited to the cases I chose to analyze in detail. I hope that the cases selected demonstrate the historical robustness of the basic political dynamics postulated and that they convey a clear sense of the potential range and practical limits of the presidency in transforming the American polity. Of course, I also recognize that a theory which encompasses the whole of presidential history is going to be exposed along a broad front, and I would count the effort a great success if it prompts the promulgation of alternatives of equal scope that explain more of the variance.

Another set of issues raised by this book has to do with the significance of secular change and the emergence of the modern presidency. Presidential leadership has never been an entirely closed system where nothing new of consequence ever happens and the patterns of the past simply repeat in lock step. Much of the analysis of *The Politics Presidents Make* is devoted to an examination of how recurrent patterns in the politics of leadership were reshaped at each of their historical iterations and to a consideration of the direction of these changes over time.

To this end, the book traces the intercurrence of the basic types of political leadership found throughout presidential history with the expansion and diversification of the institutional universe of presidential action. It shows how the proliferation of national institutional authorities and the growing independence of these authorities from one another has worked at once to make established governing arrangements more resilient and to loosen the constraints imposed on presidents by prior political affiliations. Gradually since the time of Jackson, and with increasing effect over the twentieth century, these developments have facilitated a fraying of the boundaries distinguishing the basic types of leadership. Thus, the presidency of Franklin Roosevelt, which in the standard literature marks a categorical shift to a new leadership position for presidents, appears in my analysis to mark a historical compounding of institutional resistance to presidentially led political reconstructions of American government. As the analysis extends further into the contemporary period, the significance of "the modern presidency" is revealed in a general moderation of the historic differences in the political capacities of successive incumbents.

I speculated in the last few pages of the book about what such a waning of political time might imply, but none of this is meant to suggest that patterns drawn from the more distant past no longer have anything to tell us about the politics of the present or near future. If presidential leadership, as I present it, has never been an entirely closed system, I think it has some way to go before we escape the old patterns altogether, and I harbor doubts as to whether complete escape is even a constitutional possibility. Perhaps this is where conclusions drawn from an analysis of intercurrent patterns in presidential history differ most starkly from conclusions drawn from the "modern presidency" thesis as it is found in the standard literature. I am as willing as anyone to recognize the political significance of the new institutional forms associated with "the modern presidency," but my approach to their development made me wary of the claim that they altered the politics of leadership categorically, and it led me to challenge the assumption that the institutional changes of the last fifty years are uniquely determinative of presidential politics in contemporary America. Notwithstanding all the current manifestations of the long-term trends at work muting differences among the recurrent types of leadership, I believe now, as I said then, that the most remarkable thing about presidential leadership from Carter through Clinton is how prominent these older patterns still are. By drawing forward the basic types from the beginning, my goal was not simply to trace a subtle convergence in their evolution but to reveal the extent to which our recent leaders have continued, despite all these complications, to recapitulate themes and patterns evident at the start.

A third set of issues raised by this book concerns the place of presidents in politics more generally. For some, the depiction of presidents as a blunt, disruptive force in politics misses the presidency's close connections to the other institutions of government and society and overstates its significance relative to other factors driving political change. It would, of course, be foolish to claim that presidents are the sole source of change in American politics, or to deny that a full explanation of any particular change has to take other factors into account. Wars, demographic trends, social movements, economic developments, interest pressures, and the like may, depending on the change in question, be judged as important or more important than presidents. Other political institutions—parties, courts, Congress, and so on—have also played an important part in transforming American politics. My case for the presidency is that it has been a singularly persistent source of change, a transformative element engrained in the Constitution itself. In the presidency, change is generated routinely by incumbents trying to legitimate themselves. A better understanding of these dynamics as they shift *over* time should, I think, enhance our understanding of any particular president and the factors working to define *his* times.

Far from describing some towering, all-powerful position, the depiction of the office as a blunt, disruptive force opens onto an analysis of ever-shifting leadership capacities and often paradoxical political effects. No president can avoid the problem of reconciling the order-shattering implications of the exercise of presidential power with the order-affirming purposes of the institution itself, but this means no more or less than that the negotiation of change has always been an integral part of the president's job description, a logical consequence of each incumbent's constitutional charge to assume responsibility for his own administration. Nor should this characterization be read as an endorsement of some presidential "will to power" or as a lament over the obstacles in its path. I was after some common ground upon which an institutional analysis of our perceptions of success and failure, greatness and mediocrity, might proceed, and having found it, I became both more skeptical and more appreciative of presidential leadership in all its various manifestations.

The opposite concern has also been expressed: that the book's characterization of presidents in politics is too subtle rather than too strong. Here the question is whether the analysis overstates our presidents' perceptions of their different places in the historical sequences in which I find them. All can agree, I think, that presidents are practical politicians with eyes riveted on the moment at hand, and that we should not expect them to think about history the way social scientists do. But I did not have any sense of shoehorning my examples into analytic categories. By and large, I proceeded inductively on our presidents' own quite candid articulations of their authority claims and leadership premises. The analysis assumes only that presidents will have a rudimentary understanding of their political identity as affiliated or opposed to the basic commitments of ideology and interest institutionalized by the last reconstruction, and that they will make a contingent evaluation of the current prospects for acting on that relationship. As practical and engaged politicians, presidents have an instinctive sense of these things; we hear them making such assessments constantly as a matter of course. The history that I sketch whole was fashioned incrementally, and in the moment, by successors who grappled with the legacy of their immediate predecessors and brought their own political identities to bear on new leadership situations.

But there is, as some have observed, a third side to this. One may accept my description of our presidents' political positions and leadership premises and still question the book's own premise. I say that the book is about "the politics that presidents make," but some have argued that it is really about "the presidents that politics make." The

question, as I understand it, is whether an analysis so deeply contextu-
alized can sustain any claims about the significance of the individual
presidents themselves.

This is a delicate matter for anyone interested in understanding presidents systematically. Let me venture a few brief thoughts. First, I am
not sure there is as much to the difference as might first appear. *The
Politics Presidents Make* offers an analysis of the leadership patterns
that are repeatedly produced through the American constitutional system by the peculiar structure and operation of its presidential office. In
this sense, it is about the politics that the American *presidency* makes.
This is, to be sure, a more awkward formulation, but it is one compatible with my original formulation and one less starkly at odds with the
proposed alternative.

That said, I think there is good reason to steer away from an alternative that submerges the importance of individual actors altogether.
Clearly, my analysis is meant to challenge the old myth that each
president is equally at liberty to be "as big a man as he can" and that
differences among leaders are simply matters of character and skill. But
I believe that understanding leadership contexts ultimately enhances our
appreciation of human agency, that we end up with a truer measure of
each individual effort—of its novelty and of the broader significance of
that novelty—when we take into account basic differences in the way
the leadership problem gets configured and understand what is entailed
in trying to master each configuration. I think that Grover Cleveland's
significance as a leader is sharpened when we consider the potentially
reconstructive opportunity opened to him at the outset of his second
term, that Theodore Roosevelt's creativity in office is underscored when
we consider the classic problems of orthodox innovation with which he
had to grapple, that Jimmy Carter's ingenuity in meeting the challenges
that came his way is most fully revealed when we consider the precarious political position of the late-regime affiliate. Cleveland quashed the
portends of a great departure; Roosevelt made political orthodoxy the
premise for a major breakthrough in American state-building; Jimmy
Carter stretched the boundaries of an impossible leadership situation.
These men may not have escaped the logic of their circumstances, but
neither were they mere creatures of circumstance, and their efforts had
long-term consequences for how these logics would be played out in
the future.

Finally, I think that the image of presidents as mere creatures of the contexts in which they act misses the formative role of the individuals who reach the presidency in constituting context itself. I am sometimes asked whether I think that any Democrat elected to the presidency in the late 1970s would have wrestled himself into the same corner that Jimmy Carter did. The point, it seems to me, is that Carter reached the presidency by defeating all the other Democrats contesting the office at that time. His political genius was to discover and articulate a set of premises for national action that took account of his party's difficult situation in those years and still resonated with the electorate sufficiently to carry a Democrat into office. Notwithstanding the fact that other late-regime affiliates have hit upon similar premises, there was nothing in this situation to dictate that Carter had to appear on the scene to articulate them or that a Democratic candidate had to win in 1976. I sought to show that the leadership pretensions which Carter carried into the presidency infused his tenure in office with political purpose, that they informed his actions at crucial junctures and lent political meaning to unfolding events. Carter's premises for leadership in the 1970s set up a classic case of disjunctive politics, but that remains, to my mind at least, a politics of his own creation.

I would be remiss if I did not acknowledge in closing the most obvious omission in the original text: while the book presents a typology of four kinds of leadership, it only deals in detail with three. The preemptive leaders were set aside for special treatment for both practical and theoretical reasons. The most important is that preemptive leadership does not seem to me to evolve in response to secular changes the way the other types do; it seems, rather, to be the type toward which developments in the others are tending. Be that as it may, our current incumbent has offered such a striking example of preemptive leadership that I won't try to put off the task of drawing out its characteristic elements any longer. Although the new Afterword may not substitute for a full treatment of this important subject, I hope that it serves to situate Clinton's "third way" within the book's more general analytic frame and to articulate more fully all the comparisons and contrasts contained in the original text.

Presidents of the United States

1.	George Washington	1789–1797	Federalist
2.	John Adams	1797–1801	Federalist
3.	Thomas Jefferson	1801–1809	Democratic-Republican
4.	James Madison	1809–1817	Democratic-Republican
5.	James Monroe	1817–1825	Democratic-Republican
6.	John Quincy Adams	1825–1829	Coalition
7.	Andrew Jackson	1829–1837	Democratic
8.	Martin Van Buren	1837–1841	Democratic
9.	William Henry Harrison	1841	Whig
10.	John Tyler	1841–1845	Whig
11.	James K. Polk	1845–1849	Democratic
12.	Zachary Taylor	1849–1850	Whig
13.	Millard Fillmore	1850–1853	Whig
14.	Franklin Pierce	1853–1857	Democratic
15.	James Buchanan	1857–1861	Democratic
16.	Abraham Lincoln	1861–1865	Republican
17.	Andrew Johnson	1865–1869	Union
18.	Ulysses S. Grant	1869–1877	Republican
19.	Rutherford B. Hayes	1877–1881	Republican
20.	James A. Garfield	1881	Republican
21.	Chester A. Arthur	1881–1885	Republican
22.	Grover Cleveland	1885–1889	Democratic
23.	Benjamin Harrison	1889–1893	Republican
24.	Grover Cleveland	1893–1897	Democratic
25.	William McKinley	1897–1901	Republican
26.	Theodore Roosevelt	1901–1909	Republican
27.	William Howard Taft	1909–1913	Republican
28.	Woodrow Wilson	1913–1921	Democratic
29.	Warren G. Harding	1921–1923	Republican
30.	Calvin Coolidge	1923–1929	Republican
31.	Herbert Hoover	1929–1933	Republican
32.	Franklin D. Roosevelt	1933–1945	Democratic
33.	Harry S Truman	1945–1953	Democratic
34.	Dwight D. Eisenhower	1953–1961	Republican
35.	John F. Kennedy	1961–1963	Democratic
36.	Lyndon B. Johnson	1963–1969	Democratic
37.	Richard M. Nixon	1969–1974	Republican
38.	Gerald Ford	1974–1977	Republican
39.	James Earl Carter	1977–1981	Democratic
40.	Ronald Reagan	1981–1989	Republican
41.	George Bush	1989–1993	Republican
42.	William J. Clinton	1993–	Democratic

PLACES
IN
HISTORY

Rethinking Presidential History

S UCCEED or fail, presidents are formidable political actors. They are continually remaking our politics, changing the terms of debate and the conditions of maneuver. The wonder is that we so seldom think about them this way. We know far more about the obstacles that frustrate presidents' efforts to become masters of American politics than about what those efforts do *to* American politics. The ineffectiveness of our leaders has become a consuming preoccupation; there is little stepping back to take stock of their political effects. We approach each new administration flush with ideas about what is wrong but short on explanations for the variation in what is wrought.

Taking the alternative tack, I found that historical examination of the presidency's political impact has a lot to tell us about where things stand today. My objective in this book has been to understand the different kinds of politics that presidents make. I treat leadership efforts, shortfalls and all, as politically formative; my interest lies in how they shape the American political landscape and drive its transformation. From this has come a different view of past experience and what we need to be concerned about now.

The book ranges the whole course of presidential history, retelling along the way the leadership struggles of a dozen or so incumbents.[1] I returned to the old stories to rethink fundamentals in light of what I saw as the limitations of familiar analytic strategies. The tendency has long been to compartmentalize the study of government institutions on the side of order, system, and routine in politics, to identify them with "politics-as-usual" and look outside of them for the "real" forces of change.[2] But the presidency has never fit this frame very well.[3] It conflates these categories and distinctions, and much of its political significance is lost on them. Array the stories of the presidents in succession—each in his turn endowed with broad constitutional powers and determined to exercise them in his own right—and the blunt disruptive force of this institution instantly comes to the fore. Together these stories tell of an office that regularly reaches beyond itself to assert control over others, one whose deep-seated impulse to *re*order things routinely jolts order and routine elsewhere, one whose normal activities and operations alter system boundaries and recast political possibilities.

Disruption of the status quo ante is basic to the politics presidents make and, beyond that, to the dynamics of American political development in the largest sense. Rather than filter it out as background noise, I propose to fashion an institutional analysis that brings it center stage.[4] The first step is to redirect the signposts which we use to make sense of presidential history.

The Limits of Our Search for Order

It is easy to get lost in presidential history. Each story presents itself as baldly idiosyncratic and therefore defiant of any quest for generalization. The subject matter tends at once to wander outward, encompassing the operations of the federal government as a whole, and to collapse in upon itself as a study of individuals. Patterns stretch over long spans of time, more often than not obscured by the immediate twists and turns of personality and circumstance.

To show us the order of things, scholars have divided up the history of the presidents into periods. They have grouped historically contiguous incumbents together and gleaned from the shared elements of their situations a sense of the parameters of the political system at that time. From this they derive the characteristic demands that the system places on the presidency and the characteristic resources available to meet those demands. Once the problem of political action within the period has been set in this way, presidential leadership becomes a function of relative skill at manipulating politics-as-usual.

Take, for example, Richard Neustadt's classic study of the politics of leadership, *Presidential Power* (1960). The centerpiece of Neustadt's analysis was his description of a new political/institutional system that had taken shape in the late 1940s and early 1950s. His portrait of "the presidency at mid-century" identified incumbents after Franklin Roosevelt as a distinct and coherent group facing similar challenges in political action.[5] Neustadt argued that in this period central direction and control of national affairs had become for the first time a routine imperative. Modern presidents *had* to be leaders. The prior choice of mere clerkship, of simply fulfilling the constitutional responsibilities of the office, had been rendered moot by recent, dramatic events (the New Deal and World War II) that had made crisis management a normal state of affairs and concerted action a matter of striking bargains among independent interests and institutional actors who were themselves possessed of a stubborn tendency toward gridlock. From his portrait of this new system, Neustadt derived the skills and strategies requisite to making it work, and he sustained within that frame a thematic evaluation of the performances of Truman and Eisenhower.

This was no mean achievement. Neustadt's periodization of presidential history—his distinction between modern and premodern contexts for the exercise of power—introduced a sense of coherence into the relentless succession of incumbents and raised the study of leadership efforts above the idiosyncrasies of the case at hand. But simple periodization schemes impose severe limits on the analysis of leadership, and Neustadt's was no exception. Note first that Neustadt set the modern incumbents apart from their predecessors with a mere caricature of the past. The notion of a prior age when presidents did not *have* to be leaders—an age when vital national interests were only sporadically at the fore and most presidents could rest content with mere clerkship—is nothing more than a conceit of modern times. While the imagery groups the modern presidents together on common ground and cordons them off from prior experience, the question of just how different the politics of leadership in modern times is or whether the mid-twentieth-century presidents individually share more with one another than they do with presidents in earlier periods is never really explored.

Second, in describing the system that midcentury incumbents had to manipulate, Neustadt constricted the political significance of the exercise of presidential power to what he called "operational" questions. His concern was with how presidents could make this new system work, and he evaluated their effectiveness accordingly. But Neustadt's presidents do not change the political system in any significant way. The political and institutional parameters of the system appear impervious to the exercise of presidential power; they are transformed by great external forces like economic depression or world war. Indeed, to compare Truman and Eisenhower by the same standard, Neustadt *had* to assume that Truman did not do anything to alter Eisenhower's political challenge or leadership prospects. This is really the crux of the periodization problem: to sustain comparisons within a given time frame, the systemic political impacts of successive leadership efforts must be filtered out, and no sooner are those impacts filtered out than the standards of evaluation themselves begin to ring hollow. The assumption that a system is given and that presidents make it work more or less effectively is bound to render the requisites of success elusive, for in their most precise signification, presidents disrupt systems, reshape political landscapes, and pass to successors leadership challenges that are different from the ones just faced.

Finally, and to bring this full circle, by assigning priority to those aspects of the political situation that Truman and Eisenhower shared, Neustadt elided obvious differences in the political purposes they brought to action in the moment at hand. He speaks of the "tasks" of leadership at midcentury in generic terms, but Truman and Eisenhower set out with manifestly different objectives in view. After all, one was a Democrat, the other a Republican. Truman was politically affiliated with his predecessor and out to elaborate upon the received agenda, while Eisenhower, the first Republican to come to power since the advent of the New Deal, was the leader of a resurgent opposition out to find an alternative course that could still stand the test of legitimacy.[6] To think thematically about tasks such as these, we have to be willing to break down the historical demarcations which Neustadt's analysis sets up and look back to presidents his analysis would seem to consign to irrelevance. Martin Van Buren, Andrew Jackson's vice president and successor, might be a better reference for Truman's political dilemma than Eisenhower; William Henry Harrison, the popular general who took the Whigs to their first victory over the Jackson Democrats, a better guide to Eisenhower's political situation than Truman.

Notwithstanding the limitations of the method, simple periodization schemes and modern-traditional dichotomies structure most of what we think and write about presidential leadership today. Indeed, a sampling of current opinion suggests that we are taking our period constructs more and more seriously. One leading authority describes the changes made in American government during the New Deal as the founding of a "Second Republic," a system of government so radically different from what preceded it that all prior presidential experience pales into insignificance.[7] Another writes in a similar vein that "the transformation of the office has been so profound that the modern presidencies have more in common with one another in the opportunities they provide and the demands they place on their incumbents than they have with the entire sweep of traditional presidencies from Washington's to Hoover's."[8] This segmentation of presidential history is reinforced on the other side by scholars working on earlier periods: "The conceptions of leadership of the pre-1829 presidents," writes a leading authority, "largely distinguish them from . . . latter day models. Because the first six presidents, quite simply, had different valuations of partisan motivation and of the reality of the public interest, they had different standards of executive leadership."[9]

By calling attention to the historical demarcations that currently order this field, I do not wish to dismiss the important insights that have been gained. What we have learned about the distinctiveness of the presidency in different periods and about how changes in the office have accommodated transformations in the nation at large is in fact integral to the analysis to be undertaken here. My point is simply that the politics of leadership is neither as coherent within these periods nor as disparate across them as our current approach to the subject matter would suggest, and that we stand to sharpen our insights into what is actually going on inside these periods if we resist caricatures of those outside the time frames given. Indeed, leaving the history of presidents in pieces—with incumbents in one period having little in common with, or relevance to, those in the others—would seem to be counterproductive on its face. There are only some forty-odd cases in all, and with the experience as varied as it is from one incumbent to the next, none can be dismissed out of hand as a potential source of insight into the significance of the rest.

Consider some recent incumbents. Jimmy Carter, Ronald Reagan, and George Bush may be distinguished as a group of late-century presidents sharing certain resources and constraints and pursuing certain characteristic strategies.[10] But just how similar were the leadership tasks these presidents undertook? Was Reagan simply a better politician than the others, more skilled than they at using the tools of the modern presidency? Or was he, at some yet unattended level, engaged in a different kind of politics altogether, a politics more like Andrew Jackson's than either Carter's or Bush's?

Similarly, John Adams and Thomas Jefferson shared a set of institutional resources and presumptions about leadership that distinguish them in important ways from presidents in later periods. Yet, Adams's presidency ruptured the political regime and shattered the previously dominant governing coalition, while Jefferson forged a new regime, one that would stand as the font of political legitimacy for decades to come. More curious still, Adams's shattering effect came in a rather desperate attempt to avoid national disaster and prevent his own compatriots from usurping the basic constitutional powers of his office, while Jefferson exercised extraordinary prerogatives throughout his tenure and passed power along to a hand-picked successor in the midst of a national disaster of his own making. These are stark differences in the politics presidents make. Are they idiosyncratic? Or are there other patterns at work, patterns that cut across our periods, which might help us specify the range of political possibilities further?

Multiple Orders and Political Mixes

Certainly it is no accident that the presidents most widely celebrated for their mastery of American politics have been immediately preceded by presidents generally judged politically incompetent. John Adams and Thomas Jefferson, John Quincy Adams and Andrew Jackson, James Buchanan and Abraham Lincoln, Herbert Hoover and Franklin Roosevelt, Jimmy Carter and Ronald Reagan—this repeated pairing of dismal failure with stunning success is one of the more striking patterns in presidential history, and accounting for it forces us to alter the way we have been thinking about that history. In the first place, we are prompted to think about what incumbents in very different historical periods have in common with one another and not with their immediate predecessors or successors. What conditions for leadership did the latter presidents in each of these pairs share; what could they do that their predecessors could not? Conversely, what conditions for leadership did the first presidents in each pair share; what did they do to open the door to greatness for their successor?

Note further that by accounting for the pattern in this way, we place the leaders themselves in a different light. A search for the typical effects that presidential action has in differently structured political contexts takes us behind the familiar portraits of individual incompetence and mastery. If it turns out that the "great" political leaders have all made the same kind of politics and if that politics is only made in a certain kind of situation, then our celebration of their extraordinary talents and skills will be seen to obscure more than it clarifies. Indeed, if it is the potency of the office in different situations that is being picked up in historical judgments of effectiveness, then this historiography is less a description than an extension of the politics presidents make.

Finally, no sooner do we become aware of signposts directing us toward alternative assumptions about institutional politics and presidential history than we are prompted to think about how the different patterns before us relate to one another. It will not do merely to substitute this pattern for that, presenting an alternative synthesis that tells the stories of the presidents according to a different view of order in history. Choosing one among several patterns that we know to exist is precisely what overstates the regularity and derivative character of institutional politics. At the very least, we should want to know how the recurrent pattern we have just noted has been affected by the secular changes that others have described so clearly in the operations of the government generally and in the evolution of institutional resources in the presidency in particular.

This last question points the way to a different understanding of institutional politics in all its various dimensions. When presidents act, they engage several institutional "orderings" simultaneously.[11] Three are implicit in what we have observed in presidential history already. In making them explicit, we see that each ordering has distinct institutional referents and that each frames a distinct pattern of change over time. More important still, we see that these different patterns of change overlay one another *in* time. Drawing them out together exposes the layered structure of institutional action.[12]

First, of course, there is the constitutional ordering of institutional prerogatives. It frames the *persistent pattern* of political disruption, as each new president seizes control of the formal powers of his office and attempts to exercise them in his own right. Behind that lies an organizational ordering of institutional resources. While all presidents have had the same basic constitutional prerogatives, the practical organization of institutional relationships and responsibilities has changed several times over the course of American history as national politics itself has grown more complicated. These working modes of governmental operation frame the *emergent pattern* of expanding resources and greater independence in presidential action. Finally, there is a political ordering of institutional commitments. The government's basic commitments of ideology and interest have tended to congeal institutionally around relatively durable partisan regimes, and these orderings frame the *recurrent pattern* of founding, fragmenting, and disintegrating governing coalitions and party systems.[13]

Presidents are deeply implicated in all the various kinds of changes marked along these different orderings. Distinguishing the layers thus goes a long way toward helping us specify and compare what they do to our politics. Abraham Lincoln fought a civil war and reconstructed the government's most basic commitments of ideology and interest, but he did not change the patronage-based, partisan mode of governmental operations that had organized institutional politics since the time of Jackson. Theodore Roosevelt made some extraordinary changes in this partisan mode of governmental operations, and yet in his efforts to replace the patronage-ridden, locally oriented organization of government with a more bureaucratic and nationally oriented one, he aimed at preserving commitments of ideology and interest long established by the dominant Republican coalition. Franklin Roosevelt, like Lincoln, made extraordinary changes in the government's basic commitments of interest and ideology, but he did so by elaborating principles of governmental organization that had been standard since the Progressive era.

Our historiography has picked up this differential impact but again in a curious way: it appears as the stuff of scholarly debate. Was Lincoln the great exception among nineteenth-century presidents, a founding statesman who, like Washington, towered over his age? Or was he the archetypical nineteenth-century president, master of the mundane arts of patronage distribution?[14] Was Theodore Roosevelt's presidency the "birth of modern America," or was it rather "a lot of sound and movement signifying little"?[15] Was FDR's presidency a political revolution or merely the pragmatic elaboration of a course already charted by Theodore Roosevelt, Woodrow Wilson, and Herbert Hoover?[16] As alternatives, these renderings talk past one another, each assessing institutional action along a different dimension of order in history. Once the layers are distinguished and we are no longer debating the terms of analysis, different kinds of questions immediately come to the fore, questions that seek the significance of each leadership effort more directly in the contingent mix.[17]

An analysis of these mixes dissolves the standard frame of institutional study as it has been derived from simple periodization schemes. We are no longer isolating segments of history to posit a stable system in which institutions mark order and routine; we are dividing the history up in several ways and using the different periods to juxtapose contending forces of order and change. Institutions become the arenas in which these forces converge, collide, and fold back on one another. Images of a coherent, ordered space bounded in time yield here to cross sections of discordant structures and transformative, though not entirely intractable, agents. The upshot is a radically temporalized view of institutional politics: the actor shapes and drives political sequences as the different orderings impinge on one another, and order along one dimension affects change along the next. The relationship between political order and political change becomes, institutionally speaking, a question of the reflexivities of time.[18]

Sorting and Comparing

The bulk of this work consists of a comparison of leadership efforts. By locating the presidents under examination in several different structures of action, I have, in effect, established for each a number of different reference sets. Each of these sets contains several cases that bear a family resemblance to one another along one dimension of presidential action in history. Looking at what the experiences of the presidents in each set have in common indicates what is "normal" politics along that dimension, and in this sense the experience of each incumbent is illuminated by the experiences of the others in that set. Note, however, that the several sets bring very different kinds of politics into focus. By grouping the presidents according to different ordering principles, they provide different lenses on the politics of leadership. Furthermore, each president's leadership effort retains significance as a unique and dynamic conjuncture by virtue of the incumbent's membership in several sets; his multiple memberships mark a particular historical/structural moment. The contrasting rules of action found in the different sets will be seen to inform his particular leadership dilemma, and the impact of his leadership effort will be taken to reflect the interaction of those particular elements. By playing members and sets off one another, I draw general inferences about the presidency as a position of national political action and map changes in its political range.

For an illustration of the method, consider the case of James K. Polk, president between 1845 and 1849. From one standpoint, Polk was just like every other president, out for a term to exercise the constitutional powers of his office in his own right and for his own purposes. His famous quip, "I intend to be *myself* president of the U.S.," just about says it all from this perspective.[19] The remark is a pointed declaration of an impulse that all presidents share. It directs our attention to the basic prerogatives of the presidential office (the appointment powers, the war powers, the treaty powers, the legislative powers) that incumbents put to the test to realize their ambitions within the constraints of the constitutional structure of checks and balances. We can observe here the disruptive force that attended Polk's manipulation of these powers and the inevitable frustrations he encountered from the constraints on them. In these ways, *Polk made constitutional politics.*

But Polk was also a president of the "party period," a time extending from the 1830s to the end of the nineteenth century, when political parties most thoroughly organized the institutions and practical operations of American government.[20] This periodization reminds us that presidents of the latter two thirds of the nineteenth century shared similar resources and a similar policy repertoire, and that they differed in these regards from the patrician presidents of the preparty period as well as the presidents of the more modern, bureaucratic period. Polk came to the presidency in the heyday of the party period. Indeed, he was the first "dark horse" candidate brokered by regional party leaders, and the first candidate to return a party to power after it had suffered an interim defeat. He landed in the presidency as an archetypical manager of the party machinery, and proceeded true to form to fine-tune the political/administrative system of spoils and rotation. As an operator of this patronage-based, locally oriented system of national government, *Polk made party politics.*

Beyond that, however, Polk was also a president affiliated with the dominant coalition of the second or Jacksonian "party system" (dating approximately from 1830 to 1860).[21] Indeed, he came to power in the heyday of this period also. Here Polk appears an orthodox-innovator, a stalwart Jackson Democrat leading his party at its most robust moment since its founding. Steward of the received political faith, he worked diligently to implement the program of the Jackson coalition, to adjust that coalition to changing circumstances, and to try to maintain in the process its dominance in competition with the Whigs. Thus, *Polk made Jacksonian politics.*

We have here three different reference sets for the politics that Polk made—one built on what all presidents share by virtue of the formalities of the constitutional design, another on what presidents of the same historical era share by virtue of the organization of governmental operations at the time and the distinctive institutional resources it lays at their disposal, and a third built on what select presidents in different periods share by virtue of their political relationship to previously established commitments of ideology and interest. Nothing extraordinary appears to be happening along any of these dimensions in Polk's case, but that is precisely what makes his example so useful as an illustration. Though the politics that Polk made appears in every respect normal politics or politics-as-usual, the politics in question is different in each instance. Superimpose these filters on one another, and the notion of politics-as-usual under Polk dissipates. Our attention is directed instead to the dynamics inherent in the mix. Here Polk's leadership becomes transformative, the interaction of the elements working a profound, if somewhat unwitting, change in the American political landscape.

No one the least familiar with Polk's presidency will be surprised to learn that it changed things profoundly. My objective is to explicate those changes systematically and to map them onto a larger canvas. Consider in this regard the relationship between what this president claimed to represent *in* American politics and what the exercise of presidential power routinely does *to* American politics. Polk's election as an orthodox Jacksonian Democrat—thoroughly submerged in the collective identity of his party and responsible for maintaining its integrity—rubs up uncomfortably against the independent powers of his office, the exercise of which is inherently disruptive of previously established political and institutional arrangements. For all his sensitivity to the problems this posed and for all his skill in trying to finesse them, Polk had difficulty reconciling his political legitimacy as a stalwart Jacksonian with his personal determination to be president in his own right. Stamping Jacksonian orthodoxy on the policies of American government quickly became a matter of stamping this president's personal will upon the party and the nation. Polk found himself caught in the conflicting rules informing his institutional position; exercising independent powers and attempting to maintain control over his own administration, he unwittingly but steadily undercut the contingent political premise on which he hoped to rest his greatest achievements. Thus, we discern in the interaction of different institutional orderings a logic of disruption and transformation, a logic that turned the orthodox Polk, genuinely committed to party maintenance through "equal and exact justice" to every faction, into "Polk the Mendacious," a heretic, charged by each faction with a different betrayal and responsible in the end for sending the whole Jacksonian regime into a sectarian tailspin.

The uniqueness of Polk's leadership moment is captured here in a particular conjuncture of three relatively independent institutional orderings. But because we began by sorting out these different elements, the political impact of *this* man on *his* times also stands as a signpost of more general dynamics of institutional action *in* time. As politics-as-usual falls away and the multilayered structure of this leadership moment comes to the fore, the political consequences of Polk's leadership take on a more general significance, with implications ranging the entire course of American political history.

A variety of comparisons and contrasts might be ventured to tease more general lessons out of Polk's experience. First we can compare and contrast Polk's leadership moment with that of other presidents of the party period. Polk's presidency is very much like that of Buchanan and Lincoln in terms of the organizational resources that were at his disposal in political action, but it is different by virtue of his position in the coalitional system or political regime. Unlike either Buchanan or Lincoln, Polk came to power with a potent political warrant for completing work on a long-established party agenda. There is no need to stop there. Polk's leadership moment also can be compared and contrasted with presidents in different periods who were similarly situated in a political regime—for example, Lyndon Johnson. Johnson, like Polk, was a faithful son in a long-established party coalition, and he too came to power to implement the received agenda at the most pregnant political moment for doing so since that coalition's founding. Johnson had to grapple with a dilemma that was quite similar to Polk's—the dilemma of the orthodox-innovator—but he did so at a radically different stage in the development of the presidential office and the organization of governmental power more generally.

The Polk-Johnson comparison broaches all the questions begged by the historical divisions between modern and premodern presidents that currently demarcate the study of the presidency. To what extent are the modern presidents really a group apart, sharing more with one another than with any presidents from Washington to Hoover? Just what difference did it make that Polk confronted the dilemma of the orthodox-innovator at a time of state-based patronage machines and hemispheric ambitions, and Johnson at a time of national bureaucratic power and worldwide hegemony? Just how much has the advent of "the modern presidency" changed the politics presidents make?

It should be clear by now that *The Politics Presidents Make* is neither about the order of things nor about the seamless succession of idiosyncratic personalities interacting with their own unique circumstances. It is about the institutional logic of political disruption. Though the presidency has never fit very comfortably into standard conceptions of order and regularity in politics, it is perhaps the premier example of how different sets of power arrangements are juxtaposed within government institutions and how institutional actors, by engaging all these different arrangements simultaneously, continually alter the range of political possibilities. The presidency is in this sense less the awkward stepchild of the received categories of institutional study than the guide to a new rule for understanding institutions generally. In this rendition of institutional politics, the everyday struggle of incumbents for control is itself a driving force of structural change, and standard conceptions of order in politics are but so many points of access to the ongoing political construction of time.

The picture of the presidency that emerges here is not an especially rosy one. With incumbents engaged simultaneously by very different sets of rules for venting their ambitions, the political effects of the exercise of presidential power are likely to be both willful and unintended, calculated and self-defeating. Once we discern a logic to the politics presidents make, we see just how easy it is for incumbents to get themselves, and the nation, caught up in the conflicting purposes of the institution they inhabit. Perhaps the best to be said about the presidency from this perspective is that, despite its propensity to foment debacles, there is something of enduring value to a democratic society in an office that routinely disrupts established power arrangements and continually opens new avenues of political activity for others. We might keep that value in mind as we survey past experience and identify the various leadership syndromes that have been with us since the beginning. Before we are finished, we will have to grapple with current prospects for escaping them.

CHAPTER 2

Power and Authority

FRANKLIN PIERCE isn't on anyone's list of great presidents. But neither was he what we imagine most nineteenth-century presidents to be, a mere clerk unchallenged by the duties of his office and content just to keep the machinery of government humming. Pierce came to the presidency in 1853 determined to leave his mark upon his time. In the first major test of his leadership, he threw his support behind a proposal that would radically alter the terms and conditions of national politics. With the resources of his office fully deployed, he secured that proposal—the Kansas-Nebraska Act—and inaugurated a new program for national action. In the process, he wrecked his presidency and sparked a revolution.

Pierce was a failure; yet, his story is instructive. The problem was not that he lacked the power or inclination to do great things but that he completely lost control over the meaning of what he did. His authority as a political leader collapsed in the exercise of his powers. Presidential history is littered with stories like this. As a rule, power has been less of a problem for presidents than authority; getting things done, less of a problem than sustaining warrants for actions taken and for accomplishments realized.

As most of what is written about presidential leadership takes power as the central problem, the distinction I am drawing here might at first seem strange. But consider our modern presidents. Though each has generated a long list of accomplishments, I doubt that anyone would want to use the length of those lists as the yardstick of their relative success. Successful political leaders do not necessarily do more than other leaders; successful leaders control the political definition of their actions, the terms in which their places in history are understood. The failures are those who, upon leaving office, look to some time in the distant future when people might begin to appreciate the wisdom of what they did.

Power and authority have a common source in the prerogatives granted to presidents in the Constitution and the laws, but they reach beyond these formalities in different directions.[1] Power, as I will use the term here, refers to the resources, formal and informal, that presidents in a given period have at their disposal to get things done. Presidents exercise power by husbanding these resources and deploying them strategically to effect change. Authority, on the other hand, reaches to the expectations that surround the exercise of power at a particular moment, to perceptions of what is appropriate for a given president to do.[2] A president's authority hinges on the warrants that can be drawn from the moment at hand to justify action and secure the legitimacy of the changes effected.

Why has legitimation proven such a hard nut for presidents to crack? The original rationale for the presidency offered in *The Federalist Papers* was that it would routinely direct its incumbents toward the pursuit of their highest duty to the nation. The constitutional framework cues presidents to vindicate themselves in the use of their powers.[3] They are expected to pursue "fame," undertaking "great and arduous enterprises" with an eye to establishing their legitimacy.[4]

And yet presidents are historical actors. Their words and deeds will transform the contexts in which they act, but they must act by their own lights within the context given. An old adage captures the point well: presidents, we say, want to secure *a place* in history. Echoes of *The Federalist Papers* ring clear here: presidents are driven by a concern for their reputation; they try to vindicate themselves in their stewardship of national affairs. But the old saying hints at something more: a president comes to power at a particular moment in the course of national events, and vindication turns on the prospect for securing the meaning of *that* moment on the president's own terms. The question is, how do presidents go about the task of fashioning their places in history, and how amenable are these places to being fashioned according to presidential design?

What I have called the politics presidents make encompasses both sides of the story: the president's impulse to secure a certain understanding of his place in the course of events, as well as the actual political impact of his effort to do so. I seek to show how the context-bound struggle for legitimacy informs the president's strategy for the exercise of his power, and how the political impact of presidential leadership—the particular way politics is altered—follows from the warrants the president can muster for disrupting the status quo ante. As the history reveals, more often than not the logic of disruption undercuts the agent; the leadership effort succumbs to the very changes it has sponsored. To see the logic, however, we need to know a lot more about the dynamics of presidential action in history and the political parameters of the different places presidents occupy in it.

One of the more disturbing things to be observed in presidential history is that there is little in the personal characters or political skills of those few who have mastered the legitimation problem that readily distinguishes them as a group from those who have not.[5] Some rather ordinary men have wielded extraordinary authority, and some men of great reputation have failed miserably. Political wizards have self-destructed, and successful incumbents have not always had the most salutary effects. The characters and talents of the incumbents themselves tell us so little about the political impact of presidential leadership precisely because leadership has not been a standard test in which each in his turn is given an equal opportunity to secure his place in history. The Constitution imparts to each president a similar motive and a basic challenge in political action; but, as we shall see, it leaves real historical relations of power and authority anchored in paradox.

In this chapter and the next, I pursue the impulse to fashion a legitimate place in history with an eye to these paradoxes of power and authority. What are the political parameters of a president's place in history? What are the political prospects for mastering these parameters on the president's own terms? What are the likely political consequences of the determination to do so?

Rudiments of the Leadership Problem

Presidential leadership is an effort to resolve the disruptive consequences of executive action in the reproduction of legitimate political order. Problems of historical legitimation come in a variety of forms, but all of them relate the assertion of presidential control to the disruption of past patterns of control. The core paradox that riddles the persistent striving of presidents for mastery over their places in history is that *the presidency is a governing institution inherently hostile to inherited governing arrangements.*

The roots of this paradox are not difficult to locate. They can be found in the oath of office set forth in Article II of the Constitution. Each incumbent swears both to "execute the office of President of the United States" and to "preserve, protect and defend the Constitution of the United States." In the first instance, he is charged to exercise expansive powers for independent action; in the second, he is charged to affirm the fundamental order of things. Somehow the order-shattering implications of the exercise of power have to be reconciled with the order-affirming expectations of its use.[6]

The problem of presidential action in history is compounded by the broader constitutional system in which each incumbent operates. The presidency is one of three coequal branches of government, each of which can effectively challenge the will of the others. Formally, there is no central authority. Governing responsibilities are shared, and assertions of power are contentious. Practically, however, it is the presidency that stands out as the chief point of reference for evaluating the polity as it moves through time and space; it is the executive office that focuses the eyes and draws out the attachments of the people.[7] Unity, energy, and visibility combine in the presidency to place its incumbents four-square at the intersection of the received order of things and current demands for change; and, so exposed, the president becomes the lightning rod of national politics, attracting and objectifying contending interpretations of the existing state of affairs. As the course of national politics is debated and judged administration by administration, each president will seize control of the powers of his office to try, in the face of coequal authorities, to establish order anew on his own terms.

The rudiments of the problem of historical legitimation are now in view. Presidential action in history is politicized by the order-shattering, order-affirming, and order-creating impulses inherent in the institution itself. The presidency is an *order-shattering* institution in that it prompts each incumbent to take charge of the independent powers of his office and to exercise them in his own right. It is an *order-affirming* institution in that the disruptive effects of the exercise of presidential power must be justified in constitutional terms broadly construed as the protection, preservation, and defense of values emblematic of the body politic. It is an *order-creating* institution in that it prompts each incumbent to use his powers to construct some new political arrangements that can stand the test of legitimacy within the other institutions of government as well

as the nation at large. Getting these three impulses to work together—
the political message and practical effect of each reinforcing the others—is no easy matter. That is why incumbents so often find themselves
at cross purposes. As a general formulation, however, we might venture
that to secure a place in history even roughly on his own terms, a
president must be able to exercise his power in such a way that these
order-shattering, order-affirming, order-creating impulses operate in
tandem.[8]

These dynamics did not escape the attention of the founders. Alexander Hamilton, the leading defender of presidential power, worried
openly in *The Federalist Papers* about the order-shattering impulse. He
saw "the intimate connection between the duration of the executive
magistrate in office and the stability of the system of administration."

> To reverse and undo what has been done by a predecessor is very often
> considered by a successor as the very best proof he can give of his own
> capacity and desert; and in addition to this propensity, where the altera-
> tion has been as the result of public choice, the person substituted is
> warranted in supposing that the dismission of his predecessor has pro-
> ceeded from a dislike to his measures, and that the less he resembles him
> the more he will recommend himself to the favor of his constituents.[9]

Hamilton lodged the disruptive effects of a change in presidents in
the most elementary aspects of taking charge of the presidential office.
Disruption is not the special province of the extraordinary leader; it
adheres to the most mundane tasks of running the office. Each president, Hamilton continued, will naturally want to appoint his own ministers: "These considerations, and the influence of personal confidences
and attachments, would be likely to induce every new President to
promote a change of men to fill the subordinate stations." Hamilton
could not deny that the appointment prerogative is basic to a president's
ability to fashion his own administration and exercise the powers of his
office in his own right; nor was he one to begrudge incumbents any
bold and ambitious projects they might undertake to establish their
legitimacy in the exercise of those powers. The problem as he saw it
was that in a republic, where the alteration of presidents is "the result
of public choice," these powers are also likely to promote "a disgraceful
and ruinous mutability in the administration of the government." That
is what led him to put such great stock in the constitutional provision
of a four-year term for the president and in the unlimited eligibility of
incumbents to stand for reelection. Hamilton was comforted by the idea

that a president could stay in office as long as he performed his duties well, that periodic elections might actually serve to hold a sitting incumbent to a high standard of duty and thereby extend his tenure, and that the disruptions inherent in a change of administration might thus be held to a minimum.

Note further that Hamilton linked the disruptive force of the presidency to a specific claim of political authority. Indeed, what troubled him most were the "warrants" for disruption that he thought any newly elected president would be likely to hold. Again his premise was that there is no legal limit on the prior incumbent's ability to stand for reelection and that incumbents will want nothing more than to have their actions and achievements ratified by the electorate. With these assumptions, Hamilton ventured that the election of a new president is most likely to entail the "dismission" or rejection of the standing one. New presidents were not to be taken lightly, because they would come to power with a potent political rationale for shattering the received order. They would assert that their election proceeded on the dislike of the current state of affairs; and, acting on that authority, they would be likely to try to change as much about it as they could.

Finally, consider the historical experience. The presidency has changed hands a lot more than Hamilton anticipated. George Washington established the precedent, generally followed thereafter, of a two-term limit, and the rise of a competitive party system made one-term presidents unexceptional. Only about 20 percent of our presidents have served out two full terms. About 20 percent have served less than one full term, and, taking a slightly different cut, about 20 percent have been unable for one reason or another to serve out terms for which they were elected. It is worth noting further that the Twenty-second Amendment has now formalized a strict reading of Washington's precedent that excludes some presidents from pursuit of reelection altogether. Against this backdrop, the political implications of succession run even deeper than Hamilton supposed, and they are much more complicated than he thought. The disruptions are more frequent, political relationships between successors and predecessors are not all of a piece, and power and authority are seldom as neatly aligned as in the circumstances that Hamilton postulated.

In fact, few presidents come to power upon an outright rejection of their predecessors. Many have taken office pledging to continue the course already set. Some have been expected to act as stand-ins, rendering faceless tribute to their predecessors in a kind of surrogate extension of their term. Still others, if given their druthers, would have liked to change course radically but had no clear warrants for doing so. The crux of the matter is that while all have to cope with the disruptive effects of being a president, few will locate the instrumental uses of their power on a discursive field of authority in the way Hamilton anticipated. Furthermore, while few take office that way, the situation that Hamilton anticipated and found so dangerous would seem to be the only one in which the legitimation problem is readily resolvable. Presidents elected upon the outright rejection of their predecessors will have at hand an expansive warrant for disruption. The exercise of presidential power will be relatively unencumbered in these circumstances because the incumbent is implicitly authorized by his election to constitute an alternative to the discredited past. In all other circumstances, however, presidents will find themselves at cross purposes, in one way or another disrupting a regime they do not have any clear authority to repudiate.

The very first presidential succession—from George Washington to John Adams—illustrates just how complicated the picture outlined by Hamilton in *Federalist 72* can get, and it is no small irony that Hamilton himself was deeply implicated in those complications. The second president was an affiliate of the first, and though he was skeptical of the course charted during the Washington administration, Adams came to power dutifully affirming its policies and personnel. Adams was not free to deal with his inheritance as he saw fit and take charge on his own terms. In fact, the Hamiltonians he held over from Washington's cabinet worked against his efforts to do just that, usurping in the process some of his most basic powers and turning his initial affirmation of continuity and stability into an impediment to his capacity to be a president at all. By the time Adams was ready to purge Hamilton's henchmen and stake out his own ground, he was all too deeply implicated in their controversial program, and neither they nor their strongest opponents, the Jeffersonians, were prepared to credit the legitimacy of the new order he belatedly ventured to establish in his own right.

The Priority of Authority

What is the incumbent affirming? What is he repudiating? What commitments are being betrayed? What orthodoxy, sacrificed? These questions have hounded presidents from John Adams to George Bush. Perceptions of propriety set an exacting standard for presidential action, and for all the attention we have lavished on the nuances of political skill and governing strategy, the presidency defies subtlety. The office is just too vital to the security of interests in power, and the exercise of its powers is too potent a threat to them. Presidents make choices between demands for political action in the present and existing political commitments embodied in previously established governing arrangements, and those choices are subject to ruthless scrutiny by those affected. Every affirmation is implicitly a repudiation; every commitment made, implicitly a betrayal; every new rendition of the old faith, implicitly a heresy. Any ambiguity in a president's political position will quickly be clarified by others at his expense. Any contradictions engendered in the course of acting on a position once clearly staked out will embolden and legitimize those who would oppose it.

For these reasons, the question of authority holds priority in determining the politics of leadership. Before a president can formulate a strategy for action, he needs to construe his place in history and stake claim to certain warrants for the exercise of power within it. Lincoln made the point succinctly: "If we could first know where we are, and whither we are tending, we could better judge what to do and how to do it."[10] The first thing a leader does is to situate himself in a public discourse, and construct a narrative relating what has been done previously to what he proposes to do in the moment at hand. The basic parameters of the politics of leadership are set here, in the president's initial assertions about who he is and where he sees himself fitting into the nation's history.[11]

To sustain his narrative—to confirm during the exercise of his powers his own presentments about his place in history—a president must be able to preempt the authority of others to challenge what is being done and how it is being accomplished. Concrete policy accomplishments are important to the leader's prospects in this regard, as are personal setbacks and defeats, but they are important only insofar as they bear on the story being told. The solution to the problem of implementing policy preferences—that is, garnering and deploying institutional resources strategically—has no obvious bearing on the prior challenge of formulating a credible historical project. And conversely, the implementation of a set of preferences is no guarantee that the relationship envisioned between the established order and change—the president's own imputation of meaning to his actions and accomplishments—will actually be secured.[12]

Slogans have been generated routinely over the course of the twenti-eth century to label leadership projects—Square Deal, New Freedom, New Day, New Deal, Fair Deal, New Republicanism, New Frontier, Great Society, New Federalism, New Foundation, New Beginning, New Breeze, New Covenant. The list itself suggests something of the impor-tance presidents attach to controlling the political definition of their actions in the moment at hand. But what is important about labels is what lies behind them—the political identity of the president, the war-rant he can claim for changing received relationships, and the political dynamics inherent in the historical project he proposes to undertake.

The leadership of two familiar presidents, Franklin Roosevelt and Lyndon Johnson, illustrates the different political dynamics that adhere to different historical projects.[13] Both were highly skilled, professional politicians; both enjoyed breakthrough political opportunities for the exercise of presidential power; both got a lot done; and both trans-formed American politics dramatically. An obvious difference between them, however, was their political relationship to the received order. Roosevelt came to power at one of the most desperate moments in the nation's history as the leader of the opposition to a regime in collapse. He stood beyond the old order and against the received orthodoxies. He not only proclaimed the failure of the received dispensation, he declared its most basic commitments an insufferable perversion of the "ancient truths" underlying American civilization. Johnson, in contrast, had made his way up through the ranks of a long-dominant regime. At the outset of his presidency, he pledged to continue the work of his predecessors, and his election in 1964 effectively swept aside most of the obstacles to that goal. Standing at the threshold of one of the most robust moments in the history of the nation, Johnson took as his charge the implementation of the received orthodoxy and the fulfillment of its commitments.

Roosevelt and Johnson claimed leadership authority by virtue of who they were politically and where they thought they fit into an ongoing history. Each articulated a cogent and compelling case for the exercise of presidential power; the warrants they claimed resonated loud and clear with basic features of their respective situations. But these war-rants framed different projects, and they set up very different kinds of politics. The presidents adopted different strategies in the exercise of their power, they asserted control in different ways, and they had widely divergent political effects.

From the start, Roosevelt was openly and forthrightly engaged in the displacement of the received order and construction of some alternative. The political dynamics that adhere to such a project give the president a decided advantage in controlling the meaning of his actions. With the received order in utter disrepute, the disruptions inherent in the exercise of presidential power can be sustained with little difficulty. Roosevelt's initial commitment—to restore in a new order "ancient" truths about American government that had been maligned in the recent course of national events—gave him an order-affirming message quite consistent with his order-shattering effects. Indeed, for Roosevelt, repudiation of the received order of things *was itself* a way of affirming the true order of things. This dovetailing of message and effect not only kept Roosevelt's leadership buoyant, it also liberated him from any specific commitment to a particular alternative. What actually emerged from the New Deal was, as we shall see later, only loosely related to what Roosevelt had proposed along the way, but by stiffening his repudiative stance to meet the resistance he encountered, Roosevelt was able to persevere through extraordinary twists and turns as master of the situation. In a sense, he was able to keep the ground clear of his detractors long enough for a new set of governing arrangements generally consonant with his preferences to take shape. Once this happened, the legitimacy of those new arrangements set anchor in his initial warrants for saving the government from bankruptcy and reclaiming the original conception of what American government was supposed to have been about all along.[14]

Now consider Lyndon Johnson. Johnson did not repudiate the preexisting regime or set out to replace it wholesale with another. Instead, he directed his great powers toward a purely constructive purpose: the rearticulation of the existing order at a higher level of achievement. He projected a place in history in which all the commitments of the current regime would be honored and all interests of significance to it served. Compelling as this conception was in the circumstances in which Johnson came to power, the maneuver contemplated is one that the American presidency is hard-pressed to sustain. As his warrants for action were wholly affirmative, Johnson found himself at cross purposes in exercising the powers of his office, for no sooner was the disruptive force of his program felt than he began to lose control over its meaning. To neutralize the destabilizing effects of innovation, Johnson needed to orchestrate the satisfaction of all commitments and interests. Thus, while moving ahead on long-heralded promises regarding civil rights, the containment of communism, and social welfare, he was also trying to assert near total control over each. As it turned out, the more he tried, the more his programmatic priorities became personalized; and the more personal his rendition of the received orthodoxy became, the more difficult it was for him to get the interests implicated in it to accept his package as a proper reading of their concerns. By this dynamic, the entire effort collapsed in on itself. As the President's hands-on manipulation of commitments began in fact to transform the regime he proposed to represent, the premises upon which he rested his case began to come under fire from the very interests he intended to serve. Johnson had no defense for the order-shattering effects of his actions, no response to those among the faithful who rejected his particular version of orthodoxy and charged him with betrayal, no alternative in the face of his schismatic effects but to step aside. The exercise of power left him the victim of his own policies, and turned one of the most robust moments in American history into one of the most tumultuous.

Roosevelt's order-shattering warrants had a reconstructive effect, galvanizing support for a new regime; Johnson's purely affirmative warrants imploded, shattering the regime upon which his claims to legitimacy rested. This reading of their experiences, preliminary as it is, squares in its basic outlines with similar cases found throughout presidential history. Time and again the lesson is the same: *the power to recreate order hinges on the authority to repudiate it.* The recurrent patterns of presidential politics are anchored in this paradox. The authority to repudiate is the most formidable of all political resources for the exercise of leadership. Without it, a president will have difficulty keeping the political impact of the exercise of power aligned with his own definition of the moment at hand; with it, he can undergird in a coherent public discourse the most expansive and extensive disruptions of the polity. The authority to repudiate fuses language and action, intention and effect, in the reconstruction of political order.

For better or worse, then, the American presidency has proven itself most effective politically as an instrument of negation. Too blunt in its disruptive effects to build securely on what has come before, it has functioned best when it has been directed toward dislodging established elites, destroying the institutional arrangements that support them, and clearing the way for something entirely new. Our attention to nuances of strategy and the subtleties of skill misses this. The presidency is a battering ram, and the presidents who have succeeded most magnificently in political leadership are those who have been best situated to use it forthrightly as such.

What then are the implications of the priority of authority in the politics of leadership? First, though presidential power is a battering ram, embracing it forthrightly as such is not entirely a free choice. Claims to authority in the exercise of this power are embedded in political context. Though the "great communicators" of presidential history have all been great repudiators, not all presidents can be great repudiators. Lyndon Johnson was no more free to renounce his inheritance wholesale than he was to choose to be someone else leading at a different time. Lacking the authority to repudiate, his leadership project was far more dependent on subtlety, nuance, management, and manipulation than his own blunt actions could support.

Second, the priority of authority suggests that the political effects of presidential action will be bound only loosely to the president's success in getting his own proposals implemented. Franklin Roosevelt was repeatedly rebuffed on his major policy initiatives. His initial program for economic recovery was declared unconstitutional by the Supreme Court, and the great initiatives of his second term—Court-packing, executive reorganization, and party reconstruction—all backfired badly. In light of this repeated humiliation on matters of personal initiative, it is a wonder that Roosevelt did not lose control of the situation entirely, let alone that he stands out as the most successful president of the twentieth century. Roosevelt succeeded despite stunning defeats because he remained throughout the sponsor of an alternative to a bankrupt past. Stiffening his repudiative posture throughout his first term, he forced even those who would frustrate him personally to accept the new state of affairs that was being constructed more systemically under his charge. Conversely, Johnson failed despite stunning victories because he could not distance himself from the regime his actions were transforming. Lacking the authority to repudiate any interest of significance, he deployed his powers as strategically as he could to serve all and watched in horror as each in turn repudiated him.

Finally, there is the matter of personality. To the extent that contextually embedded claims to authority are shown time and again to shape the strategies presidents deploy in the exercise of their powers, what we often take to be matters of personal character will turn out to reflect characteristics of the office under different circumstances. So convinced are we of Lyndon Johnson's perversity that we have tended to ignore his own insights into the perversity of the situation he was charged to control. Johnson did not choose the wrong strategy for exercising power; he chose the strategy that fit the best case he had for political action at that moment. When we speak about the "tragedy of Lyndon Johnson," we are speaking in the main about what happens to a president who exercises great powers without warrants for projecting his own independent course. The same is true for the opposite view, reflected in the cult of personality that has come to surround the leadership of Franklin Roosevelt. When we speak of Roosevelt as a charismatic leader we are speaking in the main about a historically contingent "charisma of office," a contextual consistency in the order-shattering, order-affirming, and order-creating impulses of presidential action.[15] Roosevelt succeeded magnificently, but it does not follow that if we could just get more people like Roosevelt into the office, the problems and dangers the presidency poses would recede.

Secular Trends

The argument as it has unfolded thus far is offered as a counterweight to any simple presumptions about free agency and self-determination that might inform current understandings of presidential leadership. It is not my purpose to absolve presidents of personal responsibility for their actions or for that matter to deny any credit due them. On the other hand, the comparison just sketched cuts equally against the old proposition that the office is as "big" (or as great) as the person who holds it and the more modern idea that the office stifles self-expression and precludes success. My point is that the test of leadership varies widely from one incumbent to the next and that what presidents do to American politics turns in large measure on which test they are taking.[16]

The fact that the political system does not take a more exact measure of the capacities of the individuals we elect—of their individual talents, their political skills, their personal characters—has led to all sorts of distortions in our politics. Some leaders have been prompted to undertake self-defeating projects, tying themselves in knots to present their actions as technically consistent with their warrants; others, who found the game rigged in their favor, have wielded an authority quite independent of the merits of their proposals. This is disturbing, and it raises another set of questions about the politics presidents make: How have the different tests changed over the course of American history? What are the prospects for escaping these primordial logics of presidential action and political change?

The picture we have drawn to this point shows a blunt, disruptive force with effects that vary through shifting structures of political authority. It speaks to persistent and recurrent features of the politics presidents make, prompting us to seek references in earlier periods for the leadership struggles of Roosevelt and Johnson. Left out of this picture are the secular or emergent developments that have affected the organization and scope of presidential power. The resources available to presidents in getting things done have changed dramatically over the course of American history. Presidents in later periods exercise more power with more independence than their earlier counterparts, and these differences render the similarities notable across periods something more akin to family resemblances.

To keep these dimensions of time in presidential politics distinct, I will call the historical medium through which authority structures have recurred *political time* and the historical medium through which power structures have evolved *secular time*.[17] Presidential leadership in political time will refer to the various relationships incumbents project between previously established commitments of ideology and interest and their own actions in the moment at hand. Presidential leadership in secular time will refer to the progressive development of the institutional resources and governing responsibilities of the executive office and thus to the repertoire of powers the presidents of a particular period have at their disposal to realize their preferences in action. The distinction will prove useful in keeping track of how the politics of leadership gets reshaped in the interaction of these structures. The object ultimately is to understand how contingent structures of authority have affected the reorganization of presidential power, and how changes in the organization of presidential power have affected the political range of different claims to authority. We will observe a subtle secular reshaping of the leadership struggles that recur in political time, a reshaping that has gradually grown more pervasive in its significance.

An elaboration of these emergent structures of power and recurrent structures of authority follows in Chapter 3. To anticipate how they bear on each other, we need only observe that the "rise" of the presidency to ever greater prominence as an instrument of American government parallels the development of a political universe which is in every way more fully organized and more densely inhabited. It is not just that the presidency has gradually become more powerful and independent over the course of American history, but that the institutions and interests surrounding it have as well.

At every stage in the development of the executive office, a progressive proliferation of organized interests and independent authorities has redounded to greater reliance on the president for central management and coordination of the affairs of state. The effect of this institutional thickening on the politics of leadership has been to make those with weak authority claims more pot⋯ and those with strong authority claims less so. The political discr⋯ ⋯ing responsibility that have gradually accrued to the p⋯ ⋯ne have bolstered those incumbents wh⋯ ⋯ight in earlier times have stymied th⋯ ⋯t action quite quickly. Conversely, the ⋯ ⋯itutional universe of presidential actio⋯ ⋯ents who hold the most compelling w⋯ ⋯making it possible for other actors to ⋯ ⋯ce to their will. The "rise" of the presi⋯ ⋯flatten out differences in the potential ⋯ ⋯s.

The implications of this are far-r⋯ ⋯is study will be devoted to exploring them. This flattening o⋯ ⋯cal prospects might not be so problematic if new warrants for leadership could be generated to take it into account. The central problem today, I shall argue, is not to be found in modern conditions per se but in the classic claims of leadership authority that have endured despite their growing irrelevance. We are witness to a mounting confusion and progressive distortion of political purposes engendered by our own attraction to the very oldest warrants for the exercise of presidential power.

When we encounter the Roosevelt-Johnson comparison again in Chapter 7, we will be fully attuned to the mix of historical patterns at issue in it, and the significance of each effort will be correspondingly altered. There we see the extent to which primordial patterns in leadership have been weakened and frayed by modernizing currents as well as the extent to which they have endured despite the counterforces at work. At the end of this study, when I speculate about the prospects for escaping the traditional and recurrent logics of presidential leadership in political time, the paradox implicit in the secular trends observed will come to bear most directly: *As the power of all presidents to get things done has expanded, the authority of those best situated to re-produce political order has constricted.* The "rise" of the presidency as an instrument of government has delimited its political range as an instrument of reconstruction.

We shall see that no president had a freer hand in constructing a new political order than the first great repudiator, Thomas Jefferson. Jefferson encountered only scattershot opposition to his course down to the very last weeks of his eighth year in office. By the time of the second great repudiator, Andrew Jackson, assaulting the old way of doing things had a very different effect, catalyzing the organization of a permanent opposition to the new course. Jackson broke with the received order and bolstered the institutional foundations of presidential power, but in the process he redivided the nation politically into two durable and highly competitive camps. By the time of Franklin Roosevelt, the president's own proposals for reconstruction were being rejected outright. The New Deal recast the political system and bolstered the institutional foundations of presidential power once again, but the new order was constructed by institutional actors who, even when they acted under the auspices of Roosevelt's reconstructive authority, thwarted his own designs. In the case of the most recent leader in this mold, Ronald Reagan, reconstruction was, relatively speaking, more rhetorical than institutional. The most successful president since Roosevelt at breaking with the past, Reagan's achievement compares with Roosevelt's as a further historical delimitation of what has traditionally been the most potent of all leadership postures.

Structure and Action

FAITH in the creative potential of men in office holds center stage in American constitutional design, and there it wrestles with fear of the degenerative propensities of republican institutions. The contest is especially intense in the presidency. A bold celebration of the energy and independence of a unitary executive, the office charges its incumbents with great responsibility for political leadership and then circumscribes them in a host of contrivances designed to control ambition and stave off the dread forces of disruption. Provisions for vigorous action press uncertainly against provisions for stabilizing the politics of the republic.

The dismal cycle of classical republican politics may have been controlled by this design, but it was not stopped. In practice, the cycle became institutionalized. Presidential leadership has worked to pull the federal government ever more deeply into crises of legitimacy before suddenly swinging things around in one spectacular display of its regenerative potential. A few incumbents, thrust to the commanding heights of political authority, have found new ways to order the politics of the republic and release the powers of the government; but they have done so by building personal parties and shattering the politics of the past, actions the Constitution originally was supposed to guard against. Moreover, each of these great political leaders—Jefferson, Jackson, Lincoln, Franklin Roosevelt, and Reagan—passed on a newly circumscribed regime, so tenacious as to implicate their successors in another cycle of gradually accelerating political decay.

The few who have succeeded so magnificently are often held up to us as exemplars of how the American political system can be made to work. Their leadership serves as a standing vindication of the possibilities open to all, and as such, they set the standards against which the efforts of the others are judged. But even if we grant that these were the right men in the right place at the right time, we might still wonder whether they really made the system work better than the others and whether our celebration of their achievements has not obscured a more disturbing reality in the operations of American government and politics. These presidents did not resolve the tension built into the relationship between the presidency and the larger political system. They did not reconcile the conflicting values of order and energy, stability and initiative, continuity and creativity. On the contrary, their leadership fused energy, initiative, and creativity in the executive only because it came upon the eclipse of stability, the suspension of continuity, and the collapse of order. These presidents soared to commanding heights not by making the system work but by building new systems, some might say entirely new understandings of constitutional government itself, and then saddling their successors with the problem of workability.

The question then is not who has made the Constitution work, but how has it worked in circumstances variously configured? This chapter details what appear to me the most salient configurations. It distinguishes four structures of presidential authority that have recurred with some frequency over the course of American history and also four structures of presidential power as these have evolved over time. These typologies will guide our exploration of the relationship between structure and agency—between political context and the efficacy of presidential action—in all its dimensions. First, we will see how the various structures of authority have informed the formulation and political impact of the leadership projects presidents undertake. Second, we will observe how these projects have interacted with one another in sequence to shape and drive cycles of political change. Finally, we will turn to the various phases in the evolution of presidential power and consider how the growing prominence of the presidency as a governing institution has recast the age-old patterns of breakthrough and breakdown.

Recurrent Structures of Political Authority

A president's political authority turns on his identity vis-à-vis the established regime; warrants for exercising the powers of the office vary depending on the incumbent's political relationship to the commitments of ideology and interest embodied in preexisting institutional arrangements. Presidents attempt to build all sorts of nuance and subtlety into this relationship, but stripped to essentials, it comes in two forms: opposed and affiliated. Leaders either come to power from the opposition to the pre-established regime, or they come to power affiliated with its basic commitments. Corresponding to these two identities are the two generic projects for political action: the leadership project of the opposition leader is to challenge the received agenda, perhaps to displace it completely with another; the leadership project of the affiliated leader is to continue, perhaps to complete, the work on that agenda.

Opposition or affiliation points up some qualitative differences at work in the political dynamics of presidential leadership. Of the fourteen presidents who have been elected twice, only four—Madison, Monroe, Grant, and McKinley—were affiliated leaders.[1] As Madison and Monroe predate the rise of a competitive party alternative and Grant gained reelection with a significant portion of his opposition under force of arms, there would seem to be even less to this list than first meets the eye. If we alter the question a bit, the facts are more striking still. The seven elected presidents who voluntarily withdrew from reelection campaigns were *all* affiliated leaders: Polk, Buchanan, Hayes, Theodore Roosevelt, Coolidge, Truman, and Lyndon Johnson.

The reason affiliated leadership is less privileged, or harder to sustain, than opposition leadership has been touched on already. The office these leaders hold calls forth independent action, disruptive of previously established political and institutional arrangements, and it demands that each incumbent establish legitimacy anew on his own terms. As the affiliated leader is beholden to received arrangements in a way that the opposition leader is not, he has more difficulty maintaining warrants for the choices he makes and the priorities he sets for himself. The opposition leader comes to power with a measure of independence from established commitments and can more easily justify the disruptions that attend the exercise of power.

Opposition or affiliation, and their attendant leadership projects—repudiation or completion—set basic variations in the politics presidents make, but they do not tell us nearly enough. Indeed, the wide range of experience encompassed by the presidents who fall into each category threatens to obscure the significance of the differences just noted. Franklin Roosevelt and Richard Nixon were both opposition leaders; Theodore Roosevelt and Herbert Hoover, both affiliated leaders. For a more discriminating view, we need to look more closely at the opportunities history presents for acting on these identities and implementing these projects.

Leadership opportunities hinge on whether the governing commitments embodied in previously established institutional arrangements are resilient or vulnerable. Do those commitments claim formidable political, organizational, and ideological support? Do they offer credible solutions or guides to solutions to the problems of the day? Or have they in the course of events become open to attack as failed and irrelevant responses to the nation's problems? Have the old solutions themselves become the problem? The more resilient received commitments are, the more authoritative the affiliated leader will be in his determination to continue or complete the work, and the more problematic the determination of opposition leaders to reverse course and challenge basic governing arrangements. Conversely, the more vulnerable received commitments are, the more authoritative the opposition leader will be in his determination to displace basic governing arrangements, and the more problematic the determination of the affiliated leader to continue.

Cross-tabulating these generic considerations of political identity and political opportunity yields a typology of four structures of presidential authority (see table 1). In each cell of this typology, the president faces a different problem of historical legitimation, and the politics presidents make is different in each case.[2]

The politics of reconstruction. In the first cell of the typology, the president heralds from the opposition to the previously established regime, and pre-established commitments of ideology and interest have, in the course of events, become vulnerable to direct repudiation as failed or irrelevant responses to the problems of the day. Thomas Jefferson, Andrew Jackson, Abraham Lincoln, and Franklin Roosevelt all came to power in this kind of situation, and while it is difficult to imagine a

Table 1 Recurrent Structures of Presidential Authority

Previously established commitments	*President's political identity*	
	Opposed	Affiliated
Vulnerable	Politics of reconstruction	Politics of disjunction
Resilient	Politics of preemption	Politics of articulation

more disparate group of personalities, it is evident that these men shared the most promising of all situations for the exercise of political leadership. These presidents constituted a politics of reconstruction. Their initial election thrust them into a kind of political interregnum beyond all semblance of legitimate political order. Opposition to the old regime held sway in the Congress as well as the presidency, and though the election returns did not convey any clear message as to what exactly should be done, they did reflect a general political consensus that something fundamental had gone wrong in the high affairs of state.

A great opportunity for presidential action was harnessed at these moments to an expansive authority to repudiate the established governing formulas. These presidents each set out to retrieve from a far distant, even mythic, past fundamental values that they claimed had been lost in the indulgences of the received order. In this way, the order-shattering and order-affirming impulses of the presidency in politics became mutually reinforcing. As the president's initial political warrants dovetailed with the inherently disruptive exercise of presidential powers, the interplay of power and authority generated its own supports for independent action. The order-creating capacities of the presidency were realized full vent in a wholesale reconstruction of the standards of legitimate national government.

Presidents stand preeminent in American politics when government has been most thoroughly discredited, and when political resistance to the presidency is weakest, presidents tend to remake the government wholesale. It is worth noting, however, that the commanding authority presidents wield at these moments does not automatically translate into more effective solutions to the substantive problems that gave rise to the nationwide crisis of legitimacy in the first place. Jefferson's response to the international problems that had plagued the nation over the 1790s proved to be a national disaster itself. Jackson's response to the economic grievances that had been festering since the Panic of 1819 prompted a panic of its own in 1833, and if his policies did not actually cause the great depression of 1837, they did little to stave off its portents. Lincoln's response to the sectional crisis of the 1850s plunged the nation into a civil war, and Roosevelt's New Deal failed to pull the nation out of the Great Depression. The fact that these presidents were not especially adept at solving the nation's problems only accents the rather sobering point that presidents freed from any connection to the politics of the past have not needed to solve these problems. What these presidents did, and what their predecessors could not do, was to reformulate the nation's political agenda altogether, to galvanize support for the release of governmental power on new terms, and to move the nation past the old problems, eyeing a different set of possibilities altogether. With old governing alliances in disarray and the new amalgam of interests thrust fresh into governmental institutions still insecure, these presidents recaptured the authority of being first, and with it a rare opportunity to recast the foundations of American government and politics.

Looking more closely at what reconstruction has entailed gives us some indication of what it takes for a president to fashion a place in history roughly on his own terms and why presidents in other situations tend to fall short. As each of these presidencies attests, reconstructing political order is a process that joins party building to an assault on the residual institutional infrastructure of the old order. These presidents were all great party leaders, but, more importantly, each stood apart from the previously established parties and appealed to the interests of a rather inchoate opposition movement to forge an entirely new one. Typically these party-building efforts are spurred on by challenges launched against the president's reconstructive ambitions through the residual institutional support left over from the politics of the past. As the president's authority to repudiate is put to the test within the government itself, the consolidation of a political coalition to support his reconstruction becomes more imperative.

These counteroffensives against reconstruction have grown progressively more formidable over the course of American political development, and the choices they have posed between capitulation or radicalization of the reform program have become ever more momentous. Only when the institutions supporting hostile interests capitulate—and the outcome of these battles even in these most fortuitous of circumstances are by no means preordained—is the dominant position of the new governing coalition secured and the politics of the past forever relegated to the realm of discredited history. Reconstructive presidents have been drawn in this way into court battles, a "Bank War," and a real civil war, and through these struggles they have penetrated to the deepest questions of governmental design and of the proper relations between state and society. By shattering the politics of the past, orchestrating the establishment of a new coalition, and enshrining their commitments as the restoration of original values, they have reset the very terms and conditions of constitutional government.

The politics of disjunction. The great irony of reconstructive leadership—that the only presidents who can effectively fuse power and authority in the reproduction of political order are those who come to office beyond all semblance of political order—is rather grimly manifested in the difficulties leaders in all other situations have had in trying to assert authority over their moments in history and refashion legitimacy on their own terms. One step back from greatness lies the very definition of the impossible leadership situation: a president affiliated with a set of established commitments that have in the course of events been called into question as failed or irrelevant responses to the problems of the day. The president in this situation constitutes a politics of disjunction. The instinctive political stance of the establishment affiliate—to affirm and continue the work of the past—becomes at these moments a threat to the vitality, if not survival, of the nation, and leadership collapses upon a dismal choice. To affirm established commitments is to stigmatize oneself as a symptom of the nation's problems and the premier symbol of systemic political failure; to repudiate them is to become isolated from one's most natural political allies and to be rendered impotent.

Presidents in this situation—John Adams, John Quincy Adams, Franklin Pierce, James Buchanan, Herbert Hoover, and Jimmy Carter are the prime examples—are often singled out as political incompetents.[3] But treated as a group, their shared situation tells us a lot about the structured political capacities and effects of institutional action. When the president can neither affirm the integrity of governmental commitments nor forthrightly repudiate them, his authority to control the political definition of the moment is completely eclipsed, and he is consumed by a problem that is really prerequisite to leadership, that of establishing any credibility at all. Radically altered conditions of governance leave the regime affiliate with little beyond his own personal dedication and his keen appreciation of the complexity of the nation's problems to justify his tenure. But when deep comprehension of the nation's difficulties and personal dedication to resolve them are elevated above all else as a premise for action, the president gets submerged in the problems he is addressing and finds himself an easy caricature of all that has gone wrong. Anything short of a miraculous solution will pass to the opposition effective control over the political definition of the situation.

Saddled with a suddenly vulnerable regime, these presidents have less authority than any others over the terms of national political debate, and they are the most severely handicapped in penetrating extant governmental arrangements. But that does not mean that they don't do anything of significance. Venting the impulse to lead at these moments has momentous political consequences. Most obviously, by their very frustrations these affiliates stigmatize the current situation as wholly untenable. Through their hapless struggles for credibility, they become the foils for reconstructive leadership, the indispensable premise upon which traditional regime opponents generate the authority to repudiate the establishment wholesale.

Beyond that, we also need to consider the exercise of power in these circumstances. The actions these presidents take on their own behalf are as disruptive of the status quo ante as any. One of the great ironies of the politics of disjunction is that presidents who come to office in these sorts of situations tend to have only the most tenuous relationship to the establishments they represent. Long-festering problems within the regime tend to throw up leaders only nominally affiliated with it, and in their efforts to address the issues of the day, these affiliates often press major departures of their own from the standard formulas and priorities set in the old agenda. The political impact of these departures is disjunctive: they sever the political moorings of the old regime and cast it adrift without anchor or orientation.

Whatever their merits, these departures suffer from a fatal flaw. They are hopelessly compromised by the rarefied claims these presidents have to justify them. The president can, of course, assert that his program is addressed to extraordinary circumstances and argue that it is at least technically consistent with his political responsibilities to the regime he represents. In fact, the reification of technique as the central justification for political action—the elevation of proper administrative methods into a political cause and the claim of special insight into the mechanics of government—is a hallmark of the politics of disjunction. But if this is the best case in the circumstances for a major policy departure, it is not for that a strong case. The technical standard of propriety immediately runs up against the incessant demands of an outraged establishment and the broadside assaults of an emboldened opposition.

Wholly inadequate to sustaining the legitimacy of innovation on its own accord, the reification of technique ushers in a nationwide crisis of legitimacy and opens the door to something far more radically different.

The politics of articulation. Beyond the extremes of a wholesale political reconstruction and a systemic political disjunction lie all those moments in political time when established commitments of ideology and interest are relatively resilient, providing solutions, or legitimate guides to solutions, to the governing problems of the day. To dismiss presidents in such situations as presiding over a stable, "normal" period of politics-as-usual is a mistake. The ambitions of opposition leaders and affiliated leaders operate continuously as formidable forces pressing the transformation of the American political landscape.

Consider the presidents affiliated with a resilient set of governmental commitments. More presidents fit this description than any other. They are the orthodox-innovators, and they constitute what we might call a politics of articulation. Orthodox-innovators stand in national politics as ministers to the faithful. They galvanize political action with promises to continue the good work of the past and demonstrate the vitality of the established order in changing times. As the font of political orthodoxy, their office is a sacred trust full of obligations to uphold the gospel and deliver the expected services in the prescribed manner.

The object of a politics of articulation is to fit the existing parts of the regime together in a new and more relevant way. The characteristic challenge is to mitigate or assuage the factional ruptures within the ranks of the establishment that will inevitably accompany even the most orthodox of innovations and agenda adaptations. The characteristic effect is that the president's particular rendition of orthodoxy sparks debilitating debate over the true meaning of the faith. The challenge and the attendant effect are repeated so often in presidential history as to highlight the inherent difficulty of making the disruptive effects of presidential action appear an affirmation of established formulas and priorities. There is simply no clear way to exercise presidential power without projecting an alternative political formation, nor to sustain change as a mere rearticulation of the established course at a higher level of achievement.

Many of the presidents in this situation will inherit a politically potent agenda but find the exercise of power on its behalf constrained by partisan divisions within the government. Like "give 'em hell" Harry

Truman, these presidents shake things up largely by blasting away at the obstacles in the path to completing the work and exhorting their followers to continue the fight. They, however, are spared the traumas that attend full implementation of another round of transformative changes.[4] Others come to power at more robust moments in the nation's political history, moments when the regime stands omnipotent in government and politics, full of promises, and strategically poised on the threshold of fulfilling its vision. These I take to be the emblematic episodes in the politics of articulation. In these circumstances, we find the presidents with the most expansive opportunities to usher the nation into the promised land, and it is they who confront most directly the underlying problem of transforming a regime they came to power to celebrate.

These were the keynotes of leadership for James Monroe, James Polk, Theodore Roosevelt, and Lyndon Johnson.[5] Each had worked his way up through the ranks of an established regime. Each came to power in the wake of a strong reaffirmation of majority party government, and no extraordinary crises distracted them from the business of completing the agenda. Relative to the other affiliated leaders of their time, they could take the greatest leaps forward along the path already traced. Each of them seized that opportunity.

These presidents cast their leadership as wholly constructive rearticulations of the received orthodoxy; no one and nothing of significance was to be repudiated. In giving full vent to the thoroughly affirmative course, their impact on national politics proved to be as profound as that of the opposition leaders who have founded new political orders by repudiating past commitments outright. The nature of the impact, however, was quite different. The great repudiators came to power freed from received political commitments and governing formulas; these great regime boosters, on the other hand, celebrated received formulas in the exercise of their transformative powers, and prior commitments pressed in on them from all sides. While the great repudiators regenerated political order through an assault on the bankruptcy of the past, these orthodox-innovators had the paradoxical effect of imploding the political order they were trying to elaborate and pulling American politics into a sectarian tailspin. It is in these eras of majority-party government, when expansive possibilities for innovation exacerbate disagreements within the establishment and accelerate debates over the true meaning of orthodoxy, that the contradictions of completion as a leadership project and the dilemmas of affiliation as a presidential identity are most fully revealed. These leadership performances take on the attributes of classical tragedy. Acting on collectively generated premises and pursing purely constructive visions of change, these presidents rupture the political foundations on which the program and the vision both rest.

It is no coincidence that Polk, Roosevelt, and Johnson all decided not to stand for reelection. A genuine and deep-seated ambivalence about the impact of leadership is built into the position the orthodox-innovator holds in national politics. Abdication or political self-sacrifice is in a sense the ultimate resolution of the tension between a president's impulse to assert his own personal control over the moment at hand and his political affiliation with the politics of the past. Premature abdication is a way of reconciling the disruptive, order-shattering effects with purely affirmative warrants; the promise of an early departure is the ultimate profession of good faith. With this promise, the president offers irrefutable testimony that the exercise of power would not, or did not, indulge any personal conceit or ambition, that power would be, or was, exercised selflessly in genuine service to the regime. The ethic of collective or party responsibility, a conundrum that haunts all affiliated presidents, gains its most genuine endorsement, paradoxically, in voluntary withdrawal.

The politics of preemption. Finally, we come to opposition leaders in resilient regimes. This is the most curious of all leadership situations. It is the one most peculiar to the American constitutional system, and the one least susceptible to role ascription. Like all opposition leaders, these presidents have the freedom of their independence from established commitments, but unlike presidents in a politics of reconstruction, their repudiative authority is manifestly limited by the political, institutional, and ideological supports that the old establishment maintains. Intruding into an ongoing polity as an alien force, they interrupt a still vital political discourse and try to preempt its agenda by playing upon the political divisions within the establishment that affiliated presidents instinctively seek to assuage. Their programs are designed to aggravate interest cleavages and factional discontent within the dominant coalition, for therein lies the prospect of broadening their base of support and sharpening their departure from the received formulas. Opportunities for preemption are never difficult to find, but the political terrain to be negotiated is always treacherous. These presidents will in effect be probing for reconstructive possibilities without clear warrant for breaking cleanly with the past, and when they probe too deeply, they get caught in a showdown crisis of constitutional proportions.

A cluster of presidents in this situation—John Tyler, Andrew Johnson, Woodrow Wilson, and Richard Nixon—stand out for attention both for their aggressive employment of the powers of their office and for their wrenching political impacts. These incumbents are the wild cards of presidential history, and they are often singled out for flaws of character. To see them as a group, however, is to observe another structured implication of the impulse to lead in American government.

Note that our two groups of leaders in resilient regimes have met very different fates. As aggressive leaders in a politics of articulation tend to use voluntary withdrawal from politics as a way of dealing with their disruptive effects, aggressive leaders in a politics of preemption tend to get themselves impeached, de facto if not de jure, for theirs. John Tyler saw his cabinet resign in protest of his exercise of power, and when he persisted on his own course, he became the first president against whom bills of impeachment were drawn.[6] Andrew Johnson and Richard Nixon faced actual proceedings; Woodrow Wilson was stripped of leadership authority in the showdown vote of no confidence that ended the fight over the Treaty of Versailles. These sorts of convulsions are indicative of the underlying political dynamics. The hallmark of the opposition leader in a resilient regime is his independence from the stalwart opposition as well as the orthodox establishment. Indeed, without that independence it is difficult to see how such a leader could rise to the presidency in the first place. Tyler, Johnson, Wilson, and Nixon each used their independence to assault established coalitions directly and to attempt to build new, personal bases of political support outside of regular political alliances (often outside of institutional politics altogether). But their order-shattering portents overreached their repudiative authority. In venturing reconstructive challenges and mounting party-building threats, they in effect put the resilience of the establishment to the test and ultimately galvanized it into an order-affirming defense of the government as it was. Out to reset national politics and government on their own terms, these presidents provoked major constitutional crises over the legitimate exercise of presidential power, crises that temporarily warded off the portents of a political reconstruction with a convulsive campaign against executive usurpation.[7]

The contrast between our two types of opposition leaders is even more revealing. It suggests just how thin the line separating towering success from de facto impeachment has been. Indeed, the constitutional crises generated during a politics of preemption appear here to be but the short side of the new constitutional arrangements generated in a politics of reconstruction. Opposition leaders intent on the aggressive use of their political powers walk that line in testing the resilience of the institutional infrastructure of the old order. The irony is that the presidents we consider great affirmed the continuing possibilities for governing under the Constitution by shattering that infrastructure and putting in place a radically new understanding of constitutional government, while the presidents who tried and failed to do the same thing are considered personally deranged and brought down on charges of gross violations of constitutional stricture.

Three Hard Cases

Classification schemes can easily take on a life of their own. My purpose is not to force every president into one box or another. These types are significant because they have each been approximated with some frequency and because their respective political dynamics have repeatedly transformed American politics in a characteristic way. Distilling general propensities, they also allow us to specify divergences and to deepen our appreciation of the diversity of historical experience.

We will have occasion to explore shadings among these types and a historical reshaping of their boundaries especially as these have been informed by changes in the organization of presidential power itself. It is also worth emphasizing that while the recurrence of each type of politics confirms post hoc the significance of the basic variables set forth, a real contest was waged in each instance, and these variables were very much at issue in the struggles that ensued. At the margins (reconstruction appeared a near thing under Woodrow Wilson), the difference between a disastrous preemption and a masterful reconstruction will turn on the political and ideological support that establishment forces can muster under siege to fight back; their resilience is tested under the challenge itself. Similarly, the difference between a schismatic rearticulation of the old orthodoxy and a systemic political breakdown (or disjunction) will turn on the political and ideological support that opposition forces can muster in mounting a broadside challenge to the old regime. A regime is only as vulnerable as the political forces challenging it are robust.

A final caution follows. Presidents are the primary catalysts of change in this scheme, but they are not automatons, programmed to fulfill these logics in lockstep. They are, rather, willful agents, more or less inclined to test the limits of their power and to act on the political world according to their own beliefs, ambitions, and outlooks. To underscore this point, I would like to draw attention to the three cases that seem to me to cut most strongly against the logics specified in these different authority structures.

Dwight Eisenhower was an opposition leader in the terms set forth here, but he demonstrated extraordinary sensitivity to the resilience of the previously established regime. The Republican party took control of Congress as well as the presidency in 1953, and Eisenhower, we now know, was personally sympathetic to conservative Republican ideals. But the new president refused to take on New Deal liberalism or Fair Deal foreign policy directly, and he carefully held the right wing of his party, zealous in its opposition to both, at bay. Eisenhower proved a master at keeping his personal and partisan political priorities hidden. He led, his admirers now say, by indirection.[8]

As master of the art of not probing too deeply, Eisenhower is, perhaps, the most remarkable of the preemptive leaders. He did not reconstruct American politics wholesale, nor did he get impeached, either de facto or de jure, in an attempt. His was an opposition carefully tuned to its own limits. He successfully cultivated his own personal independence in politics by severely curtailing the disruptive uses of his powers. Eisenhower was content to prune the radical edge off New Deal liberalism. The keynotes of his "New Republicanism"—moderation, sensibility, and accommodation—gave the GOP a new political respectability, breaking its identification with Hoover and the Depression and extending its appeal into the urban South. The result, in turn, was a singularly personal achievement. Basking in a hazy reflection of the resilience of the Democrats' regime, Eisenhower maintained his own legitimacy, but the "New Republicanism," at least as he proposed it, faded quickly as a national political alternative upon his departure.[9]

Second, consider Calvin Coolidge, an affiliated leader in a relatively resilient regime. No president was more intent on affirming the received order and none has been more successful in doing just that. Coolidge's remarkable capacity to secure his legitimacy in the face of changing times is best evidenced by his steadfast defense of "stand pat" Republicanism against virtually all challenges. His success in easing the tension between political affiliation and presidential leadership rested on his astute perception that precious little needed to be done in the circumstances at hand to vindicate his moral and material commitments and sustain his leadership position. Coolidge's withdrawal from a renomination bid in 1928, curious both for his great prospects for winning and for the surprising weakness of those supporters who sought to draft him anyway, seems to confirm this. The president was said to have sensed changes afoot in the nation that would have created a situation into which he thought he would no longer fit.[10] Taking the opportunity to abdicate just at the moment when he would have had to confront change squarely was his final, and perhaps most brilliant, assertion of control over his place in history.

Coolidge presents to us the purest historical expression of orthodoxy as a premise for political leadership, and with it, a limiting case of inaction in office. It is no mere coincidence that the president who managed to do less than anyone else during almost six years in power did better than most affiliated leaders in maintaining his own credibility. But as the limiting case of passivity in the exercise of presidential power, Coolidge is doubly interesting. For even this most orthodox of leaders found that the configuration of political power he had inherited constrained his pursuit of a "stand pat" leadership project, and he too took up the task of changing the Republican regime in order to preserve its commitments on his own terms. First, of course, there was a shake-up in the top levels of government, prompted by the scandals of the Harding administration. Then came some even more noteworthy changes in relations between the national government and society at large and between the president and the party leaders in Congress. Specifically, Coolidge undercut the political influence of stalwart party leaders in the Senate. He remade the party in his own image by deliberately accelerating a move already under foot to turn the administration of the government and the Republican party itself over to conservatives drawn directly from the business community. In the process, he unwittingly opened new ground for maneuver within the Senate, which the midwestern "progressive bloc" filled with a vengeance. Ironically, then, as Coolidge brought stalwart Republican conservatism to its fullest expression in the federal government, he rendered the Republican national organization itself something of a hollow shell. When he voluntarily withdrew from pursuit of a second nomination for the presidency, he found, much to his own dismay, that there was nothing left to stop Herbert Hoover, that upstart and curiously extra-partisan engineer who had been Coolidge's nemesis within the government all along, from simply stepping into the void he left behind.[11]

Finally there is the anomaly of Grover Cleveland. Cleveland rode to victory in 1892 on the heels of a potentially significant electoral shift. The Democrats' first sweep of all the political branches of the national government since before the Civil War, this election contained strong hints of swelling agrarian discontent with the established order of things and opened a rare opportunity for an opposition leader willing to give voice to the discontent and press the reconstructive possibilities. This, however, Cleveland steadfastly refused to do. In fact, this opposition leader found himself strangely at odds with the burgeoning new opposition movement, and the upshot was the most perplexing leadership performance in presidential history. Instead of molding the opposition into an even more potent force for change and vindicating its legitimacy, Cleveland denied it. Instead of rallying the discontented with some semblance of a programmatic break from Republican policies, he splintered the disaffected into even more extreme factions. Instead of moving the Democratic party onto new and broader ground, he effectively scuttled it as a national political alternative and left in his wake a resurgence of Republican hegemony. Cleveland's refusal to exploit the reconstructive possibilities handed the Republican party a new lease on the federal government in the realignment of 1896.[12]

The Cleveland anomaly, and the curious realignment (reaffirming the previously dominant party's hegemony) that ensued, puts the significance of presidential agency in political change in the sharpest possible relief. It reminds us that while elections may be the mainsprings of political change, it is elites who do the changing. However favorable the circumstances, basic commitments of ideology and interest cannot be reconstructed if that runs against the basic commitments of the president himself. It seems especially significant in this regard that Cleveland's reconstructive moment came at the outset of his second term and that he is the only president whose second term was separated from his first by an intervening four years. Cleveland's first-term performance was not unlike Eisenhower's. He asserted his political independence as an opposition leader and played upon divisions within the still resilient establishment to champion some popular but moderate reforms. This success kept him at the head of the Democratic party through an electoral defeat in 1888 and landed him in the White House again eight years after his initial rise to power. When the same man, still disposed by belief and background to maneuver around the edges of the Republican establishment, entered the radically altered circumstances of a Republican electoral disaster and popular insurgency, he found himself face to face with incipient forces of reconstruction. In this context, his moderation isolated him politically on the side of reaction, and his principled resistance to forging anything fundamentally new devastated the party he presumed to represent.

We cannot fail to note that while each of these three cases defies a logic outlined in the typology, each is also marked by a relative reluctance to employ presidential power aggressively in the service of political innovation. In this sense, they may be read as exceptions in support of the more general rules I have posited. By their very caution in employing the transformative powers of the presidency, they serve indirectly to elaborate the dynamics of power and authority that underlie the more general propensities we have observed. As for what they say about the potential for sustaining personal legitimacy within different authority structures, the messages cut in different ways: Coolidge and Eisenhower suggest that knowing when not to do things can be instrumental in sustaining authority; Cleveland, that denying strong expectations for change can undermine authority. The most important thing about these cases, however, is that they are exceptional. For better or worse, we should expect that the presidency will be held by individuals out to test the limits of their transformative powers.

Presidential Leadership in Political Time

The conventional wisdom that presidents and the parties that elect them carry on a difficult relationship in American government finds strong confirmation in our review of the different political authority structures for presidential action. Presidents are not, nor have they ever been, very responsible as party leaders. The institutional imperatives of the presidency lie on the side of independent political action, and that independence drives a wedge between partisanship and presidential conceptions of political responsibility. The great party leaders in presidential history have brought new coalitions to power and used their offices to consolidate new organizations. The most faithful of partisans find party service a thankless task and, however unwittingly, work to undermine the organizations they presume to represent. Whether building new parties or undermining existing ones, presidential action in politics always moves against pre-established political and institutional bonds.

But our typology also suggests something about what we have had instead of responsible party leadership: that is, presidentially driven sequences of change encompassing the generation and degeneration of coalitional systems or partisan regimes. Presidents act on American politics through personal struggles to impose an authoritative definition on their respective historical situations. In so doing, they are continually undermining the status quo ante. American politics moves through episodes of regime articulation and regime preemption in which the leader's power to respond to new circumstances is seldom synchronized with his authority to control them. What our typology represents as four distinctly configured structures for presidential leadership appears historically as interactive changes moving through political time.

The interactive relationships among the cells of our typology might be viewed along two continua, one tracking the internal disintegration of the established regime, the other, the gestation of more formidable and radical opposition to it. As a rule, successive regime affiliates will send ever more serious sectarian schisms through the ranks. Affiliated leaders tie themselves in ever more complicated knots trying to control the transformative thrust of their innovations and reconcile the conflicts within the ranks, but their personal choices are too disruptive and their personal priorities too controversial for these purposes. Caught up in the contradictions of their position as representatives of an establishment, they progressively undermine it. Each time a regime affiliate comes to power and constitutes a politics of articulation, it becomes more difficult to hold the old coalition together and stave off the spectre of complete political breakdown. The more fragmented the political establishment becomes and the farther it gets from the historical circumstances of its founding, the more ideologically attenuated and politically shallow are the prospects for defending it and the more awkward is the job of its leading defender. As the discussion of the resurgence of Republicanism in the 1890s just indicated, this dynamic is not ironclad. Still, it has been repeated several times. We see it in the progressive fragmentation of the Jeffersonian regime under Madison,

Monroe, and John Quincy Adams; in the progressive fragmentation of the Jacksonian regime under Van Buren, Polk, Pierce, and Buchanan; and in the progressive fragmentation of the liberal regime under Truman, Kennedy-Johnson, and Carter.

Opposition movements, in turn, feed on the mounting difficulties of affiliated leaders, gradually fortifying themselves with a national mission to displace the old regime altogether. Leadership in successive episodes of preemption tends in this way to become increasingly potent in tapping reconstructive possibilities. Opposition leaders—with their propensities to challenge the legitimacy of the establishment, to exploit its sectarian divisions and factional disaffections, and to stigmatize its irrelevance in the face of changing national conditions—are able to mount leadership efforts that are ever more explicit in their critique and ever more attractive in holding out hope for a more effective alternative. This dynamic may be seen in the progressively more potent challenges mounted against the Jacksonian regime under Tyler, Taylor, and Lincoln; against the Republican regime under Johnson, Cleveland, Wilson, and Roosevelt; and against the liberal regime under Eisenhower, Nixon, and Reagan.

These broadly cast temporal dynamics encompass sequences of unspecified and unequal duration, and they make no assumptions about the periodicity of electoral politics. Indeed, when it comes to explaining how different presidents get into office we need only assume the obvious: that short-term influences and chance occurrences are pervasive in the ascendance of all incumbents, elected and unelected, affiliated or opposed.[13] The politics of leadership forms an essential counterpoint to shifts within the electorate in the explanation of political change. Presidents are the critical agents interpreting the meaning of elections and translating electoral opportunities into new forms of politics.

Integrating the general patterns of presidential leadership in political time yields cycles of breakthrough, breakup, and breakdown. Tenacious in decay, political regimes are driven by their own affiliates toward flash points where the leader, struggling under the burdens of a vulnerable set of commitments, finally loses all effective warrants for action and unwittingly makes himself the foil for a wrenching reconstruction. A great repudiator then resets the clock. When Abraham Lincoln invoked the spirit of Thomas Jefferson and Ronald Reagan quoted Franklin Roosevelt, they were appealing to political identities that have little to do with the party or substantive vision of the man they were claiming as a soulmate. They were rather calling attention to these parallel moments in political time, and invoking the names of historical counterparts with whom they shared a more basic leadership project.

We have yet to escape the circuit of political time, but in each successive cycle the roller coaster has taken a slightly different loop. The basic patterns are altered and the political range of presidential leadership in all its various modes reshaped. A final assessment of these patterns, not to say an assessment of any prospective escape from the logic of change they express, awaits consideration of the other major time line of change at work in presidential history, and for that we turn to take a closer look at the secular development of presidential power itself.

Emergent Structures of Political Power

While little has been written about the political structure of presidential authority, we know a lot about changes in the political foundations of presidential power. Different types of presidential politics have been distinguished according to the extra-constitutional organization of the office. These types periodize the distinctive political and institutional resources which the office routinely makes available to incumbents in the exercise of their powers. In doing so, they also illuminate its practical working relationships with the other branches and the standard operating procedures that define routine responsibilities and bind the government together. Taken separately, these constructs tell us how the national government operated at a particular stage in the nation's development; taken together, they reveal the development of the office as it has tracked secular changes in the nation more generally. This history is summarized in table 2.

Patrician politics. A patrician politics spans the late eighteenth and early nineteenth centuries. In this period, the presidency operated most directly through interpersonal relationships among elites in the governing community, and the incumbent's most important political resource was his personal reputation within the nation's relatively closed society of notables. Patrician governance openly eschewed partisanship and organized political opposition. Government was formally treated as a deliberative process aimed at distilling a consensus among the notables,

Table 2 Emergent Structures of Presidential Power

Mode of governmental operations	Period of prominence	Characteristic presidential resource	Typical presidential strategy
Patrician	1789–1832	Personal reputation among notables	Stand as national tribune above faction and interest
Partisan	1832–1900	Party organization, executive patronage	Manipulate distribution of executive patronage to party factions and local machines as the broker for the national coalition
Pluralist	1900–1972	Expanding executive establishment attending to newly nationalized interests and America's rise to world power	Bargain with leaders of all institutions and organized interests as the steward of national policymaking
Plebiscitary	1972–present	Independent political apparatus and mass communications technologies	Appeal for political support over the heads of Washington elites directly to the people at large

and presidents acted politically as republican tribunes representing the national interest from a position above factional conflict.[14]

Partisan politics.   A partisan politics spans the nineteenth century from about 1832 onwards, encompassing a vast expansion of the polity both geographically and demographically. In this period, the presidency attained an organized political foundation in a national coalition of local party machines. Interparty conflict was the premier organizing principle in governmental operations, and the presidents acted politically as unabashed representatives of their party organization. Their most important resources were the perquisites of the executive branch—offices and services—that they could deliver to their fellow partisans in exchange for support of administration policies.[15]

Pluralist politics.   A pluralist politics spans the twentieth century through the late 1960s, a period in which America rose to world power, the national economy became interdependent, and economic interests organized nationally. The presidency in this period gained new responsibilities for managing national affairs through an expanding bureaucratic establishment. The president emerged as the nation's leading policy-maker, the one who had to negotiate complex bargains over policy with institutional elites who controlled other, relatively autonomous, centers of political power in the expanding Washington establishment. The presidency extended its political reach through this negotiating process, becoming more directly involved in the work of bureaucracies and congressional committees and directly soliciting support from major client groups in the society at large.[16]

Plebiscitary politics.   A plebiscitary politics has taken hold over the last twenty years, a period distinguished by new tools of mass communication, by international interdependence, and by intensified international competition. The selection of presidential candidates has been transferred out of the party convention to candidate-centered primary campaigns; independent candidate-centered organizations elect the party nominee; and a White House-based public relations machine manages the incumbent's political strategy. As presidents have gained their own political apparatuses, congressional careers have grown more stable and secure, and Congress has become more insulated from traditional forms of presidential influence. Using mass communications technologies, presidents now cultivate a direct political relationship with the public at large. The plebiscitary presidents routinely appeal over the heads of the elites of the Washington establishment, hoping to use their public standing to compel that establishment into following their lead.[17]

Certain general developmental dynamics are immediately discernible across these structures: the polity directly engaged in a president's leadership project has expanded over time both geographically and demographically; the political foundations of presidential action have become increasingly independent over time, the incumbent drawing upon resources for action that are ever more directly tied to the executive branch itself; the institutional universe of political action has gotten thicker all around—at each stage in the development of the office there are more organizations and authorities to contend with, and they are all more firmly entrenched and independent. Beyond this, it is also evident how these changing structures of power reshape the contingencies of political authority. Changes in standard operating procedure alter expectations for all the administrations in which the new standards operate; a change in the presidency's role in government cannot but affect perceptions of what is appropriate behavior for all those who fill it.

While much of our understanding of presidential politics and history has been built on this general pattern of secular change, it supports widely divergent political assessments. Not long ago we caught the drift of these developments by celebrating the "rise" of the presidency. The institution appeared to be coming into its own as a more democratic instrument, and on that ground it appeared to be taking by right greater directive control over our government and politics. Now we tend to lament what is perceived as a progressive degradation of the office. Starting with the original position of disinterested statesmanship envisioned by the founders and extending through two middling positions of political brokership assumed by the presidents of the nineteenth and early twentieth centuries, we see the presidency now devolving into a spectacle of sheer demagoguery, the founders' worst fear.

This book offers a more discriminating view of the matter, and a different evaluation of the current drift of the politics of leadership. In place of these images of rise or decline, let us consider in more detail how secular developments in the organization of presidential power might affect the different leadership stances that presidents adopt in political time. On the one hand, as the organized foundations of presidential power become more independent and the governing responsibilities of the presidency expand, we should expect to see the bonds of political affiliation with any previously established regime grow weaker. Ties to the politics of the past will progressively loosen as the office itself grows stronger, for a stronger office will enhance the institutional capacities of all incumbents to take charge in their own right. This waning effect of affiliation as a determinant of the politics presidents make is not to be lamented, for inherent contradictions and distinct disadvantages adhere to affiliated leadership in the American constitutional system. Anything that eases the contortions that attend it should produce a less encumbered politics and a more equal and exact test of the capacities of the incumbents themselves—their political skills, governing talents, and personal character.

On the other hand, as the larger institutional universe for political action gets thicker, we should expect to see the reconstructive capacities of opposition leaders weaken also. More has to be changed to secure a break with the past, and those adversely affected by the changes will be able to put up more formidable resistance. At first thought this waning of possibilities for recasting things wholesale from above appears cause for concern. Reconstructive leadership has served periodically to regenerate the entire political system, and reconstructive leaders have been able to convey better than any others a sense of common purpose to the political community as a whole. And yet, as much can be said for not rigging the game in favor of some incumbents as can be said for not rigging it against others. There is, after all, no telling how wise the favored incumbent will be in the exercise of this most potent form of authority. Moreover, I would venture that there is something to be gained in finally setting aside the model of reconstructive politics at least as it is taken from the past. As a standard of evaluation, it is of dubious relevance to contemporary conditions, and by discarding it once and for all, we might finally turn to thinking about leadership possibilities in new ways. To the extent that successors might be less constrained by standards of legitimacy set by their predecessors and more constrained in undertaking anything foolish, a more equal test of ideas and skills in addressing the demands of the day might well be in the offing all around.

Assuming for the moment that political time is in fact waning, can we say anything about the nature of the politics that is emerging? A glance back at our four types of authority suggests the answer, and it casts an appropriately sober light on current prospects. The weakening of political affiliation as a premise for presidential action combined with the growing resilience of established institutions portends a gradual convergence toward opposition leadership in a relatively resilient regime. Any prospective escape from political time promises to be a kind of perpetual politics of preemption with all the possibilities and dangers that leadership stance has carried with it throughout American political history.

At present, this convergence is a mere intimation. The three most recent presidencies bear ample evidence of the still pervasive influence of political time on presidential leadership. Jimmy Carter's efforts to lead the liberal regime at a time when the old solutions no longer seemed to fit the nation's new problems plunged American politics into another crisis of legitimacy. Ronald Reagan, thrust to commanding heights by Carter's flounderings, wielded his repudiative authority to reconstruct the standards of legitimate political action. George Bush followed in turn with a classic politics of articulation, playing upon the disrepute of the old liberal solutions, trying by his own lights to adjust the new regime to changing times, blaming the liberals for not implementing his programs, and scrambling against charges of heresy from keepers of the Reagan faith.

In their systemic effects, Carter, Reagan, and Bush bear a striking likeness to John Quincy Adams, Andrew Jackson, and Martin Van Buren. It is only when we look closely at all the previous incarnations of these classic forms of presidential politics and add in the new power relations of the plebiscitary period that a more complicated and open-ended picture comes into view. The full significance of the politics made by Carter, Reagan, and Bush—complete with intimations of perpetual preemption as the model of the future—lies in the peculiar mix of structures in which each acted. Thus, the Carter difference in the politics of disjunction lay in his relative political independence from and personal resistance to the old liberal establishment. The Reagan difference in the politics of reconstruction lay in the frustrations he encountered in institutional recasting, in the resort to sleights of hand and clandestine tactics to promote his new agenda (as evidenced by his budget finaglings and the funneling of aid to the Contras), and in the telltale sign of slippage from reconstruction into constitutional crisis—the devastating Iran-Contra investigations. The Bush difference in the politics of articulation lay in the initial awkwardness of his rendition of the faithful son, in the abrupt midterm reversal of his foremost pledge of orthodoxy—"no new taxes"—and in the general confusion of his political premise for reelection.[18]

An Overview

In the next four chapters I trace these recurrent and emergent patterns in the politics presidents make. Leadership in the Jeffersonian, Jacksonian, Republican, and liberal regimes is taken up in turn. Note that each of these chapters is divided into three parts. The first part considers the president who constructed the regime; the second part, the ortho-dox-innovator who rearticulated the old formulas in the greatest leap forward on received commitments; the third part, the affiliate who had to cope with the collapse of the old formulas as solutions to the governing problems of the day. Thus the reader may choose to proceed either chapter by chapter (following political time through the break-throughs, breakups, and breakdowns that mark the generation and degeneration of each regime), or part by part (following secular time through the progressive reshaping of the politics of reconstruction, the politics of articulation, and the politics of disjunction respectively).

Chapter 8 brings these recurrent and emergent patterns up to date with a look at the Reagan and Bush years. As this study closes, the progressive distortions observed in three of our recurrent forms of political leadership point us toward the fourth as a working model of the shape of things to come. I will reserve for another time a full exploration of the alternative route to this emergent state of affairs that might be traced through the wild-card presidents of the past—John Tyler, Andrew Johnson, Woodrow Wilson, and Richard Nixon. More telling at this point than the portents of a future of perpetual preemption is the evidence of lingering differences that can only be appreciated with a long glance back at the historical alternatives. The truly remark-able thing about the politics of leadership in our time is that all the forms of authority that were with us at the start are still so much in evidence. If a new world is emerging upon the disintegration of these old forms, their distorted remnants are what figure most prominently in our own.

II

RECURRENT
AND
EMERGENT
PATTERNS

CHAPTER 4

Jeffersonian Leadership:
Patrician Prototypes

Q UESTIONS of authority held sway over leadership more thoroughly in the early years of the republic than at any later time. Reasons for this are not difficult to discern. The governing community was relatively intimate, and political relations within it were highly personalized. Institutions were still relatively inchoate, and the extra-constitutional resources they made available to presidents were still quite limited. In these circumstances, variations in the particular warrants incumbents brought to the exercise of power magnified differences in the politics they made. Thomas Jefferson shows us the reconstructive authority at its most expansive; James Monroe, the proprieties of orthodox-innovation at their most labored; John Quincy Adams, the crisis of legitimacy at its most paralyzing.

Part One:
Thomas Jefferson's Reconstruction

The Revolution of 1800 was as real a revolution in the
principles of our government as that of
1776 was in its form.

ALEXANDER HAMILTON, the father of the Federalist party, opted for
the part of the spoiler in the election of 1800 and renounced
Federalist President John Adams. Adams had betrayed Hamilton's
cause; he had scuttled the party program and purged Hamilton's friends
from power. Hamilton reckoned that if Federalism was ever to regain
its proper bearings, Adams would have to be defeated and the party
rebuilt in opposition to a Jefferson presidency. "If we must have an
enemy at the head of the government," he advised, "let it be one whom
we can oppose, and for whom we are not responsible, who will not
involve our party in the disgrace of his foolish and bad measures. Under
Adams, as under *Jefferson,* the government shall sink. The party in the
hands of whose chief it shall sink will sink with it—and the advantage
will all be on the side of his adversaries."[1]

Hamilton's speculation was not entirely off the mark; Jefferson did
bring the nation to the brink of disaster. What Hamilton failed to take
into account, however, was the kind of political authority that might
redound to an opposition leader in the wake of the rupture and disgrace
of the party that had for twelve years defined the nation's most basic
commitments of ideology and interest. The advantages Hamilton expected to flow from a change in the roles of the major players were
rendered moot by changes Jefferson was able to make in the play itself.
The Federalists did try to revive their prospects by challenging Jefferson's policies. Indeed, they would keep trying for the next fifteen years.
But they never escaped the trap which Jefferson set for them.[2] Changing
national politics altogether, Jefferson turned Hamilton's prediction on
its head and made good his own vow to "sink federalism into an abyss
from which there [could] be no resurrection."[3]

Later, in the full blush of the "era of good feeling," Jefferson dubbed this political achievement a "revolution."[4] The claim has become something of a fixation for analysts of his presidency, and by and large it has proven an unfortunate one. The statement is dismissed too easily; a rhetorical flight, its debunking does more to obscure than to clarify the political impact of Jefferson's leadership.[5] The two arguments that have been offered to counter his revolutionary pretensions are themselves suggestive of the problem. In one, we find all the evidence that the rhetoric of revolution was mere hyperbole, that Jefferson was really a conciliator who did more to accommodate the previous system and maintain order than to pursue his party's radical impulses. In the other, we find all the evidence that Jefferson was indeed a radical ideologue who set the government on a truly revolutionary course and willfully threw the nation into chaos before the foolishness of his ways caught up with him.[6] Each of these arguments carries just enough weight to suggest that neither quite captures the politics that Jefferson made.

The political significance of Jefferson's leadership is to be found neither in an assessment of how much more he might have tried to do nor in the failure of things that he did try. When we tally up all that was reaffirmed on one side and weigh it against all that was repudiated on the other, the critical point simply falls between the columns. Jefferson reconstructed the terms and conditions of legitimate national government. He was one of the few presidents so situated in political time as to be able to manipulate the order-shattering, order-affirming, and order-creating components of presidential action in a consistent and mutually reinforcing way. The politics he made is distinguished by the harmonious configuration of these elements in his initial leadership posture and by the transformative effect of elaborating them in tandem. Holding reconstructive warrants for the exercise of presidential power, Jefferson secured a political formation wholly his own and largely unanticipated in prior understandings of the contending alternatives. Indeed, whatever its policy shortfalls or political accommodations, this reconstruction was to prove the most personal and unencumbered of all.

Federalist Baggage, Republican Virtue

Jefferson was the only president of the early national period to stand apart from the chain of policies that immediately preceded his incumbency, and thus he was the only one who could turn the repudiative thrust of presidential action to creative advantage in national politics. Despite his service as Washington's secretary of state and Adams's vice president, Jefferson emerged early on as the leader of a burgeoning opposition movement. Indeed, the fragile national consensus that had been garnered to ratify the Constitution degenerated so quickly that to say that Jefferson, as president, had anything so formidable as an "old order" to repudiate seems to exaggerate Federalism's prior hold on the American polity.

The problem was that Alexander Hamilton, during his years as Washington's leading minister, had locked the fledgling constitutional experiment into a tightly closed and untenably narrow community of interests. From his position in the Treasury Department, he had championed a plan to fund the nation's debt in a way that would embrace debt service as a permanent feature of the American political economy. Hamilton ventured that financing this expansive obligation would underwrite the success of the new national government for it would require the enlistment of active support from the mercantile elite that managed the lifelines of the nation's economy. By joining the fortunes of the largest seaport traders to the proficient operation of the government, Hamilton made them informal partners in it. The linkage, however, bound both parties, and it formed a network of influence strongly reminiscent of the monarchy the nation had just rejected. By tying the international traders to the government, Hamilton tied the government to policies that would guarantee the prosperity of the traders in a steady flow of British imports. Whatever Hamilton's reputation as a great modernizer, his funding scheme placed a high premium on the stability of established economic relationships and implicitly accepted the subordinate role of the United States as an agricultural exporter dependent on British manufactures.[7]

Of course, a financial system that actually secured stability in economic and international relationships might have been more valuable to the young nation than one that surged headlong onto uncharted ground. But Hamilton's policies so directly assaulted revolutionary sensibilities as immediately to envelop the new government in a controversy over first principles. Not only did the funding scheme hold grave implications for American independence, but its drastic constriction of political alternatives weighed heavily against the legitimacy of the entire constitutional experiment. These difficulties came to light as early as

1793 when British interference with American shipping prompted Congress to consider commercial retaliation against its erstwhile foe. Instantly, the government-merchant-import trade connection was placed in jeopardy, and so too were the political foundations of the young regime. In an effort to protect his fiscal program, Hamilton took the lead against retaliation and supported a negotiated settlement. The humiliating treaty which John Jay brought back from London in 1795 formalized America's subordinate partnership in the British trading system, undercut America's growing interest in trade with the rest of the world, held the development of an American home market hostage to British manufacturing, and turned Britain's enemy, France, against what appeared to be a new British ally, if not a mere dependency.[8] Hamilton secured the treaty's approval, and in the process sparked a national political conflict over the federal government's most basic commitments of ideology and interest.[9]

When Jefferson took over leadership of the opposition to Federalism, he did not so much renounce the Federalists' overweening interpretation of national power as call for a more aggressive test of national capacities. His first instincts were to assert America's freedom to trade on the high seas, to explore the potential of employing economic sanctions to protect American independence, and to rally support for the development of a home market of "arts, manufactures and population" that might eventually relieve American agriculture of its dependence on the "councils and conduct" of foreign powers.[10] But Jefferson failed to carry the day with Washington, and he had to calculate his political strategy accordingly. Realizing how potent the political opposition to the policies of Hamilton had become, Jefferson also sensed the difficulty of trying to reverse them. Writing to his chief political lieutenant, James Madison, he mounted a cogent case for the election of John Adams. The patrician mores of the day dictated deference to a senior, and repairing to the rules of gentlemanly conduct made particularly good political sense at this time. As no one would be able to challenge Washington's administration directly, there was little advantage to be had in the political situation likely to face his successor. "The President," he wrote of Washington, "is fortunate to get off just as the bubble is bursting, leaving others to hold the bag . . . As his departure will mark the moment when the difficulties begin to work, you will see that they will be ascribed to the new administration."[11]

Jefferson's prediction that the second president would have a difficult time establishing an administration on his own terms turned out to be prophetic.[12] John Adams also abhorred British domination, and he too was skeptical of Hamilton's economics; but he also abhorred the excesses of the French Revolution and feared the Republican opposition's sympathies for France. Fiercely independent, he was drawn nonetheless into the vortex of this conflict, there to propel a major political disjunction.

Privately, Adams decried the "ferment" that had come to cloud perceptions of the true interests of the nation; his personal letters scolded the American people to "awake out of their golden dreams, and consider where they are, and what they are about."[13] As a practical matter, however, he lacked the political authority to dispel popular illusions; and, worse, what authority he did have hinged on perpetuating them, at least for the time being. An overture of accommodation with Jefferson in the formative stages of the new administration was refused (as the runner-up in the electoral college tally, Jefferson had become vice president), and this confirmed to Adams the dependence of his presidency on upholding his predecessor's commitments.[14] His first fateful decision, to take the personnel of Washington's administration as his own, was a ringing affirmation of political continuity, one that tied his administration to the policies of the past, bolstered his alliance with the Hamiltonians, and acknowledged that the Jay Treaty had effectively eliminated any independent ground in national politics.[15] "I knew if I removed any one of them," he later wrote of Washington's ministers, "it would turn the world upside down."[16]

Adams's admirers are quick to point out that he crafted his role as a fellow traveler in High Federalist circles with subtlety and skill, but the fact remains that this alliance vastly expanded an already vulnerable set of governmental commitments and sorely compromised Adams's efforts to assert his independence later. As the treaty with Britain propelled the nation into a confrontation with France, Adams found himself accepting Hamilton-inspired war measures that went far beyond his own proclivities for a maritime defense. Repressive laws against aliens and government critics and an expensive new land army left him deeply implicated in High Federalist designs. By the end of 1798, his administrationwas poised for a forcible elimination of the domestic opposition and for a military alliance with Britain that would broaden the French conflict into a war of conquest against Spanish territory in the Western

Hemisphere. Adams did not fail to perceive this "profound and artful plot hatching in England, France, Spain, and North and South America to draw [him] into a decided instead of a *quasi war* and a perpetual alliance with Great Britain."[17] Nor did he miss the growing portents of a civil war at home.[18] The government and the nation were unravelling before his eyes.

Though wary of his nominal friends, Adams fell victim to their conspiracies. All along, his cabinet had been taking instructions directly from Hamilton, then a private citizen in New York. Under Hamilton's direction and against the President's explicit wishes, the leading ministers plotted to promote their real leader to effective command of the new army. They traveled to Mount Vernon to importune Washington, acknowledged by all to be indispensable as the formal if largely symbolic commander of such a force, to demand that Hamilton be named first lieutenant.[19] Washington's intervention in this matter on Hamilton's behalf shows the extent to which he remained the final source of authority even after he left office and just how far authority had become detached from the formal structure of the government. Adams capitulated to Washington's demand, but the significance of Hamilton's behind-the-scenes caper did not escape him. "I have not been so blind," he protested to a Federalist senator, as not to see the "effort among those who call themselves the friends of the government to annihilate the essential powers given to the president." Adams's grip on his office had become doubtful. "I was no more at liberty than a man in prison chained to the floor and bound hand and foot."[20]

To regain control, Adams had to move decisively against the political foundations on which his administration had been built.[21] Announcing in February of 1799 that he intended to press for peace with France, he reversed his cabinet's consensus, broke openly with the Hamiltonians, and wrenched the nation away from world war and domestic chaos. When the cabinet conspired again to scuttle his peace mission and preserve the party's war program, Adams purged it. This great reversal of party and policy, coming as it did at one of the most desperate moments in the nation's history, offers a first glimpse at the difficulties even nominally affiliated leaders have in accounting for the order-shattering impact of independent action. Adams's final assertion of independence may have saved the nation from certain disaster, but it failed to save him from political disgrace. When push came to shove and Adams seized control in his own right, his own compatriots charged him with betrayal, and he went to the nation having repudiated the very system he seemed to represent.

As Adams saw it, the Federalist party self-destructed: "The party committed suicide. They killed themselves and the national President . . . at one shot, and then as foolishly or maliciously indicted me for the murder."[22] Be that as it may, the indictment of Federalism proceeded on Adams's own actions, and from his initial alliance with the Hamiltonians to his final reckoning with the impossible breach that had developed between them and the nation, he was inextricably tangled up in their fate. When, in the first part of his administration, Adams brought the strong arm of the government down on American citizens, he made the Federalist party as vulnerable for its deployment of national power as it had been under Washington for holding national power hostage to the British trading system. During the French crisis, the federal army, the federal tax collector, and the federal judicial system were all pitted against the autonomy of the states and the liberties of individuals. Then, in his great turnabout, when Adams reversed the very policies his administration seemed to be promoting, he covered these political vulnerabilities in confusion. The fact is that he did not purge the conspirators in his cabinet until after the closely contested state elections in New York went against the Federalists, leaving him nothing to lose politically (indeed with everything to gain) by taking as much distance from his party as possible.[23] But the purge prompted a core of High Federalists to plot against Adams's reelection, and it did little to ease the minds of Republicans about his complicity in the whole chain of policies that together had made Federalism appear a counterrevolution waged on behalf of a small band of creditor-speculators and the narrow commercial interests they represented.[24]

As Jefferson had sensed in begging off the presidency in 1796, the vulnerabilities of Adams's position as a Federalist apostate redounded handsomely to the advantage of the opposition movement. The President had severed the moorings of the old regime, and that disjunctive effect had passed control over the definition of the situation to its most implacable opponents. With Federalism as vulnerable to charges of running roughshod over the limits of national power as it was to the charge of selling that power short, the Republicans proposed to clear away the whole tangle of corruptions into which the government had fallen under the "British faction" and to claim on their own behalf the retrieval of those original understandings that had brought the nation together in the first place. By 1800 they were able to join their original defense of an "American system" of commercial development to a defense of self-sufficient freeholders living in locally controlled agricultural communities. Their anti-*F*ederalism bespoke a new republican thirst for economic opportunity and looked toward more vigorous national action to promote American independence; their anti-federalism bespoke an "Old Republican" suspicion of central power and looked toward the emasculation of the national government in the cause of preserving the independence of individual citizens.

Jefferson's repudiation of the "anglomen" and his call for a return to first principles did more than steel his leadership against a course of action that Adams had already discredited. The Republican insurgency in 1800 gave vent to a whole variety of national aspirations. Its renunciation of phantom monarchists submerged stark choices about the future, but in doing so it also opened new opportunities to rework what once seemed wholly incompatible alternatives. The common cause of saving the principles of the American Revolution and resurrecting the true virtues of republican government carried a disparate and potentially overarching coalition in its train.

The Patrician as Regime Builder

As every portrait of Jefferson-the-conciliator points out, the first opposition leader to come to the presidency took no precipitate action in any of the key areas where a real "revolution" might have been made. Jefferson did not attempt to purge Federalists from the bureaucracy en masse; he did not attempt to scrap the judicial system and start over; he did not move to revoke the charter of the National Bank; he did not repudiate the national debt outright. But presidential reconstructions differ from political revolutions precisely on this point. Presidents are significant at these moments because they are not propelled along some rigid, predetermined course of action but are instead thrust to commanding heights of independent authority. With the prior state of affairs in general disrepute and the insurgent coalition unaccustomed to governing, the president takes control in a political interregnum. He stands beyond received conceptions of order, and his advantage in refashioning political legitimacy lies in extending this interregnum as long as possible.

As a rule, presidents who come into office in these sorts of political breakthroughs do not rush headlong into a wholesale dismantling of the governing arrangements of the past. They avoid actions that might spur a revival of support for the discredited cause. They cultivate their independence, and exploit the disarray in the old leadership. Reconstructive leaders seek both to broaden the political consensus around their commitment to change things and to manipulate the ambiguities that linger around their opposition to the policies of the past. The option of more radical action remains open all the while; these presidents need only stiffen their repudiative posture to meet whatever resistance might be encountered.

If Jefferson's leadership is to be set apart from others similarly situated later on, it should not be because he was inclined to finesse a frontal assault on the old governmental establishment, but because he transformed national politics so thoroughly without being forced into any make-or-break confrontation with it. Jefferson pursued the reconstruction of American government and politics relentlessly, and the regime he created in the end was profoundly different from the one he displaced. Yet, the most remarkable aspect of his transformation is how little resistance he encountered in the process from the institutions and interests previously attached to the old order. Jefferson's authority to reconstruct proved singularly disarming and all-encompassing.

Two aspects of the politics of leadership under Jefferson stand out for special attention in this regard. The first is the peculiar way in which his reconstructive project intersected with the leadership charge of the patrician tribune. Jefferson brought to the presidency an unprecedented partisan mission, one that infused his leadership with intensely ideological purposes and politicized his involvement with virtually all aspects of governmental operations. This stunning innovation in the president's political role appears at first to fly in the face of the early republican understanding of the executive as a benevolent protector of the nation's integrity, one who had to stand above the politics of faction and interest.[25] But in the aftermath of the crisis of 1798 and the political rout of 1800, the seemingly benign ideals of patrician leadership were given a uniquely liberating twist. For a moment, with Federalist heresies fully exposed, political reconstruction became the supreme duty of the national statesman, and Jefferson's intensely partisan project bespoke the highest ideals of disinterested service.

It is in the symbolic universe of Jefferson's leadership that we first discover how relentless pressure against Federalists could be applied in singularly encompassing and open-ended ways. Foremost among these symbols was the epic imagery of the election of 1800 itself, in which the man who had authored the Declaration of Independence was chosen to restore all that had been lost in the corruptions of the recent past. In this relatively closed polity of national notables, Jefferson was identified with the birth of the nation almost as much as was the recently deceased Washington; he personified first principles as no one else alive at the time could. Offering to *re*dedicate a tainted national experiment to the principles of the founding, Jefferson could stamp patently political actions with a unique claim to insight into original intent. In this way, party building and institutional reconstruction became incontestable requirements for restoring national unity, and the eradication of Federalism became the transcendence of partisan combat.[26]

Jefferson's magnanimous invocation in his first inaugural—"We are all federalists; we are all republicans"—spearheaded a campaign to turn patrician mores to the President's political purposes.[27] On its face, this conciliatory overture was a call to both sides to submerge the party spirit and to return to the consensus embodied in the principles of the Revolution and the Constitution. But if conciliation, rightly understood as a return to first principles, dictated leniency for the repentant, it did not dictate accommodation with the heretics. While openly bidding for the support of rank and file Federalists, Jefferson laid bare his implacable hostility to their erstwhile leaders in his correspondence with his lieutenants. His belligerence toward his remaining opponents—"I wish nothing but their eternal hatred"—would be echoed publically in modern times by Franklin Roosevelt at the climax of his 1936 reelection campaign—"I welcome their hatred."[28]

By enveloping his administration in hallowed norms of consensual government and by offering his party as the true home of all enlightened notables, Jefferson isolated and stigmatized diehard Federalists. In an age when it was possible to conceive of the end of party conflict, his conciliatory overture was as threatening to those who would stand by their misguided ways as it was a compelling endorsement of the most sacred governing norms of the day. Jefferson's party would know no alternative; it would be the party to end all parties; it would be itself the very embodiment of legitimate government.[29]

Jefferson's approach to administrative appointments provides a more substantive example of this disarming fusion of leadership roles. Here he found himself in the enviable position of having the partisan demands of his friends lend an aura of patrician restraint to the rather remarkable political action he took against his enemies. Initially, Jefferson upheld the common understanding that executive officers would be removed only for just cause. But while this placed him at a considerable distance from supporters who were demanding a wholesale purge, he acknowledged his partisan interests early on by declaring that all vacancies would be filled exclusively by Republicans and that political opinions actively asserted by lingering Federalists might be considered in a determination of just cause.[30] This policy effectively served notice that the conciliatory tone of the inaugural message was not meant to deny Republicans the benefits of power or to make the government safe for Federalists. In an age when the distinction between the officeholder and his office was blurry—when the opposition decried all removals as an assault on the integrity of the government as well as the official—Jefferson outpaced Andrew Jackson, the so-called father of the spoils system, in removals and replacements. Within two years of his inauguration, the President himself calculated that only 130 of the 316 offices subject to his appointment power were still held by Federalists.[31]

Beyond the felicitous blending of patrician mores with the partisan aims of Jefferson's reconstruction, the President also benefitted from the relatively inchoate character of the governmental institutions that he inherited. As a glance at the burdens of Federalism attests, the "system" which Jefferson set himself against had never sunk very deep political footings. In later reconstructions, with more broadly based interests thoroughly vested in established institutions, and those institutions more secure in their own authority, presidents would be driven toward climactic institutional battles that forced a clearer redrawing of the lines of national political conflict. In this case, however, Federalism's relatively shallow roots eased the disarming of its institutional strongholds and the incorporation of its nominal political support into a regime that was as different as it was encompassing. The insecurities of the other institutions and branches of government left Federalist stalwarts isolated to the point of irrelevance in the face of a president intent on the displacement of their regime.

When it came to getting rid of Federalists, then, the administration could take action far more dramatic than that announced in its official policy of respect for individual placeholders. Republican reform of the army, for example, preemptorily swept aside one third of the officer corps and then set out to break once and for all the monopoly held by wealth and birth on the high ranks of the army. Establishing a national military academy at West Point, Jefferson saw to the recruitment and education of a genuinely Republican officer corps.[32] Even more sweeping was the extraordinary and enormously popular decision to repeal internal taxes immediately. This action simply eliminated the internal revenue service and with it a cadre of placeholders (40 percent of the Treasury Department personnel in the field) representing one of the most visible and noxious offenses of Federalism.[33] Never again would a president be in a position to take such decisive steps in dismantling a regime with so little opposition.

The plasticity of institutional arrangements and their susceptibility to the personal will of a reconstructive leader is even more apparent in Jefferson's dealings with the Congress. According to his contemporaries, Jefferson's influence here was quite without precedent. "Never were a set of men more blindly devoted to the will of a Prime Mover or Minister than the Majority of both houses to the will and wishes of the Chief Magistrate." "The President has only to act and the Majority will approve." "Behind the curtain, [he] directs the measures he wishes to have adopted; while in each house a majority of puppets move as he touches the wires"; the "back stairs influence—of men who bring messages to this House . . . although they do not appear on the Journals, govern its decisions."[34] "The Executive as completely rules both Houses of Congress as Bonaparte rules the people of France."[35] Alert to the fact that these observations were made by Federalists and disgruntled Republicans, commentators have been intent to salvage some integrity for congressional deliberations during Jefferson's presidency.[36] But to point out that Congress often modified the President's proposals, and occasionally even rejected one, does not diminish the force of Dumas Malone's observation that "Congress not only passed virtually all of [Jefferson's] recommendations; it passed virtually no bills of any significance without his recommendation or tacit approval."[37] As Wilfred Binkley put it, Jefferson's "well-organized system [of congressional leadership] worked with almost infallible precision."[38]

It is not simply that Jefferson dominated the Congress as no president before or since but that he did so while pointedly abandoning the presumptuous formalities of executive leadership that had made Federalism look like a monarchical plot. Indeed, Jefferson made full restoration of legislative prerogatives a leading article of the Republican creed.[39] John Marshall's famous prediction that Jefferson would "increase his personal power" by "weakening the office of President" takes on special meaning when we reflect back on the difficulties John Adams had in sustaining the formal prerogatives of his office when personal political authority was being wielded outside the government by the likes of Hamilton and Washington.[40] While the patrician mode of governance was highly personalistic and hostile to powerseekers, Jefferson was able to use its norms of dutiful service to sustain a degree of personal direction never again matched.[41]

Patrician mores and inchoate institutions worked hand in hand to Jefferson's advantage in this regard. The national legislature was still in the embryonic stages of its own internal development, and it did most of its work in the rather clumsy forum of the Committee of the Whole. With the Federalist leadership displaced and the Republican national leadership removed to the top posts in the executive branch, the new Republican majorities arrived in Washington woefully incoherent and unsure of their role. Thus, Jefferson loomed all the larger as the inspiration for their action. He filled the leadership vacuum in Congress by formally deferring to congressional independence and informally indicating his preferences to legislative spokesmen of his own selection. The presumptions in his favor were magnified by the intimacy of the governing community and his personal standing within it. With control established informally, Jefferson gained an added bonus from cultivating the formalities of executive deference to Congress: when a particular initiative faltered, he simply fell back on his official position outside the fray and avoided any personal political damage.[42]

The judiciary, of course, presented a much knottier problem, one which Jefferson never satisfactorily resolved. Unlike the Congress, the judicial system confronted the President with a phalanx of Federalists guaranteed lifetime appointments. From time to time, he toyed with the idea of directly challenging the principle of life tenure with a constitutional amendment, but he conditioned such action on a groundswell of popular outrage at Federalist opinions which never materialized.[43] Meanwhile, he moved against Federalism in the courts with a succession of initiatives, each of which tested a more radical line of attack without closing off options either to support an amendment or uphold the stabilizing influence of judicial independence. First, he preemptorily swept clear the second tier of the judicial system, the federal attorneys and marshals. This gave Republicans full control of the offices which regulated access to the courts, and with it a "shield," as Jefferson called it, against the hostility from above.[44] Then, in his very first legislative initiative, Jefferson saw to the repeal of the Judiciary Act of 1801. Passed in the waning days of the previous administration, this act had allowed John Adams to appoint a number of new judges to the bench just before the Republicans took control. Political outrage at what appeared to be a transparent effort to strengthen Federalism in the judicial branch after its political defeat at the polls submerged the radical implications of repeal, but the principle of lifetime appointment was in fact being called into question by this move. To make sure that the Supreme Court did not interfere with the work of putting the repeal act into effect, the Republicans took another extraordinary step and postponed the next session of the Court for a year. Pushing the limits of constitutional interpretation still further, Jefferson then instigated a congressional experiment in impeaching the most offensive of the Federalist judges.

The impeachment strategy proved unwieldy and collapsed after an initial success. But for so brazen a deployment of constitutional procedures to serve political interests in the eradication of Federalism, this failure did remarkably little damage to Jefferson personally. Though premised on his informal endorsement, the President had studiously maintained his official posture of detachment from the business of Congress, and when things went wrong, he left others holding the bag. The difficulties surfaced in the second major test when the chief prosecutor, John Randolph, obscured whatever case he might have had against his target, Supreme Court Justice Samuel Chase, with an unbridled display of his own fanaticism for the cause. Barely able to maintain majority support among the party faithful for Chase's removal, the Republican congressional leadership suffered a serious embarrassment. Jefferson, on the other hand, simply abandoned the experiment and Randolph along with it.[45]

Much has been made of Jefferson's failure to dislodge Federalism from the judiciary, but by the standards of later court battles, Jefferson's actions appear quite radical and the Court's response rather tepid. Perhaps the most important point to be made about the federal courts under Jefferson is that, unlike their role in later reconstructions, they did not press him into a showdown over his basic political commitments. "In things that counted," observes biographer Merrill Peterson, "the courts were remarkably acquiescent to the Jeffersonian regime."[46]

The Supreme Court repeatedly ducked its opportunities to counter the new order directly. In *Stuart v. Laird,* the Court refused to challenge the repeal of the Judiciary Act of 1801, and thereby it dealt a blow to Federalist designs. In *Marbury v. Madison,* Chief Justice John Marshall did deliver a gratuitous lecture impugning the executive on Marbury's behalf and upholding in principle Marbury's claim to the office Madison had denied him. But the actual ruling dealt with a section of the older Judiciary Act of 1789, and its effect, voiding the section of that act on which Marbury's motion was premised, vindicated the Republican position in substance and dealt another political defeat to the Federalists. Moreover, while the Court in the Marbury case claimed authority to judge the constitutionality of legislation, it did not claim an exclusive authority to judge matters of constitutionality, and while Jefferson might have been irritated by Marshall's obiter dictum, he seems, like almost everyone else at the time, to have found little to object to in Marshall's understanding of the scope of the Court's charge. Marshall had, after all, left Jefferson free and clear to pursue his own interpretations.[47]

The other major "challenge" from the Court came during the treason trial of Aaron Burr, when, after Jefferson had publically proclaimed Burr guilty of conspiring to raise up an army in the West, Chief Justice Marshall seemed to go out his way to embarrass the President by having Burr acquitted. Marshall, it is said, put Jefferson on trial, mocked him with an interpretation of the treason clause so narrow that there would be little chance of conviction, and bolstered the independence of the Court in the process. Whatever points the Chief Justice may have scored for the Court in the long run, however, the personalistic character of this conflict simply did not cut very deep, and in the near term Marshall, the nation's most powerful Federalist, had little to show for setting Hamilton's murderer free. Jefferson scored an equally important point for institutional prestige by refusing subpoenas to appear at the trial. Afterwards, House leaders introduced bills to alter Marshall's narrow construction of the treason clause, and the Senate rallied to the President's support by forcing the resignation of one of Burr's co-conspirators. Massachusetts and Pennsylvania sent instructions to their congressional delegations to work for a constitutional amendment that would make judges removable by the President.[48]

The common thread running through *Stuart v. Laird, Marbury v. Madison,* and the Burr trial is not a potent judicial challenge to Jefferson's political reconstruction but a Court working to establish its own authority on the fringes of a political field thoroughly dominated by a hostile executive. The frontal assaults launched by the Court on the leadership projects of subsequent reconstructive presidents simply did not materialize here. Jefferson's battle with the judiciary might best be read, then, as a portent of things to come, an endemic problem in the politics of reconstruction that would assume far more significance for presidents similarly situated later on. Quickly, and without much effect, political attention turned away from the Burr trial to other more pressing matters. The Federalist Chief Justice notwithstanding, Jefferson's effort to recast the political regime proceeded with relative impunity.[49]

The New Republicanism

In this closely held but still inchoate polity, Jefferson acted steadily, almost methodically, to install a new political regime. He extended the Republican appeal into the heartland of Federalism, bound the nation's commercial and manufacturing interests to the stalwart southern base of his opposition movement, and established in the process a commercial republic with a country-party conscience.[50] The avoidance of precipitous action with regard to the nation's courts, bureaucracies, and financial institutions was instrumental in this regard for it helped to dispel the illusion that only Federalists respected the marketplace. And as no one placed in jeopardy by the prospect of Jefferson's success seemed capable of pushing him back onto more radical ground, the President simply claimed the entire field for his new Republicanism.

The cornerstone of Jefferson's reconstruction was a reversal of priorities in the nation's political economy. The Federalists' initial premise—support for a permanent and expansive national debt—had placed a stranglehold on domestic and international policy; Jefferson insisted on debt retirement. Broadly transformative in its implications, this policy can be seen as "moderate" only against the truly revolutionary alternative of repudiating the debt outright. Together with the repeal of internal taxes, the commitment to a schedule for extinguishing the debt placed the operations of American government on a new foundation. While a major source of government income was being eliminated, debt service was to be taken off the top of the government's remaining yield (largely now from the tariff) *before* its routine business was funded. The initial effect of this was to gut two other Federalist institutions—the regular army and the ocean-going navy—and to instigate a long, elusive quest for a "republican" defense establishment based upon state militia, seacoast fortifications, and coastal gunboats.[51]

Radical and risky, this new posture in finance and defense clearly nodded toward the provincial virtues of a decentralized agrarian republic. The trick was to sustain this commitment without abandoning the interests of other Republicans in increasing the nation's commercial freedom at home and abroad. Jefferson's new regime pressed against the different evils of Federalism simultaneously: it renounced the heresy of government centralization *and* the heresy of international dependence; it rejected the expansive peace-time debt and took a *more* aggressive posture toward the employment of national power; it liberated the localities while *using* the federal government to protect national prestige and build the home market. For most of his term, Jefferson avoided the difficulties of managing this conflation of alternatives by reaping the windfall from a boom in European trade. Swollen tariff revenues facilitated debt payments without precluding new ventures, and in this happy circumstance, Jefferson lured the nation to his cause with a host of attractions. He defended the international traders against piracy in the Mediterranean, he doubled the size of the national domain, and he anticipated a day soon when the federal government might begin to promote "rivers, canals, roads, arts, manufactures, education, and other great objects within each state."[52]

The purchase of the Louisiana Territory from France was, of course, the most stupendous achievement of Jefferson's presidency. Its significance in his political reconstruction, however, lay as much in the negotiation as in the deed itself. The initial Spanish cession of Louisiana to France posed a major crisis for the new regime. A French empire restored on the western frontier threatened the United States with dependence on a great military power for navigation rights on the Mississippi and use of the port at New Orleans. Jefferson knew that such an eventuality would virtually compel an American military alliance with Great Britain, and with that, the Republicans would be forced to capitulate on virtually all matters of principle. His tack was to use the prospect of a renewed British alliance to pressure France, all the while resisting that dismal prospect in practice and waiting for Napoleon to reckon his more immediate interests and negotiate a deal for cash.[53]

The French offer to sell the entire Spanish cession west of the Mississippi as well as New Orleans was an unexpected stroke of good fortune, but it posed some difficulties of its own. As John Quincy Adams would later observe, Jefferson's assumption of implied powers in the Louisiana Purchase was "greater in itself and more comprehensive in its consequences than all the assumptions of implied powers in the years of the Washington and Adams administrations."[54] Certainly, the leader of the party that had blasted executive usurpation under John Adams had no illusions about the fact that he lacked explicit constitutional authority to acquire new territory, let alone an acquisition as large as the nation itself: "Our peculiar security is in the possession of a written Constitution," he warned. "Let us not make it a blank paper by construction." Indeed, for a moment, as Jefferson contemplated proposing a constitutional amendment that would provide a clear ground for this sweeping exercise of power, it appeared that he might actually force a debate over the legitimacy of the action when everyone else seemed anxiously eager to accept it on its face.[55] With hints of second thoughts in France, the prospect of a delay that might jeopardize the purchase agreements became unbearable, and Jefferson decided not to let the question of propriety get in the way of the achievement.

Jefferson's immunity from the inevitable charges of hypocrisy in this action suggests the enormous weight the substantive accomplishment carried on the side of political consistency. The Louisiana Purchase harmonized the different messages in Jefferson's political project so beautifully that any dissonance on matters of technique were all but drowned out. In one stroke, Jefferson steered the Republican regime away from a forced marriage to the British Navy and toward a seemingly limitless future of independent internal development. And while the expansion westward seemed to underwrite the dream of maintaining a remote agrarian republic in perpetuity, control of the Mississippi River and New Orleans held open the prospect of building a great commercial empire. Only the Federalists, who were boxed even further into their New England corner, had reason to fear. In despair at Jefferson's triumph, they contemplated secession from the Union, oblivious to the fact that their own region was itself falling under the spell of the new Republicanism.

The reconstructive achievements of Jefferson's first term culminated in a constitutional change designed to consolidate Republican hegemony. The ratification of the Twelfth Amendment on the eve of the election of 1804 closed the only national political strategy left open to the Federalists by formally distinguishing the election of the president from the election of the vice president. In effect, this made it easier for the Republican party to exploit its growing strength as a nationwide political organization and made it impossible for Federalists to repeat their scheme of 1801. Indeed, it was a testimony to the level of efficiency achieved by the Republican organization in 1800 that Jefferson and Aaron Burr, Republicans supposed by all to be running for president and vice president respectively, tied in the electoral college vote, and it was one of the last outrages of the Federalists to try to defeat Jefferson in the House runoff in 1801 by throwing support to Burr. The Twelfth Amendment forced the battered opposition to compete with Jefferson in 1804 on the ground on which he had become invincible: the definition of a national consensus and the building of a national alliance.[56]

In party building as in recasting institutional relationships, Jefferson's political leadership suggests just the opposite of the point so often made about it. For all the emphasis that has been placed on the eternal dilemmas of presidential choice—of Jefferson's personal struggle with the questions of accommodation or reform, conciliation or revolution, partisanship or statesmanship, order or change—we have lost sight of the ease with which he negotiated these choices and the extent to which he was able to have it both ways. This was one of the rare instances in which political change actually regenerated political order. By releasing very different national interests and energies against one already failed alternative, Jefferson's first term cleared an entirely new political space. While his expansive repudiation worked to broaden the notion that Federalism, as a system of governance, was safely relegated to the dustbins of discredited history, the distance he maintained from the various alternatives fostered by his actions established a place in history that a remarkably wide range of interests could call authoritative.

Of course, not all Republicans were equally comfortable with the commodious course the President had set. Though retaining a semblance of Federalist forms broadened support for this new regime, it caused unease among many of those who had rallied to Jefferson originally in outrage against the Federalist disregard of limits on the national government. These "Old Republicans" were concentrated in the southern wing of the party, and they worried about the expansive new orthodoxy taking shape in their name. In 1805, their concern was potent enough to scuttle an administration-backed effort to resolve a long-standing controversy over claims to the Yazoo lands. Titles to these lands (located between Georgia and the Mississippi River) were suspect at best, and they were held in the main by speculators from New

England and the East. To expedite a settlement, the administration had set up a commission which recommended compensation for the claimants. That struck John Randolph, the self-proclaimed leader of the purists, as an outrage indistinguishable from the worst offenses of Federalism.

Quashing this deal was Randolph's most effective protest against the new dispensation. But as an effort to foment a schism within the ranks, it fell far short of the mark. In fact, when agitating against the Yazoo lands deal, Randolph was careful not to implicate the President or his administration directly in the charge of straying from the path of virtue.[57] Uneasy as they were, most of the Old Republicans saw good reason to identify with and to continue to provide stalwart support for this administration. There was at least as much in Jefferson's program that looked in their direction as elsewhere, and there was a new hegemonic party in the making, outside of which their concerns would have no political standing at all. That there was no alternative to Jefferson's "new" Republicanism was made crystal clear when Randolph pressed his critique more directly and found himself isolated and expelled. At Jefferson's prompting, he was defeated in his bid to remain chairman of the House Ways and Means Committee.[58]

Like Jefferson's "battle" with John Marshall, his purge of John Randolph forms an essential element of the reconstructive prototype. Both of these difficulties appear in retrospect as portents of endemic problems in the politics of reconstruction that will take on much larger significance in later reconstructive presidencies. Marshall, the leader of the residual institutional support for the old governmental establishment, and Randolph, the self-appointed conscience of the old party of opposition, presented the main sources of resistance to Jefferson's assertion of independent authority in recasting the terms and conditions of government and politics. The point is that their counterparts in later reconstructions would prove far more consequential than they in mounting such resistance; Jefferson, unlike later reconstructive presidents, rolled right past them. After a stunning first term, the central question was not whether Jefferson's new political synthesis was durable but whether it was workable.

A Leap of Faith

That the course of things had been changed decisively was brought home in 1807 when, in the face of renewed British aggression toward

American merchant ships, Jefferson refused even to submit to the Senate an agreement negotiated by his minister, James Monroe, to settle American grievances.[59] Instead of suffering terms that were all too reminiscent of the Jay debacle, Jefferson tested the Republican alternative, first with restrictions on British imports and then, in December of 1807, under hostile decrees from both Britain and France, with an embargo on all foreign trade. Initially Jefferson understood these restrictions in the traditional sense, as a way of protecting the nation's commercial resources while preparing for war. Gradually however, they evolved into something quite different: an open-ended experiment to explore the potential of economic coercion as an alternative to war. Placing immense value on testing this alternative as fully as possible ("it is the first [such] experiment, and it is of great importance to know its full effect"), Jefferson knew well that at some point his new weapon of Republican statecraft would become more burdensome to the nation than war itself.[60] He ventured to find out whether Britain could be forced to recognize American interests before the economic sacrifices of the American people became unbearable and war unavoidable.[61]

The transformation of the embargo from a prelude to war into a potential substitute for war was, of course, closely tied to the Republicans' initial premise that the nation could best protect its independence by applying economic sanctions that would force its enemies to respond to its interests. This was the option that the Federalists had never fully explored. It was the option that held equally steadfast against the Federalists' first impulse—to submit and surrender national independence—as against their second impulse—to go to war and suffer the horrors of extensive military establishments, taxes, and debt. But as a test of the nation's willingness to support a political doctrine, Jefferson's finale is little short of astounding. Using a blanket trade embargo to press the Republican alternative soon became an improvisation on the very meaning of that alternative.

The sheer scale of the national prohibitions and economic sacrifices contemplated in the embargo mocked the Jeffersonians' early claims to the virtues of decentralization. But that is perhaps the least remarkable of the challenges this policy posed as a test of Jefferson's authority. Jefferson had shown a penchant for the aggressive use of national power all along, and this was, after all, an effort to meet a national emergency in a way that would avoid the even greater burdens of war. What makes the embargo stand out as an act of leadership scarcely thinkable for us today is that it launched a frontal assault on the mainstays of the nation's economy. Instead of going to war to protect the economy, the President decided to take a giant leap ahead on his political vision of what the economy of the future should look like. Jefferson saw the international crisis as an occasion "to turn seriously to that policy which plants the manufacturer and the husbandman side by side and establishes at every door that exchange of mutual labors and comforts which we have hitherto sought in distant regions."[62] Jefferson's embargo transformed the idea of the home market (of an economy freed from dependence on foreign governments by the development of domestic manufactures and internal improvements) from a mere speculation (something that might be fostered gradually on the heels of international trade and surplus agriculture) into a priority and central justification of national action. It not only tested the resolve of the American people to persevere until Britain—rudely awakened to its presumed dependence on the American market—recognized American interests in the world; it tested the resolve of the American people to abandon that world without a fight—the world in which their most immediate interests lay—and to grasp in its place an idea of the shape of things to come.

Next to its fantastic conception as an instrument of reconstruction, the embargo is most remarkable for the political freedom Jefferson enjoyed in pressing it. The authority Jefferson wielded in his eighth year in office, while openly committed to political retirement and forcibly turning the nation's economy inside out, strains the modern imagination. Treasury Secretary Gallatin had advised the President that "a measure of the nature of the embargo . . . cannot be enforced without the assistance of means as strong as the measure itself," and Jefferson concurred. So long as "a continuance of the embargo is preferred to war (which sentiment is universal here)," he wrote back, "Congress must legalize all means which may be necessary to obtain its end . . . I am clearly of the opinion this law ought to be enforced at any expense, which may not exceed our appropriation."[63]

During the early months of 1808, Congress endorsed the President's course repeatedly with ever more sweeping delegations of enforcement powers and then adjourned with instructions that he was to use these powers until either peace was restored in Europe or either France or Britain lifted its hostile decrees. The opposition party, increasingly vehement in its renunciation of the ruinous consequences of this policy, failed to mount an effective challenge to it. Neither did doubts within the high councils of the administration have much effect. Nor, until Jefferson was virtually out the door, did the deepening factional discord within the Republican party make itself felt. For over a year, limits on the President were imposed not by checks and balances but by the relatively primitive capacities of the federal government to enforce a policy of such incredible range. There was in truth far more presidential authority here than governmental power to back it up.[64]

Making do with what resources he had, Jefferson turned the screws of economic reconstruction ever tighter. As he did, the political machinery he had put in place reasserted his case. The national election of 1808 played host to a vigorous defense of the whole record of debt retirement, tax repeal, and peaceful internal development. Despite economic devastation in the South, widespread resistance to the embargo in the North, deepening divisions within the party, and a resurgence of Federalist strength, the Republicans carried the day for the President's first lieutenant, James Madison, and, for what it was worth, maintained comfortable majorities in both houses of Congress.

The most draconian enforcement act of all was passed after the election, and it was this one that pushed the besieged New England Republicans beyond the point of further endurance.[65] In fact, the embargo had not only "re-Federalized" New England, it had squandered what strength the nation had, sparked widespread lawlessness, fomented civil unrest, and disgraced the Republic on the world stage. Finally, Congress asserted itself. Significantly, though, when Congress finally took control over policy in fact as well as in form, it failed to offer any real alternative. The moment of truth came in February of 1809, less than six weeks before Jefferson's retirement, when the administration's efforts to fix its own conditions for the end of the experiment were defeated. In a splendid anticlimax, the New England Republicans bolted from the prescribed line and changed the expiration date from June of 1809 (the time stipulated by the administration) to the very beginning of Madison's term in March. Beyond that, the administration's preferred policy alternative, a credible threat of war, was also sorely compromised. The upshot of this rebuke was the substitution of a policy of nonintercourse with Britain and France for the embargo on all trade.[66] With provisions barely adequate to save face, Congress maintained Jefferson's general strategy of commercial discrimination in principle and made it easier for the nation's traders to pursue their immediate interests in practice. Rejecting both forced modernization and war, it left to Madison the dubious honor of trying to make Jefferson's principles work in some other way.

Had Jefferson faced stiffer resistance all along, he might have seen this farewell reversal for what it was and not taken it so personally. After all, when he retired, the peculiar mixture of ideas and interests that he had stamped on the government was very much intact. The bolt of the New England Republicans masked the fact that, for all its outrages, Jefferson's experiment had fertilized a seedbed of manufacturing in their own backyard. And the stalwart loyalty of the southern Republicans, despite involving themselves in an unprecedented assertion of national authority and bringing the brunt of the economic sacrifice upon their own section, suggests nothing so much as their greater fear of armies, debt, and taxes, especially when employed at the behest of international traders. The Republican congressmen who challenged the administration line in 1809 did far more to institutionalize the new regime—to make it less a mere creature of presidential will—than to alter it. Provincial virtues *and* manufacturing interests, agrarian dreams *and* modernizing energies, economy *and* activism, peace *and* independence, internal development *and* external expansion, antimilitarism *and* commercial ambition—Jefferson had provided each with ample space within government policy to assert its legitimacy, and several administrations would stew in that achievement before another asserted reconstructive authority.

Part Two:
James Monroe's Articulation

In the path already traced

JAMES MONROE was the first president to take office free of preoccupations with the survival of the Republic. The international crises of the early national period had been put to rest with the War of 1812, and the hapless remnants of the Federalist party were smashed in their resolution. In the latter years of James Madison's presidency, the party of Jefferson had enveloped just about everyone in its overarching political consensus; it *was* the nation. In 1817, Monroe assumed responsibility for a polity that was externally secure, internally confident, and politically correct. "Our principal dangers and difficulties have passed," he enthused.[1] "Never," proclaimed his inaugural address, "did a government commence under auspices so favorable, nor ever was success so complete."[2]

This was a moment to build on the existing consensus, to complete the unfinished business, to demonstrate the constructive uses of national power; and no one was more eminently qualified to take on these tasks than James Monroe. He had worked his way up through the Republican ranks, tendering loyal, if not always stellar, service to its presidents; and he had developed strong ties to both old and new Republicans along the way. In fact, the "Old Republicans" had tried to push him ahead, urging him to compete with Madison in the election of 1808 and to take a stand for the party's original principles against the encompassing coalition that Jefferson had assembled. Monroe was tempted, but ultimately he decided to hold back.[3] Overcoming pent-up resentment about standing in Madison's shadow and recent bitterness over Jefferson's peremptory rejection of the trade treaty he had negotiated in Great Britain, he waited with stalwart patience for his rightful turn at the helm and eventually went back into national service as Madison's secretary of state and heir-apparent. The wisdom of his course confirmed, Monroe came to the presidency capping a career of dedicated service to a cause which was itself coming to a glorious culmination. With an unshakable faith in his political inheritance as the embodiment of the true principles of government, he looked forward to realizing all that this regime had anticipated and to proving it a vital, even programmatic, guide to national action in the golden age.

But the new president was also keenly aware of the special challenge such an opportunity presents. The very press of great expectations alerted Monroe to the imperatives of managing the prospective changes and patrolling the boundaries of propriety. The delicate business of protecting the integrity of a regime on the verge of fulfillment cautioned him to couple national optimism with political discipline. "In contemplating what we still have to perform," he urged everyone to bear in mind "how near our government has approached to perfection." To attain the "high destiny" which seemed to await required, above all, a firm resolve to "persevere . . . in the path already traced."[4] This in a nutshell was the burden of Monroe's charge—to lead a regime bursting with constructive possibilities in a way that would not alter anything of political significance, to change the nation without disrupting its politics.

Accustomed as we are to diminish Monroe's role in the great work of his administration and to link the political disintegration of the Jeffersonian regime to his patrician posture of benign repose, we have lost much of the enduring significance of the leadership challenge that Monroe set out to tackle. It is true that he had to pursue his course under standards of proper presidential behavior that severely limited his ability to control things, and that his hopes for this "era of good feeling" dissolved into a devastating sectarian struggle among the faithful. But it is also true that Monroe courted some of the most aggressive innovators of his day (John Quincy Adams, John C. Calhoun, Andrew Jackson) and that in spite of the spoilsport snipings of Henry Clay (who found the President's invitation to take over the War Department beneath his station), Monroe did more than any other incumbent to stamp the nation with the dreams of these young nationalists. As surely as there was an aloof Monroe who found himself powerless to alter the suicidal course of Jeffersonian politics in the 1820s, there was an engaged Monroe whose conscientious sponsorship of good works helped to blow the Jeffersonian regime apart.[5]

The Patrician as Regime Articulator

Monroe's charge was different from Jefferson's, and the difference presents us with a second prototype of the politics presidents make. Whereas Jefferson joined the retrieval of lost principles to the repudiation of recent practices, Monroe was prompted by his political identity and historical circumstances to render his leadership a purely constructive elaboration of received premises. His were the characteristic dilemmas of the orthodox-innovator: how to exercise the powers of the presidency without projecting a political alternative to what had come before; how to grasp new possibilities without impugning the existing political foundations; how to complete a long-pending political agenda without sparking sectarian dissent from those committed to the prior consensus; how to muffle the order-shattering impact of change. As a rule, the greater the leap forward along a "path already traced," the more severely the identity of the orthodox-innovator will be tested. His political authority rests in equal measure on demonstrating the old regime's integrity and demonstrating its relevance to new circumstances; his problem is that these two objects invariably grate against each other. Embracing a great opportunity to make good on long-heralded ideals, he tends to call into question the very ground on which he stands.

Monroe's effort to fashion this place in history is emblematic of the efforts of all presidents who have come to power in similar circumstances. Implementing the program, he enervated the system; carrying the party forward with a vision that synthesized received commitments and present possibilities, he left it tangled in confusion and recrimination; facilitating the implementation of new policies, he caricatured the irrelevance of the established rules; articulating received premises at a higher level of national achievement, he dissolved all sense of political coherence. And yet, while this pattern of programmatic implosion is repeated again and again in subsequent periods, the repetition alone understates our case. As later comparisons will bear out, the difference between a politics of articulation and a politics of reconstruction is cast more broadly in the contrast between Monroe and Jefferson than anywhere else.

For Monroe, as for Jefferson, the organizational norms and governing resources of the federal government in the early republic exaggerated the play of authority relations in the exercise of presidential power. Patrician mores inform both the extreme fractiousness of national politics in Monroe's articulation of Jefferson's orthodoxy and the extreme plasticity of national politics in Jefferson's reconstruction. In each case, we see reflected the relative isolation of the Washington establishment from local centers of social and economic activity, the absence of stable institutional foundations for the assertion of presidential power, and the hypersensitivity of a government of notables to the specific warrants the president brought to political action in the moment at hand.

Like other patrician presidents, Monroe came to the office less to make his reputation than to confirm and embellish it. His most precious leadership resources were his standing as the last of the fading line of revolutionary notables and as the undisputed heir to the legacy of Jefferson and Madison. Making the case for continuity in politics was his special province; cloaking change with the appearance of consistency, his most distinctive skill. Monroe may have been a bit obsessed with matters of personal countenance and proper comportment, but then he had little else to offer by way of influence and control. Sponsor of the young nationalists, the President paraded around the capital and the nation dressed in the old garb of the revolutionary era. All those who saw him were reminded in this way of his past service to the nation, and his whole personal history was brought to bear on the new projects of his administration.

Considering the highly personalistic nature of his resources, Monroe was able to act with considerable effect, especially during his first term. Take for instance his nomination of John Quincy Adams to be secretary of state. This was Monroe's first decision of political consequence, the one that set Henry Clay against him and the one with which he established the distinctive character of his administration. It was, on its face, a shocking selection. The State Department had become the sine qua non of advancement to the presidency in the Jeffersonian regime; indeed, a president's selection for the post was widely seen to designate his preference for a successor. Clay, the obvious and eager choice, had the sturdiest political credentials for the job; John Quincy was the son of the Federalist that Jefferson had driven from the presidency, and though he had been politically reconstructed, he remained on the fringes of Republican politics. Monroe accepted obvious risks in tendering Adams the appointment, but he was confident that his own personage could absorb the shock, and he was determined to clarify his broader political purposes at the outset. In truth, Monroe had fears to assuage more immediate than the revival of Federalism and concerns to address more fundamental than Clay's ambition. The greater threat to Monroe's authority lay in the resentments that were building within his party to Virginia's apparent lock on the presidency and to the presumptions in favor of a presidential succession from the State Department post. No one, least of all the new President, foresaw at the time of the appointment that Adams would be able to build so formidable a following as to continue the traditional line of advancement. In fact, the selection looked in the opposite direction, toward the fact that Adams, unlike Clay, had no political base to speak of. By tapping a diplomat whose prior service to the Republican cause lay overseas, Monroe signaled his recognition of the broad diffusion of talent and influence throughout the party, and pointedly deferred the selection of the next chief executive to the independent judgment of the rank and file. At once, he was able to acknowledge the New England Republicans as full-fledged partners in his national coalition, to open future presidential contests to other players, and to press his own best case for support among the party faithful. The appointment of Adams was a patrician's way of celebrating his party's coming of age, and by expanding opportunities for everyone else, it reduced Clay's rage to an annoying distraction that would never actually prevail over administration preferences.[6]

The point can be generalized. Throughout his tenure, Monroe employed his unique personal standing to encompass the ambitions raging within the Republican party and extort from them a semblance of political consensus and administration unity. The very image of political perfection, the President punctuated his tenure with a series of celebratory national tours; like George Washington, he conveyed through his own personage his message to the people. Then, back in the capital, Monroe would throw himself into the work of cleansing great initiatives of all hints of political disruption, refracting dissension into the appearance of unanimity, and putting a benign face on new departures. Tenacious in his efforts to obscure the political implications of innovation, he proved vigilant in keeping his administration clear of responsibility for any adverse consequences that it might have. It is not by default that Monroe stands with Washington as one of the two presidents to win reelection without opposition. He had spent four years preparing for just such a triumph, and despite impressive evidence fast-mounting to the contrary, he took his reelection endorsement as confirmation of the world of appearances he had been creating, an unmistakable sign that American government was indeed on the verge of realizing "the highest degree of perfection of which human institutions are capable."[7]

By 1821, however, appearance and reality had drifted far apart, and the President's sentiments were straining the limits of credibility. While Monroe did what he could to put a benign face on change, his personal reputation was no match for the knotty leadership challenge he so acutely perceived, and the limitations of his institutional resources for disciplining the polity were already becoming transparent. The virtual equation of his authority with a triumphant consensus had precluded his sending any clear message about the great changes that were actually taking place in the nation, and his all-too-precious pretension of standing above the fray handicapped his efforts to control the difficult political adjustments he was making. If those outside the Cabinet began to experience the "era of good feeling" as a time of aimless drift, it was not because their leader had kept himself hidden away, but because the rules of patrician statesmanship prompted him to rest the case for where he was taking the nation solely on the glory of how far it had come. While on tour, Monroe just kept telling the people that they were on the right track, as if by extending indefinitely the moment of "near perfection" he could slip them into the future without notice.[8] The shockwaves of war, expansion, economic readjustment, and democratization would not be so easily accommodated. Indeed, the transcendence of party division that Monroe was celebrating at the national level bore little resemblance to politics in the states and localities, where memories of earlier party battles lingered longer and new forms of partisan combat were already gestating.[9]

The strictures of patrician politics came to weigh on Monroe's leadership project in a way that they had not on Jefferson's. Both leaders employed the norms of disinterested service, and both aimed at the most commodious course for the interests of the nation; but their actions were politicized in entirely different ways. Where Jefferson had fused an irresistible combination of partisanship and patrician duty—of hands-on political management and deferential national service—Monroe found himself at wits' end to reconcile the competing imperatives. It is not simply that he lacked more concrete sanctions to carry his views into effect, but that the resources he did have—personal countenance and proper comportment—inhibited him from actively intervening on his own behalf. Clay saw this weakness and exploited it mercilessly. He knew that the one thing Monroe needed most to prevent was a debate about his orthodoxy. By raising that question Clay would make Monroe's control over the situation more problematic, and the more prominent the issue became, the more difficult it would be for the President to back the nation quietly into its destiny, showing the people only an ever more perfect present.

Here, the irony of the politics of articulation under Monroe comes full circle, for the scorching assaults that Clay and others began to mount on Monroe's orthodoxy fed upon the particulars of the legacy that Jefferson had bequeathed to his successors as gospel. In truth it was Jefferson, the father of the regime that Monroe came to office to celebrate, who did more than anyone else to box his faithful son into a corner. Consider first the lumpy consensus Jefferson had built against Federalist heresy. Directing action against the most extreme and distasteful of Federalist practices, Jefferson had gathered supporters on all sides of the great issues of the day. Monroe, with nothing to direct his leadership against and little organization to hold the whole together, found the supporters of Jefferson all too eager to go at each other in trying finally to resolve their outstanding differences on the issues. Movement in any direction brought sharp accusations of betrayal from those who claimed themselves to be true keepers of the Republican faith. As Monroe cloaked his actions in the rhetoric of how perfect things already were, those he needed most to convince took their cues from their own special interests in where things were actually headed, and they found themselves relatively unconstrained by the President to address the massive changes that were taking place in the economy, society, and the polity on their own terms.

Second, consider institutional relations between president and Congress. Presidential deference to Congress—the leading principle of governmental organization under the Jeffersonians—comported well with patrician suspicions of men who sought power, but it was ill-suited to the demands of managing a mature political regime. From his position as the focal point of the insurgent Republican movement, Jefferson had been able to renounce Federalism as a tyranny of executive power and still maintain, indeed enhance, presidential control over governmental affairs. But by elevating the self-effacing norms of dutiful service in the executive to the status of a sacred principle, Jefferson imposed a formidable constraint on those who would follow him. As the Congress became more self-assured in its own leadership and more elaborate in its internal organization, it began to act the part that Jefferson had cast for it.[10] With the disgruntled Henry Clay standing guard, the House took the formalities of executive deference ever more seriously and became increasingly sensitive to even the appearance of intrusion from the President. As one informed source assessed the situation in 1818, "all the effective power of the country" was being absorbed into the House of Representatives.[11] Monroe had to depend on the congressional connections of his cabinet members to generate support for his policies, and they themselves were locked in a fierce competition with each other for congressional favor.[12]

Finally, consider the institutional limits of Jefferson's single party system as they came home to roost in Monroe's triumphal elections. No sooner did the Jeffersonians succeed in clearing national politics of their rivals than national elites had to direct their ambitions through what were, in effect, radically narrowed channels for political advancement. The nation's burgeoning pool of political talent faced a bottleneck at the top.[13] There was near universal acknowledgment of Monroe's claims to preside, but there was also a near universal understanding that he would be the last to preside solely by virtue of his prior experience and national service. In the future, there would be too many with similar claims for any one to override all others. If Monroe underwrote his own claims by appointing Adams and stepping out of the process of selecting a successor, he also intensified the struggle among his followers to break through the crowd. The leading lights of the executive and legislative branches had little choice but to begin cultivating their own political followings in earnest, and as the scramble for political advantage accelerated, it mocked the consensus that Monroe presumed to represent.

Later orthodox-innovators might envy Monroe's national standing. After all, while he may have felt compelled to disavow any intention to select his own heir, many of them would feel compelled to disavow any intention to seek their own reelection; and far from being returned to power uncontested, most of those who did stand again would go down to defeat. But even here we might discern a tradeoff between authority and power. Later orthodox-innovators would bring to the task at hand far more tangible resources for seizing control and acting independently on their own behalf. As a consequence, their transformations would cut deeper into the regime they represented. In this instance, when a new generation of leaders began to use the presidency as a sounding board for the promotion of their own ambitions, there was little the stalwart tribune in the White House could do but entreat consensus more earnestly. An eager sponsor of the full flower of Jeffersonian politics, Monroe met the threat of its disintegration in public splendor and private torment.

The Benign Face of Aggression

Consider as a prime example of Monrovian leadership the President's handling of Andrew Jackson's seizure of the Spanish military posts in Florida in 1818. Jackson had been assigned by the administration to patrol the Georgia border and protect it against marauding Seminole Indians. But while pursuing the invaders across the border, Jackson decided to go to the heart of the problem and vanquish their Spanish protectors. Seizing the Florida posts was an impulsive act of war, exceeding formal orders not to challenge Spanish authority and carrying in its train the arbitrary execution of two British subjects. This de facto conquest precipitated the most portentous international crisis of Monroe's tenure, and yet the President steadfastly refused to acknowledge the stark alternatives that it presented him. Instead, he set out to move the nation triumphantly beyond them and leave it basking in glorious immunity from the political consequences of its actions.

The choices Monroe refused to make were forcefully pressed upon him by his closest advisors. On the one hand, he rejected the opinion of the majority of the Cabinet, led by Secretary of War Calhoun, that Jackson would have to be formally censured and the Florida territory returned to Spanish sovereignty in apology.[14] In the first place, such a repudiation would be certain to touch off a political explosion pitting the nation's most perfect hero—the one who had so recently routed the British at New Orleans and restored the nation's dignity—against its now nearly perfect government. Moreover, the acquisition of Florida had been a top priority on the Republican agenda from the time of the original discussions over the extent of the Louisiana Purchase. Negotiating the original purchase as Jefferson's emissary to France had been Monroe's finest hour prior to becoming president; what more could he ask for in the presidency than a chance to round it out? General Jackson was not alone in suspecting the Spanish of protecting the Seminole invaders, and although the seizure of Spanish property was an outrageous act of discretion tantamount to insubordination, it presented

Monroe an irresistible (and not wholly unexpected) opportunity to complete in short order a major piece of unfinished business.[15]

On the other hand, however, Monroe also resisted the minority opinion, pressed boldly by Secretary of State Adams, that the administration should respond to the Spanish with an unqualified endorsement of Jackson's action.[16] The integrity of republican principles, not to mention the integrity of the President himself, demanded more careful protection than that option would have afforded. As the President explained his fully reflected position to Jackson, to give unqualified support to this de facto conquest would open the administration to congressional charges of usurpation of the war power. ("The last imputation to which I would consent justly to expose myself is that of infringing a Constitution to the support of which, on pure principles, my public life has been devoted.") It would also open the door to an international confrontation. Monroe foresaw Europe standing united against the United States and mocking the presumed superiority of republican government in savage attacks on his administration's plundering. ("Why risk these consequences?")[17]

In fact, Monroe was unwilling to accept any adverse consequences at all in this affair. The leadership problem he set out to tackle was nothing less than to save Jackson, assuage the Spanish, gain Florida, moderate the domestic political debate, and wrap up the whole sordid business in a vindication of the enduring virtues of republican institutions.[18] Once he reached this assessment of the challenge at hand, there was no limit to his creativity in trying to piece it all together.

Certain facts about the events in question stood in the way of this benign synthesis, but in a moment of high anxiety and great anticipation, the President determined that it would be better to change the facts and project the proper image than to threaten good feelings with unsettling realities. A short sentence after reminding Jackson of the "pure principles" to which his public life had been devoted, the President candidly reviewed for his general the value of doctoring the record of his correspondence with the War Department so as to obscure the clear implications of the affair and turn the burden of responsibility onto the Spanish officers:

> Your letters to the Department were written in haste, under the pressure of fatigue and infirmity . . . and, in consequence with less attention to some parts of their contents than would otherwise have been bestowed

on them. The passage to which I particularly allude . . . is that in which you speak of the incompetency of an imaginary boundary to protect us from the enemy—the ground on which you bottom all your measures. This is liable to the imputation that you took the Spanish posts for that reason, as a measure of expediency, and not on account of the misconduct of the Spanish officers. The effect of this and such passages, besides other objections to them, would be to invalidate the ground on which you stand and furnish weapons to adversaries who would be glad to seize them. If you think proper to authorize the Secretary [of War] or myself to correct those passages, it will be done with care, though, should you have copies, as I presume you have, you had better do it yourself.[19]

In its assiduous assertion of the primacy of appearances, this letter brings the essence of Monroe's leadership to center stage. The point is not that he was duplicitous; few presidents would be able to escape that charge. The point is that this paragon of patrician rectitude tied himself in knots trying to prevent anyone from appearing to sacrifice anything in this affair and at the same time still grasp the fruits of power. This was leadership by absorption, soaking up expediency and wringing out propriety.

Not one to admit mistakes, much less cover them over, Jackson refused to have anything to do with Monroe's scheme. He would make his own defense in the explosive congressional investigation that Monroe had tried so desperately to forestall. In the meantime, however, the President pressed ahead, putting the best face he could on the facts at hand. In his Second Annual Message, Monroe offered the nation and the world one of his most precious and effective juxtapositions of conscience and accommodation. After a thorough review of the entire matter, he contended that Jackson had acted on his own responsibility in taking the Spanish posts, but that his actions were thoroughly justified by events in the field and, in particular, by the conduct of the Spanish officers. He observed that the posts had been returned in good speed to Spanish authority, but that the incident proved the incompetence of that authority to control the territory in question. The United States, he concluded, had suffered great injury on the Florida border over a long period of time, and it was running out of patience. It was time for Spain to review the situation "with candor" and "to take with honor the course best calculated to do justice to the United States and to promote her own welfare."[20]

Monroe's handling of the Seminole War shows him at his most agile in easing disruption without sacrificing achievement. His message put a benign face on U.S. aggression, and he moved ahead directly from there to pluck its irresistible fruits. He did not, however, enjoy the same immunity that Jefferson had in snatching the Louisiana Purchase from the ambiguities of constitutional stricture. The month-long congressional investigation of the affair, the longest on a single subject up to that time, set the pattern for the entire administration. Henry Clay, still seething with resentment over the Adams appointment, seized the occasion to vent his hostility to the administration. He was bolstered in this task by supporters of Secretary of the Treasury William Crawford who, having failed in their efforts to press their man forward for the presidency in 1816, were just as eager to showcase his independent claims on national leadership. Together they forced to the fore the question that Monroe had been so keen to submerge. Openly calling for Jackson's censure, and implicitly casting doubt on the integrity of the whole administration in the affair, they hit upon the issue of propriety and claimed that any hint of endorsing military insubordination degraded republican institutions and disgraced the American experiment on the world stage.[21] Their assault was one in a series of disputes driving a wedge between Clay and Adams, the first major divide between Clay and Jackson, the beginning of what would become an explosive relationship between Crawford and Monroe, and a time bomb ticking away in the relationship between Jackson and Calhoun.

Calhoun, Adams, Jackson, Crawford, and Clay—all leading figures of the Republican consensus and all contenders for the succession—were sent scrambling by this event, and the odd combinations spun out by it suggest a situation as schismatic in its tendencies as it was damaging to Monroe's pretensions. But these threats to present perfection would take some time to ripen. Monroe's tenure was still too fresh and the prospects of his triumph too splendid to open the floodgates of factionalism too wide. Clay's censure motions went down to defeat, the administration carrying the day. Taking advantage of Jackson's impulsive little war, Monroe had the satisfaction of completing in short order the long lingering promise of 1803. As consummated by Adams in the Transcontinental Treaty of 1819, America gained control of all of Florida, and then drew a line dividing Spanish and American claims from Louisiana to the Pacific. For the moment, the magnitude of Monroe's achievement overrode all other concerns, even Henry Clay's complaint that the Transcontinental Treaty had sacrificed the nation's clear title to Texas.

Commitments and Possibilities

The flexing of national muscle that began with the Seminole War yielded a series of advances on the world stage, culminating in December 1823 with the promulgation of the Monroe Doctrine. Acquiring Florida, staking claims to a continent, recognizing the newly independent Latin republics, and extending a benign protection for republicanism over the entire hemisphere, the President infused his message of national fulfillment and political perfection with a heady, almost euphoric, content. Later orthodox-innovators would follow suit, looking to bolster political consensus at home with impressive displays of power and influence abroad. Recognition of the Latin republics is especially telling in this respect, for the issue had been a first priority with Henry Clay, and it sustained him for several years in a bitter critique of administration reluctance.[22] Monroe was nearly as zealous as Clay for the Latin cause, but he acted in concert with Adams and kept his larger vision of political harmony at the fore. In due time, the administration swept up Clay's project along with Jackson's, transforming them both in a package boasting continental power, international prestige, and national harmony.

The cordial political reception of the Monroe Doctrine was a last reminder of the good feelings that Monroe could inspire in the nation at large.[23] Domestic difficulties were by then far advanced. It was harder for Monroe to play the rainmaker in domestic affairs if only because Congress was on firmer ground in such matters, and the fireworks set off over questions of propriety that much more distracting. Still, the President pursued his object, determined to absorb the shockwaves of internal as well as external change and to steal the thunder of his critics with actions that met their substantive concerns. To see just how thoroughly engaged he was by the task of reconciling present opportunities with regime maintenance and how fundamental the challenge of keeping innovation within the bounds of orthodoxy actually became to his leadership effort, we turn to one issue in particular, internal improvements.

Federal sponsorship of public works—primarily the building of roads, canals, and bridges—was the most delicate issue on Monroe's domestic agenda and the one on which he ultimately prided himself most for the exercise of political leadership. There can be no doubt of his enthusiasm for public works. He openly played to the new nationalist spirit in his inaugural address, calling attention to the "peculiarly strong" inducements for "completing the work of nature" at the present time. "By thus facilitating the intercourse between the States," he ventured, "we shall add much to the convenience and comfort of our fellow-citizens, much to the ornament of the country, and, what is of greater importance . . . we shall bind the Union more closely together." Monroe learned firsthand about the importance of good roads on the first of his grand tours. He warmed to the issue in response to an audience in New England, and, while traveling through upstate New York, he off-handedly ordered a party of soldiers to make some repairs on the deteriorating Plattsburgh road.[24]

Internal improvements were, of course, only one item in a cornucopia of ornaments that Monroe had in mind to bestow on this exuberant nation. Viewed along with the rest of the package—an accelerated retirement of the national debt, another repeal of internal taxes, the expansion of international trade through aggressive pursuit of reciprocal trading agreements, the rapid increase in the extent and value of public lands, the protection of domestic industry, a rebuilding and expansion of military defenses, the expansion and improvement of the physical plant of the government in Washington—it was a component of a much larger plan to cultivate the nationalist spirit within the boundaries of Jeffersonian orthodoxy.[25] This program followed closely on the heels of Madison's own expansive interpretation of the Jeffersonian faith in the wake of the War of 1812. Monroe anticipated even more activism, confident that any question of ideological boundaries would be answered by the political credentials of the President himself.

In fact, the peculiar problem with the internal improvements issue was that it had been left to Monroe as the premier symbol of Madison's own effort to uphold the doctrines of limited federal powers and states' rights and to maintain a semblance of orthodox control over the party's more zealous nationalists. Madison had been accommodating enough to swallow the establishment of a new national bank, and he had actually called upon Congress to take up the question of roads and canals. At the last moment, however, he reconsidered and decided to draw a clear line against unbridled capitulation to nationalism on the improvements issue. In his final act as president, Madison reaffirmed Jefferson's original position that although a national system of internal improvements was desirable and necessary, it could only be authorized by an explicit amendment to the Constitution. To the disbelief and disillusionment of his erstwhile admirer, Henry Clay, "Madison rejected his own bill."[26]

Thus, when Monroe took office there was no issue on which the tension between anticipation and perseverance, commitment and possibility, was more starkly displayed. The question was: had Madison drawn his line in sand? As the new president prepared to meet his first Congress, he began to sense the full burden of this question, and grew uncomfortable with his initial burst of enthusiam for improvements. Clearly troubled, he tried for a time to find a way to reconcile the nationalists' demand for public works with his own commitment to regime integrity. Unsuccessful, he determined not to repeat Madison's mistake of prompting a bill he could not sign. In a sober letter to his predecessor, he affirmed the priority of persevering in the path already traced: "After all the consideration I have given it, I am fixed in the opinion, that the right is not in Congress and that it would be improper in me, after your negative, to allow them to discuss the subject & bring a bill for me to sign, in the expectation that I would do it."[27]

Accordingly, in his opening address to his first Congress, Monroe squelched the program he had praised so effusively in his inaugural. He set out instead to reestablish the boundaries of political doctrine and forestall the development of any more divisive action on the issue.

> A difference of opinion has existed from the first formation of our Constitution to the present time among our most enlightened and virtuous citizens respecting the right of Congress to establish [such] a system of improvement . . . It would be improper after what has passed that this discussion should be revived with an uncertainty of my opinion respecting the right. Disregarding early impressions, I have bestowed on [this] subject all the deliberation which its great importance and a just sense of duty required, and the result is a settled conviction in my mind that Congress does not possess the right . . . In communicating this result I cannot resist the obligation which I feel to suggest to Congress the propriety of recommending to the States the adoption of an amendment to the Constitution which shall give to Congress the right in question.[28]

That put an end to legislation on internal improvements, at least in the near term. Clay's nationalist vanguard had no immediate hope of mustering a majority for new federal works without the President's support.

Moreover, "Old Republicans," embittered by recent nationalist indulgences, and increasingly anxious about federal encroachments into state
affairs, instantly warmed to the President's clear demarcation of the
constitutional line against federal action.

Yet, as a preemptive strike for political definition and legislative discipline, the President's leadership initiative left much to be desired. The
problem was that the nationalists, already taunted by Madison's belated
act of conscience, were not about to risk a power they were confident
Congress already possessed to the doubtful and drawn-out process of
state ratification. Controlling the House Committee on Internal Improvements, Clay turned the demand for a constitutional amendment
back on the President with devastating effect, and by the time the
congressional debate was finished, Monroe's authority to interpret the
gospel of Jeffersonian Republicanism, if not the authority of the gospel
itself, had become the central issue. The essential points were these:
While Monroe claimed the high ground of Republican orthodoxy, he
had violated the chief canon of that orthodoxy by presuming to stifle
the independent deliberations of the legislature. While Monroe had
admitted legitimate controversy over the matter in question, he had
offered no intelligible reasons or arguments to justify its exclusion from
the legislative agenda but simply gave "an historical account of the
operations of his own mind." While Monroe had refused even to debate
the rather clear bases of the constitutional authority of Congress over
the issue, he apparently had no such qualms about the limits of executive authority, for he had matter-of-factly ordered his troops to repair
the Plattsburgh road without even informing the state in question.
Finally, and most important, Monroe's position did not account for the
fact that many federal projects had previously been authorized by Republican congresses and sanctioned by presidents with presumably unimpeachable political credentials. Specifically, why did both Jefferson
and Madison sign bills authorizing and extending the Cumberland
road?[29]

Why indeed? Stung by these attacks, Monroe shot off an anxious
letter to Madison: "Be so good as to give me in detail the reasons which
justify the Cumberland road."[30] Unfortunately, Madison, on whose
authority in constitutional matters Monroe had staked so much, could
not recall the circumstances of Jefferson's action. Madison ventured
that the sage of Monticello had probably acted either "doubtingly or
hastily." He further admitted that the extensions of the road that he
himself had sanctioned had not received the attention they deserved.

Finally, he threw the matter back in Monroe's lap with a stern warning about the "serious danger" posed by enticing precedents that were, in fact, based on "inadvertence."[31]

The implications of this reply for the leadership position Monroe claimed for himself were sobering. Congress had shown itself willing and able to challenge the President on his own turf—determination of the rules of propriety. Moreover, Madison's response seemed to confirm Clay's insinuation that the President's benevolent protection of the "path already traced" was a farce, that the baggage of received principles upon which he rested his political consensus was nothing more than a wrapper for his own personal opinions, and that the authority of precedent had no claims over the combined force of interest and opportunity. To make matters even worse, Monroe found that Congress was not going to let the issue rest. Requests for separate reports on internal improvements from the secretary of war (the then ultra-nationalist Calhoun) and the secretary of the treasury (the more orthodox but increasingly antagonistic Crawford) directly challenged the President for control over his own administration.

The effect of this challenge was to spark Monroe into action and fully engage his own creative energies in defense of his leadership position. With his political project in jeopardy, Monroe thought through the whole issue once again. This time Madison's inability to provide a principled justification of past action was very much in his mind, and he felt freer to think about it by his own lights. Monroe's task was nothing less than to reclaim his own political authority, and to do this he had to repair the inconsistencies of past practice, save the reputations of his predecessors, reestablish the integrity of Republican orthodoxy in the age of nationalism, and, in the process, find some back door to the irresistible opportunities at hand.

Given the weight of this task, it should come as no surprise that the result was the longest and most tortured state paper of Monroe's tenure. The "Views of the President of the United States on the Subject of Internal Improvements" has not come down to us as a timeless example of constitutional argumentation, but it remains ripe with insight into the leadership problems Monroe had to negotiate and the kind of politics he made.[32] It was thoroughly patrician in its assertion of leadership: it met the political dilemmas of orthodox-innovation with a comprehensive treatise on the history of federal improvements policy; it rested the opinions it expressed on the political identity of the man who presented them and on the persuasive power of his exegesis on enlightened statesmen; and through some excruciating mental gymnastics, it wound its way toward an ecumenical solution that would justify innovation on orthodox ground.

Eager to head off the centrifugal forces pulling at his administration and to have his position clearly understood by his official family, the President read the entire seventy-page tome to his cabinet and indicated his intention to include the message in his third annual address. At this point John Quincy Adams, fearing the effects of another unsolicited and even more overbearing lecture from the President to the Congress, successfully argued for some relief from the bitter debates.[33] Satisfied that his cabinet would now respond to Congress according to the views he had just expressed, Monroe agreed to put the paper aside until congressional action elicited a more direct presidential response.

Much to his dismay, a national economic panic in 1819 and a series of testy congressional debates in 1820 over the admission of Missouri to statehood intervened to protract the delay. Ironically, while the economic contraction put congressional enthusiasm for public works on hold, the tensions aired in the Missouri debates over questions of states' rights and national authority directly engaged the principles Monroe had so painstakingly sought to reconcile in his paper on improvements. Now, with Congress debating those principles on its own accord and without benefit of his wisdom, Monroe found himself an anxious captive of norms about the president's proper role. He was convinced that the Missouri controversy was part of a plot to raise up new parties and redivide the nation politically, and his resolve to head off any such development, perhaps more than anything else, led him to support a compromise that would exclude slavery from the yet unorganized northern territories of the Louisiana Purchase. Monroe had a veto message prepared, and he certainly would have issued it if the Congress had interfered with the right of a new state, like Missouri, to determine its own domestic institutions. But Missouri's right to slaves was confirmed and the question of whether states admitted in the future were to be bound by the territorial arrangements set by the federal government was left ambiguous enough for the President to uphold the appearance of consensus. Monroe communicated his views in favor of such a compromise through channels, notably the senator from his home state, James Barbour. Barbour, in turn, entered the negotiations with Clay, rallied southern senators to support the compromises, and helped Monroe quell a preelection revolt among Virginia Republicans precipitated by his qualified acceptance of slavery's restriction.[34] Congress had passed to Monroe a package that finessed the indignation of the southern hot-spurs and accommodated northern opinion. Soon the President would return the favor. In his paper on internal improvement, he had already come to a position quite similar. He would support states' rights in principle, and uphold national authority in practice.

Happily for Monroe, the sectional crisis in Congress did not reverberate all that loudly in the nation at large, and the slavery issue subsided almost as soon as the compromises were hammered out. The issue of internal improvements proved far more pressing and persistent, and in the spring of 1822, Monroe was finally given an opportunity to speak his mind directly. With the economy rebounding, Congress garnered enough votes to pass a bill authorizing repairs to the Cumberland road and the construction of toll booths to finance them. In response, the President retrieved his paper on public works and revised it for formal delivery. An extended coda to his only veto, Monroe's message gained additional, implicit meaning as a belated presidential resolution of the larger issues surrounding the admission of Missouri.

On its face, the veto message met the nationalist challenge to Republican orthodoxy head on with a point-by-point refutation of its deviations from strict constitutional construction and a ringing reaffirmation of the old states' rights creed. Speaking to a younger generation with the voice of firsthand experience, the President opened with a review of the entire history of the controversy over internal improvements, commenting in turn on the true meaning of the Revolution, the Articles of Confederation, and the Constitution. He then proceeded to reject the six most obvious constitutional rationales for the authority of Congress to undertake a program of public works, elaborating upon the dire consequences that would result from looser interpretations of each. The postal clause, the national defense clause, the general welfare clause, the taxation clause, the interstate commerce clause, and the necessary and proper clause all failed to meet Monroe's test; an unbridled federal claim of eminent domain and an intrusive national police force—in short, all the power necessary for a national subjugation of the states—would, he charged, follow directly from any attempt to hedge the interpretation of these clauses for the sake of internal improvements. Monroe concluded that only by a carefully constructed constitutional amendment could the manifest benefits of a national system of improvements be realized without irreparable damage to the integrity of the states.

At this level, the message confirmed the position Monroe had enunciated in his first annual message to Congress. In doing so, it provided a pointed elaboration of his reasoning on the improvements issue for Henry Clay's edification, and offered reassurance to states like his own Virginia that had been shaken by the Missouri debates. But as Monroe now knew, leaving the matter there failed to account for the past actions of Republican presidents (how could the federal government refuse to repair a road of its own making?), and it provided precious little to feed the nationalist ambitions of a rising cadre of young Republicans. Moreover, as he had recognized in his first inaugural address, internal improvements were a prime instrument for binding the nation together, and the virtues of doing so were even more apparent after the Missouri debates than they had been before. Woven through his old Republican catechism, then, was a second and far more accommodating message.

The real problem for Monroe—and, as he set out to prove, the problem for all other right-thinking Republicans—was not the nationalist zeal for internal improvement projects per se but the ultra-nationalist (Federalist) zeal for a "system." It was the federal government's powers to construct, operate, and control as implied by the idea of a national system that Monroe found unsupportable without an amendment, and it was just such power that he found at issue in the present bill authorizing federal construction of toll booths and the federal collection of tolls on the Cumberland road. On this distinction Monroe's ringing defense of the Old Republican discipline quietly reached out a helping hand to those of more expansive national vision that it seemed at first to place in difficult straits. While insisting down the line that Congress could claim no general powers within the government's original charter over internal improvements, he took care to endorse the view that, if the federal government was to function at all, the powers it had simply to raise and appropriate money for genuine national purposes could not be limited except by the ultimate power of the people over their elected representatives. Thus, though the federal government could not "execute" a national "system" of roads and canals, it could still "cause" to be executed a seemingly endless number of national projects by simple appropriations.

Having found the saving grace, Monroe dismissed the charges of inconsistency in the behavior of his predecessors, reconciled the original construction of the Cumberland road with Republican orthodoxy, and announced his willingness to persevere on this well-traced path now that its proper boundaries had been rediscovered.[35] If Congress would just limit itself to the appropriation of the money for national improvements and leave everything else to the states, everyone could get on with the business at hand and nothing of significance would be manifestly changed.

> Having now examined all the powers of Congress under which the right to adopt and execute a system of internal improvement is claimed and the reasons in support of it in each instance, I think it may fairly be concluded that such a right has not been granted. *It appears and is admitted that much may be done in aid of such a system by the right which is derived from several of the existing grants, and more especially from that to appropriate the public money.* But still it is manifest that as a system for the United States it can never be carried into effect under that grant or under all of them united, the great and essential power being deficient, consisting of a right to take up the subject on principle.[36]

Congress responded with new internal improvement bills, each carefully crafted to comply with the President's newly articulated constitutional scruples. Monroe confidently signed each, and he used his remaining annual addresses to propose more.[37] In 1824, he even signed the General Survey Act, which was nothing if not a preparation for a system. Through this happy interchange, the President had the satisfaction of having provided the leadership necessary for holding the pursuit of a major national objective within the bounds of precedent and of showing how orthodoxy could tap national power to do good work without threatening the autonomy of the states or the integrity of the Jeffersonian regime.

But the full political impact of Monroe's tack has yet to come into view. The President's message was a valiant effort to deny the political consequences of significant action on a pressing national issue that he himself found irresistible. Its political effect, however, was to implicate him even deeper in the sectarian fragmentation of the regime he had been at such great pains to preserve. Almost eager to accept the calming salve of the Missouri Compromises and bury further debate over slavery, national elites fell all over themselves to get out in front of the internal improvements issue at the President's expense. The obfuscations of history and principle to which Monroe had been driven in his effort to render Republican orthodoxy consistent with current nationalist impulses inevitably played into the hands of all those whom he needed to convince that orthodoxy was not a sham and that the great Jeffersonian consensus was not hopelessly distended. Old Republicans now turned on him for reading a heretical doctrine of the unlimited power of appropriation into the Constitution. Nationalists continued to blast him for reading an essential doctrine of federal jurisdiction out of the Constitution. And a new radical faction, fast emerging under the leadership of Martin Van Buren, claimed for itself the lost virtues of frugality in the post-panic era. Throwing up their hands in disgust, the radicals voted for the projects, and then took over the call for an explicit constitutional amendment as the only salvation from Monroe's degradation of principle.[38]

At the very moment of his greatest personal triumph in domestic affairs, the President found himself besieged by fellow Republicans determined to explode the grand historical-political synthesis he had so carefully constructed and to destroy the defense of continuity that was making concerted action possible. Instead of holding the party together, the "Views of the President on the Question of Internal Improvements" splintered it; the President's position became a lightning rod directing the energies of those who would forge alternative coalitions. Impatience with its timidity opened a channel for common action between Clay and Adams; outrage at its nationalism opened a channel for common action between Van Buren and Crawford.

The Stalwart as Heretic

Monroe's leadership elaborated Republican orthodoxy to the point where his central claim to political authority began to dissolve in his own achievements. He had realized great national objects. Proudly he boasted to Madison that he had "promote[d] the public good in every line to which the powers of the federal government extended."[39] But there was no moving this regime forward without concomitantly dislodging it from the foundations on which it stood, and by 1822 precious few were prepared to endorse Monroe's vision of where things were (and were not) headed. Indeed, it would seem that the only one who still believed that the nation was proceeding apace on the "path already traced" was the President himself. In the end, leaders at opposing poles of Republican opinion—Martin Van Buren and Henry Clay—

found their common ground in charging the President with political heresy and holding him personally responsible for the degeneration of Jeffersonian principles. Monroe's initial leadership challenge became in the end his most conspicuous failure.

The President, of course, was "mortified" by the questions being raised about his orthodoxy. Van Buren radicals were accusing him of amalgamating the Republican party with the opposition, of compromising Republican principles with Federalist programs, and thus of reviving Federalism in Republican dress.[40] He was, he responded in protest, merely a loyal party stalwart who had done nothing more than acknowledge the irrelevance of the Federalist party and tap the opportunity to build a great national consensus on solid Republican ground.

> No allurement has been offered to the federalists to calm them down into a state of tranquility. None of them have been appointed to high office, and very few to the lowest. Their misconduct in the late war, and the success of that war broke them as a party. It has been charged to me to have reared them up . . . But in what mode? . . . Altho' I have thought that it was consistent with the principles of our government, & would promote the general welfare, to draw the people more closely together, and to leave the federal leaders without support, yet I have known that that object, without regarding other considerations of a more personal character, would be defeated if the person in this station went in advance of his own party; that he must rest exclusively on it . . . On this principle I have invariably acted, so that the charge of amalgamation is not correctly levelled at me, nor, if a merit, do I claim the credit of it.[41]

In truth, in drawing the people more closely together, leaving the Federal leaders without support, and resting all action on the Republican party, Monroe again had gone far toward completing the work of his predecessors. A single party of national consensus had been anticipated in Jefferson's first inaugural address; it had been left to Monroe to orchestrate his party's apotheosis, to transpose the Republican cause into a beneficent government of national unity. The problem was that this opportunity could not accommodate the exercise of power needed to realize its object. Monroe acted to elaborate Jefferson's vision, but unlike Jefferson, he had no enemy to assault, no scourge to eradicate, no alternative to offer. The voice of an established orthodoxy, he was constrained simply to deny the order-shattering effects of his innovations. If in the end the charges against him ring truer than the defense, it is not so much because Federalism was in fact resurgent as because

Monroe's efforts to control the meaning of the changes he had brought about were so beset by their own internal contradictions.

Monroe worked harder than any other president to articulate the case for perseverance, continuity, and consensus, but in doing so he was constantly tripping over himself to insist that his leadership was benign, that nothing of consequence was being altered. He rendered the Seminole War a matter of inevitability, internal improvements a matter of political consistency, the transcendence of party politics a matter of regularity. But the messages were too delicate for the achievements, the President's actions too consequential for their precious justifications. Monroe's path-already-traced held the nation in a time warp where past and future mingled together in perfect synthesis; if the outrageous charge of his heresy did nothing else, it dispelled this illusory world and focused the reality of change with devastating clarity.

In the end, Monroe's insistence on innovation without repudiation prompted those he sought to lead to turn on him. The disruptive side of leadership, the side that Monroe could not exploit and needed to keep hidden, twisted back on itself, imploding in a sectarian degeneration of everything that he wanted to preserve. His purely constructive leadership project unraveled as a jumble of self-denying assertions of power and self-defeating policy successes.

Part Three:
John Quincy Adams's Disjunction

Talent and virtue alone

THE DIFFICULTIES James Monroe faced controlling political definitions were dwarfed by those that confronted his first lieutenant. The election of John Quincy Adams in 1825 snapped the time-worn linkages between presidential authority and the "Revolution of 1800"; and with that break, the challenge of national political leadership shifted categorically once again. The only thing more dubious than Adams's authority to change things was his case for continuity. The fourth consecutive Republican to come to the presidency, Adams personified the regime's crisis of identity.

Adams's inaugural address described this place in history in the terms best suited for him to exercise the powers of his office. In it, his leadership problem instantly comes clear. The new President tied his prospects to two historic trends. First, he applauded the great progress the nation had made in overcoming the political divisions of the past, and he proposed to take the one last step necessary to realize the highest ideals of patrician governance: he would discard party labels altogether and run his administration solely on the basis of merit. Proclaiming the end of "prejudice and passion," Adams promised a government in which the "badge of party communion" would finally yield to "talent and virtue alone." Then, turning from politics to policy, Adams joined this bold stand on behalf of party-blind government to a humble pledge of programmatic continuity: "In . . . the promise and performance of my immediate predecessor the line of duty for his successor is clearly delineated. To pursue to their consummation those purposes of improvement in our common condition instituted or recommended by him will embrace the whole sphere of my obligation." As an indication of how those purposes might be further elaborated, Adams eyed the field of public works and urged his colleagues to find their way clear of the constitutional objections that still haunted federal action in this domain.[1]

For a loyal servant of the Monroe administration, this message was as predictable as it was proper. Still, one wonders how anyone with firsthand experience of Monroe's stewardship, least of all the former secretary of state, could have believed that the prospects for a nonpartisan consensus would be enhanced by yet another advance against the ideological boundaries of Jeffersonian nationalism. Monroe's conscientious efforts to elaborate the Republican program along nationalist lines had already made a shambles of party unity, and now, with the passing of the Virginia dynasty, the nationalist impulse could not even boast the unprejudiced voice of political orthodoxy. While the economic panic of 1819 had yielded to resurgent prosperity and the sectional conflicts of the Missouri debates had given way to the spirit of compromise, the polity that emerged from those experiences was quite different from the one upon which the Monroe administration had been premised. In this new situation, elaborating the previous line of policy in the name of national unity was simply a nonstarter.

An affiliated leader in a vulnerable regime, Adams was caught in a double bind. While he was wholly lacking in authority to repudiate the past, a simple affirmation of the received course no longer held much hope for effectively addressing the most pressing political questions of the day. Practically speaking, to build anything more on the promise and performance of his predecessor, Adams would, in effect, have had to champion an entirely new political formation; to champion a new formation he would, in effect, have had to redivide the nation politically on programmatic grounds; and by dividing the nation politically he would, in effect, have been breaking the central canons of patrician governance and Jeffersonian republicanism both, and thus undercutting the initial premise of building on his inheritance. Working through this puzzle, Adams would generate more than mere fractiousness among the faithful; he would drive a systemic political disjunction, a momentous regime shift bereft of any clear political warrants and cut loose from the old political foundations.

Like his father before him, Adams longed to dispel illusions and cut through the confusions that had overtaken the polity. But the political contradictions straddled in his initial leadership posture made clarity an elusive goal. Once in the presidency, the nation's foremost diplomat suddenly found himself possessed of "a tragic inability to make himself understood."[2] What he claimed to represent (continuity in the traditional line of political succession and the received line of national policy) bore little relationship to what he immediately came to represent (the collapse of the old consensus and the raising up of a new party). Adams exposed the bankruptcy of the regime with which he was associated in the very act of taking control of it. His leadership stalled aborning, caught in its own hapless struggle for credibility. Stigmatizing what he claimed to represent, his ambition offered an ideal target, a negative premise, for the mobilization of an encompassing opposition movement. Unable to stake out clear ground for the exercise of his powers, Adams's actions so changed the polity as to plant his successor on the most potent ground of all.

Toward a New Political Formation

Adams pursued a course in presidential leadership that not only energized his enemies but incapacitated his friends. For this, he has gained the reputation of a political incompetent as well as a failure in the presidency.[3] His insistence on patrician propriety contrasts starkly with the efforts of those all around him who were trying at the time to develop new forms of partisan engagement more attuned to the expansion and democratization of the nation. Adams's allies implored him to follow through on the implications of his rise to power and to help them forge a new political organization on his behalf. But once he had launched his administration, the new President stubbornly held himself aloof from the seemingly transparent political imperatives of his day. At midterm, when the President's supporters lost control of both houses of Congress for the first time in the nation's history, Adams's patrician resolve suggested nothing so much as passive acceptance of the inevitability of defeat.

But this view of the matter is far too simple. One problem with the assertions of Adams's political ineptitude is that they fail to take account of the political savvy and strategic cunning he exhibited in getting to the presidency in the first place. It was certainly no accident that this Federalist apostate rose to the highest office in the land along the traditional line of Republican advance. Moreover, Adams is not alone in his failure to master the kind of political situation he faced once he got to the president's chair. The political conundrum at the center of Adams's inaugural message prompts us to think about all those other late-regime affiliates who have come into office with tenuous political attachments to the regime they are supposed to represent and strained arguments for affirming its already vulnerable policy commitments. Understanding the futility of Adams's leadership effort as a certain kind of failure—a prototype of future struggles—makes it easier to credit the political prowess he demonstrated in his pursuit of power and to tap the political insights contained in the choices he actually made. The difficulties Adams faced in reconciling his position in the received order with his impulse to be a leader in his own right point to his ambition, not his ineptitude, as the engine of political disjunction in the mid-1820s.[4]

A Federalist senator during most of Jefferson's administration, Adams was one of the first of his band to see just how bleak their prospects were. "The power of [Jefferson's] administration," he wrote in 1802, "rests upon the support of a much stronger majority of the people throughout the Union than the former administrations ever possessed since the first establishment of the Constitution. Whatever the merits or demerits of the former administrations may have been, there never was a system of measures more completely and irrevocably abandoned and rejected by the popular voice. It never can and never will be revived."[5] As he tracked the Republican ascendancy in his home state of Massachusetts, Adams also found much to support in Jefferson's policies. Lured in by the administration's encompassing alternative, he put himself at odds with his own Federalist partisans on major policy questions, most notably, the purchase of Louisiana. These tensions reached the breaking point in 1807 when Adams resigned his Senate seat to protest resolutions from Massachusetts condemning the administration's foreign policy and attended the Republican party caucus to nominate James Madison for the presidency. Adams did not immediately endear himself to Republican leaders, but getting purged from the party of his father for supporting Jefferson's embargo was certainly a good start. Hounded once again by New England opposition and dismayed by the persistence of Federalism there, James Madison stepped in to rescue Adams's career. Graciously removing Adams from the difficulties he faced on the domestic political scene, he sent him into the foreign service as minister to Russia.

By the time Monroe tapped him for secretary of state, Adams had been almost nine years in foreign service. We have seen that this appointment served Monroe's interests in several ways, adding talent and geographic breadth to his administration without bringing any independent political power to it. Still a mere servant of the executive, Adams seemed wholly dependent on the good graces of the President and safely blocked from further advancement. But from his position as first secretary, Adams began cultivating a political following almost immediately, and he soon emerged as a formidable national figure in his own right. His rapid rise to political prominence within the administration hinted at some extraordinary and wide-ranging political abilities; his succession in 1825, confounding his sponsor's plan to break the traditional line of Republican advance, confirmed them.

Consider in this regard the crowning achievement of Adams's service as secretary of state: his successful campaign to head off an alliance offered by Great Britain in the cause of protecting the new Latin republics from the designs of the Holy Alliance. The idea of a British alliance at this particular time and for this particular purpose received the private endorsement of Jefferson and Madison as well as Monroe. But Adams was the one who would be held responsible for negotiating this departure from traditional Republican doctrine, and he saw as plainly as everyone else that any such move would instantly revive charges of his latent Federalism and nip his presidential prospects in the bud. Unwilling to take the fall and determined to protect his all-too-vulnerable Republican credentials in public opinion, Adams launched a one-man, anti-British crusade, trumping even the paragons of regime rectitude on this touchstone of political orthodoxy. The immediate results of his effort were the promulgation in the Monroe Doctrine of a non-colonization policy independent of Great Britain and an unstained credit for Adams to take into the election campaign.[6]

The problem was that the political hardball that Adams played to get himself elected undercut whatever advantage might have been expected from continuing the traditional line of advancement. As we shall see, Adams's brilliant political maneuvering around the promulgation of the Monroe Doctrine led to his near complete loss of control over the foreign policy of his own administration. And this was but one part of a much larger story of how his drive for presidential power in the late Jeffersonian era enervated his authority as a leader. In the short term, Adams's appeal to regularity and continuity in his succession from the post of secretary of state barely masked the scramble for power going on behind the scenes, a scramble in which he himself was circumventing established political institutions, defying his own standard of "talent and virtue alone," and playing upon emergent political divisions.

As the Monroe administration entered its final year, Adams rebuffed those who sought him out for the vice-presidential nomination of the Republican party caucus. The caucus appeared to him an outmoded piece of machinery, incapable of encompassing the vast expansion of interest and talent that had occurred since its inception. Adams confided to his agents that he would decline accepting its nomination, "even if it were for President."[7] Far from making a stand for consensus, continuity, and conciliation, he determined to take his chances along with the other five candidates boasting Republican party credentials and let the traditional vehicle for garnering party support behind a presidential ticket collapse. In so doing, he contributed mightily to the subversion of the political order with which he had become affiliated and upon which the legitimacy of his succession from the State Department depended.

The rules of political conduct that Adams had to break in order to continue the secretary of state's claim to the presidency put his leadership on an untenable double track from the start, and the tracks diverged with every new step he took. As the strengths and weaknesses of the various candidates canceled each other out, it became apparent that no one would command an electoral majority from the national canvass. William Crawford, the actual nominee of the caucus, placed fourth in the popular vote, third in the Electoral College tally. Andrew Jackson was the popular favorite, and it is worth noting that he had long been a favorite of Adams's also. William Plumer, Jr., a New Hampshire representative and Adams enthusiast, records a fascinating conversation of December 1823 in which the secretary of state assessed the candidates in the coming contest. Adams considered Jackson not only "strong" but "meritorious." He had "no hesitation in saying that he preferred [Jackson] decidedly to any of the other candidate [sic]—(He no doubt made a tacit reservation in his own favor)." Adams believed that "Jackson would administer the government with perfect integrity & disinterestedness, free from all bargains, compromises, coalitions and corruption," and this was "he added, with great emphasis, . . . more than [he] can say of either Crawford, Calhoun, Clay or Clinton."[8] These were sincere sentiments voiced by the only member of Monroe's cabinet to champion Jackson's complete vindication in the Florida campaign, but they bore little resemblance to the actions taken by the candidate who found himself second in the Electoral College tally in 1825. With the presidential contest thrown into the House of Representatives, Adams apparently lost his disgust for bargains, compromises, and coalitions. He did not allow his appreciation of the general's many talents and virtues, let alone the preferences of the people, stand in the way of his own opportunity for political advancement. The general's friends would never let him forget it.

The appeal of multiple candidates contending outside of established channels proved inconclusive, but the runoff in the House instantly rearranged political alliances. Though he had been opposed by more than two thirds of the electorate, Adams swept New England and emerged as the only candidate with a sectional block of states behind him. Putting that strength to its best advantage, he exploited cleavages elsewhere to broker the other six of the thirteen states he needed for victory.[9] Politicking one on one with the congressional delegations, Adams abruptly discarded the concern for protecting Republican orthodoxy that he had so recently displayed during the development of the Monroe Doctrine. Now playing to his previous identity, he made himself the overwhelming favorite of the remaining Federalists. Assurances to Daniel Webster, their leading figure and hitherto not much of an Adams fan, proved critical in adding three more states to his column. New York was the most impressive victory, for the Federalists in that state had shown a particular dislike for the secretary in the past.

Federalist support alone, however, was not enough to secure the election. The masterstroke of Adams's political ambition was to overcome the personal enmity that had long marked his relations with Henry Clay and to ease the way for the Kentuckian to defy a resolution from his state's legislature instructing him to support Jackson in the runoff. The history of jealousy and distrust that divided Adams and Clay stands in stark contrast with Adams's warm feeling for Jackson, but personal feelings aside, Adams had no hope of victory without Clay, and Clay, no hope of influence without Adams.[10] While Clay's direct assault on Jackson in the Florida debates effectively blocked any advance on that front, he and Adams shared many of the same views on national policy.[11] Once he was out of direct competition with Adams for the presidency, Clay warmed with anticipation of becoming first lieutenant in an administration fully committed to the nationalist program he had so long been urging.[12] Whatever the specifics of their private understanding, Adams certainly did nothing to dampen Clay's expectations, and he obviously said enough to get the most unrelenting critic of Monrovian orthodoxy to deliver him the presidency.[13]

In the immediate aftermath of this maneuvering, the gap in the middle of Adams's leadership stance widened abruptly. With a strict sense of propriety, the new President offered each of his rivals a place in his administration. His first offer, however, went to Clay, and Clay's willingness to become secretary of state made all subsequent overtures to national conciliation politically moot. Once the Adams-Clay alliance was extended beyond the House election into the composition of the top leadership positions of the administration, it projected a formidable reworking of the foundations of national power. Jackson, Crawford, Calhoun, and Clinton found common ground simply by virtue of their refusal to have anything to do with this "coalition." Meanwhile, Adams turned to others, who served to broaden and deepen the message being taken from his first appointment. With Jackson's chief rival for the political loyalties of the West in the State Department, Adams put Richard Rush, an ardent protectionist from Pennsylvania, in the Treasury. Rufus King, minister to Great Britain under the first Adams, was returned to London to replace Rush, underscoring the point that diehard Federalists would be proscribed no longer. A bit later, John W. Taylor, a leading antislavery agitator in the Missouri debates and a pivotal figure for Adams in the New York elections, won his bid for Speaker of the House. As the administration's candidate, Taylor did not exactly embody the themes of nonpartisan consensus and conciliation.[14] Indeed, the awkward proprieties of conciliation had given way on virtually all fronts to a potent distillation of nationalist sentiment extending from New England, through the Mid-Atlantic States, and outward to the West.[15] In effect, the Adams administration had shed old restraints on government action and promised to loose the full potential of federal power in the promotion of economic improvement. It was, de facto, a new political formation.

For those who might have missed these signals, Adams endowed his administration with a sweeping nationalist manifesto. He rejected the advice of some of his cabinet advisors, including Clay, who urged a moderate tone for his first annual message to Congress and cautioned against proposing too much all at once. The President knew well enough that nationalism had become steeped in controversy and that he was deeply engaged in a "perilous experiment." But he had also

witnessed firsthand the confusions engendered by half-hearted and in-
direct endorsements of the nationalist program, and he had observed
the self-defeating effect of lending support to new policies with words
that seem to endorse the fears of their most likely opponents. Another
Monroe-like reconciliation of divergent political positions would never
sustain the kind of federal involvement in economic development that
Adams now contemplated. To advance further, the nationalist program
would have to be integrated, systematized, and above all articulated for
what it was. The new President looked to "a practicability of a longer
range than a single session of Congress," and concluded that what his
experiment needed most was a forthright "avowal of general principles."[16]

With a brazen assertion that "liberty is power," Adams jettisoned the
circumspection that had marked the nationalist sentiments of his Republican predecessors. Proclaiming that the one true test of a nation's
political institutions was its capacity to build great monuments to civilization, he outlined a nationalist program of monumental proportion.
He proposed a federal Department of the Interior, a national naval
academy, a national university, a national astronomical observatory, a
national bankruptcy law, a national militia law, a national system of
weights and measures, a national patent law, and a national system of
improvements in transportation. The deep-seated fears of government
that had helped to bring the Republicans to power in the first place
were nowhere in evidence here. Indeed, Adams chided those reluctant
to follow his lead for their tendency to be "palsied by the will of [their]
constituents," and he challenged them to rise above local political resistance and embrace a truly cosmopolitan standard. The constitutional
hair-splitting that had so recently preoccupied his predecessor in his
own message on public works gave way to a rapid-fire review of federal
power and a simple conclusion: "If these powers . . . may be effectively
brought to action by laws promoting the improvement of agriculture,
commerce and manufactures, the cultivation and encouragement of the
mechanical arts, the advancement of literature, and the progress of the
sciences, ornamental and profound, to refrain from exercising them for
the benefit of the people themselves would be to hide in the earth the
talent committed to our charge—would be treachery to the most sacred
of trusts."[17]

By forging a new coalition and fortifying it with a manifesto that
dwarfed all previous interpretations of the reach of national power, the

Adams administration projected a political departure more definitive than anything since 1801. Soon, the President's cabinet advisers were traveling the country, discounting old political allegiances and hammering interest in internal improvements and domestic manufactures into a new base of political support for Adams's administration. By the spring of 1827, Clay was agitating for a convention that would bring together the friends of the administration "without regard to party denominations heretofore existing." He hoped the convention would publish an address "firm in purpose," and "form a nucleus" for a national organization.[18]

Between his drive for the presidency in 1824 and his first annual message as president in late 1825, Adams transformed the national political landscape more decisively than Monroe had done during his entire eight-year tenure. But no sooner was the revolution of 1825 announced than it collapsed, its leader seemingly paralyzed by his own disruptive force. Adams may have launched his presidency with patronage and passion, but he remained ever insistent on his inaugural pledge that his would be an administration of "talent and virtue alone." He may have argued forcefully for breaking through past constraints on federal action, but he clung to the conceit that his administration was only an extension of the work of his predecessors. No sooner did he thrust himself forward as a political leader in his own right then he assumed the posture of a disinterested manager and steadfastly refused to provide the practical supports essential to the success of the political reconstruction he had set in motion. Denying in principle what he had so aggressively undertaken, he sponsored the most partisan program in a quarter-century with the most uncompromising defense of nonpartisanship imaginable.

The Reification of Technique

Jefferson had also invoked consensual themes to justify a great departure; but, as we have seen, he never let the value of continuity interfere with negotiating that departure, nor did he ever contemplate leading an administration that would be politically indifferent to his cause. The comparison highlights just what it takes to secure a departure. It takes more than a new coalition and a new constitutional vision, more than a new program bursting with material services and supports with which to develop the nation's economy, more than political sensitivity to public opinion and skill in manipulating it. Adams had all these things; what Jefferson had that Adams lacked was a clear warrant for breaking with the past.

The political relationship Adams established between the received order of things and the changes he anticipated was as cloudy as Jefferson's was clear. In fact, the path he had blazed to get to power had called into question the most credible claim he had to make on his own behalf once he got there. As Adams acknowledged in his inaugural address, his authority remained tied to the continuity of policy and politics symbolized in his service to the Monroe administration and in his succession from Monroe's cabinet. With the order-affirming side of his leadership project still tied to confirming the integrity of the politics of the past, he simply had no justification for his own catalytic effect. Adams had fostered vast political changes, but he could not credibly repudiate recent practices, and by actively pressing a political transformation of the first order, he came up short on the question of what exactly he was trying to uphold.

Thus once he overcame the obstacles in the path of his becoming president, once he cut through the political muddle Monroe had left him, once he staked out the new political ground he wished to develop, Adams was at a loss to follow through. The order-shattering effects of his election and the order-creating implications of his early initiatives made short work of his always shaky identification with the Jeffersonian regime and cast a dark shadow over the question of who he really was.

Adams's stubborn insistence on nonpartisanship might best be understood in this light; it filled the void that had been left by his shattering all the other rules of appropriate behavior. It became the centerpiece of his leadership project, responding however awkwardly to the embarrassing uncertainty as to what about the old order his administration was trying to affirm. Adams bridged the chasm in his basic leadership posture with a reification of patrician techniques.

The twisted logic of hoisting the standard of "talent and virtue alone" and clinging to it at all cost in the face of the partisan mobilizations that he himself had instigated begins to unfold here as part and parcel of Adams's tenuous struggle for political credibility. When he held himself aloof and tried to exemplify the ideals of the patrician statesman, he was not retreating from the new politics he had made, but trying to install it on a legitimate foundation. Putting his political identity to work as best he could to bridge the gap between his ambitions and his authority, he came up with "talent and virtue alone," the broadest and most hallowed standard of the patrician mode of governance. Wrapping his hard-hitting program in an archetype of administrative rectitude augmented his leadership posture by affirming something that was as fundamental as the changes he was setting in motion. Adams's stand against partisanship fortified him with a cause more basic than his controversial policies, one that leapfrogged the appearance of personal ambition and power seeking and gave him some claim to the high ground in the battle for legitimacy.

To appreciate Adams's problem in joining the order-shattering, order-affirming, and order-creating dimensions of presidential action in a coherent leadership project is to appreciate the audacity of his course in fostering a new political formation and then defending the administration it controlled as a fortress of propriety standing *against* a break with the past. Adams's rigorous adherence to patrician principles of governmental management regardless of the personal consequences weighed in politically against Jackson's reputation for impulsive behavior. Adams's stubborn refusal to indulge in electioneering weighed in against the political threat posed by an insurgent military chieftain and the demagogic movement rallied behind him. With studied disinterest, Adams sought to cast the onus of division back upon those who were mobilizing to oppose him. In effect, he challenged those who would reject his administration to reject the governing mores of an entire generation.

All this is not to say that the dual track of Adams's leadership—at once sponsoring and denying a major political departure—ever came together to give him what he needed to succeed. Both sides of this effort looked toward a clarification of Adams's historical position as trustee of a regime whose legitimacy had become steeped in controversy, and each side cast the political alternative in the darkest light possible. But the practical business of getting the two sides to work in tandem would have defied the most skillful politician. In practice, the extreme measures Adams took to build a political foundation for the exercise of power compounded the difficulties of sustaining his central claim to authority, and the extreme measures he took to assert this claim to authority compounded his difficulties in exercising power. Looking in such radically different directions at once, Adams's leadership posture failed to cut effectively either way.

Consider once again Adams's savvy political stratagem of clinging to Republican orthodoxy in the development of the Monroe Doctrine in 1823. His adroit handling of this matter as secretary of state occasioned the first great policy controversy of his own administration, and that controversy pressed upon him both the imperatives of following through to build a new party and the problems of doing just that. Shortly after taking office, Adams was beset by several implications of his success in gaining a policy of noncolonization in Latin America that did not broach the risky question of an alliance with Great Britain and with it his own Federalist past. In the first place, the Latin republics responded to the United States' overture by inviting the Adams administration to send a delegation to a convention they planned to hold in Panama. For Adams to affirm the traditional policy of no alliances now and refuse to send a mission to Panama would be to open the door to British leadership in Latin America and render the Monroe Doctrine meaningless as a unilateral assertion of American leadership. By accepting the invitation, however, Adams would be breaking with the old policy, undercutting the consensual ground on which the Monroe Doctrine rested, and pulling himself into one of those tortured debates about the consistency of principles that he had found so debilitating during his tenure in Monroe's cabinet. Meanwhile, the British themselves were pondering the implications of Adams's bold nationalist program in light of their own increasingly deep commitments to laissez faire. Just as the Latin republics were sending signals about a possible alliance to the United States, the British decided to take their revenge for the rebuff they had received from their own overture to the United States and to show the upstart mercantilists in North America who really wielded power in world affairs. In a series of swift blows, Parliament effectively cut the United States out of its lucrative trade in the West Indies.[19]

The question of whether to send a mission to Panama exposed to all Adams's enemies the most vulnerable element of his great nationalist departure. The President, twice hoisted on his own petard, watched John Randolph, that hitherto impotent fanatic for the "Old Republican" cause, seize upon this issue and score the most devastating blows of his political career. Randolph renounced the Panama mission as a policy wholly antithetical to republican doctrines and precedents, and then working himself into a tirade of sheer madness, he tied the impropriety of the Panama mission to the impropriety of the Adams presidency itself. By the time he was finished, acceptance of the invitation from Panama had become the signal fruit of the unprincipled political bargain on which the new administration had been launched in the first place. Adams, the mastermind of the Monroe Doctrine, and Clay, the leading voice for Latin American independence, were roundly denounced as a "coalition of Blifil and Black George," a "combination unheard of till now of the puritan and the blackleg."[20]

Jefferson had faced tough questions of consistency and propriety, but generally he rolled right past them. Monroe's leadership was a constant tussle with fellow Republicans over these questions, but the President pushed and pulled his fractious band along his chosen course. The presidency of John Quincy Adams bogged down in these questions and could not budge. For the first time, Randolph's familiar charges of conspiracy, corruption, and degradation attracted a formidable band of administration opponents. Vice President John C. Calhoun and Senator Martin Van Buren immediately grasped the potential of his metaphors as standards of partisan mobilization. Their incipient opposition movement took up the devastating symbolism of the duplicitous prude and the wanton swindler and deftly joined it to outrage at the real policy debacle erupting over the West Indies trade.[21]

The outstanding issue for the President and his neomercantilist team was how best to fight back, and given the force of the onslaught, Adams's reification of patrician techniques left much to be desired as an answer. The bold nationalist departure stalled on Adams's belabored defense of the propriety of the Panama mission. The President pressed a fine distinction between allying with a European power and aligning with neighbor republics and then expostulated on that ground the thematic consistencies that tied together George Washington's original warning against alliances, the policies of the Monroe administration, and attendance at the Panama convention.[22] He met the larger political ruckus occasioned by the controversy by engaging in a newspaper debate with his vice president, properly cloaked under pseudonyms in the old-fashioned style. Meanwhile, with the President at wits' end to make himself understood and to reaffirm his commitment to continuity in national policy, his lieutenants were left to flounder in the practical business of building support for his new agenda. As Adams fought a war of words with Calhoun, his "traveling Cabinet" had to agitate the most attractive aspects of his program without benefit of the real material resources at his disposal.

Time and again the story was the same: while his opponents rode his weaknesses mercilessly, the President felt compelled to hold his most promising initiatives hostage to a defense of continuity and propriety. Consider the patronage question. Upholding the standard of talent and virtue alone did not mean just appointing some worthy Federalists to high office (a practice quite consistent with the administration's party-building efforts); it meant making an extraordinary effort to tolerate all officeholders who were not technically corrupt. With the nation mobilizing politically and redividing into Adams supporters and Jackson supporters, Adams would justify the removal of only twelve officers during his four years in office. The problems this posed for the administration were especially acute in those departments with wide-ranging field offices: in the Treasury Department, where a nest of old Crawford appointees was rallying to Jackson's cause, and in the Post Office where Postmaster General John McLean, a holdover from the Monroe administration, got high praise from Adams for his administrative talents despite his blatant hostility toward the administration and his flagrant gifts of office to supporters of Jackson and Calhoun. Going into the election of 1828, post offices and customs offices even in critical northern cities such as New York and Philadelphia were rabidly antiadministration.[23]

Repeatedly Clay and others implored the President to follow through on the party-building implications of his commitments by sweeping the departments clean of his enemies and rewarding his friends with offices. One of the secretary of state's first entreaties concerned the naval officer at New Orleans who had opposed the President's election. Clay argued the principle that once the election was decided "no officer depending upon the will of the President should be permitted to hold a conduct in open and continual disparagement of the Administration and its head." Adams acknowledged the principle as "undoubtedly correct," but argued the "difficulty and delicacy" of applying it. As there was no proof of the officer's having carried his designs into effect, "his removal would lead to the inference that I was ashamed to assign the real cause." And that real cause "would scarcely justify the removal of a man from office, in public opinion."[24]

Adams's response to Clay's urging a more aggressive use of patronage, like his response to Clay's urging moderation in the first annual address, was neither obtuse nor indifferent. Sensitivity to public opinion had been a hallmark of Adams's career from his decision to abandon the

Federalist party to his decision to defy the British as secretary of state. As President, Adams saw plainly that the potential power he held over patronage was of dubious value in the present circumstance. Whatever advantage there might be in it for securing his own political organization was negated by the effect it would have in fueling the already devastating charges of intrigue and corruption that had come to surround his administration since the moment of Clay's appointment as secretary of state.

That, after all, was the underlying message in Randolph's otherwise spurious harangue about the corrupt bargain during the Panama debates. Indeed, viewed from the other side, the lengths to which Adams had already gone to secure an independent political foundation for his presidency haunted his efforts to hoist the standard of "talent and virtue alone" against his enemies. That standard simply ignored what it could not defend, leaving the opposition to define the reality of the new political formation in its own terms. While Adams was presenting himself as the very model of patrician rectitude, his opponents pointed to the coalition he had forged and imputed to it the motives most offensive to the patrician conscience. Stories of the election intrigues that had disregarded the voice of the people in order to preserve the power of established elites and of the bargain that had delivered to Adams the highest office in the land in exchange for Clay's appointment as secretary of state made a mockery of Adams's claim to the high ground. Each of the party-building initiatives taken by Adams's administration on its own behalf helped the opposition to elaborate the theme of governmental intrigue and to undermine the President's defense of managerial integrity. The opposition newspapers denounced the administration's "traveling Cabinet" for electioneering and degrading the high offices of state. Likewise, they denounced the national convention of administration supporters, called in Harrisburg in 1827, for just what it was, "a stratagem to bring Pennsylvania over to the Adams party."[25]

For a president unable forthrightly to repudiate his inheritance and don the role of party-builder, there was no effective answer to charges such as these. In fact, the technical standard of administrative integrity that Adams put in place of party-building invited embarrassment by making each and every allegation of misconduct or mismanagement an indictment of his central claims to rule. The opposition majorities in the Twentieth Congress exploited this opportunity too. They launched a comprehensive review of the federal departments and documented their various and sundry charges of extravagant spending and malfeasance in the administration.[26] The ease with which the Jackson partisans turned the tables on the President and ran against him in the name of restoring the old virtues to government through retrenchment and reform reflects, above all else, just how vulnerable Adams's leadership claims were.

The contest between Jackson and Adams was uneven, but not because Jackson represented the politics of the future while Adams defended the politics of the past. It was uneven because of Jackson's decided advantage in doing precisely what Adams was doing, that is, joining a new political formation to a defense of ancient political mores. The issue of who (the statesman or hero) offered the greater protection to the legacy of Jefferson, and who (the political broker or the military chieftain) posed the greater threat, might well have been a wash were it not for the fact that the opposition's appeal to the preservation of fundamental values, unlike the administration's, actually authorized its party-building efforts. Adams's stand on the rarefied ground of proper administrative management undermined his new political formation and tended to rob his bold new constitutional vision of its connections to political power. At the same time, his de facto party-building undermined his appeal to administrative integrity and robbed his pledge of continuity of its connections to legitimacy. While the President was caught in the contradictions of a sweeping party program joined to a managerial defense of nonpartisanship, the opposition avoided tough policy stands and used the restoration of virtue as a magnet for pulling together disparate factions of discontent into a new opposition movement. Popular mobilization became an integral part of its call for breaking the knot of aristocratic corruption, reforming the degenerate establishment, and reclaiming the integrity of republican virtues.

We return in the end to the irony that Adams had himself assembled so many of the ingredients of a great political reconstruction. He had brought to the presidency a new interpretation of the Constitution, a new coalition, and an affirmation of fundamental principles. What he did not bring was a consistent and compelling political rationale for reconstructing the polity. Instead of each aspect of his leadership project reinforcing the message of the others and galvanizing the legitimacy of political action, they operated at cross purposes to leave him impotent and instill in his opponent the reconstructive authority he lacked.

There is little reason to suspect that Jackson or any of the other candidates contending in 1825 would have done much better. As none had a convincing case for breaking openly with the old order, none had the capacity to untangle the conundrum Adams wrestled with. Without the authority to repudiate, without the compelling logic that links saving to destroying, reconstructive programs reify propriety and render continuity a hollow shell of mere technique. Adams's struggle for credibility changed the polity profoundly, unwittingly opening the door to a political reconstruction that would destroy all that he stood for.

CHAPTER 5

Jacksonian Leadership:
Classic Forms

I N THIS second look at the politics presidents make, the three leadership types glimpsed previously appear in much sharper relief. In each case, contrasts with the politics of the patrician period reflect a secular thickening of the institutional universe of presidential action and a concomitant strengthening of the presidential office. Andrew Jackson wielded reconstructive authority for the first time since Thomas Jefferson. But those Jackson sought to repudiate reorganized themselves to contest his authority and resist his agenda, and in doing so, they pressed him to sharpen his break with the past. James Polk rearticulated Jackson's agenda to usher in a host of long-heralded regime promises, but unlike James Monroe, his counterpart in political time, Polk did so in a tightly contested universe of national party competition. The presidency's newfound capacities to command party loyalty along with the intensified demands of coalition partners for presidential services and supports framed a crystal-clear portrait of the problems and prospects of the orthodox-innovator. The politics of disjunction was also played out more sharply under Franklin Pierce than under John Quincy Adams, for Pierce's newfound resourcefulness as a party leader exploded upon an even more delicate alignment of partisan interests.

Part One:
Andrew Jackson's Reconstruction

The Bank, Mr. Van Buren, is trying to kill me,
but I will kill it!

THE JACKSON movement carried a disparate coalition of discontents into the election of 1828. Southern planters hostile to high tariffs joined northerners who enjoyed the benefits of trade protection. Northern radicals hostile to federal systems of internal improvement joined westerners with a keen interest in public works. Western debtors hostile to the National Bank joined easterners with an eye on the stability of financial markets. "Old Republicans" hostile to anything that hinted of national consolidation joined commercial interests of all stripes seeking to widen the opportunities opened by the current economic expansion. "His friends have no common principle," observed Daniel Webster at Jackson's inauguration. "They are held together by no common tie."[1]

Had the national contest been waged interest by interest, it seems certain that this unlikely assembly would have simply self-destructed. That it did not attests to the potency of the jeremiad that the Jacksonians had unleashed against John Quincy Adams. When the discontented latched onto Andrew Jackson, their disparate grievances were transformed into something more formidable than the sum of their parts. The Hero of New Orleans went to the nation in 1828 as the most celebrated victim of the old order; his defeat in the election of 1824 had become a metaphor for the chasm that had opened between power and authority in Washington. The sordid tale of the "corrupt bargain" that had denied him the presidency tapped bedrock suspicions of political privilege and elite entrenchment. It directed attention away from the fruits of the "American System" toward the architects and architecture of that system, away from the material supports the government had come to provide over the years toward the schemes of politicians too long in office and the detachment of the institutions they inhabited.

The spectacle of politicians trampling the suffrages of the people to serve their own narrow ambitions overshadowed the cornucopia of national services those politicians had so painstakingly cultivated.

The terms of Jackson's election set it apart from those that had immediately preceded it. The Jacksonians restaged the drama of 1800. As the Jeffersonians had assaulted the monarchical designs of John Adams, so the Jacksonians assaulted his son. Like Jefferson before him, Jackson was a tried-and-true defender of American freedom committed to nothing so much as breaking a knot of aristocratic corruption and restoring integrity to republican institutions.[2] Once the votes were tallied, campaign allusions to Jefferson's battle with Federalism were transformed into a more highly structured parallel. A sweeping victory for the opposition forces routed the National Republicans from control of all the political branches of the federal government. For the first time in almost thirty years, a president's impulse to fashion his place in history was released from the burdens of upholding the integrity of past commitments. If the campaign's call for a restoration of true Jeffersonian principles meant anything, it meant the disruption of current governing arrangements, and in this potential dovetailing of repudiative message and disruptive effect lay a vast reservoir of authority for independent action. With the order-shattering and order-affirming dimensions of presidential action so well synchronized in his initial claim to legitimacy, Jackson's invocation of original understandings, like Jefferson's before him, harbored the makings of an entirely new foundation for government and politics. Henry Clay caught the portent soon enough: "It was to cry down old constructions of the Constitution . . . to make all Jefferson's opinions the articles of faith of the new Church."[3]

This contingent authority to repudiate would prove to be Jackson's most formidable leadership resource. Yet, notwithstanding the parallels between these two moments in political time, Jackson did not simply repeat Jefferson's performance. Just as surely as Jefferson and Jackson stand apart from most other presidents by virtue of the kind of transformative authority they had at their disposal, they also stand apart from one another, the essential elements of their shared leadership posture being reshaped by the secular changes that intervened between their presidencies. Jackson's early course of action suggests that he would have liked nothing more than to have led in the expansive manner of Jefferson, joining his opposition stance to the consensus-building role of the national tribune. He quickly found, however, that he could not so easily disarm his rivals and consign them to political oblivion. The second transfer of power to an opposition movement proved to be less categorical than the first in terms of the control that redounded to the president over the course of political change. Quite unlike Jefferson, Jackson was forced to fight to sustain his authority.

Reasons for this difference are not difficult to discern. The years between these two reconstructions witnessed dramatic changes in both state and society. The governmental institutions that had given Jefferson such a free hand had long shed their initial insecurities. They were better organized internally, more confident of their own power and authority, and thus more resistant to presidential will. Beyond that, there were the pent-up jealousies and suspicions that had been brewing within the government of notables that Jefferson had so masterfully manipulated. The inability of Jefferson's encompassing party of national consensus to provide avenues of advancement sufficient to vent the ambitions of the burgeoning governing class it bred had been evident for years, and political elites were not about to let Jackson consolidate another. Finally, the mix of social interests implicated in any assault on established power arrangements was now more highly differentiated. A glance back at the initial Jackson coalition will attest to the expansion of the polity through virgin territories and suffrage extensions, to the development of the economy in domestic manufactures and commercial agriculture, and to the correspondingly dim prospects for holding together any overarching political consensus, even one committed to purging corruption and restoring virtue. The newfound density of American government and the far-flung diversity of the social interests it now encompassed strengthened the hand of those who would resist the president, and prompted, in turn, a more pointed and divisive test of this president's repudiative authority.

It is here—with a repudiative authority bearing down on a more robust set of institutions and a more complicated polity—that the two faces of Andrew Jackson merge into one. In the final analysis, there is no choosing between the old Whig myth of "Jackson, the demagogue"—the tyrant who disregarded all limits on executive power and ran headlong into ever more extreme and irrational policies—and the old Democratic myth of "Jackson, the liberator"—the populist insurgent who reached out beyond the elite and ushered the "common man" into a more participatory politics.[4] The battles Jackson fought in the name of the "common man" were driven, in good measure, by his own insatiable thirst for personal vindication.[5] But we come closer to the political significance of his appeals to the people by noting that personal vindication is part and parcel of the leadership drive of all presidents, and that this president in particular, despite a fearsome reputation and a heroic stature, faced open defiance from the Congress, the Court, the states, the National Bank, and even his own cabinet.

From the moment he took office, Jackson's effort to control the definition of his place in history provoked sharp, pitched battles over political commitments and governmental design. As the President stiffened his repudiative posture in response to ever more formidable resistance, each successive institutional confrontation deepened the stakes of sustaining his actions. In this way, the second reconstruction of American politics attained what we see in retrospect as a classic shape and line. Jackson's reconstruction is in fact unique in American history in that it transformed the operating mores of American government as dramatically as it altered basic governmental commitments. It not only reversed the ideological thrust of the national government and redirected its substantive uses, it also extricated the presidency from suffocating doctrines of legislative supremacy, rebuilt the political foundations of the executive office, recast the operations of the bureaucracy, and ushered in a nationally competitive party politics. For these accomplishments, each of the incumbents that followed Jackson would be vested with more formidable resources for independent action, more power than their counterparts had in the patrician era.

But the relative clarity of this result should not deceive us. The Jefferson-Jackson comparison indicates a paradox at work in the political development of reconstructive leadership. Jackson expounded upon the powers of the presidency so much more forcefully than Jefferson had because his political authority was so much more directly besieged; he overthrew doctrines of congressional supremacy and elaborated the formal prerogatives of his office because he could not simply abandon formalities and lead solely by force of his personal political appeal and national political standing. Jackson's new regime turned out to be more tightly demarcated than Jefferson's—its ideological commitments sharper and its institutional foundations firmer. But that is because Jackson found that he could not, as Jefferson had, simply smother competing sources of authority in a more expansive tack. Though his stunning performance became the touchstone of legitimacy for a new program and for more potent forms of political organization, the hotly contested party politics and the sharply delimited ideological debates that Jackson left in his wake compare to Jefferson's more encompassing handiwork as a hemming in of presidential authority in its most potent political form. The emergence of a nationally competitive two-party system—with all the newfound power and independence it bequeathed to all future incumbents alike—was but the most enduring mark of the institutional and ideological resistance encountered in the 1830s to a presidentially led reconstruction of American politics.

The Magnanimous Overture

Jackson's first annual message to Congress redeemed the promise of his election with a forthright assault on elite intrigue and institutional detachment.[6] To retrieve "the first principle of our system" and to prevent those perversions of the popular will so evident in the election of 1824, he recommended constitutional amendments that would remove the House of Representatives from any future presidential runoff and limit presidents themselves to a single term. Then, he took aim at administrative personnel so long entrenched in office that their positions were becoming a "species of property." He ventured a bold defense of the removal and rotation of executive officers, and called upon Congress to ratify this "leading principle of the republican creed" with a more extensive application of limits on terms of appointment.

With this biting indictment of the Washington establishment, Jackson stepped out in front of the regional leaders who had orchestrated his election and asserted himself as the voice of the opposition movement as a whole. Beyond that, however, his initial foray into reform was most notable for its moderation. Jackson's deepest assaults on the old order reflected his personal experience in the election of 1824 and the problems he now faced in staffing the executive branch with his own loyalists. In the rest of the message, where he dealt more directly with issues of material interest, the President indicated a willingness to incorporate a good deal of the old order within his reform project.

For those leaders who stood on the different sides of the material issues of the day, Jackson's moderation was the most threatening aspect of his message. As he maneuvered his way through the specific commitments of friends and foes alike, the President staked his claim to a reform stance that was, like Jefferson's, as open-ended about the future as it was damning of recent practice. If sustained, this bid for an encompassing reform coalition would again isolate those expounding more controversial views as radical extremists and preclude alternative political appeals. Forcing the President to narrow his compass and delimit his ground became the pervasive political motive of the next four years.

In fact, efforts to press Jackson on the scope and character of his opposition stance had begun even before he was elected. Eager with anticipation of a more sympathetic man in the White House, Georgia and Alabama had rushed ahead with plans to deny the rights of the Cherokee Indians living within the borders of their states and to take over the lands the Indians had been granted by federal treaty. Signaling in advance their willingness to resist any adverse rulings from the Supreme Court, these states gave voice to more general fears of national consolidation by judicial construction, and they rekindled the Old Republican dream of a broadside assault on federal judicial authority.[7] An even more ominous portent along these same lines came from the legislature of South Carolina. In an official protest against the tariff of 1828, it openly proclaimed the rights of individual states to nullify federal law.[8]

Jackson was hardly indifferent to the South's defiance of the nationalist impulses of the recent past. He took care in his message to nod to the principles of states' rights and the interests of his supporters. He had concluded long ago that the position of the Indians within the existing states was hopeless. Supporting Georgia and Alabama in their claims, his message urged the removal of the Indians to new territories beyond the Mississippi that Congress might set aside for their control. He also expressed his interest in modifying the tariff of 1828 with an eye toward a downward adjustment of rates. On both counts, however, Jackson steered clear of radicalism. James Monroe and John Quincy Adams had come to similar conclusions on the Indians' future within the states, and while Jackson's removal plan would have horrific consequences for the tribes involved, it was ventured politically as a benevolent accommodation to the inevitable, a way of providing for all interests concerned. Especially noteworthy in this regard is that far from taking up the charge against national judicial authority, the President proposed to strengthen the judicial system by extending its services more effectively throughout the country.[9] The President's warning against radicalism was even more pointed on the tariff issue. He went out of his way to emphasize gradualism and mutual accommodation in any reduction of rates. He explicitly endorsed the principle of protection and disavowed "all attempts to connect [changes in the tariff] to the party conflicts of the day."

It was much the same on other issues. Jackson set himself against "over-strained constructions" of constitutional authority that had recently been employed to justify federal support for internal improvements of all kinds. He was concerned about the temptation to logroll development interests into extravagant expenditures and about the overbearing power such legislation imparted to the national government vis-à-vis the states. But he was equally intent to maintain a role for the federal government in public works, and he even proposed to distribute the surplus revenues expected from the tariff to the states for such purposes. As this would, in effect, give the states a stake in maintaining the protection of manufactures, Jackson's initial repudiation of the National Republicans for their perverse constructions of national power and their expensive policies went a long way toward incorporating the core of their program into his own. Likewise with the National Bank. The Bank dominated the nation's credit system, intruded into the states without their consent, maintained extensive ties of material interest with political elites, and actively involved itself in national elections to sustain its political support. It embodied all the problems of national intimidation, institutional corruption, and political degradation against which Jackson addressed his administration, and he flatly declared the institution a "failure." For all this, however, his suggestions for reform were remarkably accommodating. He merely asked Congress to begin considering "whether a national [bank], founded upon the credit of the Government and its revenues, might not be devised which would avoid all the constitutional difficulties and at the same time secure all the advantages to the Government and the country that were expected to result from the present" one.

In all, Jackson's message sketched an enticing update of Jefferson's magnanimous overture to a new consensus. While attacking recent practice on virtually all fronts, he did not threaten any precipitous reversal of course. He offered instead to accept the general contours of the commercial republic bequeathed him by his predecessors—protective tariffs, internal improvements, national banking, and a national judicial system. He wanted to see how much could be done within that frame to counter the extravagant ambitions of the Adams years and restore to the government a country-party conscience.[10] His defense of rotation in office may have been more forthright than Jefferson's call for a politically balanced bureaucracy, but then he proposed nothing so consequential as Jefferson's immediate repeal of internal taxes. At the outset, both of these leaders laid claim to the broad middle ground of the political spectrum and employed their opposition stance to isolate dissenters at opposite extremes. The striking difference between them lay not in their political aim but in their political reception. Jackson's overture met with formidable resistance on all sides.

The Demise of Patrician Politics

A palace struggle had been going on within the Jackson administration almost from the moment the new President announced his cabinet selections. Vice President Calhoun and Secretary of State Van Buren, equal partners in forging the victorious Jackson coalition, were facing off against each other for influence over the elaboration of the new dispensation and, ultimately, for the favor of succession. While both of these leaders had been put off by the independence Jackson had shown in filling out his administration, the program Jackson outlined in his first annual message put Calhoun in especially difficult straits. As secret author of South Carolina's tariff protest, Calhoun simply could not reconcile the President's moderation with the radical resistance of his own state to national determination of tariff policy. A year of intrigue aimed at pressuring Jackson and testing his true colors culminated in a face-off at the Jefferson Day dinner in April of 1830. Calhoun's men orchestrated this celebration to showcase their states' rights doctrines, and had things gone according to plan they would have implicated the President as a supporter through his association with the event. But Jackson refused to be compromised, and his after-dinner toast—"Our (Federal) Union, it must be preserved"—underscored not only his opposition to nullification but also his insistence on drawing a line between reform and radicalism.[11]

The break between Calhoun and Jackson is especially instructive in showing how the patrician mode of governance was displaced and a new one less dependent on personal deference formed in its stead. The characteristic forms and operations of party politics emerged during the Jackson years tit for tat through a series of contests that exposed the irrelevance of older mores and the hard-pressed new imperatives of maintaining local bases of political power while in Washington. It is not simply that Calhoun saw himself as Jackson's equal in the opposition movement and refused to defer to his lead; his political base in South Carolina gave him little room to maneuver around politics at the center. When the President insisted on controlling his administration's policies himself, Calhoun severed his less important connection, the one to Jackson. The ensuing break, the first ideological delimitation of the Jackson movement, became a benchmark of the transition between patrician standards and partisan standards of presidential action.

Distrusting his vice president's loyalties every bit as much as his vice president distrusted his, Jackson decided to set up his own test of faith. He asked Calhoun to explain his censure of the Florida invasion of 1819. Calhoun's formal authority in the case was not in doubt; he had been Monroe's secretary of war and the general's superior at the time. But by asking for an explanation, Jackson was pushing Calhoun either to acknowledge that he was still a rival or to accept the position Jackson was offering as a subordinate partner in a new coalition. Calhoun responded with a patrician cry of indignation ("I cannot recognize the right on your part to call in question my conduct"[12]) and then executed a partisan maneuver of his own. He published a ringing defense of his actions in the Seminole War, and by insinuating an administration plot against him masterminded by Van Buren, he implicitly dared Jackson to try to build a party without his political support.

With the publication of the Seminole correspondence, Jackson was prompted to a more overt assertion of power and a more open acknowledgment of his partisan role. Reclaiming control, he had the vice president written out of his reform movement, and he recast his cabinet from top to bottom, purging it of all traces of Calhoun's influence. The message blasted out of the Jackson press in the early part of 1831 ended all pretense of government by elite consensus: "The supporters of Jackson are the [Republican] party . . . We recognize no subdivision."[13]

The difficulties Jackson faced in disciplining the executive branch were paralleled by the resistance he faced in Congress. Indeed, while his election victory had swept the opposition movement he led into control of both houses of Congress, Jackson found that he himself had not been given carte blanche control over either. The Senate responded to the President's call for a more representative bureaucracy by rejecting several of his initial appointments, and the House, perhaps already reflecting Calhoun's disaffection, replied to the President's interest in bank reform by reporting its full confidence in the current bank's performance.[14] Internal improvement legislation rolled out of both houses as if John Quincy Adams were still in the White House, and an unexpectedly bitter debate erupted over the Indian removal measure.

Jackson met these initial challenges quickly and effectively, but by doing so he relinquished a bit more of the patrician's pretense of standing above the fray. As with the stubborn independence of Calhoun, the independence of the Congress prompted the President into a more aggressive, and thus more openly partisan, role from the very beginning. Forced to make the Indian removal bill a test of loyalty to the administration, Jackson began to organize a congressional party identified with presidential leadership.[15] Opponents, unable to block the measure, seized upon the significance of this development. Lashing out at the "concentration of power in the hands of the executive" and the spectre of "executive despotism," they hit upon themes that would eventually be developed into the central rationale for an alternative party, a Whig organization.[16]

Next came a succession of presidential vetoes of internal improvement projects. Beginning in May of 1830 with the Maysville road, an extension of the National Road confined within the limits of the state of Kentucky, Jackson insisted that his critique of recent practice in this area not be disregarded. Careful to keep the door of accommodation open, the President reiterated that he was "sincerely friendly to the improvement of our country by means of roads and canals," and he confirmed his intention to pursue tariff reform with an eye toward providing federal subsidies to the states for such improvements. Still, Jackson had other concerns as well, and he would not permit the Congress to ignore them. He wanted to "reconcile the diversified interests of the states" and to draw a line against projects of "purely local character." The political impact of the Kentucky road veto was calculated to showcase the President's commitment to a "prudent system of expenditure" by targeting Henry Clay's home state and thus symbolically isolating the mastermind of the rule of "expedience" in constitutional construction. In its actual effect, Jackson's stricter construction would merely return the federal government to the role Monroe had outlined for it late in his administration.[17] A repudiation of excess, it still held out broad possibilities of federal action.

As if to amplify his determination not to be dismissed out of hand, Jackson sharpened his objections to the National Bank in his second annual message, and he let it be known shortly thereafter that he intended to seek reelection after all.[18] This surprisingly early change of plans, taken in conjunction with the repudiation of Calhoun, the cabinet overhaul, the Indian removal victory, and the improvements vetoes, put a sharp point on Jackson's initial leadership posture: he was intent on securing reform, and he intended to do so on his own terms. As of mid-1831, the President was still able to act on these intentions while cultivating a broad middle ground between nullification and nationalization, Calhoun and Clay. Confident of his identity as leader of the reform movement, he was committing himself gradually. He was letting the resistance he encountered define the appropriate range of reform, and thereby building a party that moved simultaneously against opposing extremes.

Jackson's drive to hold onto a broad-ranging consensus for reform culminated in his third annual message when, highlighting the pending retirement of the national debt, he took up the issue of the tariff in earnest. Calhoun had taken few southerners with him into direct opposition to the administration, but sensitivities were running high, and many expressed dissatisfaction with the new cabinet selections.[19] The President wanted to bolster his reform credentials in the region with programmatic assurances of his true commitments. In a move that anticipated more radical action during the nullification crisis of 1833, he reconsidered the threat to states' rights sentiments posed by his plan to redistribute surplus revenues, and he decided to cut tariff reform free from any implied institutionalization of a state interest in protection. Given his oft-repeated support for redistribution, this rather abrupt change was aimed unmistakably at isolating the nullifiers' appeal. Still, moderation carried the day. Notwithstanding his new signal of solidarity with the South, Jackson embraced a compromise with the nationalists on a good-faith downward revision of selected rates. The tariff of 1832 maintained substantial protection and simply cleansed away the foul odor of the 1828 "Tariff of Abominations."[20] "The people must now see," the President beamed, "that all their grievances are removed, and oppression only exists in the distempered brains of disappointed ambitious men."[21]

The Tariff Act of 1832 successfully removed a difficult issue from the upcoming presidential campaign.[22] It was the last of Jackson's consensual reform appeals to have such a salutary political effect. Indeed, it came in the midst of a series of new challenges, each calculated by

Jackson's opponents to cut into his reform consensus and push him onto more controversial ground.

The election year had begun with Vice President Calhoun's casting the deciding vote in the Senate against Jackson's nomination of Martin Van Buren as minister to Great Britain. Van Buren had volunteered his resignation as secretary of state during the cabinet reorganization to help free Jackson's hands, but he had emerged after the purge of Calhoun as the heir apparent, and his rise had tempered the enthusiasm of a host of former Jackson associates in the South and West. The Senate confirmation process aired this frustration in bitter denunciations of a man who had been confirmed just three years before for the top-ranked cabinet post. Echoing Calhoun's Seminole correspondence, the Senate dubbed Van Buren the hidden power behind the administration—the one who had worked secretly to ensure the break with Calhoun and who had manipulated the President to form his own party on the basis of political spoils. The rejection of the appointment not only scuttled plans to get the controversial first lieutenant out of the country for the election, it goaded the President into elevating him to second place on his reelection ticket.[23]

Then, in March of 1832, persistent efforts to force a confrontation between Jackson and the Supreme Court on Indian rights in Georgia finally bore fruit. With the presidential candidate of the Anti-Masonic party and the vice presidential candidate of the National Republican party jointly pressing the case against Georgia, and Georgia avowing its refusal to abide the authority of the Court, Chief Justice John Marshall joined the gauntlet and formally voided all the laws of the state dealing with the Indians. By a quirk of the Judiciary Act of 1789, Jackson was not technically bound to do anything to enforce this ruling. His determination to ignore it, however, and to press on with his removal policy sharpened the spectre of his leadership as a threat to the rule of law and tied him more closely than ever before to support of the radical states' rights position.[24]

The nationalists had been as anxious as Jackson to remove the tariff from the upcoming campaign, and they waited for that settlement before unloading their heaviest gun. In the early summer of 1832, however, everything was in place for a blanket rejection of Jackson's concern for reform of the National Bank. The House and Senate voted to recharter the institution without substantial change.[25] Prompted by Nicholas Biddle, the Bank president, and championed by Henry Clay, the presidential candidate of the National Republicans, this initiative pushed Jackson beyond all hope of controlling reform with impunity. To vindicate his initial assessment of the old Bank's failure, the President now would have to make a clean break with the single most important institutional link between the federal government and the national economy. Moreover, in taking up that challenge he would be repudiating the whole framework of government in which the Bank was embedded. As the Court had upheld the constitutionality of the Bank years before and as the only accepted grounds for a presidential veto of congressional legislation were constitutional, rejection of the Bank bill would be tantamount to open defiance of both judicial and congressional authority. In the process, it would make a mockery of the premier operating principle of the Jeffersonian regime—executive deference to the legislature. It would expose the sham of Jackson's restoration of first principles and seal the case against his presumption of a power above the law. In all, it would bring the order-shattering threat of Jacksonian leadership into the boldest possible relief.

The calculations of Jackson's opponents were richly rewarded in the President's veto message.[26] Jackson not only reaffirmed his initial assertion that the Bank had failed in its mission; he renounced the assumption of executive deference to the Court on questions of constitutionality. Then, turning to the question of executive deference to Congress, he claimed that the Bank was an agency of the executive branch, and he asserted a presidential prerogative over legislative action that affected that branch. On both sides, Jackson pressed the case for the equality of the branches. "The opinion of the judges has no more authority over Congress than the opinion of Congress has over the judges, and on that point the President is independent of both." Before he had finished, Jackson had gone far beyond questions of constitutionality to rest his veto on his own independent assessment of the political, social, and economic consequences of the proposed recharter legislation.

Yet, for all their success in pressing him onto this explosive political ground, the challenges of 1832 were calculated with a desperation that played directly to the most potent themes of Jackson's leadership project. The handling of the Bank bill, in particular, seemed to epitomize the problem that had brought this president to power in the first place—the degradation of the nation's most powerful institutions. Without missing a step, Jackson turned the blatant political calculations behind the bill back on its sponsors, and transformed an issue of dubious political advantage into another corrupt bargain (this one between Biddle and Clay) symbolizing the depth of the problems he had outlined in his initial indictment of the Washington establishment. Jackson expressed his alarm at congressional procedures that had peremptorily swept aside all the charges against the Bank, and he urged careful reflection on why Biddle would insist on recharter just before an election when the old charter "had yet four years to run, and renewal now was not necessary to the successful prosecution of its business." Having brought to light the manipulation of the issue for Clay's election drive, Jackson broadened his case against the Bank to engulf the entire Washington establishment in a conspiracy of power, privilege, and self-interest. He detailed the Bank's connections to the wealthy and influential. He described it as an unruly monopoly that had been permitted by those with a material stake in its success to run wild over the interests of the great majority. He denounced it for disregarding the rights and powers of the several states and binding the states tightly under centralized controls. Rather than unifying the nation, he claimed, the Bank had "arrayed section against section, interest against interest, and man against man, in a fearful commotion which threatens to shake the foundations of our Union."

Thus, as his enemies drew him out, Jackson stood firm and consistent on his initial warrants for leadership, and merely expanded upon the justification they gave him for independent action. He asserted sweeping new powers, but their order-shattering thrust continued to resonate loud and clear with his order-affirming pretensions. He had stiffened his repudiative stance to incorporate ever more radical claims, but he retained all along a coherent and compelling narrative about his place in history. He was still fighting to rid the government of the corruptions of the recent past. Asserting power in order to wrest the federal government from a self-interested elite and restore disinterestedness to governmental affairs needed no apology. Precedents had no standing in the face of the bankruptcy of existing institutional arrangements. The magnitude of the institutional challenges hurled at the President only underscored the need for the more drastic actions he was taking to meet them. Indeed, radicalism was Jackson's prerogative, and resistance simply an excuse for exercising it. As the establishment threw up its best defenses, Jackson's repudiative authority became a battering ram for radical change.

To be sure, a toll was extracted by the barrage of challenges hurled against Jackson in 1832. Their chief victim, however, was not Jackson; it was faith in the old virtues of institutional deliberation and the distillation of an elite consensus that had been the hallmark of patrician politics. Alerting the people to the "dangers which threaten our institutions," Jackson defied Washington sentiment for the Bank and presented his veto message as a political manifesto for popular judgment. "A general discussion will now take place, eliciting new light and settling important principles; and a new Congress, elected in the midst of such discussion . . . will bear to the Capitol the verdict of public opinion." This message fed rival party-building efforts and set the stage for a durable, programmatic division in American politics over the role of the national government generally and the presidency in particular.

The Great Repudiator

As it turned out, the Bank bill was not the last challenge hurled at Jackson in 1832. In November, at the very moment of his second triumph at the polls, South Carolina officially nullified the tariffs of 1828 and 1832 and threatened secession if federal authority were invoked to enforce the law. The temerity of this defiance, along with Biddle's electioneering efforts on behalf of a revival of the recharter issue in the next Congress, were glaring reminders that the terms and conditions of national politics remained very much unsettled.[27] No longer willing to merely react tit for tat, Jackson decided to press for a final resolution of the outstanding issues on both fronts. Testing the limits of his authority, he would throw the nation as well as the government into a frenzy of fear and confusion before the new state of affairs he was sponsoring gained legitimacy.

Jackson had to deal with nullification first, for South Carolina threatened to enforce its decree on February 1, 1833. This would prove a stroke of good fortune for the President. The nullifiers had always posed a more complicated political challenge to Jackson than the nationalists, and his stronger case for independent action was reserved for last. The difficulty was that the nullifiers' grievance against overbearing federal authority was part and parcel of Jackson's own reform message. Any showdown on the issue of state sovereignty threatened to call his own political commitments into question.

In Jackson's repudiation of the nullifiers, we see a dilemma inherent in the politics of reconstruction magnified to several times the significance it held under Jefferson. Recall that Jefferson's efforts to use his presidency to create a new Republicanism had raised the eyebrows of many of the "Old Republicans" who stood by the more radical standards of opposition voiced in 1798. The challenge from South Carolina was similar, a test of the President's true colors from those who insisted on doctrinal purity. But what was for Jefferson a family squabble easily circumvented by the purge of John Randolph became for Jackson a showdown with repercussions affecting all aspects of his leadership project. Jackson's purge of Calhoun in 1831 had failed to resolve anything, and his efforts during the nullification crisis to eliminate Calhoun as a political force in the South, the region of Jackson's greatest strength, had just the opposite effect.

To prepare the way for action, Jackson used the first opportunity he had after the election to complete his break with the nationalists' "American System" and rally all those discontented with the old order of things. His fourth annual message, delivered in December of 1832 to the rump session of the Twenty-second Congress, broadened the themes of his Bank veto—states' rights and populist democracy—to cover all the remaining vestiges of an activist government in Washington.[28] Taking the substance of South Carolina's grievance as his own, the President completely reversed his recent enthusiasm for the compromise tariff of the previous summer and proposed a new round of rate reductions that would abandon protection altogether in favor of a strict revenue standard. Then, with import revenues to be cut to the bone, Jackson went on to announce his opposition to the use of public land revenues for the support of national projects. He urged the quick disposal of land to actual settlers at a price "barely sufficient" to cover administrative expenses, and looked forward toward relinquishing the remainder to the states. Beyond this, he called for the disposal of all federal stock in private corporations; he reiterated his constitutional strictures on internal improvements; and, completely ignoring the Supreme Court's ruling against Georgia, he demanded that the Indians submit to his removal plan.

To John Quincy Adams, this plan threatened to "dissolve the Union in its original elements." Henry Clay saw it as a complete break with all that he had helped to build up: "we have no past or future . . . After forty four years under the present Constitution, what single principle is fixed?" "All is gone if the President's views are carried into effect," observed a Washington correspondent. "All is gone, which the General

Government was instituted to create and preserve."[29] The presidential battering ram was indeed poised to destroy anything and everything in its path. In his repudiation of the nationalist program, Jackson's postelection message broached no compromise and anticipated no consensus; in its unabashedly partisan call, it envisioned a political organization that would conquer the nation by dividing it. The President had all but replaced the traditional quest for a national accommodation of opinion with a new quest for an intraparty logrolling of nationally contested opinions.

But not completely. Despite the belligerent tone and radical commitments of his annual message, Jackson was not yet prepared to relinquish fully the role of national tribune. Had he simply wanted to keep the nullifiers politically isolated, his sweeping programmatic alternative to the American System might well have sufficed.[30] His immediate object, however, was to crush the southern heretics once and for all, and for this he needed the nationalists' support. Less than a week after his annual message, the President issued a proclamation as forceful in its assertion of national authority as the first was in its repudiation. Taking direct aim at the South Carolina radicals, he pronounced *"the power to annul a law of the United States, assumed by one state, incompatible with the existence of the Union, contradicted expressly by the letter of the Constitution, unauthorized by its spirit, inconsistent with every principle on which it was founded, and destructive of the great object for which it was formed."*[31] He followed up a few weeks later with a proposal to Congress, which became known as the Force Bill, granting him sweeping powers to march troops into South Carolina and compel the execution of the law even before the state had acted on its threat.[32]

The glaring disparity between the annual message and the proclamation suggests a calculation on Jackson's part that once his core supporters had been reassured on matters of policy, unionists of all stripes might still be persuaded to unite for a crushing assault on the ultimate heresy. In this sense, the annual message was issued to bolster Jackson's political warrants for the proclamation. Taken together, the two messages bid for another grand national coalition, one overarching national consensus against Calhoun and treason in South Carolina. But that calculation backfired; the reaction was horror on all sides. Far from holding the center and isolating the extremists, Jackson's double message seem to abandon the center to embrace the opposing poles. From that position, he could build neither a consensus nor a party; party-building and consensus-building, though beautifully harmonized during his first term, had begun to work at cross purposes. Determined to make his commitment to national authority as unmistakable as his commitment to states' rights populism, Jackson had championed simultaneously a complete federal disengagement and an uncompromising federal suppression. The inconsistency was magnified by debates ongoing in Congress about the nature of the federal compact.[33] For one tortured moment, the order-shattering and order-affirming impulses in Jackson's political project became mired in confusion, and his most precious leadership resource, his own political identity, was thrown into jeopardy. The leader who had come to redeem the Jeffersonian republic was bitterly denounced by the most forceful advocates of states' rights as an arch-Federalist. Those who might have supported his Force Bill were horrified by his tariff proposal; those who might have supported his tariff initiative were horrified by his Force Bill. Concerted action stalled on both fronts, and for the first time Jackson's independence in political action threatened political isolation.[34]

This is not to say that the President missed his mark entirely. With the promises of the annual message on the table, no state rose to the defense of nullification per se, and with the threat of brute force bearing down on him, Calhoun began to orchestrate South Carolina's retreat in earnest. By insisting on passage of the Force Bill as a test of the integrity of the Union and as a nonnegotiable condition for the resolution of the crisis, Jackson remained a fearsome presence behind the bizarre negotiation which followed. But while he compelled the nullifiers to capitulate, the actual terms of their surrender turned out to be a stunning reversal of what the President intended for his first postelection initiative.

Calhoun was desperate for some alternative to the President's complete vindication, and Henry Clay knew it. Only weeks after trouncing Clay at the polls and taking every southern state except Calhoun's, the President watched his two archrivals pull themselves out of oblivion on the back of his own forthright enunciation of principles. More astounding still, he saw them join each other in an alliance against him, the nationalist and the nullifier projecting a spirit of moderation and mutual accommodation against executive extremism. Clay seized the initiative, and by reversing the President's priorities, had a tariff compromise worked out with Calhoun before the Force Bill was considered. Like the President's new tariff proposal, Clay's abandoned protection in principle, but it reduced rates to the levels Jackson had anticipated only gradually, over a nine-year period. Calhoun grasped this victory for the principle of free trade, and arranged with Clay to have opposition to the Force Bill dropped. Though he accepted a tariff far less radical than Jackson's (in fact, one that seemed to guarantee protection for another decade), Calhoun gained the satisfaction of seeing the President's great test of loyalty to the Union rendered a moot tribute that moderation was forced to pay to the impulses of a tyrant.[35]

Jackson made a point of signing the Force Bill before he signed the new tariff bill. He then set out in triumph on a eastern tour that would celebrate his victory for the Union. But the political confusion in the ranks of those he had recently counted among his strongest supporters was not so easily covered over. Disarray in the fledgling Democratic party would be especially pronounced in the new Congress which, by Jackson's own words, was to bring to the Capitol the verdict of the people on the principles the President had enunciated in his Bank veto. The Senate, which had been shaky enough in its support of the President during his first term, moved completely beyond his control in the spring of 1833. In the House, which formally boasted a large Democratic majority, support for the President proved dangerously volatile. The veto had been an effective campaign tool on both sides of the Bank issue, and now with the Force Bill initiative, the whole South had been opened to alternative political appeals.[36]

Even if Jackson's pre-election veto had not been as categorical a condemnation of the Bank, the "bastard coalition" of Clay and Calhoun now rising against him blocked any possible retreat from its political implications. The stakes of breaking the recharter movement and destroying Biddle's Bank once and for all had been deepened by the frustrations he had encountered in his repudiation of radical states' rights doctrines.[37] When the national consensus anticipated by the proclamation failed to materialize and the administration's most implacable enemies joined forces instead, the partisan reconstruction anticipated in the fourth annual message became the make-or-break test of Jackson's leadership.

It was in the midst of the nullification crisis that Jackson had hatched the idea of removing the federal government's deposits from the Bank and placing them in a select group of financially sound and politically friendly state banks. This plan had several potential advantages. It not only promised to foreclose moves to renew the charter of the National

Bank; it also promised more direct supervision of banking by the executive and more direct institutional links between the presidency and state centers of political power. To complete his break with the old financial arrangements, Jackson would hold out an alternative arrangement offering federal support for commercial interests seeking new opportunities, and he would solicit in return their support in the anti-Bank crusade. Circumventing the existing apparatus, Jackson proposed an entirely new one boasting his own political and institutional networks.[38]

At first, however, few were impressed. Save Attorney General Roger Taney, Jackson's official family was united in opposition to the removal plan. Clearing the way for action in the spring of 1833, Jackson promoted his treasury secretary, the pro-Bank Louis McLane, to the State Department and recruited the anti-Bank William Duane to carry out the removal and redeposit scheme. However, when it came time to perform the mission for which he had been appointed, Duane himself began to question the President's authority to issue the removal order. He had learned that by law the treasury secretary held a special relationship to the Congress and a measure of independence from the President. As a consequence, he insisted that he would have to consult Congress on the matter prior to taking action. Risking the disarray of a second cabinet shake-up, Jackson dismissed Duane and put Roger Taney in his place. The work of removal and redeposit began in earnest in the fall of 1833.[39]

Congress proved even less accommodating. On the eve of Jackson's second inaugural, the Democratic House had passed a resolution declaring its full confidence in the safety of the deposits in the Bank of the United States.[40] In the Senate, Daniel Webster was being wooed back from his recent display of support for the administration (he had led the Senate fight for the Force Bill) to join the new Clay-Calhoun alliance in defiance of any further presidential assault on the Bank. With congressional support uncertain, and Jackson's authority to order the removal already challenged by Duane's protestations, the President made a momentous adjustment in his justification for acting independently. It was no longer the Congress that bore the verdict of public opinion, as he had claimed in the veto message; it was the President himself. Jackson's removal notice declared his own reelection the "decision of the people against the bank." The Bank had "put *the President* to the test." The President's veto had been unequivocal, and "now that the people have sustained the President . . . it [was] too late to say that the question [had] not been decided."[41]

It was precisely this claim of a popular mandate for the exercise of presidential power that galvanized the disparate strands of resistance to Jackson's leadership and forged the ideological foundations of the Whig party. And as the leadership of this new party seized upon the removal order to elaborate their portrait of executive tyranny, rumors of yet another Van Buren conspiracy—this one to transfer commercial power from Philadelphia to New York through the selection of the pet banks— ate further into the administration's southern support. The President's followers, still reeling from his threats against the nullifiers, seemed caught in an accelerating tailspin. Democratic floor leaders lost control of the administration's majority in the House and spent the next several weeks trying to end an extended and devastating debate over presidential authority. The Senate officially rejected the President's stated reason for the removal and formally censured him for abuse of power. Then they rejected Taney's appointment as secretary of the treasury.[42]

The "Panic Session" (1833–34) of the Twenty-third Congress found Jackson scrambling to refortify his troops as the proto-Whig coalition extended its reach into every state of the South and West and established itself as a truly national political force.[43] But as the race to organize the nation into rival political camps began to even out, the advantages in Jackson's leadership position became decisive. First among these was that the President's presumptions of authority vis-à-vis Congress, whatever might be said against them, were far easier to defend than the Bank's presumption of power vis-à-vis the nation at large. The Bank president, for all his clout, was no match for the President of the United States when it came to finding warrants for independent action. Jackson was a constitutional officer; and for all the controversy that surrounded his assertion of independence in presidential action, the case for the independence of the branches was there to be made. Biddle, on the other hand, was a subordinate official dependent on others for his political voice, and his apparent imperviousness to the difficulties his supporters faced in mounting a positive defense of the powers he exercised only fueled Jackson's jeremiad against institutional corruption and elite detachment.

On this score, Biddle's decision to respond to the removal order with an abrupt curtailment of loans proved a monumental miscalculation. By squeezing the nation into a financial panic at the high tide of an economic expansion, Biddle had hoped to expose the folly of the President's financial policies and to bring the government, if not the nation, to see the imperatives of recharter. But Jackson had no intention of accepting responsibility for Biddle's actions, and he simply referred all complaints about the panic back to the Bank president. Then, in another stubborn display of independence, Biddle refused an order from Jackson to relinquish control of the military pension system, bringing the payment of pensions to an abrupt halt. Jackson could not have asked for more politically potent weapons in reasserting his original mission against irresponsible institutions and power-mongering elites who defied the interests of the people. Added to the long list of charges he could now reiterate against the Bank, the panic and withholding of pensions worked wonders in reversing the tide against removal. The winter of 1834 witnessed a rally of political support for removal in the states, a sharp rebuke to the Bank from the House Ways and Means Committee, and even a personal appeal from Daniel Webster to get Biddle to release the pensions.[44]

A second factor working for Jackson in the Bank War was that he offered the only clear path to a resolution of the crisis. As President, he went about the business of implementing his state deposit scheme on his own initiative. His opponents in Congress, meanwhile, found it impossible to agree on the precise shape of a new bank charter. Held together only by their collective outrage at Jackson's assertions of executive authority, the Whigs discovered their alliance of nationalists and nullifiers embarrassingly awkward when it came to programmatic action. They could denounce Jackson's presumption of an electoral mandate from the people and endlessly lecture him about the superior claims of Congress to represent the popular will, but they could not, from that, muster support for a course that would satisfy both Webster and Calhoun.[45] For months, Jackson was left to rally his party in Congress and in the states, not only by focusing blame for the panic on Biddle but also by presenting his de facto alternative as the only path open to the restoration of order and stability. Gradually, with state after state endorsing the President's course, the reality dawned that the Bank was already dead. By the beginning of April 1834, the Democratic floor leader, James Polk, had confidence enough in his majority to ram through the House a series of resolutions upholding Jackson's authority and calling for an investigation of the Bank that would finally expose the real reasons for the panic.[46]

But there was more at work here than the Bank's mistakes and the Whigs' problems in agreeing on an alternative to the President's chosen course. Most important of all, the removal initiative and the Senate's censure turned Jackson's personal vindication into the one essential task of the fledgling Democratic party. Whatever individual Democrats may have thought about the Bank, they went into the midterm election of 1834 knowing that everything now hinged on sustaining the President, destroying Biddle, and disarming the Senate. For anyone taken with the broad vision of Jackson's fourth annual message, for anyone interested in one of the specific promises elaborated in that message, for anyone enjoying the crudest measure of presidential support in local contests for political power, there was no alternative to supporting Jackson's authority.

The President knew what his supporters needed, and he delivered it in an official protest against his censure by the Senate. Safely vindicated by the House, Jackson bluntly asked the senators why he had not been impeached. He had been accused of gross abuses of constitutional power, but had not his accusers themselves mocked the Constitution by resort to the curious device of a censure? The appropriate constitutional remedy—impeachment—was clear, and it guaranteed the accused a forum in which to defend himself against the charges and state his case. Why was the Senate so intent on denying him this forum? Did it so fear his defense and the vindication of his claims? Once the question of presidential power was recast in these terms, Jackson needed only a short coda to set the record straight and make the connections between saving the republic and destroying the Bank crystal clear. The stunning conclusion of the paper brought Jackson's whole life's story to bear on the events at hand, and reclaimed his personal political identity as the alternative to moral bankruptcy in national government.

> I have lived in vain if it be necessary to enter into a formal vindication of my character and purposes from [the resolution of the Senate]. In vain do I bear upon my person enduring memorials of that contest in which American liberty was purchased; in vain have I since periled property, fame, and life in defense of the rights and privileges so dearly bought; in vain am I now, without a personal aspiration or hope of individual advantage, encountering responsibilities and dangers from which by mere inactivity . . . I might have been exempt. If I had been ambitious, I should have sought an alliance with that powerful institution which even now aspires to no divided empire. If I had been venal, I should have sold myself

to its designs. Had I preferred personal comfort and official ease to the performance of my arduous duty, I should have ceased to molest it . . . No; the ambition which leads me on is an anxious desire and a fixed determination to return to the people unimpaired the sacred trust they have confided to my charge; to heal the wounds of the Constitution and preserve it from further violation; to persuade my countrymen, so far as I may, that it is not in a splendid government supported by powerful monopolies and aristocratical establishments that they will find happiness or their liberties protection, but in a plain system, void of pomp, protecting all and granting favors to none.[47]

Anyone in 1834 who could respond to this message was, by Jackson's definition, a Democrat. All that was necessary to secure a new order was to credit this simple declaration of faith. Though the hidden current in the midterm elections of 1834 was the continued emergence of the Whig party in all regions,[48] the manifest result was a triumph unheard of in modern times—a sixth-year surge of presidential strength in Congress. A contest that traditionally marks the ebb-tide of political control for even the most popular of presidents this time ratified the most radical departure in government and politics in three decades. Final acknowledgment of the legitimacy of this new order came in January of 1837, on the eve of Jackson's retirement, when the Senate voted to expunge its censure from the record.[49]

The New Order Takes Hold

Jackson's vindication signaled a wholesale reconstruction of American politics—one that permanently redefined the position of the presidency in its relations with the Congress, the Court, the cabinet, the states, the party, and the electorate. The executive office gained political foundations categorically more independent than it had enjoyed before, and a new regime of governmental commitments and political priorities held sway. For all this, however, Jackson left in his wake a problem as difficult as that posed by Jefferson's embargo.

Most generally, there was the question of how to deliver on the new orthodoxy of the fourth annual message. The new coalition was ripe with radical promises to special interests, but tensions among these interests still ran high.[50] More immediately, there was the question of what to do with the manifest failure of Jackson's solution to the nation's banking problem. As Congress was falling into line and as the Democratic party was gearing up to elect Jackson's hand-picked successor, Martin Van Buren, the state deposit scheme was faltering and the nation's economy was rapidly deteriorating.

In truth, Jackson had latched onto the state deposit scheme out of political necessity as much as principle. Driven on one side by a coalition of senatorial rivals dedicated to protecting the Bank from executive designs and, on the other, by his own supporters' need for a clear and attractive alternative to it, Jackson's repudiation of Biddle and Clay had melded into opposition to any national banking structure whatsoever, and the erstwhile experiment with state banking quickly became a make-or-break commitment. Unfortunately, the infusion of federal deposits into the pet banks fueled a speculative boom that was already threatening the nation with a major financial collapse. Hoping to stem the tide of this disaster, Jackson threw his support behind a gradual conversion to hard currency. For its part, the Treasury Department started choosing banks of deposit less for their political soundness than for their financial soundness and then tightened central controls over them.[51]

At this point, however, the President was forced to face the grim irony of his success as a regime-builder. In the process of moving behind his campaign to destroy the Bank, the Congress had begun to see for itself the special attractions of the new system. Democrats now decried the President's efforts to control the state banks through national regulation as tantamount to the imposition of a new national bank, and in the Deposit Act of 1836, they expanded the number of depositories and explicitly limited executive discretion in dealing with them.[52] In effect, then, Jackson had merely substituted one irresponsible and uncontrollable financial system for another.

Like Jefferson before him, Jackson left office just as the new order was taking on a political life of its own. It was left to his hand-picked successor to scuttle his failed experiment while affirming his basic course. President Van Buren grappled with this challenge in the midst of the nation's first great depression, waging a four-year battle to extend Jacksonian principles and extricate the federal government from the banking business altogether.

Part Two:
James Polk's Articulation

Equal and exact justice

THOUGH the Whigs trounced Martin Van Buren in his bid for reelection in 1840, they ended up with little to show for their first turn in the White House. William Henry Harrison's death shortly after his inauguration elevated John Tyler to the president's chair, and Whig leaders—for all their cleverness in having run a military hero they could call their own on a ticket with a disaffected Democrat—then found themselves playing host to a "mongrel." Tyler asserted his independence with Jacksonian resolve and blocked implementation of the Whig program.

Trying again in 1844, the Whigs put the legendary Henry Clay up against a second-ranked Jackson partisan, James K. Polk. When Polk eked out a narrow victory, he effectively crushed the Whigs' last hopes for their programmatic alternative. As Clay's defeat brought the Democrats back into full control of the federal establishment, the nation was poised to leap ahead along the path charted by Andrew Jackson. The resurgent Democrats had in fact joined this great "battle of the standards" with a fully elaborated program of their own, and Polk, the very image of Jacksonian orthodoxy, stood ready to stamp it on the nation indelibly.

This was not the first time that an election had signaled the impending fulfillment of long-heralded regime promises. When Polk took up the task of completing the work of Andrew Jackson, he found himself grappling with the same basic dilemmas in political action that James Monroe had. Each in his time was an orthodox-innovator, a leader thoroughly identified with a preexisting framework of political ideas and obligations and fully committed to moving forward in concert along a path already traced. Moreover, both of these presidents stood at the threshold of a golden age in regime politics. They were bolstered by the prospect of acting on commitments that held formidable political, institutional, and ideological supports. They set out to implement the policies of a robust regime, to transform the nation without changing its politics. They wanted to exercise power so as to vindicate the previously established order of things.

Like Monroe, Polk sought to smooth the transition between past and future and finesse the disruptive implications of bold national initiatives. Like Monroe, he tried to orchestrate a purely constructive leadership project, to serve all those who came under his charge, and repudiate nothing and no one of significance. Polk was fully engaged in the management of established interests, and like Monroe, he soon found himself shadow-boxing with the very real changes he had set in motion. Polk too became thoroughly caught up in his own time-warped sense of political purpose; and as his achievements began to undermine the legitimacy of the regime they were meant to celebrate, he too found himself at a loss to understand, let alone address, the political tangle he had created.

Polk and Monroe pursued parallel careers in different eras. Each had made his way in national politics as a protégé of the regime founder (Polk had been Speaker of the House under Jackson), and each had proven himself worthy through loyal service to the founder's hand-picked successor (Polk served again as Speaker under Van Buren). They encountered setbacks (Polk was defeated in a bid for reelection as governor of Tennessee in 1841), but each stuck close to the ranks. They remained men of the organization, party regulars and regime boosters. In the decades that separated their administrations, however, the organization and operation of American government and politics had changed radically. After Jackson, the power of party organizations, the nature of partisanship, and the resources available for presidential boosterism were all quite different. Thus, in this second look at the politics of articulation, we find a significant secular reshaping of the underlying leadership dynamics.

The most obvious difference is that Polk was not, like Monroe, a statesman of national reputation. The party of Jackson produced a different breed of politician than the party of Jefferson. Polk entered the most clearly articulated two-party contest of the antebellum period as the first "dark horse." A compromise choice negotiated among the major factions of the Democratic coalition at a national party convention, he pulled the various pieces of the Democratic organization together and facilitated the successful operation of the party's electoral machinery largely by virtue of his personal anonymity. Furthermore, as a party regular of the mid-nineteenth century, Polk acted according to a starkly different set of political mores. A patrician, reveling in his role as national tribune, Monroe had grasped the leadership project of the faithful son with a counsel of caution and circumspection; his reputation already established, he was at pains in office to protect and preserve it. For Polk, in contrast, attaining the presidency was the main chance; out to build his national reputation, he was determined to use his party's power as aggressively as he could to realize great national achievements. Once in office, Polk threw himself into his task with a single-minded passion that Monroe would have found offensive in the extreme. He rushed headlong to complete one agenda item after another in as uncompromising a fashion as possible. He rested his actions on the strength of his party's organization. He did not blink at the task of ordering mass removals of Whig officers to service that organization, nor did he hesitate to make extraordinary demands on his comrades to achieve his national policy ambitions.[1] Polk's political vision was unabashedly partisan, and his faith in the loyalty and political discipline of his fellow Democrats was near complete.

In part, the relative intensity of Polk's presidency reflects the imperatives of political maintenance in a fiercely competitive electoral environment. The election of 1844 marks the full maturation of the partisan mode of governmental operations as well as the high-water mark of the second, or Jacksonian, party system. As the Democrats had survived a humiliating defeat to the Whigs in 1840 and became in 1844 the first party to return to power after suffering an interim rebuff, so the Whig organization would survive the defeat of 1844 and retake control of the House of Representatives in the midterm contest of 1846.[2] These two national coalitions of local party organizations competed tenaciously at all levels of government before, during, and after the Polk presidency, and Polk's victory, the narrowest in a presidential contest to that date, appeared at the level of electoral politics as but a momentary alteration in a national balance of political power. Older, patrician ideals of transcending partisanship in national leadership gave way in this new environment to the logistics of sustaining the electoral machinery. With the Whigs ever close at heel, everything hinged on Polk's prompt orchestration of satisfactory service to each of the constituent parts of the Democratic party's fragile national majority. Polk moved swiftly and aggressively because there was simply no time to waste in priming the organization for the next electoral test.

But Polk's aggressiveness in presidential action reflects more than the maturation of party competition; it also marks a new sense of the powers of the presidential office. Polk had, after all, cut his teeth in national politics during the Bank War. As Jackson's lieutenant on the House floor, he had witnessed firsthand the emancipation of the presidency from the strictures of Jeffersonian orthodoxy. If he was more restless in the role of the faithful son than Monroe, it is because he was determined to use on his own behalf the more robust office that Jackson had bequeathed to him and to answer with great deeds the questions about his national standing that the Whigs had posed so pointedly during the 1844 campaign. In this respect, the development of the powers of the presidency did not simply keep pace with the requisites of political maintenance; it also exacerbated the tension between exercising power and holding things together. The distinctive characteristics of a politics of articulation are more sharply delineated under Polk than under Monroe for precisely this reason. It is the juxtaposition of enhanced capacities for independent action in the presidency with the more densely shaded imperatives of organizational maintenance that lends Polk's articulation its classic shape and line.

As the Polk-Monroe comparison brings to the fore these recurrent and emergent patterns in the politics of articulation, it leaves us with another developmental irony: While the new partisan professional came into office with less in the way of national standing than the old patrician tribune, his personal ambitions were fueled by a more expansive sense of presidential capacities and prerogatives. Polk would find it far easier to get things done than Monroe had, and he would get them done with far greater dispatch. But the new prospects for acting independently strained Polk's patience with ameliorating the political consequences of getting things done, and the more thorough integration of the national political system magnified the disruptive effects of what he did.[3]

A Promise of Neutral Engagement

Texas annexation was the pivotal issue of 1844, but it was hardly a new one. Andrew Jackson had been as passionate about the annexation of Texas as Jefferson had been about the acquisition of Florida. Indeed,

Jackson was one of those who believed that in settling the Florida question and negotiating the Transcontinental Treaty in 1819, John Quincy Adams had sold out the nation's clear title to Texas. Still, in the last year of his presidency, when an opportunity presented itself for decisive action on this front, Jackson held back.[4] He seemed to sense the risk of precipitous action to the national party he had just consolidated, and he dreaded the thought of dividing that party along sectional lines. Like Jefferson on the Florida question, Jackson left the dream of annexing Texas as a bit of unfinished business to be completed in due time by his faithful followers.

As it turned out, Jackson's Texas nightmare became President Tyler's political strategy. After leaving the Democratic party and being thrown out of the Whig party, Tyler seized upon the Texas issue to challenge established political alignments and press himself forward on independent ground. His call for immediate annexation threw a monkey wrench into the calculations of both major parties in the 1844 contest. Instantly, it rekindled Old Hickory's inflammatory charge that John Quincy Adams had sold out the nation's original title to Texas. Texas fever swept through the South; it gave voice to the expansionist spirit in the West, the spirit of "Young America"; and it cast a dark cloud of suspicion over the nation's most familiar political leaders. Tyler's secretary of state, John C. Calhoun, committed another of his unspeakable heresies by articulating the thought on everyone's mind and linking the Texas issue explicitly to his region's interest in slave expansion. Then Henry Clay and Martin Van Buren both hedged on their commitment. Van Buren, the nominal head of the Democratic party and again the leading contender for its presidential nomination, endorsed the idea of eventual annexation but opposed immediate action.[5]

James Polk was one of the few Texas enthusiasts in the Democratic party to remain loyal to Van Buren's candidacy up to the moment of its defeat at the national convention in 1844. He had been promoting himself for selection as Van Buren's running mate, offering to broaden the New Yorker's appeal and to help Van Buren finesse the Texas difficulty by serving in the second slot. By the same token, as a "new man" with solid links to the old leadership, Polk was perfectly positioned as a compromise choice for the top spot on the ticket when Van Buren's nomination stalled. Intimately involved in the political battles that had launched the Democratic regime under Jackson and Van Buren, and unimpeachable in his orthodoxy, Polk's leadership credentials were thoroughly and safely submerged in the evolving identity of his party. His candidacy promised to hold the old coalition together while simultaneously moving it forward intact toward an even more glorious future; it promised to parry Tyler's impetuous challenge by returning to the fold an issue that had, after all, been simmering on the back burner of Democratic politics for years.[6] With the party committed to Texas annexation, Tyler's threat receded; with Polk offering a faceless symbol of purity and continuity in party commitments, there was no need for a new organization. A fusion of past and future, the Polk campaign rearticulated traditional Democratic party purposes for a new round of national achievement.

To the Whig's derisive campaign query "Who is James K. Polk?" the Democrats gave a resounding reply, one that clearly articulated the temporal structure of Polk's leadership project as it emerged from the nominating convention. James K. Polk was "the bosom friend of Andrew Jackson, and a pure whole hogged democrat, the known enemy of Banks and distribution." He was, in Jackson's own words "consistent, orthodox and true" on "all great questions from the Panama Mission to the present day." He claimed nothing for himself, but merely assumed "a simple position as a representative of the general principles and policy of the [Democratic] party."[7]

Polk responded to this trust with a series of statements clearly acknowledging the ground on which the political legitimacy of his administration would rest. He accepted his party's nomination with an announcement that he would not stand for a second term.[8] The one-term pledge was an old Jackson standard, and though it had been quickly disregarded by the general himself, it was especially helpful to a dark-horse candidate who desperately needed to convince all the party's leaders that by electing him they would not be adversely affecting their own chances in 1848. This theme was sounded again when Polk, determined to take charge of his administration, insisted on taking it out of party politics. To avoid the kind of schismatic internal competition among lieutenants that had so sapped Monroe's strength, Polk demanded that each of his cabinet appointees make his own explicit pledge disavowing all personal political ambitions and committing himself exclusively to the success of the administration.[9] And again, even more explicitly, Polk pledged to the faithful that in patronage matters he would "know no divisions of the Democratic party," that political support would be distributed on the basis of neutrality. He would do "equal and exact justice" to every party interest.[10]

Taken together, these pronouncements of the terms upon which his administration would act added up to a declaration of benign engagement with its political foundations. With presidential power being exercised on a vow of self-denial openly taken by everyone in the administration and with patronage being distributed with "equal and exact justice" to all members of the church, Polk ventured that he could transform the nation—bringing orthodox party commitments to the full flower of policy achievements—and leave the balance of power in the established party precisely as it was at the time of the presidential nomination. The linkage Polk drew between neutral engagement in party affairs and a vigorous assertion of presidential leadership was direct and explicit. His declaration "I intend to be *myself* President of the U.S."[11] was penned in a pre-inaugural letter reiterating his determination to take himself and his administration out of all future political contention. Significantly, Polk presented political neutrality within the party fold as the very basis of his claim to the independent exercise of presidential power.

The great paradox of policy achievement and political disorientation that surrounds the Polk administration gains its enduring significance from the obvious difficulties in this approach to leadership. Polk's determination to innovate was continually rubbing up against his self-professed standards for action, and the uncomfortable choices he was forced to make between his innovations and his standards were charged directly against his definition of the moment at hand. Polk's presidency rested on a promise to reconcile the irreconcilable—personal control and political neutrality, presidential leadership and political justice, policy innovation and political maintenance.

Consider the prospects for neutral engagement as Polk articulated them: while he felt compelled to count himself out of party politics at the outset with a one-term pledge, he simultaneously felt compelled to commit himself to a superhuman feat of party management with the pledge of "equal and exact justice." If equal and exact justice meant anything, it was that neutral political engagement would be *total* political engagement. To deliver equal justice, Polk would have to orchestrate a full-service administration satisfying every faction of the faithful. Or to look at it from the other side, every faction of political significance would have to accept as just and equal whatever it was that Polk gave them, even though he himself was not only a self-effacing "dark horse" but also a self-professed "lame duck." It is here, in the very terms he set out for the appropriate exercise of political power, that the orthodox Polk—the stalwart dedicated to party maintenance through personal self-sacrifice and diligent service to every party faction—first meets up with "Polk the Mendacious"—the President charged by each faction with duplicitous manipulations and held responsible for pulling the regime apart. The efforts of this most orthodox of innovators to manage the regime he was charged to preserve unleashed systemic political schisms so destabilizing it would take a civil war to resolve them.

The Perils of Self-Assertion

Polk's betrayal of the Van Buren radicals in the formation of his cabinet is a telling case in point not simply because this first action would later be marked as a crucial step toward the momentous party rupture of the Free Soilers, but also because the whole tangled affair turned on the compulsive efforts of the President-elect to extort personal control out of outward signs of self-abnegation and an avowed pursuit of political maintenance.[12] Indeed, this episode is the classic example of the struggle of the affiliated president to reconcile the imperatives of control with the question of political justice.

Van Buren's claims on the cabinet were clear. He was the leading national figure in the Democratic party, and the leading contender for the Democratic nomination through the first half dozen convention ballots. His delegates had clinched the nomination for Polk on the ninth ballot when their own cause became hopeless, and his followers had clinched the election for Polk by patching over divisions in the New York party and carrying the state for the national Democratic ticket. This enormous debt invoked a genuine sense of obligation from the victor, but it also posed a challenge to his determination to be *himself* president of the United States. Polk's relationship to Van Buren—tinged as it was by the tension between an older, northern leader, skeptical of the new commitment to Texas, and a younger, southern leader, fully committed on all sides—confounded his stalwart determination to take control without repudiation.

Polk's overture was impeccable. On December 7, 1844, while still in

Tennessee, Polk made his first offer of office, the Treasury Department, to Van Buren's closest and most powerful associate, Silas Wright.[13] Wright declined the position (he had just been elected governor of New York), and the refusal (certainly no surprise) released Polk to form a cabinet on his own as a political unit.[14] But even as he took his first steps along this path, Polk wrote back to New York assuring Wright and Van Buren a good measure of control. Acknowledging again his great political debt to them, he asked for further recommendations and clearly indicated his intention to make a cabinet appointment of the first rank from their list.[15] In fact, the list of projected appointments that Polk presented to Jackson for review before he left for Washington not only included a Wright-Van Buren candidate, Azariah Flagg, in the Treasury slot, it contained within its careful political balance a discernible Van Buren bias overall.[16]

Once in Washington, Polk proceeded down this list with an offer of the State Department to James Buchanan of Pennsylvania. This appointment, viewed against the elevation of Buchanan's Pennsylvania rival, George Dallas, to the vice presidency, gave the administration a balance of factional representation in another pivotal state and another safe annexation man in control of foreign policy. But this first truly independent initiative left only one top position open. The political pressure on the Treasury slot mounted precipitously in the capital, and concerted drives by both those who wished to counter Buchanan and those who wished to counter Van Buren quickly merged around the selection of Robert Walker of Mississippi.[17] At this juncture, Polk began to appreciate the full weight of the difficulties posed by his avowed commitments to Van Buren. While the support for Walker reached deep into the old South (to the Calhoun faction), outward to the new West (where expansionist fever ran hottest), and even to the East (George Dallas, Walker's father-in-law, led the charge for the appointment within the administration), opposition to Flagg and the old Van Buren leadership was evident in every section, even within the New York party itself. Importantly, though, Walker had been a leader in the effort to block Van Buren's nomination at the convention, and Polk saw the wisdom of keeping his distance from southern radicalism if he could. Specifically, he wanted to confine Walker to the relatively innocuous post of attorney general, and to use the pressure for Walker to work out some other arrangements with Van Buren. It was with this recalculation in mind that Polk wrote to New York explaining the "great difficulties" that had interposed against Flagg's appointment to the Treasury post and the "great and extensive disaffection" that threatened if the concerted drive on behalf of a "distinguished individual" of the South were simply ignored.[18]

In this letter, sent ten days before his inauguration, Polk carefully pushed himself forward as a political leader determined to orchestrate the Jacksonian restoration on his own terms. He wanted to revoke some of the control he had passed to Van Buren and to sidestep the Flagg appointment, but to do so he made Van Buren another offer and sought to enlist his support in a new scheme specifically designed to hold the line against Walker. He suggested George Bancroft of Massachusetts as a compromise choice for Treasury. Bancroft had been associated with Van Buren, and though Polk had originally intended him for the Navy slot, he now latched onto a passing remark Van Buren had made suggesting that Bancroft was fit for any office. Since Bancroft was sound on Texas, Polk reasoned that he would mollify the South and West and head off the pressure for Walker. Polk then offered to meet New York's claims directly with the War Department, and he proposed either Benjamin Butler or William Marcy as satisfactory choices for war secretary. Polk was not certain that Butler would accept the War Department portfolio, since Van Buren had recommended him for the State Department, and he suggested that Van Buren intervene directly if he wanted to secure the appointment. Moreover, since Polk had received conflicting reports from various New Yorkers on relations between Van Buren and Marcy, he asked Van Buren to set him straight on the real state of affairs and, in effect, to make the decision between the two possible choices. In fact, neither Van Buren nor Wright had ever mentioned Marcy in connection with any post, and Polk's solicitation strongly suggests his own inclination toward Marcy as the safer (more conservative) and sounder (pro-Texas) candidate for the administration. In any event, he closed this pivotal letter with a portentous request for an immediate response: "Time is short and I am most anxious to hear from you before I am compelled to act definitely."[19]

The revised masterplan of February 22, 1845, bespeaks volumes about Polk's leadership. Clearly, the President-elect was pressing his own interest in securing an administration on his own terms, but he did so by turning yet another key choice over to Van Buren. As was characteristic of all Polk's grand schemes for venting his ambitions, the Bancroft/Butler plan packaged a quest for mastery with a bid for legitimacy together in a delicate balance. The plan did have a certain abstract perfection in joining political justice and party maintenance to presidential control, and in this sense it tells us as much about Polk's understanding of his charge as the ultimate result. As a practical matter, however, the plan was simply too clever for the veil of deference that surrounded it. Woven through this reaffirmation of the commitment to Van Buren was a more threatening alternative (a Walker/Marcy combination) that would, at once, represent a momentous shift in the balance of power within the Democratic party and absolve the President of all responsibility for making it. Indeed, in the high-risk, high-pressure scheme that Polk outlined for Van Buren's consideration, he actually seemed to be passing the responsibility for this alternative outcome onto the man who would be its chief victim. Whatever his actual intent, Polk's transparent calculation of his own political advantage severely tested faith in his presidency and loyalty to the party, and it was unlikely to evoke a sober response from a man who thought he had put Polk in the president's chair in the first place.

Working under a self-imposed deadline to complete the cabinet before his inauguration in early March, Polk pushed himself into action on his plan before he received Van Buren's response. On February 25 he ventured the safest move he could on his own and wrote to Butler with an offer of the War portfolio. Meanwhile, Van Buren—finding out for the first time that New York was to lose control of Treasury and that his choice for State had been demoted to the War Department—was apparently too infuriated for words and did not answer right away. As a result, Butler's immediate refusal arrived well before Van Buren's delayed response, and Polk took Van Buren's silence as sufficient warrant for further action on the plan he had outlined in his letter. On March 1—the last day before the inauguration that another offer could be secured in New York—Polk felt "compelled to act definitely" and extended Marcy the offer of the War Department.[20]

No sooner had the Marcy appointment been tendered than Van Buren's son, Smith, arrived with his father's contentious reply to Polk's letter of the 22nd. In it, Van Buren chastised Polk for capitulating to "selfish influences" and abandoning New York's clear claim to one of the two top cabinet slots. Furthermore, Van Buren told Polk that Marcy's appointment would be a "fatal mistake," and, apparently unaware of Butler's action, he personally guaranteed Butler's acceptance of the War Department. It was, of course, too late for Butler; but Polk insisted that the offense had not been intentional, and he now promised to counteract this unfortunate happenstance by turning over carte blanche control of the New York patronage—customs houses, post offices, district attorneys—to Van Buren and Wright. The next day another letter from Van Buren was delivered. This one was an apology for the first and an implicit endorsement of the Bancroft/Butler scheme. Evidently, Van Buren was as reluctant to sever his ties to the administration as Polk was loath to cross him. But as Smith Van Buren made clear in an angry lecture reviewing the implications of the Marcy appointment, there was little comfort for Polk to take in that.[21]

Despite this last effort to secure his decisions by handing more decision-making power to Van Buren, it was now evident to Polk that his masterplan for political maintenance was unraveling. The unfortunate "mishap" of March 1 had made some political slippage inevitable, but in this it also offered the President-elect a final release for independent action. As Van Buren's reaction to the Marcy appointment placed his active support for the administration in grave doubt, the impressive political support for Walker weighed in against news of New England opposition to Bancroft's appointment to Treasury. Polk could now convince himself that he had done everything he could for Van Buren, that control of the New York patronage was justice enough in the present circumstances, and that the portents of a schism in the ranks demanded that he maximize support for his administration as best he could. At the very last moment, then, Walker was invited to take control of Treasury, Bancroft was placed back in the Navy slot, and the Van Buren Democrats of New York were shut out of the cabinet.[22]

Here, then, is Polk the Mendacious as he rationalized his way from a cabinet list with a distinct Van Buren bias toward a Walker/Marcy team that clearly identified the administration with Van Buren's bitter opponents. Through a sequential recalculation of the meaning of political justice and its relationship to presidential control Polk had, in effect, built a monumental deception out of successive plans for political maintenance. He had steadfastly refused to repudiate Van Buren; indeed, with each self-assertion he felt compelled to pass some measure of control back to Van Buren. But this tangle of self-assertion and self-abnegation led Polk to a frustrating confrontation with the consequences of his own actions. Helpless, he watched as Van Buren finally repudiated him.

Van Buren spurned the offer of carte-blanche control of the New York patronage and made it known that he expected his allies to ignore Polk's overtures. When Polk visited New York, Van Buren refused to meet with him, and when Polk offered Van Buren the delicate and prestigious post of minister to Great Britain, he was again rebuffed. Flagg refused appointment to the collectorship of the Port of New York, and Butler, who accepted a position as United States attorney in the southern district of New York, turned the position into a forum for agitating against the administration.

In the end Polk got what he wanted and needed to be a leader in his own right—that is, a cabinet of new men unreservedly committed to Texas annexation. But he would have difficulty from here on being a leader on his own terms. From the moment of his break with Van Buren, Polk's central claim to political legitimacy became the subject of an incessant barrage of challenges. More sensitive to results than intentions, the Van Burenites interpreted the formation of the administration as a secret plot by the President to position himself for renomination in 1848 despite his one-term pledge, and they accused him of selling out the party to the South for the honor. Polk weathered the charges as best he could. He steadfastly refused to sever his ties to the New York radicals until they themselves formally bolted the party at the 1848 nominating convention. He kept insisting that his administration was neutral with regard to divisions in the New York party, and he vented his frustrations at the charges against him in increasingly bitter diary entries. These only seem to underscore the dilemmas of the one-term pledge and the self-delusion that political maintenance could, in fact, serve as the central premise for presidential leadership.

> The truth is *they* [the Van Buren men] are looking to the next presidential election, and nothing could satisfy them unless I were to identify myself with them, and proscribe all other branches of the Democratic party. I will do, as I have done, Mr. Martin Van Buren's friends justice in the bestowal of public patronage, but I cannot proscribe all others of the Democratic party in order to gain their good will. I will adhere sternly to my principles without identifying myself with any faction or clique of the Democratic party.[23]

The counterpart to this story in the Monroe administration is instructive. Disaffected by the appointment of John Quincy Adams to the State Department and insulted by Monroe's offer to take over the War Department, Henry Clay, like the Van Buren radicals, immediately began to agitate against the President's central claims to legitimacy. The relative intensity of Polk's manipulations and the awkwardness of his pandering to Van Buren are suggestive of the deepening systemic stakes of acting independently. But both Monroe and Polk determined at the outset to place their administrations on the most secure foundations possible, and with a firm grip on their regimes' robust policy agendas, these presidents never let the agitators carry the day. The problem was that the actions they had taken on their own behalf sparked debilitating distractions within the ranks, distractions that ate into their professed authority as ministers of the faith.

Completing the Work

The frustration of Polk's effort to take control of the Jacksonian regime without alienating vital political support was a portentous prelude to his more far-reaching efforts to take over leadership of the Jacksonian political agenda without altering the terms of political discourse that gave that agenda its meaning and vitality. As Polk sought to ground personal control in party justice and political neutrality, he also sought to ground policy leadership in strict adherence to orthodox political service. Indeed, his program recapitulated the theme of equal and exact justice with a full articulation of long-anticipated measures that, if enacted item by item as a package, would transform the nation without changing its political foundations. Polk's agenda stands as the most complete and delicately balanced scheme of programmatic party service ever conceived by any president, but as such it staked the security of each of its proposed innovations, indeed the security of Jacksonian America itself, on the riveting power of a pure and total achievement. As with the pledge of equal and exact justice, anything less than a pure and total achievement promised a political disaster.

What we find in the specifics, then, is another grand scheme that was as irresistible in its abstract conception as it was fantastic as a practical program for political action in the presidency. A pledge to return to hard money and restore the "independent treasury" reached out to Van Buren radicals and reaffirmed the cornerstones of Jacksonian finance. (Van Buren had hatched the independent treasury idea as an alternative to the failed experiment with state depositories. The implementation of the new system had been sidetracked in 1841 by the Whig ascendancy.)

A pledge to return to "tariff-for-revenue" principles reached out to the South with another orthodox tenet of Jacksonian political economy. (The tariff reduction, facilitated by the repeal of the corn laws in England, was to maintain "incidental protection" to northern manufacturers, and it was ultimately joined with a proposal for a warehouse storage system that promised to moderate the uncertainties of lower rates for import merchants.) A third tenet of Jacksonian orthodoxy, the graduated reduction of land prices, reached out to the West. (As Polk presented the case for land reform: "It is the true policy of the Government to afford facilities to its citizens to become the owners of small portions of our vast public domain at low and moderate rates.") Finally, in foreign policy, Polk reached out to the expansionists of "Young America," North and South, with equally aggressive endorsements of the "reannexation" of "Greater Texas" and the "reoccupation" of "all of Oregon."[24]

Virtually every interest of significance in the Democratic party was provided some pointed recognition in Polk's grand scheme. But just as important as these explicit commitments to a full-service administration were the implicit messages that set its boundaries. First, the idea that every interest of significance could be served, and that none would be repudiated, strongly underscored the common interest of each in providing mutual support for all. In other words, implementation of this program was to submerge the recent agitation over slavery's expansion in a renewed celebration of the central tenets of Jacksonian nationalism. Second, the idea that each interest was to be attended to in strictly orthodox terms warned against other enticing policies that could not stand the test of political purity for all. Internal improvement projects, for example, were off the plate. Finally, the prospect of delivering everything necessary to bring every interest along left open the question of what more might be done for the cause with impunity. It is especially significant in this regard that Polk's crowning achievement, the acquisition of California and the greater Southwest, entered this grand design as a mere implication of his belligerent claim to "Greater Texas." When Polk included the heretofore disputed territory between the Nueces River and the Rio Grande in his annexation plan, he effectively closed off options for the bankrupt Mexican government in settling other long-standing American claims. California became the only appropriate concession the Mexicans had left to make.[25] Polk's determination to pursue the other American claims against Mexico aggressively harbored this unspoken but obvious goal, one that would stamp his moment of orthodox service with a personal achievement of first-order significance.

In all these commitments—domestic and foreign, explicit and implicit—Polk's program carefully packaged the nation's "Manifest Destiny" as a completion of the party's historic work. Though willing to venture that Jacksonian orthodoxy could be pushed toward entirely new achievements, Polk kept the glories of the future thoroughly submerged in the methodical task of wrapping up all the old business at hand. Action was galvanized in a way that would spring the future wholesale out of clear and time-honored political commitments. Even the portentous claims to "Greater Texas" and "all of Oregon" were forced into the mold of long-pending claims—"reannexation" and "reoccupation"—that only awaited their inevitable resolution.[26] More fundamentally still, Polk's approach to Manifest Destiny reflected a Jacksonian preoccupation with securing and perpetuating the world of the past itself. The consistency of the entire package is to be found in its summary conception of freedom. Each of Polk's policies bespoke the same "true policy" that the purpose of the federal government was to "afford facilities" for citizens to become independent owners of "small portions" of a vast public domain. The President set out to realize this vision not only by consolidating the old policies but by extending the Jacksonian regime across the continent, and guaranteeing it in perpetuity through unlimited access to new space.[27]

It is equally clear, however, that Polk's leadership project left precious little play for imperfections in the process of policy innovation itself. Party loyalty was the key to the program's success, but though few presidents would find party discipline in Congress stronger, this scheme demanded more than a series of favorable party votes. To maintain political alliances through aggressive policy leadership, each proposal had to be geared to all the others. The sequence, pace, and symbolism of the initiatives would have to be assiduously controlled and coordinated with heated foreign negotiations so that the sectional paranoias and the ideological heresies they harbored individually would continually be held in check. Mutual self-interest had to remain at the forefront so that reciprocal party obligations could be reinforced. Put another way, the failure of total presidential control over the meaning of each and every innovation promised to bury the prospective political synthesis in an explosion of self-interest that would contaminate the orthodoxy of whatever achievements were gained. Though "consistent, orthodox, and true," the planned orchestration of services became, at the practical level of interest manipulation, more grist for debilitating charges against Polk the Mendacious.

This time the breakdown of Polk's grand design came in the guise of a betrayal of the West.[28] The President moved forward immediately and simultaneouly with his claim to "all of Oregon" (extending north to the 54°40′ parallel line) and "Greater Texas" (extending south of the Nueces River 150 miles to the Rio Grande). The pledge to get "all of Oregon" unleashed a tidal wave of popular enthusiasm in the Northwest. Unfortunately, however, Great Britain refused to play according to presidential plan, and while Van Buren Democrats joined the northwesterners in belligerent support of 54°40′, a peace movement, spearheaded by Calhoun, spread across the South out of fear of an impending war over the Oregon boundary.[29] Polk was willing to use the belligerence of the "fifty-four forty or fight" faction to counter the peace movement and to prod the British into coming to terms; but when negotiations with Mexico collapsed, he had to face the implications of British rejection of his Oregon claims.[30] Polk might have accepted, even promoted, an "inevitable" war with either Britain *or* Mexico, but a war with *both* Britain and Mexico would risk losing everything that was now in sight.

A skirmish with Mexican troops on the Rio Grande in early May of 1846 provided a timely pretext for claiming that Mexicans had shed American blood "on American soil" and thus for declaring to Congress that a state of war existed "by the act of Mexico herself."[31] Then, in early June, when the British finally renewed their initial offer to settle the Oregon boundary at the 49th parallel, Polk called for the advice of the Senate as to whether to accept half of what he had promised or to press a claim that would now risk a war on two fronts.[32] By asking for the Senate's advice prior to sending over a treaty for approval, Polk in effect passed responsibility for the resolution of his political difficulties onto the upper house. Like passing his responsibility for his cabinet selections onto Van Buren, this was another all-too-clever retreat from pure and total achievement, and the dubious call for a defense of American honor against Mexican aggression only partially covered it over. While the war with Mexico all but announced a jingoistic drive west to California, the anger of unfulfilled expectations (and the real political embarrassment of northwestern politicians who had been led by the President to agitate for "all" of Oregon in the first place) was left to fester.[33] In a situation in which legitimacy hung delicately on perceptions of equal and exact justice, it appeared that a northern war had been sacrificed for a southern war, and on this ground northwesterners first became attuned to Van Burenite charges of willful deception on the part of the administration.[34] Polk had stumbled on British determination and western pride, and even as he gained a huge chunk of the Oregon territory, his grand orchestration of mutual services struck an ominously discordant note.

The shortfall from pure and total achievement in domestic legislation amplified western discontent.[35] Polk pressed hard on northwestern Democrats to make up for expected eastern defections on his downward revision of tariff rates. In doing so, he not only held out the promise of land reform, he also kept silent about a legislative initiative brewing among representatives of the South and West for improvements on the Great Lakes and Mississippi River system. The northwesterners swallowed their pride over Oregon, threw their support behind tariff revision, and openly anticipated a lucrative policy alliance with the South. But once the tariff was secure, Polk vetoed the internal improvement bill. Not only was this bill a clear and insufferable offense to Jacksonian dogma in general, it was a particular insult to the eastern radical element. Support for internal improvements had been conspicuously absent from Polk's program, and perhaps even more important, the expense it entailed now presented a direct threat to the prospects for Polk's orthodox financial and trade package.[36] Needless to say, however, western politicians had more at stake here than the purity and consistency of Polk's principles, and to make matters worse, Polk's promised land reform failed to get through the increasingly hostile congressional thicket. Burned three times in matters of interest, westerners began to abandon the counsels of mutual restraint. The President's efforts to bring the war with Mexico to a quick and triumphant conclusion provided them an opportunity to strike back in self-defense with their own declaration of political principles.

The war was in fact only a few months old, but Polk sensed the need to expedite the harvest of the fruits it promised. All along, Polk's war objectives had been veiled in pretense. Presumably the war was being fought because the United States had clear title to "Greater Texas," because Mexico had refused to make good on the long-standing claims of American citizens, and most important, because of Mexican aggression on United States soil. On August 8, 1846, however, the President formally asked Congress for a two million dollar appropriation as an advance for "settling all our difficulties with the Mexican Government" and for making a downpayment on "any concessions which may be made by Mexico" in the "adjustment of the boundary between the two Republics."[37] This proposal to pay for Mexican land was Polk's first unmistakable declaration that the United States was engaged in—perhaps had consciously provoked—a war for territorial aggrandizement in the Southwest. And with it, the latent issue of the 1844 campaign manifested itself with a vengeance. Faced with growing antislavery agitation at home and Whig opposition to the war effort, northern Democrats—East and West—now perceived unequal treatment in the administration's handling of interests, intolerable duplicity in presidential action, and an insufferable southern bias in national policy. They desperately needed some way to defend the Democratic regime to their constituents and to deflect charges of selling out their section's interests.[38] Together they took aim at the South, forced the uncomfortable political realities of the present to the fore, and exploded the President's benign synthesis of past and future.

Importantly, their vehicle steered clear of outright opposition to the war or the administration. The agitators merely attached a condition to their support for the President's proposal to buy peace and land. Introduced by David Wilmot, a Van Buren Democrat from western Pennsylvania, this Proviso guaranteed the exclusion of slavery from any new lands acquired from Mexico. The initiative was spearheaded by James Thompson (also a western Pennsylvania Democrat), Preston King (a Van Buren radical from New York), John Wentworth (a leading Democratic advocate of the internal improvement bill from Illinois), and Jacob Brinkerhoff (an Ohio Democrat who had been roundly criticized by the administration for his opposition to certain provisions of the tariff bill deemed hostile to the West). An appropriation bill with the Wilmot Proviso was passed in the House. The bill failed in the Senate when an effort to remove the Proviso was successfully filibustered.[39]

The Wilmot Proviso endorsed the crowning achievements of Jacksonian nationalism with a gross distortion of the received terms of Jacksonian discourse, and its sponsorship directly implicated Polk's leadership in an assault on the received foundations of Jacksonian politics. Polk had again provoked others to acknowledge the political changes he had tried to submerge in the pursuit of innovations formally consistent with the commitments of the past. A master manipulator of the abstract scheme, he again found himself at a loss when confronted with the real political consequences of his own actions. He confessed to his diary that he found the connection between slavery and making peace with Mexico "difficult to conceive." He denounced the Proviso as "worse than useless." It was a "distraction" from the business at hand, irrelevant to any practical settlement of the Far West, and virtually guaranteed "to destroy the Democratic party." Behind the budding free soil movement he saw scheming politicians and desperate presidential aspirants selfishly pursuing their own personal ambitions.[40] What he failed to perceive, or at least could not acknowledge, was how thoroughly his own schemes had transformed the political calculations of all others.

Between Past and Future

Between the spring of 1845 and the summer of 1846, Polk had delivered the independent treasury, tariff reduction, the warehouse storage system, Texas, and Oregon. Awaiting peace with Mexico, he was also securing American control over California and the greater Southwest. The scheme may have been fantastic, but Polk almost pulled it off. On the resilience of the Democratic alliance, he had raised a near-perfect monument to Jacksonian nationalism.

By 1847, however, political cartoonists were portraying "the house that Polk built" as a house of cards.[41] Even as he was raising the monument, Polk was progressively weakening the joints that held the whole edifice together. There it stood, more fully articulated and more precariously balanced than ever before.

During the remainder of his term, sectarian wrangling over what to do with Polk's achievements began to overtake the clear distinction between orthodoxy and heresy on which their legitimacy rested. In the Alabama Platform of 1847, a budding southern rights movement responded to the Wilmot Proviso with a declaration that denied the federal government the authority to prohibit slavery anywhere in the new territories. Moderates in the West warmed to a third alternative, popular sovereignty, which would allow the people of the territories to decide the issue for themselves.[42] Congress lingered over these differences in debilitating debates about the precise formula to be used in establishing civil authority over its new empire, and as it did, the politics of the future began to eclipse the politics of the past. Whigs and Democrats might continue to compete section by section, state by state, but politics at the center of the nation was now driving the sections farther apart. Neither party, considered as an instrument of national government, offered a solution to the new issues of the day. Increasingly they were being perceived as part of the problem.[43]

Inevitably the President was drawn into the new controversies he had sparked.[44] The position he ultimately adopted bore final testimony to his determination to deny the political consequences of his actions and to force the transformative political changes he had instigated into a pattern of policy consistent with past practice. Pressed on the territorial question, Polk took his stand on behalf of the Missouri Compromise of 1820; and while the contending alternatives each more or less explicitly called the legitimacy of the Compromise into question, he worked as best he could to ground legislation in the principle of extending the old Missouri line to the Pacific.[45]

It is fitting that this last stalwart stand for innovations that could pass the test of consistency with the past sparked charges of betrayal from the South, completing the panoply of interests who rejected Polk's politics of aggressive maintenance. Just before the congressional adjournment for the 1848 presidential campaign, northern Democrats and Whigs succeeded in passing a bill which provided a territorial government for Oregon with an explicit free soil provision. Southern Democrats and Whigs demanded a presidential veto, and for the first time the central political preoccupation of the next decade was squarely joined. Faced with a choice between leaving one of his great achievements unsecured or endorsing a principle he deemed heretical, Polk resolved to sign the bill. He would not leave the Oregon territory without a government, but neither would he endorse free soil principles. Orthodox to the end, he chose to reprimand the heretics on both sides, and for that his premises were rejected by southern agitators as they had been already by eastern and western agitators.

Polk sent a special message to Congress justifying his endorsement of the Oregon bill and warning agitators in all sections not to read too much into it. He had accepted territorial legislation with a free soil provision, he explained, because the exclusion of slavery was, in this instance, consistent with an extension of the old Missouri line to the Pacific.[46] The message pointedly avoided any affiliation with free soil principles, and yet the President's signature on the bill just as clearly rejected the Alabama Platform. The Whig press blasted Polk's final betrayal to Democrats across the South and carried the cry of "Polk the Mendacious" to victory in 1848.[47]

Polk's schismatic political effects make the tenacity of the regular party machinery in the election of 1848 all the more remarkable. The President had ridden party power through the fertile fields of Jacksonian orthodoxy and onto rugged new terrain, but when he stepped off, the engines were running hot as ever. Democrats and Whigs used the President's achievements to spin out new issues on which to compete, and the decentralized character of their organizations facilitated the delivery of different—often contradictory—messages to different sections.[48] The northern insurgents, nominating Martin Van Buren as the candidate of their Free Soil party, could hope for little more than to tilt the balance of national power and show the defeated Democratic machine that they were a force not to be ignored.

So as Jacksonian politics disintegrated at the top and the bottom, the resilience of the old party machinery extended the operations of an increasingly moribund regime.[49] There was no recovery from the sectarian turn of the mid-1840s. The national achievements and political shortfalls of Polk's presidency had hollowed out the old rules of appropriate national action. The disorientation in national politics and national party purposes that Polk had precipitated gave way to a patch-up operation; and the new formulas spun out to deal with his handiwork would sink the nation further into a crisis of legitimacy.

Part Three:
Franklin Pierce's Disjunction

No grandeur of enterprise and no urgent inducement
promising special favor will lead me to disregard
those lights which experience
has proved to be safe.

THE blunt force of presidential power does not admit much strategic fine-tuning, and the more delicate the situation, the less subtle the instrument is likely to prove. Presidents who by dint of circumstance have to grope to explain the disruptive effects of their actions find the meaning of those actions clarified by others at their own expense. Herein lies the explosive political significance of Franklin Pierce. A late-regime affiliate, tenuously attached to a political regime which was itself vulnerable on its most basic commitments of ideology and interest, his warrants for leadership were elusive in the extreme, and the actions he took on his own behalf were instantly subject to devastatingly simple interpretations from others as to the real state of national affairs. Perhaps the most colossal failure in presidential history, Pierce's impulse to lead would catalyze one of the most profound transformations of the American political landscape.

Pierce first comes into view as a shadow of James Polk. He was another dark horse of the party period, another faceless representative of Democratic orthodoxy, another Jacksonian president determined, in spite of his obscurity, to lay claim to the powers of Old Hickory. But between the Democrats' choice of Polk—a second-rank party leader to be sure—and their choice of Pierce—a figure on the distant fringes of national politics—the problems of affiliated leadership in the Jacksonian regime had been so magnified as to suggest a different kind of challenge altogether. Once the old party agenda had been enacted and the old party coalition pushed to take on new commitments, it became far more difficult to draw a line between orthodoxy and heresy in national Democratic politics. Pierce assumed power at a time when the central premise of affiliated leadership—upholding past commitments and continuing along the established course—was all but exhausted as a warrant for further change. Anything more than a simple affirmation of the status quo ante threatened to pull down the entire regime in sectarian warfare.

Thus, Pierce began to fashion his place in history one step removed from Polk's full-service program and the hands-on manipulation of coalition interests that went with it. He faced a challenge that was really prior to an assertion of leadership. First and foremost he had to figure out how to establish credibility for taking any action at all.

In this regard, Pierce's futile four-year struggle for credibility points back beyond Polk to a similar struggle for credibility in the late-Jeffersonian era. If the politics of leadership in the Jacksonian period are not all of a piece, neither are they entirely idiosyncratic. As Polk and Monroe shared the dilemmas of orthodox-innovators, Pierce shares with John Quincy Adams the impossible challenge of making something of the broken pieces their predecessors had left behind. Pierce and Adams both found themselves pressed between the political exhaustion of the old governing formulas and their own nominal identification with them, and for each of these late-regime affiliates the mere act of asserting political control threatened to expose the bankruptcy of the entire system of political control. The basic structure of the legitimation problem was so perverse in these instances that these presidents could no more affirm the past than repudiate it. Whether they withheld their power to change things or asserted it, they would be committing political suicide.

The outstanding question is how the relative independence of the post-Jackson presidency and the enhanced resources of executive power in the party period recast leadership in this impossible situation. To be sure, Pierce had none of the trappings of patrician statesmanship, and little of Adams's reputation for national service. He was a mere creature of the organization that nominated him. But he came to an office that now had some real clout behind it, and that inspired dreams of building a great reputation within it. When Pierce brought the weightier tools of the Jacksonian presidency to bear on this most fragile of circumstances, the political impact of the impulse to lead came into much sharper relief, and the disjunctive effect of presidential action gained a classic shape and line. Pierce met the delicate question of his own legitimacy with a greater capacity for self-assertion, more room to maneuver, and more blunt force in action. Once it became clear that a political explosion of unprecedented proportion was in the making, Pierce threw himself into the center of it with an offer to carry the nation to safety on wholly new ground.

Reassembling the Old Party

The political ground for Democratic leadership in 1852 had been narrowed significantly by the Democrats' response to their loss to Zachary Taylor and the Whigs in the presidential election of 1848. This defeat alerted the party managers to the importance of those sects that had become disaffected from the stalwart nationalism of Jackson and Polk, and it spurred them to try to repair the damage. In 1850, congressional Democrats came to the aid of a faltering Whig coalition and supplied the critical votes necessary to secure the passage of a legislative package that promised, finally and conclusively, to settle the issues that Polk had left in his wake. This incongruous series of measures, collectively labeled the "Compromise of 1850," offered a new orthodoxy of sorts, a premise for regime maintenance and continuity in public policy. Some hoped that it would isolate both free soil and southern rights elements and lead to the formation of a new Union party. But those seeking to keep the Democratic standard alive preempted that dream and turned the Compromise into a contract for holding the fractured parts of their old party alliance together. Free soil and southern rights extremists were asked to acquiesce in the new terms of sectional accord in return for the enhanced prospects of retaking control of the federal government and participating in the distribution of its benefits.[1]

With the Democratic organization revitalized at the ideological extremes of national opinion, Jacksonian nationalism was effectively gutted as a substantive foundation for presidential action. The nominal leader of such a reassembly would begin pretty much where Polk had left off, sitting atop a boiling caldron of self-interest and mutual suspicion. In this circumstance, it came as no surprise that the Democratic convention of 1852 failed to muster a decisive rally behind anyone with influence enough to really take charge in a new incarnation of majority party government. This time, the leading lights of the party kept the nomination proceedings locked in a stalemate through forty-eight ballots. The break for Pierce on the forty-ninth saved the convention from dissolution, but no one, not even the Democrats themselves, knew Pierce very well.[2]

A New Hampshire attorney who had been refusing political offices for a decade, Pierce had not even been placed before the convention until the thirty-fifth ballot, when Buchanan supporters from Virginia became desperate for anyone who might prevent the renomination of their rival, Lewis Cass. But the "new man" from the granite hills proved to be a rare find indeed. He had entered the House of Representatives under Jackson and retired from the Senate in 1842 to cultivate his law practice. His most notable national service had been as a brigadier in the Mexican War, after which he once again retired from public service to a lucrative private life as a New Hampshire notable. The unofficial leader of the Democratic party in a state with a marginal claim to national significance, his reputation rested on two recent feats: holding New Hampshire for Cass in the face of the Free Soil threat in 1848 and then holding his state party to the terms of the Compromise of 1850 against challenges to the provision for the return of fugitive slaves.[3]

The appeal of this record was symptomatic of the tenuous state of the Democratic alliance. Here was a stalwart Democrat who was far removed from the political intrigues that had gripped the Democratic regime over the past eight years and unidentified with any personal program or higher purpose. Here was also a New Englander, one who had recently demonstrated respect for the South and yet one who might ease the return of the Free Soil Democrats by symbolizing the party's respect for the region of their greatest strength. Here, in fact, was the perfect representative of the new party consensus, one who could tap the broad electoral appeal of the "finality" of the Compromise of 1850 on the question of slavery and suffer its shallowness as a foundation for further action without much affect on anyone else. The critical letter Pierce wrote for his friends to use in pressing his name at the Baltimore convention highlighted his uniquely inoffensive availability. It contained only one pledge: to uphold the terms of the Compromise against "any time-serving policy."[4]

By 1852, then, expedience had eclipsed enthusiasm on all fronts. The bond between the regime and nation hinged on a suspect compromise. The bond between the majority party and its candidate hinged on the prospects of a benign intercession from one of its most marginal figures. The bond between the candidate and the nation rested on a solitary pledge that nothing would be done that might disturb the delicate political handiwork of the recent past. Success in reassembling the Democratic coalition on these terms left Pierce the steward of an enervated regime. Tenuously positioned in a governmental establishment that had just welcomed back its most myopic sectarians, he would find it extraordinarily difficult to justify acting on his own behalf. Somehow he needed to reconcile his own awkward position within the old order with the awkward position of the old order in the nation at large.

The Reification of Technique

On the surface, the Democrats' electoral strategy in 1852 was a stunning success. Pierce carried 27 of the 31 states, for a hefty 250 out of 296 electoral votes. In the process the Democratic party claimed huge majorities in both houses of Congress. But as with many other electoral college landslides, support for Pierce was more apparent than real, and his victory anything but a mandate for action. Once he had endorsed the Compromise of 1850 and pledged resistance to all further agitation on the slavery issue, the candidate simply let the party regulars mobilize their voters as best they could. Meanwhile, the Whig coalition crumbled. Its southern wing, disaffected from antislavery agitators in the North and not yet ready to join the southern Democrats, "sullenly stayed home."[5] The Democratic landslide was a triumph of mere survival.

As Pierce had done little more than ratify the work of those moderates in the Senate who had divined the terms of the sectional accord two years before, it is possible that he might have enhanced his postelection prospects best by immediately taking a second bow to the center and placing the full largesse of his office at their disposal.[6] Senator Stephen Douglas, a rising star of the Democratic party from the West and one of the chief architects of the Compromise, would have been an obvious target for such an overture. But Pierce had more in mind for himself than a clerkship to Douglas; and, once elected, he set out in Polk-like fashion to demonstrate that he *himself* could be president of the United States. It must be said that certain aspects of the election of 1852 argued against a deferential bow to the center. Pierce had actually received less than 51 percent of the popular vote. He had not won the presidency because moderate national opinion had rallied to his standard but because the Democratic managers had delivered on their promise and brought the party's most extreme elements back into the fold. To these elements, the Compromise of 1850 remained a source of apprehension rather than inspiration; the payoff for their reluctant acquiescence was yet to be determined.

Sensitive to his precarious position, Pierce was moved by the election's display of renewed faith in the party that had elected Van Buren and Polk. However shallow that faith might be, he was not about to dismiss it in the vague hope that centrists of all different stripes might unite in a national coalition government. To stand with the moderates now and just abandon the extremes was to reject the proven wisdom of the regulars in reassembling the old electoral coalition. The victory of 1852, viewed in the harsh light of the defeat of 1848, seemed to render the President's initial task transparent. Pierce decided to reach out to those who had swallowed their fears and their pride to acquiesce in the new orthodoxy of the Compromise. His first job would be to complete the party restoration that the election campaign had set in motion. He would perfect the old political machinery, heal the wounds of 1848 once and for all, and demonstrate thereby the enduring vitality of the Jacksonian regime.[7]

In this bold bid for leadership, Pierce held himself aloof from the moderate Senate Democrats and set out to secure the political apparatus of Jacksonian governance under his own auspices. Success in this endeavor would have made short work of the credibility problem. It would have allowed a still obscure figure from a minor state to meet the new Congress as the truly indispensable man—the real genius behind the party's revival—and to assume control of national affairs as a political leader in his own right. If all went according to plan, Pierce would establish his claim to wield the powers of the Jacksonian presidency on his own terms and, in 1856, carry the Democratic party forward on the basis of his own accomplishments. The question was: did any interest of significance care enough about Pierce's success to make this scheme work? Had not the new President tapped the limits of his coalition's national strength and coherence by simply letting the party leaders elect him? As it turned out, the prospect that these leaders might withhold their mutual suspicions in order to enhance Pierce's personal authority was pure delusion. They had no intention of following their own creation. Pierce quickly found that he had no independent claim to the office of Andrew Jackson, and that by asserting his independence at the outset he had robbed the alternative tack—a humble bow to senatorial power—of any possible advantage.

Given Pierce's obscurity in the annals of presidential history, it is worth emphasizing that it was his insistence on leadership—not his abdication—that drove the systemic political disjunction of his tenure. And in considering his initial approach to leadership, two comparisons are especially helpful. Pierce's standard for breathing life into the old Democratic machine was, of course, the party standard plain and simple. He set out to provide equal and exact justice to every Democratic faction. But that had proven difficult enough back in 1845 when Polk had clear and potent programmatic inducements arrayed behind that standard to keep the various factions working together. Now with the old program implemented, with sectarian divisions festering, and with the facade of party consensus masking a struggle over first principles, the appeal to the party standard rang hollow. In these circumstances, restoration of the old coalition became a purely mechanical exercise, one that could work only if all talk of national issues was excluded. Infusing the old operational standard with programmatic content drawn from the vital political questions of the 1850s was a sure way to cut short any repair of the party apparatus and scuttle in an instant the revival of the old regime. This left Pierce to replay the consequences of Polk's patronage distribution as farce. His only hope was that everyone would just forget the most pressing issues of the day and support his presidency.

But Pierce's quest to perfect the political machinery of Jacksonian democracy cannot be dismissed out of hand as hopelessly misguided. There are strong parallels between his invocation of the theme of "equal and exact justice" to reconstitute party government and John Quincy Adams's invocation of "talent and virtue alone" to reconstitute patrician government. Both these presidents compromised their control over the really explosive issues of their presidencies by raising a standard for action that those issues had already rendered politically vacuous. To be sure, these were very different, even antithetical, standards; the similarity is that they were the incontestable operational standards of government in their day and that by taking hold of them, both of these late-regime affiliates elevated technique over substance. Adams's insistence on purest patrician standards in government saddled him with officials in powerful positions who were actively working for his opponents. Now Pierce would impale himself on a standard of pure party service that was completely divorced from the central issues that gripped his party's ranks. Why?

The answer is that, in the absence of any programmatic consensus, the only readily apparent warrant for affiliated leadership is managerial propriety. The reification of technique vents the exercise of presidential power in an enervated regime; it is the last remaining premise for action, the final refuge for leadership ambitions when all substantive action threatens to indict the old formulas and derail the entire polity in sectarian warfare. The reification of technique may cripple the president by encompassing under its umbrella interests bent on contradictory courses of action, but more important for the president's precarious hold on authority, it repudiates nothing.

In Pierce's case, this initial bid for credibility collapsed on the notorious problems of harmonizing the Democratic factions in New York. Pierce knew that if healing the wounds of 1848 meant anything, it meant forgiving those Free Soil heretics who had abandoned their insurgency, returned to the party fold, and supported the Democratic ticket in the election of 1852. Thus, the President offered all party factions in New York an equal measure of presidential favor. Much to his dismay, however, many of the state's Democrats who had remained loyal in 1848 refused to forgive the bolters and share the booty. For these "hardshells," there was no justice at all in equal treatment. The Democratic party in the state disintegrated at a touch, and the Whigs swept the state's elections in 1853.

The New York hardshells gained confidence in their defiance of the President's patronage policy from their keen understanding of southern sensitivity to any implication of special favor for the Free Soil elements. Southerners' suspicions of unequal treatment were already running high. They perceived lax enforcement in the North of the fugitive slave laws they had extracted from the Compromise of 1850, and they had turned to Pierce in 1852 to redress this "injustice."[8] The New Yorkers could short-circuit the President's efforts to submerge the substantive political conflicts of the day under orthodox procedures by appealing their local grievances to radical southern rights advocates in the Senate.[9] If Pierce chose to move against the hardshells in defense of returning Free Soilers, he would place the Senate's judgment of his leadership in jeopardy when it came time to confirm his New York appointments.

Hardly insensitive to this dilemma, Pierce clung to the hope that the crisis might be weathered through sheer perseverance. But when the hardshell collector of the Port of New York persisted in open rebellion against direct orders to share the offices at his disposal equally with the other New York factions, the President demonstrated his resolve and made a whole new round of appointments. The new selections would still stand the formal test of equal and exact justice if anyone still cared to check. The problem was that the hollowness of that standard was now exposed for all to see. An electoral debacle in a pivotal state and the hardshell agitation of their grievances with southern radicals in Washington mocked Pierce's determination to prove himself through independent action. If, after reviewing the whole dismal affair, the Senate did in fact withhold support for the President's second-round choices, the rebuke to his leadership pretensions would be fatal.

Pierce's initial assertion of leadership had worked like a stick in a snake pit. In his efforts to clear some ground from which he might address the Senate on his own terms, he had, in effect, placed himself at the mercy of the Senate; more portentous still, he had placed the Senate at the mercy of the most dangerous vipers of all, the southern radicals. Claiming that they had been short-changed by the distribution of patronage in their own region, this small but potent band of senators took up the hardshells' charges of special favor to the Free Soil element. They plotted their revenge by characterizing the distribution of patronage in the North as a heightened level of commitment to the faction they dreaded most, and they challenged their more moderate southern cohorts to extract a new level of commitment to their region's interests as well. When the President met the Senate for the first time in December 1853, the Democratic party was already a shambles, and Pierce's bid to present himself as his party's leader already a manifest failure.[10] He had no more control over the meaning of justice in the 1850s than Adams had over the meaning of virtue in the 1820s.

Divining an Appropriate Course

The Democratic party had been forged by Jackson in pitched battle against the National Bank. It had accepted Van Buren's independent treasury plan as the orthodox alternative to a national banking system, and it had implemented that alternative during the Polk administration. Now, during the booming prosperity of the 1850s, the party appeared to have solved conclusively the central problem which had brought it to life. As Pierce surveyed the scene looking for something else to do, two prospects, each far removed from the central issue contested at his party's founding, vied for his attention.

One was railroad development. An explosion of interest in rail linkage between the Mississippi River and the Pacific coast followed directly upon Polk's conquests. So too did an explosion of competition for federal favor in support of one route or another. Pierce was hardly indifferent to this new enthusiasm, but for an administration eager to establish its bearings on orthodox ground, the most daunting challenge appeared to be that of holding the contending interests to some standard of propriety. The President made clear his view that the federal power to construct (or aid in the construction) of a road in the territories, "though not embarrassed by that question of jurisdiction which would arise within the limits of a State," was still of "doubtful propriety." Then he asked Congress to review the whole issue of the federal government's role in internal improvements. Without consensus on the proper course of action there could be no escape from the "constant strife, the suspension of the powers of local enterprise, the exciting of vain hopes, the disappointment of cherished expectations." The implications of an unbridled competition of interests on this issue, and perhaps worse, the prospect of forcing an executive choice among those interests, prompted the President to counsel patience and caution. "It is, I trust, not necessary to say that no grandeur of enterprise and no urgent inducement promising special favor will lead me to disregard those lights or depart from that path which experience has proved to be safe, and which is now radiant with the glow of prosperity and legitimate constitutional progress. We can afford to wait, but we cannot afford to overlook the ark of our security."[11]

The other great prospect was further territorial acquisition; and, by comparison at least, it seemed to place the President on far more solid ground. While some of the original issues of Jacksonian politics (finance) had been settled, and others (internal improvements) remained intractable, the call of Manifest Destiny suggested near-endless possibilities for bold executive action. As the Democratic platform of 1852 had been loud and clear in its defense of the Mexican War and its territorial gains, any offer to continue along the path that Polk had blazed for the party had at least a prima facie claim to orthodoxy. Pierce trumpeted this cause in no uncertain terms: "The policy of my administration," he told his inaugural audience, "will not be controlled by any timid forebodings of evil from expansion."[12] The contrast to his caution on railroad development could not have been more striking.

Now expansion may well have been the one course consistent and true to the path already traced, but it was Polk's course, and it had already proven a controversial extension of the main road blazed by Jackson in banking and finance. Getting the reassembled party of Jackson back on Polk's track was not nearly as straightforward a task as the President's bold declaration suggested. Indeed, Pierce hit on the difficulty himself. When his inaugural message turned from the glories of expansion to a review of the nation's narrow escape from calamity, it seemed as if he was crediting the "evil forebodings" he had just been at pains to dismiss.

> We have been carried in safety through a perilous crisis. Wise counsels, like those that gave us the Constitution, prevailed to uphold it. Let the period be remembered as an admonition, and not as an encouragement, in any section of the Union, to make experiments where experiments are fraught with such fearful hazard. Let it be impressed upon all hearts that, beautiful as our fabric is, no earthly power or wisdom could ever reunite its broken fragments.[13]

Pierce's determination to negotiate a course true to both the Compromise of 1850 and to a revival of Polk's expansionist agenda suggests once again his audacity in the face of the most rarefied of warrants for political action. He could rightly claim that no faction of the party had opposed expansion per se, that the "perilous crisis" with which Polk had saddled the nation was due to the absence of a consensus on how the new territories were to be governed. As the Compromise of 1850 had settled that question by endorsing popular sovereignty in the Mexican cession, he could claim further that all objections to continuing along the course Polk had blazed had been removed. But for all that might be said on behalf of this position, it was, at best, a rather precious one for supporting bold new actions at the national level. Everything hinged on bolstering the integrity of a compromise that many of the President's nominal supporters eyed apprehensively; and, as we have seen, bolstering the integrity of the Compromise had come to hinge on the success of a patronage policy that was itself aimed at gaining support from the polar extremes of national opinion. If the idea of simply forgetting the factional discord exacerbated by Polk's expansionist policy was a weak premise for restoring the old party machinery, so much more so was the idea that a party restored on that basis might revive the expansionist fever of the Polk administration and continue innocently along the course that had fractured it in the first place.

During the early months of the administration, while Pierce was trying to secure the coalition that had elected him, he was also trying to secure a purchase of Cuba from Spain and an extension of the southwest boundary further into Mexican territory. Far from working in tandem to bolster his pretensions, these domestic and foreign initiatives immediately began to work at cross purposes, unraveling the whole fabric of national politics into a string of sectarian convulsions. As conservative New Yorkers alerted the South to the President's indulgence of free soil elements in the distribution of patronage, Stephen Douglas—the moderate whose power and prominence had been conspicuously ignored in Pierce's bid for independence in party leadership—eyed with alarm Pierce's appointment of James Gadsden as minister to Mexico. Gadsden, a South Carolinian active in the promotion of a southern rail route to the Pacific, had been given instructions to purchase a vast extension of the southwestern border, including, though not limited to, lands deemed critical for his rail corridor. To Illinois's champion of a northern rail route from Chicago to San Francisco, Gadsden's appointment was an ominous portent indeed. Congress had recently frustrated Douglas's efforts to clear a corridor for the railroad he wanted by refusing to organize a territorial government in the remaining portion of the old Louisiana Purchase through which it would have to pass. As this Nebraska territory was still formally subject to the Missouri Compromise of 1820, it appeared to be closed to slavery, and the prospect of organizing free territory for the sake of the northern rail route was not the stuff to engage southern interests. In this circumstance, Pierce's Mexican initiative left Douglas more anxious than ever to secure southern support for his Nebraska bill, and the heightened sensitivity to antislavery sentiments in the North made southerners more insistent that there could be no organization of the Nebraska territory without an explicit repeal of the Missouri Compromise.[14]

The Congress which Pierce had hoped to meet with proof positive of his political credibility gathered in December 1853 to a host of horrors. Gadsden had gotten bogged down in negotiations and was slowly realizing that the most he would receive would be a paltry strip of land on the southwest border—his southern rail corridor plain and simple. Douglas was desperately searching for a way to organize the Nebraska territory to keep his northern route alive and slowly realizing that there was no alternative to repeal of the Missouri Compromise. Pierce was anxiously awaiting the Senate's verdict on his appointments, anxiously watching the leader of the Senate from the West negotiate a dreadful experiment with the leaders of the Senate from the South, and anxiously hoping that he might yet have a vast new empire in the Southwest to place at the feet of the powerful upper house. For a time, Douglas himself resisted the reopening of the issue he had so brilliantly settled a few years before. He clung to the interpretation that the two great sectional compromises were different solutions to different problems— that of 1820 binding on the Louisiana Purchase, and that of 1850 binding on the Mexican cession. Even so, he had a powerful incentive to let himself be persuaded gradually by the southern view—that the Missouri Compromise of 1820 had been superseded by the Compromise of 1850, that popular sovereignty in the territories was the new rule everywhere, and that, therefore, the older restriction no longer applied anywhere. Early in January 1854 Douglas proposed that the Nebraska territory be organized without reference to slavery at all. This solution was technically in accord with the Compromise of 1850 but not a definitive repudiation of the 1820 restriction. While the southerners had implicitly accepted this solution by electing Pierce in 1852, they had been offended by the President's northern political strategy in 1853, and they were now in a position to hold out for something more. The repeal of the insulting doctrine would have to be transparent, indicating in no uncertain terms that slavery could become established in the lands from which it had hitherto been explicitly excluded.[15]

As Douglas was convincing himself that this final step would be nothing more than a symbolic change in the position outlined in the bill he just proposed, Pierce tried to head off the dread choice between supporting the demands of the party leaders and upholding his national pledge not to reopen the slavery issue. Had he not just informed Congress that he would not be moved from the safe course, no matter how grand the enterprise or how compelling the special inducement? For a moment, in mid-January 1854, he and his cabinet stood firm against endorsement of the Missouri repeal, suggesting instead a judicial determination of its constitutionality.[16] Then Douglas with his cohort of southern collaborators went to the White House to clarify the situation for their leader.

When this powerful group of senators came to secure Pierce's support for a Nebraska bill with an explicit repeal provision, they were, in effect, offering him a chance to save his administration. The President's effort to secure his leadership on his own terms had crumbled with the New York debacle, and there was little reason to doubt that the men who visited him had it in their power to complete his ruin. The new Senate had already proven itself keenly sensitive to hardshell attacks on the administration's patronage policies. It had rejected the chief spokesman for that policy, Robert Armstrong, for the position of public printer. This initial test of administration strength did not bode well for the pending consideration of the second-round appointees at the New York customs house, and a call for papers concerning the fiasco of the first round had already become the subject of heated congressional debate.[17] Adding to the prospects for disgrace, Gadsden's disappointing treaty for the purchase of territory on the southwest border was about to be forwarded to the Senate for review. Could Pierce afford the implication of opposing a northern rail route while sponsoring what was, in effect, the southern route? If he rejected the senators' overture, he would stand alone against simultaneous charges of free soil sympathies and southern sympathies. His policies would be repudiated in both sections, and he would lose all remaining credibility in the party. If, on the other hand, he signed onto the Missouri repeal, he might still prove himself a leader, albeit now on the Senate's terms. He might start afresh as a full partner in a new governing coalition.

What, then, of the President's credibility in the nation at large? What of his multiple pledges to resist the "time-serving policy," to uphold the established terms of sectional accord against all special inducements, to keep the issue of slavery closed? The twists and turns of the consistent course kept running back to this ominous portent of an outright betrayal of the President's sole commitment to the country as a whole. At best, the senators offered corollaries to the President's pledge, corollaries that heaped new layers of subtlety on the already highly refined foundations of his leadership. And yet, for one looking out from the center of this knot of contending interests, these subtleties promised to work wonders. If the Compromise of 1850 had in fact been meant to supersede the Missouri Compromise as a solution to the territorial question everywhere and if the restriction of 1820 had for all intents and purposes already been lifted, then Pierce's promise to uphold the finality of the later settlement would not be at issue if he chose to sign the Nebraska bill. Rationalized in this way, the repeal was not at all what it seemed at first thought to be—a new and startling departure; it was a mere formality, a matter of cleaning up old business; technically, there was no "reopening" of the old controversy. Through these arguments the real repudiative thrust of the Missouri Compromise repeal seemed to dissipate. The old formula could be discarded with impunity after all. The Nebraska bill could be transformed into the only appropriate and consistent path, the one that vindicated the work of the immediate past and affirmed the promise of presidential support to each and every faction.

The arguments may have been subtle and the rules of appropriate action obscure, but the choice was clear. Pierce decided to stand with the party leaders and repudiate the Missouri Compromise rather than appeal to his national pledge and repudiate his party's leadership. It was one of the most momentous presidential choices in American political history. In part, it reflects the palpable force of party ties in the organization of American politics at midcentury. In part, it reflects Douglas's standing as an architect of the Compromise of 1850 and the harsh realities of Pierce's political situation early in 1854. In part, it reflects Pierce's faith in the potential of the office of Andrew Jackson to carry the hard choice, and his dream of rebuilding the great party Jackson had fashioned on new ground. In all these particulars, it appears a Hobson's choice. The New York appointments were confirmed, and the President, suddenly reborn as a full partner in this myopic community of sectarian interests, got a second chance to make his mark.[18]

Toward New Political Formations

Both in its bearing on the legitimation problem and its impact on national politics, Pierce's bargain with Douglas bears a striking resemblance to John Quincy Adams's bargain with Henry Clay. In each case, profound inconsistencies in the twin imperatives of presidential leadership—exercising power and maintaining legitimacy—drove a nationally wrenching political disjunction. In each case, the entire Washington establishment became vulnerable in an instant to broadside charges of systemic corruption and moral bankruptcy.

The Jacksonian difference, however, is not to be missed. Unlike the Adams-Clay alliance, Pierce and Douglas were not paralyzed by the political implications of their pact. Marshaling all the resources of the presidency in the party state, they muscled their program through.

The four-month battle to pass the Kansas-Nebraska bill ranks high on the list of the Congress's most bitter contests. Salmon Chase, a free soil Democrat from Ohio, inaugurated the Senate debate with a stunning indictment of the administration's claim to national authority. Issuing the "Appeal of the Independent Democrats in Congress to the People of the United States," he arraigned the Nebraska bill as "a gross violation of a sacred pledge," and an "atrocious plot" by the slave power to exclude free laborers from the national domain. He castigated Douglas for relinquishing all principle to his interest in a railroad and Pierce for discarding at first opportunity his promise that he would suffer no shock to sectional comity during his term as chief magistrate. He warned of "imminent peril" to the Union, and called upon the nation to resist this "enormous crime" "in whatever mode may seem expedient." In an instant, the idea that a slave power conspiracy had taken hold of the federal government became an ideological force of national rather than merely factional significance.[19] Instead of perfecting the old political machine, Pierce had, with his first legislative commitment, sparked a political revolution.

The President was quick to make it clear that the Kansas-Nebraska bill was "the policy of the administration," that dissent would not be tolerated, and that patronage recognition now hinged on support for it. The Senate debate raged for weeks, ending on March 3 with a sweeping 37–14 victory for the Douglas-Pierce alliance.[20] The free soil Democrats in the House, however, were not impressed. In fact, the Democrats' overwhelming House majority (159 to 76) virtually collapsed upon consideration of the measure. A vote to kill the bill by transferring it to the Committee of the Whole rather than the Committee on Territories passed on March 21, 110 to 95.

Presidential power moved into the breach, and throughout March and April Pierce and Douglas worked tirelessly to save the measure. It would take nineteen roll calls just to bring the Nebraska bill to consideration, one to open the Committee of the Whole and eighteen to postpone consideration of all the bills in front of it on the committee's calendar. Gradually, the resources of the Jacksonian presidency— patronage pressure, newspaper propaganda, floor management—made themselves felt. Initially, 66 of the 90 northern Democrats stood against this northern Democratic president. But by May 8, the lines of support had been bolstered sufficiently to permit the roll calls to proceed. Passage was secured late that month, 113 to 100. About twenty strays had been coaxed back to the fold; forty-four northern Democrats voted in the affirmative. With nearly solid southern support, that was enough. Forty-two northern Democrats remained openly defiant.[21]

This triumph for the powers of the Jacksonian presidency shattered the Jacksonian political system beyond repair. Far from proving his credibility, Pierce's success in the exercise of power made his leadership the focal point of a nationwide crisis of legitimacy. To northern disgust with "the slave power," it added a national disgust with patronage-wielding politicians.[22] More immediately, the Nebraska controversy infected the administration's stalwart appeal to Manifest Destiny. The Gadsden treaty was mutilated by an outlandish combination of forces: free soilers outraged by power-thirsty southerners, southerners disappointed by the meager size of the deal, and a scattering of other interests aggrieved by the specific terms of the land grants. After outright defeat of the original measure, 9,000 square miles of the small amount of land that Mexico had agreed to cede was actually abandoned by the Senate in a compromise move to salvage the rest.[23]

Bold action on the Cuban front also fizzled under the pressure of the renewed sectional agitation. In late February, Spain had seized an American cargo ship, the *Black Warrior*, and Pierce had grasped the chance to channel the nation's rage along the tried and true path of defending national honor. In a short but firm message to Congress, he demanded that this stain be removed. He requested that provisional war measures be taken, and punctuated American impatience with a direct warning about the significance of Cuba to U.S. commercial interests.[24] Then, in a stunning display of the impact of the Nebraska debates, the President abruptly pulled back. With northern Democrats tying the Cuban initiative to the southern interest, Manifest Destiny was forced to take a back seat to the central task of defending the new Nebraska orthodoxy. Pierce abandoned the southern hotheads rallying in Congress to meet the Spanish threat and in effect pulled the teeth out of his own proposal. And, on the day he signed the Kansas-Nebraska Act, he issued a stern warning, later followed up in a presidential proclamation, against the private filibusters being organized in Louisiana for the purposes of "freeing Cuba."[25]

Pierce's shift back to the negotiating table in search of an amicable purchase of Cuba and his August proclamation against filibustering signaled his concern about the impending national referendum on the Nebraska bill. Between January and May the President had put his credibility in the nation on the line. In the fall of 1854, the nation rendered its verdict. Revenge for the broken pledge of 1852 brought defeat to the Democratic party in every northern state except New Hampshire and California. The party's huge majority in the House was wiped out. And this time, it was not the old Whigs who were to take over but a strange assortment of new elements with no apparent stake in the old alignment of political forces. The President's second bid for leadership credibility ended in unmitigated disaster. He had failed to prove himself to the Senate on his own terms, and failed to prove himself to the nation on the Senate's terms.

As the whole intricate argument for consistency in action collapsed, it took everything the administration proposed to represent down with it. Sectional comity could not survive the repeal of the Missouri Compromise, the nationalist appeal of Manifest Destiny could not survive the renewed sectional agitation, Democratic power in the North could not survive the charges of a southern conspiracy to dominate the federal government, and Pierce could not survive his complicity in this shattering of the old order. At midterm, the unraveling that he had set in motion began to take on a life of its own. While the Kansas-Nebraska Act did not, by itself, guarantee that the Republican party would ascend to dominance out of destruction of the old alliances, the new Republican leadership secured their claims on the future by exploiting the consequent vulnerability of Pierce administration commitments.[26]

Just as the midterm election returns were coming in, word leaked to the press that a new policy statement on Cuba had been issued by Pierce's ministers in Europe. As if to counter the President's recent retreat from belligerence, Pierce's ministers played to the fear of the southern hotheads that the slaves in Cuba might peremptorily be freed, and on the basis of that impending threat to American security, they bluntly called upon Spain to sell Cuba or have the island seized. Though unauthorized and quickly disavowed by the administration, the ministers' proclamation, the Ostend Manifesto, exposed the soft underbelly of the administration's expansionist commitments. Pierce's overzealous ministers had turned the nationalist appeal of Manifest Destiny on its head and saddled his administration with a degenerate doctrine of naked aggression employed at the service of the slave interests. The new Republican movement rallied to its censure.[27]

More dramatic still was the prima facie indictment of the alleged orthodoxy of the Kansas-Nebraska Act. Pierce's legislative triumph on behalf of the principle of popular sovereignty in the territories had mobilized rival bands of land speculators nominally boasting slave and free soil interests into a confrontation on the fields of Kansas. Missourians on the Kansas border invaded the territory to force a radically proslave constitution on Pierce's governor. The free state element refused to recognize this government and moved to set up one of their own. As the Missourians prepared for a second invasion to protect their handiwork, it became apparent that popular sovereignty was fueling anarchy. By Pierce's own standard, none of the contending factions could claim legitimacy. The Republican movement surged into the void left by the manifest bankruptcy of the administration's new formula for territorial governance.[28]

The distillation of the Republican movement as the national political alternative was the dominant aspect of the final years of Pierce's presidency. Defined against the outrage of the Ostend Manifesto and the anarchy of "Bleeding Kansas," free soil became something more than another interest; it became a first principle upon which the redemption of the nation's honor and the integrity of its institutions might be pegged. Pierce's new formula, like John Quincy Adams's before him, appeared to magnify the problem. Unable to control the changes they had instigated, these presidents became their chief victims.

But unlike Adams, Pierce continued to fight back. His spirited refusal to credit the virtual collapse of his leadership at midterm stands as a final tribute to his unflagging determination to claim the office of Andrew Jackson. Now taking aim at the "prevalence of heresies in direct antagonism . . . to the authority of law," Pierce threw his hat into the ring for a second presidential nomination.[29] In this third and last bid for support, he would actively counter the spectre of his party's bankruptcy, boldly defend established power against those who would destroy it, and desperately try to erase the stigma of his own disgrace.

In 1855, for the first time, Pierce's sense of purpose stood out clearly from the twists and turns of other politicians' handiwork. He called attention to the momentous stakes at issue for the nation in upholding his chosen course, and defined the mission of what was emerging de facto as a new Democratic party. The Missouri Compromise, he explained, had been "stripped of all moral authority" in the debates of 1850. The Kansas-Nebraska Act, he declared, upheld a principle fundamental to the constitutional compact: "No portion of the United States shall undertake through assumption of the powers of the General Government to dictate the social institutions of any other portion." The government that had opened Kansas according to this principle would bring the power of the federal government to bear there on the side of law and order. It would resist the Missouri invaders as well as the treasonous pretensions of the free soilers. In all, Pierce wrapped his administration in the rule of law and defined the party of the Kansas-Nebraska Act as the home of all true "friends of the Constitution." He branded its new enemies uncompromising disunionists bent on civil war.[30]

The Democratic party would write these sentiments into a winning platform for 1856, and it would invoke them in one form or another for the next seventy-five years. But in considering this, Pierce's most constructive achievement, it is important to remember who these "friends of the Constitution" were. First, they were decidedly different from the friends of Andrew Jackson. Holding onto a mere remnant of Old Hickory's northern base, this new Democratic party was fully hostaged to southern power and shorn of majority status in the nation at large. Second, these "friends of the Constitution" were not friends of Franklin Pierce. Once the North had rejected him, the South found it had little further use for him, and the party that Pierce had so desperately sought to lead became increasingly anxious to get rid of him. His four-year campaign to demonstrate political credibility ended with a concerted drive by those who had called him to power to bury all memory of his tenure. The Democratic convention of 1856 was an anybody-but-Pierce affair.[31]

Republican Leadership: Stiffening Crosscurrents

THIS THIRD look at the politics presidents make is marked by stiffening crosscurrents along our secular and political time lines of change. The long Republican era straddles the heyday of party politics and the emergence of the more pluralistic politics of the industrial era. Each of the leadership postures we have been tracing now appears more complicated and internally conflicted, with new conditions for the exercise of power reshaping its range. Lincoln's reconstruction was the most disruptive and penetrating to date, but in recasting basic commitments of ideology and interest he had to grapple with the stubborn persistence of the organizational forms and institutional operations of nineteenth-century party governance, and this delimited his control over the process. Theodore Roosevelt set out to affirm received commitments of ideology and interest and to demonstrate their vigor in the face of the vast economic and international changes of the industrial era, but rearticulating the Republican regime for a new round of achievement entailed recasting the underlying mode of governmental operations. As Roosevelt began to displace the old party politics with a bureaucratic politics better suited to the management of Republican interests in an industrial society, he became embroiled in an explosive confrontation with the coalition whose capacities for governance he was seeking to demonstrate. The chapter ends with an examination of Herbert Hoover, a president caught in an economic calamity that indicted the Republican regime's most basic commitments of ideology and interest. Hoover, however, was fully attuned to the presidency's new role as the font of policy leadership in a pluralist polity. His ability to set a new course in public policy vastly outstripped the best case he could make for doing so.

Part One:
Abraham Lincoln's Reconstruction

> As our case is new, so we must think anew and
> act anew. We must disenthrall ourselves,
> and then we shall save our country.

THE POLITICS of leadership under Lincoln presents a curious juxtaposition of the monumental and the mundane. At one angle we glimpse the awesome figure of a statesman who would secure a break with the past more fundamental than any since the American Revolution itself; at another, we see a mid-nineteenth-century party professional with a talent for distributing patronage. Fixing a subject who can slip in the blink of an eye from hopelessly romantic to ruthlessly realistic is no small challenge, and Lincoln scholars have responded with densely shaded portraits of the man and his times. Our object, however, is somewhat different. To see how Lincoln recast the politics of leadership, we need to sort out the elements that the biographers have so subtly blended. When the emergent and recurrent patterns are plotted and the implications of this conjunction drawn, Lincoln's leadership stands as a reliable signpost of the changing shape of political possibilities.

The emergent pattern. The realist's rendering of Lincoln in his mid-nineteenth-century context shows us a man who bears virtually no resemblance to prior reconstructive leaders. He comes into focus as the archetypical politician of the party period—a self-made man-on-the-make working his way through established channels. The radically different institutional universe through which Lincoln rose to prominence marks the historical distance separating him from the political masters of the early part of the nineteenth century, and it is here that an emergent pattern in the politics of reconstruction begins to come clear.

A prairie lawyer of humble origins, Lincoln most impressed his friends with his consuming ambition.[1] He turned to the Whig organization in Illinois to vent this ambition, and by setting his sights on winning elections and controlling offices, he established himself as one of the leading party managers in that state. In a revealing speech delivered early in his career, Lincoln explicitly warned his generation against following the example that their fathers had set in politics. He urged them to disavow the path of revolution and institutional reconstruction, and called instead for "cold, calculating, unimpassioned reason" in dealing with the political questions of the postrevolutionary era. The mission of the emergent political class, he argued, was to preserve, indeed to revere, the institutional framework their fathers had put in place. The current generation had no higher duty, he believed, than to frustrate the "towering genius" of the future who would disdain the "beaten path" and set himself "boldly to the task of pulling [the old institutions] down."[2]

True to this understanding of his calling, Lincoln stood as a Whig candidate for the legislature in 1832, 1834, 1836, 1838, and 1840. He was a Whig presidential elector in 1840 and 1844, a Whig nominee for Congress in 1846, and as late as 1855, a Whig contender for the Senate. He kept his distance from the Liberty party in 1844 and the Free Soil party in 1848, and he moved only belatedly into the Republican ranks, one of the last holdouts in an already moribund Whig machine.[3] He first gained national attention in high Republican circles in the course of losing his second bid for a Senate seat in 1858. Pressing himself forward as a compromise choice for the Republican presidential nomination in 1860, he was nominated on the third ballot and elected with a minority of the popular vote.

In this context, Lincoln appears as a Whig-Republican counterpart to Polk and Pierce. He was a party professional in a polity run by party professionals. These men managed organizations designed for constituent service. The organizations themselves were rife with checks on independent action and resistant to claims of personal authority. It is true that Lincoln, unlike Polk or Pierce, ultimately brought a new party to the presidency, but he had none of the heroic posture of Jefferson or Jackson (or, for that matter, of Washington or William Henry Harrison). Jefferson and Jackson each carried into the executive office a history of national service that personalized their party's cause and instantly identified it with the cause of freedom. In contrast, Lincoln's prior national service pales even in the face of more comfortable midcentury comparisons; he could match neither the legislative record of Polk nor the military record of Pierce. Like other dark-horse candidates, his identity as a presidential candidate was fully submerged in the collective identity of his party, and even after his election to the presidency, he never achieved more than a modicum of acceptability within its ranks.[4]

To pursue these comparisons a bit further, consider the fact that Jefferson and Jackson, by their very election, each dealt a death blow to the previously dominant political organization (Federalists and National Republicans respectively). The party that opposed Lincoln, in contrast, not only survived his election, it made steady and substantial progress toward recovery over the course of his administration.[5] Indeed, at the very first national referendum on Lincoln's performance, the election of 1862, the Democrats demonstrated the wherewithal to deliver a stunning blow to his administration. Castigating the President as an abolitionist dictator and war criminal, they overturned Republican congressional majorities in the five most populous states and took the governorships of New York and New Jersey outright.[6]

Even better as an indicator of the state of presidential politics in the party period is the treatment Lincoln received from his fellow Republicans. While Jefferson and Jackson each pressed showdown confrontations with rival factions in their own ranks and forged organizations in which they were virtually unassailable, Lincoln endured merciless public denunciation from those who had placed him in power. Hardly less virulent than the Democrats, Republicans dubbed their first president a dictator, a hopeless incompetent, an unmitigated failure, and, at the penultimate moment, a political liability. He was surrounded by unsolicited advice and hounded in new institutional forums. No one seemed the least intimidated by the special war-making powers granted the President under the Constitution. Republican governors asserted their own war powers, organizing in 1862 "to act in common on the means to influence the president."[7] Republican congressmen declared their branch the "arbiter and regulator of the War Powers" and organized a special committee to oversee Lincoln's conduct of the war.[8] A concerted drive to dump Lincoln from the Republican ticket mushroomed in the first half of 1864, and when that failed in its objective, a new party was formed, the Radical Democrats, sporting the Republican standard bearer of 1856, John Frémont.

As we have seen, avenues of resistance to presidential direction had been proliferating steadily over the course of the nineteenth century, as had the resources available for resistance. It had become a matter of course over the past twenty years for parties to turn on their own chief executives. The realist rendering underscores the fact that the war crisis did not break this emergent pattern. If anything, it magnified and accelerated it. With party-politics-as-usual very much alive under Lincoln, there is really no wonder at all that he was so beset by political difficulties.[9] His would be the most institution-bound reconstruction yet.

Still the question remains: how is it that a mere party regular trumped the achievements not only of Polk and Pierce but of Jefferson and Jackson as well? How do the operational continuities and organizational evolution of the presidency in the party state of nineteenth-century America illuminate what was, after all, the most extraordinary administration in American history? Before abandoning the realist frame as hopelessly misleading on the most obvious point, we should consider some crucial linkages.

The first lies in the extraordinary act of secession itself. Coming fast on the heels of Lincoln's election, the secession crisis bore ultimate testimony to the eclipse of personal authority in the party presidency and boldly displayed the growing resourcefulness of those determined to resist presidential direction. Certainly, there could be no more profound public humiliation of a man duly elected leader of the nation by constitutional procedures than that which Lincoln received at the hands of the South in the fall and winter of 1860. He was dubbed an "ass," a "chimpanzee," a "mobocrat," an "abolitionist." He was seen as an "illiterate partisan," a scourge of the "Black Republican" juggernaut, a sectional vigilante implacably hostile to the interests of the South. He was so thoroughly dehumanized as to appear a mere piece of the political machinery, a cog in an apparatus bent on destroying the region's most basic institutions.[10] Calculating their loss of influence in national affairs, the deep southern states did not even wait for Lincoln to assume office before taking decisive action on their own behalf. They peremptorily withdrew from the Union, established their own confederation, and dared the incoming President to try to mount an effective challenge to their institutions. Despite his best efforts at reassurance, Lincoln's presidency simply had no standing in half the nation.

The second connection between Lincoln's woeful lack of personal authority and the extraordinary transformation he effected mirrors the first. It is one of the singular ironies of this crisis that the withdrawal of southern representatives from Congress bolstered the relative power and position of the Republican organization, releasing it to govern exclusively in the region of its greatest strength and giving it a degree of control over the Congress denied by the election itself.[11] The Republican party was born with a full cadre of Lincoln-like managers already on hand. With their mobilizing skills fine-honed by prior years of experience in the Democratic and Whig organizations and their political machinery already in place when Lincoln took office, the national party leadership was well poised to marshall the vastly superior material resources of the North to meet the demands of a civil war. Its persistence in this task was proven in the face of incredible military bungling; in the end, it ground the South into submission on the field of battle by sheer tenacity. In December of 1864 Lincoln could boast to Congress that "the national resources . . . are unexhausted, and . . . unexhaustible." "We are *gaining* strength, and may, if need be, maintain the contest indefinitely."[12]

The North's mobilization was the collective effort of an integrated political organization. Indeed, as it deployed manpower and materiel, the Republican political machine continued to hold Lincoln "responsible" for the war, and, not unlike the South, to subsume his authority as but one part of its apparatus. As one northern party cell put it, "He has no army, he has no navy, no resources of any kind except what the people give him . . . The Republican organization, in all its principles, in all its practices, and by all its members, is committed to the preservation of the Union and the overthrow of the Rebellion. It is the power of the State and the power of the Nation."[13]

No personal authority but extraordinary systemic power—that is the portrait of Lincoln's presidency rendered exclusively within the context of mid-nineteenth-century political operations. These twin insights penetrate deep into the mysteries surrounding both the towering success and the agonizing travails of this administration, and they provide an indispensable guide to the political development of presidential leadership more generally. But as revealing as it is, realism of this sort has its limits, and to appreciate those limits we need only consider what this portrait asks of Lincoln himself.

The hallmark of realism in the assessment of Lincoln's leadership lies in its emphasis on his special talents in distributing the patronage. "The secret of Lincoln's success is simple," David Donald has written. "He was an astute and dexterous operator of the political machine."[14] In truth, relative skill at playing the game of nineteenth-century power politics is just about the only consideration that an assessment of the presidency rendered in its midcentury political context offers for distinguishing one leader from another. Because Lincoln so clearly stands out from the pack and because patronage distribution is the one organizational imperative that ties all midcentury presidents together, Lincoln's talents on this score might appear self-evident. And yet the distinction is more easily asserted than established.

How, to select just one example, should we compare Lincoln's appointment of Simon Cameron as secretary of war with Polk's appointment of William Marcy? Presumably a key appointment for both of these wartime presidents, each in its own way backfired badly. Polk manipulated his fellow partisans aggressively to get the appointment of a man he wanted, but he had to deal with a fractured party coalition as a result. Lincoln took the opposite tack. To stave off a conflict in the ranks, he accepted a man he had been at pains to avoid. Indeed, Cameron rebuffed a direct request from Lincoln to drop his claims on the cabinet, and Lincoln, in finally accepting the appointment as inevitable, saddled his administration with incompetence, insubordination, and national scandal.[15] Which leader, then, was the more masterful? Who gained the most control? The closer we get to the notion of relative skill in tackling the standard organizational challenge of midcentury leadership, the more Lincoln's distinction unravels into something less readily explicable: his relative immunity from the inevitable frustrations and inherent limitations of the patronage game.[16]

In the end, then, the realist portrait of Lincoln-in-context simply leaves intact the core insight of all the romantic myths that surround him: there is a difference in kind here that goes beyond all considerations of relative skill in manipulating party patronage and playing power politics as usual. Lincoln did not transcend the pitfalls of party leadership, nor did he escape the charges of hypocrisy and double-dealing that so routinely sapped the strength of the executives in the mid-to-late nineteenth century. Yet, he is unique among presidents of the party period in successfully orchestrating radical shifts in national policy without succumbing to the operational limitations of the office at the time. He not only sustained himself in a polity contemptuous of his leadership, he successfully transposed a northern consensus for the preservation of the Union into a revolutionary force for wholesale transformation of the nation. The romantic—sensitive to this point—

reminds us of the grandeur of Lincoln's soul, the essential purity of his message, the underlying constancy of his principles.[17] The realist—finally pushed to articulate something beyond patronage skill—falls back on the old saw of pragmatism. But when pragmatism is understood to encompass the poet's "negative capability," a capacity to accept uncertainty, mystery, and doubt "without any irritable reaching after fact and reason," the difference between realism and romanticism begins to blur.[18]

In either view, something fundamental about Lincoln's leadership remains inscrutable. We have isolated but we have not yet penetrated a form of political control less obvious than the force of personality but more potent than the power of patronage, a form of control that kept Lincoln abreast of his friends and on top of his foes as they pushed and pulled one another across uncharted ground.

The recurrent pattern. If the historical organization of political power cannot explain Lincoln's distinction as a political leader, closer attention to the political contingencies of institutional authority might. Indeed, our realist rendering—no personal authority but extraordinary systemic power—begs examination of just what kind of authority Lincoln did wield. We begin to make some headway on this score by adding the perspective of political time, in which authority structures recur, to the realist understanding of politics in secular time, where power structures evolve. At this alternative point of access, Lincoln's leadership embodies all the characteristic elements of a politics of reconstruction, and the comparisons implicit in the realist rendering are inverted. That is to say, despite the striking absence of a commanding personality in the White House and the hard-pressed reality of organized power in the party state, the basic political structure of Lincoln's leadership authority was of a piece with that of Jefferson and Jackson and different in kind from that of Polk or Pierce.

For all the political and institutional encumbrances that would come to complicate his leadership after he gained the presidency, there is a delicious irony in the clarity with which Lincoln, on his way there, expounded upon the most potent of all leadership postures. The coincidence is not accidental. Never were conditions more favorable to a candid and thorough presentation of the ground for leadership—to setting forth in words the central claims of a politics of reconstruction—than they were for an opposition leader in the late 1850s and early

1860s. Jefferson and Jackson had brought to the presidency national reputations that made any further elaboration of their political purposes superfluous. Polk and Pierce avoided the palpable risks of any elaborate explanation of their political purposes by tapping their party's historic identity. But Lincoln, a professional politician making his way in the ranks of a new organization that was itself conspicuously lacking in charismatic figures, was nothing without his talent for explicating for his party what Jefferson and Jackson personified in theirs. This Lincoln did in 175 speeches between 1854 and 1860.

The mere fact that campaign debates propelled Lincoln from relative obscurity to national prominence in Republican circles is then an important sign of the times. Arrayed against Stephen Douglas in a contest for the Illinois Senate seat in 1858, Lincoln was fortuitously positioned as an underdog challenging the "little giant" of the dominant coalition. With no comparable record of achievement to boast, he asserted himself against the leading architect of the current state of affairs by explaining the national mission of the new opposition party he proposed to represent. A forceful presentation of the standard Republican line, his message gained him national party attention as much for being unexceptionable as for being eloquent. Among all contenders for the Republican presidential nomination in 1860, Lincoln alone would go to the Chicago convention with no distinctive ideological identity among the factions contending within the ranks.[19]

The most important speech of Lincoln's 1858 senatorial campaign came with his acceptance of the nomination. Here he presented a general sketch of a place in history, describing in detail "where we are, and whither we are tending." He took his bearings from the handiwork of Pierce and Douglas in passing the Kansas-Nebraska Act, and then carried forward Salmon Chase's galvanizing charge of a slave power conspiracy to circumvent all limits on the expansion of that offensive institution. The dire implications of the repeal of the Missouri Compromise, Lincoln argued, had been compounded by Roger Taney's decision in the Dred Scott case and by President James Buchanan's support for a proslavery constitution in Kansas. All told, the Democrats had constructed an "almost complete legal combination—a piece of machinery so to speak"—aimed at breaking down all restrictions on slavery and, ultimately, at authorizing its spread throughout the Union. In this, he saw evidence of a party design, "a concert of action, among its chief bosses, from the beginning." "When we see a lot of framed timbers, different portions of which we know have been gotten out at different times and places and by different workmen—Stephen, Franklin, Roger, and James . . . and we see these timbers joined together, and see they exactly make the frame . . . in *such* a case we find it impossible to not *believe* that Stephen and Franklin and Roger and James all understood one another from the beginning, and all worked upon a common plan or *draft* drawn up before the first lick was struck."[20]

Concerned that Douglas might use his recent differences with Buchanan to deflate the Republican critique, Lincoln was at pains to portray his opponent as a captive of his past policy commitments. That Douglas had broken with the Buchanan administration on the Kansas issue hardly mattered at all, he argued. The part Douglas had played under Pierce in setting the machinery of the slave power conspiracy in motion had rendered him a "caged and toothless" opponent of its subsequent development.[21] Only a political opposition firmly committed to stopping the expansion of slavery and ensuring the ultimate triumph of free labor principles could redeem the nation from the disgrace of 1854 and set it back on the road the founders had charted. The Republican party, Lincoln observed, was composed of "strange, discordant and even hostile elements" come together with one great object in view: to reverse the policy of Douglas and his collaborators and return the nation to its proper course. The Democratic party had so perverted the nation's true purposes that nothing short of a frontal assault would suffice to reclaim original principles.[22]

Lincoln's reading of the great events of his day—his definition of the moment at hand—made repudiation of the received course of national affairs the ultimate affirmation of the nation's true principles; it rendered the order-shattering implications of leadership fully consonant with its order-affirming pretensions. This had been Lincoln's theme from the moment he learned of the repeal of the Missouri Compromise: "Our republican robe is soiled and trailed in the dust. Let us repurify it and wash it white in the spirit, if not the blood of the Revolution . . . Let us readopt the Declaration of Independence, and with it, the practices, and policy which harmonize with it . . . If we do this, we shall not only have saved the Union; but we shall have saved it, as to make and keep it, forever worthy of the saving."[23]

In taking up this task, the Republicans of the 1860s echoed the message of their namesake, the Republicans of the late 1790s: established power arrangements represented a dire perversion of original purposes; apostates of the dominant machinery (Stephen Douglas in the late 1850s, John Adams in the late 1790s) had been hopelessly compromised by their participation in it; ordinary conflicts of interest had to be suspended; first principles had to be retrieved; the present course of national affairs had to be arrested and reversed. The historical parallel was stock in trade for Lincoln.[24] In a letter declining an invitation from Boston Republicans to speak at a Jefferson Day dinner in 1859, Lincoln related the story of a fight between two drunkards which ended in each having wrestled himself out of his own coat and into that of his opponent. "If the two leading parties of this day are really identical with the two in the days of Jefferson and Adams," he observed, "they have performed about the same feat as the two drunken men." As the old seat of the Federalist empire prepared to celebrate Jefferson's vision of "free government," the region of Jefferson's greatest strength was emerging as the "vanguard of returning despotism." Ironically, the stakes of the struggle against the "so-called democracy of today" were to "save the principles of Jefferson from total overthrow in this nation." "We must repulse them," Lincoln declared, "or they will subjugate us."[25]

As Lincoln became better known, he had to resist more actively the efforts of his fellow partisans to identify him with one or another of the factions contending within the opposition movement itself.[26] Avoiding too close an association with the radical wing, moderate wing, or the conservative wing of the Republican coalition had an obvious strategic advantage for a dark-horse candidate, but Lincoln gained far more for his independence than that. On the positive side, he caught the expansive authority generated by the interplay of the different impulses at work within the Republican movement. His rhetorical stance tapped the party's different ideological currents as mutually reinforcing themes, and he established a leadership posture more plastic than any of its parts. He delivered a radical indictment of the current regime. ("Either the *opponents* of slavery, will arrest the further spread of it . . . or its *advocates* will push it forward, till it shall become alike lawful in all the states, old as well as new—North as well as South."[27]) He offered a conservative defense of slavery's restriction. ("We stick to, contend for, the identical old policy adopted by our fathers who framed the Government under which we live; while you [southerners and Democrats] with one accord reject, and scout, and spit upon that old policy, and insist on substituting something new."[28]) Finally, he charted a moderate course for reform, one that would recognize the constitutional right of slavery in the states in which it existed and insist only on stopping its further expansion. ("I wish to make and to keep the distinction between the existing institution, and the extension of it, so broad, and so clear, that no honest man can misunderstand me."[29]) Lincoln insisted only on pointing the nation down the road to freedom; he promised only the "ultimate" extinction of slavery and the *eventual* triumph of free labor principles. He was committed to overthrowing the slave power conspiracy and to reaffirming the principles of the Declaration of Independence, and he made clear that the latter was contingent on the former; but he left the implications of these commitments open to the play of events. How far he would go in reenacting first principles would be determined by how much resistance he faced in arresting the present course.

Lincoln installed the reconstructive trope—repudiation-as-affirmation—at the heart of the newly empowered opposition movement. From this, he would gain his independence in political action, and with it he would exert a decisive measure of presidential control. The purity of message and the constancy of principle that the romantic finds so distinctive in Lincoln's leadership hinged on this underlying consonance in the order-shattering, order-affirming, and order-creating elements of his political posture. In elaborating the case for change out of the evolving imperatives of restoring legitimate order, resistance would become his resource, and radicalism his prerogative.

Similarly, the fabled "pragmatism" of Lincoln's leadership appears here as a political contingency. His famous refrain, "My policy is to have no policy," would surely have been a counsel of aimless drift rather than an artful assertion of political control had it not been tied to an open-ended case for shattering existing power arrangements. To truly break free of "the dogmas of the quiet past"—to continually readjust thinking and actions to the demands of the situation as they unfold—a president must have an expansive warrant for disruption, one that holds independent ground for action through continuous and open-ended assaults on the status quo ante. Pragmatism worked for Lincoln because legitimate order and radical change were virtually synonymous in his basic leadership stance. Pragmatism was not Lincoln's secret insight into politically appropriate action in the American presidency; rather, pragmatism proved an effective stratagem for Lincoln because he operated within the contingent structure for action in which it was most appropriate, the one that maximized presidential independence from the received governing formulas. The authority to repudiate gave Lincoln's pragmatism its range and vitality.

Saving the Union, Destroying Slavery

On August 20, 1862, Lincoln responded to critics of his handling of the slavery issue in a letter to Horace Greeley published in the New York *Tribune*. No statement is more widely cited to exemplify his moderation and pragmatism in political leadership, and yet none better exemplifies the radical independence and transformative logic of his reconstructive stance.

> My paramount object in this struggle is to save the Union, and is not either to save or destroy slavery. If I could save the Union without freeing any slave, I would do it; and if I could save it by freeing all the slaves, I would do it; and if I could save it by freeing some and leaving others alone, I would also do that. What I do about slavery and the colored race, I do because I believe it helps to save the Union; and what I forebear, I forebear because I do not believe it would help to save the Union.
>
> I have here stated my purpose according to my view of official duty; and I intend no modification of my oft-expressed personal wish that all men everywhere could be free.

This pragmatic approach to the root cause of the rebellion is curious on several counts. First, Lincoln's earlier actions on the question of slavery moved in a very different direction. Indeed, by the time of his inaugural, when he first implored the South to reconsider its threat to destroy the Union, he had already determined to do more than simply save it. The Union had to be saved on Republican terms, terms that would make it "forever worthy of the saving," and that entailed, at the very least, a steadfast resolve to redeem it from its fall from grace in 1854. As President-elect, Lincoln had instructed Republicans in the rump session of Congress to stand firm against Unionist John Crittenden's compromise proposals to ease the secession crisis or any other measure that might yield the party's position on the expansion of slavery in the territories. He would not permit the Republican party to "become a 'mere sucked egg all shell and no meat,—the principle all sucked out.'" At the moment when the choice was most starkly posed, setting a course for the "ultimate" extinction of slavery took precedence over all competing expedients aimed at preventing civil war. "The tug has to come," Lincoln observed, "and better now, than any time hereafter."[30]

Second, it can be readily observed that Lincoln's pragmatism on the matter of slavery did less to delimit his war policy than to extend a presidential prerogative over virtually all possibilities. No doubt, the President was thinking strategically in August of 1862. He wanted to rally national opinion to a standard of his own by clarifying his independence from extremists on the left and right and by establishing an attractive center of moderation. The striking thing about the *Tribune* statement, however, is that it turned moderation into something wholly indeterminate. Rather than staking out a middle position along the line between conservative restoration and radical revolution, Lincoln took the entire line for himself and equated the political center with faith in his official judgment as to what needed to be saved, what destroyed, and when.

Taking aim at those radical antislavery critics in the Republican party who had been blasting away for months at his qualms about abolition, Lincoln implied that he simply could not decide the fate of the institution according to his "oft expressed personal wish that all men everywhere could be free." Rather, he had to decide it as a president, "according to my view of official duty." But then he all but exploded the distinction between radicalism and conservatism by proclaiming that in his view "official duty" did not constrain radical action but actually authorized it. Thus, as Lincoln pulled himself away from his antislavery critics by placing his role as an agent of constitutional government before his own understanding of the morality of the case, he also pulled himself away from the constitutional arguments of the antiabolitionists. He implicitly rejected the two central claims of the conservatives, denying both their premise that any attempt by the federal government to free the slaves must be itself a revolt against the Constitution and their conclusion that the war could be prosecuted lawfully only on behalf of the Constitution "as it is" for the restoration of the Union "as it was." Lincoln asserted instead that his constitutional responsibility to restore the Union might well work a radical change in the Constitution itself. In fact, this August statement of purpose was the first public proclamation that the President actually had the authority to free all the slaves, and thus that he could, if he so chose, transform the Union fundamentally in the name of saving it. Lincoln insisted, in other words, that he could make a revolution without any sacrifice of constitutional scruples—that at some point, revolution actually might become his constitutional duty.[31]

Finally, it remains to be observed that the wily ideologue who had chosen conflict over compromise on slavery in the winter of 1860–61 was professing openness and independence about a foregone conclusion in the summer of 1862. At the very moment that Lincoln was setting himself apart from the Republican radicals and declaring the salvation of the Union his sole object, he had, in fact, already determined to heed the radicals and make the Civil War a revolutionary struggle.[32] An Emancipation Proclamation had been drafted and approved by the cabinet weeks before Lincoln announced his "paramount object" with its pretense of official indifference to the question of slavery. To be sure, Lincoln would pursue emancipation as a military necessity warranted by his constitutional position as commander-in-chief and aimed at undermining the forces in rebellion. Following the third option outlined in the *Tribune* statement, he would free slaves only in areas that, after a three-month notice of his intent, persisted in open defiance of the government of the United States. Nonetheless, he would now drive his armies against the bulwark of southern culture and pit the two economic and social systems supported by the Constitution in a death struggle.[33]

In this light, the *Tribune* statement declaring slave liberation a legitimate instrument of war and anticipating emancipation as a military necessity to "save the Union" appears a deft bit of posturing meant to ease (and further blur) the transition between the restoration of the Union and the wholesale reconstruction of the South. To prepare the nation for this imminent transformation of Union war aims, Lincoln set out in August to trump the faction that had been espousing this program all along, to transcend its political base, and to temper its radicalism with a preservative purpose. Stratagem was heaped upon stratagem in a magnificent display of the art of political persuasion. Indeed, Lincoln issued his August statement on a calculation that it would be best to wait for a significant military victory before announcing his real intentions about slavery. Marking time until he could take on that evil institution from a position of strength on the field of battle, he not only strained the truth in his paramount object statement, he also called into question the entire argument about military necessity.[34]

On all these counts, pragmatism in the service of saving the Union appears something of a ruse. It lured challengers of all stripes into the President's web, and then bound them there in a seamless logic of saving and destroying. Lincoln's basic leadership posture defied the extremes of conservatism and radicalism by pressing a rather uncompromising claim to being both at once, and we should remember that this same posture girded the political leadership of Jefferson and Jackson as well. These presidents countered their detractors, neutralized their attacks, and fine-tuned the art of political persuasion by constructing a discourse impervious to the essential contradiction of presidential action in history. For each of them, repudiation *was* affirmation, disruption *was* restoration, destruction *was* salvation.

There was nothing at all mysterious about this in Lincoln's case. He had warned the South from the beginning that its intentions would backfire with devastating effect. Far from staving off the order-shattering threat posed by the Republican party's election victory, the counter-threat of secession would, he argued, only fuel the forces of destruction. "Such of you as are now dissatisfied," he had observed in his inaugural address, "still have the old Constitution unimpaired, and, on the sensitive point, the laws of your own framing under it; while the new Administration will have no immediate power, if it would, to change either." Secession would not only bolster the power of the antislavery party (giving it carte blanche control over the federal government), it would also bolster the authority of the antislavery President (turning him into an extrapartisan protector of the integrity of the Union). "*You* have taken no oath registered in heaven to destroy the Government," the President warned, "while *I* shall have the most solemn one to 'preserve, protect and defend it.'" And who could say what would become of the "old Constitution" under the extraordinary strains of the ensuing civil war? On this score, Lincoln could assure his dissatisfied countrymen that "the certain ills you fly to are greater than all the real ones you fly from."[35]

Failure to reckon Lincoln a president in his own right was indeed a fatal flaw in the South's calculations. For just as surely as its rejection of this inaugural plea laid bare a total eclipse of the authority of the man, it also exposed the fearsome charisma of the presidential office itself. By acting on their perception that Lincoln was a mere pawn of an organization bent on revolution, secessionists gave him the authority to make that revolution on his own terms. Challenging Lincoln to vindicate his oath of office, the South provided him the independent warrants to fashion the Republican party's latent revolutionary ambitions into the only appropriate course for the nation to pursue.

One can only imagine what would have become of the windfall of political control that redounded to the Republican party with the secession of the South without this windfall of independent authority that redounded to the obscure man it had placed in the White House. For all the organizational resources at its command, that party was still new in power. It was nominally headed by a regular politician of dubious personal standing, and it was ideologically hostaged to a pertinacious band of moralists impervious to the North's own resistance to its plea for racial justice. Formal power alone would have been a mixed blessing at best for such an assembly. Lincoln gave it something more. His commitment to crush the rebellion "by all indispensable means" harnessed the power of the Republican party to the constitutional authority of the American presidency.[36] This recasting of the Republican movement gradually came to be reflected in the adoption of the "Union party" label; and with this change, Lincoln, the party regular, gained some of the trappings of a party-builder in the mold of Jefferson and Jackson.[37] The Union party label acknowledged implicitly that Lincoln had a leadership role apart from the organization that had elected him and that he carried a broader political movement in his train.

With this broader political movement in mind, let us take stock of Lincoln's tenacity in holding the nation to a logic where the destruction of order was synonymous with the saving of it. The leader who stood before the people in 1860 was very different from the one who sought their endorsement again in 1864. Lincoln first ran for the presidency on the Republican ticket with a radical from Maine. He was then the candidate of an avowedly antislavery party, but, as such, he was at pains to assure the slaveholders of the border states and the South that he would uphold all of their constitutional rights and guarantees. Four years later, Lincoln was the candidate of a "Union" party, running with a Tennessee Democrat on the ticket; but from that more inclusive posture, he was at pains to secure a far more radical platform committed to the abolition of slavery once and for all by constitutional amendment. It is difficult to find any point in this transition at which the President carried an issue decisively, and yet the resistance he encountered only served to bolster his transformative authority. With each rebuff, he became more radical and more independent; his position more encompassing and more formidable.

March 1861. Lincoln began his inaugural by repeating his assurances on the question of slavery in the South. "I have no purpose, directly or indirectly, to interfere with the institution of slavery in the States where it exists. I believe I have no lawful right to do so, and have no inclination to do so." The South ignored him and the war came.[38]

July 1862. Lincoln implored conservative congressmen from the border states to accept his plan for gradual, voluntary, and compensated emancipation. The Union armies, he observed, were disrupting slavery everywhere they went. The institution was doomed by mere "friction and abrasion." He urged the border states to examine the "unprecedentedly stern facts of our case," and accept the implications of the war. The sanctity of slave property, he ventured, was a principle hanging by a thread, and a "decision at once to emancipate *gradually*" was the only hope for gaining compensation for the loss. The border congressmen ignored this plea and rebuffed the program.[39]

September 1862. Lincoln proclaimed his intention to emancipate slaves in those areas still in rebellion three months hence. If there was a measure of political subtlety in this—taking decisive action only in areas over which the federal government had no actual control—it was lost on the Democratic party. Now mobilized against presidential dictatorship, northern opposition saddled the administration with serious midterm losses.[40]

January 1863. The final Emancipation Proclamation was issued with a provision for mustering blacks as soldiers into the Union armies. "The colored population is the great available, and yet unavailed of, force for restoring the Union." But immigrant workers in northern cities resisted conscription, denounced Lincoln's war for Negro freedom, and rampaged against northern blacks. Leading Democrats launched a peace movement to negotiate an end to the war and pave the way for their final overthrow of the Lincoln dictatorship.[41]

June 1864. Lincoln was nominated by a Union Party committed to a constitutional amendment to abolish slavery. A few days later, the House rejected the abolition amendment.[42]

The yield from all this rejection and frustration became evident the instant Lincoln was reelected on the Union party ticket. Though he had been rebuffed at virtually every turn, the President did not wait for the new, more solidly Republican Congress to assemble before moving to secure his Emancipation Proclamation. He took the Union party platform as a mandate for immediate action and had the rump session of the old Congress reconsider the abolition amendment previously rejected by the House. With patronage in one hand and his familiar refrain in the other ("My chief hope [is] to bring the war to a speedy close"), he cajoled the necessary Democratic votes to his side and, on January 31, 1865, reversed the verdict on the most radical solution to the fundamental question.[43]

Lincoln's steady approach to this monumental achievement had less to do with the organized features of the polity in the party period, tenacious as they were, than with the national upheaval and political disarray that attended his rise to the presidential office. The Republican organization harbored an unprecedented concentration of power, but it was never more potent than when it was modified in the course of events into a more inchoate extension of the President's national leadership posture. Like Jackson's one-man party in the Bank War, Lincoln's phantom Union party took its warrants for action from the resistance he encountered, and just kept battering away at the obstacles thrown in its path. Ever more expansive in its sweep, Lincoln's battering ram, like Jackson's, never really won anything decisive until it had laid waste to the institutional bulwark of the old order. "If the people across the river had behaved themselves," he commented on the eve of the congressional passage of the Thirteenth Amendment, "I could not have done what I have."[44]

Reconstruction

We have taken stock of the emergent and recurrent patterns that structured the politics of leadership under Lincoln, but we have yet to consider the full significance of their conjunction. Lincoln's reconstruction was typical in its dovetailing of order-shattering and order-affirming impulses, but its distinctive shape and character quickly came to the fore when he tried to create order anew. Lincoln's struggle to control the terms of restoring the South draws forward the pattern of secular change that we have been tracing through each successive reconstruction of American politics. For all that he shared with Jefferson and Jackson in his transformative posture and all the systemic power he had at his disposal to trump their claims to revolutionary action,

Lincoln's reconstruction remained the more encumbered for the obstacles to rebuilding order in the party state. The government had never penetrated so deeply into the affairs of the nation; power had never been so closely bound to organizations with a life of their own; and the authority to reconstruct had never operated so far removed from the personality of the president himself.

That Lincoln was forced to maneuver around organizations he never fully controlled should already be apparent. A delimitation of the ground for wielding reconstructive authority was part and parcel of the thickened institutional universe in which he acted. Shorn of all personal authority for imposing his will, Lincoln's leadership, even more than Jackson's, depended on his constitutional position. He was continually reaching back to his oath of office to reassert himself and he relied heavily on his role as commander-in-chief to justify his actions.[45] The relative formality of his case underscored a degree of institutional intermediation of presidential will not seen in prior reconstructions. From start to finish Lincoln's margin of freedom on the crowded field of political action was dictated by the often sorry decisions of his generals on the fields of battle and the outcome of engagements that were largely beyond his control. ("I claim not to have controlled events," Lincoln wrote in a somewhat different context, "but confess plainly that events have controlled me."[46]) In the meantime, as his armies mediated his will, Lincoln had to maneuver his way around another organization, the tenacious political machine that had thrust him into office in the first place. At his most effective, Lincoln rode herd on the Republican party. He paced its power, imparting his own meanings to the events it encountered and the actions it took. It remained all the while an independent force he had to reckon with.

The relative density of institutional politics in the 1860s made itself felt on several fronts in Lincoln's reconstruction. Its impact is notable first and foremost in the operational independence and organizational efficiency of the Republican congresses. Lincoln, of course, boasted a Whig pedigree in addition to his Republican party credentials and his Union party aspirations, and for this he was perfectly content on grounds of both procedure and substance to ratify most of what the Republican-controlled legislature chose to do. But the oft-invoked image of Lincoln as "a Whig in the White House" does not quite capture the developmental significance of congressional initiative during his reconstruction.[47] The truly remarkable thing is how proficiently these congresses delivered the goods and the extent to which the new order emerged de facto as a creation of the Congress. These congresses produced, with virtually no active involvement from the White House, the most durable elements of what would become the new Republican regime.

Under pressure to finance the war, Congress trashed the strict discipline the Jacksonians had imposed on the national government and instituted a new regime of national banking, national borrowing, national currency, and protective tariffs. And while Lincoln remained fixed on the battlefields of the South, Congress was continuously extending the Republican party's hold on the North. Attractive new services delivered under federal auspices stamped the Union with the spirit of national improvement. The Department of Agriculture Act, the Morill College Land Grant Act, the Homestead Act, and the Union Pacific Railroad Act heralded a wholly new dispensation in governmental affairs. Taken along with the war emergency legislation, these measures substantially altered relationships between American society and the federal government in commerce, finance, industry, and agriculture. Though the implications of these changes for presidential leadership would not be felt for some time, the Republicans in Congress were facilitating the development of a truly national economy and fueling organizational developments that eventually would crowd party politics itself. Seeds were planted here that would gradually blossom into a new, more pluralistic form of politics in which the leaders of private-sector organizations would bargain over the shape of national policy with the leaders of government.[48]

Of course, with Congress a full and equal partner in this reconstruction, the potential for conflict over the range of congressional and executive authority was as ominous as their potential for cooperation was revolutionary. Lincoln could rely on congressional initiative for getting things done across a wide range of mutually shared goals, but these goals were never fully coincident, and Republican congressmen reshaped the politics of reconstruction by challenging and delimiting their president's role. Indeed, the Whig boast of mutual respect between independent branches of the federal government, each acting within its proper sphere, quickly ran up against the reality of overlapping responsibilities; and for Congress, at least, the counsel of institutional self-control applied only to the other side of Pennsylvania Avenue.

Consider the partnership of president and Congress on the issue of emancipation. When Congress passed territorial legislation overturning the Dred Scott decision, Lincoln signed it. When Congress passed war emergency legislation confiscating rebel property, Lincoln signed it. When Congress passed blatantly radical legislation abolishing slavery in the District of Columbia, Lincoln negotiated some of the fine points and then signed it. But when Lincoln attempted to assert his own control over the meaning of the war, Congress balked. Two such moves in the first year of the rebellion set the pattern. The first involved the promotion of a Democrat, George McClellan, to the command of the Army of the Potomac; the second, the reversal of an edict issued by a Republican general, John Frémont, emancipating slaves within the military district of Missouri. The McClellan appointment fueled Republican charges that Lincoln was untrustworthy; the Frémont reversal fueled charges that he was dictatorial. By the end of the year, Republicans were not only echoing the attacks of the Democrats against the administration, they were taking action to secure their interests. In their Committee on the Conduct of the War, they set out in effect to destroy McClellan and secure more radical army leadership in his stead.[49]

As the sparks over McClellan and Frémont indicate, there was more at issue between Lincoln and the Republican Congress than constitutional jurisdiction. These conflicts were in fact early manifestations of an organizational dilemma that would gradually swell and come to a head over the most profound order-creating challenge of all—the reconstruction of the South. At issue was the awkward relationship between the sectional party that had elected this President and the national party that the President set out to fashion on his own terms once in office. The historian Michael Holt may have overstated the point a bit when he claimed that "Lincoln almost from the moment he was elected set out to destroy the Republican party as it existed in 1860."[50] But even when we acknowledge the many mutual advantages to be drawn across the porous lines that separated the Republican organization and the Union party cause, it is clear that Holt caught something basic in the politics of this reconstruction. Like the reconstructive presidents before him, Lincoln used the independent powers and prerogatives of his office to fashion his place in history in terms largely unanticipated by preconceptions of the political alternatives. In this instance, however, that entailed something more than it had in the past: it meant altering an up-and-running engine of change. The newfound limits of the politics of reconstruction are most clearly evident in the difficulties Lincoln encountered in that task.

There is no need to deny the vast field of action over which the interests of the Republican party and the Union party coincided—or the vast difference between Lincoln's course and that pursued by his Union party running mate after his assassination—to appreciate how seriously the success of his Union party would challenge the preexisting Republican organization. The problem is a familiar one, but its antecedents—Jefferson's confrontation with John Randolph over the shape of the new Republican party, and Jackson's confrontation with John Calhoun over the shape of the new Democratic party—suggest nothing so much as a progressive magnification of an inherent difficulty. All reconstructive leaders have to deal with a disillusioned element that had been integral to the party's initial insurgency. But whereas Jefferson dealt with an individual crank within his ranks and Jackson dealt with a regional leader who wielded significant power within his initial coalition, Lincoln dealt with the organization that had made him what he was. Republicans were no more willing to suffer the independence of presidential action in politics when it threatened to alter their organization than were the Democrats or the southern states when it threatened theirs. As Lincoln proceeded to remake the Republican party in his own image, he risked a devastating confrontation with what was after all the sine qua non of his presidency. If his expansive warrants for shattering old political and institutional arrangements buoyed him in this contest, his dependence on the organizational foundations of his power delimited his advance.

Lincoln could not have survived without the support of the Republican party, but neither could he have safely afforded to rest content with it. That in a nutshell was the problem. Indeed, one of the immediate aims of the Union party was to fashion a more secure political base for a president who, after all, had been elected in 1860 with less than 40 percent of the popular vote. Taking advantage of disruption and disarray at the margins of the old alliances, Lincoln's Union party looked southward for support, first to the border states, where Republican strength was weak, and then, with the progress of the Union armies, to the South itself, where the Republican party was nonexistent and its prospects nil. The President's constitutional position as commander-in-chief became the lifeline of this new party. Its flagship was his polyglot cabinet, its political machine was his Union Army, and its ideology, as we have already seen, carefully elevated unionism above the destruction of the institutional bulwark of the old order, slavery, thereby leaving open the question of the precise shape of things to come. Meanwhile, the political base of the Republican party remained lodged in the northern tier of the nation, where opposition to slavery and enthusiasm for the new age of national improvement ran hottest. This party was as implacably hostile to the South and the Democratic party as they were to it, and the war only intensified the mutual animosities. Had Lincoln been successful in institutionalizing his Union party in place of the one that had elected him, he would have significantly altered the ideology and interests of the then-existing Republican organization. But from their center of institutional power in Congress, the Republicans fought tenaciously and not without effect to hold Lincoln to their standard. They challenged his control of the political machinery of the Union Army, they pushed him to sharpen his commitments in national policy, and they resisted his overtures to southern unionists and War Democrats.[51]

The tension between these two kindred parties, one organized and powerful, the other inchoate and largely symbolic, was first manifested in the struggle to control the pace of emancipation, with the President determined to move more slowly and to resist action based solely on the morality of the case. But in the wake of the Emancipation Proclamation and the steady advance of Union armies in 1863, the contest shifted ground and got tangled up in a host of thorny organizational problems. When attention focused on the terms for the restoration of the southern states, the President showed himself more willing to move quickly and to take what support he could find for the Union in occupied rebel territory. Lincoln's Proclamation of Amnesty and Reconstruction in December 1863 accelerated this shift by resolving some old bones of contention and showcasing new ones. By the standards of six months prior, this was a radical document; by those of six months hence it was decidedly out of step with advanced Republican thinking.[52]

Lincoln's December proclamation was radical in preempting the revival of slavery in those areas of the Confederacy that had been exempted from his prior emancipation edict because they were already held by Union forces. He made the abolition of slavery an absolute condition for restoration of the Confederate states, and in doing so he linked the Republican party and the Union party in a way that would prove critical during the difficulties ahead. But even as they relished these prospects, congressional Republicans could see problems in the President's terms for restoration. Lincoln would pardon all but the highest-ranking participants in the rebellion if they would take an oath of allegiance to the Constitution and the Union and agree to abide by the acts and proclamations regarding slavery made by the government during the war. Furthermore, a state government could be restored to the Union with full and equal standing under the President's plan provided that a mere one-tenth of the number of voters that had cast ballots in 1860 were willing to take the same oath and participate in the reorganization of a government that recognized emancipation. Finally, a military government, working directly under the authority of the President, was to oversee this transition.

To be sure, Lincoln had crafted his message carefully with overtures to both conservative southern unionists and Republican congressmen. He suggested on the one hand that the new state governments might shape their own policies toward the former slaves so as to ease the social and economic dislocations attending their emancipation; on the other, he reminded all concerned that Congress, through its control over the readmission of its southern members, would have its own say on conditions for restoration. The December proclamation is in this sense one more mark of Lincoln's determination to assert control over the terms of political change by keeping the precise shape of things to come open-ended. But the deeper he plunged into the problems of reconstructing the polity, the more abrasive the political and organizational thicket became. The Republican party had provided the core of his support as he drove the Union Army into the heart of southern society; now he had to rely on that army to build Union party support in the rabidly anti-Republican South, and that support would have to be acceptable to the rabidly antisouthern Republican Congress. The several points of resistance to this design threatened to arrest the whole project; Lincoln's control became most problematic just as his leadership claims were becoming most encompassing. Retaining mastery over the meaning and effect of the amnesty proclamation as it wove its way through these multiple levels of institutional intermediation put Lincoln's reconstructive authority to its most severe test.

The political tangle that developed in Union-occupied Louisiana shows what he was up against.[53] Over the summer and fall of 1863, Lincoln had grown increasingly frustrated with the apparent inability of the Louisiana Free State Committee to get on with the task of reconstructing the state government on its own initiative. A speedy reconstruction of this state was, he believed, essential to demoralizing the remainder of the Confederacy and hastening an end to the fighting. But the delay raised even deeper concerns, for conservative planters in areas of Louisiana under Union control seemed determined to form a government under the old state constitution that would profess loyalty to Washington but retain slavery. Direct presidential pressure to prompt the Free State Committee into action had failed, as had equally pointed efforts to discredit the planters' designs. Finally, Lincoln intervened officially by making his commanding general in New Orleans, Nathaniel Banks, "master of all" and ordering him to reorganize Louisiana as a free state with all due speed. When Lincoln issued his December proclamation outlining a general program of presidential amnesty and reconstruction, he had the Louisiana case (and the planters' designs) very much in mind, and he hoped to present a new government in Louisiana as the model for his more general program.

Banks did give Lincoln what he wanted most—a government without slavery. But he proved a poor conduit for what Lincoln needed most—freedom to maneuver around the issues that separated the Republicans in Congress from a potential unionist coalition in the South. Lincoln's order making Banks "master" of the situation left a bitter taste in the mouths of radical leaders in New Orleans, and their frustrations were vented in Washington through Salmon Chase, the treasury secretary. Chase was tying his own incipient drive for the 1864 Republican presidential nomination to mistrust of Lincoln among congressional radicals and to the vast pool of treasury patronage his department commanded in every port city under Union control. Far from galvanizing Republicans in Congress and unionists in the South behind his plan, Lincoln's Louisiana experiment touched off resistance in one area which then reverberated in the other, driving deeper divisions within each. Banks precipitated the trouble by reversing an earlier endorsement of the date the Free State party's leaders had set for holding a constitutional convention and calling instead for an election of officers under the old constitution as a first show of strength for the proemancipation forces. The general had voided the slavery provisions of the old document by military fiat, and he certainly would have voided the election returns had the proslavery faction won the election. But his decision to delay the calling of a convention that might formally eradicate slavery and specify the political and civil rights of the freedmen was seen by the radicals of the Free State movement as an overture to the conservative planters and a betrayal of the Republican cause. Banks was already vulnerable on this ground because he had previously authorized a system of contract labor that severely restricted the civil rights of the freedmen. His call for early elections prompted the radicals to break the Free State movement in two and field their own ticket in the upcoming contest. When the moderate slate of state officers boasting Bank's support carried the day and the radicals came in third behind the planters' slate, the alarm bells sounded loud and clear in the halls of Congress.

Of all the contingencies on which the fate of the Union party in the South hinged, the weakest of all was Lincoln's administrative apparatus. The President was at the mercy of subordinates hundreds of miles away who dealt with the most sensitive political questions of the day with little direct supervision; and with military controls, intrapartisan maneuvering, and local electoral politics all tangled together, interpretations of presidential intent began to take on a life of their own.[54] For all the clumsiness of his political maneuvering, Banks remained Lincoln's best hope for a speedy reconstruction; and, with the war still raging, speed remained a presidential priority. So Lincoln stood by the white loyalist government Banks had given him in Louisiana. Meanwhile, the radical leader of the Free State party, William Durant, began to feed congressional fears of presidential reconstruction with a steady stream of reports from the scene. Through these reports, all the pieces of a monstrous threat to the Republican cause began to fall into place: free elections appeared no more than a pretense for military despotism; a commitment to construct pure republican constitutions appeared to have been shelved for the political expediency of action under the tainted old slave constitutions; the old planter class appeared resurgent; an indigenous Free State movement appeared to have been betrayed in the formation of a new Union party; and the President seemed determined to gain the electoral votes of any Union party government he could form, regardless of the price extracted by the implacable enemies of the Republican party.

There was countervailing evidence, to be sure. Lincoln had actually acted to preempt a conservative counterrevolution in Louisiana. He had saved emancipation from planter designs, and subsequently he had worked from afar (to no avail, as it turned out) for a black suffrage provision at the state constitutional convention. But intraparty opposition to Lincoln had moved into the open during the winter and spring of 1864, and with suspicion of presidential reconstruction already in the air, Durant's version of developments in the field merely stiffened Republican resolve to assert congressional authority and take control of the terms and conditions of southern restoration. As the election year unfolded, efforts to dump Lincoln as the party's candidate in the upcoming election surfaced on a variety of fronts. Secretary of the Treasury Salmon Chase, the darling of the radicals, finally came out of the closet to mount a direct challenge to Lincoln's renomination. John Frémont, whose emancipation edict Lincoln had reversed in the first year of the war, took the field as a third-party candidate and blasted Lincoln's usurpatious policies from the left as the Democrats blasted them from the right. And Benjamin Wade and Henry Winter Davis fashioned a pointedly antiadministration program in the guise of a congressional alternative to presidential reconstruction.

The Wade-Davis bill, presented to Lincoln on the last day of the congressional session in July, was designed for the short-term purpose of taking Lincoln's reconstructed governments out of the upcoming presidential contest, and a longer view toward providing time for making the yet unfathomable adjustments necessary to ensure that reunification with the South would be safe for the Republican cause. Instead of having reconstruction follow directly in the wake of army conquests as Lincoln had planned, Congress opted for a long period of federal domination and contemplated an extended reform effort during peacetime. Specifically, it demanded a loyal citizenry constituting 50 percent of the number of voters in 1860 (rather than the President's 10 percent) as a basic condition for forming a new government, and then it allowed only those who could take an "iron clad" oath of *loyalty during the rebellion* to elect delegates to a constitutional convention. During the interim, the federal government would control the situation through a provisional civil governor (rather than Lincoln's military governor), and certain basic civil rights for the freedmen would be guaranteed.

In responding to the Louisiana experience, Congress had in effect drawn a line against the Union party design, and when the Union party's presidential candidate pocket-vetoed the Wade-Davis bill, the Republicans' worst fears appeared to be confirmed. As the veto fueled the revolt in the ranks, a worried Lincoln tried his best to patch over the breach. In a belated explanation of his action, he commended the Congress for outlining a sound idea that some states might well wish to adopt, but said that he did not want to tie himself to one fixed plan of action. Of course, tying the President to a fixed plan of action was the whole point of the congressional initiative, and for a moment this vintage piece of Lincolnian leadership only made things worse.[55] Furthermore, Lincoln, always careful to lodge his actions in the Constitution, rested his veto on certain provisions of the bill pertaining to abolition of slavery, claiming that Congress did not have that authority and that, short of a constitutional amendment, only the commander-in-chief could authorize such action.[56] This constitutional argument for presidential reconstruction proved too much for the radicals to bear. Hoping to spark Republican resentment into a stampede against Lincoln, Wade and Davis published a searing manifesto of opposition to his "dictatorial usurpations" of power. Appealing to "The Supporters of the Government," they condemned the President's Louisiana regime as "mere oligarchy, imposed on the people by military orders under a form of election, at which generals, provost marshals, soldiers and camp followers were the chief actors." Lincoln's presidency, they concluded, had become a "studied outrage on the legislative authority."[57]

These wounds were raw, and the issues being contested very much unresolved, at the time of Lincoln's assassination. The Union party platform skirted the issue of reconstruction. The President went to the nation committed to saving the Union and abolishing slavery. Indeed, if there was a saving grace in Lincoln's explanation of his veto of the Wade-Davis bill, it was his pointed reminder to Republicans of his firm support for the constitutional amendment that would abolish slavery once and for all. It is not too much to suggest that Lincoln survived the party rebellion against his reconstruction policies because on this ground—saving the Union and destroying slavery—he remained irresistible. Both sides ultimately accepted a stalemate on reconstruction in order to fight this common cause during the campaign. The Wade-Davis manifesto actually helped in this regard, for no sooner did it appear than Republicans began to realize that they themselves had made the Democrats' case, that their tirade against Lincoln's dictatorial usurpations was "the most effective Copperhead campaign document" of all.[58] There could be no question that Lincoln was preferable to George McClellan, the Democratic nominee, when it came to destroying the old order, and to seal the political truce for the final election drive, Lincoln's Army covered its recent sins in Louisiana with a timely act of devastation. The surrender of Atlanta on September 2, 1864, after a politically debilitating summer of siege, kicked the bottom out of the Democrats' peace platform, and with victory for the Union forces now certain, the "Radical Democrat" John Frémont withdrew for fear of splitting the antislavery vote.[59]

In speculating about how things might have turned out had Lincoln lived out his second term, it is best to be cautious. There is certainly good reason to believe that a disastrous confrontation like the one that later ensued between the Republican Congress and Andrew Johnson could have been avoided. Indeed, Lincoln had continued his self-paced move toward the radicals in the early weeks of his second term. In the days before his death, he was contemplating the virtues of both a slower-paced reconstruction and of limited black suffrage. The rift between him and his fellow Republicans had less to do with principles than with strategic calculations, and by holding open the precise shape of things to come, Lincoln had kept the lines of accommodation clear as to the proper scope and timing of change. There is virtually no intersection between the drift of his administration in these last days and Johnson's efforts to rebuild the national coalition of the Democratic party.[60]

On the other hand, none of these observations permit us to dismiss the knotty organizational and operational problems that left Republicans and Unionists stalemated over reconstruction in 1864.[61] A successful reconstruction of the South would have required at the very least a mode of governmental operations quite different from that which prevailed during the middle years of the nineteenth century, and for all that Lincoln did to revolutionize the federal government's basic commitments of ideology and interest, there is nothing to suggest that he was inclined to challenge parties per se as the central organizing mechanism of governmental affairs. Thus, when he urged the selection of Democrat Andrew Johnson to run for the vice presidency on the Union party ticket in 1864, Lincoln did less to resolve than to accentuate the problem of working a reconstruction of the South through the instrumentalities of a party state. Just as the spectre of a new Union party straddling the sectional divide ran up against core Republican commitments in 1864, that spectre would run up against core Democratic commitments under Johnson's leadership in 1865. Both encounters suggest that the Union party was an aberration of the war with slim prospects for guiding reconstruction and anchoring a new order in its aftermath. Irresistible as a force for saving and destroying, it had neither the power nor the authority to recast all that it had shattered.

Lingering questions about the prospects for Reconstruction under an extended Lincoln administration might be easier to live with if we consider the politics of reconstruction as it had been in the more distant past and as it was yet to be in the more distant future. As Andrew Jackson had given his party little choice but to be what he said it was, Franklin Roosevelt would be forced through frustration to give up on party organization altogether as the political foundation of his reconstruction. The push and pull between Lincoln and the Republicans, with all its synergy, all its antagonism, and all its potential for mutual accommodation, sits comfortably between these poles, a reliable signpost of the changing shape of political possibilities.

Part Two:
Theodore Roosevelt's Articulation

Making an old party progressive

THOUGH Theodore Roosevelt proudly placed himself in the "Jackson-Lincoln tradition" of presidential leadership, he was also the first to admit that such comparisons left him short.[1] As steward of a nation that was flush with prosperity, heady with imperial triumphs, and rock solidly Republican, Roosevelt knew that he was an awkward match with those who rode into power on the heels of national upheaval and political disintegration. "If there is not the great occasion," he observed, "you don't get the great statesman; if Lincoln had lived in times of peace no one would have known his name now."[2]

Scholars writing later in full view of the Great Depression and World War II put the point more starkly. By the early 1950s, historical interpretation had come close to dismissing the presidency of the "first" Roosevelt as a lot of "sound and movement signifying little." No less an authority than Elting Morison speculated that historians might finally dub him the leading figure of another "era of good feeling." Busy with the sheer joy of life, the era of Theodore Roosevelt appeared, like Monroe's, all but devoid of the "massive formulations" and "great releasing statements" that mark the truly meaningful points of departure in American development.[3]

Morrison's allusion caught something basic in Roosevelt's leadership, but his speculation about the direction of subsequent opinion proved wide of the mark. Theodore Roosevelt may not have met the New Deal standard of greatness, but neither could he be dismissed out of hand.[4] To be sure, a Roosevelt reconstruction failed to materialize in the early years of the twentieth century; still, there was a Roosevelt departure, and we appreciate that departure today as no less momentous than "the birth of modern America."[5]

This dissonance in interpretations of Roosevelt, not to mention the dissonance in Roosevelt's interpretation of himself, alerts us again to the stiffening crosscurrents of order and change that reshaped the politics of leadership during the Republican era. As in the case of Lincoln, the politics Roosevelt made can slip in the blink of the eye from the monumental to the mundane. From one angle, we catch the essential continuity of his administration with those before and after; at another, we see changes that reset the very standards of evaluation. More interesting still, the developmental dynamics at issue in the contending assessments of these two leaders are inverted. While Lincoln's leadership left the organizational forms and institutional operations of party governance very much intact, it reset within that frame the government's basic commitments of ideology and interest and ushered in a wholly new political regime. Theodore Roosevelt, on the other hand, dedicated his presidency to defending and confirming the commitments of an established political regime, but within that frame, he negotiated the first major departures from the institutional forms and routine operations of American party governance. As Lincoln acted to construct a new political order within established forms of political organization, Roosevelt acted to elaborate the commitments of an established political order at the threshold of a new era in the organization of power relationships.

Only Andrew Jackson made a clean break along both the organizational and political time lines of order and change. Only in that one instance did a categorical change in the underlying mode of governance coincide with a change in the government's basic commitments of ideology and interest. The point is not simply that the leadership postures so clearly delineated throughout the Jacksonian era become more complicated thereafter, but that they were stretched in ways that flatten out the most obvious differences among them. Lincoln, we have seen, was more encumbered than earlier reconstructive leaders by the radically thickened institutional universe in which he acted. Roosevelt, on the other hand, was emboldened by secular changes at work in the nation to wage the most aggressive campaign for political maintenance yet. Roosevelt grasped the potential of the industrial era for building new kinds of governing institutions and expanding the domain of presidential power, and he harnessed that potential to the cause of rearticulating the commitments of the established regime at a higher level of achievement. Eventually Roosevelt grew so emboldened by his success in staking out new ground for national action that he seized the role of party-builder itself and attempted a wholesale political reconstruction of his own. In this instance, then, the implications of change along the secular time line of emergent power structures would seem simply to cancel out the implications of change along the political time line of recurrent authority structures.

These observations capture the drift of the analysis here. Roosevelt's leadership reveals a weakening of the constraints of political time on the politics presidents make. As such, it stands as a benchmark of the impact of modernity. Yet sorting out the different layers of presidential politics actually becomes more helpful as we encounter the more complicated mixes of the twentieth century. Nowhere are the counterpressures at work in reshaping the politics of leadership more dramatically displayed than in the twin struggles of the Roosevelt years: the first, a restless engagement while in the presidency with the leadership posture of the faithful son; the second, a fitful, postpresidential effort to throw off the shackles of lifelong affiliations and stand independently as a great repudiator. If Roosevelt's decision to change leadership robes demonstrates anything, it is that even the most popular of the orthodox-innovators could not simply revamp his leadership project at will.

The story of Roosevelt's leadership is not the story of the breakdown of the distinction between an orthodox-innovator and a great repudiator. On the contrary, it is the story of Roosevelt's sensitivity to the political stakes of maintaining that distinction and of the frustrations he met when he finally chose to cross the line. Roosevelt opened several new avenues for independent action in the presidency, but what he achieved in the way of expanding governmental capacities in the industrial era did not erase the conditions for political leadership imposed by his affiliation with the Republican regime. The opportunities and constraints encountered along the political and secular time lines of change were still quite different. Thus, as surely as Lincoln, with virtually no personal authority, pressed the most expansive warrants for independent action imaginable in the presidency, Roosevelt, the most charismatic figure to come to the presidency since Andrew Jackson, committed political suicide in his effort to leapfrog the limits of his initial warrants for action and assume a more Lincolnian posture.

In this light, it might be useful to retrieve Morrison's allusion to another era of good feeling at the dawn of the twentieth century. By changing the company Roosevelt usually keeps in political analysis, this allusion helps to bring his leadership struggles more into line with the distinctive political problems he faced. Treated not as a peremptory dismissal of Roosevelt's (or James Monroe's) performance but as a reminder to attend to the contingencies of political time, it invites us to understand Roosevelt's leadership as something else rather than something less.

Conjured up in the image of a modern-day James Monroe, Roosevelt is illuminated in ways that comparisons to Andrew Jackson, Abraham Lincoln, and Franklin Roosevelt miss. TR was, first and foremost, a regime booster. Like Monroe, he had worked his way up through the ranks of the dominant coalition of the day. Once in the presidency, he was, like Monroe, torn between his perception of the great possibilities for national action that had opened at one of the most robust moments in American development and an equally keen appreciation of the imperatives of political maintenance. Like Monroe, he sought to vindicate the overwhelming dominance of the established coalition with purely constructive responses to changing conditions. Within those limits, he sponsored another "awakening of American nationalism," and in the process he too stretched his regime's political consensus to the breaking point. Why? Because in exercising the powers of his office, Roosevelt, like Monroe, found himself at cross purposes. Both of these presidents had to juggle their abiding faith in the commitments of the established political order with their stubborn determination to be presidents in their own right. They kept tripping over the problem of how to forge something new without destroying anything of significance, how to innovate without repudiating received commitments, how to affirm continuity with the immediate past while still negotiating a significant departure, how to transform the nation without changing its politics.

For all his efforts to resolve these dilemmas, lifelong political allies would charge Roosevelt, as Monroe himself had been charged, with betrayal and heresy; scholars would charge him with "evasion and compromise."[6] The charges, however, are symptomatic of the field on which these presidents tried to lead. The real interest lies in the efforts of obviously talented politicians to master the challenge presented them. If we stick to the presidential years, we might venture that Theodore Roosevelt is unmatched in presidential history for his mastery of orthodox-innovation. Far more powerful than Monroe, he employed his national reputation more aggressively to prod the political establishment he wished to preserve to a higher standard of performance. Roosevelt showed how a president of high public standing could make himself the controlling agent of a revitalized party agenda. Compared with the other orthodox-innovator we have observed in action, James Polk, Roosevelt was also more circumspect and self-confident. He recognized the danger of abstract schemes and rigid designs and insisted instead on a reform program that could stand the tests of "practicality" and "efficiency." Even at his most belligerent, TR was less driven than Polk by a need to prove himself, and he was more open to collaboration and incremental adjustments.

Roosevelt trumped Monroe and Polk in the politics of articulation by building into the presidency itself new resources for executive action. To the power afforded him by party organization, he added extrapartisan modes of governance more responsive to the issues being raised by a new era of social and economic organization. In building national bureaucracies and in bargaining directly with private-sector leaders, he gained room to maneuver around the problems of orthodox-innovation that Monroe and Polk never had, and he used this newfound freedom brilliantly to juggle his zeal for the exercise of leadership with his abiding commitment to regime maintenance. Roosevelt extended the reach of presidential concerns in government, he forged a more broad-ranging and independent foundation for national political action, and he passed to his hand-picked successor an office significantly recast in its powers and responsibilities. It is little wonder that when he had finished, he thought he had successfully finessed the paradox of his initial leadership situation.

As it turned out, he was wrong. Like others who struggled faithfully to control the disruptive consequences of vigorous presidential action, Roosevelt ultimately set up the very explosion he had been at such pains to avoid. When, at the pinnacle of his powers, he bowed out of a second run for the presidency and encouraged the amiable William Howard Taft to stand in his place, he merely passed to someone else the political consequences of his own actions. Roosevelt pressed his boldest departures in national policy with a heroic vow of political self-sacrifice, but that was not enough to hold things together. No one would have been able to reassemble all that Roosevelt's reforms had disrupted, and when Taft faltered, Roosevelt came face to face with the precariousness of all that he had achieved under the old formulas.

It was then that he decided to transcend his initial leadership posture. Roosevelt's calamitous decision to abandon orthodox-innovation and don the mantle of a great repudiator shows us the flip side of his painstaking and self-denying struggle to exhort an organizational shift in governmental operations out of dutiful respect for the established political regime. In the incongruous role of the insurgent party-builder, he made crystal clear the whole host of inferences we have drawn from the experiences of Monroe and Polk: that innovation, however orthodox, is inherently destabilizing; that the purely constructive leadership project is an illusion; that the affiliated leader cannot assume independent ground without ultimately embracing the role of the heretic; that the only way ever to be president in your own right is to become yourself a great repudiator and set yourself directly against the bulwark of received power; that political disruption parallels presidential significance. Roosevelt's insight was not simply that new achievements do not rest securely on old foundations, but that to save the handiwork of his presidency he would have to reconstruct its political base.

Roosevelt's decision to act on this insight might be taken as the first truly modern conceit of presidential politics, for it is in the modern period that the growing power of the office begins to rub hard upon ascribed roles and to cause the classical boundaries around different leadership projects to fray. The premise that Monroe and Polk accepted implicitly, but that modern presidents with their enhanced powers tend to question, is that a leader cannot simply make himself over at will. By indulging the conceit that he could, Roosevelt clarified the more stubborn reality. Emboldened by his enormous personal popularity and bolstered by his prior ingenuity in expanding the realm of independent action in the presidency, Roosevelt's finale exposed the limits of personal choice in adopting a leadership posture at the turn of the twentieth century. The political dilemmas of orthodox-innovation were not resolved at this juncture in American development, much less superseded; they were only more explosively revealed.

The Loyal Agitator

Roosevelt had the kind of star quality that Republican organization men would have preferred to leave shining in splendid isolation. He had been promoted for the vice-presidential nomination in 1900 by machine politicians in New York who were anxious to get him out of the state house in Albany. On the receiving end of this deal, President McKinley and his political manager, Mark Hanna, were little more enthusiastic about having a "mad man" so close to the throne, and, for a time, they resisted the move.[7] Still championing reform, Roosevelt was too independent to be embraced with open arms; still basking in the glory of his Cuban adventures in the Spanish-American War, he proved too popular to be held at bay.

McKinley admirers are quick to point out that much of what Roosevelt would actually accomplish in the presidency was anticipated by his predecessor and that in substance, if not in style, it might well have been accomplished anyway had McKinley not been assassinated. But even as this accidental president made good his pledge to "continue absolutely unbroken" the policies of his former chief, he brought to the presidential office a personal history in the Republican party that set his efforts apart from those of his predecessor.[8] Roosevelt still harbored that original Republican impulse to use the party organization as a foundation on which to agitate for the moral improvement of the nation, and he embraced change as part and parcel of his party's fundamental purpose.

Ever careful to put first things first, Roosevelt stuck close to the path of regularity. He made his way within the Republican ranks with due respect for maintaining the integrity of the organization; party loyalty was the cornerstone of his career. Roosevelt was conspicuous in choosing party service over personal interest in 1884 when he refused to join kindred Republican moralists in their bolt from the party nominee, James Blaine, to the Democrats' reform candidate, Grover Cleveland. The same can be said of his decision in 1900 when, against his own grim judgment of the prospects, he sacrificed real power in New York for the impotence and isolation of the vice presidency.[9]

But as respectful as Roosevelt was of the integrity of the Republican organization, he found his chief political concerns in the limits that party government had encountered in the industrial age. Carefully he cultivated those concerns into a national reputation as a reformer, and one way or another, he always ended up a thorn in the side of the men he was chosen to serve. Benjamin Harrison implicitly acknowledged Roosevelt's identity as a loyal Republican of independent mind when he appointed him to his first federal office as civil service commissioner, and Roosevelt returned the favor by demonstrating a pesky resolve for ferreting out corruption in the administration's manipulation of patronage. Boss Platt supported Roosevelt as a candidate for New York's governorship because he was just about the only Republican in the state who was both respectable enough to counter the party's recent record of corruption and dependable enough to respect the organization despite its sordid record. Roosevelt lived up to his bargain and never went after the machine directly. But his zeal for reform in other areas left Platt anxious to find relief. Things did not change much after McKinley's assassination. Despite assiduous efforts during his early years in the presidency to assuage the fears of his party's leaders and to prove himself responsible in the exercise of power, Roosevelt watched Mark Hanna mount a drive to block his bid for his party's presidential nomination in 1904. The efficiency with which Roosevelt outmaneuvered Hanna and gained a resounding election victory in his own right showed to all who might have doubted it that this was a "wild man" who knew how to use the organization as well as the best of the professionals.

Roosevelt framed the leadership project of his presidency historically, focusing on the changing relationship between the Republican party and the nation at large.[10] He appreciated that the Republican party had never stood on more solid ground than it did at the moment of McKinley's assassination. It had attained a lock on national power unseen since the days of the Jeffersonians. The opponents of the Republican party, in Roosevelt's view, had been proven "utterly and hopelessly wrong" on all the great issues on which they had tried to mount a contest—union, slavery, currency, industrial development, and international expansion. What disturbed him was that during the 1890s the Republican party had abandoned the "radical" posture that was its birthright in national politics. The "foolish, ill-judged, mock radicalism" of Democrats, populists, and socialists had pushed the Republicans to take up the fight for right from a dangerously conservative and defensive position. Now basking in the full glory of its power and success, the party risked what Roosevelt called "fossilization," that is, a disastrous identification with the forces of reaction against the plain people to whom Lincoln had originally appealed. If it was to continue as a vital governing instrument, protecting and nourishing the inestimable benefits of its rule, the Republican party would somehow have to retake the offensive. It would have to meet the new governing demands posed by the national organization of the economy and the rise of America to world power. It would, in other words, have to respond creatively to the new issues raised by the very fruits of its own policies. "I am not advocating anything revolutionary," Roosevelt insisted. "I am advocating action to prevent anything revolutionary."[11]

Looking back on it, Roosevelt would summarize his presidency as an effort to make "an old party progressive" again. This was no small challenge. When he came into office, there was neither an irresistible party faction pressing for change nor a long-heralded agenda of great regime promises waiting to be implemented. Reinvigorating so conservative an establishment was an especially tricky business; distinguishing an aggressive defense of this regime from an outright attack on it was not an easy task for Roosevelt's fellow partisans. His determination to get the Republican party moving again ran directly against the grain of the "stand pat" orthodoxy of those he himself dubbed "the leaders," and it lent his rearticulation of regime interests and ideals a distinctly belligerent cast. Bolstered by unprecedented prosperity and an international triumph of imperial proportions, the "standpatters" saw little need for agitation, and with their lock on congressional power, they threatened to label even this most sympathetic innovator an opponent contemplating the destruction of everything they valued.[12]

Still, Roosevelt's position was not as untenable as it might at first appear. His appeal for the revival of a forgotten tradition of Republican radicalism may have been lost on the Old Guard, but it was not really directed at them. It was aimed at those whose faith in the regime needed bolstering. The years between the radical inception of the Republican regime in the 1860s and its conservative reincarnation in the 1890s had, in fact, witnessed a profound transformation of the economy and the society, and with it had appeared all sorts of heretical assaults on the existing order of things. Prior to 1896, when elections were less predictable and the balance of party power in government very much unresolved, creative responses from the national government to address the issues of the day had been stifled, and discontent had simply been left to fester. Thus, when the Republicans finally rendered their political opponents impotent in the national government, they found that virtually everything they held dear had been thrown open to public debate. If there was little immediate political pressure to do anything in particular, there was a vast store of popular concern that something or other be done. In this context, the orthodox-innovator faced a fairly open field for championing new forms of government action and at the same time for asserting an enlightened control over the appropriate boundaries of innovation. A little reform might go a long way toward countering the spectre of "fossilization," stamping the existing order with the higher virtues of flexibility and responsiveness, and furthering the cause of stability and political continuity.

Rather than turn a cold shoulder to reform ideas, Roosevelt set out to make them "respectable."[13] This meant that he would remain something of a thorn in the side of "the leaders," but there would be nothing new in that. Certainly, the Republican leadership was strong enough to swallow a little preventative medicine, and Roosevelt could always counter their resistance by whipping up public enthusiasm for action. In all, a belligerent stance, properly understood and sensitively managed, might work a significant departure in national policy with political impunity for all concerned.

The "progressive position" that Roosevelt sought to stake out for himself and to establish for the Republican regime as a whole was then to be a "conservative-radicalism."[14] Believing that William Jennings Bryan was "half right" in his quest for justice, Roosevelt also believed that conservatives had to lead that quest because the real radicals could not be trusted to preserve in the process all that the existing regime had achieved.[15] From this followed a host of familiar perplexities: How exactly does one take the offensive without shattering the defense, how exactly does one change the face of established power without challenging its integrity, how exactly does one lay claim to ideas hitherto deemed heretical for purposes of bolstering orthodoxy? Can politicians allied in power walk together along the fine line between a higher order of things and a different order of things? In dealing with such questions Roosevelt took his bearings from Edmund Burke ("There is a state to preserve as well as a state to reform," he would say), and in trying to act in that spirit of discrimination, he placed the delicate distinctions emblematic of all orthodox-innovators at the very center of his leadership project.[16]

Tending the Foundations

Whenever Roosevelt presented his reform proposals, he drew a distinction between "constructive" and "destructive" action. He stood on the side of "achievement" rather than the side of "negation, criticism, and obstruction." He wanted to "build up rather than tear down." His object was to "uphold the foundations" while "building a more lofty superstructure."[17] The importance of these rhetorical distinctions are manifest in virtually every issue that Roosevelt touched, and nowhere did they figure more prominently than in his approach to the "foundationstone" of the Republican regime, the protective tariff.

Beginning in its earliest days in power, the Republican party had worked to raise an imposing tariff wall around the American economy, and over the previous twenty years in particular the protective tariff had been vaunted by the GOP as the key to prosperity. The tariff also supported an impressive electoral coalition of industrial and labor interests, and in national elections that coalition delivered indispensable votes to the Republicans in the rich and populous states of the northeast. By the turn of the century, however, the Republican success story was beginning to bring new political pressures to bear on the very policy on which it had been premised. In the first place, the nation's rapidly expanding productive capacity was fomenting a scramble for new markets outside the United States. In the bidding for these markets, prospective trade partners found themselves in a position to demand tariff concessions, and they threatened to counter American resistance to concessions with special discriminations of their own against American goods. At the same time, midwestern Republicans were beginning to resist what they perceived as the adverse effects of the corporate consolidation of industry. They boasted the "Iowa idea" linking the nation's protective tariff directly to the overweening power of the trusts, and they took tariff reform as the solution to the new problems posed by monopoly capital.[18]

Roosevelt would juggle the ideas and interests swirling around the tariff question for seven years without changing much of anything, and then, just as the issue was getting too hot to handle, he would step aside and toss the issue of reform into the lap of his hand-picked successor. Though at one time he had identified himself with free trade principles, Roosevelt's tariff policies followed closely the precedents set by his predecessor, the arch-protectionist William McKinley. McKinley had distinguished himself in Congress as one of the chief architects of the tariff wall, and as president he had shown little inclination to reverse his course and press for a major downward restructuring of rates. For all the grousing about the issue, he knew that the bulk of American manufactures still depended almost exclusively on the home market. After the Spanish-American War, however, McKinley did become more sympathetic to the difficulties faced by producers looking for new outlets overseas. In his last years, he began to call for a more aggressive use of special reciprocity agreements with prospective trade partners. Roosevelt picked up this solution to the trade problem and pressed for special tariff arrangements on a variety of fronts.

The results were modest at best. ("I have tried once or twice to make such openings . . . and have had to fight tooth and nail to get either Democratic or Republican Senators to so much as consider the treaties I have sent in, and generally they have rejected them."[19]) Republican conservatives who might otherwise have appreciated this tack as a way to expand trade without relinquishing the principle of protection were so fearful of the Iowa idea that all they could see in reciprocity was an opening wedge for structural reform. Moreover, when reciprocity involved agricultural imports, the erstwhile free traders of the South and the West suddenly took the lead for protection. Roosevelt had no harder task during his first term than gaining a modest 20 percent reduction of duties on imports from the nation's own dependencies in the Caribbean and the Pacific.[20]

Nowhere were Roosevelt's stalwart sympathies more boldly underscored than in his reaction to these defeats and half-measures. He not only defended the "foundationstone" of the regime, he defended its chief defenders against the assaults of his personal loyalists. In one of his more remarkable protests, Roosevelt scolded William Howard Taft, then the governor general of the Philippines, for reproaching the leader of the protectionists in Congress, Rhode Island Senator Nelson Aldrich, after the Philippine trade agreement failed to pass the Senate.

> You are unjust to Senator Aldrich. My experience for the past year and a half . . . has made me feel respect and regard for Aldrich as one of that group of senators, including Allison, Hanna, Spooner, Platt of Connecticut, Lodge and one or two others, who together with men like the next speaker of the house, Joe Cannon, are the most powerful factors in Congress. With every one of these men I at times differ radically on important questions; but they are the leaders, and their great intelligence and power and their desire to do what is best for the government, make them not only essential to work with but desirable to work with. Several of the leaders have special friends whom they desire to favor, or special interests with which they are connected and which they hope to serve. But, taken as a body, they are broad-minded and patriotic, as well as sagacious, skillful and resolute.[21]

In this case, Aldrich had in fact supported the administration. Philippine exports posed little threat to eastern manufacturers, and the senator thoroughly enjoyed forcing the presumably low-tariff westerners to take the lead in defeating the bill. In general, however, Taft was quite right to peg Aldrich as an opponent of reciprocity; and, as we shall see, this would not be the last time that the supposedly more progressive Roosevelt would urge his supposedly less reform-minded protégé to respect his party's arch-conservatives.

Much as he himself respected the "leaders," Roosevelt could not afford simply to ignore the pressures for reform. As the one official who had to "reckon with the temper of the party as a whole," he was tormented by the "ugly fact" that between the Aldrich protectionists and the Iowa-idea reformers a dangerous rift was brewing within the Republican ranks.[22] On the eve of a western trip that was critical to his preparations for the 1904 Republican convention, Roosevelt called Aldrich and other leading Republican senators to a meeting at his home in Oyster Bay. Foremost on his mind was how to handle the budding western interest in the Iowa idea.[23] In a speech given in Indiana, the President outlined the compromise. While mounting a strong defense of protection, he called for a commission of experts that might recommend incremental rate adjustments where necessary.

> We need to devise some machinery by which, while persevering in the policy of a protective tariff, in which I think the nation as a whole has now generally acquiesced, we would be able to correct the irregularities produced by changing conditions, without destroying the whole structure. Such machinery would permit us to continue our definitely settled tariff policy, while providing for the changes in duties upon particular schedules which must inevitably and necessarily take place from time to time as matters of legislative and administrative detail. This would secure the needed stability of economic policy which is the prime factor in our industrial success, while doing away with any tendency to fossilization.[24]

This was not only a classic statement of the leadership posture of the orthodox-innovator but also a classic statement of Roosevelt's particular solution to the problem of orthodox-innovation. Through the construction of new administrative instruments, Roosevelt offered to take conflicts brewing within the ranks into new institutional forums within the executive branch, there to hammer out with experts any changes that might be needed and to limit their disruptive political consequences. The tariff commission idea had in fact been hatched by McKinley himself to shepherd his sharply protective tariff bill through Congress in 1890. Surely Aldrich and the other leaders would remember that. Moreover, Roosevelt had gone directly to the people and told them that something new could in fact be done about their concerns. Surely midwestern Republicans would appreciate that.

But ingenious as his designs were, Roosevelt could not make the tariff issue go away with speeches and good intentions, and the closer he got to the 1904 campaign, the more concerned he grew about the risks of action. "There is no need for revision at all," he wrote testily about this time:

> I believe that business would be better off if we could have it understood definitely that for the next four or five years there would be under no circumstances a revision, and that our policy in consequence was absolutely stable. But there is a strong sentiment for revision. There is an equally strong sentiment against it. It may well be that the attempt to revise the tariff will split the Republican party wide open and insure defeat. It may be that failure to make the attempt will insure its defeat . . . We have to fight straight on the tariff issue this time. We cannot promise revision. All we can say is what I have said, namely, that whenever necessary it is to be revised, but that the Republican party should revise it.[25]

Accordingly, Roosevelt accepted the Republican presidential nomination in 1904 with a message that denounced those who would "uproot and destroy the protective system." Again he argued that only those firmly committed to the view that protection was "definitely established" as the nation's policy could be trusted to undertake any change in the tariff.[26]

But would those so committed undertake a change? Just after his landslide victory Roosevelt decided to feel out the party leaders on the tariff reform "to be sure that I go right up to the breaking point but not beyond it."[27] He was having "great difficulty on the tariff business" in December 1904 as he prepared to outline the reform program he had just promised the nation. "I am not meeting a material need but a mental attitude," he reasoned. "What I am concerned about is to meet the expectation of the people that we shall consider the tariff question, and the need of showing that the Republican party is not powerless to take up the subject."[28] Powerlessness, however, is precisely what Roosevelt ultimately demonstrated. He bargained away his proposal for a special commission to report on the tariff in return for conservative support of his much-heralded initiative on railroad regulation.[29]

Trading away a threat to expose the foundationstone in return for conservative support for other administrative reforms that might be built upon it was another astute move for a leader determined to fashion a great departure without changing fundamentals. Roosevelt had used this troublesome issue to his best advantage by gaining some much needed leverage with the Old Guard, and he could now use that leverage to bind the West to the regime in a host of other less dangerous ways. Moreover, Roosevelt got what he really wanted all along, a way of avoiding any action on the tariff for the next "four or five years."

In the interim, of course, the issue continued to fester. In the fall of 1907, as Roosevelt prepared to confront the Old Guard on a host of other reforms, his thoughts turned to the tariff once again. This time it was not prosperity that advised against any tampering with rates but the rumblings of economic distress. About to unveil his most radical message yet, he still thought it best to wait until after the next election to address the issue of tariff reform.

> The one way we can be absolutely certain of getting bad times is to have the Republican party undertake to revise the tariff next winter. If we had meddled with the tariff before this we should have had bad times already. If we escape a panic now, as I hope and believe we shall, the present check will be ultimately a benefit; and then, immediately after the next election, I think the Republican party should undertake the revision, not that there is any great need of it, but because public sentiment demands it.[30]

On the tariff issue, then, trimming is what Roosevelt did best. He juggled his commitment to action on the tariff until he had one foot out the door, and when he finally did embrace it as his own issue, it was to give Taft's nomination a much-needed boost. Taft, Roosevelt argued, was the Republican party's surest bet for tariff revision: "The Republican party ought to and will go into the next election committed in good faith to taking up the revision of the tariff immediately afterwards, I believe. If the reactionaries can get for their standard bearer some good man like Knox, or Cannon, or Hughes, you can say goodbye to tariff reform; for such a man, however excellent personally, would be nominated by the interests that mean to have a reversal of the policies for which Taft and I stand."[31]

But even at this late date, well after his political relations with the Old Guard had broken down, Roosevelt offered Taft the same advice he had given him in 1903. After securing his protégé's election, he urged him to work with, rather than against, the conservative protectionists who formed the core of the old Republican establishment. Roosevelt had endorsed Taft's effort to turn the tariff into the centerpiece of the promise to continue the Roosevelt reforms, but when Taft indicated that he would open the fight for revision by supporting the western progressives in their upcoming battle against Joe Cannon's new bid for the House speakership, Roosevelt balked. Indeed, TR joined Elihu Root in heading off the President-elect and preventing any such breach with the Old Guard. He helped arrange a meeting between Taft and Cannon where the new President agreed to support the reactionary Speaker in return for the Speaker's pledge of support for tariff reform. A similar arrangement seems to have been reached with Aldrich in the Senate.[32]

Taft knew firsthand that by 1908 Roosevelt had himself exhausted the strategy of working reform through the Old Guard and that if he was to make good on his pledge to continue the Rooseveltian initiative, he would have to take a different tack. When, on Roosevelt's advice and against his better instincts, Taft ultimately made his peace with the conservatives, he sold himself short.[33] Instantly, he relinquished his claim to leadership of the rising, Roosevelt-inspired progressive wing of the party; and the progressives, finally out from under Roosevelt's moderating hand, fueled their insurgency with cries of Taft's betrayal. Well they might, for the conservative's tariff bill turned out to be travesty of reform. The dreaded party schism quickly became a reality anyway, and when Taft faced Roosevelt afterward, he was de facto a leader of the forces of reaction.[34]

Uplifting the Superstructure

Roosevelt's orthodoxy in tending to the foundationstone of the Republican regime was but a premise for vigorous action and far-ranging innovation on other fronts. In Roosevelt's reading of the American Constitution, the presidency carried more authority and greater opportunity for independent action than any comparable institution found in the great states of Europe. As a president, he saw himself the steward of the people free to do just about anything on their behalf that was not expressly forbidden him by law. Full use of the potential of the office to serve the nation was not a choice, in his view; it was a duty.[35]

Roosevelt did not claim to have invented this "stewardship theory" of the presidency. To him, it merely explicated the leadership posture that had been assumed by presidents like Jackson and Lincoln. Even here, however, the most remarkable thing about Roosevelt's exercise of power is his sensitivity to the political responsibilities it carried. Roosevelt was ever careful to balance what he saw as the potential of his office to electrify politics with what he saw as his responsibility to guarantee that change proceeded in an "orderly" fashion.[36] "I have just as much trouble preventing the demagogues from going too far," he wrote, "as in making those who are directly or indirectly responsive to Wall Street go far enough."[37]

Roosevelt scorned Jackson's impulsiveness and he spoke conscientiously of the differences between Lincoln's "leadership in adversity" and his own leadership "when all things flourish."[38] His preoccupation with Lincoln went far beyond the usual Republican gesticulations to the savior of the Union and the founder of the regime. Lincoln was a model leader in Roosevelt's eyes, but one whose example he dared not follow too closely. Lincoln stood in Roosevelt's mind as a constant reminder of the contingent character of leadership possibilities and of the historicity of legitimate presidential action. In revealing what it was possible to achieve in the gravest of circumstances, Lincoln's example cautioned Roosevelt that he himself had been given a "lesser" or "lighter task." In revealing the primacy of the fight for right, Lincoln's example carried to Roosevelt a stern warning against demagogic self-indulgence. In underscoring the peculiar circumstances in which the great destructive forces of his office could be unleashed in a truly heroic manner, Lincoln's example urged Roosevelt to demonstrate the virtues of patience, temperance, and self-restraint.[39]

Roosevelt repeated the admonition that context sets the boundaries of dutiful service as if he constantly needed to remind himself of that fact. "At times, a great crisis comes in which a great people, perchance led by a great man, can at white heat strike some mighty blow for the right—-make some long stride in advance along the path of justice and of orderly liberty. But normally we must be content if each of us can do something—not all that we wish, but something—for the advancement of those principles of righteousness which underlie all real national greatness, all true civilization and freedom."[40] This keen sensitivity to doing only what was appropriate for the moment suggests that Roosevelt saw himself as something of a constrained giant in the presidency.[41] Yet, the overriding facts of the case are that Roosevelt flourished along with the regime he protected. Poking and prodding those reluctant to change things to a higher level of achievement were what he did best.

Like the great orthodox-innovators who preceded him, Roosevelt tapped the strength of the established regime most effectively when asserting American power in international affairs. With the results of America's muscle-flexing war with Spain confirmed by the election of 1900, the major political question of the recent past had been answered conclusively so far as Roosevelt was concerned. The nation's destiny had become manifest once again. There could no longer be any doubt that America was to be a major player among world powers. The constructive work at hand was to demonstrate to all concerned that the nation would play its part effectively.[42]

To this end, Roosevelt determined to do some muscle flexing of his own. Not unlike Polk, he moved simultaneously north and south, pressing Great Britain to settle a boundary dispute between the United States and Canada and recasting claims of hemispheric hegemony to protect the United States' interests in Latin America. With regard to the latter, Roosevelt expanded upon claims first set forth by Monroe and then significantly recast by Polk. His own corollary to the Monroe Doctrine was, he said, designed to bring old precepts into line with our "growing and changing conditions" so that our neighbors to the South would remain free to develop "onward and upward." America's Latin neighbors were less sanguine about Roosevelt's assertion that the United States had special rights of supervision over Central and South America, but in making the case, Roosevelt staked out a pivotal position for the nation in the balance of world power.[43]

Roosevelt was at his boldest in putting his vision of American world power into effect. He consummated a revolution in Panama, secured exclusive American control over the long-anticipated isthmian canal, and began a "constructive" improvement of unrivaled proportions. Lest the rest of the world not get his message, he pressed, along with his canal project, an unprecedented peacetime program of "upbuilding the Navy" and later celebrated his achievement by sending his Great White Fleet on a world tour. After all, he warned, reluctance to back up the nation's riches with military power would "invite destruction."[44]

When building in concrete and steel—when building the Panama Canal or building a world-class Navy—Roosevelt projected a relatively straightforward relationship between presidential initiative and the evolving commercial interests of the Republican regime. To be sure, consummating the Panamanian revolution, agitating for more battleships, and sending the fleet around the world were not uncontroversial acts. But presidential power directed outward was suffered with relative impunity on the Republican front at home. Moreover, this party had always had a soft spot for great public works projects. That enthusiasm was evident on the domestic side of Roosevelt's agenda as well as on the foreign. Along with building the canal and building the Navy, Roosevelt promoted vast irrigation works to develop the West.

Roosevelt's ambitions on the domestic side went far beyond public works, however. He believed that the most important challenge before him was to construct a managerial capability in the federal government commensurate with the scale and scope of the new economy the Republicans had shepherded through the years.[45] As he told the editor Albert Shaw, the "methods of government for regulation ought by rights to proceed step by step with the development of new business conditions."[46] Building a federal superstructure that would "uplift" the moral tenor of the nation's economic activity was, in his view, a task not only compatible with support for the existing foundations of power, but one absolutely essential to protecting and preserving them.

It was in the course of this effort that Roosevelt negotiated the first major departure from the nineteenth century's more narrow, party-based forms of presidential action and forged the broader, more pluralistic structure that would become predominant over the course of the twentieth century.[47] Supplementing party organization here and displacing it there, he opened several new avenues of executive action. Roosevelt established a more direct relationship between the presidency and the public, a more direct relationship between the presidency and the leaders of national organizations (business and labor) in the private sector, and, through his expanded national administrative arm, a more direct role for the presidency in the promulgation and management of national policy.[48] His office became a "bully pulpit" used to rouse popular support for presidential initiatives on selected topics. It became a more autonomous center of governing, able to tap the professional expertise and administrative capacities of an expanded executive establishment. And it became a new forum for negotiating complex bargains with the leaders of other national institutions, public and private. Roosevelt all but announced this new state of affairs in the way he met the first great challenge of his presidency, settling the anthracite coal strike of 1902. Bringing the leaders of industry, labor, and the federal government together for the first time, Roosevelt held himself up as first among equals in industrial affairs. The strike became an occasion to make a pointed public display of the usefulness of the executive office in resolving the disputes now endemic to a nation of interdependent economic interests.[49]

While these innovations constituted the most important departures in governmental organization and political procedure since the Jackson era, they were more than merely a functional adaptation to the governing imperatives of a new era. The meaning and content of Roosevelt's response to industrialism was inextricably bound up with his earnest quest for a *Republican* response. He sought to fashion innovations that would serve his twin purposes: to respond to demands for change *and* to maintain established political commitments. In this regard, the bluster from the bully pulpit screened a painstaking, hands-on management of ideas and interests. Roosevelt was continually balancing the message of "the people" to "the leaders" against the message of "the leaders" to "the people." He manipulated each into a program he could safely call his own.

There was more to this than mere trimming, although, as we have seen from his handling of the tariff, that was certainly part of it. In fact, however, Roosevelt's whistlestop endorsement of a tariff commission was but one aspect of a far more intricate bit of political management touching a host of interconnected issues. The "Iowa idea" had tied tariff revision to antitrust sentiment. But by the winter of 1902–3, Roosevelt had already pressed his own initiative on the trusts. He had insisted on the creation of a powerful Bureau of Corporations at the heart of the newly created Department of Commerce and Labor, and he had carried the day by publicizing Standard Oil's opposition to the proposal and compelling Republican lawmakers to confront the true depth of public hostility to corporate power. The new bureau, with its power to investigate and, at the President's discretion, expose corrupt corporate practices, was the pride of Rooseveltian reform in the early years.[50] Thus, when Roosevelt went west to the people and delivered the message of "the leaders" who had recently caucused at Oyster Bay, he did more than mount a staunch defense of the protective tariff and more than endorse a tariff commission to consider any adjustments that might be necessary. He also staked out his claim to national leadership on the trust question.

First, he pointedly separated what the Iowa idea had connected. He denounced the "revolutionary and destructive" implications of trying "to reach the trust question by means of the tariff."[51] Then, he took the "anti" out of trust regulation. "I always hate to have them called anti-trust laws or anti-corporation laws because they are not designed to hurt any corporation, they are simply designed for such regulations and controls as will prevent the doing of ill."[52] Finally, he reiterated his promise that the national government would "assume power of super-vision and regulation of all corporations doing an interstate business," and as evidence of that commitment he cited, among other things, the establishment of the Bureau of Corporations.[53]

This scrupulous management of ideas and interests, complete with the key distinction between preserving the foundations and building a more effective superstructure, is the hallmark of Roosevelt's leadership. As his tariff commission idea looked toward preserving the protective principle, his Bureau of Corporations provided a vehicle for the control of business that would not be *anti*trust. Each proposal promised bold and substantive action, but the changes anticipated were to be wholly affirmative. Through the expansion of national administrative capaci-ties, the regime was to gain a capacity to respond decisively to the issues of the day without suffering adverse affects on any of its basic commit-ments. On trusts, tariffs, railroads, and natural resources, Rooseveltian state-building reached out one hand to the people (offering a palpable sign of governmental attention to their concerns) and the other to the leaders (with a promise to relieve the incipient conflicts brewing within the party coalition). Through the enlightened councils of administration experts and the political judgment of a loyal Republican president, bold action was to be reconciled with stability and the old order accommo-dated to the new age.

There were, however, some obvious points of tension in the execution of this project; and as Roosevelt showed just how much could be accomplished on the terms he set forth, he brought those tensions into the very center of national politics. The President asked for the con-fidence of both "the leaders" and "the people" as he expanded his own powers and built a state apparatus that would, in effect, have a sub-stantial amount of autonomy in reshaping the ideas and interests on which it drew. The extrapartisan politics Roosevelt was designing to serve his party's higher purposes was therefore susceptible to being interpreted by any aggrieved element of the party as an independent, personalized politics designed simply to aggrandize the powers of the presidency itself. Roosevelt's intense manipulation of ideas and interests at the top inevitably added to the political pressures on all sides of the Republican coalition, so that by the time the great steward of Republican hegemony left office, his dream of a party revitalized under the banner of progressive reform had given way to a much harsher reality. The bureaucratically managed consensus had broken down; political confrontation and sectarian division had become the order of the day.

Even at the height of his powers, in 1905–6, Roosevelt's bargaining with Republican leaders in Congress proved bruising. Especially brutal was his effort to deliver on his campaign promise to strengthen national railroad regulation through the Interstate Commerce Commission. As we have seen, the President in 1905 treated tariff reform as "a matter of expediency," and willingly bargained it away to garner conservative support for his railroad regulation initiative.[54] The agreement worked effectively enough in the House where Speaker Joe Cannon facilitated action on a bill the President liked, but in the Senate, Nelson Aldrich seemed to go out of his way to embarrass the President and expose his leadership project as a sham. First, the senator pushed Roosevelt to embrace a proposal more radical than that which he had originally recommended by handing control over the railroad debate to a southern Democrat. Then, Aldrich forced Roosevelt to accept the inevitability of defeat unless he abandoned the radicals and deferred to the Republican leadership on a compromise proposal that was more conservative than the one he had originally supported. In accepting the compromise, Roosevelt claimed a great victory for moderation against both extremes. And yet Aldrich had made his point. He had let the reformers indict themselves as too radical for his party's conservatives, and he had pushed Roosevelt to indict himself as too conservative for the truly reform-minded. The first move threw into question Roosevelt's dependability as a party leader; the second, his credentials as a steward of the people against the "interests." Robert La Follette, the emergent leader of the Republican progressives, was disgusted by the President's waffling; Roosevelt himself became embittered toward the Old Guard.[55]

Then, in the first half of 1907, the West opened its own attack on the President's managerial pretensions. The program in question, resource conservation, was the thematic centerpiece of the entire Roosevelt reform effort. The conservation initiative aimed to end the unrestrained destruction of the nation's resources and to begin, under the auspices of administrative experts working in new national bureaucracies, the constructive management of resources to ensure their long-term productivity.[56] The program depended on the President's using his discretionary authority aggressively to cut through the intense conflicts of interest that arose over access to natural resources at the local level. Roosevelt pushed this authority to its limits. He had his special Commission on Department Methods investigate the inefficiency of the old land office; he employed the Secret Service to uncover fraud and political corruption in land sales; he removed more and more public land from sale; and he created more and more national forests under the stricter supervision of his new Forest Service Bureau. Budding western resentment of the new national controls culminated in a standoff between the executive and legislative branches after the midterm elections of 1906. Early in 1907, Congress passed a rider to the Department of Agriculture's appropriation bill forbidding the creation of new national forests except by act of Congress, but Roosevelt, with the bill on his desk awaiting his signature, issued an executive order that added twenty-one additional forests. The President's claim that he could do anything except what the law explicitly forbade came down here to a blatant act of bad faith, and for this, a sizeable western bloc signaled its readiness to join the already sizeable eastern bloc in denouncing "executive despotism." In retaliation, Congress took aim at Roosevelt's superstructure and scuttled the work of his Commission on Department Methods, his Inland Waterways Commission, and his National Country Life Commission. Furthermore, it formally restricted his use of the Secret Service. When, on the eve of his departure, Roosevelt publically denounced this last action as congressional protection for criminals, Cannon rallied an overwhelming majority in the House to formally rebuke him.[57]

Finally, there was the precarious dependence of Roosevelt's political project on the regime's economic performance. The President had urged the people to "feel the pulse of prosperity" before contemplating radical reforms, and he had urged "the leaders" to accept reform as a stabilizing influence. The economic downturn in the fall of 1907 tore simultaneously into both sides of his message and cut the ground out from under Roosevelt's whole case for orthodox-innovation. The business community came down hard on the President, blaming his reforms and the broader movement his reforms were fueling for inciting the economic panic.[58] Roosevelt, genuinely worried about the economic situation and stung by an attack that labeled him the nation's leading economic "destroyer," finally faced an unbridgeable chasm between his political reputation as a reform agitator and his political intentions as a regime booster. "I am well aware," he commented in the midst of the panic, "how difficult it is to get people to understand what is said or to read what is said. The yellow press has endeavored to misrepresent me by stating that I have not gone far enough in attacking the dishonest rich. It is the so-called conservative press, the capitalist press, that has misrepresented me by stating that I have gone too far."[59]

The potential for cooperation with Congress vanished with the panic. Speaker Cannon, disgusted with the President's treatment of business during the crisis, finally gave up on him; and Roosevelt, embittered by the conservative attack on him, reached out to the "innocents" who bore the brunt of corporate greed. The proposals he ventured at this juncture for social justice, business regulation, and judicial restraint lit a fire under the fledgling progressive movement and sent his party's conservatives into an advanced state of rage.[60]

Roosevelt's uncertainty about the political effects of his own handiwork was revealed at this stage in the way he qualified his counterattack in his private letters. Casting the blame for the panic squarely on irresponsible financial speculators, he worried that his reform efforts might well have precipitated the economic instability a year or two sooner than would have been the case otherwise.[61] Moreover, during the political stalemate that ensued over further reforms, Roosevelt became quite lenient in his private bargains with economic leaders. In various negotiations with representatives of J. P. Morgan, he moved quickly to bolster New York City's banks against the demands of their depositors. He called off the Justice Department from its pursuit of a Bureau of Corporations investigation of International Harvester, and he guaranteed United States Steel immunity from prosecution in a dubious buy-out of the Tennessee Coal and Iron Company. The one legislative achievement of his last Congress that gave Roosevelt genuine satisfaction (indeed it was one of the few recommendations from the imposing reform package that Roosevelt had sent up on which Congress took any action at all) was the Aldrich-Vreeland Currency Act to provide for a more elastic currency in any future panic. On this issue,

Roosevelt stood by Aldrich against a virulent assault from his party's progressive wing.[62]

From beginning to end Roosevelt saw himself as a president who could put to rest the "well defined opinion growing up among the people that the Republican party had become unduly subservient to the so-called Wall Street men."[63] But throughout his administration, he wavered on the question of how much of the problem was mere attitude and how much was substantive. He acted as if he could go as far as he wished in challenging the opinion so long as he did not do too much to disturb the reality, and by the time he left office, American politics was thoroughly caught up in his confusion of purposes. Ironically, on the day that the House censured Roosevelt for abusing the Secret Service, the more conservative Senate publicly criticized him for allowing the merger of Tennessee Coal with U.S. Steel in violation of the antitrust laws.[64]

Commitments and Betrayals

For all the political furor and personal recrimination that gripped the Republican party during Roosevelt's last months in office, it is easy to forget the saving grace upon which it was all premised. Roosevelt had anchored his reform agitation in an act as clear in its recognition of his responsibility to the regime he represented as it was stunning in its self-denial: he had pledged not to stand for reelection in 1908. Roosevelt's pledge, unlike the one Polk had made in 1844, was not ventured from a position of weakness when it was crucial to gain the support of disappointed contenders for the nomination in the upcoming election campaign; it was made, rather, a moment after he had won the largest landslide victory to date. The difference is considerable—Roosevelt could never be construed as a mere creature of the party organization—but this should not obscure the more fundamental point. For an orthodox-innovator determined to lead, the promise of abdication was still the ultimate justification for self-assertion.

Attuned to the tragedy of Roosevelt's future as a progressive leader, scholars tend to look upon this pledge to step aside as the biggest mistake of his political career.[65] And yet, from the vantage point of the leadership project he was pursuing in the presidency, it might be better appreciated as a brilliant political overture to the exercise of power in his own right. An affiliated leader, genuinely dedicated to regime maintenance but determined to use an overwhelming election victory to enact his own vision of appropriate change, Roosevelt did exactly what he had to do to demonstrate that he was exercising power in good faith. The abdication pledge was a standing refutation of the inevitable charges of power-mongering, and, at the same time, it was a license to press the powers of the presidential office emphatically. It gave the weight of self-sacrifice to the idea of aggressive maintenance; it held personal ambition to the vision of building a superstructure that would enhance, not displace, the existing foundations; it promised to preserve the integrity of the regime in exchange for a real chance to lead it.

Long into his elected term Roosevelt could have changed his mind (as Jackson had) and had a second nomination for the asking. He said, of course, that he wanted to uphold the two-term tradition, but technically there was no reason to take the three and half years he had served of McKinley's second term as his own first. There was more to it than that. As he reasoned the case in the wake of his surprise announcement:

> Suppose that there was no third term tradition in our government, and none of the valid reasons (as I regard them) against a third term; it would yet be true that in 1908 it would be better to have some man like Taft or Root succeed me in the Presidency, at the head of the Republican party, than to have me succeed myself. In all essentials of policy they look upon things as I do; but they have their own ways of thought and ways of expression, and what they did and said would have a freshness which what I did and said could not possibly have; and they would be free from the animosities and suspicions which I had accumulated, and would be able to make a new start and would have a much greater chance of achieving useful work. After eight years in the Presidency, not only is it unwise for other reasons to re-elect a man, but it is inadvisable because it is almost certain that someone can be found with the same principles, who, from the mere fact that he is someone else, can better succeed in putting those principles into practice.[66]

This statement touches the bedrock of Roosevelt's solution to the political disruptions engendered by his leadership. From it, we can make some sense of the curious course he pursued in 1908, when after agitating for his most radical reform proposals and coming to a Jackson-like confrontation with the congressional leaders, he helped persuade Taft not to press the attack but to pull back, to make peace with the Old Guard, and to continue reform by working with its most stubborn opponents. Roosevelt certainly wanted a successor who would protect and embellish his program, but it seems just as clear that he did not want someone who would merely pick up the battle where he had left off. Ever protective of the regime he led, he never thought of tapping one of the leaders of the emergent insurgency in the progressive wing of the party to carry on his work. He looked, instead, to two conservatives, Root and Taft, men who could be trusted to preserve the fruits of Republican power and hold reform to the standard of political practicality.[67] Taft was someone who shared Roosevelt's original premises, and one whose "new start" might retrieve those premises. Thus Roosevelt urged Taft to begin by going back to where he himself had begun, to try to manipulate the same interests in the same way. It was in this sense that Roosevelt reckoned a prospective Taft presidency even better than another term for himself. Taft could do what Roosevelt could not: repeat his own performance. Moreover, with such a man waiting in the wings, Roosevelt could embrace his last years without fear of the "animosities and suspicions" he was inciting. He could revel in his confrontation with the Old Guard, he could venture a reform program that he knew stood no chance of enactment, and he could go out the undiminished leader of the progressive forces at work in the nation. He could do all this, because he had confidence that Taft would set things straight again and start the process over.

Considering the extended coda to Roosevelt's leadership effort in this light, two points stand out for attention. The first is that as surely as Roosevelt wished Taft all the success he himself had enjoyed, he set him up to take the fall. What Roosevelt wanted Taft to do, he himself had already failed to do. That is, for all his self-consciousness about the political challenge of his presidency, Roosevelt had not transformed the superstructure of the Republican regime without instigating a concomitant change in its foundations.[68] It was a comforting idea—that after bringing the internal agitation within the Republican party to a dramatic climax, the President could pass the regime on intact by merely stepping aside and putting in his place someone who would retrieve the original premises of his actions. But it was also a preposterous idea. The political consequences of Roosevelt's increasingly militant call for reform could not be so easily finessed. In his public posture, he had all but sanctioned the insurgent movement against the Old Guard. More than anyone else, Roosevelt had given the burgeoning forces of "progressive" reform the stamp of political legitimacy. Unwittingly, he had jolted the regime's defenses and unhinged its politics. Thus, when Taft heeded his mentor's advice and pressed reform with an eye to "practicality," he brought Roosevelt face to face with the limitations of his own designs.

Part and parcel of this setup were Roosevelt's Lincolnian standards of judgment. He was thoroughly convinced that his had been a "lesser task" than Lincoln's and that it had resulted in "an ordinary kind of success." He told himself he had done nothing more than what "most of us can do" if we would only choose to do it.[69] Securing Taft's election and passing on a party that appeared not only intact but rededicated to constructive action only confirmed Roosevelt's convictions that he had mastered the political challenges of his presidency, and that in asking Taft to do the same thing he was not asking anything extraordinary. This belief, in turn, nurtured a host of more dangerous delusions, especially when Taft's efforts to maintain the momentum for reform in alliance with the Old Guard succumbed to the deep schisms within the ranks. One of these delusions was that Taft was to blame for the debacle: "I do think that we had the Republican party in a shape that warranted the practical continuance of just what we were doing. To announce allegiance to what had been done, and to abandon the only methods by which it was possible to continue to get it done, was not satisfactory from my standpoint."[70] Another of Roosevelt's delusions was that he could put things right again.

Roosevelt's initial impulse in reentering politics in 1910 was to save the Republican party from certain ruin. ("The administration has . . . wholly failed in keeping the party in substantial unity, and what I mind most is that the revolt is not merely among political leaders, but among the masses of the people."[71]) At first, saving the Republican party meant trying to bring the various factions together to support Taft again in 1912. To rally the party, Roosevelt took a swing through the West, preaching moderation, and then turned back East to preach the virtues of reform. The tour demonstrated that he still had great personal appeal, but it failed to stem the tide of disaster for the Republicans in the midterm elections. After that, saving the party entailed mounting a challenge to Taft's renomination and heading off the dread portents of a Democratic victory in 1912.

To this end, Roosevelt entered the presidential primaries to rally the party's rank and file to his own candidacy. Then he watched Elihu Root manage the Republican national convention on Taft's behalf. The message behind his primary sweep was ignored, his challenge dismissed. Nothing could have been better calculated to convince Roosevelt that "the Republican party had become pretty nearly hopeless"[72] than this rejection of him by "the leaders" in defiance of the will of "the people." He now reasoned that he had not betrayed his party, but that the party leadership had betrayed him. The time had finally come to take on that organization directly—to destroy it and build in its place a party that would give full field to his vision of constructive reform.[73] Here was the chance to do something truly extraordinary—to save by destroying—and Roosevelt seized it.

The second point to be made about Roosevelt's insurgency is that he failed to displace the Republican party for the very same reasons that he had failed to regenerate it from within: Roosevelt's vision of appropriate action was so intensely personal, so subtle in the distinctions it drew, and so thoroughly tied up with traditional Republican commitments that it was virtually impossible for anyone to see the stakes of the contest as he saw them. Roosevelt had once reminded Joe Cannon of "how incapable the average man is of drawing any distinction even of the broadest kind."[74] Now he proposed to return the nation to the constructive path he had charted in his presidential years and stave off the destructive impulses of the Democrats by himself destroying the very foundations of his own constructive achievements. As Roosevelt reasoned his way out of the guise of the orthodox-innovator and into the guise of a great repudiator, he toyed with the notion that what he was doing in founding a new party was exactly what the founders of the Republican party had done. "We should have a new party for practically the same reasons that in '56 it became necessary to break up the old Whig party and ultimately beat the Democratic party with the Republican organization."[75] He told himself that, like Lincoln, he had finally come to one of those crossroads in national affairs where a great crisis was unavoidable and truly heroic deeds had to be performed in the cause of moderation. And yet, even as he "stood at Armageddon" and prepared to "battle for the Lord," Roosevelt knew that this parallel was a weak one. "I am under no illusion about it" he wrote to a Justice Department official. Urging this officer to stay at his job rather than join the crusade, Roosevelt confessed: "It is a forlorn hope . . . Probably all the men who are with me in this fight will suffer more or less because they are with me and will gain nothing. Thank Heaven! I think I can conscientiously say that I myself will suffer most and gain least."[76]

Roosevelt had good reason to despair at the prospects for building a new party in the manner of the Republicans of 1856. Pieced together out of the sectarian wranglings within the dominant coalition, the coherence of the Progressive party under his lead was hopelessly compromised at every level. Up and down the line, the distinctive identity of the new organization hung on Roosevelt's increasingly personal vision of appropriate change. While all sides seemed to agree that certain fundamental commitments had been betrayed, there was little agreement as to what fundamental commitments separated one organization from another. For Roosevelt, Taft's ultimate act of betrayal—the act that finally prompted Roosevelt to mount a direct challenge for the Republican nomination—was to press the antitrust suit against U.S. Steel that he himself had let pass. While Taft counted the steel suit as one of his irrefutable progressive credentials—as a sign of his willingness to move against big business where even Roosevelt had hesitated—Roosevelt saw it as an insufferable personal insult. Taft had not only stabbed him in the back, he had failed utterly to respect the fine line Roosevelt had so painstakingly drawn in the steel case between constructive and destructive action.[77] In Taft's view, Roosevelt's final act of betrayal was to endorse judicial recall. More than anything else, this bit of "demagoguery" prompted Taft to stay in the presidential race against Roosevelt even when it was clear that he would be playing the part of the spoiler. For Taft, Roosevelt's assault on the Republican establishment had broached an assault on the rule of law itself. The problem, for Taft, was not that Roosevelt was a progressive; Taft's charge against Roosevelt was precisely the same as Roosevelt's charge against Taft. Each claimed that the other had crossed the critical but invisible line between constructive and destructive action.[78]

The confusions of purposes became even more pronounced when Roosevelt took hold of the insurgent progressives. Taft may have betrayed the progressives in signing a mockery of tariff reform, but Roosevelt also betrayed the progressives. He waffled in his condemnation of Taft's tariff, he refused to sanction a vigorous antitrust plank in the Progressive party platform, and his rather complicated notions of how to handle each of these critical reform issues passed both over to the Democrats. (Roosevelt's campaign was financed by Morgan interests, for alone among the candidates, he promised to avoid antitrust assaults on corporations and continue his staunch defense of regulated monopoly.) Important Progressive leaders, Robert La Follette most conspicuous among them, were outraged when Roosevelt peremptorily took over an insurgency he had previously refused to endorse and then set about tempering its positions. These progressives registered their commitment to real change by supporting the campaign of Woodrow Wilson. Still other Progressive leaders, like William Borah of Idaho, left Roosevelt feeling betrayed, for while they pushed him to challenge Taft for the nomination, they stood by their commitment to the Republican party and refused to support the formation of any new organization.[79]

By the time of the campaign, then, Roosevelt had turned the Progressive party into a personal organization to vent his frustrations with the self-evident failure of purely constructive action. The effect may have been cathartic but it was also self-defeating. The campaign gave him a chance to say "the things that were deepest in his heart and that he believed he would never have a chance to say,"[80] but this was just the kind of political self-indulgence he had resisted all his life. Even as he demonstrated his tremendous personal appeal, the negative result—defeat for Republicans and a sweeping victory of the Democrats—ran up against everything he had wanted progressive leadership to be.

Perhaps the greatest of Roosevelt's political achievements was that all three of the major candidates in 1912 claimed to be progressive reformers.[81] This was no mean accomplishment given the stand-pat conservative note on which he had taken the presidency in 1901. But Roosevelt himself reckoned it a dubious triumph. How, he wondered in his postmortem on the election, was he to build a new party when all the parties in the contest were claiming the same ground? After all he had gone through to speak in his own voice and offer leadership in his own terms, he had to admit that his terms were not all that different from his opponents'. For all that he had done as president and as party builder, Roosevelt had fashioned an insurgent force with nothing to repudiate.

> Unfortunately, it is not with us as it was with the Republicans in '56 after their defeat. We have not the clear cut issues as to which we take one side and our opponents the other side . . . in consequence it is a matter of incredible difficulty to shake loose from the old parties many men who profess adherence to our principles. Wilson and Taft both fervidly announce themselves as Progressives, and as regards most of our principles they make believe to be for them, and simply to disagree with us as to the methods of putting them into effect.[82]

Roosevelt's experiment with reconstructive politics was short-lived. He quickly gave up on his Progressive party and, after an appropriate interval, moved back to the Republican fold. To see him as a failed reconstructive leader, a lesser light standing between Abraham Lincoln and Franklin Roosevelt, is a mistake, however. The pressure he applied to the distinction between rearticulating a regime's purposes and reconstructing it wholesale tells us more about the development of the politics of leadership than the failure of his reconstructive crusade itself. As an orthodox-innovator rubbing hard against the boundaries of a politics of articulation, Roosevelt holds an important place between James Polk and Lyndon Johnson. There he stands as a reliable signpost of the changing shape of political possibilities.

Part Three:
Herbert Hoover's Disjunction

> We have not feared boldly to adopt unprecedented
> measures to meet the unprecedented violence of the
> storm. But, because we have kept ever before us these
> eternal principles of our Nation, the American
> Government in its ideals is the same as it was when
> the people gave the Presidency
> into my trust.

HIS PRESIDENCY linked by happenstance to a national economic catastrophe, Herbert Hoover chafed at the thought that the American people would have no other recollection of him. Determined to set the record straight in his memoirs, he cast the linkage a great misfortune which had sidetracked an otherwise vital reform effort. Carefully, Hoover sorted out his "reform and development activities" from his measures to combat the Depression. Cataloging the extraordinary range of his concerns in the first area, he conveyed a sense of what might have been had his efforts not been so tragically "interrupted."[1] Here was a man of unique experience, high achievement, and broad national vision, one who under other circumstances might well have risen to the reform standard of his hero, Theodore Roosevelt. Here also was the pathos of one so gifted to find himself in 1929, less than a year into his presidency, the steward of an intractable crisis that mercilessly crushed the highest hopes of a great life of public service.

Whatever might be said for this assessment, its implications for a general understanding of presidential leadership are worth some reflection. Recall that Theodore Roosevelt himself had just the opposite complaint about his own place in history. By his lights, the real misfortune for a man of high ambition and broad vision was to lead at a time "when all things flourish." Believing that great presidential leadership could only be spawned by a great national crisis, Roosevelt was haunted by the thought that, but for the absence of such a challenge, he might have risen to the standard of *his* hero, Abraham Lincoln. Then, of course, there is the example of Hoover's successor, Franklin Roosevelt. Hoover and FDR grappled with the same crisis, but the latter was able to turn it to his political advantage and to emerge from it the master politician of the twentieth century. Why then was the onset of the Great Depression a great misfortune for Hoover and not a great opportunity? What precisely is the relationship between great national crises and great presidential leadership?

Recent reassessments of Hoover's intentions and actions demand that we specify answers to these questions carefully. The revisionists have taken direct aim at popular images of Hoover's incompetence, and they have dispelled the myth of an intransigent, laissez faire ideologue hostaged to business interests and impervious to the plight of the American people. The Hoover we know about today is more like the Hoover of the memoirs. He was indeed the leading political innovator of the 1920s and a worthy heir of the progressive legacy of Roosevelt and Wilson.[2] No friend of the "fatalists" who believed that natural laws ruled the marketplace like a dispensation of Providence, he was the most prominent advocate of a "New Era" in thinking about the nation's political economy. From his position in the Commerce Department, Hoover promoted the newly emerging science of economic management, and though the fates would defy him, he believed that government had a positive role to play in controlling the dismal cycles of boom and bust.[3]

This new appreciation extends beyond the great promise of Hoover's prepresidential career to encompass the unprecedented steps he took to counter the effects of the Depression itself. Even as the economic crisis engulfed his presidency, Hoover remained active and methodically tested a range of different responses. Far from ignoring the severity of the situation, he employed the metaphors of wartime to combat it and became the first American president to meet a downturn in the business cycle with massive governmental interventions. Far from being shocked into paralysis, he secured virtually all his major proposals, including some critical departures from past practice. Far from standing fast against innovation, his administration anticipated much of what would occur during the early years of the New Deal.[4]

Finally, we know that while Hoover's policies did not bring recovery, neither did those of his more celebrated successor. Again, why would one great innovator fail so miserably and the next succeed so brilliantly?

To the extent that Hoover revisionism adds credence to the "great misfortune" thesis, it makes an especially powerful case for political time in the explanation of presidential possibilities. Notwithstanding Theodore Roosevelt's longings and Franklin Roosevelt's example, Hoover's experience highlights a dismal half-truth in the commonplace that great national crises spawn great political leaders. Not only does it remind us that a crisis tends to cut two ways—crushing one incumbent while elevating the next—it strongly suggests that the outcome turns rather bluntly on the incumbent's political identity vis-à-vis the established regime. Despite his considerable efforts and manifest achievements, Hoover had little more success in political leadership than James Buchanan, for, like Buchanan, he was inextricably tied to the governmental commitments that events were calling into question. With political warrants wholly inadequate to controlling the meaning of his actions in the moment at hand, Hoover became the foil for a resurgent opposition bent on a general repudiation of the established regime. Actions addressed to the crisis, even those that marked dramatic departures from past practice, were reduced to symbols of the political bankruptcy of the old order. The most visible representative of a vulnerable regime, Hoover was caught in the impossible leadership situation.

The structural insight implicit in the "great misfortune" thesis is that no Republican president is likely to have survived the legitimation crisis that gripped the old order in the Great Depression.[5] And yet, carrying the thesis beyond that requires utmost caution. A more dubious implication is that the Depression stifled what otherwise might have been another great reform presidency. We have good reason to doubt the proposition that the mere continuation of "Republican prosperity" would have supported another round of reform like the one delivered by Theodore Roosevelt. Speculation about what might have been, had Hoover not encountered the Great Depression, must turn on more than an appreciation of his talents, achievements, and ambitions, if only because Theodore Roosevelt's own leadership effort had real political consequences for the prospects of another Republican reformer in the presidency. Hoover could no more repeat Roosevelt's performance than Taft could, for Roosevelt had generated schismatic divisions over reform that now ran deep within the Republican ranks. The fates of John Quincy Adams and Franklin Pierce are especially relevant here, for they alert us to the general pattern among ambitious late-regime affiliates.

These presidents tend to tread on the most brittle political ground, and their most forceful actions precipitate debilitating political crises quite independent of wars or depressions.

When Hoover's experience is tuned to the plight of other late-regime affiliates, the recent revisionist accounts suggest something quite contrary to the great misfortune thesis. These comparisons suggest that the Depression did more to extend than to contract Hoover's lease on political creativity. When his accomplishments are set against the backdrop of recurrent and emergent patterns in the politics of leadership, speculation about what he might have done becomes more dubious but analysis of what he was able to do becomes more interesting. In this frame, the most remarkable thing about the national calamity that engulfed Hoover's presidency is not that it crushed his leadership, but that it kept him going.

Hoover took charge of a political regime wracked by decades of sectarian controversy. In the full blush of prosperity, he crafted a leadership posture as delicate as it was ingenious; committed to innovation, it hovered innocuously over a regime bereft of political consensus. It is especially significant in this regard that the collapse of Hoover's control over the political definition of his actions preceded the collapse of the economy. Like that of his counterparts in political time, Hoover's initial leadership posture proved so delicate that it crumbled immediately before the demands of his own supporters.

The onset of the Depression certainly did not help Hoover resolve this typical legitimation problem, but it did open up new possibilities for a modern president already caught in its grip. The policy achievements Hoover extorted from the dismal logic of his political situation appear in this light as benchmarks of the secular evolution of the executive office. Though politically crippled even before the Crash, Hoover could draw afterwards on the widening responsibilities of the presidency in managing the nation's economy and on the undercurrent of expanding institutional resources that came with them. The broader purview of the presidency in the pluralist polity enhanced his independence in political action and grounded a succession of presidential initiatives on crisis management pure and simple. Though he never regained control over the meaning of his actions, Hoover was a far more powerful political agent than his counterparts in political time, and with this power he forged a substantive response to the charges of regime bankruptcy that was all his own.

The irony behind the crosscurrents of change structuring Hoover's leadership is that this president ultimately did far more to meet the crisis than his feeble political warrants would permit him to recognize. Hoover's boast on entering the presidency is painfully familiar: he wanted to tap the unrealized potential of the old regime without undermining its essential integrity, and he claimed special knowledge of the administrative techniques necessary to get the job done. True to the end to his technocratic discipline, he asked the American people to stay the course in 1932 and to reject "so called new deals which would destroy the very foundations of the American system."[6] The fact is, however, that while Hoover was invoking his rarefied rules of appropriate action, he was also recasting basic regime commitments. Indeed, under the pressures of the moment, he reworked the old rules so thoroughly that today some wonder about how much of a break the New Deal actually represented. While at one level Hoover was being crushed for his scruples in a politics of disjunction, he was at another level displaying striking independence in making things up as he went along. Not only was he prepared to defy his self-professed standards of appropriate action (Franklin Pierce had done that much), he was able to continue a largely personal course, and in the end to point the government in a new direction from which it would not depart even after he himself had been thoroughly repudiated.

The Reification of Technique

The Republican party might well have elected any of the candidates who offered themselves for its nomination in 1928. As it basked in the euphoria of boom times, the Democrats decided to gamble on running a Catholic for president. Al Smith threatened to mobilize urban, ethnic, working-class voters against Prohibition, but with that he also threatened to alienate other traditional Democratic constituencies. Republicans had little reason to fear defeat and even less awareness of the broader agenda that Smith's urban Democrats might harbor.

As it turned out, however, the GOP made an unusual choice in 1928. Indeed, one would have to go back to John Quincy Adams to find a contender as politically formidable for his service in the federal bureaucracy or as intent on positioning himself as an apolitical administrator. Like Adams, Herbert Hoover ran for the presidency after serving eight years as the most dynamic figure in the cabinet, and again like Adams, his murky personal history in party politics bespoke an awkward, attenuated relationship to the regime he proposed to serve.

Prior to entering into federal service, Hoover had cultivated a public reputation wholly outside national politics. Trained as a geologist, he made his first career as a mining engineer in Asia, and a second as a businessman. He was living in England at the outbreak of World War I, and there he took charge of efforts to provide emergency relief for Belgium. The Belgium relief effort earned him an international reputation as a great humanitarian, and it opened the doors to a new career in public service. Still, Hoover's path into national politics was anything but straightforward. A nominal Republican in the early years of the century, he jumped ship in 1912 to support Theodore Roosevelt's Progressive campaign. Then moving even further afield, Hoover took his first government post from Woodrow Wilson, the Democrat who had landed in the White House by virtue of the Republican party split. He served Wilson loyally and effectively as one of many leaders drawn from the private sector into the emergency apparatus of wartime administration. Added to his other laurels, his service in the cause of victory made him an obvious contender for a presidential nomination in 1920, albeit one of uncertain political affiliation.

Though the Democrats sought him out as a possible nominee that year, Hoover returned to the Republican fold. GOP stalwarts welcomed their new star back to the ranks, but once Hoover made it clear that he would not campaign for the honor of their nomination, they quickly turned to safer prospects. Hoover was simply too undependable in his loyalties for the politicians who controlled the Republican party in 1920. Memories of the support he had given to President Wilson's call for the election of a Democratic Congress in 1918 were still fresh. Indeed, those memories would linger on until 1928 when the Old Guard launched an even more concerted effort to block his impending nomination.[7]

The old Adams standard of "talent and virtue alone" echoes loud and clear throughout Hoover's resumé, and in the Progressive era that standard resonated among reformers in a way that it had not before. Engineer, businessman, humanitarian, administrator—Hoover's life story read like a chapter of the larger progressive crusade to supersede the limitations now evident in party governance and recast the government to meet the new demands of an industrial age. It is notable in this regard that Adams, as Monroe's secretary of state, staked his claims to the presidency on a traditional line of advancement, while Hoover, as secretary of commerce under Harding and Coolidge, blazed an entirely new one. The "Wonder Boy" took control of a young department that had fallen on hard times under Wilson, and, to the surprise of many, he turned it into a showcase of the potential of administrative action, technical expertise, and governmental management of the economy. With Hoover's vision of the new "American System" that the Republicans might build in the postwar era and with Harding's promise that Hoover would have a hand in all the important economic matters before the administration, the Commerce Department became the very center of federal activity in the Republican era.[8] Hoover could not have given a more fitting tribute to Theodore Roosevelt, the President who had overseen the birth of the department in 1903.

The scandals of the Harding administration left Hoover's beacon beaming all the more brightly in national politics. But what exactly did he envision? In large measure, Hoover's "New Day" confirmed and extended the reform program of Roosevelt's presidential years. Yet, Hoover had been sensitized by the difficulties progressive presidents had encountered in enacting their visions, and he came to believe that thus far the underlying faith of each in direct government action had led down a series of blind alleys. As an alternative, he adopted a less overtly political approach toward change. He met the challenge of reform one step removed from Theodore Roosevelt's hands-on manipulation of the issues and interests contending within the Republican coalition. He was less interested than Roosevelt in bringing the message of "the leaders" to the people or the message of "the people" to the leaders. His reliance on managerial expertise was more finely honed, his faith in administrative action plain and simple, more complete.

Hoover championed a version of indicative planning where government experts would gather information and share it, along with their interpretation of its implications, with the leaders of new associations of economic actors. His would be an activist state, offering vital technical services and encouraging the organization of trade associations that might use those services to coordinate private action. Moreover, his ideal state would employ a full range of countercyclical interventions to stabilize the postwar marketplace. Notwithstanding the resistance of his more conservative colleagues on this score, Hoover thought public works expenditures, marketing cooperatives, tax manipulations, and monetary adjustments were all fair game as instrumentalities for smoothing out the business cycle and promoting more orderly growth. The special challenge Hoover set for himself was to manage all this prospective federal activity so as to protect freedom of action in the private sector and in local government. He rejected direct interference in enterprise as a violation of the sacred American promise of equal opportunity, and he celebrated American government's traditional decentralization as a bulwark against unbridled bureaucratization. Thus, if his vision of an American system of "ordered liberty" was more technically sophisticated than earlier progressive reform programs, it was also more ambivalent about the exercise of governmental power. Less statist than Theodore Roosevelt's New Nationalism, less formalistic than Taft's neo-constitutionalism, and less regulatory than Wilson's New Freedom, the New Day simply had less to say about the real choices to be made in reconciling a historical legacy of individualism and private initiative with the evolution of industrial society.[9]

Hoover's program moved sharply in opposing directions. While his faith in national administration heralded the promise of a continuously managed economy, his faith in the established regime led him to place a premium on voluntarism and local autonomy. Acutely sensitive to TR's experience, he was all the more sensitive to the danger of a powermongering executive. He felt that without a firm specification of limits, the government's acceptance of new responsibility for the nation's economic performance might easily get out of hand and start calling into question the integrity of the political regime it was all meant to serve. The techniques for intervention that Hoover stipulated were meant to clarify the legitimate ground for political action; the problem is that his attachment to method per se tended to obfuscate matters of substance. What exactly was the relationship between the established order and the political changes he proposed to effect? It was difficult to say. One political analyst tearing into the ambivalences of Hoover's position in 1928 put it this way: "The central fact militating against Candidate Hoover is that many people cannot understand what he stands for."[10]

Take, for example, Hoover's use of the term "reconstruction." A key word in his political vocabulary, it seems calculated to evoke a parallel between the scale of the postwar adjustments he contemplated in the 1920s and the scale of the postwar adjustments Republicans had contemplated in the latter half of the 1860s. If anyone missed that point, they had only to listen to his inaugural address. There the new President spoke boldly of building "a new economic system, a new social system and a new political system."[11] But the order-shattering portents of re-constructions past were absent here. The real political genius of Hoover's method was that it promised to render this wholesale trans-formation of systems thoroughly bloodless. Behind the monumental changes he projected was a technician's faith in "cooperative manage-ment."

Cooperative management sanctioned a government that would be assertive and transformative without threatening one that might be aggressive or coercive. The concept projected an extrapartisan, pluralist politics where executive officers, armed with the authority of expert knowledge and the power of public opinion, would seek to persuade labor leaders, business leaders, leaders of local communities, and the like of their best interests in the larger society in which they had all become inextricably connected. The government would employ its bu-reaucratic resources to prod, educate, and guide the private sector. By respecting private initiative, however, the government would also steer America clear of the bureaucratic domination and encroaching collec-tivism that was consuming Europe. Cooperative management promised to reconstruct the "American System" by repudiating ignorance, waste, duplication, and inefficiency and by affirming order, control, stability, and standardization.[12] The opponents of this reconstruction were ab-stractions; its objectives admitted no real losers. To vanquish its enemies was simply to make the existing machinery run more smoothly.

The initial success of this bid for leadership reflects plainly on the state of the Republican regime as Hoover found it. Though his obfus-cation of the relationship between the political order he represented and the political changes he contemplated would prove devastating once he got to the presidency, it was instrumental in getting him there in the first place. Hoover's call for reconstruction may have stirred little en-thusiasm, but for a Republican leader in the age of Coolidge, the call itself was something of a bold stroke. Read loosely, it comported well with a number of different political positions now uncomfortably ar-rayed under the Republican umbrella. It sidestepped both the impotence of old-line western progressives and the chilling indifference of stand-pat Republican conservatives, staking out what ground for political action was still left between them.

Most notable about Hoover-the-politician was how he cultivated his independence in Republican circles. While he bespoke a late-regime affiliate's characteristic faith in perfecting the machinery of the old order with the appropriate administrative techniques, he tapped through that faith some prominent themes in the progressive reform movement. During his stint in the Commerce Department, Hoover developed a public relations network to promote his vision. He used magazines, news stories, and local Hoover Clubs to project an image of himself as an effective manager of the nation's economy. The reification of administrative techniques as a strategy for leadership was thus built into Hoover's public persona. His public relations apparatus joined his administrative method to the promotion of his political ambitions; the Hoover Clubs made good politics synonymous with good administration. An apparatchik's version of TR's "bully pulpit," the public relations machinery offered Hoover a more refined way of rallying the people to a more sterile cause; it looked toward bringing the pressure of mass opinion to bear in government on behalf of an apolitical, scientific approach to the nation's problems. The herald of the New Day made himself the can-do master of those difficult, complicated questions that ordinary people might not understand. By 1928 Hoover had cultivated a personal following among rank-and-file Republicans strong enough to withstand the hostility of the Old Guard and the doubts of old progressives. Soon the "Wonder Boy" would wonder if he not been "oversold."[13]

A master administrator of the modern age, Hoover showed how independence from the traditional centers of party power could now be exploited openly and built into a political following that the traditional party leaders simply could not resist. The presidency was the only elective office Herbert Hoover ever contested or held, but he was never considered a dark horse. Coolidge's famous quip—"That man has offered me unsolicited advice for six years, all of it bad"—suggests something of the candidate's relations with the party leadership in 1928. But Coolidge proved unwilling to act on his words and take issue with the call for a "New Day."[14] Hoover was simply too formidable.

Hoover's awkward relations with Republican party regulars are but the last of many ambivalent relationships underlying his leadership project. Not only did Hoover flourish despite Coolidge's coolness, he returned the sentiment with kindness. He praised his predecessor time and again during the 1928 campaign, and in the face of scarcely veiled hostility from the party stalwarts, he persistently professed his faith in party government. Curious on its face, there was more here than cynicism in the pursuit of power. For Hoover to praise the accomplishments of the Coolidge administration was, after all, tantamount to praising his own handiwork. He could enthuse over a platform to "maintain and continue the Coolidge policies," for his own ideas had been nurtured within them. There was, in other words, no substantial divergence between Hoover's commitment to a New Day and the commitments of the old regime he proposed to serve. For all that his call to action might grate against the stand-patters, the candidate did not contemplate any material break with the past, and he prided himself on knowing the distinction between the constructive and the destructive path. With all the changes he contemplated safely submerged in matters of mere technique, Hoover never let his independence get in the way of his broader claim to acceptability.

Thus, for all his apolitical sensibilities, Hoover took the field in 1928 as an earnest booster of the Republican regime. Hoover's leadership project covered deep political divisions within the coalition, and his call for a New Day mustered what enthusiasm there was for a completion of the work of the 1920s. In his party's best traditions, Hoover went to the people affirming both the creative potential of the national government *and* the "genius of modern business." He proclaimed a new economics of prosperity *and* he mounted a stalwart defense of the foundationstone of tariff protection. If Hoover's professions of faith in party government ring hollow, the reason must be found in the state of the Republican party itself. It was ripe for takeover by an administrative upstart for, in truth, there was not much else left to it. The leadership that had managed to reassemble a victorious coalition behind Harding in 1920 had since endured a national scandal, another consolidation of power by an unelected president, and another progressive bolt in 1924. By 1928, the Republican administration *was* the Republican organization, and Hoover, the leading Republican administrator, simply absorbed them both into his technocratic crusade.

The Bugaboos of Appropriate Action

The most important issues which Hoover catalogued in his memoirs as matters of "reform and development"—tariff revision, water power development, and agricultural marketing—were, in fact, matters of crisis management from the very beginning of his presidency. The prosperity of 1928 was far from complete, as he well knew. By the time of his inauguration, the nation's agricultural sector was in the throes of a depression already several years old. To his credit, Hoover set out to address the problems of the farmers immediately after his inauguration. In this quick start, we glimpse the weaknesses of Hoover's leadership posture under conditions that he fully expected to confront; from it, we see political prospects so dim that the advent of the Great Crash seems something of a saving grace. Hoover's subtle views on the proper relationship between political order and political change may have helped him carry overwhelming Republican majorities in the election, but they failed—quite apart from the great industrial contraction—to leave him any substantial ground for the exercise of political leadership.

Not unlike Theodore Roosevelt, Hoover addressed the farmers during his presidential campaign with a tactic of bait and switch. He promised bold new action on their behalf, and he even aligned himself with the basic thrust of their more recent reform ideas. In keeping with much of the new thinking in agricultural circles, Hoover thought it was high time that farmers received some of the benefits of the protective tariff. He also recognized that the agricultural sector, composed as it was of a large number of small and independent producers, would need special support from the government if it was to act effectively in an increasingly organized marketplace.[15] Still, Hoover opposed the farmers' favored methods. He found their proposals, most notably the various versions of the McNary-Haugen bill, counterproductive in their prospective effects and misguided in their resort to government price fixing. Coolidge had already vetoed two different version of this scheme, and those actions fully accorded with the advice Hoover had given him. The new President was determined to demonstrate to the farm community that the more voluntarist and cooperative methods he had employed at the Department of Commerce were equally suited to agriculture.[16]

Hoover's farm program had two parts.[17] One part called for tariff reform. The President wanted a "limited" revision of rates, one that would provide more protection for agricultural imports but avoid further increases in industrial schedules. Indeed, Hoover's proposal hinted that industrial rates might already be too high. In addition to the call for limited rate revision, he asked Congress to authorize him to adjust any rate on the schedule at his discretion and to strengthen the Tariff Commission to provide him with the technical information necessary to carrying out revisions on a case by case basis. With a stalwart defense of protection in principle and a specific promise of more protection in one area, Hoover asked his fellow partisans to expand administrative capacities and to give him the flexibility to manage more effectively the foundationstone of the Republican regime.

The other part of Hoover's farm program was a proposal for a federal Farm Board. This board was to sponsor, support, and advise agricultural cooperatives that would be owned and controlled by the farmers themselves. Financed by a revolving fund to be administered by the board, the cooperatives would provide a variety of services to the various commodity producers, including the removal and disposal of temporary surpluses to their collective advantage. Fulfilling his promise to do something positive for farmers, Hoover's Farm Board nonetheless stopped well short of any endorsement of their own proposals for overseas dumping, price fixing, and production controls. At best, his plan was something the western progressives might work with as they continued to promote their own ideas. Senator William Borah, one of the progressive leaders, had rallied impressive support for Hoover in the West with the understanding that the first order of business in a Hoover administration would be to call a special session of Congress to deal with the nation's agricultural crisis and that the candidate meant to take action in accordance with progressive views.[18]

In truth, Hoover's proposals for agricultural reform and farm relief mixed conservative and progressive sentiments in equal doses. As in his approach to tariff reform, here too he hoped to get both sides to agree to transfer the agricultural question "from the field of politics into the realm of economics."[19] But at this late date in the Republican era this all-too-familiar formula was far too precious for the political weight it had to carry. In the sectarian wrangling that exploded upon the special session of Congress that Hoover called in April 1929, his much touted methods were reduced to so much bugaboo.[20]

More attuned to the President's promise of bold action than to his scruples about direct governmental controls, the Senate, with Borah in the lead, shelved Hoover's Farm Board and passed another version of the farmers' favored reform scheme. In his very first initiative, Hoover locked horns with his party's progressive wing. While promising to study the Senate's plan, the new President held the line for voluntarism in the House, where the Republican majority had more than a paper presence. The dismal state of party affairs came into view soon enough, however, as the Senate refused to endorse a conference committee report more favorable to the President's scheme than to its own. With this, the progressive senators moved into open opposition to the administration, and stayed there. They placed full responsibility for the pending action on Hoover personally and detached themselves from what they saw as the inevitable failure of federal action without significant governmental controls and guarantees. Once the terms of future relations were clarified in this way, an agreement to try something was eventually worked out. In June 1929, the President, now shorn of his progressive support, celebrated his first victory for the "American System."

Submerged in the progressives' attack on Hoover's Farm Board was the opposition of the established agricultural commission houses. Mocking the President's pretensions to the preservation of private initiative, these entrepreneurs pointed out that he was in fact supporting a massive intrusion of government into the marketplace, one that directly threatened the very existence of the businesses already operating there. There was no more conservative support for the fine distinctions of Hooverian reform than there was progressive support, and as the tariff debate unfolded, the absence of political support for Hooverian techniques took an even larger toll.

More attuned to the President's stalwart defense of protection than to his call for limiting revision solely to agricultural imports, the Old Guard defeated a progressive-sponsored resolution upholding Hoover's carefully considered stipulation. From then on the special session turned into a political debacle as the legislators negotiated a general upward revision of rates. Horrified by the spectacle, Hoover decided not to confront his party directly on matters of first principle. He took his stand for a more disciplined politics by defending the administrative provisions of his bill and insisting that whatever schedule the Congress agreed to had to include his strengthened Tariff Commission as well as the flexibility provision authorizing him to revise individual rates.[21] With this, conservative and progressive Republicans both joined forces against him. Acting in concert, they defeated the flexibility provisions, denouncing them as a presidential encroachment on congressional prerogatives. The special session ended in stalemate on the tariff and predictions of the imminent collapse of the Republican party.[22]

The tariff issue was debated for another six months in the regular session of Congress that convened immediately thereafter. As finally signed, the Smoot-Hawley Tariff of 1930 contained a significant upward revision of rates, the President extracting his flexibility provisions from a tie-breaking vote cast in the Senate by his vice president. For this victory, Hoover paid an enormous price. Tied from the start to the dubious cause of protection, he signed a bill that, on balance, worked to the decided disadvantage of agriculture. Moreover, with the European economies already strained to pay their war debts to America, the new round of protection threatened to fuel a burgeoning international economic crisis.

The President might have believed that he could gradually undo the damage caused by the new schedules by using his new authority over rate adjustments, but his faith in administrative action to correct legislative abuses was sadly misplaced. In the short term at least, the war-ravaged European economies would bear added burdens in selling goods on the American market, accelerating the debt crisis. The Tariff Commission not only acted slowly on a rate-by-rate basis, but for all the talk about scientific methods, it worked without clear standards in judging the validity of any given rate. The President, who had pledged to take the most divisive political issues into the realm of economic science, was instead caught up in self-perpetuating political controversy. Perhaps most damaging of all for a leader who had claimed the authority of expertise, one thousand members of the American Economic Association signed a petition denouncing the new tariff as a portent of national and international calamity.[23] A debacle that would haunt the administration to the end, the tariff became, in the short term, the central policy issue in the midterm rout of the Republican majorities in 1930.

Clearly, then, the fabled Hooverian techniques were under siege well before the gloom of the Great Depression took hold of the rest of nation. The lines Hoover had painstakingly drawn between cooperation and coercion, between private initiative and governmental interference, between politics and administration, between interest and science—all the fine distinctions of his American System gave way in their first encounter with the political divisions of the dominant coalition. With them went much of Hoover's control over the meaning of his actions. In light of the disastrous political toll extracted by the special session, it is difficult to escape the conclusion that the President first met the stock market collapse of October 1929 and the ensuing panic as something of a new lease on political leadership.

Two Hares in the Hat

Far from being poised to repeat Theodore Roosevelt's performance, Hoover, at the moment of the Crash, was repeating the debacle of William Howard Taft. First actions had devastated Roosevelt's immediate successor, shattering the party he presumed to lead. They had similarly scuttled the leadership premises of John Quincy Adams and Franklin Pierce. But, when the real trouble started for Hoover, his prospects began to look up. Suddenly, he appeared buoyant.

Though already bereft of defenders in the halls of Congress, this late-regime affiliate had formidable resources to draw on in meeting the economic crisis. His program for countercyclical stabilization boasted the most advanced economic thinking of the day, and he had spent eight years in the Commerce Department cultivating that program. He also had the good will of formidable leaders outside of Congress. Powerful men in business, labor, and the federal administration offered an alternative constituency for presidential leadership in a pluralist polity, and the economic downturn made this an especially timely constituency to have on hand. It was to these leaders, as well as to the leaders of state and local governments, that Hoover now turned to help him take charge of national affairs.

Within weeks of the stock market crash, the President was holding widely publicized conferences with magnates of all sorts and announcing precedent-shattering initiatives to meet the emergency. These conferences served several objectives. First, they were designed to boost the nation's confidence. Taking action to bring things under control and gaining the cooperation of the leaders of American industry in the process was a masterful bit of public relations that played directly to the political identity Hoover had so long been projecting. Beyond that, the conferences stimulated private action on common objectives and helped maximize the effect of the government's countercyclical efforts.[24] For a moment, everything seemed to be falling into place. Business leaders promised to increase their investments and maintain wages; the Federal Reserve Board agreed to expand the money supply; Congress moved to reduce taxes and expanded dramatically its appropriations for public works; the governors agreed to support even more public projects on their own initiative.[25]

In all, a comprehensive program of cooperative management held center stage in the fall of 1929 and on into the first part of 1930. "The most interesting phenomenon of the day," one reporter remarked, "is not business depression but the repression of depression."[26] Hoover was pointedly discarding the government's traditional laissez-faire response to economic crises and just as proudly affirming private initiative and the limits of federal intervention. The brilliance of his performance made the results all the more conclusive. The business leaders who had agreed to expand investment and maintain wages failed to convince the others in their sectors to follow suit. Soon they found themselves looking for a way out short of a direct reversal of their public pledges of cooperation. Maintaining wage levels ultimately came at the price of scaling back working hours and laying off laborers.[27] Then, the nation's first-line banks failed to live up to expectations. Instead of using the Federal Reserve Board's new terms to expand credit, they used it to bolster their own positions against bad loans.[28] The tax cuts were offset by the tariff increases, and the public works projects took too long to gear up to have much of an impact. Meanwhile, the Farm Board succeeded in buoying prices temporarily, only to stimulate more production and increase the downward pressures.[29] No sooner was Hoover's system fully deployed than the limitations of its much touted strictures on governmental control were fully exposed.

At midterm, then, aggressive efforts to demonstrate the creative potential of the old regime devolved into defensive efforts to protect it against the impending threat of more fundamental changes. The off-year elections had gone badly. For whatever they were worth, the once-imposing Republican majorities in Congress vanished, and disgruntled progressives began to contemplate the prospects of forging a new opposition movement in alliance with the incoming class of Democratic reformers. As the final session of the old Congress convened, Hoover was poised to step into a political crossfire.

Just then, however, Hoover pulled a second hare from the hat. In his second annual address, he announced that the causes of America's distress lay overseas, and that the solution lay in international negotiations.[30] Hoover took a third lease on leadership from America's new-found prominence in world affairs.

Hoover used his position as a world leader to considerable effect. The centerpiece of his initiative was a moratorium on the payment of war debts, and an agreement to that effect was hammered out with European leaders in the spring. Stopping well short of the cancellation of the debts, Hoover's tack in the matter bypassed both the call for outright repudiation of the debts abroad and the unacceptability of repudiation at home. Successfully finessing this impasse, the moratorium was to prove the greatest single accomplishment of Hoover's term. Initially, even his critics hailed it as a "far reaching and most praiseworthy step."[31]

Hoover negotiated this triumph on the world stage while Congress continued its ravaging of his all-too-precious leadership posture at home. No sooner had the progressives exposed the bugaboos of Hoover's farm program than they turned attention to another of Hoover's pet interests, water power development. Like the farm program, water power was an issue of vital concern to rural America; and as with his farm initiative, Hoover sought to seize the lead on the issue while keeping federal action within his rules of appropriateness. His vision bore fruit in the summer of 1930 with the commencement of his greatest public works project, the Boulder Dam. Hoover's design for a comprehensive water development project on the Colorado River included many services to several states, and promised to support itself through the sale of "falling water" to private and municipal power companies.[32] But the President was not the only Republican with bold ideas about how to harness water power. Senator George Norris, a leading progressive from Nebraska, proposed an equally ambitious project for the economically ravaged Tennessee Valley in 1931, only this time the federal government was to do more than simply sell its falling water to power companies to cover its costs. Norris wanted the government to assume more direct responsibility in the production, distribution, and regulation of the power generated. The President, generally supportive of a project for the Tennessee Valley along the lines of his Colorado project, vetoed the Norris bill as a species of socialism. With that, Norris emerged as the champion of the people's interests; Hoover became the sellout to the power companies.[33]

As the progressives seized from the President leadership over water power development, the new reform-minded urban Democrats mounted a challenge to Hoover's support for the working man. Hoover's prepresidential record on labor boasted federal initiatives to stimulate full employment as well as opposition to labor injunctions. As President, he would take further pride in landmark pieces of legislation on each issue: the Federal Employment Stabilization Act of 1931 and the Norris-LaGuardia Anti-Injunction Act of 1932. But by 1930, Hoover was locked in a battle with Democratic Senator Robert Wagner of New

York for control over labor issues. The stabilization act was, in fact, one of three labor initiatives Wagner had offered to the lameduck session of the Seventy-first Congress, and with the spectre of federal unemployment insurance already looming on the legislative horizon, Hoover feared the extent of Wagner's grand designs. When another of Wagner's proposals, this one to revamp the federal government's employment services, began to move through Congress, Hoover tried unsuccessfully to derail it with his own substitute. In the end, he vetoed the bill on a technicality, trumping up an argument about the costs of delay in changing from one administrative system to another. With the head of his own Emergency Committee on Unemployment favoring the Wagner scheme, this bid to maintain a semblance of control over labor issues came at an enormous price. It made Wagner, not Hoover, the true friend of the working man.[34]

The spate of presidential vetoes that attended the adjournment of the Seventy-first Congress in March 1931 brought to the fore the full meaning of the President's message from the previous December.[35] To assert that the nation's economic woes lay in the international political economy, was, for Hoover, to argue that American institutions were fundamentally sound. Bold actions to meet the crisis had to be taken with a mind toward the preservation of the enduring virtues of these institutions.[36] Insurgent Republicans and reform Democrats were beginning to break down the distinction that Hoover had always been at pains to uphold, the distinction between elaborating the "American System" and replacing it. Recent electoral reversals made the collapse of that distinction an even more potent threat. Seizing the initiative on the world stage, and drawing new lines of defense around established governing arrangements at home, the President straddled a widening breach.

After the Seventy-first Congress adjourned, Hoover canvassed pledges of support for his moratorium agreement, informally guaranteeing its ratification in what promised to be an even more difficult meeting in December.[37] He was not anxious to meet the new Congress any sooner. Though Democrats and progressives demanded that he call a special session over the summer of 1931 to consider the moratorium, Hoover, with his pledges in hand, would have none of it.[38] The Congress had already shown its indifference to his determination to keep bold action within the bounds of appropriateness. A special session would only bring more headaches. Hoover intended to savor his world triumph as best he could. "I do not propose to call an extra session of Congress," he said in May 1931. "I know of nothing that would so disturb the healing process now undoubtedly going on in the economic situation. We cannot legislate ourselves out of a world economic depression; we can and will work ourselves out."[39]

The Precedents of Wartime

Leaving the American people as much freedom as possible to "fight their own battles in their own communities" was not, Hoover admitted, the "easy way" out of the crisis. Still, he insisted, it was "the American way."[40] Great principles were at stake in ensuring that the governmental response to human suffering was technically correct, and Hoover was nothing if not a master-craftsman of the technically correct response. The crisis was deepening; Hoover's reputation as a reformer was collapsing; his political support was evaporating. And yet the President kept himself going with new initiatives that by his own lights were still consistent with his rules of appropriate action.

As the summer of 1931 dragged on, Hoover could see that something more would be needed to save his administration and the larger Republican regime it existed to preserve. There were signs aplenty that a "healing process" was not under way and that the American people were getting tired of hearing about what their cherished principles forbade their government to do. It was becoming increasingly clear that his "American way" would not survive his political defeat. The question was, could he save himself from defeat without destroying his American way?

In an emergency meeting with the nation's bankers in the fall, Hoover gave voluntarism one last try. He threatened direct governmental control of the nation's finances along the lines of the War Finance Corporation of the Wilson years unless a voluntary association of creditors was formed immediately to administer relief to solvent banks that were experiencing difficulties. But even the bankers were becoming impatient with the President's precious precepts about appropriate action. Much to Hoover's surprise, they discounted the prospects for voluntary cooperation and asked for the threatened federal action. Hoover promised to comply in the upcoming Congress if voluntary action undertaken immediately failed to have the desired effect.

Under these terms, terms which doomed the experiment before it began, the bankers agreed to form the National Credit Corporation.[41]

The near-immediate failure of the corporation angered the President and further tainted his administration. At a time when many who needed relief most saw the bankers as the source of their problems, Hoover had once again placed his faith in the power of the old financial houses to bolster the economy. Not only did the bankers fail to get the job done, they reinforced the image of a president hostaged to the money changers and impervious to the plight of the common people. Again Hoover's central claim to legitimacy, his American way, appeared more a part of the problem than the solution. As the technocratic pretensions of Hoover's initial leadership posture were stripped away, the ideology and interests that they protected became increasingly vulnerable.

Nonetheless, the President rebounded. If there was anything for Hoover to salvage from the banker's debacle, it was a rationale for transcending his own discipline. Now not even the most stalwart conservative could accuse him of having failed to explore the full potential of private initiative to meet the deepening crisis. Hoover was free to acknowledge the limitations of voluntarism in meeting the extraordinary demands of the Depression and to propose direct governmental intervention as the only recourse left. This new Hoover, the one unveiled in his annual message of December 1931 and the one who would go to the people for support in 1932, was one willing to adapt pragmatically with "the shifting battle against the depression" and to "adopt new measures and new tactics as the battle moves on."[42] In this final bid for credibility, it became markedly more difficult to find the system the President was proposing to preserve.

Hoover's still considerable power at this moment derived from his indispensable role as the nation's chief policy maker, and he drew his warrants for action directly from the intractable state of national affairs. He began to act in accord with the precedent and guide of wartime experience. "We are engaged in a fight upon a hundred fronts," he declared. The fight was "just as positive, just as definite, and requir[ed] just as greatly the moral courage, the organized action, the unity of strength, and the sense of devotion in every community as in war."[43] The resurgent Democrats had no intention of blocking the President in this fight, or, for that matter, of taking responsibility for his actions. The new leaders of the House and Senate pledged their cooperation, and the "kissing bee" Congress delivered on requests for the moratorium, for easing Federal Reserve requirements, for a strengthening of the Federal Home Loan Bank system, and for currency reform.[44]

The centerpiece of Hoover's new program was the Reconstruction Finance Corporation. Recommended in his annual address in December 1931, it was enacted in January. By the late spring, the President was contemplating significant amendments to the corporation's authority, and after a bitter and extended debate in Congress, these were incorporated into the Emergency Relief and Reconstruction Act of July. The initial bill had been modeled closely on the War Finance Corporation of the Wilson Administration. The federal government was to expand vastly the credit available to financial institutions and railroads and take direct control over the administration of these resources to stimulate the economy. The July act trumped this initial governmental intrusion into the private sector with even more penetrating extensions of federal authority. The RFC was authorized to provide loans to states for direct relief on the basis of need, to provide new funds for self-liquidating public works projects, and to offer loans to institutions promising to stabilize agricultural prices. Direct loans to industry were provided through the federal reserve banks. In their recognition of federal responsibility for economic recovery and relief from distress, these two measures all but dispensed with the strictures of voluntarism and local initiative that had marked Hoover's earlier efforts.[45] Indeed, they embraced principles Hoover's American System seem to proscribe. There would be no turning back.

Why, then, was the President unable to capitalize on this departure? If the problem was ideological rigidity plain and simple, there would have been no departure at all. The fact is that Hoover had built a substantive record to back up his pretensions to pragmatism in the 1932 campaign. Successive experiments to bolster the faltering economy had been formulated and tested in turn, and while each had been carefully controlled, they ultimately broached a direct assault on traditional governing arrangements. New lines of action had been opened after each previous position proved wanting. Hoover might be guilty of being too methodical and too intent on giving each new step a fair trial before trying something else, but it is important to keep in mind that what he proposed in the winter of 1931 was a radical step beyond what he had proposed just a few weeks before, and what he proposed in the spring of 1932 was a radical step beyond what he had come to accept in January. To dismiss Hoover as a conservative ideologue and ignore his precedent-shattering pragmatism gets us no farther than praising Lincoln as a pragmatist and ignoring his order-shattering ideology.

Much the same can be said about another common charge, that the initiatives of 1932 were simply "too little too late." To be sure, these measures provided, at best, only a momentary pause in the downward spiral, but there was far more to this political disjunction than such a broadside dismissal can explain. For all his intervention in the economy, Hoover became almost as vulnerable to the charge that he was doing too much as he was to the charge that he was doing too little. In the 1932 campaign Franklin Roosevelt himself argued that Hoover had given the nation too much government and his program was busting the budget.[46] Finally, to give them their due, the innovations of 1932 were just the kind of departures from past practice that one associates with great political reconstructions. Their scale and purpose laid a rich seedbed for further experimentation (just the kind of experimentation that would take place in the early New Deal), and they were well-timed to take something new to the people in the upcoming election.[47]

Far more problematic than the measures themselves was the absence of political supporters willing to credit Hoover's creativity. To be sure, Congress passed the President's measures, but it also robbed them of all claims to authority. A budding coalition of Democrats and progressives sat in judgment on the meaning and significance of the President's innovations, and while they disagreed widely among themselves, they were quite effective in denying Hoover any positive role.

The initial debate over the Reconstruction Finance Corporation, for example, submerged the significance of Hoover's departure in talk of another bailout for bankers and millionaires. Then, in the spring when the President endorsed direct relief, he was undercut by the Speaker of the House (soon to be the Democrats' vice presidential nominee), John Nance Garner. Garner abruptly abandoned his recent defense of a balanced budget and substituted for the Hoover bill a measure so loose in its provisions for lending that even some of its supporters openly hoped for a veto. In this way, the climax of the great relief debate came not when the President signed the precedent-shattering measure he had supported, but a few days before when he vetoed Garner's handiwork as an extravagant and imprudent departure from established principles.[48] Finally, there was the nightmare of administering the relief measure. Though Gifford Pinchot, an old Bull Moose Republican now serving as Pennsylvania's reform governor, had been agitating to get federal relief for his state for over a year, the RFC rejected his initial applications. The agency argued that its funds were limited, that they were available to the states only as a last resort, and that state-by-state comparisons indicated that Pennsylvania had not done as much as other states in tapping its own resources. Throughout the summer and fall of 1932, applications from Pinchot showing the dire state of affairs in Pennsylvania and rejections or partial actions from the board painted a stunning portrait of administration niggardliness in the face of widespread human suffering. Though Pennsylvania would eventually get more than any state save Illinois and twice as much as the next, Michigan, it was Pinchot who had the last word on the meaning of the administration's actions. In the final stretch of the 1932 election campaign the Republican governor charged the Republican president with "giving everything possible to the big fellow and as little as possible to the little fellow."[49]

For all this, however, there was something even more fundamental at work in Hoover's failure to capitalize politically on his boldest initiatives. What enabled the opposition to set the terms of debate and to cast Hoover in the worst possible light was Hoover's own disposition toward the vast changes he was now willing to set in motion. Hoover himself would never accept the notion that his actions were opening the door to the displacement of the old order and thus he could never link his initiatives with the promise of constructing a new one. A "new" Hoover openly indicting the old regime was hardly even tenable, for the Hoover that everyone knew had been touting the great potential of that regime his entire public life. He could no more assault the received formulas directly than call his entire political career into question. The war metaphor itself was meant to help the President finesse this dilemma. Wars might be understood as extraordinary events whose purpose was to defend cherished values. Extraordinary measures might be needed to win them, but they were abnormal, and care had to be taken so that the system might return to its proper functioning after the victory. For Hoover, legitimacy remained tied to the way things had been, or at least to the way they had been evolving, before the onset of the present crisis.

It was this understanding of his warrants that Hoover attached to his boldest initiatives and carried into the presidential campaign of 1932. In accepting the Republican nomination for a second term, Hoover curiously boasted that while he had "ventured unprecedented measures to meet the unprecedented violence of the storm" he had not changed anything of significance.[50] He defended his record by saying that his innovations were designed to ensure that "when this emergency is past, our governmental, social, and economic structure [will be] functioning as before."[51] (This from the man whose inaugural address had envisioned a new economic system, a new political system, and a new social system.) Hoover's best case for measures that were altering de facto relations between state and society was that they had headed off any truly fundamental changes. For all that he was doing, Hoover went out of his way to make it clear that he was *not* offering any new deals to the American people.

> I therefore contend that the problem of today is to continue these measures and policies to restore this American system to its normal functioning, to repair the wounds it has received, to correct the weaknesses and evils which would defeat that system. To enter upon a series of deep changes, to embark on this inchoate new deal which has been propounded in this campaign would be to undermine and destroy our American system.[52]

Hoover's inability to take the final step in innovation and repudiate the system he was transforming served his critics well. As the war metaphor touted his identity as leader and booster of the Republican regime, it undercut the political effect of the very real changes he was setting in motion. Certainly his new American System had become, if it had not always been, every bit as inchoate as the New Deal he now denounced. In "repairing the wounds" of his American System, in "correcting its weaknesses," and in "meeting the evils that would defeat" it, Hoover was in fact just making it up as he went along. Except for the rhetoric, anyone in 1932 who took the time to look for the American System that Hoover had heralded in 1928 would have to conclude that his own policies had already acknowledged its bankruptcy and that he had set a course for something else.[53]

Hoover would later lament the people's failure to appreciate the significance of his policies, and yet he was the first to deny it. The crosscurrents of change in the politics of leadership left him with an impressive string of policy successes, all of which added up to one colossal political failure. Significance eluded his many achievements because from first to last Hoover was unable to embrace forthrightly the changes that came with them. Back in 1928, reconstruction had been a slogan without substance in Hoover's political vocabulary; now it became an unfolding reality about which he could not speak. Back in 1928, proper techniques had held open the promise of dramatic change; now the promise was that his techniques would keep all this change from becoming too dramatic. Venturing his innovations without the slightest hint of betraying the ground just left behind, Hoover denied the significance of his own deeds. He was drawn to distinctions that left him politically isolated and his actions obscure. Shorn of any repudiative thrust, his most important measures assumed a meaning quite at odds with their effect and became a stalwart's defiance of anything substantially new.

Of course, both presidential campaigns of 1932 were a conceptual muddle. As Hoover's sought to defend a system that he had already dispensed with, Roosevelt waffled on critical issues—tariffs, big government, and balanced budgets—that held in their resolution the shape of things to come. In 1932 Roosevelt was blasting the Hoover administration for its extravagance as well as its callousness and proudly reclaiming for the Democrats the Jeffersonian gospel of economy in government. And yet, Roosevelt's muddle was really quite different from Hoover's, and for all that Hoover enjoyed pointing out specific contradictions in his opponent's positions, the President understood the potency of the Roosevelt difference instinctively. What distinguished Roosevelt was not so much the changes he proposed as his general disposition toward change. Hoover's stern warnings against the destructive force of the opposition now mobilized against him were not misplaced. Roosevelt's call for a "new deal" was nothing if not a forthright indictment of old governing arrangements and the claim of an expansive warrant to displace them.[54] "It is not the change that comes from the normal development of national life to which I object," Hoover protested, "but the proposal to alter the whole foundation of our national life."[55]

CHAPTER 7

Liberal Leadership:
Fraying Boundaries

I N THIS fourth look at the politics presidents make, we encounter what would seem to be the logical limits of each of the leadership postures we have been tracing. Franklin Roosevelt, Lyndon Johnson, and Jimmy Carter, each emboldened by the conceits of the modern presidency, pressed hard against the boundaries of their political authority and in doing so blurred the distinctions among the familiar forms. In Roosevelt's reconstruction, we mark the gnarly problems of breaking with the past in the emergent pluralist polity. Challenged by these problems to test the outer boundaries of the reconstructive stance, Roosevelt ultimately dissolved the distinction between a political reconstruction and a reification of technique. Lyndon Johnson blurred the distinction between rearticulating received premises and reconstructing American politics wholesale. We see in his leadership how the expansion of presidential power bears on the capacity to manipulate established interests and commitments, and how the very intensity of that manipulation began to dissolve the practical meaning of affiliation in presidential leadership. Jimmy Carter, a president whose genius lay in filling out the contemporary frame of plebiscitary politics, used his direct relationship with the American public to press the logical limits of the politics of disjunction. With a heady sense of his ability to build his own political support, Carter went far beyond what other presidents had done in the impossible leadership situation. Combining direct appeals to the people with a technocratic approach to solving the liberal regime's mounting problems, he resisted some of the regime's most basic commitments, declared the existing order bankrupt, and mounted his own case for structural change.

Part One:
Franklin Roosevelt's Reconstruction

> Rulers of the exchange of mankind's goods
> have failed through their own stubbornness
> and their own incompetence, have admitted
> their failure, and have abdicated.
> Practices of the unscrupulous money changers
> stand indicted in the court of public opinion,
> rejected by the hearts and minds of men . . .
> The money changers have fled from their
> high seats in the temple of our civilization.
> We may now restore that temple
> to the ancient truths.

FRANKLIN ROOSEVELT was the candidate with "clean hands" at a moment when failed policies, broken promises, and embarrassed clients were indicting a long-established political order.[1] Agitating for a rout in 1932, he inveighed against the entire "Republican leadership."[2] He denounced them as false prophets of prosperity, charged them with incompetence in dealing with economic calamity, and convicted them of intransigence in the face of social desperation. Declaring their regime morally bankrupt, he campaigned to cut the knot, to raise a new standard, to restore to American government the ancient truths that had first inspired it.

We have to range far afield of the mid-twentieth century to find a leadership stance as simple as this in its basic claims or as firm in its grasp of the moment at hand. Roosevelt asserted a form of political authority wielded by only a few presidents before him, and they are scattered widely over the past. The interesting thing is that when we do locate those other leaders who, like FDR, promised to restore in a new order the ancient truths lost in the indulgences of the existing one, our first impressions of his commanding position quickly give way to more nuanced perceptions. These backward-looking comparisons draw out an emergent pattern in the politics of reconstruction. They show how the essential elements of this leadership posture have been reshaped by the secular development of American government and politics, and with that, they turn our attention to the complications and contextual slippages newly insinuated into its characteristic claims.

Take Roosevelt's simple assertion that he was a candidate with "clean hands." Nothing is more basic to the reconstructive stance. Yet, it is readily apparent that, for all the egregious failures of the old Republican regime, staking out an identity independent of received commitments had now become a relatively involved undertaking. In the first place, Roosevelt was not like Andrew Jackson, a party unto himself; nor was he, like Abraham Lincoln, the candidate of a new party. The party that was to nominate him for the presidency carried the baggage of a hundred years of national history; the candidate himself saw it as little more than another name for "the same reactionary doctrine."[3] Thus, while Roosevelt assumed what has always been the most potent of all leadership postures, he was confronted immediately with new problems of following through. He uttered those fateful words "a new deal" in an institutional universe for reconstruction that was in every way more densely inhabited and firmly entrenched than it had been for past presidents similarly situated in political time.

Roosevelt addressed this initial complication head on. Hearing his nomination on the radio, he flew to the Democratic convention in Chicago to accept it in person before the party assembly. No nominee of a major party had ever done this before, and Roosevelt opened his address by pronouncing the act "the symbol of my intention." He told his party that the critical state of the nation's affairs called for candor in speech and action, and that candor required cutting through received rules of appropriate behavior on all sides. The party of a "new deal," he declared, would reach out to "nominal Republicans whose conscience cannot be squared with the groping and failure of their party leaders." Just as surely it would part company with "nominal Democrats who squint at the future with their faces turned toward the past, and who feel no responsibility to the demands of a new time." As he had broken with tradition in coming to accept his nomination personally, so Roosevelt urged all Democrats: "Let it be from now on the task of our Party to break foolish traditions."[4]

Roosevelt had moved none too quickly to snatch his extraordinary opportunity out of the clutches of established institutional arrangements. He had been nominated on the fourth ballot with all the usual equivocations of traditional convention deliberations. His flight to Chicago parried the thought that he might be tied through his party to the politics of the past, and its stunning display of the independence of a modern nominee crystalized in an instant a profound change in traditional relations between candidates and the organizations they were nominated to represent. Roosevelt characterized the old formality of sending a delegation of the party to inform the candidate of his nomination after the convention a silly ritual rendered obsolete by modern means of communication and transportation. But there was more to the traditional procedure than that. It was a way of inviting the nominee to take the charge of leadership *as it had been offered,* and it thus served as a safeguard of the party's own integrity. Roosevelt pressed himself forward quite literally on the wings of modernity to take charge of the party on his own terms; as he held himself above old attachments that might prove uncomfortable, he challenged Democrats to pull themselves out the torpor of their history and grasp his own personal standard. In effect, he told the organization that selected him that he planned to reconstruct it along with the rest of the old regime.[5]

On the face of it, the story of Roosevelt's acceptance speech tells of newfound independence in national political leadership. And yet, as subsequent events would confirm, the meaning of modernity in this reconstruction lay as much in the conceits of independence as in the displays. Roosevelt's rhetorical cleansing of the Democratic party in Chicago heralded the messiest party-building design of any political reconstruction yet, and the institutional obstacles he faced in party-building were but a signal of the difficulties that would press in on his reconstruction from all sides. Independent national organizations now operated continuously in virtually every sphere of political and economic life, and this raised the stakes of reconstructive politics in a variety of interrelated ways. It deepened the social and economic implications of any concerted effort to recast power arrangements at the center; at the same time, it fortified other centers of institutional authority with the wherewithal to generate a steady stream of alternatives to Roosevelt's course; ultimately, it pushed Roosevelt into an untenable constitutional position as he struggled to follow through on his reconstructive project. Buried in the modern drama Roosevelt so carefully staged that day in Chicago was a first encounter with the distinctive challenge of his presidency: breaking with the past in an emergent pluralist polity.

The bold new claims that Roosevelt kept making on his own behalf take on a distinctive coloration in this light. They suggest the magnitude of the obstacles in the path of reconstructive leadership as much as the new resources he was able to tap; they portend a curious disconnection between the leader and the changes taking place under his authority as much as they do his newfound independence. Just as surely as Herbert Hoover had been buoyed in the midst of a nationwide crisis of political legitimacy by the expanded policy-making role of the president in the pluralist polity, Roosevelt found himself surrounded with interests and organizations more resistant to his efforts to reconstruct that polity wholesale. Just as surely as Hoover delivered changes more fundamental than he could acknowledge, Roosevelt demanded a change more fundamental than he could deliver. Like other reconstructive leaders, Roosevelt would steadily expand his leadership claims in order to outflank resistance as he encountered it. But the challenge of maintaining control over a systemic reordering of public and private power at this new place in history quickly broached the logical limits of even this most expansive of leadership postures. By the outset of his second term, Roosevelt's bid for control had so overreached itself that the crucial linkage at the heart of the reconstructive stance—the equation of radical change with the reaffirmation of ancient truths—began to dissolve.

Of course, in 1933, little thought was being given to the limits of Roosevelt's leadership. As one adviser read the situation on the eve of the inauguration: "No political party at Washington [is] in control of Congress or even itself . . . There [is] no cohesive nationwide sentiment behind any fundamental policy or idea today. The election was an overwhelmingly negative affair."[6] To all appearances, the break *was* clean. Roosevelt had taken the presidency in an interregnum; thrust beyond the old order, he appeared free to refashion the polity at will.

He did not miss his cue. Steadfastly defying the complications in his reconstructive stance, Roosevelt reached down to the foundations of American government and politics and joined the immediate task of economic recovery to the idea of a more permanent alteration in relations between American government and American society. His acceptance speech in Chicago identified the New Deal as "a workable program of reconstruction."[7] In the most important policy statement of the campaign, he spoke of recognizing new "economic rights," and of building a new "economic constitutional order."[8] In his published post-mortem on his election victory, Roosevelt said that "our political life clings too much to the political machinery of the past," that "we are a generation overdue in political and economic reconstruction."[9] In his second fireside chat, Roosevelt reminded his listeners that the goal was not simply relief or recovery but "to prevent the return of conditions which came very close to destroying what we call modern civiliza-tion."[10] The word "New" in New Deal, he wrote a few years later, meant that "a new order of things designed to benefit the great mass of our farmers, workers, and businessmen would replace the old order of special privilege in a Nation that was completely and thoroughly disgusted with the existing dispensation."[11] Not since Lincoln had an American leader grasped such an opportunity to think anew and act anew, and not since Jackson had the field for independent political action appeared so wide open.

Roosevelt's sense of the reconstructive moment intensified as his presi-dency progressed. "The more I learn about Andy Jackson," he wrote in the latter part of 1934, "the more I love him."[12] It is difficult to imagine two presidents less alike in personal temperament. Roosevelt was a pragmatic, engaging, and buoyant gentleman schooled in the eastern establishment; Jackson, a moralistic, vindictive, and tortured soldier hardened on the frontier. Yet the kindred relationship that Roosevelt began to feel with Old Hickory at about this time was born of a sense of their shared political situation. The summer of 1934 had witnessed the first clear signs of discontent with the New Deal, and in August some of the favored interests of the old order (old-line Demo-crats prominent among them) formed the American Liberty League as a first line of political resistance.[13] With the League arrayed against the New Deal in the midterm elections and friend separated from foe, the Jacksonian frame of national politics came back into sharp relief. The 1934 election returns gave Roosevelt an extraordinary popular endorse-ment—actually expanding upon his initial rout of Republicans and reactionaries. But shortly thereafter, more formidable support for the old order began to flex its muscle within the government. The Supreme Court peremptorily swept away the most important work of the New Deal reconstruction to that time. It was now Roosevelt on one side boasting overwhelming popular support, and standing against him, a bulwark of interests and institutions determined to defend the old ways.

For Roosevelt after the Court challenge, as for Jackson after the recharter of the National Bank, the choice was either to abandon the commitment to reconstruct or to radicalize it.

Roosevelt used the Jackson analogy to kick off the election year of 1936. "History so often repeats itself," he told his audience at the Jackson Day dinner in January. "An overwhelming proportion of the material power of the Nation" had arrayed itself against him, as it had against Jackson. "Hollow and outworn traditionalism" had shaken its finger at them both. "It seemed sometimes that all were against [them]—all but the people of the United States."[14] Roosevelt savored each parallel, defiant as ever of the differences that had emerged over the intervening hundred years of national development.[15]

But then, just as he prepared to do what Jackson had done so long ago, those differences began to take their toll. The party that Roosevelt had enjoined to don the mantle of his New Deal simply refused to give up its foolish traditions on demand. His was not, like the party of Jackson, a mere extension of his personality, and to prove the point, modern Democrats called an abrupt halt to his efforts to remake their organization. As for the material powers arrayed in opposition, Roosevelt did not face a single, conspicuous, overweening corporation but a densely organized corporate economy. Destroying the latter was unthinkable, and therein lay a new and even more formidable line of defense against a leader determined to make things over. True enough, a new majority of farmers, laborers, and businessmen was ripe for mobilization just as it had been in Jackson's day. But fashioning a new political coalition for these interests now meant parceling out power to national farm organizations, national labor organizations, and national business organizations. Roosevelt's allies in this reconstruction were less dependent and thus less dependable; his opponents, less dispensable and thus more secure. The measure of independence afforded Roosevelt by modern conditions was more than matched by the demands this nationally organized society imposed on his extra-modern leadership project.

Reflecting back on earlier efforts, we see that Roosevelt was triply constrained in wielding the reconstructive authority in a pluralist polity. He could not stand alone like Jackson had and claim with simple innocence that his battles were the people's battles. Nor could he fall back on any single, overpowering concentration of national political energies like that which had supported Lincoln's far less personal political appeal. Nor could he, like both of these, destroy outright the key institutional supports for his opponents' power. The Roosevelt reconstruction was neither a personal triumph over all comers (Jackson) nor a skillful pacing of an irrepressible vanguard party (Lincoln). His authority operated further removed than before from control over the terms and conditions of the reordering of government and politics. His reconstruction unfolded as a more systemic process, curiously decoupled from his own personal will. The most significant political leader in twentieth-century America, Roosevelt repeatedly went down to personal defeat, leaving others to compose an order of their own out of the wreckage of his much grander ambitions.

The more we pursue the historical reshaping of reconstructive politics under Franklin Roosevelt the less satisfactory become our commonplace understandings of the dynamics of presidential history in general and the making of the "modern presidency" in particular. From his flight to Chicago in 1932 to his order creating the Executive Office of the President in 1939, Roosevelt appears at first an extraordinarily skillful politician successfully garnering new leadership resources from modernity and methodically forging from them the foundations of presidential government. Roosevelt's America was growing ripe with nationally organized interests and independent authorities, and modern American government was becoming increasingly dependent on the directive capacities of the presidency. We see him expanding these capacities categorically, foreclosing the option of a "clerkship" presidency, and institutionalizing executive leadership in a new, presidentially driven system of government.[16] And yet while the forging of the "modern presidency" during the New Deal imparted a critical margin of new power and independence to all future incumbents alike, a careful reading of past experience suggests that it delimited Roosevelt's own. The New Deal was about recasting basic commitments of ideology and interest in American government, and for that it relied on a leadership stance that long preceded the proliferation of nationally organized powers and independent authorities. More to the point, this burgeoning of interests and authorities in modern America did not serve to bolster Roosevelt's transformative ambitions, but, on the contrary, served to strengthen the countervailing forces within the government and to undercut his personal control. If Roosevelt is a prototype of the "modern president," it is only because when he tackled specifically modern concerns like managing the organized interests of industrial society or rationalizing a bloated federal bureaucracy he met with frustrations that would prove commonplace among his successors. Like the forging of an organized political opposition under Jackson, the forging of the institutions of the modern presidency under Roosevelt marks a hemming in of what has traditionally been the most potent leadership posture.

Others have cautioned against attributing Roosevelt's distinction among modern presidents to some extraordinary skill in political leadership.[17] Looking back to previous reconstructive breakthroughs, we see that his decisive edge lay more precisely in his political identity as an opposition leader standing steadfast against a vulnerable regime. Roosevelt did no more important work during the New Deal years than to cultivate this identity and exercise the prerogative it afforded him to hammer relentlessly against the bankruptcy of the received order. That was what opened the door to a rush of new ideas and interests, that was what kept his presidency buoyant in the face of one reversal after another, that was what gave meaning to his landslide elections, and that was what forced those who would frustrate him personally to acknowledge and ultimately accept the new state of affairs he had sponsored. The irony in the making of the modern presidency during these years is that at each step of the way it reflected new encumbrances on the battering ram of reconstructive authority. From the flight to Chicago to the establishment of the Executive Office, the modern tools and claims that Roosevelt bequeathed to future incumbents were fashioned in grudging recognition of the organized powers and independent authorities that were circumscribing his extra-modern political warrants. These new imperatives of accommodation dogged all aspects of his leadership project until finally his extraordinary claims to independence were corralled into a new organizational form—the "modern presidency"—far more respectful than Roosevelt himself of the power and independence of everyone else. Roosevelt's political achievement was to extort from modernity a measure of legitimacy for radical change in basic governing commitments; the "modern presidency" emerged as the achievement of those who resisted him.

Roosevelt's Discipline

Roosevelt concluded his first inaugural address with a hard-hitting cadence about the importance of discipline. The new President urged "sacrifice for the good of a common discipline," "a disciplined attack on our common problems," "discipline and direction under leadership." Curious on its face, Roosevelt enveloped within this appeal something even more remarkable: a plea for indulgence, of Roosevelt himself and the requisite adjustments in the Constitution that might be needed to obtain "action in this image."[18]

While Roosevelt was adamant about the importance of discipline, few at that time or since have been able to find in his leadership any such thing. Further exploration of the impact of modernity on Roosevelt's political project helps to unravel this paradox. Part of the problem is figuring out what Roosevelt meant by discipline. He hints at a general set of commitments, "a common discipline," through which broad authority might be claimed for action in the moment at hand. He suggests that these commitments impose a certain duty or regimen, galvanizing the people for "discipline and direction under leadership." He implies that these commitments might release the leader from more formal restraints on presidential action in order to pursue a "disciplined attack" on the nation's problems. These different meanings of the term drew out the requisites of acting effectively at the historical juncture Roosevelt described in the earlier parts of his address. The President made his appeal for discipline after he had declared the old leadership bankrupt; they had lost all "vision," and "where there is no vision the people perish." He said that his vision would release the nation from the received dispensation, that it would save the people by implementing afresh the ancient truths. In this, Roosevelt, like Jefferson, Jackson, and Lincoln before him, determined to let the legitimacy of a new ordering emerge out of his extraordinary warrants for shattering the received order and building anew upon the principles on which the government was first founded. He claimed expansive authority for transformative change by couching a thoroughgoing repudiation of the order that presently existed in an order-affirming logic. Discipline meant nothing more or less than adherence to the logic of this reconstructive trope, the political grammar of saving by destroying.

Sustaining this discipline in modern America presented no end of difficulties, however, and perhaps that is why Roosevelt was so insistent about it. Strange and starkly contrasting alternatives surrounded him from the outset, and mastering the particular choices presented through the simple reconstructive logic strained that logic almost beyond recognition. When contemplating a basic change in established power arrangements in industrial America, nothing was simple or straightforward.

No sooner did Roosevelt repudiate Hoover's "American way" then he was besieged by questions about what exactly he proposed to replace it with. The questions themselves suggest a heightened level of uncertainty about fundamentals in the ideologically charged world of the 1930s. At the time of Roosevelt's inauguration, designs for imparting coherence and direction to the state were crowding in on one another as never before, and with a whole host of cosmopolitan alternatives implicated in any decisive change, debates about where Roosevelt might lead the nation proved especially difficult to control. In his first three months in office, Roosevelt launched one program (the Tennessee Valley Authority) that Hoover had rejected as a "piece of socialism," and another (the National Recovery Administration) that Hoover had rejected as a species of "fascism."[19] Socialism, fascism, capitalism, communism—these were the terms of candid talk about the direction of national affairs in the 1930s, and they were constantly shoved in the face of the leader who had promised candor to America.[20] Frances Perkins relates the story of a young reporter who confronted the President directly with this field of choices and asked him to declare himself explicitly. After rejecting each of the labels presented him, the President asserted blankly: "I am a Christian and a Democrat—that's all."[21]

No president so fully authorized to change things had ever faced so stark an array of alternatives, and Roosevelt was never so steadfast as in his refusal to embrace any one of them. He appears in this light to have evaded the momentous questions of his age, to have been impervious to the choices before him; he was intent only to affirm American traditions. His self-definition suggests the antithesis of design, or to put it more generously, a pragmatic application of familiar values to the political exigencies of the moment. Perkins herself reads Roosevelt's response in this benign fashion. His ambitions, she argued, were essentially American, and his political achievements merely pushed our politics "a little left of center."[22]

Much the same conclusion can be drawn from Roosevelt's disposition toward the other set of choices confronting his New Deal, the burgeoning field of progressive reform alternatives. Confronted with all the various reform ideas that had been percolating through American government over the previous thirty years, Roosevelt again refused to commit himself. Much to the frustration of those competing to control the nation's new direction, he embraced all and kept his options open. He lent a sympathetic ear to nationalists and internationalists, budget balancers and deficit spenders, planners and regulators, corporatists and trust-busters, voluntarists and statists, centralizers and decentralizers, economic realists and social idealists, scientific managers and partisan enthusiasts. In the end, all these contending "progressivisms" would make themselves felt in New Deal policy. For all Roosevelt's eagerness to elaborate the ideas of reformers and launch new reform experiments, he appears in these matters inconsistent in his choices, indifferent to the competing claims being asserted in his name, and bereft of any particular transformative vision of his own.[23]

Between all the designs he rejected and all the designs he embraced, Roosevelt's discipline seems to just melt away into a broth of truisms about American national politics.[24] Therein indeed lay new limits on the reconstructive stance. And yet, to leave the matter at that misses the point entirely. Little can be gained from fixing the boundaries of Roosevelt's leadership if we do not first reckon with its extraordinary potency. Assessing the transformative punch that made the New Deal one of the few decisive departures in American government and politics forces us back to Roosevelt's initial premises for leadership, premises that transcend these contemporary frames of reference altogether.

The commonplace that Roosevelt was a pragmatist tells us far more than we realize in this regard. Historically, the pragmatic approach to policy questions has not signaled the absence of something else, but the presence of something quite rare. A president can be a pragmatist only to the extent that he commands political independence from the existing state of affairs and asserts an expansive warrant for discarding received political formulas. Those presidents who have pursued a political alternative most doggedly have not been those with grand designs or comprehensive policy packages, but those least closed off to rethinking political relationships by the shape of things as they find them. Their stubbornly open-ended approach to the shape of things to come does not foreclose options on change but protects and nurtures them. Pragmatism in this sense—skepticism toward received conceptions of the alternatives and willingness to entertain different formulas—harbors radicalism as the president's prerogative. Roosevelt was less the archetypical American leader than a leader of this particular type. If the political premises he brought to action were familiar, they were also quite extraordinary. He flatly asserted both the ethical bankruptcy of the recent course of national development and the need for a thoroughgoing reformulation of first principles. It is in just this sense that his discipline defies the cosmopolitan and progressive labels that surrounded it. It was Jeffersonian in the sense that Jefferson's declaration "We are all federalists, we are all republicans" aimed to displace the received alternatives altogether. It was Lincolnesque in the sense that Lincoln's refrain "My policy is to have no policy" set the course for a second American revolution.

Roosevelt's self-definition "I am a Christian and a Democrat" took in the historical context in which it was offered in this way. Christian sentiments reverberate throughout New Deal political rhetoric, a reminder of the pervasive influence the social gospel has traditionally played in American reform. But when Roosevelt invoked these sentiments in the 1930s, they hit their targets with the authority of Jesus Christ himself. He employed them at once to stigmatize the received course, to set his leadership apart from it, and to tie his vision back to fundamentals. Christian sentiments framed ruthless images of the degenerate regime Roosevelt sought to displace. He stood against the "money changers." He would "apply social values more noble than mere monetary profit," and cleanse the temple of the stewards who had disgraced it. "Their efforts had been cast in the pattern of an outworn tradition. Faced with the failure of credit they have proposed only the lending of more money. Stripped of the lure of profit by which to induce our people to follow their false leadership, they have resorted to exhortations, pleading tearfully for restored confidence. They know only the rules of a generation of self-seekers."[25]

Roosevelt led off with an uncompromising declaration of his single most important commitment: to discard the premises currently undergirding the American political economy.[26] Change was possible, indeed imperative, he claimed, because the values that currently held sway in American government were not the values on which American civilization really rested. Roosevelt reassured the people of the essential soundness of their system of government by insisting that different values, his values, were the original and fundamental ones. His contention was that these "ancient truths" could not be abandoned without risk to our national identity, and that they could not be reaffirmed without a basic alteration of received arrangements. To restore them now was, in other words, a reconstructive task of the first order.

Roosevelt proclaimed the "falsity of material wealth as the standard of success" and punctured illusory "standards of pride of place and personal profit." "These dark days will be worth all the cost," he said, "if they teach us that our true destiny is not to be ministered unto but to minister to ourselves and to our fellow men."[27] The sentiments were as familiar to Americans as Christian morality itself, but this was no run-of-the-mill critique. Once stated in the desperate circumstances at hand, there would be no retreat short of political suicide from the transformative ambitions it encompassed. Roosevelt would, in fact, be driven by these initial commitments in directions he scarcely contemplated at the outset. His radically open-ended assault on the old elite set in motion a radical recasting of the social foundations of the American regime.[28]

The "Democrat" side of Roosevelt's self-definition was also elaborated early on. Again the point of reference was Hoover's impossibly narrow conception of the "American Way." In Roosevelt's hands, American values did not constrain the nation to rest its fate on the machinations of the bankers; on the contrary, they demanded attention to the whole range of economic interests and social concerns. The new "economic constitutional order" that Roosevelt promised was one that would reach out to the "forgotten man at the bottom of the economic pyramid" and directly engage all actors in the marketplace.[29] As he put it just after his election:

> There have been administrations in the life of the country which have represented only a part of this great union of interests, and, unfortunately, at times, a very special and narrow interest . . .
> The interests of labor and industry cannot be promoted at the expense of agriculture; neither can capital reach a condition of true prosperity without at the same time offering a more legitimate share to labor. Any neglected group, whether of agriculture, industry, mining, commerce, or finance, can infect our whole national life and produce widespread misery. My administration shall be devoted to the task of giving practical force and necessary legislative form to the central fact of contemporary American life, viz., the interdependence of all factions, sections, and interests of this great country. I believe in a higher conservation which seeks to provide work and economic security to the mass of the people in order that they may be free to live and develop their individual lives and seek happiness and recognition without inflicting injury upon their fellow citizens.[30]

On inspection, then, Roosevelt's seemingly evasive self-definition, like his seemingly oblique call for "discipline," concentrated all the elements of a classic reconstructive project. The order-affirming, order-shattering, and order-creating impulses of presidential action were synchronized to propel, through both words and deeds, a concerted break with previously established commitments of ideology and interest. While familiar national values were invoked to lend legitimacy to this break, Roosevelt's claim was that those values had been lost in the indulgences of the old order. Redeeming them at this moment would mean far more than tilting politics a little left of center; it would entail reconstituting the national government around an entirely new political center.[31] To be sure, Roosevelt reached out to all interests to join him in this reconstructive task. He would, in fact, reach out to the managers of credit first of all. But his repudiative posture harbored potent warrants for redistributing power away from the favored interests of the old order, and as the bankers themselves were the first to realize, his commitments to other, previously marginalized interests changed the terms of dealing with everyone.[32]

By the foreign and domestic standards of the day, this discipline was elemental and crudely political. There is no need to make it more than it was, only to identify it as something recognizable enough in the range of stances that presidents have struck that its effectiveness can be evaluated amid all the more substantive choices now pressing in upon it. In the 1930s, the reconstructive discipline would prove to have less purchase on the particular choices the president made than it had for others before, but understanding Roosevelt's premises in this way raises several cautions for evaluating what actually happened.

The first is simply that Roosevelt's reassurances affirming transparent American values should not be taken as prima facie evidence that he lacked transformative ambitions. When Roosevelt deflected stark cosmopolitan alternatives in favor of ancient truths, he was not abdicating a transformative role for himself but pressing the best case he had for transformation against an especially heavy bombardment of nonstarters.[33] So much commentary has exposed the limits of Roosevelt's order-shattering commitments that we have generally failed to appreciate the importance of order-affirming assurances to presidential reconstructions. Given the near constant press of foreign designs, it might better be said that nothing was more critical to negotiating a decisive break with the politics of the past in the 1930s than that it be understood as resolutely American. Roosevelt's avowed commitment to address the interests implicated in the Depression in radically new ways invited foreign comparisons and compounded the difficulty of sustaining this classically American reconstructive authority. As it turns out, it was the vagueness of Roosevelt's order-affirming assurances, not the weakness of his order-shattering commitments, that proved to be the real Achilles' heel of his leadership project.

A second caution: while Roosevelt relied on the penetrating simplicity—the transparent legitimacy—of the reconstructive discipline, he was thrown back for practical instruments on a set of reform formulas that were anything but uncomplicated. Progressivism was the irresistible source of reform ideas for the New Deal. It was the voice of the people against the interests, the gospel of social improvement through governmental action, the democratic response to corporate capitalism, the authority of experts, the promise of economy and efficiency. If nothing else, Roosevelt's personal history beckoned him to realize the progressive reordering that had eluded both his cousin Theodore Roosevelt and his mentor Woodrow Wilson. And yet, as Herbert Hoover's experience had recently attested, progressivism had become over the years a rather sticky smorgasbord of competing enthusiasms. Attractive as it was overall, it was harder than ever to arrange on a single plate. Progressives were at odds among themselves on basic questions about the proper direction of reform, and progressivism could as easily justify resistance as support for any particular course that Roosevelt himself might choose. When a national policy had to be set, the progressive ideal of administrative rationalization proved sorely lacking as a cohesive political force and the experts could be counted on only to debate the issue from scattered positions all over the political map. Before we conclude that Rooseveltian reform lacked the depth of vision possessed by other reconstructive leaders—Jefferson, Jackson, or Lincoln—we might consider the fact that in this reconstruction, unlike those others, the dominant reform impulse of the day defied efforts to galvanize political change in any particular direction. Between his substantive promise of "work and economic security to the mass of the people" and the competing voices of progressivism, Roosevelt had all he could do to wield his expansive political authority and carry on, in the name of reform, a sustained assault on established power arrangements.

A final caution is that while the reconstructive discipline offers a wider field to pragmatic action than any other leadership posture, it is never purely pragmatic. The pragmatism of Roosevelt's leadership is easy to exaggerate because his approach to the designs contending for his attention was enigmatic and also because virtually all the choices he made were sorely compromised by others. It is certainly true that

Roosevelt was least successful when he was least pragmatic, but the more important point is that the upshot of this reconstruction was a good deal less ideologically charged than Roosevelt himself.

One of the great advantages of the political grammar of the reconstructive stance is that it can accommodate broad strategic turns on matters of policy without obscuring the leader's commitment to change. There were some astounding turnabouts on policy over the course of Roosevelt's first term, but he emerged in 1936 more implacable than ever in his resolve to displace the received political order and secure a broad-based alternative. Throughout his reelection year, he expanded upon his earlier repudiations of Herbert Hoover and the Republican leadership. "The challenge faced by this Congress," he said in his annual message in January of 1936, "is more menacing than merely a return to the past—bad as that would be. Our resplendent economic aristocracy does not want to return to that individualism of which they prate . . . Give them their way and they will take the course of every autocracy of the past—power for themselves and enslavement for the public."[34] In accepting his party's nomination for a second term, Roosevelt spoke of economic dynasties that had come to regiment the people, their labor, and their property, leaving the average man today to confront "the problem of the Minute Man." The fight, he said, was "to *save* a great and precious form of government." "These economic royalists complain that we seek to overthrow the institutions of America. What they really complain of is that we seek to take away their power. *Our allegiance to American institutions requires the overthrow of this kind of power.*"[35] By the fall of 1936, Roosevelt was taking on all the sinister "forces of selfishness and of lust for power." He intended for his second term to do more than "match" these forces; he intended to "master" them. Roosevelt's defiance—"I welcome their hatred"— openly proclaimed sentiments that Jefferson had left to his personal letters.[36]

This campaign has been criticized for its failure to prepare the nation in a more concrete way for the difficult constitutional questions that would arise in the reconstructive initiatives of the second term.[37] Nonetheless, Roosevelt's words were blunt and uncompromising, and they clearly anticipated a decidedly unpragmatic turn. More important still, the President's relentlessly repudiative rhetoric left an indelible imprint on his overwhelming reelection victory, effectively silencing direct challenges to the legitimacy of the new state of affairs he had sponsored.

Curiously, as Roosevelt prepared to risk the enormous political capital he had earned in the campaign with a final bid for mastery over those who had threatened the security of his new regime, it was his opponents who opted for the more pragmatic approach and seized from him control over the institutional forms through which the new regime would be accommodated.

Holding fast to a political discipline that had proven its potency time and again in galvanizing the reconstruction of American government, Roosevelt was able to tap the still formidable advantages it afforded over the foreign and domestic choices pressed upon him. But as the very stridency of his rhetoric might suggest, that discipline had to be stretched to cover the new universe of institutional action in which it now operated. There was nothing so clear or straightforward in Roosevelt's stance in 1936 as destroying a bank to save liberty or destroying slavery to save the Union. As the old argument for saving through destroying reverberated through the now interdependent interests of industrial America, it became at once more encompassing and less pointed. The broad truths to be affirmed melted into truisms, as actually doing away with any of the institutions they implicated became more problematic. Jackson and Lincoln could marginalize the institutions inhabited by those whose interests and values they sought to repudiate; Roosevelt's targets had to be abstracted from the institutions they dominated. He raged against economic royalists and judicial incompetence, but he did not propose to do away with corporate capitalism or the Supreme Court, and to the extent that he was understood to be threatening the destruction of such institutions, he exposed the precariousness of his claims to saving anything fundamental.

This weakness in Roosevelt's reconstructive stance was foreshadowed in his first inaugural address when he linked his appeal for discipline to a plea for indulgence in manipulating constitutional formalities. As would become increasingly clear, one of the "truths" Roosevelt was determined to retrieve was the mythic intention of the founders to keep the basic framework of American government flexible. No one had put the case for reconstruction quite that way before, and Roosevelt would find this rather slippery ground for radical action. A less than reassuring affirmation of fundamentals, the argument for flexibility in constitutional interpretation is easily unhinged in the pursuit of transformative changes. We need only reflect back on the difficult struggles Jackson and Lincoln waged against charges of despotism to appreciate the importance of having the order-affirming pretexts for radical change more firmly in hand. Roosevelt's counterparts had boasted far clearer conceptions of constitutional government as they went about altering received governmental arrangements, and their substantive referents for saving through destroying were far more tightly specified. Could Roosevelt's "ancient truths" stand the test of his ambitions and protect his reconstructive project against the inevitable accusations of constitutional usurpation and one-man rule? Would the more technocratic nostrums of progressive reform cover the shortfall? How much of this extra-modern discipline would the interests and institutions of modern America absorb before rendering the whole idea of a presidentially led political reordering insufferably un-American?

The Collapse of the NRA

Three and a half months after taking office, Roosevelt announced passage of "the most important and far-reaching legislation ever enacted by the American Congress." The National Industrial Recovery Act climaxed that breathless special session known as the "Hundred Days" with "a supreme effort to stabilize for all time the many factors which make for the prosperity of the Nation, and the preservation of our standards."[38] Roosevelt's rhetoric heralded what was indeed the single most ambitious initiative for reconstruction he sponsored during the New Deal.[39] The National Recovery Administration anticipated a wholesale reorganization of the nation's industrial relations, and in doing so it put Roosevelt's transformative discipline to a severe first test.

Thinking ahead to what would happen later in the New Deal, we might consider the NRA merely an overture to reconstruction and a rather typical one at that. Consistent with the early initiatives of previous reconstructive leaders, the NRA deflected immediate pressures for more divisive and destabilizing action and sought instead to build the confidence of all interests in the New Deal departure. It was the administration's alarm over the Senate's passage of Democrat Hugo Black's bill mandating a thirty-hour work week for labor that set it moving in earnest toward its own program for industrial recovery. Facing down the first major initiative of the special session to address the unemployment problem, as well as the threat of a general strike if the initiative failed, administration forces bottled up Black's bill in the House and then displaced it altogether with a more flexible and commodious proposal.[40] Its National Recovery Administration was designed to reach out to industry as well as labor and to sponsor new forums of cooperation that would ease the antagonisms of the marketplace. The NRA echoed conspicuously Hooverian themes of voluntarism, associationalism, industrial self-help, and cooperative management. It acknowledged the interests of labor with promises of collective bargaining; it acknowledged the interests of large corporations with promises of relief from the antitrust laws; it acknowledged the interests of smaller entrepreneurs with promises of continued protection against unfair trade practices; and it acknowledged the interests of planners with promises of governmental control and direction. It held in its balance a presidential bid for national unity in industrial policy.[41]

And yet no president had ever attempted to change so much so soon. No mere overture to reconstruction, the NRA was, just as the President billed it, the main event. It is noteworthy that Roosevelt had originally thought that this kind of initiative would be out of place in a special session devoted largely to emergency action. He had hoped to wait and, more in the manner of other reconstructive leaders, let the situation sort itself out a bit more before crafting a program so sweeping in its transformative ambitions.[42] Since congressional support for the Black bill had made it impossible to wait without risking serious offense to labor or industry, overture and main event were folded together in a program whose reconstructive implications were far more radical than its encompassing political vision would admit or, as it turned out, long sustain.

The NRA aimed to stabilize production. In its original, pre-Roosevelt formulation, it was an industry-sponsored proposal for "business syndicalism backed by police." But the amended version that was approved by the Roosevelt administration and enacted by the Congress contained novel provisions for bolstering the purchasing power of consumers, and these carried in their train a host of potentially radical ideas.[43] The first was that the federal government should become an active partner in controlling the industrial relations of the nation, rather than a mere policeman; the second was that those relations should be orchestrated according to the executive branch's holistic view of national priorities.[44] The federal executive was to help business trade associations negotiate and enforce uniform operating codes appropriate to their particular industries. The codes were to establish a floor under the downward spiral of prices, and to provide industry-appropriate standards of minimum wages, maximum hours, and working conditions. In addition, the codes were to guarantee that workers could organize and bargain collectively without employer interference. Though the act did not elaborate the point, the code-making scheme implied a significant redistribution of power within as well as among business, labor, and the state. For NRA enthusiasts, the program embodied the ideal of a socially benevolent economy in which mass interests would be directed democratically by government administrators. Among skeptics, the controlling ideas seemed to come in equal measure from Moscow and Berlin.[45]

Behind the dreams and horrors inspired by the NRA were three assumptions about order and change in the American regime whose fate would determine the federal government's new claims to partnership "rights" in industrial relations.[46] The first assumption, and the only one Roosevelt could still reclaim by the spring of 1935, drew out the repudiative implications of the recent presidential campaign. It held that the people had rejected the old thinking about the American political economy and that the election had authorized a radical departure. Reminded of just how directly the NRA would repudiate the myths of laissez faire, Roosevelt responded: "If that philosophy hadn't proved to be bankrupt, Herbert Hoover would be sitting here right now."[47] The second assumption, and the one most dramatically refuted in the spring of 1935, was more affirmative, but also more speculative. It ventured that the Constitution offered the Congress and the chief executive sufficient authority and flexibility to oversee, implement, and, if push came to shove, impose a new order of productive relations on industry. There was a broad precedent for this in the mobilization for World War I, and a more specific one in railroad-labor relations. But 1933 was not wartime, and Congress's provisions for the NRA were woefully underspecified. Two years after it was inaugurated, the industrial code scheme would be rendered null and void by the Supreme Court.[48]

Yet, the NRA was moribund well before that. The program collapsed upon its third assumption, the one about how order was to be reconstructed. The plan's success hinged on workers and businessmen accepting the government's recognition of their interests in a spirit of mutual self-sacrifice—that is, with a willingness to forego the exercise of some of the market power each had developed over the years in order to serve the administration's own more complicated priorities.[49] This reliance on the cooperation of the program's principal clients was magnified at the very outset when Roosevelt, fearing uncontrolled spending on the part of the government itself, hived off the massive public works provisions of the NIRA into the conservative hands of the Interior Department and left the NRA to jump start a consumer-driven recovery by its own devices.[50] Roosevelt's disciplinary authority had a heavy load to carry at the NRA. It was his commitment to reconstruction that held together the diverse economic, social, and political interests arrayed under the initiative, and he was the one left floundering by the near immediate collapse of the program's operational integrity.

The political logic of the NRA demanded, first, that prices be held down long enough to allow consumer demand to catch up, even at the risk of reduced profits, and, second, that a modicum of competition be kept alive under the new cooperative arrangements. Both goals hinged on the ability of the code-making authorities to restrain the impulses of the program's business clients. Yet, in the frenetic days of code-making that followed the initial appearance of the Blue Eagle, program administrators were overwhelmed by the enormity of their task, and they came to depend on the most powerful businesses to hammer out standards for their industries. No sooner did it become apparent that pricing policies in the new codes would restrict entry to the marketplace than weaker businesses turned against the program. When program administrators made moves to redress these initial imbalances, the support of more powerful corporations softened. Within six months, business support, both strong and weak, large and small, was scattering to cries of centralization, regimentation, and dictatorship. Public investigations of NRA pricing policies followed fast on the heels of rising business disaffection, and this steamrolling of discontent forced the President to move in and clean house early in the fall of 1934. By that time, the damage was near complete, and the prospects for rededicating the program to free market principles and fair competition were grim.[51]

Meanwhile, the program's other major clientele, industrial workers, had trashed Roosevelt's hopes for the NRA on their own. The endorsement of collective bargaining rights contained in section 7a of the act was a cornerstone of the strategy of a consumer-driven recovery: bargaining wages up would fuel consumption. Yet, the program fell short of union interests per se in its vagueness about how collective bargaining would be exercised. Labor leaders, intent on fostering autonomous organizations, demanded that labor representation be determined exclusively by a simple majority of the workers employed by the company.

Business leaders, equally intent on maintaining their own power through company unions, insisted on principles of voluntarism and proportional representation. This issue split the NRA so severely that Roosevelt had to step in to reimpose a semblance of order. The program's administrator, Hugh Johnson, had come down hard on the side of proportional representation, and any other decision by the President would have further damaged the program's already precarious administrative integrity, not to mention its business support. But even as Roosevelt was endorsing Johnson's position and reassuring business, workers were exercising their independent powers to disrupt productive relations nationwide. Embittered unions mocked the NRA's pretensions to the restoration of order, stability, and productivity by striking, throwing industrial America into a heightened state of class conflict, all the while keeping the attention of reformers in government riveted on the issue of majority rule. Startled by the intensity of the storm but still concerned to maintain industry support for the New Deal, the President sought to bolster labor's position further without actually yielding on proportional representation. Specifically, he moved to strengthen the enforcement of labor's claims through a National Labor Relations Board that would operate within the existing NRA framework. But this accommodation to the contending interests proved no more effective in controlling the course of reform than did his retreat from de facto cartelization.[52]

As the NRA's complex priorities succumbed to the independent power of the program's major clienteles, a political embarrassment of Hooverian proportions seemed in the offing. Roosevelt had encompassed under his personal authority a set of starkly conflicting interests, confident that his reconstructive discipline could reorder and stabilize relations among them. He found, however, that he could neither contain, transform, resolve, nor ignore the hard choices they presented him. Eighteen months after announcing the most important and far-reaching legislation ever passed by the American Congress, the NIRA had proven itself to all concerned just one more link in the chain of broken promises. To the left, the "New Deal" seemed to be nothing more than "the Old Deal in high gear." To the right, it seemed to be "absolute state socialism." To skeptics of all sorts, NRA had come to mean "No Recovery Allowed."[53]

Roosevelt appeared to drift as his new order collapsed around him. Progressive voices for industrial reform, newly fortified in the halls of

Congress by the midterm election, were fast at work on new initiatives more fully attuned to the failures of the President's program.[54] But Roosevelt held himself aloof from these efforts and committed himself instead to a salvage operation. "The fundamental principles and purposes of the [NIRA] are sound," he declared. "To abandon them is unthinkable."[55]

The NRA was still the centerpiece of the Roosevelt reconstruction, and Roosevelt was loath to renounce it, even at the risk of abandoning his position at the forefront of political change. In February 1935, he requested a two-year extension of the program in modified form. With all its problems, he argued, it was the only alternative to chaos.[56] What saved Roosevelt from the dubious prospect of having to stick with that argument was not the midterm bolstering of congressional support for reform (convenient as that would soon prove to be); it was the distillation of even more formidable resistance. Early in May the United States Chamber of Commerce, a key prop in NRA support, openly declared war on the New Deal.[57] Then at the end of the month, the Supreme Court added the authority of law to the assaults of the businessmen and unanimously declared that the President's alternative to chaos had itself no legitimate claims to order. While the NRA was disintegrating from within, the President had floundered; but as soon as it was declared unconstitutional, he bounced back, galvanized the overwhelming reform majorities in Congress, and nailed down the basic commitments of what would become the new liberal regime.

Close observers at the time recognized that the Court's decision in May 1935 was "the President's best piece of luck during his first term, for it spared him the uncomfortable necessity of lying in the bed he had made."[58] The insight is worthy of elaboration, for it is counterintuitive on its face. How could a president be made more effective politically by having the centerpiece of his program declared unconstitutional by the unanimous verdict of the nation's highest court, liberal and conservative justices alike? Roosevelt was able to get up out of the bed he had made because, far from denying his distinctive claim to political authority, the Supreme Court's action revived it. The Court released the President from the burdens of reconciling irreconcilable interests and defending the operations of a moribund program in the manner of a leader bound to past commitments. More than that, it dramatized the far more penetrating warrants for political action that had brought him to power in the first place. The voiding of the NRA codes turned the embarrassments Roosevelt had encountered in trying to deliver a new dispensation into a clear case of the intransigence of the old dispensation. On the eve of the "second hundred days," he was again blasting the bankruptcy of previously entrenched ideas and interests, defending the legitimacy of radical change, and promising to reconstruct the very terms on which American government operated. He was moving neither left nor right; he was making an extraordinary return to where he had started.

A few days after the Court's action, the President declared the voiding of the NRA codes "more important than any decision probably since the Dred Scott case."[59] He warned that the invalidation of the NRA threatened the whole concept of the New Deal, that the Agricultural Adjustment Act and the Securities Act had been made vulnerable to the same lines of argumentation. The question now was not simply whether there would be industrial codes but whether the nation would be forced to retreat to the principles of the discredited past. Indeed, the Court would push the federal government back beyond the Hoover days to the "horse and buggy" days. It threatened a "perfectly ridiculous and impossible situation." There would be no way to "move ahead," no hope of gaining "control over social and working conditions throughout the country." Roosevelt reckoned the Court's decision "the best thing that has happened to this country for a long time." It clarified for all concerned the stakes of support for a New Deal, and left him to hammer at the critical point.

> The issue is this . . . Is the United States going to decide, are the people of the United States going to decide that their Federal Government shall in the future have no right under any implied or any court-approved power to enter into a solution of a national economic problem . . .

> Shall we view our social problems—and in that I include employment of all kinds . . . from the same point of view or not; that the Federal Government has no right under this or following opinions to take any part in trying to better national social conditions? Now that is flat and that is simple.

> Can we go ahead as a Nation with the beautiful theory [that] . . . 'business can do anything it wants and [that] business is going to live up to the golden rule . . .' It is a school of thought so delightful in its naivete.

The NRA decision became a pivot around which the Court and the President, moving in starkly contrasting directions, framed the remainder of Roosevelt's first term. Initial press reaction to the President's attack on the Court was sharply negative, and yet between the spring of 1935 and the spring of 1936, the justices added credence to Roosevelt's words with a string of adverse decisions that voided far more than the relatively unpopular NRA.[60] Meanwhile, Roosevelt let the nation slip onto new political foundations. Passage of Senator Robert Wagner's National Labor Relations bill had become inevitable by this time, and sometime between the blast from the Chamber of Commerce and the voiding of the NRA codes by the Court, Roosevelt accepted the fait accompli. Belatedly, he threw his support behind a measure that would provide a government enforcement mechanism guaranteeing employer noninterference in labor organization and majority rule for union representation within government-certified bargaining units. In doing so, he implicitly acknowledged that industry was indeed irreconcilable to the kind of changes to which he had committed his administration and that all hopes for securing a new order now hinged on tying down a partnership between government and labor.[61]

With the Court negating the first New Deal, the presidential battering ram cleared the way to a second. Capitalizing on his new offensive against the intransigence of the old order, Roosevelt held Congress in session throughout the summer of 1935. In a rush, social security legislation, bolstering amendments for the Agricultural Adjustment Act and the TVA, a farm mortgage moratorium, a coal stabilization act, new relief legislation, and a wealth tax transformed the landscape of American government and politics. Notably, nothing on this list of leading reforms (or in those of the first part of 1936, like the Rural Electrification Act and the Soil Conservation and Domestic Allotment Act) tested the personal authority of the President to discipline interests in the way the NRA had. Roosevelt refortified his leadership position by underwriting a host of discrete interests and ideas, each under its own guiding lights. The closest thing to a new discipline to be found in these months lay in the juxtaposition of new supports for previously marginal constituencies and a more determined governmental thrust against previously established economic power. Stiffer banking regulations, the breakup of utility holding companies, the strengthening of the Securities and Exchange Commission—that was what remained of progressive business policy once the contending enthusiasm for a corporate commonwealth collapsed with the NRA. Proponents of these less accommodating forms of business control had been vying for the dominant voice in New Deal regulatory policy from the very beginning.

With the indifference industry had shown to the far more ambitious ideals of government planning, and with stark lines being drawn against the New Deal by the Chamber of Commerce, Roosevelt yielded to these old progressives and called their ideals his own.[62]

The Making of a Modern President

Roosevelt continued his frontal assault on the old order through the election campaign of 1936, and he gained in the process an overwhelming popular endorsement of the changes he had sponsored. Political opposition to the New Deal was virtually wiped out. Immediately after the election, the President moved to consolidate his achievements and recast the government in a way that would secure the dominance and future elaboration of his liberal social commitments. Like Jackson in 1833, Roosevelt set out to force submission, concentrate control, and attain mastery.

The result was stunning and relentless humiliation. During 1937 and 1938, Roosevelt was defeated in his effort to pack the Supreme Court, defeated in his effort to gain control of the new executive establishment, defeated in his effort to purge the conservatives from the Democratic party. His personal ambitions were deflected across the board, and his designs for the new order were replaced at every turn with arrangements that accommodated the authority and independence of the very institutional actors he had sought to bend to his will. The awkward edifice known as "the modern presidency" was premised on this systematic denial of Roosevelt's own proposals. Roosevelt did not aspire to the position offered him; he was forced into it.

A glance back at prior reconstructions reminds us that these gross slippages in political control are not entirely without precedent. Indeed, each successive reconstruction has demonstrated increased political resistance to the president's personal will. Had not Jackson's victory tour after the compromise settlement of the nullification crisis hidden a scattering of his postelection support and the political revival of his arch enemies? Had not the Democratic gains in the midterm elections of 1834 and the final expunging of Jackson's Senate censure in 1837 hidden a formidable reorganization of national political opposition during the Bank War? The point remains, however, that Roosevelt would have been delighted with such an outcome. His second-term initiatives yielded no victory tours, no electoral gains at the crucial six-year mark, no final expungements, no reclarification of national party divisions. His frustrations went deeper even than Lincoln's, for Roosevelt's differences with his own party pushed far beyond questions about the strategy and timing of change. In fact, common ground between them was fast disappearing, and an impasse over ultimate ends threatened as the President's quest for national controls rubbed up against the institutional bulwark of race relations in the South.[63]

How are we to make sense of Roosevelt's acute political estrangement at the very moment when his new regime was being consolidated? An important clue lies in the collapse of the NRA during his first term. When the program Roosevelt touted in 1933 as the centerpiece of his reconstruction fell apart in 1934, his reconstructive project was resurrected by other institutional actors on ground that he was, at best, reluctant to tread. Indeed, up until the final moments of the legislative process, Roosevelt had been an unhelpful witness to what would become the critical political shift in New Deal regime construction—the shift from the NRA (and business) to the Wagner Act (and labor) as the cornerstone of the new ordering. While the making of the liberal order had proceeded apace under the general auspices of Roosevelt's reconstructive authority, the terms that he himself had set for change had not only been frustrated by those opposed to a New Deal but disregarded by many of those most friendly to it. The Rooseveltian battering ram had provided the opening to a second New Deal, but the new order was provided by the Congress.

This dynamic was elaborated during the second term. Each of the stunning defeats administered to Roosevelt personally were accompanied by equally significant recognitions by the victors of the legitimacy of a new state of affairs. The Supreme Court took its cues from the election returns. Working in the privacy of its own chambers, it had decided to reverse its opposition to the New Deal well before the President's Court-packing plan was disclosed.[64] Indeed, the Court helped defeat the President's plan—a plan that threatened to terminate judicial independence and subordinate the Court to the presidency—by accommodating in the midst of the battle the content and style of New Deal legislation. Similarly, while the central targets of the party purge survived and thwarted Roosevelt's quest to become master of his own party, they took care to avoid campaigning as opponents of the President or the already-enacted policies of the New Deal.[65] Finally, while in 1938 the Seventy-fifth Congress rejected the President's plan for subordinating the new national bureaucracy to the chief executive, the Seventy-sixth passed another, more modest proposal in 1939 to help him manage the newly expanded federal establishment.[66]

The pattern to be gleaned across the eight years of the New Deal reconstruction draws forward a pattern evident across successive episodes of reconstruction. What we observe is a systematic decoupling of the reconstructive process from the personal will of the reconstructive leader. Although thwarting the President's own designs, Court, Congress, and party accommodated the New Deal in an order that contained Roosevelt's quest for mastery and preserved traditional prerogatives. In the second term, it was *their* pragmatic adaptations that scuttled *his* more programmatic vision.

These observations help to unravel the most obvious problem confronting anyone trying to come to terms with Roosevelt's political leadership: how could a president suffer so many resounding defeats on his major political initiatives—from the voiding of his initial program by the Supreme Court to the failure of the party purge—without completely losing control of the situation? The decoupling phenomenon suggests two factors at work in this puzzle: one, tied to the historical development of the reconstructive stance, has rendered the president's personal assertion of control progressively more problematic; the other is the residual and yet still formidable advantage that clings to this leadership stance vis-à-vis all others in legitimating change. Roosevelt's resilience in the face of stunning defeat testifies to the distinctiveness of the central claim that he brought into office. His basic leadership posture identified him with the building of an alternative to a bankrupt regime, and he used that posture effectively enough to challenge old arrangements and cut off all paths of retreat from a political reconstruction on new liberal ground. To understand why Roosevelt's presidency did not simply disintegrate in the face of his second-term reversals, why radically new commitments of ideology and interest were accommodated in the end, and why censorious charges, sensational defeats, and even another late-breaking recession did not hamper his nomination or election to an unprecedented third term, the residual authority of his extra-modern, reconstructive stance remains crucial.

This leaves us to consider the secular development within that stance: the extent to which this great force of negation was further detached from control over the process of recreation. Historically, the delimitation of the reconstructive authority has followed the secular thickening of the institutional universe of political action; the proliferation of independent centers of power and authority has brought a simultaneous deterioration of the president's personal political control. The historian James Patterson hit on the point in a passing comment on Roosevelt's campaign to purge his conservative opponents from the Democratic party in the 1938 primaries. Responding to scholars who trace the failure to recast that party more thoroughly under the liberal standard to problems in Roosevelt's own performance, Patterson argues forcefully that success was precluded by the resilience of the two major parties' organizations. Conservative Democrats were firmly ensconced in their own local fiefdoms. They showed little inclination to follow Roosevelt, but neither did they have any intention of leaving the party they had so long dominated at its moment of greatest power to join conservatives in the Republican organization. Republicans, despite a dismal performance at the polls, were equally disinclined to abandon their own organization. More revealing still, Roosevelt was himself dependent on support within the established Democratic organization to carry out his party-building designs. He needed and expected help from liberal Democrats within the states in which he was actively trying to purge conservatives, while they, on their own part, proved reluctant to intercede on his behalf against their fellow partisans and disturb the local party machinery within which they worked. "The purely organizational side of politics," Patterson concludes, "was too strong for sudden change from the top."[67]

Secular changes on the "organizational side of politics" have magnified the obstacles in the path of reconstructive leadership in several different ways. Most obviously, more organizations must be changed to secure any break. Furthermore, these organizations are more independent institutionally. Finally, when it comes to actually controlling matters of institutional reconstruction, the president himself is increasingly more dependent on a larger number of progressively more independent actors.

Consider in this regard the stern lesson in modern American politics administered to Roosevelt by organized labor during the Court battle. Roosevelt had good reason to expect labor support in the high-risk ventures of his second term. The AFL and CIO had suppressed their suspicions of each other and rallied to Roosevelt for the 1936 election.[68] Labor contributions to the Roosevelt campaign had helped offset the loss in business support incurred in the wake of the "second hundred days."[69] Moreover, Court-packing seemed a natural for organized labor: its hostility to the judiciary was primal, judicial action on the Wagner Act was pending, and the Court's opposition to New Deal legislation in general seemed crystal clear. Just to be sure, Roosevelt held new labor legislation hostage to a victory in Court-packing. He wanted the rival labor organizations solidly behind him in his final rout of judicial independence.

But grateful as the nation's labor leaders may have been for a sympathetic voice in the White House, they were hardly in the President's pocket, and Roosevelt came up short when they set his personal stakes in the Court battle against their own. The AFL, fearful that the President might throw his full weight behind the CIO, did give the Court plan its official stamp of approval. Still, its powerful Carpenters' Union affiliate remained strongly opposed, and with the internal unity of the organization in doubt, AFL leaders held back from any aggressive lobbying effort for the President on Capitol Hill. The official endorsement of the CIO was similarly conspicuous in its failure to follow through with a show of support where it would count most. Their leader, John L. Lewis, saw nothing pressing in the Court bill as long as the Wagner Act was law, and he preferred to devote his energies to using the Wagner Act and exploring its implications. He might have bargained with the President to help push judicial reform in exchange for an endorsement of the rights of workers in their sit-down strikes, but at that moment Roosevelt could ill afford to test the patience of Democratic regulars by piling upon his own controversial Court plan a radical quid pro quo to the workers' insurgency.[70]

The failure to rally a decisive show of labor support for the President in the first weeks after the Court plan was announced proved critical, for in mid-April the Supreme Court upheld the Wagner Act and Roosevelt lost all leverage with his most powerful ally in the fight. Indeed, the institutional roles were suddenly reversed. By continuing to insist on judicial reform even after the Court changed its tune, Roosevelt indicated that he wanted something more than judicial acceptance of New Deal programs. The implicit goal—subordination of the judiciary—posed a threat to labor almost as severe as the old system of labor relations in which the judiciary had exercised supremacy. The Court, in effect, underwrote the independence of labor organizations from the President along with its own.

The executive reorganization controversy, coming fast on the heels of the Court battle, offers another variation on this theme, for in its wake came a near universal drive among institutional actors to secure independence from presidential controls.[71] When Roosevelt first announced his intentions to reorganize, there was general agreement that something had to be done to restore order to the federal establishment. The helter-skelter proliferation of New Deal agencies with their far-flung constituencies was in Roosevelt's view the Republican's strongest potential issue in the 1936 campaign, and though they failed to press it, he took steps in the spring of that year to head it off.[72] By January 1937, he was ready with a report to Congress and a list of recommendations that would "set our house in order."[73] But general agreement that something had to be done proved as shallow as it was broad. Once it became clear that Roosevelt's intention was less to economize than to formalize spending programs initially addressed to the emergency, the bipartisan conservative coalition forged during the Court battle intensified its opposition. And when it became clear that the plan would insulate the programmatic commitments of the New Deal from congressional influence and consolidate the entire executive establishment under new presidential controls, organized support for the President, both inside and outside the government, turned tepid. Roosevelt wanted to build new departments, to limit the independence of the regulatory commissions by moving their policy-making role into the departments, to bring the budgeting, accounting, auditing, and planning functions of government all within the direct personal supervision of the President, to assume a near-unilateral authority to reorganize the executive branch. These changes would have provided his new regime a measure of organizational coherence and institutionalized a capacity for concerted action, and just as surely no organization or leader affected cared to sacrifice its own autonomy to these goals.[74] Labor organizations, the Catholic Church, and even Robert Wagner himself turned against the President's plan.

In the executive reorganization controversy we see most clearly how the social and economic forces prompting the President to claim supremacy within the federal establishment worked to deflect his effort to attain it. A centralization of governmental controls under the president may have been the best hope for ordering the organized interests of industrial America in their newly acknowledged state of interdependence, but the Constitution's stipulation of coequal branches stubbornly bolstered the independence of these interests. Once the President's reorganization plan went down to defeat as a dangerous assault on basic constitutional guarantees, a path opened to resolve the dilemma of how to manage the new regime. The shadow form of the reorganization proposal that was passed by Congress the next year recognized the President as first among equals in tackling the problems of administrative management. But while Roosevelt got the institutional independence he needed to service the new regime, everyone else got the independence they needed to prevent him from controlling it.[75] There were to be no new departments, the independent regulatory commissions were to remain independent, accounting and auditing functions were to remain separate from the newly enhanced presidential role in budgeting and planning, and discretionary reorganization authority was limited. In the end, Congress joined the common concern of all organized interests in protecting themselves from executive authority to a general recognition that new responsibilities would have to be borne by the president in negotiating national policy through this burgeoning organizational maze. The New Deal reconstruction ended on this note, with Roosevelt establishing the Executive Office of the President on the terms that Congress had set.[76]

The idea behind the modern presidency as it was actually constructed in the New Deal was to compel Roosevelt to continue bargaining and compromising. The idea implicit in his own proposals suggested something very different. They embodied the quest for presidential mastery promised in the 1936 campaign. Bargaining and compromising, though often seen as the essence of Roosevelt's skill as a political leader, had indeed been forced upon him all along. That something more would be needed to consolidate his new regime was the great insight of his second-term initiatives. It is in Roosevelt's failure to break out of the bargaining mold that we locate the impact of modernity on the politics of reconstruction.

The Logical Limits of the Reconstructive Stance

To rest this matter solely on the "organizational side of politics" is to leave out the most mysterious aspect of the detachment of this president's reconstructive authority from his actual political control. Roosevelt was no innocent in this process, naively playing Andrew Jackson in a polity grown resistant to Jacksonian claims. At the crucial juncture, he carefully tuned his designs to the managerial concerns of the new organizational polity and thereby made himself the nation's leading decoupler. As he took up the reconstructive initiatives of his second term, Roosevelt abruptly jettisoned the reconstructive language that had served him so well in his first.

On the face of it, the Court-packing and executive reorganization initiatives reveal a single-mindedness of purpose in redesigning basic constitutional relationships unrivaled by any president. Roosevelt was, in fact, proposing changes in the governmental frame quite unlike any that had been contemplated before. That he failed in the end to get what he really wanted is perhaps less striking than the fact that he could not even talk about what he wanted in the terms in which everyone else understood it.[77] Explaining this calls for some speculation, but we are not without certain guides.

Consider the constitutional arguments mustered by Roosevelt's counterparts in political time. Jefferson's quest for mastery rested on a formal celebration of executive deference to Congress; Jackson's rested on a forthright claim of the equality and independence of the presidency from the other branches; Lincoln's rested on a forthright defense of the integrity of the Union. Different as they were from one another, these arguments had several things in common. In the first place, each of these presidents claimed to be retrieving a true reading of the Constitution from the clutches of a degenerate understanding. Second, each claimant recognized that this true reading was a critical issue—if not *the* critical issue—in the larger political controversy in which he was engaged, and that he was rejecting the received orthodoxy. Furthermore, for each of these claims there were clear, if not conclusive or incontestable, referents to draw on within the basic constitutional frame. These presidents were not asking for flexibility in adapting received understandings to new conditions; they were forthright in arguing for an altogether different interpretation of the Constitution. It might be added that the Constitution proved flexible in each instance because the radical principle of change being asserted was not entirely foreign to it.

Roosevelt's heavy reliance on the flexibility of the Constitution is especially telling in this context. Squaring the requisites of mastery over his new political economy with an original understanding of the Constitution put him on ground far more precarious than that which had undergirded his predecessors. Given the scale of his undertaking, mastery entailed prima facie recognition of presidential supremacy, and that was something the basic constitutional frame was especially hard-pressed to accommodate. And in the unlikely event that anyone needed to be reminded of the danger, foreign affairs in the 1930s were sure to keep the senses alert to any seizure of executive power.

In this light, it is easier to understand why Roosevelt fudged the presentation of his second-term program for reconstruction; why he abandoned the repudiative rhetoric of the 1936 campaign; why he presented measures that would, in effect, subordinate both the judiciary and the Congress to the executive as housekeeping measures aimed at improving efficiency; why he insisted that these measures were fully in keeping with received practice and simply denied that there were any serious constitutional questions at issue at all. "This program rests solidly upon the Constitution and the American way of doing things," he asserted in the presentation of his executive reorganization plan. "There is nothing in it which is revolutionary, as every element is drawn from our own experience either in government or large-scale business."[78] The gap between this bland assertion that there was nothing of first-order significance at issue in this proposal and the substance of the proposal itself was glaringly obvious from the start.[79] There was also an enormous difference between this kind of presentation and one that would have argued the case forthrightly on constitutional grounds, rejecting the previously dominant reading of the document and substituting a definite alternative deemed truer to its real spirit. Roosevelt seemed to go out his way to pull the transformative punch out of these proposals. The strident (if somewhat abstract) reconstructive rhetoric of 1935 and 1936 failed him in 1937 when he championed the proposals that gave it substance. The classic grammar of reconstruction was abandoned for a washed-out form of progressivism, an "American way of doing things," as if suddenly the President had no more in mind than Herbert Hoover. The fundamental truths on which his fundamental changes were to be forged had in fact become a mere riddle of truisms.

When Roosevelt's repudiative authority came up against the separation of powers, it touched the outer boundary of the most expansive leadership posture, and in trying to break through that boundary Roosevelt fell back upon a bland reification of technique. To package his bid for executive control of the newly empowered bureaucracy as advanced progressive thinking on administrative rationalization, Roosevelt appointed a blue-ribbon panel of administrative experts and let their authority mediate his desires. To rationalize his intention to appoint more judges to the bench, he argued that he wanted to facilitate the work of the entire system of federal courts by improving efficiency and easing the burdens on older justices.[80] He was nonplussed when his fellow Democrats failed to rally to this standard. "We gave warning last November that we had only just begun to fight," he said after the unveiling of his Court-packing plan. "Did some people really believe we did not mean it?"[81] Roosevelt boasted the confidence of Andrew Jackson in his refusal to bargain over Court-packing or to accept the Court's accommodation to the New Deal as a de facto victory. Time and again he repeated, "The people are with me, I know."[82] But for all this, the deterioration in his reconstructive stance could not have been more conspicuous. Supremely confident of popular support and ready to go head to head with Court and Congress, Roosevelt curried public confidence in his quest for mastery by turning a proposal for radical constitutional change into a bloodless technical adaptation. In the blink of an eye, he slipped from the strongest case for political leadership to the most lame:

> In striving to make our government more efficient, you and I are taking up in our generation the battle to preserve that freedom of self-government which our forefathers fought to establish and hand down to us. They struggled against tyranny, against non-representative controls, against government by birth, wealth or class, against sectionalism. Our struggle now is against confusion, against ineffectiveness, against waste, against inefficiency.[83]

Roosevelt was at his least effective when he spoke the language of modernity. His appeal to organizational efficiency was woefully inadequate to his reconstructive ambitions. The ridiculousness of this tack for seizing control of the judiciary was fully exposed when the Chief Justice informed the Congress that the Court was fully abreast of its work and did not need the assistance of additional judges.[84] When Roosevelt continued to insist on the measure, the duplicity of his initial presentation fed the charges of constitutional usurpation that its careful progressive packaging seemed designed to forestall. Indeed, the Senate Judiciary Committee damned the proposal for being "presented to the Congress in a most intricate form and for reasons that obscure its real purposes," and it interpolated those "real purposes" freely from "the condition of the world abroad" and the dangers of "autocratic dominance, by whatever name it may be called." The Court's acceptance of the New Deal served, so far as the committee was concerned, to render the President's insistence on judicial subordination "a needless, futile, and utterly dangerous abandonment of constitutional principle."[85] Likewise, progressive rhetoric failed to shield Roosevelt from the wildest sorts of speculations about the true intent of the executive reorganization measure. The spectre of European autocrats so haunted this "dictator bill" that Roosevelt was ultimately compelled to issue a sober public disavowal of any intention to assume the position of dictator.[86] Congress then completed the ideological decoupling that Roosevelt had begun. Drawing upon an alternative reorganization plan presented by experts from the Brookings Institution, Congress took over the progressive ideals of administrative efficiency and mounted its own defense of the Constitution against the arbitrary view of executive power it found so offensive in the President's proposal. Scuttling the President's design, it used his rationale to implement its own program.[87]

Roosevelt's technocratic appeal can be dismissed as a strategic blunder, as a cunning bit of gamesmanship too clever for its own good, only if we assume that the Constitution really did have stronger supports to offer him in this quest to consolidate the liberal regime. Otherwise it will be seen that his consolidation initiatives did not fail because he presented them so lamely; rather, he presented them so lamely because the requisites of bringing order to the sprawling social commitments of his new regime so overreached the strongest warrants that he had. At the pinnacle of his power—when he was just about to secure his extraordinary work—Roosevelt reached the limits of his authority to change things. From there, it was difficult to see where his quest for control could find order-affirming assurances commensurate with the order-shattering changes it had come to entail. The President chose not to mount a candid defense of his constitutional reordering because the institutional changes he contemplated could gather little support from any corner of the basic constitutional frame.

Roosevelt's preoccupation at the outset of his second term was with clarifying new lines of institutional control. These were intended to run outward from the presidency to nationally organized economic actors and social interests that the New Deal had acknowledged as interdependent. This concern reflected at once the encompassing character of the changes he had sponsored, the absence of any other dependable source of security or coordination for his social commitments, and his own commitment to a further elaboration of the liberal program.

Roosevelt had used his freedom from received formulas to justify a radically new kind of polity, a new "economic constitutional order"; but as this political transformation radiated through power relations in all realms of American society, it finally reached the one formula, the old separation of powers, that it could not challenge outright.[88] The independence of the Congress and the Court flew in the face of the social interdependence of the interests that Roosevelt sought to build into the operations of the national government, and at that level of design conflict, there were no constitutional claims to be brought to bear to break the impasse.

The gap between the constitutional division of powers and the requisites of consolidating a social democracy yawned so wide at the outset of Roosevelt's second term that in order to tie the new liberal regime together with an order-affirming logic the President had to indulge the ultimate conceit. He attempted the most radical of all reconstructions of American government by simply defining the constitutional questions away in an appeal to flexibility. In truth, this ruse only revealed the extent to which the substance of his reconstruction had made his own leadership position within the constitutional frame awkward. Of all the lapses newly insinuated into the reconstructive discipline, this one proved the most consequential. It played into the hands of those who would scuttle Roosevelt's consolidation initiatives seriatim in their own ringing affirmation of ancient truths, it narrowed the ground between the strongest and the weakest of presidential claims, and it built into the modern presidency itself a set of aspirations at odds with the foundations of its legitimacy.[89]

Part Two:
Lyndon Johnson's Articulation

Let us continue.

T HE "TRAGEDY of Lyndon Johnson" is a drama without parallel in modern American politics. It is the story of a master politician who self-destructed at the commanding heights, of an over-arching political consensus shattered in a rush of extraordinary achievements, of a superpower that squandered its resources in a remote conflict with people struggling on the fringes of modernity. Incredible and yet still fresh in our memories, devastating and yet still formative of our present debates, the Johnson presidency remains one of the great riddles of our time.

Answers to this riddle have tended to chase each other back to a restatement of the original question. Some have attacked Johnson himself; others, the ideas he drew upon; most, some combination of the two. We now know so much about the character flaws in this man and the logical flaws in the prevailing wisdom of his day that either alone might tell the whole tale. But that itself is the problem. Anger and frustration with Johnson's days in power rage just beneath the surface of these explanations, and it is no easier to tell now than it was then if liberalism at high tide really got a fair trial or whether it was done in by the insecure and imperious personality in the White House. Was Lyndon Johnson a ruthless and cynical manipulator of power, consumed by his own insatiable quest for political control and public approval? Or was he really a true believer, a faithful son of Franklin Roosevelt, Harry Truman, and John Kennedy, an innovator whose frustrations indicate that the particular orthodoxy bequeathed to him had been misguided all along? Unable to see beyond these alternatives, we just continue the old debate.

To clear this impasse we need to break our fixation on the most idiosyncratic features of actor and context and think about Johnson's

325

leadership project in more generic terms. Notwithstanding its many distinctively modern features, the tragedy of Lyndon Johnson is a drama that admits several parallels. After all, Johnson was not the first incumbent to work his way up through the ranks of a dominant political regime and then preside over the most decisive electoral triumph since its founding. Nor was he the first to wrap great ambitions in a pledge of continuity, to act on a vision framed by the commitments of his immediate predecessors, or to orchestrate transformative changes to the discipline of an already-charted national destiny. Johnson was, in fact, one of several presidents who, by dint of political identity and leadership opportunity, felt compelled to synthesize past and future, to fuse standing commitments and current possibilities, to affirm his orthodoxy in the very act of transforming the nation.

Johnson summarized his leadership project poignantly in his initial charge to the nation: "At this moment of new resolve . . . let us continue."[1] A classic statement of the leadership premise of a politics of articulation, Johnson's overture invites comparisons with presidents similarly situated in earlier periods, presidents who, like him, had an expansive political opportunity to elaborate received governing formulas. How, we might ask, have such leaders fared generally? What common problems have they confronted in trying to exercise power in their own right and to define their place in history on their own terms? Have efforts to harmonize orthodoxy with extensive innovation proven politically tenable in *any* circumstances? Once Johnson's leadership project has been situated in political time and his encounter with the conundrum of orthodox-innovation reflected back on other encounters drawn from the past, the particulars of his experience appear in a different light. Through them we see how *this* episode in the politics of articulation was reshaped by the more modern arrangements of political and institutional power in which it took place.

At the farthest reaches of our search for Johnson's counterparts in other historical periods we encounter the unlikely example of James Monroe. By the standards of Johnson's day, the instrumentalities of leadership in the first "era of good feeling" were quaint. The presidency had come a long way from the time when an orthodox-innovator would tackle a perplexing political issue by sitting himself down to write a comprehensive treatise on the subject, as Monroe did in trying to pull together the contending positions within the Republican party on the question of internal improvements. And yet, this relatively benign patrician tribune was the first to bring an established regime to the gates of its promised land and invite the nation to celebrate its triumphant consensus. In this, Monroe and Johnson were two of a kind. Consummate insiders, they were acutely attuned to the demands of received doctrine and the play of the political factions under their charge. Regime boosters, they were so taken with the prospect of managing the whole so as to fulfill everyone's expectations that they fell victim to their own dreams.[2] Let us not forget either that Monroe underwent a political transformation in this context that prefigures Johnson's own, a transformation from the keeper of the one true faith into the unwitting betrayer of all manner of faithful followers.

Monroe's was the pristine form of the leadership problem that Johnson would come to know all too well. With little more than his national political identity and his belabored orthodoxy to put on the line, this stalwart Jeffersonian was at pains to sustain authoritative control over a moment of near perfection and to prevent the rush of expectations from exacerbating conflict over the true meaning of received commitments. Echoes of Monroe's discipline for fulfillment ring loud and clear in Johnson's assessment of his prospects: "We have enough to do it all." But "we need to appeal to everyone to restrain their appetite."[3] Both these presidents embraced an expansive opportunity to do good works plain and simple, and they both proceeded to tie themselves in knots trying to finesse the adverse consequences of their actions for everyone of political significance.

Solid policy achievements are the trademark of the orthodox-innovator. The problem is that when a concerted leap forward in policy does not carry with it an equally thoroughgoing indictment of past practice, it tends to get caught up in a debilitating debate over precisely what kind of future the past really anticipated. In these circumstances, the president's achievements tend to undercut the legitimacy of his entire undertaking. At each successive incarnation of this problem in our nation's history, the incumbent has had more potent political resources at his disposal; he has enjoyed incrementally greater independence in political action; and he has taken on a broader range of governing responsibilities. But far from helping to resolve the underlying dilemma, these secular changes have elicited increasingly convoluted responses. When the critical issue is the authority of the president to change the regime he is presumably in office to affirm, added increments of power and responsibility only force the inherent contradictions to the fore.

The power that makes it possible to contemplate greater achievements also makes those achievements more disruptive, and the adverse consequences of achievement are felt that much more forcefully by the members of the faith who are implicated in them. Over the course of American history the struggles to sustain the leadership project of the faithful son have only grown more intense; added increments of presidential power have only made the results that much more convulsive.

To trace the emergent pattern within the politics of articulation, recall how James Polk heaped symbols of self-denial atop his aggressive assertion of the powers of the Jacksonian presidency. Polk's bid for leadership began with a deep bow to the existing foundations of national politics: he forthrightly renounced any intention to build his own base of political power once he came into office. Taking himself out of all future political contention before he was even elected, he then reached out to the old Jackson coalition with a program that promised to realize the interests of each and every faction. In his zeal to erect a monument to orthodox Jacksonian priorities, however, Polk intended to do more than merely underwrite the interests of others. He set out to be *himself* president of the United States. Manipulating the operational norms and political resources of the Jacksonian presidency, he took control of the interests under his charge and employed them in a transformation of the nation that was all his own. While Polk was pressing Congress to enact his full-service agenda, he was simultaneously pressing a war that would crown the old program with personal achievement. In the end, the politics he came to power to celebrate was unhinged by his exercise of power, and the monument he built to Jacksonian orthodoxy had no more resilience than a house of cards. Polk acted on a program delicately crafted and subtly balanced to transform the nation without changing its politics; what he demonstrated was just how blunt and disruptive the instrumentalities of presidential leadership are.

Recall also how Theodore Roosevelt chafed at the sober responsibilities of regime maintenance and ultimately came to a resolution that was even more awkward and explosive. Roosevelt entered the presidency eager to forge new forms of executive power and to promote administrative regulation of the economy, but these ambitions rubbed hard against his equally acute perception that the moment was not ripe for reconstructive politics. Dutifully, he crafted his new administrative state to harmonize with received formulas and embellish the existing foundations of Republican power. Once elected in his own right and freed to pursue this project more aggressively, Roosevelt immediately announced that he would not run again and submerged all hint of personal ambition in cultivating a successor who might sustain and elaborate his program of state-building and party maintenance. All went pretty much according to plan until he left office and the unwieldy superstructure he had created began collapsing in on the foundations on which he had placed it. Faced with Taft's failure to sustain his vision of purely constructive action, Roosevelt reconsidered his self-sacrificing pledge to step aside and took a momentous step beyond the boundaries of orthodox-innovation. Finally seeing that the handiwork of his presidency could only survive if national politics was placed on a different foundation altogether, he donned the mantle of a reconstructive leader and returned to national politics in the unlikely guise of a political insurgent. In the end, he not only failed to save his own handiwork, he failed to recast its foundations as well. His insurgency accelerated the collapse of both.

This pattern of presidential leadership and political change subsumes much of what we have attributed in Johnson's case either to the psychological profile of the man or to the liberal regime's peculiar enthusiasms. At these seemingly robust moments, presidents characteristically undercut the ground upon which they stand. The efforts of very different sorts of men to reconcile orthodoxy with expansive innovation has consistently turned out to be self-defeating. The presidents who have done the most to embellish established regimes have in the process also thrown them into a sectarian tailspin. Thus, much of the attention we have turned inward on *this* man and *his* times might better be redirected outward toward general questions about presidential action *in* time. How was this familiar leadership dynamic reestablished in the Johnson presidency?

The particulars of Johnson's case draw forward a trend already established. From Monroe to Polk to Theodore Roosevelt, the emergent pattern in the politics of articulation shows that as the powers and responsibilities of the presidential office have grown, they have come to compete more fiercely with the humilities of regime service and personal self-effacement that are the trademark of the political project of the faithful son. Enhanced resources for independent action and greater national responsibilities strain patience with the demands of regime maintenance, rendering this leadership posture progressively more distended and internally conflicted. These strains culminate logically as well as historically in the "tyranny of benevolence" established by Lyndon Johnson. The consummate insider of the post-New Deal period, Johnson rose to an overweening position of power in the "modern presidency."[4] It is little wonder that he self-destructed in a burst of thoroughly orthodox innovations or that he belatedly withdrew from office in the hope of salvaging his credibility. The interesting speculation is whether Johnson's struggle did not, both by its example and by its actual political effects, finally gut the whole idea of a faithful son in the American presidency.

Johnson's leadership had it all—a Monroe-like appeal to a truly overarching national consensus, a Polk-like determination to deliver on each and every commitment, the urge of Teddy Roosevelt to act himself like the founder of the regime. But where Theodore Roosevelt had equivocated, Lyndon Johnson plunged ahead. The Republican Roosevelt had wrestled with the distinction between his situation and Lincoln's, and throughout his term in office he stubbornly resisted his ambition to do what Lincoln had done. Johnson had no such ambivalence. He was determined from the start to use his presidency to trump the political achievement of his mentor, Franklin Roosevelt.[5] The fact that the first Roosevelt belatedly abandoned the strictures of orthodox-innovation and waged his own reconstructive crusade actually helps underscore Johnson's elaboration of the historical pattern. Throughout his long and twisted odyssey, TR remained acutely sensitive to the distinction between articulating and reconstructing the received premises of national politics, and when he finally ventured to abandon the first posture and adopt the second, he clearly understood that he was making a momentous choice, the most fateful choice of his political career. Lyndon Johnson had little use for the distinction at all. His was the more thoroughly modern conceit that differences among leaders hinge less on the nature of the historical project at hand than on the amount of power and skill that might be brought to bear in executing it.

Johnson's presidency pressed harder than ever against the line separating an articulation of received premises from a reconstruction of them. Indeed, with civil rights agitation already at high tide, Johnson could hardly have avoided recognizing that at this moment effective political leadership would go hand in hand with a "shattering of the political and social structure."[6] What the other orthodox-innovators had struggled in vain to deny was for this one a self-evident fact of his circumstances, and in championing civil rights, Johnson took steps along the road toward political and social reconstruction beyond which the whole concept of an "orthodox" innovator would lose its distinctive meaning. And yet Johnson held back from the final step; he was nothing if not a regime affiliate. With the order-shattering prospects of his leadership in full view, the only thing separating the politics of reconstruction from the politics of articulation was Johnson's sense of his political authority to discard old formulas, to "think anew and act anew" on all the questions before him. He persisted at this boundary, trying to encompass initiatives that were manifestly reconstructive in a more general program devoted to upholding the old formulas and affirming continuity. He would not dispense with the politics of articulation and wage a reconstructive politics on its own ground; he would not abandon the role of orthodox-innovator. He would manipulate received formulas into radically new governmental commitments, but he would not—seemingly he could not—liberate himself from them. When they crashed in on him, it was with the unprecedented force of the revolutionary changes he had sanctioned.

In opening his elected term, Johnson bid adieu to the past: "Is our world gone? We say farewell. Is a new world coming? We welcome it."[7] This fond farewell presaged a difficult parting. Rather than rejecting the old order outright, Johnson insisted that its passing follow naturally upon its very premises; rather than taking his distance from all prior commitments, he welcomed a new world fully committed on all sides. While accepting the order-shattering implications of presidential leadership, Johnson determined that no interest of political significance at the moment of his political ascendance would be adversely affected by them. His new world was simply to transcend the old in a final redemption of its long-heralded promises. Johnson's presumption that the political system might be shaken to its foundations and the received dispensation still reaffirmed in its wake pushed the divergent impulses of the politics of articulation to their logical extremes. This is what lends his leadership its special significance in the range of presidential experience. The upshot—a leader pilloried for his time-warped sense of purpose, and a polity wrenched between orthodoxy and social revolution—so exposed the absurdity of faithfulness and orthodoxy as premises for the exercise of power that any further elaboration of the historical pattern is difficult to conceive.

Stalwart Confidence and Modern Angst

Johnson recalled his relationship to Franklin Roosevelt in the most intimate terms: "He was like a daddy to me always."[8] Johnson's political career featured several "daddies," sponsors who opened the doors of power and helped him through. Still, none offered him what FDR offered. Roosevelt gave Johnson a political identity, and Roosevelt's presidency became for Johnson the standard for thinking about the prospects for presidential leadership generally.

In 1935 Roosevelt appointed Johnson, then a 26-year-old congressional aide, director of the National Youth Administration in Texas. Two years later, when Johnson entered a special election to represent Texas's Tenth congressional district, his connection to Roosevelt and the New Deal was just about his only claim to distinction. Johnson showed how valuable that chip could be. With the Court-packing controversy already in the air, he placed himself foursquare behind the President. He presented himself in the campaign as the very model of filial loyalty and instantly distinguished himself in a large field of New Deal supporters as "all out, one hundred percent for Roosevelt."[9] When he went to Congress in 1937, Johnson was the only member actually elected on a pledge to support the President in his battle to reform the judiciary. He was already the "perfect Roosevelt man."[10]

As it turned out, however, 1937 was not only the year that Johnson's political identity fused with the work of Franklin Roosevelt; it was also the year that Roosevelt faltered and the New Deal stalled. No sooner had Johnson claimed as his birthright the role of the faithful son than he witnessed firsthand the failures of the father. The impact of this event on his understanding of presidential politics and his own place in political history would prove profound.[11] In his presidency, Johnson would reshape the leadership posture of the orthodox-innovator with an abiding faith in the New Deal vision and a deep-seated cynicism about the exercise of power generally. His political identification with the New Deal fused with the lessons of lived experience to generate a perverse combination of stalwart confidence and modern angst.

It is hardly a wonder that Johnson had less patience than Theodore Roosevelt with drawing fine distinctions among leadership postures; from the perspective of a congressman rising to power during Franklin Roosevelt's second term, those lines were already quite blurry. A large part of the explanation for Johnson's straddling the treacherous boundary between articulating and reconstructing the received premises of national politics is to be found in the frustrations he saw Roosevelt encounter during the New Deal reconstruction itself. Confusing results in the first instance bred a confusion of purposes in the second.

In the first place, Roosevelt's setbacks had left New Deal liberalism insecure at its party base. When Johnson assumed the presidency in 1963, liberalism still rested on the awkward political foundations forged for it in the wake of the Court battle. The bifurcation of the Democratic party along northern liberal and southern conservative lines anchored Johnson's conception of political history, a conception in which completing the work of the past would require a good deal of work on the foundations themselves. Second and more curiously still, once the prospect of his finishing Roosevelt's work came into full view, Johnson was led to rethink his whole approach to the reconstructive tasks yet to be completed in light of the reversals Roosevelt had suffered. As the historian William Leuchtenburg has put it, "If Johnson sought to emulate Roosevelt, he also attempted to avoid his predecessor's mistakes."[12] As Johnson saw it, doing what Roosevelt had failed to do argued for shelving Roosevelt's political stance altogether. Roosevelt's problems in reconstruction became Johnson's justification for sticking to an alternative leadership posture, the one that he had learned and successfully nurtured in the intervening quarter-century of political gridlock.

The nation went into World War II with the new majority party split into liberal and conservative camps. When it emerged, Roosevelt was dead, liberalism was becoming synonymous with support for labor unions and civil rights, and conservatives, opposed to both, had reconsolidated their hold over the southern wing of the Democratic party. The postwar political order kept New Deal liberalism simmering on a stalemate and built instead on a newly emergent consensus over containing communism and maintaining the nation's newfound military and economic preeminence.[13]

The implications of all this bore down with particular force on a "perfect Roosevelt man" still trying to make his way in Texas politics. Not yet ready to sacrifice himself to a cause, Johnson adopted a strategy for survival and made a tactical overhaul of his political credentials. Repackaging himself to run for the Senate in 1948, he disavowed the labels that had distinguished him from most other southerners for so long. To call him a "New Dealer" was really a "misnomer," he now protested. He proved the point by opposing most of Truman's "Fair Deal," supporting the Taft-Hartley Act's curtailment of union powers, embracing the Cold War with his own special brand of Red Scare hysteria, and inveighing against liberal overtures to the civil rights of black Americans.[14] For all this, however, Johnson went to the Senate a southern moderate. He stood steadfast against all threats of outside interference in local affairs, but he was reluctant to mount a direct defense of racism. He was respectful of the political boundaries set by the South's peculiar institutions but still willing within those bounds to cultivate the fruits of federal activism, both international and domestic.[15]

At the far reaches of his drift from identification with the New Deal, Johnson's relations with the liberal reformers in the Democratic party soured. In the 1950s, however, a moderate Republican controlled the presidency, and Johnson's career flourished. The very embodiment of the status quo, he became the master mediator of political gridlock during the Eisenhower administration. He learned how to finesse the political divisions that riddled this awkwardly structured regime, and he brokered the interests of its various factions brilliantly. Johnson could see little advantage in rekindling the old reform impulse. He refused to use his position as Democratic leader in the Senate to help the liberals cultivate a post-New Deal alternative to Eisenhower's "New Republicanism." Much to their frustration, Johnson held himself aloof, maintaining that "the American people [were] tired of wrecking crews."

> They want builders—people who can construct. They will entrust their affairs to the party that is constructive. They will turn their backs on the party that is destructive. If we go forward as positive Americans and not negative oppositionists, I am convinced that the time is not too far distant when the Democratic party will again be in the majority.[16]

It was in this spirit that Johnson turned his eyes toward the presidential election of 1960 and began to work on his national image. He was never more impressive in maneuvering over the political terrain of the post-New Deal era than in 1957 when he fielded a civil rights initiative from the Eisenhower administration that was all but guaranteed to break the Democratic party apart. Not only did Johnson hold his party together, he secured passage of the bill; and not only did he boast the most significant civil rights law since Reconstruction, he retained his position as the South's first choice for the presidential nomination.[17]

Still, Johnson's hopes that the national party would reward him for the services he had rendered in Congress went unfulfilled. The heavy-handed compromises that facilitated his feats of legislative leadership did little to alter his reputation as a trimmer in the minds of northern reformers, and indeed the liberals were disheartened when John Kennedy offered him the second spot on the national ticket.[18]

But Kennedy desperately needed to build support for his campaign in the South, and by 1960 Johnson was apparently desperate to escape the Senate. Hailing from the rival regions of Democratic strength, the two of them made a textbook team of regime managers. Both moderates, they straddled the great divide within their party and juggled the boldest platform commitment ever on civil rights with a stubborn determination not to lose the support of its most passionate opponents. With impeccable Cold War credentials and a vaguely tinged New Deal promise to "get the country moving again," they squeaked out a narrow victory. In effect, they had united the Democrats in the common cause of bringing the Republican intercession to a close.

Johnson's career came full circle suddenly with Kennedy's trip to Texas in November 1963. By this time the civil rights movement had become a mass insurgency bursting the channels of containment that Kennedy and his predecessors had so carefully cultivated. With the assassination in the South of a northern president committed to moderate reform, the political knot that had defined Johnson's career since the late 1940s loosened to the point of unraveling. Remarkably, he did not resist. He made his southern heritage a motor force rather than an impediment to decisive action on civil rights and reached out to an insurgency that threatened to break the back of all that he had held together in national politics for so long.

Johnson found his bearings for this undertaking instantly. "Do you realize," he exclaimed after meeting with Kennedy's advisors on the evening of the assassination, "that every issue that is on my desk tonight was on my desk when I came to Congress in 1937?"[19] In his very first thoughts as President, Johnson traced the leadership challenge handed down to him—completing Kennedy's program—back to the political stalemate that had pushed him on his long journey away from New Deal liberalism. There he made the final connection between *his* political history and the nation's political history. By pressing forward Kennedy's agenda in the areas of civil rights, aid to education, fighting poverty, and the like, Johnson saw himself reclaiming his original political identity and taking up the "old reforms which had been crying for action since Franklin Roosevelt's time."[20] Who better than the "perfect Roosevelt man" from Texas, the southerner whose liberal faith had abided all along, to break the crippling stalemate in the nation's political reconstruction and unite the nation at long last behind the unrealized liberal consensus?

Johnson's invocation—"Let us continue"—carried the political burden of these multiple meanings. Most of what Johnson took over from Kennedy was not Roosevelt's agenda at all; it was the post-World War II agenda of containing communism, maintaining economic growth, and managing civil rights agitation. James Monroe, James Polk, Theodore Roosevelt—all the great orthodox-innovators—had embraced programs somewhat removed from the central concerns of the founders of the regimes they served. Each took their inspiration for a second round of national achievement from initiatives cultivated by more immediate predecessors, new policies designed to keep the old regime vital and to vindicate it in a new era. Like these others, Johnson saw in the received agenda the chance to build a loftier superstructure on the old foundations: "In our time," he ventured, "we have the opportunity to move not only toward the rich society and the powerful society, but upward to the Great Society."[21]

But in a more profound sense, the connection back to the New Deal was exactly right. The civil rights insurgency was forcing resolution of the political impasse that had been reached in 1937–38. Breaking that impasse meant more than simply embellishing the existing social and political structure; completing the unfinished business of the Roosevelt reconstruction would entail overhauling the entire structure that had been built up in the interim. Civil rights was not just one more policy on the old agenda; it was the one policy guaranteed to affect everything else. Johnson perceived this. "There is really no part of America where the promise of equality has been fully kept," he acknowledged. "In Buffalo as well as Birmingham, in Philadelphia as well as Selma, Americans are struggling for the fruits of freedom." In the final analysis, "it is not just the Negroes but really all of us who have to overcome the crippling legacy of bigotry and injustice."[22]

It is here that Johnson's firsthand experience of the reconstructive politics under Roosevelt would seem most critical in determining how he handled the practical dissolution of the distinction between articulating and reconstructing, completing and discarding, the received premises of national politics. Johnson's sense that Roosevelt had miscalculated in 1937 confirmed his judgment in 1963 that doing what Roosevelt had failed to do would require a different approach to leadership altogether. When his thoughts returned to the Roosevelt administration, Johnson not only redeemed his abiding faith in the liberal vision, he also reconfirmed the virtues of the wholly affirmative, purely constructive politics he had cultivated under Eisenhower. At one and the same time, he connected his place in history to Roosevelt's, reached out to the forces of insurgency mobilized around him, and self-consciously rejected everything distinctive about the reconstructive stance in presidential leadership.

Johnson tied the shortfall in Roosevelt's performance directly to the repudiative posture the President had adopted in the election of 1936. "When people did not like what Roosevelt was doing, he called them economic royalists and moneychangers. He said they had met their match and would meet their master. It was like people fighting and spitting at each other."[23] As Johnson saw it, the great political victory of 1936 went up in smoke in 1937 because of all the antagonisms Roosevelt's leadership stance had engendered.[24] Roosevelt's "wrecking crew" approach to change had been a colossal mistake, or so it seemed to Johnson. That is what had turned liberalism into the precarious and stalled agenda of the past quarter-century, or so it seemed to Johnson.

The irony, of course, is that Johnson's careful assessment of Franklin Roosevelt's frustrations in the New Deal reconstruction led him back to a leadership stance that was decidedly inferior. The first Roosevelt, the Republican Roosevelt, could see the matter more clearly: the purely constructive stance was to be adopted only for a "lesser task." Truly great achievement demands a greater distance from established commitments and formulas. Viewing the matter through the blurry lenses of the New Deal reconstruction, Johnson, in effect, embraced a leadership task tantamount to Lincoln's, all the while arguing the *superiority* of the stance that Theodore Roosevelt had adopted in grudging recognition that his was not, like Lincoln's, a reconstructive moment.

Significantly enough, there were other connections that might have been made. For example, Johnson did not connect Roosevelt's repudiative posture in the election of 1936 to the Supreme Court's extraordinary reversal from opposition to support of the New Deal. Nor did Johnson connect FDR's repudiative posture to his unusual capacity to survive the whole series of devastating second-term reversals with his political authority still intact and to go on to win an extraordinary third-term victory. Nor, to look at it the other way around, did he connect Roosevelt's reversals to the fact that the Court-packing and executive reorganization initiatives had actually been *shorn* of their repudiative force and packaged rather duplicitously in consensus values plain and simple. These alternative insights might have helped Johnson appreciate and tap the liberating effect of the reconstructive stance. From them he might have taken greater distance from received formulas. He might have used the impending social and political revolution as an opportunity to rethink *all* commitments. But these insights simply failed to resonate with Johnson's political experience. Roosevelt's reversals in reconstructive politics and Johnson's subsequent success as a manager of the regime in Congress came down hard on the side of his particular assessment of the flaws in Roosevelt's political performance. Johnson looked back from the mid-1960s to the mid-1930s to identify a leadership situation similar to his own in which a great opportunity for constructive work had been derailed by the President's refusal to assuage the disruptive consequences of change. Roosevelt had shown Johnson the "terrible power" of the presidential office, and what he saw cautioned him to try to wield it in a way that everyone could feel good about.

We diminish these perceptions by psychoanalyzing them. If Johnson confused leadership stances that were once clearly delimited, his decisions merely accelerated a historical blurring of the differences that was already well advanced. And if Johnson chose wrong, he had a lifetime of affiliations pulling him away from the repudiative alternative and toward the wholly affirmative approach to the order-shattering work at hand. Here was a man of the South who longed to relieve his section of the nation of the crippling burdens of racism, a man of the New Deal who longed to fulfill the unfulfilled promise of Franklin Roosevelt, a man of the Cold War who respected the commitments of Harry Truman, a man who had led with Dwight Eisenhower in a spirit of cooperation, a man who succeeded Kennedy with a solemn pledge to continue. And then, just when Johnson might have been expected to step out of these shadows and stake his own claims to the presidential office, the Republicans took the wrecking-crew approach for themselves, and standing in the shadows became for Johnson more comfortable than ever.

All of Johnson's connections to the past were forced to the fore in

1964 when Barry Goldwater accepted the Republican presidential nomination. With Goldwater in the field as the repudiator of the hour, Johnson was unbridled as the redeemer of promises already made. Every Goldwater outrage prompted him to a more expansive celebration of the constructive legacy of the New Deal and the resilience of the post-New Deal political order. Every thrust engendered a stronger defense of the foundations: "We have so much to preserve and so much to protect."[25] Though impotent in the final tally, Goldwater's insurgency had perverse effects on Johnson's presidency. By rallying white southerners to the Republican banner, it thrust Johnson ever closer to the civil rights insurgency, to the unfinished business of Roosevelt's purge, and to the political urgency of orchestrating a liberal reconstruction. But by simultaneously casting Johnson in the role of the defender of the established regime, it underscored his confidence in the resilience of the old formulas for solving the nation's problems.

Johnson relished the fact that his popular vote margin over Goldwater surpassed that of Roosevelt's victory margin in 1936.[26] His landslide seemed to prove the folly of Roosevelt's repudiative stance in 1936 and the superiority of a purely affirmative posture in the pursuit of radical change. The "perfect Roosevelt man," Johnson had acted to correct what he saw as the one serious flaw in his mentor's leadership posture and to set himself on what he thought was a course toward an even more perfect performance. In truth, however, Johnson had prepared for the political and social revolution at hand with the most explicit and elaborate defense ever made of a path already traced. He had celebrated the hopes and achievements of his predecessors; he had offered the fruits of past labor as the only reasonable source of solutions to the nation's problems; he had campaigned *against* any "radical departure from the historic and basic currents of American thought and action." "We must decide," he had said in the keynote speech of his campaign, "whether we will move ahead by building on the solid structure of achievement created by forward looking men of both parties over the past thirty years. Or whether we will begin to tear down this structure and move in a radically different direction." In opposing Goldwater and anticipating an overarching national consensus unrivaled since the days of Monroe, Johnson pledged that he would *not* "shatter the foundation on which our hopes for the future rest." "Too many have worked too hard and too long to let this happen now."[27] Trouncing Goldwater gave Johnson unprecedented political power, but affirming received commitments held hostage his political independence in exercising it.

In retrospect, we can see that for all of Johnson's fascination with Franklin Roosevelt, he had made Roosevelt's experience far more accessible than it actually was. When he took Roosevelt's presidency as his standard and reflected his own political history back on it, he turned the very distinctive kind of politics Roosevelt had made—the politics of reconstruction—into something ordinary and fungible. Roosevelt, in Johnson's view, had made some serious "mistakes," and he had suffered some serious reversals. In these ways FDR appeared to Johnson to be rather like the other presidents he had known. From this vantage point, there was no Roosevelt difference apart from the size of his victory margins and the sheer number of policy successes he was able to extort from them.[28]

With these as Johnson's standards of judgment, the lessons of lived experience turned very dark indeed. Leadership became a desperate calculation to avoid some crippling exposure and to stave off the inevitable paralysis. A 15-million-vote margin of victory in 1964 was small comfort for someone who had watched Roosevelt's margins turn to smoke within weeks of the landslide of 1936. As Johnson calculated it, 2 or 3 million of the votes he had received could be tossed off to Goldwater's fanaticism, and "I could be down eight million in a couple of months."[29] Nor was there much comfort in great policy accomplishments because each extracted a cost against the standard of more. Speculating in 1967 that his grandchildren would be proud of what he had done for blacks and what he had done "to see it through in Vietnam," Johnson calculated that "the Negro cost me 15 points in the polls and Vietnam cost me 20."[30]

Acting in this way at the fraying boundary between articulation and reconstruction, Johnson turned presidential leadership into a game of one-upmanship in the exercise of power. He wanted to "go the distance" and if possible to do Roosevelt one better along the way.[31] But this was not a liberating challenge; it was a frightful one. Johnson was haunted by the knowledge that trouble lurked around every corner, and that he could not possibly anticipate, let alone cover, all of its sources. He might correct Roosevelt's "mistakes"; he might even surpass Roosevelt's "achievements"; but there was no real escape from Roosevelt's "fate." No one escaped. Everyone, even Roosevelt, made mistakes; everyone, even Roosevelt, suffered serious reversals. It was only a matter of time. Johnson presented his Great Society as an opportunity for the nation to replace its old preoccupation with quantity—"How much?"—with a higher concern for quality, and to make "leisure a welcome chance to build and reflect."[32] And yet in the Johnson presidency "there was no time to rest." Getting things done was the only standard, "How much?" the consuming preoccupation.[33]

By making Roosevelt an exception to prove the rule about presidential leadership, Johnson not only flattened the playing field of presidential politics, he also boxed himself into a corner. He made his extraordinary opportunity to transform the nation an existential test of skill, but he coupled exuberant optimism about the nation's future with a deep-seated fatalism about his own. No matter how much power a president had, no matter how popular he was, the forces conspiring against him were likely to prove overwhelming. The only real test of the man was the strategic challenge of manipulating fate. As Johnson took his historical bearings, his supreme confidence in the legacy of the past dovetailed with a desperate insecurity, and his abiding faith in the liberal reconstruction unfolded in rampant cynicism. Johnson refused to chase anyone from their high seats in the temple of American civilization, and yet he "knew from the start" that he was "bound to be crucified" any way he moved.[34]

"Having the Power, We Have the Duty"

"Power?" Johnson quipped. "The only power I've got is nuclear . . . and I can't use that."[35] The outburst captures the leadership dilemma of the orthodox-innovator in the acute form in which this president dealt with it. Exercising the independent prerogatives of the presidential office instantly brought to Johnson's mind the terror of ultimate destruction. Committed on all sides, the resources at Johnson's disposal to realize his objectives were a source of frustration, their order-shattering effect somehow ill-suited to the task at hand.

In truth, there will never be enough power in the presidency for an incumbent to make good on a purely constructive leadership project, and it is unlikely that there will ever be another president stretched so thinly by a determination to use great power to do just that. Lyndon Johnson was a full-service president who had at his disposal an alignment of political resources, institutional resources, economic resources, international resources, and military resources unmatched in the annals of presidential history. The problem is that in a full-service presidency, where no interest of political significance is denied a modicum of legitimacy, resources turn fickle; the exercise of power consumes authority. Committed to a wholly affirmative result, Johnson could not rest content to let anyone carry the brunt of change. If he was unimpressed with his great resources, it was because he was, in Wilson Carey McWilliams's apt phrase, "tyrannized by his sense of his duty."[36]

First among Johnson's duties was the containment of world communism. Little wars of dubious provocation figure prominently in the work of the great orthodox-innovators. James Monroe had the Seminole War, James Polk had the Mexican War, and, somewhat more vicariously, Theodore Roosevelt had the Spanish-American War. Behind the dubious provocation in the Gulf of Tonkin in 1964 was Johnson's hope that he too could fight a little (or, in the parlance of the times, a "limited") war. Indeed, next to the task of getting Congress to endorse his resolve to fight in Vietnam, nothing was quite so important to Johnson in 1964 as making the whole affair appear a matter of little consequence for anything else.[37]

But Johnson's war was different from the start. Each of the others was a kind of political adventure, a national projection onto the world stage of robust confidence and newfound independence. In the 1960s, however, America's preeminence on the world stage was well-established, and its international mission firmly fixed in all corners of the globe. Muscle flexing in the cause of containing the communists was not a spirited adventure; it was a sober and open-ended obligation. At issue was Johnson's will to uphold the foundationstone of the existing order of things. "The integrity of the U.S. commitment is the principal pillar of peace throughout the world," Secretary of State Dean Rusk reminded the President in the fateful summer of 1965. "If that commitment becomes unreliable, the communist world would draw conclusions that would lead to our ruin and almost certainly to world war."[38] The President himself had said as much just a few months before at Johns Hopkins University. "We are in South Vietnam because we have a promise to keep . . . We are also there to strengthen world order. Around the globe, from Berlin to Thailand, are people whose well-being rests, in part, on the belief that they can count on us if they are attacked. To leave Vietnam to its fate would shake the confidence of all these people in the value of an American commitment and the value of America's word."[39] The defense of Vietnam was the most firmly rooted of all the commitments this thoroughly committed President had to manage.

Like Polk, Johnson pressed his foreign war in conjunction with a comprehensive domestic program. But in his thinking about his package as a whole, Johnson expressed personal aspirations that were quite different. As Polk saw it, the domestic program was essentially a holding action making good on the old promises; the foreign war was the source of great personal achievement. As Johnson saw it, the foreign war was the holding action, and implementing the domestic agenda the true achievement. "I do not want to be the President who built empires, or sought grandeur, or extended dominion. I want to be the President who educated young children . . . who helped the poor . . . who protected the right of every citizen to vote."[40] "The guns and the rockets, the bombs and the warships" were to Johnson "a witness to human folly." "Necessary symbols," they were not really "impressive at all." What impressed this old New Dealer was "a dam built across a river" and the "electrification of the countryside." In this sense, the sober, unquestionable duty of defending South Vietnam was always something of a distraction calling Johnson away from doing the constructive work of politics "on a scale never dreamed of before."[41] And yet *as a duty*, defending South Vietnam also served Johnson's larger purpose. It stood as an ever-present reminder of his respect for the received order of things. With all the momentous changes Johnson was setting in motion in domestic affairs, meeting this foreign obligation anchored his political identity as a stalwart affiliate of a robust regime. Just as the Gulf of Tonkin Resolution had stolen the wind from Barry Goldwater's sails in the campaign of 1964, the "limited," "low key" war of 1965 temporarily underwrote Johnson's Great Society. Handled "undramatically" and as a "natural consequence of our determination to meet our commitments," it promised to silence right-wing critics of the liberal agenda and to carry the Left along.[42]

Pledging himself to an "adequate" and "sufficient" response to aggression in Southeast Asia, Johnson was both resolute and wholly uninspired in the exercise of his most terrible powers.[43] He committed the nation to the defense of South Vietnam with restrained words and actions thoroughly contrived to do no more than necessary to sustain the principle that lay behind that commitment.[44] Johnson remembered all too clearly the charges of betrayal that Truman had suffered after the fall of China and the right-wing stampede that had sidetracked the liberal program after World War II.[45] Instead of challenging the Right to do it again, he followed Truman's subsequent course and incorporated the interests of the right wing as one of his own. Undersecretary of State George Ball urged the President to take his distance from received formulas in Vietnam, to weigh the imponderable costs of actually winning against any calculation of prospective gains, and to think about ways of getting out gracefully. Vice President Hubert Humphrey advised the President to consider his great election victory a release from old concerns about right-wing opinion, and to cut his losses in Vietnam.[46] But to do so Johnson would have had to explain to the nation's foreign policy establishment why this domino was less strategically important to the containment of communism than previously thought; he would have called into question a course set by the three presidents before him and, with that, his own pledge of continuity; and he would have countered the opinions of the senior counselors he had retained from the Kennedy administration, counselors who, with varying degrees of hawkishness, argued that there was no graceful way out and that the U.S. obligation had to be upheld in a credible fashion. To cut his losses, Johnson would have had to plead, against all appearances, that he did not have the power to "do it all," and he would have sparked a national debate about just what should be done and what foregone. At a moment of seemingly limitless possibilities, he would have been testing his authority to challenge a principle that no one, not even those who urged caution, seemed to doubt. If Johnson was determined to avoid Roosevelt's repudiative posture in 1936, so much more so was he determined to avoid any hint of betraying the established regime's most politically resilient precept.

The trick was to manage the war, and by upholding this cornerstone of the politics of the past, to enhance the legitimacy of other commitments that were far less firmly established and much more obviously transformative. One was the order-shattering commitment to civil rights; the other, the order-creating commitment to building a Great Society. In addition to their record of stalwart support for the containment of communism, Truman and Kennedy had left to Johnson a legacy of symbolic support for the civil rights of black Americans and an elaborate domestic policy agenda. The case for continuity could therefore be pressed simultaneously on all three fronts. Johnson turned the Civil Rights Act of 1964 into a monument to Kennedy's memory, and his uncompromising stand on its behalf secured what Kennedy never expected—passage of his entire proposal intact.[47] Johnson went to Independence, Missouri, to sign the controversial Medicare bill of 1965 and turned that labored compromise into a monument to Harry Truman's far more sweeping commitment to national health insurance.[48] But herein lies the crucial difference. While Truman and Kennedy had acted on their commitment to the containment of communism, their commitment to civil rights and an expanded liberal agenda were still largely matters of talk. Having the power, Johnson had the duty to make good on the whole package.

As sure as he was that the commitment to containing communism was unquestionable, Johnson saw that there was no resisting the obviously reconstructive idea of civil rights. This idea stretched back in time beyond the postwar political consensus to the mass conversion of blacks to the Democratic party during the New Deal, back beyond that to the debates of the Civil War era, and back beyond that to the founding of the Republic itself. "We have talked long enough in this country about equal rights," Johnson declared. "We have talked for a hundred years or more. It is time now to write the next chapter—and to write it in the books of law."[49]

Woefully compromised by his predecessors and still unrealized, the liberal commitment to civil rights had never fit very comfortably into the political consensus that Johnson had determined to preserve, and there were few illusions about the difficulty of managing the separate lines of national development now converging. Johnson knew that his southern brethren would charge him with treason for making the cause of civil rights his own. His advisers lectured him about the prospective white backlash in the North.[50] He also knew that "if [he] didn't get out in front on this issue they [the liberals] would get [him]."[51] To his credit, Johnson kept the moral imperatives at the forefront, and he never gave the liberals or the more moderate Republicans a chance to doubt his resolve. It must be said that the watershed Voting Rights Act of 1965 followed close on the heels of the loss of five southern states to Goldwater and that the significance of a potentially large southern black electorate was not lost on liberal Democrats. But if there were political as well as moral imperatives for reconstruction in this instance, Johnson pressed ahead even when the political calculus was less straightforward. A third legislative initiative, this one on housing, followed close on the heels of passage of the Voting Rights Act. Johnson proposed open housing legislation in 1966, and he pursued it tirelessly even in the face of ghetto riots in the North and outright rejection in Congress. He secured the bill in 1968, the most difficult year of his presidency.[52]

It is readily apparent that the two most resolute commitments of Johnson's presidency—the one to Vietnam, the other to civil rights— held in their balance the order-affirming and order-shattering elements of presidential action. And yet it is also evident that these commitments failed to reinforce each other and underwrite the legitimacy of a new order as in a classic politics of reconstruction. Johnson was not affirming some distant, mythic past while pursuing his social reconstruction; he was pursuing his social reconstruction while affirming an immediate and all-too-real commitment to a preexisting order of things. Rather than meshing together, his twin commitments were rather precariously balanced against each other, and rather quickly they began to move past each other. Instead of elevating the President above prior conceptions of the political alternatives, they tended to rivet him to very different conceptions of the alternatives. In effect, Johnson had taken aim at the past without gaining any distance on it; his orthodoxy in foreign affairs worked to neutralize the liberating effect of his reconstructive initiatives in domestic affairs. For all their clarity, the order-shattering and order-affirming elements in his leadership posture did not bolster his independent authority or immunize him from the inevitable charges of betrayal; they drew him deeper into the conflicts within his ranks. With his resolute defense of the cornerstone of the old order and his equally resolute pursuit of the cornerstone of a new one, Johnson led himself into a time warp where he became vulnerable to charges of betrayal on all sides.

But this takes us too far too soon. Johnson may have had a keen sense of fate, but he had not gotten to where he was by capitulating to it. For decades he had employed his energy and skill to considerable effect in struggling against the inevitable, and this struggle intensified during his presidency. It was the political symmetry of his commitment to communist containment abroad and his commitment to social justice at home that provided his opening. Johnson held in a momentary balance two political orthodoxies whose contentious stalemate had defined his entire career. The commitment to Vietnam weighed in against something that Johnson had worried about at every stage of his political life, a "stampede" from the right wing. The commitment to civil rights weighed in on the other side against something else he had lived with all along, dismissal by the eastern liberal establishment.

Johnson took his inspiration for the Great Society from these countervailing poles. With his two most resolute commitments weighing against each other, he moved quickly to pour on a special cement of his own creation, a "healing" and "building" concoction that might bond the whole before the faultlines at the base had a chance to shake things apart.[53] In Johnson's hands, the Great Society became more than just an extension of the old liberal orthodoxy; it became a vehicle for superseding the antagonisms that had been exacerbated by that orthodoxy. The Great Society was to alleviate conflicts between North and South, black and white, labor and capital, left and right—all the conflicts that had riddled liberal politics since its inception. Johnson gambled that he could hold the balance of forces long enough to slip the nation past these conflicts and into his own vision of the future before the real disruptions of war and social revolution began to bite.

The Great Society bore the burden of Johnson's order-creating ambitions, and it was a heavy burden indeed. The task was to bring the blessings of abundance home to a nation engulfed in world responsibilities and racial insurgency, to prevent the demands for change from colliding with the imperatives of maintenance, to solidify a broad-based consensus behind a synthetic package. To this end, Johnson studiously avoided Roosevelt's tack. He did not, as Roosevelt had, try to purge the Old South from the Democratic party. Instead, he bent over backwards trying to prove that the benefits of their staying in would far exceed the dreaded costs. Nor did he, as Roosevelt had, rail against Wall Street and the economic royalists. Instead, he sought a partnership with business in the politics of growth. Johnson's "party for all Americans" was to be just like Monroe's, a party which no American would want to oppose. He offered tax rebates to business, higher minimum wages to labor, safer mines to miners, job training to the unskilled. He offered food stamps to the hungry and higher subsidies to the farmers. Urban America got mass transit and Model Cities, rural America got comprehensive resource planning and Appalachian redevelopment, suburban America got safer cars and cleaner highways. The elderly got health care, the young got education assistance. Outdoor enthusiasts got parks and conservation, indoor enthusiasts got public broadcasting and high culture. If the War on Poverty is emblematic of the Great Society as a whole, it is because it was a war to be waged without enemies. "Why anyone should hate an anti-poverty program, I don't know," Johnson replied to its critics.[54] This program was conceived as an economic development measure, a boon to business; it was also a job-creating measure, a boon to labor; it was a race-neutral measure, a "substitute for the high emotional costs of fighting race prejudice"; it would benefit the South as well as the North, attacking rural as well as urban poverty; it was a hedge against white backlash, a new prop for the aging ethnic-based political machines of urban Democratic mayors.[55]

With his vast powers fully deployed, Lyndon Johnson went to the Congress in January 1966 the mastermind of a fabulously productive balance of contending pressures and commitments. The previous year had been spent doing what Johnson did best, finagling disparate forces of order and change into a grand concert of thoroughly constructive action. "We will not permit those who fire upon us in Vietnam to win a victory over the desires and intentions of all the American people." "I believe," he concluded triumphantly, "that we can continue the Great Society while we fight in Vietnam."[56] In the parlance of the times, the President had pledged "guns and butter." But for Lyndon Johnson it was much more than that. It was the old and the new, the welding of the past to a more glorious future; it was a triumph of orthodoxy and innovation, a perfect graft onto the government of the political identity of a regime stalwart. All the pieces were in place, ready to explode.

The Nightmare of Political Management

In a classic politics of articulation, presidential leadership is neither so penetrating as to reach to first principles nor so shallow as merely to reify technique. It aims at a middle level of political management; it is a hands-on manipulation of received interests and priorities. The management problems engaged here, while always intractable, are especially instructive to observe in the intimate and pristine environs of the first "era of good feeling." John Quincy Adams relates the story of a meeting late in the Monroe administration between the President and William Crawford, the secretary of the treasury whom Monroe had held over from Madison's cabinet. Crawford, one of the three cabinet officers then vying for the succession, had come to the White House to get approval for a list of political appointments. When Monroe objected to the choices, the secretary turned petulant. The President responded with equally sharp words to remind Crawford of his proper place. Then in a fury, Crawford moved to strike the President with his walking stick.

Monroe grabbed the fireplace tongs to block the impending blow, and threatened his secretary with forcible eviction from the White House. Crawford left; Monroe never met with him again.[57]

Such are the torments of the orthodox-innovator. Tensions between Crawford and Monroe had been building for years. The secretary had been considered a possible alternative to Monroe for the presidency in 1816, and he stayed on in Monroe's cabinet as the self-appointed conscience of the Old Republicans and the self-designated successor to the presidential chair. It can hardly be said that Crawford wanted to push the nation in a direction dramatically different from the one that Monroe was pursuing, but his transparent ambition and independent standing made him a constant source of irritation. Indeed, his not-so-subtle promotion of his own future at the President's expense made him a prime mover in the disintegration of the grand coalition that Monroe was trying to preserve. For all this, however, the most revealing aspect of their final confrontation may be what Monroe ultimately did about it. Upon reflection, he decided that it would be impolitic to actually remove Crawford from office for his insubordination and treachery. With the outcome of the election of 1824 still in doubt, Monroe thought it better to keep the incident under wraps than to give any appearance of choosing among the faithful.[58]

As Monroe's assertion of his prerogatives as president made him a target for Crawford, so Polk's had make him a target for Van Buren. Teddy Roosevelt was spared a bit by Mark Hanna's death, but by the middle of his elected term Nelson Aldrich was filling the bill precisely. Orthodox-innovators determined to exercise power in their own right and to define their place in history on their own terms have no more potent adversaries than those among their followers whose authority to interpret the faith differently cannot be denied. In the Johnson administration, this syndrome took the form of the "Bobby problem." From the start Robert Kennedy posed an ever-present threat to Johnson's leadership claims, and there was little the President could do about it.

The "Bobby problem" is a structural condition. It stems from the unavoidable tendency for the orthodox-innovator to personalize his rendition of received commitments as soon as he sets his administration in motion. From then on, he becomes fair game for all those he has tried to encompass within those commitments. Some of the alternative leaders of the regime will have had a different mix of priorities all along.

Most will merely adjust their understanding of orthodoxy as events unfold and pass off any adverse consequences of the president's policies to his obviously misguided understanding of the true faith. Meanwhile, the president finds himself locked into the particular course he had articulated in his initial quest for consistency with past commitments.

Consider the predicament of the orthodox-innovator against the plain confessions of a reconstructive leader. Lincoln's candid admission that he could not control events but that events had controlled him describes the nightmare of all those who come to power to affirm a previously prescribed course of action. Aiming from the start at a full orchestration of interest services and political commitments, the orthodox-innovators are not so free to adjust to the situation as it unfolds. Indeed, unexpected events threaten all they are trying to hold together. The pragmatism that we celebrate in Lincoln and Franklin Roosevelt is a luxury forfeited in leadership projects that are as elaborate in their doctrinal claims of consistency as they are in their schemes for maintaining balance among established political interests. To stave off disaffection, the orthodox-innovator begins with a hands-on management of interests and reaches for complete control of the entire situation. Recall Monroe's urgent plea to Andrew Jackson to doctor his report of the invasion of Florida so as to assuage the political fallout. Recall Polk's bitter despair when his ostensible allies insisted on connecting slavery with his efforts to make peace with Mexico. Recall Theodore Roosevelt's shock during the panic of 1907 when Republican conservatives and business leaders implicated his reforms—reforms he had pursued ostensibly to underwrite their long-term interests—in fomenting instability. Uncontrollable events are a cause for high anxiety for these leaders; the orthodox-innovator has no good defense against the unexpected.

The nightmare of interest management was compounded for Lyndon Johnson by the paradoxes of modernity. More powerful than his predecessors, he also encompassed more interests than ever before in his delicate balancing act. Indeed, at times the task forces he set up to study national issues seemed to be creating new interests around presidential initiatives of their own accord. Interest for interest, the legions Johnson was gathering together were more organizationally independent of presidential control than ever before. The President's service-oriented posture drew him into a position of dependence on a greater variety of independent actors and magnified his susceptibility to a wider array of uncontrollable actions. Turning the Democratic party into a "party for all Americans," Johnson offered virtually everyone the favor of presidential support and virtually guaranteed that no one could be counted upon to support his whole package.[59] Indeed, the package was all the more precariously stretched in its political presumptions for being socially encompassing in its resolves and penetrating in its economic effects. How was Johnson to maintain the appearance of consensus?

Johnson's response to this dilemma was to try to stifle alternative voices of authority. To protect his world of appearances, he had to control the real one completely. Polk's demand that each of his cabinet appointees take an oath foreswearing presidential ambitions during their term of service was but a prelude to Johnson's efforts to silence all dissonance within the ranks. Johnson is notorious for his suspicion of the loyalty of his subordinates and his obsession with unauthorized leaks to the press, but with his unprecedented exposure on questions of legitimacy that is hardly a wonder. By 1966 he was fully drawn out by the balance of his commitments. His commitment to the civil rights movement had run up against the traditional southern base of the Democratic party, his commitment to affirmative action in federal contracts and hiring had run up against the traditional labor union base of the Democratic party, his commitment to a war on poverty had run up against the traditional machine base of the Democratic party, and his commitment to the defense of South Vietnam was fast running up against his commitment to the civil rights movement and the Great Society. Preserving these balances was Johnson's only hope for sustaining his definition of the moment at hand, and the prospect of their unraveling called forth a desperate effort. In trying to uphold his rendition of the faith, Johnson ended up trying to crush the prime repositories of that faith.

We need not recount all the prior instances of deceit, intimidation, and duplicity we have encountered in presidential history to recognize that Johnson did not invent these tools of presidential management. What he did do was to employ them on a scale commensurate with the scope of his undertaking. As he was tyrannized by his sense of duty, so much more so was he driven by the task of fulfilling it to tyrannize over others, and as he tyrannized over others, he sapped all honor out of the duties of the faithful son.

Hubert Humphrey provides a clear case in point. A politician of independent national standing, Humphrey was widely perceived at the time of his nomination for the vice presidency to be the very model of "the modern liberal."[60] But Johnson seemed to want him on the ticket as much to neutralize him as a threat as to tap his liberal credentials. Johnson seemed to go out of his way to humiliate Humphrey. Up to the moment he selected him, the President kept the vice-presidential hopeful in doubt as to his intentions. He urged Humphrey to prevent a southern walkout from the 1964 party convention, as if to test his willingness to put loyalty to Johnson's consensus ahead of his own political identity.[61] Long the embodiment of liberal integrity in support of civil rights (a Humphrey speech on civil rights had helped spark the southern walkout from the 1948 Democratic convention), Humphrey was encouraged to negotiate a compromise on the floor of the convention between the Mississippi Freedom Democrats and the regular racist delegation. In doing so, he all but relinquished his independent claim to the high moral ground in national politics.

Humphrey's travails with Johnson's consensus did not end there. In 1965, a week after Johnson appointed him chairman of the President's Council on Equal Opportunity, the vice president began to voice his objections to the administration's war policies. For that, Johnson not only shut him out of future National Security Council deliberations, he immediately began rethinking the responsibilities he had bestowed on Humphrey in the area of civil rights as well. The vice president soon found himself shut out of deliberations in this area, too. Pressed by Attorney General Nicholas Katzenbach to transfer the coordination of civil rights policy to the Justice Department and by moderates and conservatives to take the spotlight off enforcement activities, Humphrey was imposed upon to relinquish his leadership of the administration's civil rights program only eight months after he assumed it.[62]

This same impulse to neutralize competing voices of orthodoxy is evident in Johnson's gutting of the National Committee of the Democratic party. This faithful son, desperate to sustain his own rendition of orthodoxy, savaged the organization that more than any other embodied the ideas he had come to office to celebrate. He slashed the budget of the National Committee, diverted its traditional fundraising and patronage activities into the White House, and left the apparatus to atrophy under the auspices of a thoroughly humiliated chairman, John Bailey.[63] As Rowland Evans and Robert Novak caught the drift of Washington opinion in late 1966, Johnson "was afraid that if he replaced Bailey with a tough-nosed political manager, the National Committee might be built into a power center capable of challenging the

White House. This is, of course, preposterous, but to non-northern Democrats that National Committee had always represented a center of big-city power politics. And with the Johnson and Kennedy wings of the party more than ever suspicious of each other, Mr. Johnson apparently [did] not want to give the committee any independent power of its own."[64]

Looking back we can see that for all of Johnson's sensitivity to the difficulties of sustaining his presidency on his own terms, and for all his ruthless resolve to meet that challenge, his ability to manipulate the faith effectively was remarkably short-lived. During the first half of 1965, the major Great Society initiatives were enacted alongside an extended administration review of the appropriate policy response to the war in Vietnam. But for this deft bit of policy management, the impending commitment to fighting a ground war in Asia might well have jeopardized safe passage of the domestic program.[65] Before the year was out, however, Johnson confronted the hard-pressed realities of his course. By December 1965, his economic advisers were already urging a tax increase in order to sustain the whole package without adverse economic effects. Johnson overruled them. He accurately perceived that such a proposal would force Congress into a debate over his priorities, and that any choice among them would cost him dearly. He was not about to sponsor the dismantling of the political synthesis he had just set in motion by raising questions about whether "progress at home" could be made while "obligations abroad" were being met. Manipulating economic reports to have things break his way, Johnson let the whole bundle of commitments run on automatic pilot. The budget resolves of 1966 echoed the State of the Union message, insisting that there was no need to "halt progress in the great and vital Great Society Programs in order to finance the cost of our efforts in Southeast Asia."[66] Playing for the breaks posed the lesser risk to Johnson's political authority.

Unfortunately, the administration's optimistic forecasts for 1966 underestimated the costs and economic impact of the war, and domestic price inflation became an issue of increasing concern over the course of the year. Early in 1967, the President acknowledged the problem and proposed a 6 percent surcharge on personal and corporate taxes to meet the "unusual expenditures" associated with the war and regain control of the economy. But much as he had suspected, Wilbur Mills, the conservative chairman of the House Ways and Means Committee, red a tax increase to finance the war without concomitant cuts in nestic spending. The President, still determined to keep his leadership oject intact, held out against these cuts, and action against inflation was stalemated until the middle of 1968 when, in the midst of an international gold crisis and rampant speculation, the administration capitulated to Mills's terms and a 10 percent tax surcharge became law.[67]

The year 1967 featured classic signs of the unraveling of a politics of articulation: Democrat Wilbur Mills took aim at the Great Society, Democratic Senator J. William Fulbright took aim at the orthodoxy of containment, and former Attorney General Robert Kennedy prepared to pronounce his judgment on the results from his current position as senator from New York. Johnson was proving no more successful than Polk as a master manipulator of the regime's commitments; the difference was that the transformation of the orthodox Johnson into Johnson-the-Mendacious shook American politics with unprecedented force.

In thinking about the impact of modernity on Johnson's leadership project, the effects of television call for special attention. There is no denying that television enhanced the independence of the President. It allowed him to communicate directly to the people and made the old party apparatus more dispensable. But television also enhanced the independence of everyone else and made them less dependent on presidential favor. The use of the media by the civil rights movement in Selma in early 1965 is perhaps the leading example of how television brought new pressure to bear on the task of interest management. The movement refused to be treated as an interest like any other or to accept the Civil Rights Act of 1964 as sufficient recognition of its concerns. After the initial victory, the leaders stepped up their agitation to keep the civil rights issue at the forefront of political attention, and with television cameras exposing the brutality of Selma officials against peaceful marchers, they propelled the Voting Rights Act to the top of the national agenda. Beyond this effect of pushing the administration forward on its avowed commitments, television also magnified every dissonance between the President's commitments and actual events. It brought ghetto riots into the homes of voters who had selected a president pledged to revive the cities, student protests into the homes of voters who had selected a president pledged to educate the young, and the physical destruction of war into the homes of voters who had selected a president pledged to "save" South Vietnam.[68]

But there was more than modern technology at work in undermining Johnson's managerial pretensions.[69] Try as he might to manipulate and intimidate them, Johnson had to contend with independent spokesmen and authoritative leaders everywhere he turned. From his promotion of civil rights to his promotion of high culture, Johnson found himself enhancing the authority of men over whom he could exert little personal control.[70] The poet Robert Lowell led the way in June of 1965, declining an invitation to the White House Festival of the Arts with a public protest against the administration's foreign policy.[71] "A Call to Resist Illegitimate Authority" was published in the *New York Review* in October 1967 with the names of 121 liberal intellectuals attached.[72] Civil rights leader Martin Luther King, Jr., had made an independent judgment of Johnson's leadership package earlier that year and publicly threw his own weight against the war in Vietnam.[73]

Then there were the independent experts securely ensconced in the nation's universities who debated the presumptions of the administration's experts with all the detachment afforded them by their professional authority and all the objectivity afforded by their lack of policy responsibility. The economist Milton Friedman intruded upon the scene with a frontal assault on his discipline's guiding theoretical premises. Weighing in against the administration's more orthodox economists, he opened a debate about the wisdom of the experts Johnson had been relying upon.[74] The professional detachment of the national press corps established another standard of independent political authority, and here Johnson's heavy-handed efforts at management backfired badly. Resentment between the White House and the press paralleled the deteriorating political situation. In November 1963, Walter Lippmann had hailed Johnson as a "bridger of unbridgeable chasms," but by March 1967 he was denouncing him for misleading the nation with "false historical analogies . . . [and] dangerous illusions of omnipotence."[75] Johnson himself dated the general turn in press opinion and the stampede of charges of a "credibility gap" to Lippmann's shift.[76] The coup de grace from the press would be delivered by Walter Cronkite early in 1968 when, in a special broadcast on the Vietnam War, he ventured on his own authority an interpretation of the Tet Offensive that devastated administration claims of light at the end of the tunnel.[77]

Johnson was acutely vulnerable to these barbs because his political authority was so thinly stretched around his various commitments. The point is not that things went badly (that, as we have seen, is the norm rather than the exception). The point is that Johnson's consensus was so precariously poised among contending interests that he could not afford to have anything go wrong. Johnson had "read about all the troubles Lincoln had in conducting the Civil War."[78] He believed that, like Lincoln, he had chosen the middle course between two extremes, and Lincoln's example suggested to him that perseverance in the face of adversity would be rewarded. Had he not refused to sacrifice the Great Society for Vietnam? Had he not refused to sacrifice Vietnam for the Great Society? In fact, however, Lincoln's moderation did not rest on finding a middle way between the extremes; it was premised on an overriding opposition to received governing arrangements and an affirmation of values that had presumably been lost in the existing order of things. When things went badly for Lincoln, he tightened the screws of change and foreclosed paths of retreat from wholesale reconstruction. When things went wrong for Johnson, he found himself equally vulnerable on all fronts; shorn of the premise that he could be all things to all people, he simply stepped aside. In the end, it was his path that was cut off. He was caught in the crossfire of demands that more be done on behalf of one or another of the commitments that he pulled in his train.

> I felt that I was being chased on all sides by a giant stampede coming at me from all directions . . . I was being forced over the edge by rioting blacks, demonstrating students, marching welfare mothers, squawking professors, and hysterical reporters. And then the final straw. The thing I feared from the first day of my Presidency was actually coming true. Robert Kennedy had openly announced his decision to reclaim the throne in the memory of his brother. And the American people, swayed by the magic of the name, were dancing in the streets. The whole situation was unbearable for me.[79]

The Final Affirmation of Faith

Johnson's decision not to run for reelection in 1968 caught the nation by surprise, but it gave him precisely what he needed most at the time, the restoration of a semblance of credibility as a faithful son who was simply doing his duty. Abdication has always been the ace in the hole for orthodox-innovators facing up to the dilemmas of interest management. Polk made his announcement on the eve of his nomination so as to keep the party machinery primed for his dark-horse campaign. Theodore Roosevelt made his announcement right after his landslide victory at the polls so as to assure his party of his benign intentions in the upcoming drive for reform. We now know that Johnson had this option in mind from the start. All along, he had kept an announcement of this sort in his pocket, perhaps hoping that he could sustain his consensus without it and that he would not need to sacrifice himself in order to underscore the integrity of his commitments.[80] It was not until March of his reelection year, with his party in open revolt and Robert Kennedy entering the field against him, that he offered it up as certain proof of his honorable intentions. By this late date, the act had all the overtones of a tragic withdrawal, but the subsequent lift in the polls indicated more than that. It was a release from the debilitating siege of the White House, a momentary retrieval of initial leadership claims, a final bid for control over the situation.[81]

That the situation to that date had moved far beyond Johnson's managerial capacities was indicated in the political reception of the two key events leading up to his withdrawal. The Tet Offensive of January 31, 1968, proved in the end to be a military victory for the allied forces. Not only was the enemy's assault on the cities of South Vietnam decisively turned back but the elite troops of the Vietcong were left severely weakened. Never had the South Vietnamese Army performed so well nor had enemy hopes for prevailing militarily ever suffered so sharp a reversal. But this news got lost in what proved to be a managerial fiasco for the administration.[82] Political handling of this "limited" war had long entailed manufacturing a world of appearances. The enemy's military potential had been systematically understated, and unsupportably optimistic projections of "progress" and "light at the end of the tunnel" had become routine. The President was unable to gain credit for his military victory in 1968 because he was unable to credit the scale and scope of the uprising itself. The enemy offensive indicted his carefully managed and wholly uninspired approach to the war, and left his whole line of argumentation about what the nation was up against a shambles. The only one who lost more credibility than the Vietcong in late January was Lyndon Johnson himself.[83]

The same message was reaffirmed a month later when the President snatched defeat from the jaws of another nominal victory. On March 12, 1968, the antiwar candidate Eugene McCarthy polled 42 percent of the vote in the New Hampshire Democratic primary, compared with the 49 percent attracted by the President himself in a difficult write-in vote. Even though Johnson was not an announced candidate and had not campaigned, the protest vote instantly dispelled the appearance of his invincibility. The vote for McCarthy was an embarrassing sign of just how much Johnson's exercise of power had eviscerated his claims to political authority and just how vulnerable his leadership had become. Especially devastating was the fact that the New Hampshire protesters were divided on both sides of the substantive issue of the day. In fact, more hawks than doves had supported McCarthy against Johnson. The issue was not war or peace; the issue was Johnson's handling of his commitments.[84]

Johnson announced his withdrawal from the presidential race on March 31 at the end of a televised announcement of a change in America's war aims.[85] In the main part of his message he informed the nation that he had rejected a request from his generals for another major escalation of troop strength and that he was pressing for a negotiated settlement instead. He explained his decision not to run for reelection in a follow-up news conference. He reasoned that if he took this new policy into Wisconsin and subsequent party primaries and did battle directly with Kennedy and McCarthy, his motives might be called into question, and he might jeopardize whatever gain the change in policy might yield. Taking the high road of personal withdrawal, on the other hand, would underscore his disinterested service to the nation and prove that his pursuit of the cause had always been in earnest. Thus, Johnson kept hopes alive for a retrospective understanding of his actions and perhaps also for the imponderable political rewards that might follow more immediately from a major diplomatic breakthrough. "I'm not sacrificing anything," he insisted to a reporter. "I think that if I do not have the aura of a political campaign around me, that my efforts might be a little more fruitful." Then, he reminded the press of his original leadership aims: "Some of you refer to my actions as consensus. I do think now is the time . . . to remove yourself [sic] from any selfish actions."[86]

Johnson's withdrawal message did little to arrest the sectarian turn in national politics that had precipitated it. The touchstones of the prior consensus—the containment of communism, the incremental expansion of the welfare state, and an economy managed by the federal government to secure stable growth—had all been thrown open to question by his concert of action on all fronts, and the questions were pressed with increasing fervor in the tumultuous campaign that followed. Yet, it is important to add that Johnson's fracturing of the liberal regime did not yield any firm resolve to reverse course. The unraveling of his administration is typical of the politics of articulation in that the only consensus to emerge from it was that the President had failed to manage the regime's commitments effectively. Anger directed at Johnson was eventually defused to candidates who promised to do similar things more effectively. The President himself did not present the military decision of March 31 as a reversal or an indictment of his prior aims but as a way to continue, to see the commitment through in Southeast Asia. Furthermore, none of the major candidates, Democrat or Republican, repudiated that commitment directly.[87] The point could be expanded beyond the war policy. With all the tumult of this election year, Lyndon Johnson was far more vulnerable than the foreign and domestic commitments that he had impressed upon the nation.

This message was conveyed in part by the appearance of a "new," more moderate Richard Nixon whose successful presidential campaign in 1968 held back from a frontal assault on liberalism's achievements and promised simply to "bring us together again" under the Republican banner. The point was made even more dramatically by Hubert Humphrey, the nominee of a Democratic convention that had featured the disintegration of Johnson's consensus on national television. At the time of the convention, Humphrey was perhaps the only politician of national significance over whom Johnson still wielded control. The stalwart Democratic nominee continued to bear the full weight of his affiliation with the policies of the administration through the month of September, and the burden proved crushing. Humphrey's campaign was shaping up as a complete disaster. His party's apparatus was financially broke and organizationally in ruins, the liberal coalition was divided against itself, the insurgent candidacy of George Wallace was fueling old southern racism into a nationwide backlash against liberalism. Finally, Humphrey decided he had nothing to lose by formally distancing himself from his discredited chief. On September 30, he made a televised policy statement on Vietnam. He said that if elected he would stop the bombing of North Vietnam as "an acceptable risk for peace," but would "reserve the right to resume the bombing" if the government of North Vietnam were to show "bad faith."[88] There was no change in basic commitments in this message. Indeed, questions immediately arose as to whether there was any significant change in policy implied by the statement at all.[89] The force of the message lay in Humphrey's public assertion of independence from Johnson in interpreting received commitments. Humphrey wagered correctly that he did not have to repudiate the commitment to Vietnam per se, he only had to repudiate his faith in Lyndon Johnson.

Having taken his distance, Humphrey's campaign started its long surge back from the abyss. No sooner did he indicate his determination to speak about the old commitments in his own voice than the voters responded. The liberal coalition began to coalesce once again, and the Wallace insurgency began to fade. Still gaining on the weekend leading into the election, Humphrey's loss by a hairbreadth seems less attributable to the vulnerabilities of his liberal commitments than to the association with Johnson that had set him so far back. It was Johnson, the hapless manager of orthodoxy and innovation—not the Democratic party or the regime it had built—who took the rap for the sectarian unraveling of liberalism in 1968. "The only difference between the Kennedy assassination and mine," Johnson lamented, "is that I am alive and it has been more tortuous."[90]

Part Three:
Jimmy Carter's Disjunction

There is no reason why we should have a horrible,
bloated, confused, overlapping, wasteful,
inefficient, ineffective, insensitive,
unmanageable bureaucratic
mess in Washington.

LYNDON JOHNSON left in his wake a sectarian politics clinically diagnosed in academic political science as "interest group liberalism."[1] As orthodoxy, liberalism was on the defensive, but the organizing impulses it had unleashed continued unabated, and government institutions pursued a rule of expedience in dealing with the seemingly ubiquitous pressures from issue-based lobbies. Democratic congresses decentralized their operations to cultivate client services and resist presidential designs.[2] Republican presidents probed the weaknesses of the liberal order, but accepted—and, for a time, even elaborated upon—its commitments.[3]

With their regime hanging on as an expedience for their clients, the Democrats' surge back to complete control of the federal establishment in 1976 did little to dispel the doubts about liberalism as an authoritative guide to solutions for the problems of the day. With more commitments than ever to defend and less national resolve to muster on their behalf, their victory merely forced to the fore the question of exactly what they intended for the nation in the post-Vietnam, post-civil rights, post-Great Society era. Core Democratic constituencies harbored expansive demands for another round of social reform, but in the inflation-wracked, oil-shocked economy of the 1970s, any plan for carrying forward the work of the past was bound to strain the already fractured ranks of their national coalition. Meanwhile, within the Republican party, hard-line conservatism was resurgent and pulling the organization back into a more repudiative posture. When the lost cause of the Goldwater Republicans sprang back to life under Ronald Reagan in the mid-1970s, it rode a wave of discontent with the established order of things that was missing in 1964. Promises of restoring American preeminence on the world stage, of breaking the back of bureaucratic paralysis at home, of releasing individual initiative from excessive taxation and regulation were now offered in condemnation of a faltering liberal project.

Jimmy Carter, the leader of the Democrats' resurgence, understood exactly what was at stake for liberal government in the 1970s. He challenged the liberal regime to take the test that circumstances had thrust upon it and candidly acknowledge that its old solutions were now a part of the problem. He insisted that changes in the economic and international climate had shifted the task of liberal political leadership categorically and that a simple, straightforward rearticulation of received premises would no longer do. He reassembled the broken pieces of the party of Roosevelt and Johnson with a critical eye focused on the task of rehabilitating the beleaguered system of governance they had bequeathed to his new day. With a studied distance from the establishment he proposed to lead, he exuded an extrapartisan competence, a can-do, problem-solving approach to power that promised to make the old regime work almost in spite of itself.[4] Carter was a nominal affiliate of a vulnerable regime projecting a place in history in which liberalism would prove its vitality through hard-nosed readjustments of its operating assumptions.

The recurrent pattern. Though the challenges facing liberal government in the mid-1970s were unique, the politics of leadership under Jimmy Carter proved painfully familiar. On his way to office he set up a test of leadership that no president has been able to pass, and his performance followed the pattern among late-regime affiliates with grim consistency. In fact, Carter's initial bid for office echoes all the rarefied claims these presidents have ventured over the course of American political history. When he stretched to articulate new warrants for political action—warrants that might reconcile his affiliation with the old order with the growing skepticism about its commitments at this new place in history—he hit upon matters of administration and procedure.[5] Like John Quincy Adams, Franklin Pierce, and Herbert Hoover, he rested his distinctive claim to authority on the reification of technique.

John Quincy Adams had held out a standard of "talent and virtue alone"; Carter asked, "Can our government be competent?" "Can our government be honest and decent and open?"[6] "Why not the best?" was his campaign theme. His most solemn pledge to the American people was that he would never knowingly tell a lie.[7]

Franklin Pierce had thought that if he could just repair the machinery that had serviced the old regime in the past, he might be able to revive some version of the programmatic agenda it had supported. Though Pierce's machinery was party-based and locally controlled, whereas Carter's was bureaucratic and nationally controlled, Carter shared Pierce's premise that the best hope for the old program lay in first fixing up the apparatus itself. And just as Pierce's leadership project had engaged the Jacksonian regime a step removed from the full-service orchestration of interests and policies provided by James Polk, Carter's engaged the liberal regime a step removed from Lyndon Johnson's no-holds-barred implementation of the liberal agenda. What Carter set out to show was that "there is no inherent conflict between careful planning, tight management, and constant reassessment on the one hand, and compassionate concern for the plight of the deprived and afflicted on the other."[8] Against the burgeoning conservative insurgency, Carter insisted that "the problem is not that program goals are unworthy; it is not that our public servants are unfit. What is at fault is the unwieldy structure and frequently inefficient operation of the government; the layers of administration, the plethora of agencies, the proliferation of paperwork. If we are to succeed in other substantive policy areas, government must cease to be an obstacle to our efforts."[9]

Herbert Hoover had boasted the potential of scientific management and professional expertise to supersede Republican politics-as-usual. Technical competence was his solution to the complicated problems confronting the old regime, and with it he promised to guide the nation into a "New Era" of Republican prosperity. Carter updated these claims as well. Like Hoover, he had a background in engineering, and also like Hoover, he had a disdain for old-style party politics. Carter's appreciation of the managerial challenges at hand had been sharpened at meetings of the Trilateral Commission, a seminar sponsored by David Rockefeller that brought together elites from Japan, Europe, and the United States to discuss the emergent new order in world affairs.[10] His policies were fully attuned to the changing shape of competition among nations, to the growing interdependence of the world economy, and to the domestic implications of world resource constraints. He took this message to the people, treating them to truly mind-boggling accounts of the task at hand:

> The future is pressing on us in such an inexorable way, in such a complicated interrelated way, that we need for political leaders to have an understanding of what is going to occur inexorably and inevitably, on the one hand, and what options we still have open to us. We need to have analyses made by complicated procedures using electronic data processing, computer models, so that we can see the interrelationship between foreign trade, the quality of the ocean, environmental deterioration, utilization of energy, the wasting of commodities, food shortages . . .[11]

Carter argued that American government was not prepared to deal with problems in this way. A new politics was called for, one that would dispense with the tired bickering of the old parties, transcend special interest pressures, and generally authorize smart people to generate public policies in the national interest. As he told the National Wildlife Federation, "Now is the time when professionals, like many of you, and scientists, like me, need to be in the most enviable possible posture in our government."[12]

Comparisons between Jimmy Carter and Herbert Hoover became a staple of political commentary in the late 1970s. Politicians and commentators alike derided the President as "Jimmy Hoover."[13] They chided him as a Democrat in name only, one who was displacing the old Rooseveltian faith in the potential of government with a consuming interest in the "machinery of his government and the monitoring of all its details."[14] It was said that he led "like a problem-solving engineer" rather than a man of great vision, and that his promise of competence had only deepened the nation's "crisis of competence."[15] Eventually he would be charged with doing for the Republicans what they could not do for themselves—"making his own name a synonym for mismanagement and expunging memories of Herbert Hoover's dawdling at the onset of the Great Depression." "A long line of Republicans," it was predicted, "will henceforth run against Jimmy Carter."[16]

More often than not, these assessments cast Carter as just another political incompetent and rendered his reification of technique a blunder plain and simple. Certainly, there is more to it than that. To take the dismal results of the leadership of Carter and Hoover as prima facie evidence of their political talents is to assume that presidents who have fared better played on the same field of political authority. For all that

Carter shared with Hoover, this assumption seems to miss the point. Once we acknowledge that the playing field for the assertion of political leadership is not level, and observe further that Hoover and Carter shared elements of a leadership situation unlike that of any of the presidents that came between them, the parallels in their experiences begin to speak to more fundamental dynamics of structure and agency. From this perspective, the similarities reflect the powerful effects of political time on the quest for national authority and help us sort the politics of leadership into patterns that recur across broad stretches of history.

These two former engineers swept aside the stalwarts of their old and fractured parties because there was little resolve left in those old parties to stop them. They carried the nation by promising technocratic relief from tensions building within the establishment because, short of a broadside challenge to the legitimacy of the regime itself, technical mastery of the situation in all its complexity was the best hope for solving the nation's problems. The reification of technique, for all its weaknesses vis-à-vis other leadership postures, is prominently displayed among late-regime affiliates because nothing is quite so effective in submerging the difficult issues of substance that tend to accumulate among the commitments of long-established regimes or in galvanizing broken coalitions for another round in power. These politicians reify technique because more basic commitments of ideology and interest have already been thrown in question and because received formulas can be neither affirmed without qualification nor forthrightly repudiated. This leadership stance recurs in presidential history because outmoded regimes have an institutional staying power and because the technocratic appeal has a momentary resonance in one that is lingering on in disarray.

Note further that the Carter-Hoover comparison speaks to the question of structure in a particular way. When commentators were not targeting Carter personally as the source of failure, they tended to point instead to the organization and operation of contemporary American government.[17] The trials and tribulations of the Carter presidency thus became manifestations of the "contradictions and complications of the modern presidency."[18] But this assessment too appears a bit wide of the mark. Not only has the modern presidency failed to provide a consistent test of leadership skill, but Carter came to power in what has proven to be an impossible leadership situation time and again since the presidency of John Adams. Failure in this light is the least remarkable aspect of his performance, and its explanation is largely independent of modern conditions.

Carter's leadership tracks the age-old pattern among late-regime affiliates in its unraveling as closely as it does in its initial premises and pretensions. Locating the salvation of the nation in the machinery of the government, Carter was unable to anchor his leadership project in any bedrock of constituency support. He landed in Washington tenuously attached to a governing establishment that itself appeared dangerously out of step with the most urgent questions of the day, and like his counterparts in political time, he struggled haplessly in that awkward position just to bring his credibility as a national leader into focus. In this sense, we might say that Jimmy Carter began where Lyndon Johnson had left off, with a credibility gap. Whereas Johnson's career as liberalism's booster had run headlong into a confrontation with its own achievements, Jimmy Carter's career as liberalism's problem-solver got stuck on its initial premise, spinning about in the problems without ever really establishing credibility at all.

Finally, and most importantly, the political impact of Carter's hapless struggle for credibility also followed true to the old pattern. Acting on his precious formulas for rejuvenating the machinery of liberal government, Carter placed himself at the center of dissension over the substantive commitments of the national government. When he challenged received domestic priorities, he encountered fierce resistance from within the ranks; when he elaborated them, he encountered equally fierce assaults from the insurgent opposition. When he challenged old foreign policy priorities, he encountered fierce resistance from the insurgent opposition; when he elaborated them, he encountered equally fierce resistance from within the ranks. Caught between the problematic expectations of his liberal constituents and the mushrooming critique of the insurgent conservatives, the man who had promised to make liberal government work again became the leading symbol of its collapse. Initiatives heralding the revitalization of the old order served instead to stigmatize it as utterly barren of hope for the future, and Carter's search for credibility yielded the precise opposite of what he intended. Indicted by its own standards, Carter's leadership offered a prima facie case for an even more decisive break with the past. He became a caricature of the old regime's political bankruptcy, the perfect foil for a repudiation of liberalism itself as the true source of all the nation's problems.

The emergent pattern. There is no denying that modern forms of politics and governance reshaped the politics of disjunction under Carter in important ways, but to see how requires a bit more sorting through the relevant comparisons and contrasts. Comparing modern presidents with their counterparts in political time yields three general observations: first, that modern power relations exert a subtle rather than a decisive influence over the politics of leadership; second, that the effect itself is a countervailing factor in the recurrent patterns; and third, that the impact of modern forms and procedures is not all of a piece but varies under different structures of political authority. For Franklin Roosevelt, a president who came into office with the most expansive of warrants for independent action, modernity proved to be something of a constraint. As we have seen, the proliferation of independent actors throughout the political system, and their resilience in the face of his repudiative authority, introduced all sorts of complications and slippages into his initial leadership pretensions. Jimmy Carter, on the other hand, came to power with what have traditionally been the most constricted warrants for independent action. For him, modernity had just the opposite effect; it expanded his range. As we shall see, by drawing on the enhanced institutional resources of the presidential office itself and by exploiting the political fragmentation in the rest of the governing environment, Carter was able to press the case for technical competence to the very brink of venturing reconstructive claims of his own.

Put another way, what marks the Carter disjunction as distinctively modern is the relative weakness of his affiliated status as a constraint on his actions. Abstracted from history, Carter's tortured relationship to the Democratic establishment might evoke longing for some ideal of "responsible" party government. But that ideal world never existed in America. The relevant record to draw on is that of John Quincy Adams clinging stubbornly to hollowed-out norms of propriety, Franklin Pierce caving in to the disastrous designs of the party leaders, and Herbert Hoover grasping after hobgoblins of ideological consistency. Let us review Carter's struggle to escape the dismal political implications of his affiliated status in this light.

Note that *each* of these late-regime affiliates began with an attenuated political relationship to the establishment for which they would be held responsible in office. Adams and Hoover were candidates of dubious orthodoxy, at least as perceived by stalwarts within the ranks. Pierce was an obscure figure far removed from the center of national political action. Carter was as obscure a figure as Pierce and as mugwumpish in his politics as Adams and Hoover. Note further that each of these leaders reflected in his own candidacy the severe strains that had come to weigh on the old orthodoxy, and that, once in office, each had to wrestle with the meaning of his affiliation to it. The emergent pattern to be discerned among them on this score should now be clear: with each successive incarnation of the politics of disjunction, the incumbent has proved himself less deferential to the politics of the past and has pressed more vigorous departures from established formulas. Late-regime affiliates have been able to mount progressively more formidable assaults on the boundary condition of their political identity because the resources of their office have become progressively more expansive and the institutional foundations of their action progressively more independent. Carter, the most resourceful of them all, commands our attention precisely because he pressed this logic of institutional independence to its outer limits.

Recall first how John Quincy Adams wrestled himself into paralysis over the question of his affiliation with the old order. On the face of it, Adams had assembled all the elements of a major break from the political muddle of the "era of good feeling": he had shoved aside the old selection procedures to make his own bid for the presidency; he had forged an alliance with Monroe's most outspoken critic, Henry Clay; he had put together a new coalition of Federalists and Nationalist Republicans; he had fortified that coalition with a ringing political manifesto. But for all the evidence that he was building a wholly new political formation, Adams was at a loss when it came to using his office to follow through. Rejecting Clay's advice, he refused to purge his enemies from the administration or to wage the manifestly partisan battle in which he was engaged on partisan ground. He felt constrained to keep his warrants for action locked up in standards of appropriate behavior that his own quest for power had done so much to discredit. By wrapping his administration in traditional claims of continuity in the line of succession and hallowed norms of proper administration, he undercut the dramatic changes he had set in motion to take control in the first place. At the same time, the actions he had taken to gain control undercut his assertions about administrative propriety and political continuity.

Franklin Pierce's struggle with the meaning of his affiliation with the old order took a somewhat different turn. Initially, Pierce promised to stand by the work of his predecessors and accept the received solution to the slavery issue as final. Unfortunately, his efforts to repair the political machinery of the Jackson coalition without reference to slavery and get on with the old agenda collapsed almost immediately. Within months of his inauguration, his commitment to keeping the dreaded issue closed portended his own isolation and impotence within the Democratic ranks. Unwilling to accept this fate, Pierce grasped the second chance offered him by the party leadership. He forged a coalition with Stephen Douglas, and he threw the resources of the Jacksonian presidency behind a measure that would radically alter the received terms of regime legitimacy. He secured the new program, packed the federal government with its supporters, and then called on all "friends of the Constitution" to rally to his new standard and defeat the forces of revolution rising against him. Pierce did not hesitate to take action on his own behalf even when that action entailed a forthright break with formulas he had presumably come to power to uphold. By the middle of the nineteenth century, loyalty to the party had supplanted loyalty to predecessors as the standard of political affiliation, and Pierce's efforts to assert the party standard unleashed the resources of the presidency to secure one of the most momentous and controversial policy departures in all of American political history.

Hoover's struggle for credibility cut even further into the constraint of affiliation with the politics of the past. He tied his action neither to the standards of his predecessors nor to the evolving standards of the party leaders. He offered expertise in the management of the nation's economy as a standard in and of itself, and his cultivation of local "Hoover Clubs" responsive to that standard gave him an independent political base from which to launch his drive for his party's nomination. Though Hoover's early initiatives set off an explosion of sectarian infighting that mocked his managerial pretensions, the onset of the Depression provided a showcase for them. The presidency was now the font of policy leadership, and Hoover, the nation's policy leader in a time of crisis, put his own limits on change in the old formulas. Indeed, as his departures became progressively more substantial, the meaning of his affiliation with Republicanism came to reside largely in his own ideas and beliefs. Hoover sought to take credit for extraordinary actions addressed to the emergency, but the more he did, the more insistent he became that these actions did not entail any fundamental departure from his original commitment to the "American Way." He boasted that his emergency measures actually would guard against any permanent or fundamental break with the tried and true methods of doing things. The fact was that these fundamentals existed largely in the machinations of his own mind. Affiliation boiled down to preserving Hoover's way of doing things.

This subtle undercurrent of political effacement in the affiliated status of the late-regime insiders culminates in the Carter presidency. Indeed, Carter went so far in challenging the constraint of political affiliation that on the most basic question of political identity—is the president an affiliate or an opponent of the established order?—he succeeded in making himself one of the most difficult of all presidents to classify.[19] Less of a political apologist than Hoover, Carter put a far more critical spin on his technocratic resolves. He took his cues from the nation's problems as he saw them at the moment, and displayed little apparent concern for political history, ideological consistency, or party responsibility.[20] His initial assessment of current conditions raised serious questions about the establishment built by the party he presumed to represent. His midterm reassessment called for permanent and fundamental changes in the existing order of things and placed him on a collision course with the nation's leading spokesman for liberal priorities in government. Before he was defeated by Ronald Reagan, he had in fact turned those priorities on their head. In all, the travails of "Jimmy Hoover" mask the brazenness of a "Jimmy Jackson" who challenged the ties that bound him right up to the moment the Democrats nominated him for a second term.

This overlay of emergent and recurrent patterns leaves us with two conclusions. The first finds a common lesson in the experiences of FDR, LBJ, and Carter. Looking at this group, there is no denying that the modern presidency instills in its incumbents a powerful conceit that the playing field of political leadership is level, and whatever evidence we can mount to the contrary, there is also no denying that this conceit is itself a potent corrosive. Carter's challenge to the boundary condition of affiliation in political leadership, Lyndon Johnson's challenge to the practical distinction between articulating and reconstructing an established regime, and Franklin Roosevelt's technocratic challenge to the logical limits of the reconstructive stance itself all speak to the same point: the boundaries that have framed the politics of leadership in its various modes since the beginning of presidential history are being frayed on all sides.

The more telling point, however, is that these boundaries have yet to give way. When we consider the stark contrasts to be drawn among the presidents in this modern grouping and the similarities that tie each to distinctive sets of leaders in other historical periods, it is apparent that notwithstanding secular changes in the institutional foundations of presidential power, classic differences among leadership stances still hold sway. Despite the force of the countercurrents supporting Carter's pretensions to independence, there were severe limits to his impulse to dissolve the distinction between affiliated leadership and opposition leadership, limits which the conservative insurgency exploited to saddle him with the liberal label and repudiate the regime wholesale. Carter flirted with the language of repudiation, but, as we shall see, the authority was never his.

We are left in the end to ponder the still decisive difference between Franklin Roosevelt, a modern president who pressed reconstructive claims to such extremes that he ultimately fell into his own reification of technique, and Jimmy Carter, a modern president who pressed the case for technique to the brink of making his own reconstructive claims. Just as surely as Roosevelt did not succumb to the stunning failure of his technocratic appeal but persevered as a legitimating force for a new political order, Carter did not extricate himself from the burdens of his affiliated status but was pegged with responsibility for the plight of his enervated regime. The transformative political effect of these two leadership efforts suggests that modernity is still but a complicating factor, and that in the main, the politics presidents make continues to recapitulate the basic patterns and sequences evident from the start.

The Sound of the Trumpet

Of the many tests that Jimmy Carter set up for himself as a political leader, the most telling of his strengths and weaknesses was the promise of clarity. Carter took his text on this matter from 1 Corinthians: "If the trumpet be given an uncertain sound, then who shall prepare themselves for the battle?"[21] His actions bore witness to his faith. When it came to explaining to people who he was and what his campaign was all about, Carter proved himself inexhaustible. He had a position on every conceivable topic, and he carefully punctuated each commitment with a trademark tag: "You can depend on it."

The upshot, however, was decidedly mixed. Like all the other tests Carter would impose upon himself, the test of clarity quickly came back to haunt him. Carter's ability to take his case directly to the people, and his personal determination to put it to them as forcefully as possible, only amplified the static in his leadership posture. Like other late-regime affiliates, he had extremely subtle claims to make about what he represented politically and offered quite complicated explanations of what he intended to do in government. The more he attempted to elaborate and clarify his position publicly, the more dissonance people heard, and by the end of the 1976 primary campaign, he was already stamped indelibly with a debilitating reputation for "fuzziness." It is little wonder that clarity would prove one of the leadership qualities most admired in Ronald Reagan;[22] the "Great Communicator" of the 1980s was a product of Carter's tortured efforts to make himself understood.

Although Carter failed to achieve clarity, he still achieved something remarkable in his presentations to the public. Even as he drew out the inherent political tensions in the leadership position of a late-regime affiliate, he pressed the limits of that position and stretched its political range. As one interviewer put it, "Every politician emphasizes different things to different audiences," but "in your case . . . you seem to have several faces."[23] Indeed, on his way to the presidency, Carter cultivated a variety of starkly different, even antithetical identities—outsider/insider, conservative/liberal, populist/technocrat, opposition leader/affiliated leader—and in the near term at least, he gained from this "an uncanny ability to influence how people interpreted him."[24] As the early charges of fuzziness bear out, these antinomies were never reconciled. And yet, in a political situation stubbornly resistant to blunt claims and simple explanations, Carter showed how a modern campaign could juggle a whole host of widely divergent messages. What he gained in the process was a measure of political independence from the implications of each message that others would have to reckon with.

Fuzziness notwithstanding, Carter had some good reasons for believing that his message would ring more clearly than anyone else's in the presidential contest of 1976. In the first place, he stood to make the most of the best argument the Democrats had going for themselves that year. The national prospects of the beleaguered party of Roosevelt had brightened considerably against the sordid record of scandals and exposés that had come to wrack the Republican intercession. With the resignation of Vice President Spiro Agnew, the long exposé of the Watergate crimes, the resignation of President Nixon, and the pardon of Nixon by the successor he himself had appointed, the Democratic party found itself the alternative to a national disgrace. And of all the Democratic contenders that year, Carter packaged this alternative in the starkest possible contrasts with the current state of national affairs. He was a clean-living, plain-style, Bible-reading populist, an "outsider" with no connections whatever to the current state of affairs in Washington. His ministry of moral regeneration and the restoration of virtue heralded the contingent premise of the Democratic resurgence with Jackson-like resolve.

Furthermore, as a candidate from the deep South, Carter's bid for the Democratic nomination also packed a potent instrumental logic that the party leadership could not afford to ignore. Like Franklin Pierce, Carter hailed from the region of greatest erosion in his party's national support. The Republicans had by now made deep inroads into the Democrats' old southern base, and Carter, a former governor of Georgia, offered to bring that region back to its old standard without at the same time alienating the party's now vital civil rights constituency. The prospect of reclaiming the solid South would facilitate a triumph of expedience over enthusiasm unrivaled among party leaders since the Democratic convention of 1852 chose that obscure ex-senator from New Hampshire in the hopes that he might bring the bolting Free Soilers back to the party of Jackson and Polk.

Finally, and most importantly, there were internal weaknesses in the Democratic party organization that helped Carter craft his message in an intensely personal way. He would never have had the chance to present the nation with his high standards of clean living if it were not for the vastly expanded system of primary elections for the selection of delegates to the party convention. A drive to displace the traditional party managers from control over the nomination machinery had rumbled out of the Democratic debacle in Chicago in 1968, and by 1976, the substitution of these new plebiscitary procedures for the older internal party controls was near complete. In effect, the Democratic convention was opened to any candidate who might mobilize popular support on his own behalf, and that meant that even the darkest of dark-horse candidates could remain the master of his own message. Though he was the most obscure contender elected to the presidency since Franklin Pierce, Carter would not have to depend on the party leaders for his voice, nor would he be beholden to them for his selection. Acting independently and on his own behalf, he bypassed the party establishment to fashion his own appeal; taking his case directly to the people, he sharpened his Jackson-like resolves in an extended series of public contests against the leading lights of the Democratic establishment.

Carter's drive for the White House revolutionized the political art of self-presentation and set the mold for the plebiscitary politics of our day. His was an "autobiographical" campaign which blurred received images of the Democratic party to project a national political identity that was wholly idiosyncratic.[25] Carter was a "loner." He was a southerner. He was a farmer. He was a scientist. He was an engineer. He was a governor. He was a born-again Christian. He was a businessman. He was a Trilateral technocrat. He was a populist. He was an idealist who wanted, in the post-Vietnam era, to elevate respect for human rights into a leading principle for the conduct of foreign policy; he was a realist who had concluded that government had its limits and could not solve all problems. He was a budget balancer who appreciated the virtues of the free market and burdens of government regulation, but he was also an environmentalist, a consumer advocate, a welfare reformer, and a friend of national health insurance. He was neither implicated in nor beholden to the current state of affairs, and yet he looked forward to the new spirit of honesty, trust, and cooperation that might be established between a president and a Congress once again united under the Democratic banner.[26]

Carter was nothing if not something different. Throughout the primary season, he exploited his remoteness from his party and its institutional centers of power and turned detachment from the establishment into his most distinctive political asset. Probing deep beneath the general public revulsion against the Watergate crimes, he was able to speak to uncertainties that had come to surround the Democrats' own alternatives. Moral degeneration in the executive was but a point of departure as Carter drew attention to more generalized problems of "mismanagement" riddling the entire government. By keeping these general problems in view, he compelled the party that had built that establishment to indulge a crusade against it.

Carter charged categorically that government in Washington had become a "horrible, bloated, confused . . . bureaucratic mess"; that the nation's tax system was "a disgrace to the human race"; that the welfare system was a "failure" in "urgent need of a complete overhaul."[27] He was running for the presidency because he felt that the American people needed "new voices, and new ideas and new leaders." He wanted to "strip away the secrecy," and expose "the unwarranted pressure of lobbyists." He thought it was time for "comprehensive" reform and a "thorough" housecleaning.[28] For a President who would have such a hard time getting others to understand him, Carter's critique was devastatingly simple: "We know from bitter experience that we are not going to get the changes we need by simply shifting around the same group of Washington insiders." "There is one major and fundamental issue. And that is the issue between insiders and outsiders."[29] Is there any wonder he made clarity his issue?

Up to the time of the Democratic convention, Carter's drive for the presidency went pretty much as he had planned it. As he vented popular disillusionment with political insiders and entrenched special interests, the stalwarts of the Democratic party found themselves unable to settle on a single voice. The more they floundered, the more it became apparent that liberalism could no longer take the political offensive on its own terms. Carter delivered the coup de grace in the Florida primary in March. In these precincts the Democratic party confronted the even more fearsome heresies of George Wallace, and the liberal wing of the party yielded Carter the field in hopes that a moderate southerner would knock Wallace out of contention once and for all. Stopping Wallace, however, made it all the more difficult for anyone else to stop Carter. His Florida victory gained him a respectability within the ranks that the late-breaking "anybody but Carter" drive simply could not counter. With this key southern state added to his earlier victories in Iowa and New Hampshire, Carter stood as the only Democratic candidate who had proven his appeal in all sections of the country.[30]

After Florida, Carter would win some and lose some, but no single alternative would emerge. Slowly but steadily, the Democratic party capitulated to his carefully crafted siege. Mounting an independent, populist critique, Carter succeeded in making himself "a liberal to liberals, a moderate to the moderates, and a conservative to the conservatives."[31] In the end, Richard Daley, the old machine mayor of the city of Chicago, and Leonard Woodcock, the liberal president of the United Automobile Workers, both came to believe that he was the perfect candidate for the times.[32]

But therein lay the dissonance that would muddle the Jackson-like sound of Carter's trumpet. Support from the likes of Daley and Woodcock was, of course, critical to the success of any Democratic contender, but the more of it Carter won, the more mysterious his political position became. He had claimed the high moral ground of detachment from a debased establishment, but he had to cultivate well-established interests to carry him to victory in November. For all his populist outrage, he had been bidding all along for the leadership of an old governing coalition, one whose substantive commitments ran deep through Congress and the bureaucracy and then outward to powerful constituents in the nation at large. For all his insight into the importance of clarity—for his extraordinary success in overcoming obscurity to emerge as the most distinctive Democrat in a distinguished field—he found himself at his moment of triumph straddling both sides of the most basic of all questions of political identity. "All of a sudden," he later despaired, "whether I wanted it or not I inherited the Democratic party."[33]

Carter's belated protestation of indifference to the prize he had fought so hard to win is understandable, for taking over the leadership of the Democratic party caused him "horrible trouble."

> That was the biggest problem we had. To go into the position as the titular head of the Democratic Party, the head of the ticket, compelled by fairness to campaign with local and state congressional candidates, not only removed the lonely, independent candidate image depending on the voter only, but it was also a reversal of what I had been during the primary season. It contributed to the claim that I was a person of mystery and that I was fuzzy on things, that I changed my positions. I could never resolve that question.[34]

Flashes of the candidate's struggle to control the implications of his opposition stance and toe the line of the regime affiliate appear here and there throughout the campaign. Take for instance the line of attack he tested before a labor gathering during the Ohio primary. Beset by the anybody-but-Carter forces and tossing around for a new stump speech he charged that:

> My critics . . . want to stop the people of this country from regaining control of their government. They want to preserve the status quo, to preserve politics as usual, to maintain at all costs their own entrenched, unresponsive, bankrupt, irresponsible political power.[35]

This frontal assault is revealing not only because it drew out the full repudiative implications of Carter's leadership stance but also because Carter immediately pulled back. Alarm swept through the campaign leadership as the press elaborated upon the meaning of this attack.

Carter spokesmen equivocated, affirming the candidate's respect for the Democratic party and its leading lights. The charges of bankruptcy were dropped from all future speeches.[36]

Preventing these divergent identities from crashing into one another became even more difficult during the general election campaign. Consider what happened when, at the end of a sensational interview with *Playboy* magazine, the candidate lumped Lyndon Johnson together with Richard Nixon: "I don't think I would *ever* take on the same frame of mind that Nixon and Johnson did—lying, cheating, and distorting the truth."[37] Republicans in Texas seized upon this statement, and urgent messages from Robert Strauss, the chairman of the Democratic National Committee and a Texan himself, told of a firestorm of outrage developing among Democratic elites which had placed the election in that state in jeopardy. Again an impression had been created that Carter was indifferent to the organized base of his political support, and again the candidate hastened to pull his repudiative punches. Indeed, so eager was he to mend fences and save Texas that he indulged his own distortion of the truth in order to set things right. He intimated that he had never actually made the remark about Johnson at all, backing down only when reporters threatened to call him on the record and demolish his whole case for truth-telling in the court of national opinion.[38]

The high stakes of these occasional missteps make it all the more important to understand how Carter managed the tensions in his basic leadership posture. Despite the very real difficulties he encountered as a party leader and the deep misgivings he came to have about the role later, he had prepared for this task from the start, and he got pretty much what he wanted. The "mistakes" themselves suggest his purpose: to cultivate a double message that would accommodate the party establishment even as it asserted independence from it. The trick was to lay siege to the liberal regime without threatening to destroy it outright, and to retain thereby a warrant for leading it, burdens and all, after it had capitulated.

Winning the Democratic nomination did not change Carter's tune, it merely drew out these subtleties. He selected a running mate with solid liberal credentials, but then carefully cautioned the Democratic convention that "government has it limits and cannot solve all our problems." He reminded his fellow partisans that he had "always been a Democrat," but in the next breath, he reminded everyone else that he had "never met a Democratic president."[39] Perhaps the most effective use of dual identity in the campaign came at the official kickoff on Labor Day. Carter chose not to go to Detroit, the heartland of organized labor and the traditional place for Democratic candidates to begin. He chose FDR's southern retreat at Warm Springs, Georgia instead. His break with tradition was thus also a return to tradition. Warm Springs was the perfect symbol for a candidate who wanted to reunify an old alliance and at the same time take his distance from its most powerful constituent groups.

To keep the lines of accommodation open while pressing on with his siege, Carter was at pains to prevent his devastatingly simple assessments of what was wrong from wandering into equally simple assessments of what should be done about it. Indeed, when he came to the question of what was to be done, the most important thing Carter had to say was that there were "no easy answers" to the questions his campaign was raising. "I think it's just as misleading to give a simplistic answer to a complicated question as it is to avoid the issue." Or, "My answers might be complicated, and might present both sides of a question . . . [but] they are complete." Or, "I'm not an ideologue, and my positions are not predictable . . . I've tried to analyze each question individually; I've taken positions that to me are fair and rational, and sometimes my answers are complicated." Or, "I am still searching for answers to complicated questions. I have always avoided trying to give simplistic answers for reasons of political expediency."[40]

Responses like that, following up a critique that was sharp and categorical, sealed Carter's reputation for "fuzziness." And yet he stuck by the "no easy answers" theme, invoking it repeatedly throughout his four years in office.[41] It is not difficult to understand why. "No easy answers" was the ideological linchpin of the whole project. It held together all the different identities Carter had encompassed. Addressed at once to the lack of enthusiasm for the party within the nation and the lack of enthusiasm for the candidate within the party, it staked out a position which both the party and the nation could credit. With "no easy answers," Carter kept his distance from the old coalition while at the same time deflecting any frontal assaults on the establishment it had built. With "no easy answers," he joined his critique to his reification of technique.

This point was drawn out as the press became more insistent on calling Carter to account for the starkly contrasting messages of his basic leadership posture. When reporters spoke of political contradictions, the candidate spoke of fine-tuning machinery. The general rhetoric, one interviewer observed, was "anti-Washington, anti-big government, anti-big spending," but the specifics of the program called for "more on education, more on transportation, more on the cities, more on welfare, more on health, more on housing, more on jobs, more on Social Security." Carter responded: "I'm not anti-Washington. I'm not going to disrupt anything when I get here to Washington . . . I never said I wanted a small government. I want one that, when it performs a function, does it well and performs a function in ways that alleviate the problems of those who have not had an adequate voice in the past."[42] Or take another instance. The candidate had said that he was a "conservative on spending and a liberal on human welfare." How exactly was he going to reconcile these divergent impulses? "How," Carter was asked, "can you be a liberal on human welfare, which requires the expenditure of usually a great deal of money, and conservative on spending?"

> I would . . . continue . . . with the same attitude toward government management as I did as governor. We maintained a balanced budget, we had strict budgeting rules . . . I think for the first time in any government [we implemented] zero based budgeting, where we automatically weeded out old and obsolescent programs. We established renewed priorities every year to make sure that we spent the money or other resources on the things that were of the highest need in that particular year. We reorganized the structure of government to make it simple and manageable. We invested state funds on a competitive bid basis, and I think I ran the Georgia government as well as almost any corporate structure in this country is run.[43]

In statements such as these, Carter resolved the apparent contradiction between his populist opposition to the establishment and his institutionalized connection to it in talk of bloodless mechanical contrivances that might improve the operational efficiency of liberal government. His reification of technique took a monumental indictment of the stifling weight and moral decay of the federal government and turned it into a problem of administrative management that competent engineers might solve with a little institutional tinkering. There was a difference, Carter maintained, between attacking bureaucrats the way the Republicans did and "releasing them from bureaucratic chaos" as he planned to do. With hopes pinned on the perfectibility of machinery,

Carter offered to save the old regime from its own self-destructive impulses and to eliminate as much as possible the need for substantive choices among the commitments it encompassed. It was precisely because there were "no easy answers" to the challenges facing the established regime that the nation needed a president smart enough to tackle complicated trade-offs with technical expertise.

The promise of making the engines of power run more efficiently carried Carter along a rocky road to election. Ambivalence toward the candidate ran high in all quarters, and the dissonant sounds in his trumpet took their toll.[44] What began as an enormous lead in the polls all but vanished by election day, and Carter's narrow victory cast an early cloud over his credibility as an effective manager of his party's interests.[45] Still, the "no easy answers" theme worked wonders. It kept the old Democratic coalition in tow without undercutting the outsider's critique, and it landed Carter in the presidency with a whole host of different identities to manipulate. For those not yet willing to pronounce liberal government a hopeless failure, as well those still eager to press ahead with one or another of the items on the old agenda, the discordant tones of Carter's message were laden with hope for "the best."

The Shakedown

The Speaker of the House, Thomas P. O'Neill, dubbed Carter's first hundred days in power more productive than any he could recall since the presidency of Franklin Roosevelt.[46] The Senate Majority leader, Robert Byrd, exclaimed that in 27 years in Congress he "had never seen such tremendous legislative achievement" as the Ninety-fifth Congress had realized under Jimmy Carter.[47] On the eve of his renomination by the Democratic party, Carter himself boasted that "there is not a President in modern history, including Franklin Delano Roosevelt and Lyndon Johnson, who has had a better record of support from the Democratic Congress" than he had.[48] Exaggerated to counter grim perceptions to the contrary, these protestations of regime vitality capture an important truth. For all the attention that has been lavished on Carter's inexperience with the ways of Washington and his incompetence in making the government work, he still got a lot done. He was well within the ballpark of legislative performance for modern presidents, and like them, he had notable accomplishments to boast all along the way: the creation of the Department of Energy, government reorganization, the Panama Canal treaties, the normalization of relations with China, the creation of the Department of Education, the overhaul of the civil service system, two energy conservation packages, the negotiation of a strategic arms limitation treaty, the deregulation of transportation and banking, stiffer regulation of strip mining and off-shore drilling, the Egypt-Israel accord, a renewed commitment to national defense.[49]

How then do we account for the sense of hopelessness that gripped this administration during its first year in power and never really let go? The great attraction of arguments about Carter's lack of skill and experience is that they preserve our faith that anything is possible in the presidency if only the right person is in the job. And yet if Carter's leadership holds any enduring interest at all, it must be because he so earnestly pressed his particular conception of the possibilities and still failed monumentally. The first year's unraveling was about premises, not about skill; it was about the challenge that Carter had posed to the established regime and the test of legitimacy he had thrust upon it to gain the presidency in the first place.[50] Granting that someone more familiar with the ways of Washington might not have even tried to do what Carter tried to do, the problem that calls for our attention still remains locked in the leadership project he came to office to execute.

Carter's struggle for credibility in office produced a rapid, almost systematic shakedown of his authority as a national leader because his political pretensions simply could not survive the disruptive impact of his exercise of presidential power. To understand this, we need only consider the relationship between what he proposed to affirm and what he proposed to change. Carter had diagnosed a political regime in deep trouble, one that would have to alter radically the way it worked in order to meet the problems of the day. Yet, he came to power to rejuvenate that regime rather than repudiate it, to save it rather than destroy it. As the order-affirming and order-shattering dimensions of this project had virtually the same referents, Carter convened a politics in which he could not win for winning. To make his critique credible, he would have to offer potent prescriptions for changing the way the government did business. But the more potent his prescriptions, the harder he would have to fight his ostensible allies to secure them; and the harder he had to fight to administer his remedies, the more elusive his case for the vitality of the regime would become. Earnest in the pursuit of his objectives, he could not but drive the disjunction between the regime and the nation beyond repair. The very relationship that Carter sought to carry on with the political establishment served to magnify the problems he had ostensibly come to Washington to resolve.

About a month after the election, Carter's chief pollster, Patrick Caddell, advised him to consolidate his political support. The margin of victory had been narrow, and the Carter vote had proven alarmingly "soft." Caddell saw clearly that Carter's leadership pretensions had "no anchor."[51] "Before you can lead the country," the pollster cautioned, "you have to have the credibility to lead the country."[52] The logic was irrefutable in principle, and yet for Carter it only crystalized the problem. Credibility in leadership is inherently elusive when the basic question of political identity has been so carefully fudged. Caddell was asking his boss to consolidate a position that was itself a delicate balance of contradictory messages. The candidate had cultivated the position of one who was of-but-not-in the established regime, and efforts to reinforce that identity promised only to deepen the tensions within it.

Taking up Caddell's challenge, Carter did just what one might expect of him. He moved simultaneously on opposing fronts, cultivating at once his credentials as an affiliate and his credentials as an outsider. On the one side, he tapped into a vast reservoir of talent that instantly becomes available to a president-elect from the Democratic party. Not only did Carter put in place a group of department managers who could relate to the Washington establishment on the most intimate terms, he also disavowed the recent practice of direct White House control of all administration business. He proclaimed a return to the principles of cabinet government and collective decision-making, and asked only that his collaborators rise to his standards of competence and personal integrity. Carter's choices drew heavily on people who had served in second-tier positions in the Johnson administration, many of whom he had met at David Rockefeller's seminar on the governing problems of the 1970s. Cyrus Vance, Johnson's deputy secretary of defense, became the new secretary of state; Harold Brown, Johnson's Air Force secretary, became the secretary of defense; Charles Schultze, Johnson's budget director, became chairman of the Council of Economic Advisors; Joseph Califano, Johnson's domestic affairs advisor, became secretary of health, education and welfare; Michael Blumenthal, a trade negotiator in the Johnson State Department, became secretary of the treasury.[53]

Carter's team was so thoroughly conventional, so eminently respectable, and so well connected that he and the band of Georgians he gathered at the White House appeared the odd men out. Reviewing the list, Hugh Sidey predicted that "grafting the head of this Administration to its body is going to be one of the most fascinating bits of political surgery of this century."[54] Others could not help but wonder what had happened to the candidate who had claimed to be different, the one who had implied that his administration would not be just more of the same old thing and who had told the people repeatedly that they could count on him to keep his word. Carter had promised "new faces" and "new ideas." His campaign manager had underscored that pledge by stating flatly that if his boss picked Cyrus Vance or Zbigniew Brzezinski for the high posts in foreign policy, he would consider his efforts a failure and quit.[55] (Brzezinski, a Columbia University professor who had helped Rockefeller organize the Trilateral Commission, was appointed Carter's national security advisor.) To some, the identity crisis that would grip this administration over the course of its first year in power was already apparent. "The last laugh," wrote William Greider, "is on those who thought Carter might have the nerve or the political vision to break cleanly with the past. Instead he has revived it."[56]

But Greider was only half right. Those who took the symbolism of those formative weeks as seriously as the substance could see that even as Carter was making his overture to the Democratic establishment, he was also fortifying his best defense against it. Caddell had advised Carter to "give the people the visible signals that are needed to understand what is happening," and Carter responded with an elaborate media display of the dramatic changes he was making in the tenor of the government.[57] A walk to the White House after the inauguration, a fireside chat from the White House library with the President clad in a cardigan sweater, a morning flight to Pittsburgh to sympathize with the victims of the winter's cold and nation's gas shortage, a series of town meetings to keep in touch with the concerns of the common folk—all the events and decisions of Carter's first weeks in office looked toward expanding the reservoir of popular faith in his intention not to get taken in by politics as usual but to stand apart and change it. Bypassing Washington, this "strategy of symbols" staked claims to authority in government as an extension of the President's personal relationship with the people themselves.[58]

His credibility bolstered on the inside and the outside, Carter was ready to exercise the powers of his office. Though he had been willing to tap the same old managers, he made it clear at the outset that he was not about to let them manage the same old policies. Lingering economic worries dampened whatever enthusiasm the President might have been able to muster for expensive social initiatives in the old mold, and tensions began to build as the new President countered the traditional Democratic enthusiasm he had incorporated into his administration with his own mugwumpish insistence on budgetary restraint.[59]

The problem manifested itself immediately in the development of his welfare reform proposal. Carter had pronounced the nation's welfare system a failure time and again, and his promise of a prompt and comprehensive overhaul was a first test of liberalism's ability to save itself by revamping its old programs. Unfortunately, Joseph Califano, the Great Society visionary whom the President had authorized to develop a plan, found it difficult to meet his charge of revitalization under the President's chief stipulation: no increase in cost. Much to Carter's dismay, Califano insisted that little in the way of constructive reform could be accomplished by merely reorganizing the existing machinery. He contended not only that reforms consistent with the President's chief stipulation would hurt the very groups he and his party ostensibly meant to support, but that any such proposal would prove a nonstarter politically. "At zero-cost," he said in a heated exchange with the President, "we are retaining so many inequities that we would be shot out of the water."[60]

In confrontations like this, the antinomies so precariously balanced in Carter's leadership posture were sent crashing into one another. If those who thought that Carter might break cleanly with the past were put off by the appointment of managers like Califano, those who took comfort in the appointment of such men were soon put off by Carter's stubborn determination to resist their policy recommendations. There was to be little room for laughter on either side. By the summer of 1977, Califano had finagled a compromise welfare plan that simply hid most of the cost increases. The administration never showed much interest in the measure, however, and Congress quickly saw through the charade. The long-heralded "Program for Better Jobs and Income" failed to make it to the floor, and relations between Califano and the White House degenerated in a tangle of mutual suspicion.[61]

While Califano was sparring with the White House over what constituted a politically acceptable welfare reform proposal, a test of what

Carter's leadership posture might achieve in Congress was already under way. Just four weeks into his term, Carter announced his intentions to review federal commitments to the construction of local water projects with an eye to a "prudent and responsible use of the taxpayer's money and to the protection of the environment."[62] The review resulted in a decision to cut nineteen of these projects from the budget for 1978. On its face, this is hardly the stuff of extraordinary national leadership, but Carter had calculated the impact of this initiative with a precision reminiscent of Andrew Jackson's veto of the Maysville road. He wanted to hit the nerve center of politics-as-usual, and he did.

In fact, this Jackson-like declaration of war on extravagance placed the disjunction between the President's personal appeal to the nation and his political support in the government in the starkest possible light. As he later wrote in his memoirs, "The issue of the water projects was the one that caused the deepest breach between me and the Democratic leadership."[63] For Carter, the projects were a prime example of the wasteful and unnecessary expenditures inherent in the old ways the government did business. The cuts offered him a well-founded and much-needed opportunity to demonstrate at the very outset of his term what he had been saying all along: that an outsider with no attachments to established interests and routines could bring a thrifty discipline to the national government without threatening anything really significant. Carter targeted one of the most notorious and deeply entrenched pork-barrel systems in the government—one that had sustained the Army Corps of Engineers in the good graces of the Congress for well over a century—because he wanted to express his commitments "very clearly" at the outset and to redeem his promise to free the national interest from its subordination to special interests.[64]

Of course, Congress saw the matter quite differently. Carter's initiative was received on Capitol Hill as an ignorant, irresponsible, and politically pretentious assault on the bread and butter of congressional careers. Its transparent purpose was to enhance the President's public identity as an outsider and populist reformer, but its chief victims were those upon whom he depended most directly for support in government. The sorry fact was that no interest of political significance in Washington cared much for Carter's idea of changing the way the government worked. Though at times the President felt more "at home" with the Republicans in Congress than with his own partisans, they were not about to make his case for regime vitality.[65] And though the

Democrats had overwhelming majorities in both houses of Congress, Carter's promise of a more disciplined machine did little to stir their enthusiasm. Core Democratic constituencies—labor unions and civil rights groups—found the President's concerns tangential to their own; and, to make matters worse, Carter's formulas for revitalizing the machinery threatened governing arrangements that over the years had come to underwrite congressional careerism. The Democrats on Capitol Hill had piled up victory margins far in excess of their strange new affiliate in the White House, and the bureaucratic largesse he targeted for his new discipline was a valued instrument of their newfound security.

The Senate leadership took up the challenge and pressed the confrontation. A group gathered at the White House on March 10 and denounced the administration's water projects initiative in no uncertain terms. Then, by a vote of 65 to 24, they reinstated most of the projects in a presidentially sponsored public works bill. Though the President retained enough support to sustain a threatened veto, 35 Democratic senators stood ready to defy him. There was little more support in the House, where the majority also voted to restore the cuts. As word went out from the Capitol that Carter's resolve to end politics-as-usual was placing his administration's major legislative goals in jeopardy, Speaker O'Neill began to look for a compromise position. No less irritated than anyone else by the President's initiative, O'Neill was alarmed that so wide a breach between the Capitol and the White House had been opened so early in the game. He called Carter with a deal that would split the difference, continuing half of the projects and deleting the rest.[66]

Nothing has contributed more to Carter's reputation for political ineptitude than his reluctance to bargain in the manner of an experienced legislative leader like Lyndon Johnson, and yet Carter's acceptance of O'Neill's deal on the water projects suggests just how inapplicable the old rules of bargaining were to his purposes. Carter took from O'Neill what he thought was a victory in principle and moved to limit the damage to his working relationship with the Democratic leadership. But when on August 8 he signed a public works appropriations act funding ten of the projects he had been seeking to kill, he compounded the damage.[67] The deal settled nothing. It did little to heal the wounds that had been opened by the initial assault, and by accepting projects he had already declared wasteful and unjustified, Carter appeared to be backing away from a test of leadership he himself had set up, in order to mollify the establishment he had come to power to change. "It [the compromise] was accurately interpreted as a sign of weakness on my part," Carter admitted in his memoirs. A year and a half later, he did veto a public works bill with many of these same water projects included, but by that time the pattern of fighting battles he could not win for winning was already well established. "It was rewarding to prevail even though almost every Democratic leader lined up against me, but the battle left deep scars."[68]

As the welfare reform debacle was sowing the seeds of bitterness between the White House and the liberals in the cabinet and as the water projects controversy was calling an abrupt halt to Carter's honeymoon with Congress, the Bert Lance affair began to strip the President of his special relationship with the people. Like the water projects fight, the Lance affair is most remarkable for the devastating symbolic force it packed into matters that were, nationally speaking, of substantive insignificance. The administration's "scandal" amounted to an investigation of financial indiscretions by the director of the Office of Management and Budget that had occurred before he had assumed office. When the President's initial premises got tangled up in the affair, however, a matter of minor embarrassment quickly exploded into a major crisis of credibility. The Carter administration was nothing if not something different, and Carter's campaign had wrapped the pledge to be different in standards of conduct so stringent that any human foible could present a prima facie indictment of the whole enterprise. As he put it on the day of Lance's resignation: "A lot of the problem has been brought on Bert Lance by me, because of the extraordinary standard that we have tried to set in government and the expectations of the American people that were engendered during my own campaign."[69] For at least one administration intimate, the indictment of the administration's self-professed standards in the Lance affair became "the single biggest turning point in the Carter presidency."[70]

Bert Lance was the President's most trusted friend in politics, and the Office of Management and Budget was, as Carter well knew, "key to the entire process of budgeting and reorganization."[71] Carter did not hesitate when it came to filling the post on which all hopes for rethinking liberal priorities and revitalizing the machinery of liberal government were pegged.[72] Lance was as close as anyone came to being the indispensable man in Carter's leadership project, and Carter was not about to let him be run out of town by those who seemed to resent the very idea of cleaning house and readjusting priorities. But his resolve in this matter could not have been more unfortunate. The exposé of loose banking practices on the part of the man in charge of the bureau-cratic machine indicted Carter's own high standards of conduct in the very area in which he had asserted a special competence and a distinc-tive reform purpose. Nothing could have jammed the gears of the Carter presidency more completely, and once the unraveling of presumptions started, it was difficult to stop.

The Lance exposé inverted the administration's whole understanding of its place in the Washington establishment. The insiders were unmask-ing the outsiders in this affair, and in trying to make sense of that reversal, the White House fell into a defensive posture, hopelessly con-fusing the whole insider/outsider distinction.[73] Interpreting the revela-tions and media attention as evidence of the Washington establishment's deep-seated hostility to upstart Georgians in the White House, Carter's intimates fashioned a palace-guard response all too reminiscent of the kind of politics they initially had proposed to eradicate. Carter read the results of the comptroller's special investigation into Lance's banking practices as a legal brief on the question of criminal misconduct and declared that he saw nothing in the record of overdraft endorsements and special privileges to justify Lance's removal. On August 18 he pronounced his friend fully exonerated and told the nation that he was in fact "proud" of him.[74]

Neither the press nor the Senate could let the matter rest there. The press tore into the President's pretense to a higher morality by invoking at every possible occasion the standards he himself had articulated. When he had asked "Why Not the Best?" was he not promising some-thing more than technical innocence of criminal wrongdoing? Had he not warned his subordinates at the very outset that he would not tolerate even the appearance of impropriety? Had he not told the American people that any continuation of the cronyism and whitewash tactics of the recent past would do irreparable damage to the nation?[75] Meanwhile, the Senate, embarrassed by what the special investigation implied about its own confirmation proceedings and stunned to hear the President read the report as an exoneration, set up another investi-gation of its own. With the Senate pursuing more questions about Lance, and the press relentless in its pursuit of Carter's handling of the matter, the storehouse of good will that Carter had so carefully cultivated in the nation at large began to slip away. Between mid-August and mid-September, the President's overall popularity fell from 66 percent to 54 percent; Lance's resignation at the end of the month left just 24 percent of the public willing to give the President "strong" support, little more than half of what it had been in the spring. Memories of this affair would fade quickly; but looking back on it, pollsters saw permanent damage. In George Gallup's year-end assessment, it was all the more evident that a "serious rupture" had occurred in "the bond of trust . . . between [the] administration and the public it serves."[76]

As the symbolic supports of this administration began to crumble, it became increasingly difficult to cast the Carter difference in a flattering light. Attention turned to the apparent inability of the outsiders to deliver on the technocratic promise of solving problems and making the government work. As it happened, Lance's resignation came at the climax of a bitter debate in the Senate over an issue that the President had declared the most pressing problem of all, the nation's dependence on foreign oil.

Carter's energy program, submitted to Congress the previous April, was the centerpiece of his first-year agenda. Carter had proclaimed the attainment of energy security the "greatest challenge that our country will face during our lifetime," and he went on to declare that goal the "moral equivalent of war." A seemingly intractable problem, Carter turned the quest for energy security into the showcase demonstration of his new politics.[77] The issue focused all the principles of policy leadership that he had enunciated during his campaign. National resource management was a multifaceted problem, one that demanded a comprehensive view of many complicated and interdependent issues. It was also beset by conflicts among some of the most powerful interests in Congress. ("Congress is disgusting on this particular subject," he vented to his diary.[78]) It demanded a leader who knew how to put the long-term interests of the nation above all else. On this issue, as on so many others, Carter was aware that no one would like what had to be done. He called upon the people to uphold his course and help him resist the Washington lobbies, so that everyone would bear a fair share of the burden.[79]

Carter's proposal delivered pretty much what he promised. It was an intricate, holistic package, a hard-hitting, comprehensive plan generated without the usual interference from politicians or special pleaders. Carter had hoped to circumvent the intense counterpressures that had previously stifled effective action in this area by developing a proposal secretly within the offices of the executive branch. By springing the package upon Congress wholesale and whipping up popular support, the President sought to overwhelm the entrenched resistance and propel a concerted drive for decisive action. He stated his challenge in no uncertain terms, declaring energy planning a "test of the character of the American people and the ability of the President and the Congress to govern this nation."[80]

Speaker O'Neill, sensitive as always to what was at stake for Carter's credibility, worked wonders to give him what he wanted. He cleared the tracks for the measure in the House and handed the President an initial victory in August. By that time, however, Democratic senators were in no mood to cooperate. The fact that the President had not consulted the relevant leaders in the original formulation of his proposal only added salt to already festering wounds. Not about to be taken for granted, the senators gave a full hearing to their own deeply divided opinions on this subject, and sent only a vague semblance of the original pieces of the administration's program to the conference committee that opened in October.

Still convinced of the "paramount importance of developing an effective energy plan this year," Carter canceled plans for an overseas trip so as to monitor the work of the conference.[81] He tried at this point to strike a conciliatory tone, and publicly disavowed any intention of turning the conference into a "contest of wills" between himself and the Congress.[82] But the meeting of the minds deadlocked, and after eight months of effort and four appeals from the President to the nation at large, the White House had to concede at the end of the session that it had failed to win agreement on an energy package it could accept.[83]

This embarrassing deadlock would continue on through 1978, with the administration reaping a stern judgment of the "ability of the President and the Congress to govern the nation." The "moral equivalent of war" was met by doubt, delay, and extended stalemate. The promise of a new politics that would restore confidence in the government was frustrated, and as the old politics of interest drove the new politics of technocratic management into the trenches, the administration found itself in another battle it could not win for winning. Through sheer persistence, it finally broke the impasse in October 1978, and for those who still cared to look, the residue left over from the original plan was still quite remarkable. The second session of the Ninety-fifth Congress closed with a phased decontrol of natural gas prices, new automobile regulations, new public utility regulations, new home construction standards, new home appliance standards, new environmental controls, and incentives for the use and development of alternative energy sources. And Carter's accomplishments in this field did not end there. A year later, a second round of energy proposals, this one addressed specifically to the oil shocks rolling out of the Iranian revolution, would produce even more impressive results.[84] All told, Carter's achievements in the field of energy conservation provided the central piece of evidence that he would take to the people in 1980 to show that his long struggle had not come to naught and that a "new foundation" had in fact been laid for the American political economy.[85] By then, however, the cause of reconstructing foundations had become more clearly the province of the Republicans, and Carter was scrambling to convince his fellow Democrats that he had not really sacrificed their old priorities to his new base assumptions.

But let us return to the first-year shakedown. When Carter entered 1978, there was still one leadership pretension he had brought to power that had yet to be put to the test, and there was still one item left on the initial agenda that promised to show it off in the best possible light. Having identified himself with consumer issues during his campaign and having nurtured consumer legislation over the course of his first year, the President kicked off his second with a final push to establish a consumer protection agency. Polishing up his credentials as a liberal reformer, Carter prepared to fight one of the good old fights in the best of Democratic traditions.

Consumer protection was not exactly what the old Democratic constituencies had in mind when they thought of liberal reform. There was little here for labor or the cities. But Carter, like all ambitious presidents, was seeking new sources of political support to revitalize his party's base.[86] Along with his endorsement of environmentalism, Carter's enthusiasm for consumerism looked toward reviving the faith of middle America in the Democratic standard. Indeed, the idea of a consumer protection agency seemed a perfect bridge between the old liberalism of providing for the socially disadvantaged and a new liberalism attuned to middle-class concerns about the quality of life. After all, the regulation of business had been redirected toward consumer concerns during the final years of the New Deal, and the consumer movement itself had had its inception during the Johnson years. By the time Carter assumed office, support for a separate agency of consumer protection was arrayed along a broad front. New "public interest" lobbies mobilized support, the nation at large appeared sympathetic, and the Democratic leadership in Congress was solid. And if all that was not enough, consumer protection also offered Carter a bridge between liberalism and governmental discipline. It gave him a chance to prove himself a liberal reformer while at the same time emphasizing his aversion to waste, duplication, and new governmental spending. "I am strongly opposed to the proliferation of new agencies," he had said during his campaign, "because it adds on to an already confused federal bureaucratic structure. But this agency [a consumer protection agency] is different." Carter would tout the consumer protection agency as a cost-saving reorganization aimed at consolidating a number of regulatory activities currently spread throughout the federal government under one roof.[87]

In sum, the battle for the consumer protection agency had all the markings of a great victory, one that might wipe away the grim memories of the first year and place Carter's own distinctive stamp on liberal reform. But it never made it out of the House. Opposition was fueled by a business establishment newly mobilized in politics to lay the blame for its own faltering performance on the governmental activism of the late sixties and early seventies. Consumer protection was a critical test for both sides: for Carter it presented a much-needed opportunity to demonstrate the continued resilience of liberalism in a new age; for business it presented a much needed opportunity to expose liberalism's vulnerabilities. There was no contest. Seizing upon the crippling effects of bureaucracy on private initiative, business's political action groups turned the issue against the administration with crushing effect. Dubbing the proposal a prescription for more red-tape and bureaucratic bumbling, they made Carter's neoliberalism appear more of a symptom than a solution to the problems the liberal regime had engendered.[88] Suddenly, the President's own critique of undisciplined governmental expansion and unnecessary interference in the market was taken over by his fiercest critics, and the fine distinctions he had been at pains to draw between himself and the old liberal establishment were erased. While this most distant of Democrats was alienating the liberal establishment by his neglect of its traditional priorities, he found himself inextricably linked to it by a no-holds-barred assault on all that that establishment had wrought. All told, Carter's liberalism-with-a-difference had no ground to hold in the sectarian controversies that wracked American politics during the 1970s. It was as vulnerable to conservatives for being more of the same as it was vulnerable to liberals for being different.

Toughing It Out in the Modern Presidency

Far from restoring confidence in liberal government, Carter had made himself the leading cause of skepticism.[89] White House intimates protested that there was much more to the first year than met the eye, but what met the eye were the issues large and small on which the President had staked his authority as a political leader. Over the course of that year virtually every claim Carter had brought with him into office had been tested and discredited. His overhaul of the welfare mess, his defiance of pork-barrel politics in Congress, his new morality in government, his new politics of energy management, even his revival of liberal reform—all showed him floundering in his own standards. It is hardly a wonder that charges of incompetence began to ring loud and clear.

But that, it must be added, is the standard plight of late-regime affiliates: putting their faith in the machinery of government, they accelerate the political disintegration at its foundations. Nothing exposes a hollow consensus faster than the exercise of presidential power, and no consensus is more hollow than one built on a reification of technique. Only when the charges of incompetence are rooted in this recurrent pattern of near-immediate unraveling does the extraordinary range of Carter's leadership effort begin to come to the fore.

Recall that it was at just such an impasse that Franklin Pierce finally capitulated to the party leadership in the Senate. Having failed in his first year to repair the old machinery and revive the old agenda, Pierce abandoned the electoral vow that had brought him into the presidential office, grasped the second chance Stephen Douglas offered him, and tried as best he could to make his way back into the good graces of the Democratic organization. Not so Jimmy Carter. Senator Edward Kennedy of Massachusetts, not unlike Stephen Douglas in his role as spokesman for the old regime, marched to the White House in Carter's second year with the latest liberal enthusiasm in one hand and an implicit threat of pronouncing the beleaguered President a failure in the other. But there was no Carter-Kennedy alliance to recapitulate the

Pierce-Douglas disaster. Faced with Pierce's choice, Carter opted to resist. He defied the condemnation of the liberal establishment, sharpened his original critique, and took his chances with the people at large. Shorn of his initial leadership pretensions, he indulged the conceit that the liberal base of the Democratic party was "illusory," that he could cut himself loose from the traditional foundations of Democratic support and still persevere.[90]

The break between Carter and Kennedy was foreshadowed by the first of what would be three major efforts to rehabilitate the President's original leadership project. Each of these "rebirths" would reassert Carter's political identity as a responsible manager of the nation's business willing to face the hard-pressed realities of the day, whatever the political cost.[91] At each of these junctures, the President would jettison a bit more of the baggage of affiliated leadership, and fortify his determination to stand alone with institutional resources drawn directly from the presidential office itself. Carter could reject Pierce's choice because he had an institutional alternative that simply did not exist in Pierce's time. His was a thoroughly modern assessment of political possibilities, an assessment that in the final reckoning the party would be whatever its president wanted it to be.

The "rebirth" of Jimmy Carter was first announced in the spring of 1978. White House advisor Hamilton Jordan candidly admitted that efforts to get the President's message across and gain credit for his accomplishments had thus far come to naught. "We did a lot in the first year," he protested, but "because we're being measured against some unrealistic goals we set for ourselves . . . we are found lacking." Of all the negative perceptions of the administration that had begun to take hold, the one that grated most was the belief "that Jimmy Carter is not tough and that he is not competent." To turn that perception around, the administration had decided to redeploy "the appropriate political resources of the presidency." The White House staff would be reorganized and strengthened; the cabinet would be brought under stricter controls; the congressional liaison operation would be beefed up to discipline defectors from the President's line; interest-group support would be mobilized more effectively through White House coordination; and the President himself would get out of Washington more and put himself back in touch with the people. The administration, Jordan reported, had learned the hard way that the party in Congress was too fragmented for its leaders to deliver the kind of political support the

President needed. Now that the illusion of collective responsibility had been dispelled, the administration was being recast to give the President more personal control and political independence. Jordan thought that with the instruments of presidential power reorganized, the people finally would see the "real" Jimmy Carter: "He is very tough, and he is very competent."[92]

Carter's toughness was being heralded in public just as private negotiations with Kennedy were heating up over how to fulfill the Democratic party's platform commitment to a national health insurance plan. Carter insisted that any comprehensive health plan be phased in piecemeal as the nation's economic performance permitted, and he punctuated Jordan's words with stubborn resistance to Kennedy's desire to commit the government up front to eventual implementation of the whole package. Indeed, over the first half of 1978, the President was as adamant about disassembling the senator's comprehensive program for health insurance as he was about preventing the rest of the Senate from disassembling his own comprehensive program for energy security. In both cases, the administration was hanging tough for the new politics of responsible management against ostensible political allies touting more traditional forms of party and interest representation.

This, of course, was not the first time the President had tried to affirm traditional Democratic priorities without really going to bat for them. As he had on Califano's welfare reform initiative, the President tried with health care to finesse the enthusiasm of his liberal allies while demonstrating a new conservative discipline to the nation at large. Kennedy saw the stakes for what they were and accepted his charge as keeper of the liberal faith. He went to the White House in July boasting formidable support from organized labor and promising that if the President got behind his health plan, this core Democratic constituency would deliver the votes in the midterm elections to secure action in the next Congress. The President was not impressed. He did not see the votes in Congress, he had no inclination to fight for them, and he saw little prospect that labor would be able to deliver the goods at midterm with an angry tax revolt afoot in the nation at large.[93] Carter knew he had to do something, if only because his commitment to national health insurance had been critical to his gaining the support of the United Auto Workers and its formidable political machinery during the primaries. But he was not about to saddle himself with Kennedy's program, even in the face of the united union support the senator had assembled behind it. When Carter informed Kennedy of his intention to go public with general guidelines for a phased-in approach conditioned on the strength of the economy, Kennedy called an impromptu press conference and denounced the administration's plan as a sham before it was even unveiled. With AFL-CIO President George Meany at his side, the senator charged the President with misreading the public mood, with failing in his leadership role, and with scuttling a party promise.[94]

Kennedy and Carter both sensed the conservative turn in national opinion, but Carter refused to accept Kennedy's invitation to "sail against the wind," and Kennedy refused to allow a Democratic administration to abandon liberal priorities. When fully joined, this battle would go far beyond differences over health insurance. The administration's budget outline for 1979 told the tale. In the first of what would be three "austerity budgets," Carter asked Congress to increase defense spending (to meet a Soviet military buildup) and to cut social spending to pay for it. In effect, the administration was setting in motion a double shift away from liberal policy priorities, one away from the orthodox domestic agenda that liberals still prized, the other back to a Cold War orthodoxy in foreign policy that most liberals had renounced in the aftermath of the Vietnam War.[95] Kennedy met that challenge at the midterm convention in December 1978.

> There could be few more divisive issues for America and for our party than a Democratic policy of drastic slashes in the federal budget at the expense of the elderly, the poor, the black, the sick, the cities, and the unemployed. We cannot accept a policy that cuts spending to the bone in areas like jobs and health, but allows billions of dollars in wasteful spending for tax subsidies to continue and adds even greater fat and waste through inflationary spending for defense.[96]

The Carter White House had the midterm convention securely wired before it met, but Kennedy knew his audience, and the administration could not prevent the party elite from cheering his defiance and encouraging his challenge. It is worth observing that the Congress had just enacted the Humphrey-Hawkins Full Employment Act, a ringing reaffirmation of liberal orthodoxy that had been carefully and thoroughly gutted of all practical policy effect. Democratic elites clutched the old symbols because when forced to commit there was little else they were willing to give their old constituents. Kennedy monopolized these symbols, leaving Carter to take the rap for slapping the constituents in the face. The President had the power, but Kennedy spoke with the voice of authority.

The contest for leadership of the Democratic party was another of those battles the President could not win for winning. To jump ahead through several of Carter's rebirths, Kennedy would press his challenge right up to the presidential nominating convention, and even though Carter again had the votes locked up long beforehand, Kennedy's speech to the delegates would again steal his show. In the interim, as Kennedy charged the President with betrayal, incompetence, and failure, Carter tried to make the best of a bad situation and turned the challenge into an opportunity to demonstrate that eerily timeless attribute of toughness on which he now staked so much. It was Vice President Walter Mondale who had the last word at the midterm convention, and he used it to reiterate the administration's position that "the most important social program" was the anti-inflation program because without it all other social programs were doomed.[97] Six months later when polls began showing that Democrats preferred the keeper of their faith in the Senate to their responsible manager in the White House by a margin of two to one, Carter was still convinced that the senator's political base was illusory, and he pointedly dismissed the threat of a Kennedy challenge with a tough "I'll whip his ass."[98] Even in the middle of 1980, with the nation sliding into recession, the President stood aloof as Kennedy's campaign pledged 12 billion dollars in emergency relief for urban unemployment. Taking a hard line, Carter said only that he would "work with the mayors within the framework of fiscal discipline and non-inflationary contributions to resolve any unanticipated problems" that might arise.[99] By projecting an image of "toughness" in the face of the Kennedy challenge, Carter sowed the seeds for the charges of "meanness" that the Reagan camp would harvest during the general election campaign.

By then, however, Carter had been reborn several times over. The second, and most wrenching, of his rebirths came during that dismal summer of 1979 when the aftershocks of the Iranian revolution hit the nation in the form of severe gasoline shortages. With the Kennedy challenge building what seemed irreversible momentum and his presidency continuing to unravel, Carter suddenly seized the nation's attention. Canceling an already scheduled speech on the energy crisis, and then abruptly suspending all business as usual, the President mysteriously retired to Camp David. From there, the administration announced an impromptu summit on domestic policy. Leaders of every sort were called to the mountain retreat to help the President reassess his presidency in light of the deepening popular malaise. Meanwhile, the nation, rapt in a drama carefully orchestrated to build the suspense, awaited the diagnosis.[100]

Carter reported his finding on July 15, the third anniversary of his nomination by the Democratic party. As always, he admitted his failures candidly. He knew the people were frustrated, and he wanted to address their anxieties head on. Accordingly, his speech broached problems far more profound than any he had hinted at before. The President spoke of disloyalty in his cabinet and of a Congress that was still "twisted and pulled in every direction by hundreds of well financed and powerful special interests." He had now seen firsthand how "every extreme position" was "defended to the last vote, almost to the last breath by one unyielding group or another." Dismal as this assessment of the federal government was, however, Carter had come to see that the degenerate morés of the Washington establishment were only symptoms of a larger problem. The "fundamental threat to American democracy," he said, lay in society itself, in a popular culture that "had come to worship self-indulgence and consumption." Carter had concluded in effect that before he could deliver on his initial promise of making American government as good as the American people, he would have to lead the people themselves back to the path of virtue. He told them that he was about to unveil a stern new discipline for energy conservation, and he asked that they accept the challenges it posed as an opportunity. He was offering them a chance to take stock of who they really were, a chance to reverse course and regain their proper bearings, a chance to retrieve the values of hard work, self-denial, and sacrifice to the common good that had made their country great.[101]

Carter made no pretense of affiliation with the existing state of affairs in this message. By this time, he had rejected Hoover's choice as well as Pierce's. He was not speaking of preserving the tried and true principles of the received regime or of negotiating a temporary emergency departure from the norm. Instead, he was speaking bluntly of the bankruptcy of the entire system. He reached back to a mythic past to retrieve values lost in the indulgences of the current system in order to guide a permanent and fundamental reordering of extant priorities. The crisis of confidence speech was a presidential declaration of independence, and while it did not exactly galvanize a reconstructive movement, it did propel the President toward truly reconstructive action. In a sense, Carter had rediscovered John Adams's choice. Like the second president at his moment of greatest crisis, Carter in his most dramatic public moment sought to dispel the golden dreams of the contending parties, and force the nation to confront the situation squarely. Like the second president, he chose to purge his administration of his disloyal partisans and turn their world upside down. Kennedy, the keeper of the faith, already rejected for the part of Stephen Douglas, responded in kind by taking a page from Alexander Hamilton's script of 1800 and opting for the role of the spoiler.

Of course the trappings of modernity were everywhere in the execution of this maneuver. Carter did not simply purge his cabinet of its most recalcitrant members, he reorganized the White House staff as well, this time reintroducing the once-disparaged position of chief of staff to further tighten hierarchical controls. And, while he tightened some controls, he loosened others. The single most important effect of the summer's reshuffling was to place a new manager in charge of the powerful but formally independent Federal Reserve Board. William Miller, prized by the administration as a team player but blamed by Wall Street for runaway inflation, was shifted from the Fed into the Treasury Department, where he replaced Michael Blumenthal, believed by the White House to be one of the worst examples of cabinet disloyalty. The administration then turned to "the choice of Wall Street," Paul Volcker, to manage the nation's banking system. Volcker, it seems, was fully attuned to the President's recent call for national discipline and sacrifice, for he set about reversing forty years of Democratic precedent in monetary policy with just those goals in mind. Determined to shock the nation out of its inflationary spiral, the new chairman discarded traditional principles of fiscal management, replaced Keynesian orthodoxy with a heretical concern for controlling the money supply, and in effect let interest rates seek their own levels.[102]

It is one of the singular ironies of Carter's leadership that in his most forceful appeal to the people against the establishment he put himself at the mercy of his own technocrats and destroyed his populist, Jackson-like pretensions. Between the fall of 1979 and the fall of 1980, as the central bank engineered an election-year recession, the Democrat in the White House stood silent. Carter had anticipated a tight money policy (though certainly not the revolutionary policy he got), and he found it difficult to object when his own appointee led the charge he himself had opened against self-indulgence and mindless consumption. Only in the final weeks of the campaign, with the prime rate up again to 14 percent and the Carter campaign desperate to rally traditional Democratic support, did the President try to distance himself from the new policy and begin to question its wisdom. In October 1980, the Jackson-like sound of Carter's trumpet amounted to impotent protestations that the Fed was wholly independent of the executive branch ("just like the federal judiciary") and a personal judgment that its present policies were "ill-advised."[103]

After imposing an austerity program that privileged inflation over unemployment as the nation's most important economic problem, after purging the liberals from the administration and sponsoring a conservative revolution in monetary policy, Carter's leadership came completely unhinged. The cabinet shake-up in the summer of 1979 and the great policy departure it set in motion left the boundary between responsible policy management and a wholesale reconstruction of priorities quite blurry. But the political resources Carter had employed to assert this new measure of independence had proven as fickle as they were formidable. The lift the President had gotten from his dramatic Camp David summit was immediately undercut by his decision to clean house. In calling for resignations Carter did not question the talent or managerial competence of the administrators under his charge; the purge marked the full extent to which the terms on which he had originally assembled his team had changed. It was a blunt demand for subordination to presidential will, and its victims were outraged by the new strong-arm tactics. Their resentment of the President's treatment reverberated through the party's ranks, and the exposé of more disarray in the administration sent Carter's stock tumbling to record lows.[104] Standing alone in the modern presidency, Carter was now little more than a creature of events riding a roller coaster of ups and downs. He might manipulate crises to project a momentary semblance of control, but then the bottom would fall out and he would have to wait for another opportunity to start rebuilding his credibility all over again. The seizure of American hostages in Iran, an event dubbed by one astute observer "a sheer gift of circumstances," became in the end the main chance.[105]

The taking of the hostages in early November 1979 occasioned the third rebirth of the "real" Jimmy Carter. Again the President gave voice to the frustration of the American people. "I've got to give expression to the anger of the American people," he confided to his advisors. "If they perceive me as firm and tough in voicing their rage, maybe we'll be able to control this thing."[106] Again the President suspended business as usual. He canceled plans to debate Kennedy in the primaries and removed himself from partisan politics. Leaving aside the "fundamental threat" to American democracy he had outlined just a few months before, he rededicated his administration to this single mission, freeing the captive Americans. Again, he turned away from the Washington establishment and inward upon the resources of the presidential office. While Secretary of State Vance urged the traditional course of diplomacy, caution, and restraint, National Security Advisor Brzezinski seized upon the possibilities of the moment and captured the imagination of the White House. "This is the first big test of the Carter presidency," he argued. "It is a crisis for sure but it is also an opportunity, a chance for the President to show the world that he is capable of handling a crisis of international implications. A chance to show American resolve."[107] When push came to shove, Brzezinski's position prevailed, and Vance resigned.[108]

Carter lost no time making the hostage crisis the one big test of his leadership. Addressing the AFL-CIO on the twelfth day of the crisis, he deftly set aside all talk of his administration's record on the labor front, and turned instead to a review of the issue on which his political identity as a responsible manager of the nation's affairs could now be more firmly projected. He spoke of the hostages as national heroes who had "reminded us of the basic facts and principles which are fundamental to our existence as a people." He pledged "firmness," "patience," and "perseverance" in his efforts to gain their release. He reviewed the actions he had taken to meet the challenge, and, last but not least, he claimed full vindication for his unrelenting three-year campaign for energy security.[109] As the election year dawned, the only issue that Carter permitted to compete with the hostage crisis for his or the nation's attention was the Soviet invasion of Afghanistan. That, in the President's view, was "one of the most serious threats to World Peace since the Second World War,"[110] and with it, his turn back to Cold War orthodoxy accelerated rapidly.

At the beginning of 1980, Carter was sweeping away three years of frustration and declaring that now there were only "two major questions that our Nation must resolve."[111] Neither had much to do with the nation's seemingly intractable domestic problems, but for a time it looked as if Carter had finally defined a situation in which he was in full command of his office. The political effect was immediate. Any hopes Kennedy might have had of actually taking the Democratic nomination were crushed. Sequestered in the White House to resolve the crises of the hour, the President was politically unassailable. Indeed, crisis management became a kind a campaign in itself. As the White House announced doctrines, embargos, freezes, boycotts, immigration regulations, and draft registration, political leaders were invited up to pledge their support and bear witness to Carter's toughness and competence under pressure.[112] More important still, Carter's new command of the subject matter of national politics took much of the substance out of Kennedy's critique. As the hostage crisis vindicated the President's effort to place energy security over social reform in domestic politics, the Soviet invasion vindicated his drift back to a Cold War defense policy.[113] The reversal of political fortunes was astounding. Carter's popularity soared twenty points in one month. Democrats who over the summer had preferred Kennedy by two to one were now preferring Carter, and by March 1980 his margin was two to one.[114]

Over the long haul, of course, these matters came to look quite different. The problem-solving president sets the stiffest possible standard for success in political leadership, because sooner or later he has to solve a problem. Carter had struggled under the burden of such self-imposed tests for three long years; and, like all the others, the hostage test came back to haunt him. By the time of the Wisconsin primary on April 1, the President's fortunes had begun to sag again, and pressures to do something had become unbearable. There was a suspicious announcement of progress on the hostage front on the very morning of that election, and Carter's victory that day made his nomination all but certain. But no sooner did the announcement prove a false hope than the White House was deluged with charges that it was manipulating the hostage issue for political advantage. Exasperated, the administration finally opted for a military rescue, but that too broke down.

It might be tempting then to conclude that modernity had very little impact at all in reshaping the politics of leadership for this late-regime affiliate. Like the other "rebirths" of Jimmy Carter, this last one came to naught. Far from releasing the administration from the frustrations of the previous three years, the hostage crisis became the most frustrating predicament of them all, and as such it stood as a devastating election-year metaphor for the entire four years. That metaphor was reinforced on November 2, the Sunday before the general election, when the President suddenly suspended his campaign and rushed to the White House on late-breaking news of progress on the hostage front. As it turned out, there was little new to report, and the beleaguered incumbent had to go on national television one more time to acknowledge that freedom for the captive Americans was not in fact imminent. In Robert Strauss's view: "No question that Sunday was the magnet that pulled it all together. Reagan had not really been able to do that . . . it still needed something, and that was the absolute spark when [Carter] went on television that day."[115] Patrick Caddell confirmed this judgment as he read his last sampling of opinion. Undecided voters were breaking overwhelmingly for the Republican, wiping out in a Reagan landslide the slim hopes Caddell had held out for Carter's chances.[116]

But it would be slighting of the modern presidency to rest the matter there. The mere fact that there was an outstanding question about Carter's leadership on the Sunday before this election should tell us something about the impact of modernity on the politics presidents make. Profound changes in leadership possibilities had, in fact, been worked throughout Carter's several rebirths. He had wrenched the liberal government away from received liberal priorities. He had prevailed in his bid for renomination in the face of a direct challenge from the leading light of the liberal establishment. And most remarkable of all, he had turned the prospect of a reconstruction from within—a political achievement unprecedented in presidential history—into something of a crap shoot. In November 1979, Carter made one radically narrow and remote challenge—the freeing of hostages—a make-or-break test of his competence as a political leader. This challenge was largely unrelated to the frustrations this administration had encountered over the previous three years and unrelated as well to the substantive changes the administration was then setting in motion. Even with the nation tumbling into recession, with the administration wallowing in Hooverian images of economic mismanagement, with Reagan gaining momentum, and with traditional Democratic constituencies tepid in support of their president, the general election rushed to a close with the possibility still open that Carter might pull off a "surprise" on the hostage issue. The truly astounding thing about leadership in the modern presidency is that had the military rescue in April worked or had Tehran been willing to move in that last week of the campaign, Carter might have been able to vindicate his leadership and all that it implied for the reversal of Democratic priorities in government. On this one remote and narrow issue, he might actually have confirmed himself the hard-headed manager of all the nation's problems and turned a crushing metaphor for frustration on all fronts into a leading symbol of the virtues of toughness and perseverance in the face of adversity. The modern presidency harbored this chance for Jimmy Carter, the chance to manipulate fate and escape political time.

Affiliation and the Authority to Repudiate

Can regime priorities be recast from within? Can the traditional boundaries of political identity be stretched so far that the distinctions that have defined leadership projects since the beginning no longer hold meaning? Are modern incumbents free to make their own politics, indifferent to matters of affiliation or opposition, affirmation or repudiation, continuity or reconstruction? Jimmy Carter's presidency posed these questions in their starkest form yet; the collapse of his initial political project had prompted him to unprecedented defiance of its traditional boundaries. And yet, after four years of pushing against the limits of affiliated leadership, he was compelled to fall back. Accepting his renomination by the Democratic party, Carter acknowledged what Kennedy had proven the night before: "I'd like to say a word to Senator Kennedy. Your speech before this convention was a magnificent statement of what the Democratic party is and what it means to the people of this country and why a Democratic victory is so important this year. I reach out to you tonight, and I reach out to all those who supported you in your valiant and passionate campaign. Ted, your party needs [you] and I need you."[117]

Time and again and with increasing forcefulness, Carter had broached the prospect of outright repudiation of the politics that Kennedy represented. But even in defeating Kennedy and setting a new range of independence for an affiliated leader, he failed to resolve the problem that had dogged his assaults on the old politics from the Ohio primary of 1976 to the crisis of confidence speech in 1979. Each attack had generated new confusions over his political identity and new threats of his political isolation. Carter emerged victorious in the summer of 1980, but the party he took charge of was still not his own; the boundaries of affiliated leadership had been pushed to new limits, but they were not successfully crossed. There was no escape for Carter because there was no new premise for further action, no forthright accounting for what he had done to Kennedy's party, no warrant that could address the concerns of that party and the problems of the nation as well.

Without a compelling definition of his own, Carter had to admit that he could neither remake his party as he wanted it to be, nor stand alone, sui generis, in his leadership pretentions. In the general election campaign, the President's first—and, as it turned out, most difficult—challenge was simply to convince the party faithful that he really was "proud to be a Democrat." The first step was to acknowledge that the Democratic party was not illusory, and that it was Kennedy who defined it. Formally at least, the Carter camp deferred to the priorities of the Kennedy campaign and took on a party platform that not so subtly repudiated its own economic program. At Kennedy's insistence, the party reaffirmed the old policy of privileging unemployment over inflation as the chief economic concern, and it pledged the 12 billion dollars in emergency unemployment relief that Carter had previously denounced as irresponsible. To add insult to injury, Kennedy demanded as a price of his support that the President assume his campaign debt as well.[118]

Needless to say, this final "rebirth" of the "real Jimmy Carter" lacked the spirit of the original. Carter was no party regular, and his reaffirmation of the legacy of Roosevelt and Johnson at every campaign stop sounded as fuzzy as his 1976 efforts to trumpet the repudiative themes of Andrew Jackson. Meanwhile, Carter's idea of a "new foundation" was being scooped by Ronald Reagan in a familiar fashion. Nothing irritated the President quite so much in 1980 as Reagan's own invocation of the memory of Franklin Roosevelt. And yet it was Reagan, not Carter, who found the Jacksonian message in Roosevelt's words—Reagan, not Carter, who laid claim to the authority of the reconstructive leader. In his acceptance speech at the Republican party convention in Detroit, Reagan put the case for a new foundation in the blunt, uncompromising terms that lay just beyond Carter's reach: "The major issue in this campaign is the direct, political, personal, and moral responsibility of the Democratic Party leadership—in the White House and in the Congress—for this unprecedented calamity which has befallen us."[119]

Carter's affiliation may have been suspect among loyal Democrats, but his opponent needed no convincing. Reagan rode that theme hard, taking from it the charisma of a great repudiator. At that moment, it did not take much to expose "no easy answers" as no answer at all.

THE
WANING OF
POLITICAL
TIME

CHAPTER 8

Reagan, Bush, and Beyond

They called it the Reagan Revolution and I'll accept that, but
for me it always seemed more like the Great Rediscovery: a
rediscovery of our values and our common sense.
RONALD REAGAN

There's a general thrust, and President Reagan set that . . .
We're not coming in to correct the ills of the past, we're
coming in to build on a proud record that has
already been established.
GEORGE BUSH

AD RONALD REAGAN not played the part of the great repudiator so broadly and George Bush not rendered the travails
of the faithful son so poignantly, it would be easier to endorse
the prevailing view that the politics of leadership is dramatically different now than it was two hundred years ago. But recent presidents have
offered such gross caricatures of the classic leadership postures that the
received wisdom gets the problem exactly backwards: the real worry
today is not that presidents are departing from traditional leadership
roles, but that they still think about their places in history in the same
old ways. After two hundred years of national development, they are
still trying to make the same kinds of politics.

American government has evolved in ways scarcely contemplated in
the early years of the republic, and the resources of modern presidents
dwarf those of their predecessors. But modernity has not altered our
presidents' political purposes correspondingly. Lacking new premises,
they adopt leadership projects and political stances that modern developments would seem to render obsolete.

It is true that recent presidents have crafted their leadership around
very different political warrants, and that the rules of appropriate po-

litical action have changed radically from one incumbent to the next; but for all the variation, the old claims to legitimacy just keep getting recycled. The exercise of presidential power today spins out parodies of nineteenth-century prototypes. Jimmy Carter, Ronald Reagan, and George Bush did not take the same test of skill at the bar of the modern presidency; rather, by claiming distinct places for themselves in an unfolding political drama, they constructed national politics in ways that bear an eerie, almost surreal, resemblance to that constructed in turn by John Quincy Adams, Andrew Jackson, and Martin Van Buren. When leadership is understood serially, as a successor's effort to secure a place in political history that was reconfigured by his predecessor, the impact of modernity is marked in the degrees of distortion in the patterns that have been with us since the beginning.

We have come to assume what stands most in need of historical analysis: the significance of changes in the organization of American government and politics. The impact of such changes has been subtle and cumulative, but we have conceptualized it in ways that consign more distant points of reference to irrelevance and limit our commentary to a kind of running critique of the latest techniques. We write about the "post-modern presidency" and the "plebiscitary presidency," showing how different the politics of leadership is now from the way it was a few decades ago.[1] But these newly emergent power arrangements tell only part of the story; the clock at work in presidential leadership has continued to tell political time. By cordoning off the most recent presidents from their predecessors and trying to glean from their performances a sense of how the newest politics works, we not only miss the durability of older patterns, we limit our insight into the very changes we are analyzing.

What alternatives do we have when we insist on using contemporary references to make sense of Ronald Reagan's rendition of reconstructive politics? One is to ignore it, to submerge the distinctive thrust and political impact of Reagan's leadership in a more general exposé of politics-as-usual in the contemporary period. When Theodore Lowi, for instance, assessed the new rules of action implicit in "the way the presidency is now built," Reagan became just another case in point; the Reagan presidency was, for Lowi, a prime illustration of all that is wrong with the new "plebiscitary" politics.[2] As Reagan's experience does not directly contravene certain broader lessons that can be gleaned from the experience of his immediate predecessors, the Reagan difference can in this way be minimized, if not dismissed outright as illusory.

Generally considered, Reagan's performance does provide an archetype of the new strategy of "going public," the Iran-Contra affair does verify judgments drawn from Reagan's immediate predecessors that something fundamental is wrong in the way the presidency relates to the rest of American government, and Reagan's resilience in the face of difficulty does confirm the rule that nothing is quite so important to political survival in the plebiscitary period as a growing economy. There is no denying the significance of the political and institutional developments on which such assessments rest. The problem is that these assessments offer little insight into what is most important about the Reagan presidency—what it did *to* American government and politics, and how it did it. It is difficult to account for the extraordinary impact of Reagan's leadership within the norms of plebiscitary politics, for those norms submerge the presidency in the larger system of governance and filter out its persistently disruptive force. The rules of the "plebiscitary presidency" have been formulated as a single, overarching explanation of popular frustration with, and political failure in, contemporary leadership. As such, they present us with an indictment of modern conditions per se. On inspection, however, the failures turn out to be as varied as ever, and considerable significance still adheres to the differences in what contemporary presidents actually produce. Whatever the limits of the Reagan reconstruction, no president in recent times has so radically altered the terms in which prior governmental commitments are now dealt with or the conditions under which previously established interests are served.

The other way of assessing Reagan within contemporary frames of reference is more sensitive to the exceptional character of his leadership, and its insights run directly counter to the first. In attending to the outstanding features of Reagan's performance, many commentators were prompted to applaud Reagan himself and indict what was thought about the office just prior to his ascendance. They challenged the familiar conclusion that the system had changed in ways that made success near-impossible. Judging Reagan against the "failed presidencies" of Johnson, Nixon, Ford, and Carter, they revived the notion that the office is "as big as the man." In this scenario, Reagan became the very model of the kind of leader needed to make this system work; his relative success became a standing refutation of the charge that something fundamental had gone wrong; his performance became a confirmation of older beliefs that the system is sound and that the problem is simply getting the right person into the office.

Journalists were the first to strike these themes. As Hugh Sidey declared on the occasion of Reagan's second inaugural, "The idea that the job was too big for one person has little currency now. The notion, so popular only a few years ago, that one man could not make a difference has been pushed aside . . . We enter these next four years with the knowledge that the presidency works."[3] Richard Reeves was even more pointed: "Reagan had come into the oval office at a time when the man in it . . . was declaring political bankruptcy and important voices outside it, in the press and the academy, were decrying the end of leadership. They were wrong. The new President made the system work . . . The leader was an extraordinary man."[4] Soon such assessments could be found just about everywhere. In 1988 Stuart Eisenstadt, Carter's domestic policy advisor, confessed: "It now appears that a mortal can handle the job [of president] and be successful."[5] Louis Fisher, a leading constitutional scholar, put it this way: "Reagan showed that a person with a good mandate, good speaking skills and a targeted agenda can make the system work."[6] And this theme insinuated itself into the political science literature generally. Larry Berman opened his leading collection of essays on this note: "That there was any Reagan impact . . . attests to the President's leadership skill . . . Reagan demonstrated that the demands of the presidency need not engulf the occupant of 1600 Pennsylvania Avenue. He was, above all, psychologically suited for the job."[7] As Paul Peterson and Mark Rom reported it, the "good news" coming out of the Reagan years is that "in most respects the American political system seems to have worked."[8]

Problems with this reading go deeper than those of the first. Most obviously, Reagan's distinction as a leader is blurred here by the very standard used to measure it. The notion that Reagan made the system work flies in the face of what the Iran-Contra revelations said about how the system was working and how this president was handling the job. Even more disturbing, perhaps, is what happens to the sober lessons of the recent past in this reading. Institutional problems that were once thought to be overwhelming recede before the cult of the great man. In fact, because Reagan is presumed to have tested himself in the same system and at the same basic tasks as his immediate predecessors, his leadership can be set apart from theirs only by endowing it with certain inscrutable attributes—political skills, communication skills, personal charisma, ideological commitment—and it is but a short step from there to the conclusion that the absence of those qualities explains why all the others fell short. A final and related concern is that commentators who advanced the case for Reagan's "success" against the backdrop of Carter's "failure" did less to expose than to extend the workings of the system. In what must be considered the ultimate tribute to the potency of the reconstructive authority, astute observers of the American presidency were moved to accept Reagan's own interpretation of his place in history. The final triumph of the great repudiator lies here, in having us take over his presentments about the meaning of his leadership.

Reagan's leadership was both more of the same and something wholly unexpected. There is really no choosing between these lines of argument; the question is whether we can proceed beyond them. Recognizing that Reagan did something extraordinary for a contemporary president does not refute the charge that something fundamental has gone awry in the operations of the presidency more generally. Locate his efforts on a larger historical canvas—plot it against recurrent and emergent patterns in the politics of leadership—and the achievement and the problem come together with new significance.

Reagan pressed warrants for leadership that have fused new orders in American government and politics repeatedly over the course of our history. But the resistance he met was unprecedented. The stiffer reception to these classic leadership claims fits the general pattern we have drawn across prior reconstructive episodes: a pattern of greater institutional resilience in the face of these presidents' order-shattering authority, of an ever thicker government that can parry and deflect more of their repudiative thrust. These backward-looking comparisons mark the Reagan Revolution as a signpost of the waning of political time. They draw our attention to the deteriorating rhythms of the very oldest claims to legitimacy. The most effective political leader to come to the presidency in the last fifty years is also the least effective leader to wield what historically has been the most potent form of presidential authority.

This is of no small consequence for assessing recent problems and current prospects. As we grapple today with the Reagan legacy—with the hollowness of his central claims and the grim irresolution of his promised catharsis—it is especially important that we discard the shorthand history that has so long informed our analyses of the politics of leadership and consider more carefully the lessons we draw from the past. In 1981, the blunt, disruptive force of reconstructive leadership proved itself as politically arresting and systemically wrenching as ever, but never has it produced so distended a result. Once we control for a situation in which extraordinary changes are to be expected, the bizarre effects of acting the great repudiator in the contemporary period come quickly into sharp relief. In Reagan's rendition of the classic reconstructive stance, as in George Bush's rendition of the faithful son, we see that our present problem is not modernity per se; it is the failure, after two hundred years of political and institutional development, to transcend the very oldest standards of legitimacy in the exercise of presidential power. Nothing has proven more problematic in recent years than our presidents' insistence on the authenticity of warrants that have grown specious with age.

Ronald Reagan as a Reconstructive Leader

There is no mistaking the kind of authority Reagan claimed for himself. He came to power in circumstances that recalled the great reconstructive crusades of the past.[9] An economic crisis had highlighted the accumulated burdens of the old regime and indicted its political, institutional, and ideological supports. The Republicans took control of the Senate for the first time in twenty-eight years, and, with the Democratic party in disarray, the administration quickly fashioned a working majority in the House of Representatives. The election of 1980 thrust Reagan beyond the old order into a political interregnum. It did not convey any clear message as to what exactly should be done; but it did give voice to widespread discontent, and it underscored the new administration's assertions that something fundamental had gone wrong in the affairs of state.

Reagan needed no prompting to take the part of the great repudiator.[10] His administration opened with a broadside assault on the ruling formulas of a bankrupt past: "In the present crisis, government is not the solution to our problem; government is the problem."[11] This message would be hammered relentlessly over the next eight years, each blow directing the presidential battering ram against the institutions and principal clients of the liberal regime.[12]

To stoke the order-shattering thrust of his leadership, Reagan offered an equally belligerent reaffirmation of first principles. True to form, he reached back to the ancient truths of a mythic past and offered the nation no alternative but to accept a radical change of direction:

Isn't our choice really not one of left or right, but of up or down? Down through the welfare state to statism, to more and more government largesse accompanied always by more government authority, less individual liberty, and ultimately, totalitarianism, always advanced as for our own good. The alternative is the dream conceived by our Founding Fathers, up to the ultimate in individual freedom consistent with an orderly society.[13]

When the going got rough, as it did in the recession of 1981–2, the great repudiator responded in kind:

We're going through a period of difficult and painful readjustment . . . but there is no alternative. Some of those who oppose this plan have participated over the years in the extravagance that has brought us inflation, unemployment, high interest rates and intolerable debt.[14]

As for creating order anew, Reagan promised to "put the Nation on a fundamentally different course," one that would regenerate all that the pundits were saying was lost forever. Nightmarish projections of the future were to be dispelled; Carter's "no easy answers," the journalists' predictions of national decline, the economists' prophecy of a new age of limits and individual sacrifice—all were forthrightly rejected. By releasing the creative energies of the private sector from their government shackles, Reagan promised to reset the clock, to make it once again "morning in America."[15]

Devastatingly simple and viscerally seductive, Reagan's reconstructive posture quickly earned him distinction as a "Great Communicator," the most masterful politician in the presidency since Franklin Roosevelt.[16] It is hardly a wonder. Opposition leaders with expansive warrants to change things typically exercise a disarming control over political definitions. Not the least of Reagan's accomplishments would be to equate liberalism itself with illegitimacy and to force the party of liberalism to search on his ground for some new identity, a "New" Democratic party.[17]

The difficulty comes not in explaining Reagan's fame as a master of rhetoric and a communicator of ideas but in trying to square that with his other reputation for wandering into incoherence, misstatement of fact, and fantasy during his more extemporaneous remarks. Taking account of the latter demands careful specification of what lay behind Reagan's charismatic appeal. The starkly contrasting images suggest the extent to which the distinction of "Great Communicator" really applies to the message, not the messenger.[18] Trained as an actor, Reagan relied on the script. He brought the reconstructive narrative to life once again, but he was not, in the parlance of contemporary analysis, a "personal president" at all. Political identity, the cornerstone of presidential leadership in political time, evolved in his hands into a role to be performed.[19]

Had we targeted the reconstructive message and traced its effectiveness back through similar contexts in presidential history, we might have found Reagan's presentation of it a bit less stunning and the prospects of playing Andrew Jackson at the end of the twentieth century a bit more sobering. Far from trying to make the system work, Reagan set about forging a wholly new system, and with it a different understanding of constitutional government itself. He harnessed presidential power to the task of sweeping away a degenerate order and reaffirming ancient truths; he ventured a wholesale change in governing formulas and a reordering of political priorities. Reagan pressed a classic politics of reconstruction at a time when fulfilling such an objective would have to cut more deeply through the economic fabric of the nation and rearrange more lives than ever before.

One of the reasons Reagan's rendition of the classic reconstructive stance played out so perversely is that the President and those around him were driven by a modern conceit: they thought that the rise of the presidency to a position of overweening prominence in government and virtual independence in politics had made the office a potent instrument for imposing change wholesale on both. As we have seen, the politics of reconstruction has paced the rise of presidential government in a paradoxical way, with progressive complications and newfound slippages. Over time, political reconstruction has in fact become less presidential; reconstructive outcomes have gradually been decoupled from the personal will of the reconstructive leader himself. Jefferson, the least encumbered practitioner of reconstructive politics, was virtually unchallenged until the last weeks of his second administration in his control over the reordering of the American regime. Jackson, challenged on all fronts, prevailed by sheer grit against a steady bombardment of challenges from Congress, Court, cabinet, and states, and still his opponents institutionalized themselves into a permanent opposition. A testy division of labor between president and Congress marked Lincoln's reconstruction, and it was the Congress that produced the most durable and constructive elements of the new order. The New Deal reconstruction saw President Roosevelt repeatedly go down to defeat on his major reconstructive initiatives, the new order constructed by others out of the wreckage left from his grand designs.

Decoupling accelerated under Reagan. Unlike his counterparts in political time, this reconstructive leader tried to work his will in government through the airwaves of television. His repudiation of the old order was beamed out to the people, its bludgeoning force to be redirected by them back upon the fortresses of Washington.[20] The order-shattering thrust of Reagan's leadership thus came to operate in a realm dangerously disconnected from the larger realities of political power and institutional organization. When his withering assaults on liberalism's failures hit the realities of late-twentieth century governance, their regenerative promise dissipated into mawkish truisms woefully inadequate to the challenge of following through.[21] Under the great force of Reagan's negation, the government careened beyond the old order and out of his control.

With the national government and the national economy meshed together even more tightly than in the 1930s, Reagan's dreams of a wholesale reordering driven by the president moved past mere conceit and raced toward self-delusion. During 1981 Reagan repeatedly reminded his listeners of what would be demanded of the government to launch his "New Beginning" successfully. The program's principal elements—the domestic budget cuts, the defense budget increases, the tax cuts, the monetary discipline, the deregulation of business—each anticipated wrenching changes. On top of that, they were said to be mutually interdependent as well.[22] The promise of regeneration was held together by precarious presumptions about the prospects for implementing and coordinating all the elements and some unbridled speculation about the catalytic effects of their interaction.

Calculating these prospects, a leader less taken with the dream of a wholly new order of things might have hesitated. Budget Director David Stockman, the mastermind of what he himself dubbed the "Rosy Scenario," saw them clearly enough.[23] As he looked out from the White House onto the complex networks that connected congressional committees to the national bureaucracy and integrated both into state and local economies, he began to despair at the chances for concerted, holistic action. It seemed that the election had changed very little after all; an abrupt shift in party control no longer shook the old governing arrangements as it once had. The new Republican-dominated Senate was only marginally more amenable to the President's designs than the Democratically dominated House.[24] The problem was not divided party government—the Democratic House and the Republican Senate warring with each other over the President's priorities—it was the institutional independence of the Congress, House and Senate alike, and its members' determination to have their concerns met whatever the President proposed. When it came to setting limits on change, senators seemed to feel even greater responsibility (or culpability) than the House members, for they were the ones who acted most decisively in 1981. Stockman realized early on that the administration's reconstructive vision rested on a fantasy. The program, he said, "implied a stunningly radical theory of governance. The constitutional prerogatives of the legislative branch would have to be, in effect, suspended."[25] "The Congress felt that as a co-equal branch of government, it had the right to 'mix and match' . . . What they didn't realize was that . . . the Reagan Revolution had all along required of them one thing: complete surrender."[26]

Congressional abdication to the executive in the degree demanded by this program is virtually unknown to the modern presidency, at least in peacetime. Even in the tumultuous spring of 1933, it was glimpsed only momentarily. The president who came closest to wielding the kind of control that Reagan's program presumed was the first reconstructive leader, Thomas Jefferson. Never since has Congress proven so organizationally inchoate and politically malleable, and even in that instance, presidential control rested on a formal celebration of congressional prerogatives. Assuming a Congress more pliant than any since the very earliest days of the Republic, the Reagan reconstruction found itself fighting a hidden, as well as a manifest, enemy. As it targeted the destruction of the liberal regime, it placed itself on a collision course with modernity. To dislodge established commitments of ideology and interest in the traditional fashion, the Reagan administration had to take on all the systems and processes that had evolved over the course of the twentieth century to represent social interests, protect institutional prerogatives, and stabilize the management of a polity that was nationally integrated and internationally interdependent. The distance between Jefferson's world and Reagan's was marked by the emergence of governmental norms and institutional modalities that had no place for the classic reconstructive stance. Wielding a political authority still quite capable of sustaining a radical disruption of established routines, Reagan's encounter with the accouterments of modern American government spun out a series of grim ironies.

(1) First, while the administration was possessed of the conceit that history was repeating itself and a political opportunity like that facing Roosevelt in the 1930s was at hand, it felt compelled from the start to act in ways that belied the difference.[27] One of the hallmarks of prior reconstructive episodes, even the New Deal if we consider the ecumenical thrust of the NRA, was the impulse of the leader to cast the widest possible net in the initial reform program and let unfolding events sharpen the imperatives of making the break more decisive. Indeed, resistance, when it surfaced, was something of a resource for the reconstructive leader, a spur to more radical change. In Reagan's reconstruction, however, there was little patience for an accommodating overture; the prospective resistance foreclosed any long, drawn-out exposé of just how much might have to be changed. As Stockman saw it, the only hope for success lay in taking maximum advantage of whatever political disillusionment and disarray the election had created; reconstruction would have to come immediately and all at once.[28] "My motivation for [such an] inhuman schedule was grandiose," he confessed. "I reckoned that the 'window' for successfully launching sweeping change in the national political economy would be exceedingly brief. Then a deteriorating economy and the resurgent political forces of the status quo would quickly overtake the new administration. In combination, the two could blow apart the tenuous budget equation that held the supply-side program intact."[29] "The strategy [in the Spring of 1981] was to bring all the power of the Great Communicator to bear on [the Congress] and shove our budget cuts down their throats."[30]

So it was that this administration tried to squeeze its reconstruction into the standard rhythms of modern American government. The "honeymoon period," the time when modern presidents have ordinarily tried to set their own course, became a time when this administration would try to undo most of what the modern presidents had hitherto presumed.[31] If the early months of the Reagan administration evoked Rooseveltian images of the "100 Days," there was a sneaking suspicion among its architects that, unlike Roosevelt, 100 days might be all that Reagan would have to deliver his new order. From the start, the administration's ambitions were held hostage to the normal operations of the government it was assaulting. Move it or lose it was the sentiment of the hour. "I was just racing against the clock," complained Stockman. "And when you decide to put a program of this breadth and depth out fast, you can only do so much. We didn't add up all the numbers."[32]

Even in those early months, when the administration was fully mobilized to the charge of "break with the past," Stockman's confrontation with extant governing arrangements dealt harshly with his budget calculations.[33] The assumptions of the "Rosy Scenario," as loose as they were in theory, proved too rigid to survive the perilous course of implementation. The administration simply failed to achieve reductions in the domestic budget of the magnitude that were required to compensate for its other priorities in lowering taxes and increasing defense expenditures. On the one hand, it became increasingly apparent that the projected future reductions that would need to be made in the domestic budget could not be had without cutting into entitlement programs such as Social Security. On the other hand, it was made crystal clear that this part of the liberal regime's "social safety net" was stubbornly resilient to election returns.[34] In May of 1981, Reagan's new Republican Senate voted 95–0 against an oblique suggestion from the administration that a proposal to revamp the Social Security system might be in the offing.[35] In effect, this scuttled all real hope for the success of the grand design. With its friends as attached to the old formulas as its foes, the Reagan Revolution led the nation into an all-consuming sea of red ink. Stockman was the first to admit that the numbers used in passage of the administration's program were of dubious authority. Between what the administration demanded and what the Congress—Republican and Democratic members alike—was willing to give, the program could pass the modern test of "adding up" only by deceit or self-deception.[36]

That a recognizable version of the Reagan program was enacted in a rush, despite the numbers, attests to the distinctive standards on which this administration rested its case. Unlike his immediate predecessors, Reagan was not beholden to specifically modern criteria of appropriateness. His most potent political resource was his authority to repudiate. That contingent authority unlocked the charisma of the presidential office, harmonizing its order-shattering, order-affirming, and order-creating impulses. Trumping the authority of the numbers with the disarming entreaties of Andrew Jackson, Reagan urged the nation to take a leap of faith.[37]

Appealing for passage of the administration-backed budget bill of 1981 over the bill offered by the House Budget committee, Reagan employed this authority to dismiss talk of alternatives. "It may appear that we have two alternatives," he said in a televised address to a joint session of Congress. "In reality, there are no more alternatives left . . ."

> [The House Budget Committee's measure] reflects an echo of the past rather than a benchmark of the future. High taxes and excess spending growth created our present economic mess; more of the same will not cure the hardship, anxiety and discouragement it has imposed on the American people.[38]

When faced with the hard-pressed realities of national budgeting in the late-twentieth century, Reagan turned his plan into a necessity by casting the republic as a dream.

> The poet Carl Sandburg wrote, "The republic is a dream. Nothing happens unless first a dream." And that's what makes us Americans different. We've always reached for a new spirit and aimed at a higher goal . . . Who among us wants to be first to say we no longer have those qualities, that we must limp along, doing the same things that have brought us our present misery.[39]

Three months later, a 25 percent tax cut, phased in over three years and skewed to benefit those with the means to stimulate productive investments, was rammed through Congress on similar imperatives after another televised invocation of the classic reconstructive trope.

> In a few days the Congress will stand at the fork of two roads. One road is all too familiar to us. It leads ultimately to higher taxes. It merely brings us back full circle to the source of our economic problems, where the government decides that it knows better than you what should be done with your earnings and, in fact, how you should conduct your life. The other road promises to renew the American spirit. It's a road of hope and opportunity. It places the direction of your life back in your hands where it belongs.[40]

The bargains, compromises, and sleights of hand that actually carried the Reagan program through Congress at the height of the President's influence made it all the more imperative that the administration sustain the initiative and force a more workable accommodation to its new priorities over the long haul. But even before the end of the first year, the administration was a spent force so far as reconstruction was concerned. There was to be no second thrust as there had been for FDR in 1935; the Reagan Revolution turned out to be a single-jolt affair. As the initiative returned to Congress and subsequent White House budgets were declared dead on arrival, the administration found itself engaged in trench warfare. In the end, the most potent weapon Reagan could muster in his crusade against the domestic priorities of the liberal regime was the prospect of the long-term havoc to be wreaked on the modern economy by the ballooning budget deficits he had created. Failing to actually dislodge the commitments of the old order, the Reagan administration created a monumental governing problem that would keep them suppressed long into the future.

(2) While modern American government thwarted Reagan's ambitions, it also magnified his effects. Reagan was able to transform the terms of national government so thoroughly within the space of a single year only because he had the tools of the modern presidency at his disposal. Consider for example the national budget. The routine budget-making responsibilities of the modern presidency gave Reagan immediate access to the working structure of the government as a whole, and when he used his reconstructive authority to slice through the complexities of the budget process, he was able to cut deep into routine operations of government in a remarkably short span of time.

The existence of a national budget not only enhanced the order-shattering possibilities, it also drew out the implications of the confrontation between modernity and this kind of leadership authority. The working standards of the modern presidency, like the working standards of modern American government as a whole, remain historically and structurally irreconcilable with the Jackson model of forcing reconstruction from on high. Its institutions form a new layer of government bequeathed to incumbents as tools to routinize political management of governmental affairs. The national budget, first introduced into American government in 1921, was in fact the premier institution of the modern presidency, and from its debut, it engaged the chief executive in a complex managerial relationship with the Congress.[41] The Reorganization Act of 1939 (the act in which the modern presidency first took recognizable form) recast national budgeting considerably, but that act was itself a victory for interests and institutions determined to prevent a reconstructive leader from consolidating his new agenda entirely under his own command and completing his break with the past. The design of the modern presidency, as it emerged from the New Deal, deflected Roosevelt's drive for presidentially controlled government; it held the president to a more accommodating role vis-à-vis the Congress and the interdependent interests of the new political economy. This message was reinforced in the sweeping reforms in national budgeting enacted in the mid-1970s in which Congress moved to counter the threat of an "imperial" presidency by centralizing its own procedures.[42]

The institutions and procedures of national budgeting had been designed and redesigned to thwart the unmediated imposition of presidential will and to force deliberation and compromise. They could become instruments of a presidentially driven political reconstruction only if their operations were subverted and the standards of legitimacy on which they rested were trashed. The budget battle in 1981 juxtaposed two very different standards of national action—one modern and managerial, the other transhistorical and unrepentantly disruptive. David Stockman documents the confrontation. The reconciliation process in the formal budget procedures "underscored the complexity of altering dozens of different kinds of spending mechanisms that had evolved over the decades. And it showed that the institutional management and scorekeeping tasks of plenary budget subtraction were nearly insuperable."[43] To use the congressional budget process as an instrument of reconstruction, the administration had to corrupt it, for better or worse distorting the purposes for which it had been set up.[44] Committee chairmen expressed "genuine alarm" that "the product of the committee system can be cynically discarded in favor of substitute legislation written in some downtown hideaway."[45] But their protest was no match for the authority of the great repudiator; Reagan took over the reconciliation procedure in the congressional budget process and turned it into a vehicle for the imposition of his will. The norms of congressional management were discarded, and with the tools of congressional management redeployed under the President's reconstructive warrants, the administration rejected the handiwork of the House committees and rammed through its alternative.

This subversion of the instrumentalities of modern American government was documented even more fully during Reagan's second term in the Iran-Contra revelations. Here again institutions formally designed to foster deliberation, coordination, and management were redeployed to very different ends under the guiding light of this president's expansive political warrants. This time the corruption assumed constitutional proportions.

The Iran-Contra operation aimed to cut through the obstacles that stood in the way of realizing three of Reagan's foreign policy concerns.[46] The President wanted to free the remaining hostages in Lebanon, but he was blocked by his categorical ban on bargaining with terrorists. He wanted to provide military support for the rebels fighting the government of Nicaragua, but he was blocked by explicit congressional prohibitions. He was also interested in opening some channel of communication with moderates in Iran, but he was blocked by his own administration's "Operation Staunch," which sought to impose an international arms embargo on that country. To address the President's concerns without publicly broaching the difficulties they raised, staff personnel of the National Security Council (another component of the Executive Office of the President) conceived and coordinated a governing regime of their own. Through a series of secret arms deals with the Iranians, they sought to establish relations with a hostile power, to use Iranian influence to pressure the terrorists in Lebanon to release hostages, and, by diverting the profits from the sales to the Contras, to support counterrevolution in Nicaragua. The staff's operation was conducted wholly outside the pale of the law, overriding not only the policy prohibitions of Congress but all the other procedural formalities that had been designed with cooperative management in view. The staff circumvented arrangements designed to hold the President accountable for the foreign policy of his administration, to limit the involvement of the Security Council in the actual implementation of foreign policy, to force White House deliberation with the Departments of State and Defense, to promote a consistent foreign policy throughout all parts of the government, and to keep the Congress abreast of new initiatives. Unable to get his goals enacted within the terms set forth in modern structure and procedure, the reconstructive leader, in effect, sponsored an alternative government that operated independently within his own offices.

That these revelations did not lead directly to impeachment proceedings is further testimony to the relative weight of the two standards of legitimacy that warred with each other during this administration.[47] Reagan's reconstructive warrants left him curiously untouchable in the face of a scandal with constitutional implications of the first order. Though his administration mocked the first principles it was presuming to regenerate, the Congress showed extreme reluctance to take Reagan on directly.[48] Commentators who had sought to describe this curious deference before invoked the metaphor of the "Teflon President."[49] For reasons that no one could quite fathom, nothing seemed to stick. But Reagan's protection did not come from some mysterious modern tech-

nology; it rested on the residual potency of one of the oldest constructions of political authority. Reagan had effectively cast himself as the
leading symbol of hope for salvation from a bankrupt past, and, even
in contemporary America's "politics of high exposure," no one cared
to take that on.[50] He was held to a different standard by virtue of the
politics he had made; he survived because in the political world he had
constructed, he was a leader with impeccable intentions who occasionally made mistakes.[51]

(3) Not the least of the ironies spun out by this confrontation between
modernity and reconstructive leadership is its confirmation of the pervasive influence of modern bureaucrats and their norms. The actions of
national administrative managers shaped the fate of this reconstruction
as none before. Budget Director Stockman, mastermind of the first-year
victories, stunned the nation before that year was out by confessing that
the political ambitions of the Reagan administration had no foundation
in principles of good government management. In the case of the hostages and the Contras, the initiatives of staff personnel working independently within the Executive Office of the President so departed from
managerial norms as to bring the entire administration to its knees.

In other instances, where the exercise of bureaucratic power was
perfectly legal and managerial norms were more fully adhered to, the
complications introduced into reconstructive politics were more subtle
but more profound. For instance, with President and Congress scrambling for cover in the face of a volcanic explosion in the national debt,
effective control over the fate of the Reagan Revolution passed out of
the hands of politicians and into the hands of the Federal Reserve
Board, an administrative instrument charged to stabilize the operations
of the nation's economy. The Fed had been structured from its inception
to work largely independently of the president and the Congress, and
with the inability of the elected branches to resolve the powerful order-
shattering thrust of the Reagan program, that became a weighty complication indeed. From beginning to end, the custodians of the nation's
financial system toyed with the Reagan reconstruction; reacting to it
with their own managerial purposes in view, they drove its friends and
foes alike to distraction.

In 1981, as the administration was enacting what became in effect a
massive increase in governmental expenditures and a major tax cut, the
Fed was applying the brakes, and in the fall the economy entered its
second recession in twelve months. This was not entirely unexpected or

even unwelcome by the administration. It wanted inflation under control before its new stimulus package took effect, and it counted the principles of Chairman Volcker's new monetary discipline an integral part of its own program. As the downturn seemed to be running the normal cycle back toward revival in the early months of 1982, the White House looked forward to a recovery that would vindicate its tax cuts and sweep it through the midterm elections with the kind of extraordinary political endorsement it needed to bolster its reconstructive ambitions. But it did not work out that way. Instead of working in tandem, the monetary policy of restraint collided with the fiscal policy of expansion.[52] The Fed continued to act out of concern for the inflationary pressures pent up in the government's new budgets and refused to let up. As Volcker held tight on the money supply, interest rates soared upward, and the recession cut deeper.

At first, outraged leaders in Congress and concerned insiders in the Reagan White House threatened legislation that would strip the Fed of its independent power.[53] In the end, they reacted much as other politicians of the modern period had in similar straits, and deferred. Rather than try to change the Fed, the President changed his program, agreeing to a "mid-course correction" that included the first of what would become a series of tax increases. The Fed's stiff discipline during the spring of 1982 and the tax bill of that summer snuffed out what hope remained for a political resurgence of the revolutionary fervor of 1981. The midterm elections followed the ordinary course of losses for the party of the incumbent president. The recession lingered through the fall and on into winter, sending unemployment up past 10 percent and Reagan's approval ratings down into the mid-30 percent range.

When the Fed was most zealous in implementing the monetary policy that Reagan had hailed in principle, it undercut the Reagan Revolution politically; then, when zeal for combatting inflation gave way to alarm about the dimensions of the recession, the Fed reversed itself and called a halt to the revolution in principles. Even as it was forcing moderation on the question of taxes, the Fed was beginning to take steps to moderate its own course as well.[54] During the summer of 1982, the new experiment in monetary policy was quietly terminated. Instead of controlling the money supply and letting interest rates seek their own level, Volcker gradually turned back to the old policy, the policy roundly repudiated by Reagan and his monetarist advisors, of targeting interest rates and manipulating the money supply to attain them.[55]

The Fed played fast and loose with the tax and monetary principles of the Reagan Revolution, but when it finally threw its support behind the remaining part—the massive spending stimulus—it saved the Reagan presidency. The recovery kicked in just in time for the President's reelection campaign. Even in facilitating the recovery, however, the Fed had to deal with the implications of the stalled political agenda. As the yield from any given rate of taxation would no longer get the boost provided in the past by inflation, expected increases in federal expenditures threatened to drive the government ever further into debt. To finance the deficits, Volcker kept the economic revival on a tight leash, and the real rate of interest (the rate that takes account of inflation) remained high.[56]

In the middle years of the Reagan presidency, the modus vivendi worked out between the gridlocked politicians in the White House and Congress and the economic managers at the Fed proved to be as disturbing as it was awkward. It is not simply that the Reagan program accelerated the decline of organized labor, that it hastened the collapse of marginal farms, and that it further marginalized the urban poor. That much might have been expected given the administration's belief that prior commitments were clogging up the works and that the interests the government served would have to be thinned out in order to release the creative energies of the nation once again. More disturbing was what happened to that regenerative promise, the promise of setting the nation on a robust "new course" for future development. The "boom years" of the Reagan administration witnessed a decline of the nation's export industries, a flood of foreign products into the American marketplace, a ballooning trade deficit, the empowerment of foreign creditors in the high affairs of state, a speculative binge in real estate and construction that threatened the savings and loan industry with insolvency, and a burgeoning consumer debt as ominous as that facing the federal government itself. In the fall of 1987, a stock market crash unprecedented since 1929 threatened the entire financial system, and the Fed, faced with impending disaster, rushed in with new supports to keep the system sound.[57]

What then are we to make of Reagan's pretensions as a reconstructive leader? Time and again we have had occasion to take note of the sober side of the politics of reconstruction. Despite their many political advantages, reconstructive leaders have never been especially adept at solving the problems that brought them into office in the first place.

But one of the things that has distinguished these sorts of leaders from their less fortunate predecessors is that they have not had to solve those problems. What they were able to do instead was to transform the nation's governing commitments and the ways in which political problems were dealt with institutionally. In the past, reconstructive leaders have been able to dislodge old commitments, to reorient the government for political action along a different course, and to move the nation beyond the old problems toward a different set of possibilities altogether.

Like other reconstructive leaders, Reagan closed off a prior course of development. Beyond that, however, these comparisons reveal the distinctive limits and peculiar success of his efforts. Reagan fell far short of the mark in revitalizing national government around his new priorities and opening a more productive course for development. For all that the New Beginning changed the terms and conditions of national politics, it proved far less successful than the New Deal in reconstructing American government. The institutional commitments of the liberal regime, though battered and starved, were not decisively dislodged, and their "entitlements" would continue to determine the range of political possibilities. Meanwhile, the problems of stimulating productive investment and enhancing international competitiveness emerged more imposing than ever from the Reagan shock treatment, and new demands of the very sort that Reagan had sought to repress—demands for government action in health care, environmental regulation, and education—continued to mount. Reagan's most prominent legacy, the national debt, weighed against the economic miracle he had promised from the private sector as much as against the public-sector initiatives he had renounced, and the two reconstructive ideas on which he had rested his new course—the monetarist discipline and the supply-side stimulus to invest—appeared all the more dubious after the recovery took hold.[58]

Yet, it is also the case that the New Beginning succeeded where the New Deal had failed: it generated an economic recovery. For all its limitations in establishing new governing formulas, this administration did appear to solve the immediate problem that brought it to power in the first place. The American economy emerged from the 1982 recession growing with a low rate of inflation, and Reagan in 1984 was perfectly positioned rhetorically to take full credit for that achievement.[59] Adopting the strikingly modern boast of having restored stable economic growth, Reagan was able to paper over the limitations of his extra-modern campaign to reset the political clock. In fact, the recovery of the mid-1980s submerged reconstructive ambitions in conventional economic wisdom and substituted the old pattern of government spending and consumer consumption for the new course he had heralded.

The two sides of this story—the economic success and the political failure—tell the same tale. Both point to the new modalities of American government that parried the order-shattering thrust of Reagan's leadership and transformed classic reconstructive ambitions into a singularly modern achievement. The collision of these forces, however, left an unsettling legacy. By bringing permanent pressure to bear against programs that maintained formidable political and institutional support, Reagan's assault threatened to keep the government suspended in the crisis of legitimacy it was meant to resolve. Republicans and Democrats alike would find themselves hard pressed to come up with a credible case for governing in the new world Reagan had created, and what made that task especially difficult is that Reagan's reconstructive authority served less to open political possibilities in modern America than to short-circuit them. This great repudiator left his successors to search for a new course of action with radically diminished prospects for doing much of anything at all.[60] Modernity may have tilted the balance in reconstructive politics, giving the final victory to the Monster over Andrew Jackson manqué, but it proved an exceedingly costly contest all around.

George Bush as the Faithful Son

When George Bush invoked the spirit of Harry Truman to spur his 1992 reelection drive, Democrats were quick to take offense.[61] What could a Greenwich-born, Yale-educated conservative possibly have in common with that liberal midwestern haberdasher? What could Reagan's successor possibly have in common with Roosevelt's?

But Bush was not thinking about anything so obvious as Truman's background, his personality, his party, or his ideological commitments. He was thinking about Truman's place in a political sequence and about the leadership project that Truman had tagged to that moment. He was thinking about Truman's come-from-behind vindication of the regime-founder's commitments and priorities.[62] Overall, Truman's leadership stance during the 1948 presidential campaign struck Bush as a parallel moment in political time. If Ronald Reagan could reclaim the leadership warrants of Franklin Roosevelt, why shouldn't Bush follow in turn and reclaim the leadership stance of the faithful son? If Truman could win election as Roosevelt's loyal successor facing off against a "do-nothing" Republican Congress, why couldn't Bush blame the Democratic Congress for stalling the Reagan agenda and preventing Reagan's rightful heir from completing the work he had begun?

That Bush identified himself in the end with the most celebrated modern-day exemplar of the leader-as-faithful-son was less a surprise than a disappointment. From the moment he signed on as Reagan's vice president, Bush found himself engaged in an extended debate about his political identity. Had that ambiguity been manipulated to transcend the traditional limitations of the faithful son, creating in its place a premise for leadership that was both new and distinct, his presidency might well have proven worthy of the appellation "postmodern." But in his reelection drive as before, Bush only toyed with these possibilities. At the crucial junctures, he refused to strike out in a new direction. When the going got rough, he repaired to the same time-worn standard of legitimacy that affiliated leaders have had thrust upon them since the days of John Adams. From the early talk about his failure to articulate his own vision for the nation to this last appeal to "give-'em-hell Harry Truman," Bush made himself a parody of the all too familiar dilemmas of the orthodox-innovator.

The faithful-son theme of the 1992 campaign was a reprise of the warrants Bush had claimed for himself throughout 1988.[63] Back then, he said, "We don't need radical new directions, we need strong and steady leadership. We don't need to remake society, we just need to remember who we are."[64] On taking office in January of 1989, he remarked that "we're coming in to build on a proud record that has already been established."[65] These themes echoed sentiments that loyal successors have invoked since the beginning of our constitutional history. But Bush's rendition of the president-as-faithful-son never really rang true. In his quest for authenticity, he appropriated a classic leadership role, but it was one that has grown progressively more problematic as the presidential office itself has grown more independent. The historic significance of his leadership effort lies in its dismal confirmation of what all presidents should know by now: that the political premise of affiliated leadership is utterly exhausted.

As we have seen time and again, affiliated leaders work at cross purposes. They are at an inherent disadvantage when it comes to exercising the powers of their office in their own right and defining legitimacy anew on their own terms. In its basic outlines, the Bush presidency followed distressingly true to form. He accepted his nomination for the presidency in 1988 with a belligerent pledge to uphold the Reagan orthodoxy: "The Congress will push me to raise taxes, and I'll say no, they'll push, and I'll say no, and they'll push again. And all I can say to them is: Read my lips: no new taxes."[66] In his campaign Bush asked, "Who can you most trust to continue the Reagan revolution?"[67] Content to defend the existing order at home, Bush was soon looking to the rest of the world as the arena in which he would create something new, "a new world order." He vented the powers of his office most dramatically in the Persian Gulf, fighting another of those splendid little wars that affiliated leaders seem to find so irresistible. But international muscle-flexing has never proven a sufficient distraction from the dilemmas of regime management, and Bush's case proved to be no exception. From the outset, it was clear that he would not be able to govern within the terms of his initial pledge of orthodoxy in domestic affairs, and a year and a half after his inauguration, he disavowed his commitment on taxes. For this, he was charged with a monumental betrayal of faith, and his presidency ended up fracturing the coalition it had come to power to serve.

If there is anything remarkable in the particulars of this case, it is the exaggeration of the familiar patterns to the point of caricature. By the time he was finished, Bush had turned faithfulness into a national joke. If Reagan's posture as the great repudiator broached new heights of irresponsibility by ignoring the resilience of the institutional relationships he set out to reconstruct, Bush's efforts to uphold the Reagan orthodoxies broached new heights of irresponsibility by denying the independence now built into the institution he took over. The overweening prominence of the presidency in contemporary American government and the unfiltered exposure of the leader in modern politics make short work of the self-effacing discipline of the affiliated leader. The political position Bush staked out in national affairs was recast under modern conditions to appear, wittingly or not, as cynical in the extreme.

It is instructive that this latest effacement of the leadership posture of the faithful son first came to light through the contemporary process for the selection of presidential candidates. The primary elections are the cornerstones of the plebiscitary presidency. They strip away the veneer of party unity and expose the individuality of each candidate.

As contemporary selection procedures force party leaders to compete with one another in the open, they prompt them to differentiate themselves publicly and to boast of their independence of mind. Pitting potential party spokespersons against one another in public combat, these procedures undercut the credibility of the candidate's affiliation with anything other than him- or herself. Bush put a finer point on this than most. Back in the 1980 primary season, when he was staking his claim to moderate Republican ground and trying to put as much distance as he could between himself and his chief rival for his party's nomination, he repeatedly denounced Reagan's program as the "free lunch approach," "economic madness," "voodoo economics."[68]

Having played hard by the rules of the primary contest, Bush found it to difficult to negotiate a graceful retreat to the old rules of party regularity. The charge of voodoo economics figured prominently in his political persona from then on. He acknowledged the problem immediately after his nomination as Reagan's vice-presidential running mate: "I know people will be saying 'he said this and he said that.' But . . . I'm simply not going to dwell on the differences."[69] Still, the charge was thrown back at him, and after his convention conversion, it raised new questions about his personal integrity and true identity.[70] Before the 1980 campaign was over he was heard muttering: "God, I wish I hadn't said that."[71] Bush's initial repudiation of Reagan's ideas dogged him again in 1988 when he sought to run for president as Reagan's heir and protegé, and it surfaced again in 1992 when he sought to repent for the apostasy of his first term in the presidency and to return to Reagan orthodoxies for a second.[72] An enduring source of embarrassment, "voodoo economics" encapsuled Bush's enigmatic relationship to Reagan personally and became emblematic of a much larger credibility problem that would define his presidency. From start to finish, Bush was in one way or another trying to explain away some former self and render some prior course consistent with his current commitments and affiliations.

The most sympathetic explanation was that Bush hated campaigning and felt it had little to do with governing. The campaign was the price of gaining power, another scripted performance Bush had to give in order to get to the one office where he could play himself.[73] The problem was that in fashioning authority for the exercise of presidential power, Bush went farther than most to imply that publicly professed beliefs had no more standing than a calculation of momentary advantage. Willing to detach his political identity from his own personal history for the purposes of a campaign, he reduced identity to nothing more than the role a politician happened to be adopting at a particular moment for purely tactical purposes. Leadership is not that easy, especially not in the age of the so-called "personal president," and Bush found it difficult to straighten things out once he was in office. During his four years in the presidency, he was continually tripping over the question of who he really was.

On reflection, Bush's exposure on the issue of political identity seems more typical of the plight of a late-regime affiliate than of one who, like Harry Truman, came to power on the heels of the great repudiator himself. His fumbling over the question of who he was and where he stood recalls the likes of Jimmy Carter and Herbert Hoover, presidents who were stuck with an orthodoxy that no longer held out solutions to the nation's problems and who struggled with received formulas in a fitful search for credibility. Bush got even less out of his affiliated posture than his proximity to the Reagan Revolution would lead us to expect, and that suggests another factor working against his leadership claims as Reagan's faithful son.

It is not simply that the modern presidency accentuates the independence of the office, that it strips away the ties that bind politicians together, that it sets up an especially ruthless exposé of the affiliate as a leader at odds with his constitutional charge to be president in his own right. Just as important, affiliation played perversely for George Bush because Reagan's performance as a reconstructive leader was itself so severely constricted. As the Reagan Revolution emerged unresolved from its own collision with the political and institutional modalities of late-twentieth-century governance, there was that much less political authority for his successor to extract from his association with it. As one Bush aide put it: "It was awkward to follow Reagan and claim success. We couldn't say we'd be cleaning up the Reagan mess. We would just have to do it without talking about it."[74]

In Bush's case, as in Reagan's, we see how contemporary renditions of the classic leadership postures have gotten cut short, how in contemporary settings the variables structuring traditional differences in the politics presidents make tend to collapse in upon one another, how the deterioration of one leadership stance accelerates the deterioration in the others, in short, how political time has been short-cycled. The norms of affiliated leadership fail to guide presidential action when the predecessor boasting reconstructive warrants has left the old congressional politics and the pre-established bureaucratic institutions substantially intact. In these circumstances, the loyal successor might well wonder which commitments are more resilient—the old ones still in place or the new ones still struggling to take hold. What are the nation's priorities when the reconstruction turns out to have been largely rhetorical? What does the premise of continuity actually entail when recent rhetoric and policy have diverged so widely? The "vision thing"—the repeated calls for George Bush to stake out his own terms for the exercise of presidential power—suggests something of the profound impatience of modern American politics with the givenness of the commitments of a regime affiliate. The expectation that every president will articulate a personal vision of his own for the exercise of power is strikingly contemporary; it is modernity's exhortation to candidates to discard the traditional burdens of affiliation and step out of the traditional roles.

There were some strong hints of just such a stepping out in the way Bush tackled the first challenge of affiliated leadership—modifying the received agenda and rearticulating the relationship among its parts so as to adjust it to the demands of changing times. In taking up this familiar task, Bush had the words exactly right: time and again throughout the 1988 campaign, he reminded his listeners that "we have unfinished business." By the historical standards of affiliated leadership, however, the agenda on which Bush promised positive action was intriguing. He reached back beyond Reagan's reconstruction of federal priorities to revive some of the very commitments that Reagan had sought to bury. A good deal of his "vision" was constructed not of innovations drawn from the new orthodoxy with which he had belatedly identified himself but of innovations drawn from the old orthodoxy that Reagan had presumably repudiated. Bush promised that the federal government would tighten environmental regulations, broaden Medicaid coverage for the poor, subsidize child care, "fully fund" Lyndon Johnson's Head Start program, attend to the burdens of paying for college, improve standards in elementary and secondary education.[75]

These promises suggested a resurfacing of the old Bush. They bespoke the moderate Republican of the prior establishment, the one who knew that once elected he would face a Democratic Congress, the erstwhile insider who might yet establish a more cooperative, bargaining relationship with his former colleagues on Capitol Hill.[76] In another sense, these promises were just more strategic posturing. They were aimed mainly at the suburban voters who had grown anxious about the Reagan agenda even as they had supported Reagan himself. Bush was address-ing their concerns with "the quality of life." The point is that in the post-Reagan era, Bush could neither recall his former self nor act stra-tegically without offering an implicit indictment of his predecessor's priorities. Beneath the numbing belligerence of his tax pledge something new was being insinuated into affiliated leadership after all: while claim-ing to build on his inheritance, he was in fact also recognizing the limits of the Reagan reconstruction and pushing against the boundaries of his ascribed role as heir. When he tried to clear his own ground, Bush used "words Reagan could scarcely be imagined to have uttered" and made promises that, if enacted, would veer sharply off the course set by his predecessor.[77]

But Bush gave few clues about the significance of this turn, and his priorities began to blur in the uncertainties that surrounded his depar-ture. When Bush insisted, as he did throughout the 1988 campaign, that "we are the change," when he anticipated becoming known as "the Education President" and "the Environmental President," when he asked his inaugural audience to feel the "New Breeze" that was sweep-ing the world, when he appealed to the Democratic leadership of the House and the Senate saying "this is the age of the offered hand," when he promised the nation a "kinder," "gentler" America—when he said these things, he was actively obscuring the relationship between past and present thrust upon him by his affiliated status. At such times, Bush presented the connection between the changes he anticipated and his commitment to continuity in a way that promised to supersede the dilemmas of orthodox innovation. At such times, he appeared to be more his own man than Reagan's, a president ready to establish legiti-macy anew on his own terms. Ready but not willing. Though he signed a new civil rights bill, a new clean air bill, a disabled Americans bill, a transportation bill, and oversaw a gradual retightening of economic regulations, Bush went out of his way to make it clear that he had commitments on all sides of these issues. Close observers reported that he was "elevating irresolution to an art form and inventing new ways of disconnecting political rhetoric from performance."[78]

Bush's overtures to independence were, of course, as risky as they were potentially liberating. If the promise was something new—that a contemporary president might step outside the bounds of his affiliated status and cultivate his freedom of received orthodoxies—the danger was that he would provoke the same old reaction—devastating charges of heresy and betrayal from the faithful. The tragicomedy of the Bush presidency played out his reading of these tradeoffs. As virtually all affiliated leaders, no matter what they have chosen to do, have provoked charges of betrayal, and as the development of the presidential office has placed an ever higher premium on independent action, one suspects that Bush had everything to gain by testing the opportunities for liberation. There is no need to speculate about what was lost by clinging to orthodoxy. Bush's determination to avoid the risks proved disastrous.

That Bush chose to stake so much on orthodoxy cautions against the notion that the residual attractions of abiding by ascribed roles are simply fading away into insignificance. Illusory as they turned out to be, these attractions were still strong enough for a prospective president of the 1990s to compromise the powers and possibilities of his administration at the very start. No doubt, orthodoxy offered Bush something definite and familiar with which to fashion his place in history. Moreover, as his natural tendency toward moderation made his orthodoxy suspect on its face, he was perhaps not entirely unreasonable in his concern to reassure the conservative base of the party that Reagan had bequeathed to him.[79] Finally, it must be admitted that a serious testing of any alternative would have called for considerable subtlety in presentation and execution, a quality never easily insinuated into the exercise of presidential power.

Bush's public profession of his political faith at the Republican national convention in 1988—after he had already won his party's nomination—was anything but subtle. His airtight pledge on taxes moved in exactly the opposite direction, bluntly foreclosing the possibility of doing what even Reagan himself had done repeatedly over the past seven years. Seldom in all of American history has a leader so thoroughly sacrificed his capacities to address the most pressing problem facing the nation in his own right and on his own terms. One thinks of John Adams taking Washington's cabinet as his own and holding his presidency hostage to the Jay Treaty, or of Franklin Pierce pledging to uphold the Compromise of 1850 and committing himself to say nothing new about the most explosive issue of the day. But such comparisons only draw attention to the opportunity Bush squandered for testing the leadership potential of the modern presidency. Bush's choice was not foisted upon him. Determined to avoid the risks of independence, to hold onto the ascribed role, and to prove his faith, he embraced a fate over which he had more control than anyone before.

Indeed, we know now that Bush's unconditional pledge of orthodoxy was hotly contested by his own advisors long before it was made. Robert Teeter, Bush's pollster, and Richard Darman, a top legislative strategist in the Reagan administration who would become Bush's budget director, objected sharply in successive drafts of the convention speech. They recognized immediately that the pledge on taxes would undercut Bush's capacities to govern. They argued further that it held serious and adverse implications for the nation's economy and that these must override any short-term electoral advantage it might provide. They observed that the case in favor of such a pledge was dubious even from a short-term tactical standpoint because the public already believed that Bush was less inclined to raise taxes than his opponent. Finally, they warned that given the existing state of economic affairs the pledge would almost certainly have to be broken, and that when it was broken it would wreak incalculable damage to Bush's political credibility.[80]

Those on the other side—Peggy Noonan, a Reagan speechwriter on loan to the Bush campaign, and Roger Ailes, Bush's media consultant—had little patience with the prospective problems the pledge might cause for the candidate once he got elected. They were concerned primarily with the dramatic structure of the campaign, with creating the appropriate images, and with casting Bush in the most authentic light possible in the moment at hand. They argued that, more than anything else, Bush needed to sharpen his image, that he needed to "say something definite." They warned that if he did not set the terms of his campaign at the outset, he would end up battling the media to establish his message.[81] Those most concerned about clarifying Bush's political identity prevailed, but it is difficult to imagine a less inspired victory. Drawing out their candidate's differences with the "tax and spend liberals," Bush's handlers left him hopelessly adrift in the commitments of his predecessor. Instead of exploiting the ambiguities of Bush's relationship to Reaganism and trying to fashion something new and distinct for him, they stamped him with an authenticity wholly detached from any candid assessment of his prospects as a national leader.

The debate over when the Bush administration would break its pledge on taxes and how the President would handle the political fallout began immediately after his inauguration.[82] Not insensitive to the impending embarrassment, the President held out as long as he could, perhaps hoping that as the deficit situation deteriorated further his reversal would seem more appropriate. Despite his overtures of a new cooperative partnership with the Democratic Congress, Bush scuttled the work of a bipartisan commission that had been formed to come up with a deficit reduction plan, and in effect blocked any concerted attack on the problem for another fateful year. Reality triumph over orthodoxy on the next round. In the summer of 1990, Bush agreed to put the question of taxes back on the table.[83] By that time, the economic recession had made the implications of a tax increase as ominous as the mounting budget deficits had made it imperative.[84]

The budget plan hammered out in the summer of 1990 in negotiations with the Democratic leadership in Congress not only raised new revenues but promised new controls on spending as well.[85] Had Bush never made his tax pledge, had he not prompted Republicans throughout the nation to distinguish themselves from their opponents on that issue,[86] the story of this deal might have been written as a victory for continuity and consolidation of the Reagan agenda. In fact, the administration held out for concessions that obligated the Congress to maintain the policy priorities of the Reagan Revolution largely intact. Even when Congress chose to ignore the new strictures, Bush might have carried the day, for this new evidence of Democratic irresponsibility would have played directly to his Trumanesque crusade for reelection. But Bush had made the tax pledge the linchpin of his and his party's credibility, and when he pulled it out, the reaction was swift and predictable. The reversal put Republicans in far more difficult straits than Democrats, and Bush's fellow partisans rose up in revolt, charging their leader with the "big lie." "I don't want to use the word 'betrayed,'" said Senator Malcolm Wallop of Wyoming, "But people feel they are victims of some ill-conceived actions."[87]

These events dovetailed with an accelerating crisis in the Persian Gulf, and Bush's triumph on that front is especially notable for its coincidence with what would prove to be his moment of greatest difficulty at home. All along Bush had been cultivating a concern with foreign policy that contrasted sharply with his performance on the home front. Certainly there is nothing inherently "postmodern" about Bush's interest in foreign affairs. Faced with the political dilemmas of managing a received agenda, orthodox-innovators have traditionally found the rest of the world a more hospitable realm in which to demonstrate the robust confidence of the nation and to exercise the great powers of their office. Their muscle-flexing wars punctuate our history. Neither have affiliated leaders been reluctant to turn their order-creating ambitions abroad. Bush's "new world order" recalled the boast of the Monroe Doctrine, the drama of the Truman Doctrine, and the symbolism of Theodore Roosevelt's Great White Fleet.[88] If no orthodox-innovator ever went as far as Bush to let foreign policy appear a substitute for hands-on management of the domestic agenda, this was a conceit of the modern presidency fully in keeping with his moment in political time. As Carter had exaggerated the importance of technocratic skills in tackling the complex problems of national governance and Reagan had exaggerated his ability to sweep away the old problems and establish a new order of things in their place, Bush exaggerated the ability of his aides to manage domestic problems while he directed his attention elsewhere.

But it must also be said that no orthodox-innovator has ever made quite so spectacular a show of prowess in world affairs as Bush did during the crisis in the Persian Gulf. In a remarkable display of American leadership in his new world order, Bush pieced together against Iraq an international coalition of some of the most unlikely allies, paid for their actions with foreign money, and with the television cameras rolling, made surprisingly short work of the liberation of Kuwait. If there is an irony in Bush's performance in the war with Iraq, it may be that this stunning demonstration of how effective he could be made all the more irritating his apparent inattention to domestic affairs and the disarray in his domestic commitments. Perceptions on both sides of the Bush presidency tended toward extremes, the foreign policy preoccupation and domestic policy indifference evoking an especially awkward caricature of the leadership posture of the faithful son.

So it was also with Bush's response to charges of betrayal brewing within the Republican ranks. By the spring of 1992, Republicans were attacking their president for heresy every bit as fiercely as Democrats were attacking him for clutching a failed orthodoxy. To add to his difficulties, the mercurial figure of Ross Perot was agitating against the entire government for the gross neglect it had shown to the nation's domestic problems. Affiliated leaders have had two sorts of responses when, like Bush in 1992, they have found themselves besieged on all sides by challenges to their chosen course of action: they mount a defense of their course or they abdicate. Leaders as different as John

Adams and Franklin Pierce took the first route, and for a moment at least it seemed that Bush might do the same. As he had put it at a news conference in 1990 soon after his announcement that the question of a tax increase would be on the bargaining table after all: "I'm presented with new facts. I'm doing like Lincoln did, think anew. And I'm thinking anew . . . We have got a major problem facing this country. And I have the responsibility, leading the Executive Branch, to get things moving to a solution."[89]

The arguments were clear enough: a president has a constitutional responsibility to chart his own course, and modern presidents in particular need to be able to free themselves of received dogmas in order to address the complex and rapidly changing affairs of state with candor and vigor. But in the end Bush did not press his case for independent action. Indeed, when Patrick Buchanan, a Reagan speechwriter and political commentator, entered the 1992 Republican primaries and forced the President to respond to the charges of heresy and betrayal, Bush retreated. He did not, like John Adams, purge those who refused to follow his new initiative. He did not, like Franklin Pierce, throw himself back into the ring to vindicate his chosen course.

Neither did he abdicate, or not exactly. A favorite method among orthodox-innovators for dealing with the charges of heresy, abdication lets personal sacrifice speak for itself about the incumbent's sense of his responsibilities to party and nation and to the integrity of his decisions in the face of the competing pressures. Bush made no such sacrifice. He withstood the charges of heresy in a singularly self-effacing manner. When Buchanan presented himself as the true defender of the faith and blasted Bush's apostasy on everything from taxes to civil rights, the President confessed his sin. He had made a mistake in agreeing to raise taxes.[90] Refusing both to defend his chosen course and to formally step aside, he pled guilty to the charges, reaffirmed his faith in orthodoxy, and turned his clearest act of independence in domestic affairs into an error never to be repeated again.

Perhaps Bush was acting strategically. Was it the spectre of Ross Perot rather than the Buchanan challenge that prompted his retreat from independence back to the Republican party base? While Buchanan never threatened much more than embarrassment, Perot introduced a new and wholly unpredictable element into the electoral calculus. Whatever, Bush's self-denial at this juncture turned into something more akin to self-mockery. The general election campaign of 1992 featured a kind of surrogate abdication, albeit one bereft of the dignity of the real thing.[91] It is not simply that Bush handed the Republican national convention of 1992 over to his critics on the far right of the party. (Carter's capitulation to the liberals at the 1980 Democratic convention was just as awkward.) Bush went beyond that to confirm the view that his course had in fact been misguided. He promised that if he was reelected he would dismiss his entire economic management team and turn the domestic policy of his second term over to James Baker III, his campaign director, secretary of state, and all-around fix-it man of the previous twelve years. Bush's reelection campaign was nothing so simple as Harry Truman's crusade against the "do-nothing" Congress control-led by his opposition. He went back to the nation to campaign against his own policies as well. He had come a long way from his repudiation of voodoo economics, but at every turn he managed to get himself more and more tangled in the role of regime affiliate. At the final juncture, Bush could retake the leadership posture of the faithful son only by repudiating his own administration. He had become an affiliated leader opposed to himself, an opposition leader who had spent the last twelve years in the White House.

Bush's confusion of political identity with political strategy became something of a cliché during his years in office. As the commentator Russell Baker summed up the 1992 campaign, Bush "ran under so many identities it was hard to keep track of who he was from day to day."[92] What Baker hit upon was not only a fatal flaw but also a missed opportunity. The mere fact that Bush could manipulate so many differ-ent identities suggests something of the plasticity of ascribed leadership roles in contemporary American politics. Instead of shifting from one persona to another as the strategic calculations of the moment dictated, Bush might have used this newfound freedom to fashion something that was both definite and distinctive; he might have used the tools of the modern presidency to make the office his own. As it happened, the President found exactly the opposite potential in modern presidential politics. Loosening up the old identities, he turned the whole problem of identity over to his handlers and got himself lost in their strategies.

Once lost, authority for political leadership is difficult to recover. Ultimately, Bush made the pursuit of power its own justification; on this alone, could he boast credibility in 1992. Looking forward to the campaign, he declared simply: "I am prepared to do what I have to do to be reelected."[93] The mark of his mettle and his commitment to the job was his determination to win. Even when trying to assess what went wrong in the 1992 election, the principals got it backwards: the Bush campaign "never had a message," complained Vice President Dan Quayle, because "that takes a strategy."[94]

The Prospects for Perpetual Preemption

It is tempting to inveigh against the evolution of American government and politics. Certainly, the current state of affairs leaves much to be desired. But in our frustration, we run the risk of targeting the wrong problem and embracing unreflected alternatives. We are witness to the waning of political time, to the practical disintegration of the medium through which presidents have claimed authority for the exercise of their powers since the beginning of our constitutional history. The choices at hand are imposing, but the prospects are not necessarily bleak.

The old tropes die hard. Even at this late date, it is difficult for presidents to resist recycling the traditional claims of authority. These claims resonate with authenticity; they are familiar, and in the modern world, that alone is comforting. By continuing to indulge them, however, our presidents have misled us; they have concealed what the changing conditions of power and responsibility demand. As a result, the standards of appropriate action are more confused now than ever before.

Rather than rail against modernity, we must insist that the presidency come of age. A candid reading of the history of the presidents—one that is shorn of nostalgia for "great" leaders or the lost arts of "true" statesmanship—suggests that it is time to let go of the old standards. As the traditional leadership postures have deteriorated into mere roles to be performed, their recent exponents have demonstrated nothing so much as their perversity. If we would but reckon with their irrelevance, we might discover that the waning of political time has opened more possibilities for our leaders than it has foreclosed.

There are of course many paths to the future, some less hopeful than others. Two in particular strike me as especially troublesome. One, of course, would be to indulge the old claims further, to wait for a president to recall the themes of past greatness and take these as the marks of a truly great leader. It seems to me that doing so at this point merely invites some great repudiator to fill the empty truisms of the classic reconstructive stance with a substance that seriously undermines the checks on power that the Constitution still affords. Another path might be to insist that presidents adopt techniques proven elsewhere and strike a more businesslike pose. But appeals to technique have never delivered on their promise in presidential leadership; they do not support the relentlessly disruptive, and thoroughly politicized, force of this institution. The idea of the president-as-business-manager flies in the face of everything we know about the exercise of presidential power and much of what we still have to gain from its inherent hostility to order and routine.

Ross Perot's appeal in the early part of the 1992 campaign managed to broach both of these prospects at once, and in that it might be taken as emblematic of current confusions. In his broadside assault on politics-as-usual, Perot offered a businessman's vision of the alternative. His was a model of executive efficiency that had no clear place for the Congress and little apparent use for the separation of powers. More curious still, when he withdrew from the race abruptly in July of 1992, Perot explained that the thing he most feared was that he might prove "disruptive."[95] Here was a man who instigated a wild-fire movement for change, professing that the last thing a leader ought to do was to disrupt things; here was a leader who valued businesslike management above all else and fomented a mass insurgency to attain it.

We need to think more carefully about how we want to tap the power of the presidency as an engine of political change, about how its inherently disruptive force might best serve democratic politics in contemporary America. The stakes are such that any guide to the possibilities at hand should draw on the whole of our experience. As we have traced the politics of leadership over the course of American history, we have seen how two of the four variables that have traditionally oriented a president's place in history have gotten crowded out by secular developments in American government and politics. The vulnerability of established governing commitments has been limited by the proliferation of interests and authorities throughout the government as well as by the organizational resilience of the institutions that defend them. This itself argues for finally discarding the idealized reconstructive catharsis as a premise for leadership. At the same time, affiliation with received formulas has been undermined by the increasing independence of the office in politics and government. The accumulation of governing responsibilities in the executive and the detachment of its political foundations from those of other actors and institutions argue strongly for discarding this premise also and with it the self-defeating strictures of the leadership posture of the faithful son. If presidents will now assert independence of received formulas more equally and fashion their own coalitions accordingly, the gain should more than compensate for the loss.

There are historical precedents for this emergent state of affairs, and their attraction, I admit, is not self-evident. What is sketched here hints at a secular convergence toward opposition leadership in a resilient regime. The typology of political authority structures outlined in Chapter 2 designates this a "politics of preemption," and the presidents who have illuminated this category in the past certainly give reason to pause. These are the wild cards of presidential history, and the range of their experiences has been especially broad. It encompasses administrations as diverse as Dwight Eisenhower's and Richard Nixon's, Andrew Johnson's and Woodrow Wilson's. If these are guides to the future, the prospects are anything but routine.

Of all the types of politics that presidents make, the politics of preemption is the least susceptible to role ascription. Its hallmarks have been the cultivation of independent political identities, the exploitation of ad hoc coalitions, and the high risk of suffering the ultimate disgrace of impeachment. We need to become better attuned to how this kind of politics has played out intermittently in the past, but more than that, we need to consider how it might play differently as a perpetual state of affairs. How might presidents learn to act when the opportunities for fashioning legitimacy anew no longer swing so radically from one to the next? A case should be made for this emergent situation, lest we simply overlook the potential.

A state of perpetual preemption offers reasonable prospects for presidents to get things done and shake things up, but little hope for disarming potential critics. There are strong incentives for each president to build his or her own political support for the exercise of power, but in all likelihood the resort to clandestine tactics will be met with exposure and disgrace. A state of perpetual preemption ultimately favors pragmatism, that is, a vigorous assertion of freedom from established dogmas. With presidents more consistently independent of received formulas, the pragmatic stance can become a less episodic feature of our national leadership. Moreover, a state of perpetual preemption ultimately favors deliberation. The experimentation that goes along with the pragmatic stance will have to become more collective, for no president will be able to tramp roughshod over the authority and independence of everyone else. Over the course of American history, political reconstructions have already become less and less a creature of presidential will, and presidents acting within these emergent parameters should become even more wary of the prospects for imposing their designs wholesale. But as the waning of political time prompts candid recognition that change can no longer be imposed holistically from the top down, it should also prompt recognition that American government and politics must be continually reconstructed and that fashioning a reputable place in history now entails finding solutions to problems collectively.

A sober reading of this emergent state of affairs calls for vigilance and determination in the prosecution of wrongdoing and irresponsibility. The threat of impeachment figures prominently in the politics of preemption, and it has also figured more prominently in our recent experience. It needs to be rethought in that light as a vital, and more accessible, tool of constitutional government. The hope, however, is that the exhaustion of the old premises does not signal the exhaustion of all legitimate premises; that we may yet see a "personal president" and a "post-modern" presidency. If we do, it will be unmistakably different from recent experience, for the presidents of the modern period have yet to tap the potential for something new.

Modern presidents have more freedom than ever to resist the traditional roles. Notwithstanding recent caricatures, leadership chances have actually become less determined from one administration to the next, and each president now has a more equal opportunity to exercise the powers of the office in his own right. Once shorn of the roles ascribed to them in political time, leaders will in fact have little else to rely upon but reason, talent, ideas, and character. The politics they make will have to adjust to a world in which warrants for change can no longer simply be assumed and terms for the exercise of power are no longer simply given. This is the untapped promise of modern American government: not some dismal politics-as-usual, but a politics that is less familiar and more open-ended. Success may not be any more frequent in this imaginable future, but failure will be less ordained. More importantly, success when it comes, will come as it should, to presidents who make the case for change on the merits of their proposals, garner popular support, and keep their hands clean.

Our recent leaders have confused hard-hitting leadership with more strident appeals to outmoded political standards. A constructive escape from the patterns of the past, one that credits the incumbent's sense of responsibility and enhances democratic politics, will not be automatic. The accelerating breakdown of the old identities and the tendency of contemporary politics toward full disclosure may have hollowed out the old leadership projects, but what is sketched here as a possible escape is no more than an intimation, and no more likely than some far less attractive alternatives. If we are to realize it, our leaders will have to formulate new warrants for the exercise of presidential power, and we will have to reject those who merely recycle the old ones. Reagan and Bush have shown us not only that the old premises lead nowhere but also that a more open-ended politics cannot emerge so long as presidents are rewarded with office for invoking the same standards of legitimacy that have been with us since the beginning. Their failures were failures of political imagination, an inability to see past the possibilities of the great repudiator and the faithful son.

Bill Clinton is neither, and he faces no more difficult or important a task than projecting a credible alternative. It must be said that as the first Democrat to take office in the post-Reagan era, Clinton comes to the politics of preemption as a matter of course. Indeed, after Reagan's Roosevelt and Bush's Truman, it is a wonder that his promise of a "New Democratic party" was not identified more closely with the moderating themes of Eisenhower's "New Republicanism." If that indicates recognition that Clinton is no Eisenhower, or that none of the old models are appropriate to the task at hand, we can all be grateful. In his early months in office, Clinton has shown an inclination to exploit the collapsing distinctions among the old roles: he is an opposition leader forthrightly committed to a change of course; he is a Washington booster who seeks a concert of action with party and Congress and substitutes the hands-on orchestration of established interests for frontal assaults and confrontations; he is a technocrat who professes strict adherence to the stern discipline of the numbers and little interest in who is to blame for current maladies.[96] Whether Clinton will fashion all this into a presidency that supersedes the old standards or merely flounder in the muddle is the question of the hour, but it is only one of the questions that needs to be posed. Another, more important one is whether we will remember how the old standards work and demand something better.

Afterword: Bill Clinton's Moment in Political Time

W HAT ARE we to make of the Clinton presidency? He was
the first Democrat to enter the White House in sixteen years,
the first president in twelve years to find his own party in
control of both houses of Congress. "Change" was the mantra of his
rise to power. As it turned out, however, the most significant change to
occur during Clinton's first term was the one his leadership was most
obviously meant to avoid. A stunning Republican sweep in the 1994
elections broke the Democrats' long hold on congressional power. It
rekindled the ideological fervor of the Reagan Revolution and reduced
a humiliated president to public protests that he had not been rendered
completely irrelevant to the future course of American politics.[1] Few
imagined at that time that Clinton would emerge from this crushing
indictment more secure in his message and more attractive in his appeal
than he had ever been when his own party controlled the Congress.
And now, as commentators hail Clinton as the first Democrat since
Franklin Roosevelt to be elected to a second term, the question of what
his bizarre incumbency says about the American presidency—or American politics more generally—looms large.

A good part of the answer may be found in the particular kind of
change that Clinton has been after. All presidents talk about change,
but what they have in mind varies widely from one to the next. When
Ronald Reagan spoke about change, he stood in open condemnation
of a governing regime in collapse. Linking the prevailing liberal establishment with a then-pervasive sense of impending national ruin, he
demanded a categorical break with liberalism's guiding assumptions
and promised to restore legitimacy to government through a thoroughgoing reconstruction of its basic commitments of ideology and interest.
George Bush took a very different view of the matter. As an affiliate of
Reagan's, he did not propose to break with his inheritance, but to

"build on a proud record that ha[d] already been established." When the Democratic challenger of 1988, Michael Dukakis, called for change, the Bush campaign countered: "We *are* the change," meaning that the Reagan Revolution was an ongoing political project, that Dukakis's "change" would be a retreat back to a discredited past, and that the task at hand was to complete a transformation already in progress. Bill Clinton came to power with something else in mind again. He was not, like Reagan, the great repudiator of a governing regime in collapse; nor was he, like Bush, the faithful son of an unfinished revolution. A Democrat seeking the presidency in the post-Reagan era, he spoke of change as finding a "third way."

To talk about a third way in 1992 was to acknowledge the Democrats' three consecutive losses to liberal-bashing Republicans and to attempt to adjust the Democratic alternative to the new political realities that had been created by the Reagan Revolution. The objective was to dispel the aura of illegitimacy that had surrounded the Democratic party's posture in national politics since the Carter years, to redefine the choices at hand so that Republicans no longer offered the only response to discredited liberalism. As leader of the Democratic opposition, Clinton did not hesitate to peg the nation's problems on twelve years of Republican rule or to commit himself to a "new course" that would "put people first." But the not-so-subtle subtext of Clinton's opposition stance was his independence from received Democratic identities. By rejecting the "liberal" label outright, by turning a cold shoulder to familiar icons on the left, and by proclaiming himself the leader of a "New" Democratic party, Clinton actively tried to dissociate himself from the standard which Reagan had so effectively driven from the field and to take the discussion of alternatives beyond what he called the "stale, failed, rhetoric of the past."

Bringing to power different kinds of political projects, presidents set up different sorts of political contests. Each project contains a distinctive claim to leadership authority, one with its own characteristic capacities and vulnerabilities. Note first how winning the White House as a post-Reagan Democrat has redounded to Clinton's advantage in charting his own course. He has been far freer to maneuver around and between received political commitments than either Bush or Carter were. Where orthodox innovators and late-regime affiliates are constantly being called to account for their doctrinal purity by partisans within their own ranks, Clinton's ranks have been relatively quiescent in holding him to any standard of consistency with established party priorities.[2] At the same time, Clinton's leadership has had none of the clarity we find in great repudiators like Reagan. He has attempted in several ways to assert a more positive role for the federal government in the economy and the society, but lacking the authority to challenge fundamentally the terms in which legitimate national government has come to be understood in the post-Reagan era, he has made little progress in redefining them. His leadership has been preemptive rather than reconstructive. While suggestive of a new middle ground, his third way has, as a practical matter, been located on a field largely defined by his opponents, and this has infused his opposition stance with an indeterminate, seemingly ad hoc character.

The distinctive thing about preemptive leaders is that they are not out to establish, uphold, or salvage any political orthodoxy. Theirs is an unabashedly mongrel politics; it is an aggressive critique of the prevailing political categories. These leaders bid openly for a hybrid alternative. Their leadership stance provides them with considerable license to draw policy positions and political commitments from different sides of the issues of their day and to promote their recombination in a loosely synthesized mix. Herein lie the characteristic strengths and weaknesses of the stance. Preemptive leaders are well positioned to exploit those schisms within the ranks of the dominant coalition that affiliated leaders are so much at pains to assuage, and by doing so, they can appropriate much of the field of action staked out by those who built the regime they are challenging. But the political contest is joined as their purposeful blurring of the received identity of their own party runs up against their opponent's stake in keeping that older identity intact. The characteristic risk in leadership of this sort is that in trying to chart a third way the president will appear to be wholly lacking in political principles; that in exploiting the indeterminacy of his opposition stance, he will be branded unscrupulous and cynically manipulative.

The third-way appeals of preemptive leaders have been heard throughout American history. Richard Nixon and Woodrow Wilson offer the most striking parallels to Clinton's circumstance. Like Clinton, each first reached the presidency in a three-way race which featured a major schism within the dominant party, and they each won with about 40 percent of the popular vote. Once in office, all three adopted amalgamation strategies designed to reach out to disaffected groups recently affiliated with their opponents. The objective, of course, was to prevent these groups from drifting back to their old allegiances and to secure a real majority for the president by reelection time. The effect was to submerge the matter of their prior political identity into what became essentially an independent political appeal.

Preemptive leadership does not, however, depend on a 40 percent victory.[3] Dwight Eisenhower, the first Republican to come to power after the New Deal reconstruction, remains the most successful of our preemptive leaders to date. His criticisms of the Truman administration, while often harsh, were of far less importance politically than his rejection of the stalwart Republican alternative in foreign policy and his determination to steer a pragmatic course in domestic policy that would recognize the resilience of New Deal innovations. Grover Cleveland, the first Democrat to win the presidency after the Civil War reconstruction, was particularly candid about the preemptive character of his leadership. Determined to woo northern capitalist support to his southern agrarian party, he avowed that "the transfer of executive control from one party to another does not mean any serious disturbance of existing conditions."[4] Zachary Taylor, a military hero of the Mexican War who was elected by the antiwar Whigs, went so far in distancing himself from the received political identity of his party as to brand himself the "No-Party" candidate. The preemptive thrust of third-way leadership can also be found in some of our accidental presidents: John Tyler, the disaffected Democrat who was elected vice president by the Whigs in 1840, and Andrew Johnson, the disaffected Democrat who was elected vice president by the Republicans in 1864. All of these presidents were opposition leaders in the sense that they rode into power with parties opposed to a previously dominant regime. But each was careful to assert his independence from the alternative thought to be harbored by that opposition party and to project some new accommodation with received priorities.

As this grouping suggests, efforts to chart a third way in American politics have been marked not only by extraordinary variety, but also by extreme volatility. Preemptive leaders appear as wild cards in presidential history; they intrude sui generis into our national politics with inconsistent and often explosive effects. One needs to look carefully for patterns emblematic of this type of leadership. They are, however, there to be found, and each helps to illuminate the Clinton presidency as it has unfolded to date.

First, we might simply note the strong association of preemptive leadership with hyphenated party labels that convey the independent, hybrid appeal of the effort. Taylor's "No-Party" brand of Whiggery, Andrew Johnson's "War-Democrats," Cleveland's "liberal-reform" Democracy, Wilson's "progressive Democracy," Eisenhower's "Modern" Republicanism, the "new" Nixon with his "new" or "silent" majority—these along with Clinton's "New" Democrats all exemplify political identities carefully crafted to sidestep preestablished conceptions of the alternatives and to reach out beyond the president's traditional party base to some new and largely inchoate coalition.

It can be observed further that the third-way appeals of preemptive leaders have proven quite effective electorally. Like Clinton, Cleveland, Wilson, Eisenhower, and Nixon, all won two presidential elections. In fact, no opposition leader elected to office in the first instance and surviving his first term has failed to win a second. This record stands in stark contrast to that of affiliated leaders, who often withdraw from reelection bids and seldom win them.[5] The contrast attests to the greater freedom of action among opposition leaders relative to affiliated leaders in crafting their own political positions.

But it can also be observed that the third-way alternatives of preemptive leaders have not proven very durable in American politics. These "neo" parties with their hybrid agendas have held only a loose grip on the terms and conditions of national politics, and their champions have wielded only a temporary influence over its future course. Eisenhower was a personal success; Wilson gave a virtuoso performance; but the alternatives posed by these leaders have not cut deeply enough into the political, institutional, or ideological bedrock of American government to sustain themselves over the long haul. There is, moreover, a disturbing pattern to be found among those who pressed these alternatives most aggressively. Under Tyler, Andrew Johnson, Wilson, and Nixon, the third way degenerated into personal and constitutional tests of wills and culminated in a devastating collapse of presidential authority. The line between independence and isolation in this leadership stance has repeatedly proven a thin one.

The fact that no third way has ever outlasted the president who articulated it presents Clinton with a challenge of historic proportions as he begins his second term. Nothing would more clearly mark this preemption as something extraordinary—or more strongly suggest a special affinity between modern American politics and preemptive appeals—than to find Clinton, in the year 2001, passing power on to a hand-picked successor pledged to continue his course. But before we turn to speculation about the future, we might pursue a bit further the patterns of the past. In considering the special challenges of preemptive leadership, we find that problems that may at some level be thought common to American leaders generally appear among these leaders in a particularly pronounced and emblematic form. At issue in each is the temporal and political structure of preemptive leadership as it thrusts certain sorts of difficulties to the forefront and sustains a political contest around them.

One of these has to do with the policy records which these presidents accumulate. While often quite impressive in retrospect, these records have been riddled in their own time with questions about their authenticity. The reason for this is not difficult to discern. These presidents are challenging their opponent's exclusive claim to the definition of legitimate national government by appropriating much of their opponent's national agenda in a modified form. The preemptive character of the third-way appeal involves a good deal of "playing against type" and poaching on the policy terrain staked out by those the president is challenging. These incursions characteristically provoke battles over issue ownership, over who can speak and act authoritatively on the prevailing issues of the day.

Scholars have long noted Richard Nixon's Disraeli-like dreams of coopting his opponents' agenda, but only recently have they begun to reckon seriously with the liberal legacy of his administration. Liberals in the 1970s were loath to credit his administration's record, and conservatives did not quite know what to make of it. Still, considering Nixon's domestic initiatives and accommodations—in incomes policy, monetary policy, affirmative action, social security, health care, economic management ("I am now a Keynesian"), and environmental regulation—and considering also his overtures to détente in foreign policy, it might not be too much to claim that the Reagan Revolution targeted a set of Nixon-era commitments even more directly that it did Great Society commitments.

Reaction to Nixon's Family Assistance Plan, a proposal that would have transformed the nation's approach to poverty from a policy of providing welfare into a policy of guaranteeing income, suggests something of the difficulties that arise when preemptive leaders "play against type." The plan was pitched to Nixon by Daniel Patrick Moynihan, the resident liberal in his administration, and it reflected the classic third-way combination of critique and accommodation. The administration judged the received welfare system a mess and a failure, but its proposal accepted, and in sweeping ways elaborated upon, the received principle of federal responsibility to provide for the poor. While conservatives like Arthur Burns professed shock and disbelief at the proposed new commitment ("It ran counter to everything I knew about Richard Nixon"), liberals convinced themselves that the proposal could not be the progressive innovation that it seemed to be but must be a covert "attack on the poor."[6] One of the most progressive welfare initiatives ever proposed by an American president succumbed in this way to the disorientation and suspicion aroused by the president's confounding of received political identities.

We know, of course, that few presidents could meet any strict standard of ideological consistency. What stands out here, however, is the brazenness with which preemptive presidents maneuver around the ideological spectrum, zigzagging in their policy commitments and crafting hybrids that confound the standard labels.[7] The relative freedom with which they shift their ground and act on all the different sides of the political divisions of their day is a constant source of provocation to their opponents. The Family Assistance Plan may have nodded to established liberal priorities, but it nested in a host of other commitments—to "law and order," to an end to "forced" busing, to a "New Federalism," to an "honorable" settlement in Vietnam—that made it difficult for those on the receiving end of the administration's policies to fathom the "real" Nixon. In their most clever manifestations (one thinks of the impact of Nixon's affirmative action initiative on the coalition of union labor and African Americans in the Democratic party), third-way initiatives threaten to divide the political base of the previously dominant party by putting its different factions at odds with one another.[8] It is no wonder that the keepers of the faith respond by branding these initiatives wholly instrumental and by charging their initiators with obfuscation. Nor is it surprising that efforts to pin these leaders down tend to drive toward institutional showdowns.

Woodrow Wilson's experience is perhaps most instructive in this regard, for his success in helping to implement a progressive legislative agenda is now regarded as one of the great programmatic feats of presidential leadership. Even in this instance, however, we find that questions about the reliability of the president's commitments and the authenticity of his achievements form the strongest and most persistent line in criticisms of his leadership. The 1912 election campaign itself echoed with charges calling into question Wilson's claim to be a progressive leader. The critics pointed to the reactionary character of Wilson's historical writings, to his long-standing opposition to Bryan's leadership of the Democratic party, and to his sudden, belated conversion to the progressive cause. "It must not be forgotten," warned one California progressive, "that Mr. Wilson offers his presidential nomination without apology for the past."[9]

Leading progressive commentators reacted with similar skepticism to Wilson's early years in power. The New Freedom legislation, a stunning achievement to be sure, appeared a bastard to these keepers of the faith. *The New Republic,* which would grudgingly endorse Wilson in 1916, questioned the integrity of any accomplishment worked exclusively through the Democratic party caucus in Congress and elaborated upon the implications of Wilson's decision to have progressive policies sifted through the reactionary elements contained in that body. In Herbert Croly's summary judgment, Wilson's progressive hybrid was "either too vague and equivocal to inspire sufficient energy of conviction, . . . or a progressivism with its eyes fastened more on the past than on the future."[10] Wilson, it was charged, had repeatedly sacrificed progressive principles "on the altar of Democratic resurrection" and contaminated progressivism by mixing it with antithetical ideals more truly representative of his party's real character.[11] These observers granted that Wilson had proven himself a masterful politician, but warned that his progressivism would prove "short-lived and insincere" and that his leadership would turn out to be a smokescreen masking the resurgence of a political organization whose hostility to the values of all true reformers was visceral.[12]

Such concerns spread as Wilson's presidency unfolded. *Collier's Weekly* charged that "the first frame in which [Wilson] sets an idea for inspection is inevitably a conservative one. His progressivism consists in that, when the old-time remedy fails, he will sometimes dare the new."[13] *The Nation,* though initially quite taken with Wilson's conservative brand of progressivism, became increasingly disillusioned by what it saw as his readiness to capitulate to the most expedient course.[14] As time went on, and Wilson's propensity to zig-zag became more pronounced, Progressives and Republicans stopped trying to make any ideological sense of his course at all, and simply charged him with crass opportunism. Recognizing that he had, by 1916, completely stolen the Progressives' thunder and brilliantly preempted the Republicans' challenge, *The Outlook* derided Wilson as "too flexible," too willing to be "on both sides of an issue," too quick to court public opinion, too devoted to "playing it safe."[15] By late 1917, Wilson's reputation as a political gadfly was so firmly fixed as to appear a source of humor among his own supporters: "It is quite important," one Massachusetts admirer admitted, "when quoting an opinion of President Wilson's to state the date."[16]

All told, the third-way programs of preemptive leaders are apt to be portrayed as so many clever tricks played upon a public not fully attuned to the difference between a subterfuge and the real thing. Clinton's first term has proven classic in this regard. Liberals have worried incessantly about their president's willingness to capitulate to Republican priorities on issue after issue. At times, the president seems even to have surprised himself by the out-of-character thrust of his course. In promulgating his 1993 budget, for instance, he reportedly lamented to his staff "I hope you're all aware we're all Eisenhower Republicans."[17] In his public posture, however, Clinton has not been shy to take President Reagan's objective as his own achievement—"The era of big government is over"—or to trumpet his preemption of Reagan's message with his third way—"Today we can declare: Government is not the problem, and government is not the solution."[18] Whatever Clinton's true leanings, the overriding feature of his first term is that its major policy accomplishments—the deficit-reducing budget of 1993, GATT, NAFTA, the crime bill, and the welfare overhaul—all "played against type," that is, contrary to the positions presumed to be held by liberalism's traditional constituents.

Republicans, meanwhile, have been at their wits' end to deny the authenticity of Clinton's commitments to what they consider the mainstays of their own agenda. The debate over the crime bill of 1994 was a particularly clear case in point. Clinton, determined to erase any doubt that a Democrat could be tough on crime, endorsed provisions for the death penalty, for stiffer court sentencing ("three strikes and you're out"), and for putting 100,000 new police officers on the street. Republicans, however, pointed to other provisions of the bill to insist that the president's initiative was not the hard-nosed assault on urban ills that it pretended to be, but was in reality a covert liberal conspiracy, a weak-kneed "hug-a-thug" program wrapped in an empty, cynical display of new police uniforms. This challenge to the integrity and reliability of Clinton's policy commitments was later taken up in Bob Dole's election campaign, where the president was repeatedly charged with offering a "wink-and-nod conservatism" and with carrying out a "rearguard action" aimed at bringing in "through the back door" discredited liberal solutions to the nation's problems.

Republicans have good reason to question Clinton's motives. Just as liberals in the early 1970s found Nixon's hybrid unsettling to the Democrat's national coalition, Republicans today understand the danger which Clinton's success at "triangulation" poses to their future political prospects. Preemptive leaders never propose to do exactly what their opponents would do, and their hybrid initiatives become all the more potent politically when they push those opponents to articulate purer (and more radically divisive) expressions of their ideas. Clinton's claim that his approach to crime was "tough but smart" captured perfectly the preemptive tactic of indicting the party whose issue is being stolen. His victory on the crime bill not only made good his claim to speak with authority as a leader in the fight against crime, but also succeeded in identifying his opponents more closely with a controversial gun lobby. Presidents so adept at taking over the message of their opponents leave those opponents little choice but to go after the messenger.

A second, more difficult, problem repeatedly encountered in efforts to chart a third way has to do with "signature issues." With so much of their political project aimed at accommodating their party to prevailing norms and at exploiting ambiguities in their own opposition to those norms, preemptive presidents have been prone to put down a marker that will serve to establish the distinctiveness of their course and in Grover Cleveland's oft-quoted words, "Make the party stand for something." The fate of the third way as a political alternative tends, in this way, to turn on the outcome of one particularly bold policy initiative—Tyler and Texas, Taylor and immediate statehood for the southwestern acquisition, Cleveland and the tariff, Wilson and the League of Nations, Clinton and health care. In each case the president stepped forward with one clearly transformative policy commitment, a commitment that conveyed a clear difference between his third way and the received line of public policy. Instantly, all concerned understood the high stakes riding on the resolution of this one issue.

One reason third-way alternatives in American politics have lacked durability is that the initiatives on which much of the distinctiveness of these alternatives came to rest were all derailed. Instead of isolating the opponents of these presidents, the signature issues have tended instead to isolate the presidents themselves. This pattern of failure in preemptive leadership is suggestive of the underlying resilience of the older political categories and associations which these presidents were at such pains to submerge in their initial rise to power. The fact is that preemptive leaders do best when they play at the margins of change where the political implications of their core commitments can remain ambiguous. An initiative which bids for a clear definition of the third way offers an occasion to air the whole problem of definition which lies at the heart of this leadership project. In seeking to redress the central weakness in their leadership stance, these presidents tend instead to draw themselves out where they are most vulnerable.

With his novel approach to post-war internationalism, Wilson took his stand for something truly original, but he was, in the end, unable to rally any solid base of political support for it. With Texas annexation, Tyler pressed an explosive issue which the established parties had previously conspired to finesse and submerge. But no sooner did he advance it than he found one of the old parties (the Democrats) making assurances that it would finally take the issue as its own, so long as the man who had articulated it was discarded and his threat to their party coalition defused. Cleveland is perhaps the most interesting case in point for he, like Clinton, chose for his signature initiative an issue that had long been on his party's political agenda. Alert to the fact that his early years in power had given core Democratic constituents little to rally around, Cleveland acted to reignite his party's fervor for his administration by devoting his entire annual message in 1887 to the old Jackson standard of tariff reduction. But tariff reform in the 1880s, like health care in the 1990s, was a party orthodoxy carefully repackaged for the new times. Cleveland's message was a brilliant synthesis which cast old reform sentiments around new political realities. He presented tariff reform as an issue whose time had finally come. It was now a practical matter essential to business expansion in a new age of capital shortages and government surpluses; it was now a consumer issue from which all would gain. Determined to give his party its long-sought-after reform, Cleveland was, at the same time, anxious to preempt the arguments of its critics. Defusing the ideological connotations of reform and refocusing the matter on the economic problems of the day, the message culminated in the now-famous admonition: "Our progress toward a wise conclusion [of the tariff issue] will not be improved by dwelling upon the theories of protection and free trade. This savors too much of bandying epithets. It is a *condition* which confronts us, not a theory."[19]

Clinton was equally determined to present his party's long-standing commitment to health care as a practical idea whose time had come and to submerge its traditional ideological connotations in a practical response to current conditions. Unfortunately, his effort to detach the initiative from the big-government, tax-and-spend, formulas of the discredited past drove him to embrace a program of mystifying complexity, and his bid to present the goal of universal coverage as a strategy for reaching other goals of cost control and budget balancing never rang true.[20] The problem for Clinton and for Cleveland was that they were so clearly trying to have it both ways, to nod to traditional coalition partners while at the same time embracing newly established governing priorities. This ambiguity was all their opponents needed to make short work of the bid for a clear and compelling definition of their third way. Dismissing the subtleties of design and presentation, the Republican opponents of Clinton and Cleveland grasped the signature issue as proof positive of the unregenerate character of the president's politics. The signature initiative became an occasion for stripping away the veneer of "newness" around the president's party and for identifying him as an all-too-clever representative of the same old thing.

All of this points to one final difficulty repeatedly encountered by preemptive leaders. We have noted the highly individualized quality of these leadership efforts, but what remains to be appreciated is the radically personalized nature of the political contests they provoke. Preemptive leaders set up a political struggle in which their own personal code of conduct takes center stage. While other presidents might be labeled weak, directionless, or even incompetent, these presidents are often judged moral degenerates, congenitally incapable of rising above nihilism and manipulation. Their very skill at preemption is seen to reveal a fundamental and dangerous character flaw.

Nixon's reputation among his critics as "Tricky Dick" is perhaps too well known to deserve much elaboration. Less likely to be remembered is Wilson's reputation as "our reversible president": "He changes—he moves—he shows another side—or turns completely about."[21] At issue in such characterizations were the president's stunning shifts on major issues of public policy, issues that would ultimately come to include party reform, civil service reform, trust regulation, the tariff commission, Panama Canal tolls, preparedness legislation, "special legislation" for farmers and workers, and, most famously, peace and war. Concerns about Wilson's instrumentalism, his apparent willingness to take whatever position seemed most expedient, deepened after 1914 as the president stiffened his determination to find his own way through the Democratic, Republican, and Progressive divisions of his day. His cooptive changeability came to be ascribed to a "vacillating," "uncertain," and "infirm" character.[22] He was labeled "politically unstable" and "mentally inconsistent."[23] By 1915 Theodore Roosevelt, the nominal leader of the Progressives, and Henry Cabot Lodge, the stalwart Senate Republican, were so concerned about Wilson's success in preempting their alternative appeals that they opened a backstairs campaign aimed at undermining the president's authority through character assassination. Roosevelt described a weak and self-serving man. He mercilessly derided Wilson's "adroit, unscrupulous cunning, his pandering to those who love ease . . . his readiness to about-face, his timidity about any manly assertion of our rights, his lack of all conviction and willingness to follow every gust of opinion." His "soul," Roosevelt charged, was "rotten through and through"; he hadn't "a thought for the welfare of the country; or for our honor; or for anything except his own mean personal advancement."[24] Lodge echoed these diatribes, charging that Wilson was "shifty," "furtive," and "sinister," a man whose "passionate absorption in himself and his own interests and ambitions" overshadow all other considerations. As Lodge makes clear in his memoirs, Wilson went into the fight over the League of Nations with this reputation for willful deceit, unbridled self-promotion, and false idealism already firmly fixed among his opponents.[25]

Similarly, to sustain their charge that Clinton's "New" Democratic party is really a ploy masking a rearguard defense of liberalism's "leftist, egalitarian, redistributionist impulses,"[26] the political Right has had to press the central issue of the Clinton presidency far beyond ideology. There has to be some explanation for Clinton's repeated forays onto conservative ground, some accounting for how a man could use the presidency to deny his party's true leanings and pose as something else. The "character issue" has been seized upon in this context, a political context in which the received definitions of liberal and conservative, of Democrat and Republican, of Left, Right, and Center have all been placed in contention by the president's third-way appeal. The details of

Clinton's personal life are presented as evidence of the contention that the man has no standards at all, that he is wholly lacking in principles. Showing us an executive who has never cared much about the truth, who has proven incapable of standing by any commitment, and who has no higher purpose than his own self-indulgence becomes, in this context, a way of preserving the particular version of the truth which these keepers of the faith wish to promote: the one in which the Democrats remain a desperate party of discredited ideas and debased leadership, while the Republicans remain the only legitimate exponents of national solutions.

As preemptive leadership seems to encourage opponents to engage in character assassination, we might expect that nothing would be more valuable to a president engaged in it than an unimpeachable character. In fact, it has proven especially helpful for an American president pursuing a third way to have some independent claim to national authority, one that lies wholly outside the rough and tumble of the political struggle in which he in engaged. Eisenhower is the leading modern case in point. Bringing to office a national reputation that lodged his trustworthiness on ground quite independent of his hybrid politics, he all but shut down any questions that might have been raised about his standards or principles. The recent enthusiasm for General Colin Powell also suggests the greater resonance of a third-way appeal in a figure who appears to stand above or outside of politics. A general who had difficulty deciding which party he belonged to but who came up with policy stands that sounded remarkably Clintonesque, Powell seemed for a time to have it all: Clinton's politics with personal integrity. Another example of military reputation undergirding preemptive leadership with a nonpolitical appeal may be found in the nineteenth century in the "No-Party" politics of General Zachary Taylor.

Grover Cleveland is again a particularly interesting case, for he, like Clinton, constantly battled charges of personal immorality, from his fathering of an illegitimate child, to Tammany-inspired rumors about perverse sex romps through the woods around Buffalo, to press speculation about his belated White House marriage to a much younger woman, to the widespread belief that he was infected with syphilis. Cleveland's genius was to counter these charges of personal immorality by making the issue of his day the immorality of the federal government and by billing himself as the only man with the courage, honor, and independence to cleanse government of *its* corruptions. As his enemies,

Republican and Democrat, sought to deny him the authority to make any moral claim whatever, they steeled him to undertake exactly what they most feared: moralistic governmental reform. "Our stock in trade," Cleveland confided to his secretary of state, "is absolute cleanliness."[27]

Cleveland's insistence on moral reform has much to tell us about Clinton's early years in power. His example of countering personal liabilities with a prominent commitment to clean up the government underscores the importance of a decision which Clinton made at the very outset of his first term to let his own commitment to campaign reform take a back seat to more immediate prospects of forging a cooperative legislative partnership with fellow Democrats in Congress.[28] Clinton's rationale for this choice was straightforward: the Democrats held majorities in both houses of Congress, the Clinton campaign had made much of the potential of united party government to break what was then perceived to be the "gridlock" of divided government, and the last Democrat in the White House, Jimmy Carter, was widely perceived to have squandered his opportunity for leadership by antagonizing his party leaders in Congress. Interestingly, Clinton was not the first preemptive leader to make this very choice. Woodrow Wilson did precisely the same thing in 1913. He abruptly dropped his commitment to civil service reform in order to seize the opportunity to lead the Democratic party in Congress. The problem was that Clinton shelved the Cleveland strategy of government reform without gaining the critical advantage that Wilson had enjoyed in pursuing the alternative. Wilson entered into a partnership with a congressional party only recently in power, one that was desperate for presidential patronage and receptive to the prospect that presidential leadership might expand the party's national base and make its newfound prominence more secure.[29] Clinton entered into a partnership with a congressional party that was forty years in power, one that had grown comfortable with its institutional majority and relatively indifferent to the political calculations of presidents.

It would appear, then, that during his first two years in office, all of the contingencies that might affect the outcome of a third-way appeal in American politics were running against Bill Clinton: He did not have a congressional majority he could oppose (the Cleveland model); he did not have a congressional majority he could lead to greater security (the Wilson model); and he did not have any independent claim upon which he could rest his authority as a national leader (the Eisenhower model). Identifying these contingencies and their bearing on the distinctive strengths and weaknesses of preemptive leadership goes far toward unraveling the great curiosity of the Clinton presidency, for it now appears that the massive repudiation of the president's party at mid-term was the best thing to happen to Clinton during his first two years in office. To make sense of this, we need only recall that preemptive leaders instinctively strive for political independence and that nothing thwarts independence in the American presidency like responsibility for a congressional party that has grown comfortable in its own power. So long as Clinton was saddled with a Democratic Congress, he ran a high risk of appearing as Carter redux. With a revived Republican Revolution at his heels, however, he was fully liberated to exploit the moderating, mongrel appeal of classic preemptive leadership.

But let us not lose sight of the larger point. Just as the charges of incompetence leveled against Jimmy Carter have figured prominently in the experiences of all late-regime affiliates and the charges of betrayal leveled against George Bush have figured prominently in the experiences of all orthodox innovators, the charge of fatal character flaws leveled against Bill Clinton figures prominently in the experiences of our preemptive leaders. Clinton as "Slick Willie," Nixon as "Tricky Dick," Wilson as "a sham," Cleveland as a "libertine" and "moral leper," Andrew Johnson and John Tyler as "mongrels"—all these characterizations taken together suggest that worries about the authenticity of commitments and the trustworthiness of character are engrained in a politics of preemption. Such concerns are readily provoked by the unabashed efforts of preemptive leaders to establish a political hybrid, and exploiting them has proven the political response favored by those seeking to discredit these efforts.

This observation is not meant to suggest that these charges and characterizations are fabricated out of whole cloth for purely political purposes or that they have no foundation beyond the politics of the moment. It might just as well be said that slick and tricky men rise to power when the nation most wants them, when it is fed up with ideologies of all kinds and casting about for someone who is fast and loose enough in his commitments to generate the mixture it is yearning for. It was ventured in 1992, and resoundingly confirmed in 1996, that people knew all about Clinton's character and voted for him anyway.

If the attraction of a leader like Ronald Reagan is that, politically speaking, he seems to represent the genuine article, the attraction of leaders like Wilson, Eisenhower, Nixon, and Clinton, is that, politically speaking, they do not. Their appeal lies in the promise of muting differences, bridging principles, and combining doctrines.

Several different scenarios are currently in play for Clinton's second term, but one, it seems safe to say, is not. Though Clinton is the first Democrat since Franklin Roosevelt to win a second term, he finds himself today in command of a very different moment in political time. With the clear example of preemptive leadership presented in his first term and the rather unambitious agenda for the second outlined in his reelection campaign, it is apparent that we are not on the road to a major political reconstruction. Clinton's leadership, like that of all other preemptive leaders before him, seems likely to continue its highly individualized course, and the political contests it engenders are likely to continue to highlight the intensely personalized nature of the effort. Indeed, the political question of the moment seems to be whether Clinton's presidency will end peacefully as Eisenhower's did or convulsively as Wilson's and Nixon's did.

In this regard, two scenarios seem especially worthy of comment for their bearing on the larger themes explored in the chapters of this book. One is that Cinton will, in the end, trump the record of prior preemptive leaders: that he will not only end his term with his authority intact but that he will also pass power onto a designated successor who is committed to the pursuit of a third way. Though no third way to date has outlasted the president who articulated it, one does not have to stretch to credit this as a possibility in the current instance. Clinton has been extraordinarily adept at exploiting the technological capacities of the modern presidency to synchronize his message with the complex movements of public opinion and keep his political identity plastic. The heir apparent is already in view and well positioned to step into that role. And the failure of the Republicans to capitalize on the virtual collapse of Clinton's authority in the middle of his first term is suggestive of the difficulties they will continue to face in challenging his third way during the second. We may look back on Clinton's second term to say that he played the classic sequence of preemptive leadership in reverse and that, having survived the stunning collapse of his authority midway through his first term, he was in a stronger position than others of his type to meet the challenges of his second. The historical significance of such an outcome would be to indicate a further erosion of the regime structure that has marked American political development since the time of Jefferson. It would confirm the emerging prominence of preemptive leadership as a hallmark of the evolution of the modern presidency, a form particulary resonant with governing in the contemporary era.

But one cannot, at the present moment, dismiss the possibility of a very different result, one that recalls the historic connection between preemptive leadership and constitutional crises that strip the president of all authority. The many investigations now swirling around Clinton suggest at least one important downside for him in the Republican congressional victories of 1994 and 1996. The wellsprings of potential constitutional crises appear particularly full at this writing, and the prospects of Clinton completing the profile of the typical preemptive leader are all too real.[30] Another colossal collapse of Clinton's political authority and the election of a Republican committed to moving the nation down a more orthodox road would confirm a course of regime development even more rigid than the chapters of this book would lead one to expect.

It is, of course, possible, even likely, that we will look back on Clinton's leadership to see both a typical moment in a familiar political sequence and another indicator of long-term secular trends. All the more reason, then, to ponder the contextual and historical resonance of current concerns about Clinton's ability to weather his second term. This administration has offered nothing to ease concerns about preemptive politics' most worrisome tendencies. Whatever the endgame, it seems likely that the classic problems inherent in this type of leadership will be a staple of American politics long into the future.

January 1997

Notes · Index

Notes

1. Rethinking Presidential History

1. The history of the presidents is a venerable but long abandoned genre of scholarship. Recently there have been calls to revive it, but what has been produced thus far are largely compendia for general reference. Sidney Milkis and Michael Nelson have paved the way with *The American Presidency: Origins and Development, 1776–1990* (Washington, D.C.: Congressional Quarterly Press, 1990). This able work is all the more significant because, as its authors point out, it is "the first comprehensive one volume history of the presidency to be written by political scientists in more than fifty years. Not since Wilfred Binkley first published *The Powers of the President: Problems of American Democracy* has a similar effort been undertaken" (p. xi). The historian William Goldsmith begins his multivolume compendium on a similar note: "I discovered in the rich literature . . . that there was no satisfactory book or set of books which presented the growth of presidential power in its historical context." *The Growth of Presidential Power: A Documented History,* 3 vols. (New York: Chelsea House, 1983). Rexford Tugwell's *The Enlargement of the Presidency* (Garden City, N.Y.: Doubleday, 1960) is the last exception to Goldsmith's rule. Partial histories and period treatments abound, as we shall see. One with a strong analytic bent that promises through later volumes to take in the whole of presidential history is Aaron Wildavsky and Richard Ellis, *Dilemmas of Presidential Leadership: From Washington through Lincoln* (New Brunswick, N.J.: Transaction Books, 1989). Another that includes presidents in a broader historical survey of American leaders is Bruce Miroff, *Icons of Democracy: American Leaders as Heros, Aristrocrats, Dissenters and Democrats* (New York: Basic Books, 1993).

2. To put a fine point on it, "social history" was born in a rejection of the history of the presidents. In his classic critique of "The 'Presidential Synthesis' of American History" Thomas C. Cochran called upon historians to "sweep away the presidential structure" of history so as to attend to the underlying forces of change. *American Historical Review,* 53, no. 4 (July 1948), pp. 748–759.

3. Arguably, no institution has suffered more as a subject for inquiry by being pressed into such a frame. The appearance of these categories for institutional analysis did more than relegate the history of the presidents to the dustbins of outmoded scholarship; it also turned the presidency into a backwater of

theoretically informed research in political science. Political scientists have found it more difficult than historians simply to turn their attentions elsewhere, but about the time of the behavioral revolution, the study of the presidency became notorious in professional circles as an analytic swampland. Congress, far more amenable to the prevailing assumptions of institutional analysis, was the institution of scholarly choice. "The eminence of the institution," wrote Aaron Wildavsky of the presidency, "is matched only by the extraordinary neglect shown to it by political scientists." *Perspectives on the Presidency* (Boston: Little, Brown, 1969), p. ix. John Manley wrote that the literature "reflects the worst of all possible worlds: it is neither empirically rich nor revealing of how the Presidency affects who gets what, when and how in the United States." "The Presidency, Congress and National Policy Making," in *Political Science Annual,* Vol. 5, ed. Cornelius Cotter (Indianapolis: Bobbs Merrill, 1974). For similar sentiments see Hugh Heclo, *Studying the Presidency* (New York: Ford Foundation, 1977); George C. Edwards III and Stephen J. Wayne, *Studying the Presidency* (Nashville: University of Tennessee Press, 1983); George C. Edwards III, "Studying the Presidency," in *The Presidency and the Political System,* ed. Michael Nelson (Washington, D.C.: Congressional Quarterly Press, 1988), pp. 29–45.

4. In his masterwork, *Leadership* (New York: Harper and Row, 1978), James MacGregor Burns also places conflict and change at the center of study. See esp. pp. 36–41. This work is seminal and it provoked much of what is presented here. Still, Burn's distinction between "transactional" and "transformative" leadership (p. 4) is addressed to the study of leadership generally, and despite its considerable range, I found the distinction difficult to sustain in the study of American presidents. I have opted for a more specifically institutional/structural approach. In this book the presidency is treated as a singularly persistent force driving the transformation of American politics, its impact varying with the political and institutional context.

5. Richard Neustadt, *Presidential Power: The Politics of Leadership* (New York: Wiley, 1960); also Richard Neustadt, "The President at Mid-Century," *Law and Contemporary Problems,* 21, no. 4 (Autumn 1956), pp. 608–645. In this early article, Neustadt is especially clear in describing how periodization helped him delimit his analytic ground. "This is an effort to look at the Presidency *operationally,* in working terms, as an instrument of governance in the middle years of the twentieth century; as man-in-office, that is to say, in a time of continuing 'cold war,' spiralling atomic discovery (and vulnerability), stabilized 'big government,' and stalemated partisan alignment . . . This calls for an examination of the President at work within the Presidency in a setting bound on the one hand by the final phases of the last World War and on the other by the unknowns of the next decade" (p. 600).

6. That Eisenhower had a political purpose different from his Democratic predecessors' is the point of departure for Fred I. Greenstein's counterpoint to Neustadt, *The Hidden-Hand Presidency: Eisenhower as Leader* (New York: Basic Books, 1982).

7. Theodore Lowi, *The Personal President: Power Invested, Promise Unfulfilled* (Ithaca: Cornell University Press, 1984).

8. Fred I. Greenstein, "The Need for an Early Appraisal of the Reagan Presidency," in *The Reagan Presidency: An Early Assessment* (Baltimore: Johns Hopkins University Press, 1983), p. 3. A more fully developed statement of the modern presidency perspective can be found in Fred I. Greenstein, "Continuity and Change in the Modern Presidency," in *The New American Political System*, ed. Anthony King (Washington, D.C.: American Enterprise Institute, 1979), pp. 45–86.

9. Ralph Ketcham, *Presidents above Party: The First American Presidency, 1789–1829* (Chapel Hill: University of North Carolina Press, 1984), p. 228.

10. See Samuel Kernell's update of Neustadt's analysis, *Going Public: New Strategies of Presidential Leadership* (Washington, D.C.: Congressional Quarterly Press, 1986). Also Richard Rose, *The Post-Modern President: George Bush Meets the World* (Chatham, N.J.: Chatham House, 1988).

11. The more elaborate statement of this perspective on institutional analysis, from which I have drawn freely in this prologue, is Karen Orren and Stephen Skowronek, "Beyond the Iconography of Order: Notes for a New Institutionalism," in *The Dynamics of American Politics: Approaches and Interpretations*, ed. Lawrence C. Dodd and Calvin Jillson (Boulder: Westview Press, 1993).

12. In choosing these three familiar orderings, I do not mean to suggest that they exhaust the possibilities or to preempt efforts to distill others. For another effort to sort out the different historical dimensions of presidential politics see Bert A. Rockman, *The Leadership Question: The Presidency and the American System* (New York: Praeger, 1984).

13. These patterns have all been glimpsed discretely through various "syntheses" of American history that have competed for our attention over the years—the "presidential synthesis," the "organizational synthesis," and the "realignment synthesis" respectively. On the presidential synthesis see Cochran, "Presidential Synthesis." On the realignment synthesis see Richard L. McCormick, "The Realignment Synthesis in American History," *Journal of Interdisciplinary History*, 13 (Summer 1982), pp. 85–105. On the organizational synthesis see Brian Balogh, "Reorganizing the Organizational Synthesis: Federal-Professional Relations in Modern America," *Studies in American Political Development*, 5, no. 1 (Spring 1991), pp. 119–172. These are, in a sense, the building blocks of my analysis. I am especially indebted to the work of Walter Dean Burnham on the realignment synthesis and to the work of Louis Galambos on the organizational synthesis. But rather than choosing one pattern and describing the significance of institutional action solely along that dimension, I distinguish the *different* structures engaged by *each* incumbent and attend to the politics in the mix.

14. Compare Carl Sandberg's classic one-volume edition, *Abraham Lincoln* (New York: Harcourt Brace, 1954), with David Donald's pathbreaking article "A. Lincoln: Politician" in David Donald, *Lincoln Reconsidered: Essays on the Civil War Era* (New York: Random House, 1961), pp. 57–81. These contrasting evaluations will be explored further in Chapter 6, Part One.

15. George Mowry, *The Era of Theodore Roosevelt and the Birth of Modern America, 1900–1912* (New York: Harper and Row, 1956); Introduction to

The Letters of Theodore Roosevelt, Vol. 5, ed. Elting Morison (Cambridge: Harvard University Press, 1953), pp. xiii–xiv. These assessments are discussed further in Chapter 6, Part Two.

16. See for example Albert Romasco's review essay, "Hoover-Roosevelt and the Great Depression: A Historiographic Inquiry into a Perennial Comparison" in *The New Deal,* Vol. 1, ed. John Braeman, Robert Bremmer, and David Brody (Columbus: Ohio State University Press, 1975), pp. 3–26. These different aspects of FDR's leadership are explored in Chapter 7, Part One.

17. For a statement of the potential value of integrating electoral alignment perspectives with a study of presidential leadership, see Jerome M. Clubb, William H. Flanagan, and Nancy H. Zingale, *Partisan Realignment. Voters, Parties, and Government in American History* (Beverly Hills: Sage, 1980). The pioneering work in this regard is James Sundquist, *The Dynamics of the Party System: Alignment and Realignment of Political Parties in the United States* (Washington, D.C.: Brookings Institution, 1973). See also Walter Dean Burnham, "The Politics of Repudiation," *The American Prospect,* 12 (Winter 1993), pp. 22–33. For a work that explicitly integrates the organizational and constitutional "layers" of presidential politics, see Jeffrey Tulis, *The Rhetorical Presidency* (Princeton: Princeton University Press, 1987).

18. I draw the term "the reflexivities of time" from Mark Elchardus, "The Rediscovery of Chronos: The New Role of Time in Sociological Theory," *International Sociology,* 3, no. 1, pp. 35–59.

19. Polk to Cave Johnson, December 21, 1844, "Polk-Johnson Letters," ed. St. George Sioussat, *Tennesse Historical Magazine,* 1, no. 3 (September 1915), p. 254. Polk's statement is taken up at length in Chapter 5, Part Two.

20. On the party period generally see Richard L. McCormick, "The Party Period and Public Policy: An Exploratory Hypothesis," *Journal of American History,* 66 (Summer 1979), pp. 279–298. Also see my own description of nineteenth-century American government as a "state of courts and parties" in *Building a New American State: The Expansion of National Administrative Capacities, 1877–1920* (New York: Cambridge University Press, 1982).

21. Richard P. McCormick, *The Second American Party System: Party Formation in the Jackson Era* (Chapel Hill: University of North Carolina Press, 1966); Richard P. McCormick, "Political Development and the Second Party System," in *The American Party Systems: Stages of Development,* ed. William Nisbet Chambers and Walter Dean Burnham (New York: Oxford University Press, 1967).

2. Power and Authority

1. The term "authority" figures prominently in Richard Pious's, *The American Presidency* (New York: Basic Books, 1979). Pious revived the term as a counterpoint to the Neustadtian tradition which had identified power so closely with efforts of incumbents to husband the informal resources of leadership. When Pious reintroduced the notion of authority, it was to reclaim the significance of constitutional formalities in the politics of leadership. This was

an important move, but it is a bit different from what I have in mind. I am trying to get at aspects of authority that are submerged in the formal/informal distinction and cut across it.

2. James G. March and Johan P. Olsen point to perceptions of appropriateness as an emergent standard in a more general reorientation of the study of institutions. *Rediscovering Institutions: The Organizational Basis of Politics* (New York: Free Press, 1989).

3. James W. Ceaser, *Presidential Selection: Theory and Development* (Princeton: Princeton University Press, 1979), pp. 62–87.

4. "Federalist No. 72," in Alexander Hamilton, James Madison, John Jay, *The Federalist Papers,* ed. Clinton Rossiter (New York: Mentor, 1961), p. 437.

5. The most significant effort to describe the politics of leadership thematically as a reflection of character is James David Barber's *The Presidential Character: Predicting Performance in the White House* (Englewood Cliffs: Prentice Hall, 1972). For an important demur along the lines of the argument being set forth here, see Jeffrey Tulis, "On Presidential Character and Abraham Lincoln," in *Rethinking the Presidency,* ed. Thomas E. Cronin (Boston: Little, Brown, 1982), pp. 87–102; I would extend Tulis's query about how Lincoln fits into the Barber scheme to include Andrew Jackson. Also see, Michael Nelson, "James David Barber and the Psychological Presidency," *Virginia Quarterly,* 56, no. 4 (Autumn 1980), pp. 650–667; and Michael Nelson, "The Psychological Presidency," in *The Presidency and the Political System,* ed. Michael Nelson (Washington, D.C.: Congressional Quarterly Press, 1988), pp. 185–206. Barber adapts a more systemic and historical view in *The Pulse of Politics: Electing Presidents in the Media Age* (New York: Norton, 1980).

6. The ambiguity of the oath of office reflects a deeper tension in the relationship between executive power and the rule of law generally. For a penetrating study of the inherently extra-legal character of the executive power as it has been accommodated to modern constitutional government, see Harvey C. Mansfield, Jr., *Taming the Prince: The Ambivalence of Modern Executive Power* (New York: Free Press, 1989).

7. "In every large collection of people there must be a visible point serving as a common center in the government, toward which to draw their eyes and attachments." *The Federal Farmer,* quoted in *The Complete Anti-Federalist,* ed. Herbert J. Storing (Chicago: University of Chicago Press, 1981), p. 310; also Mansfield, *Taming the Prince,* p. 253.

8. In *The Discourses,* (New York: Modern Library, 1950), p. 182, Niccolo Machiavelli described the imperatives of reconciling the order-shattering impulse of leaders with an order-affirming purpose this way: "He who desires to reform the government of a state, and wishes to have it accepted and capable of maintaining itself to the satisfaction of everybody, must at least retain the semblance of the old forms; so that it may seem to the people that there has been no change in the institutions, even though they are entirely different from the old ones."

9. "Federalist No. 72," p. 436.

10. Abraham Lincoln, "Speech at Springfield," June 16, 1858, in *The Collected*

Works of Abraham Lincoln, Vol. 2, ed. Roy P. Basler (New Brunswick, N.J.: Rutgers University Press, 1953), p. 461.

11. On a related theme see Richard E. Neustadt and Ernest R. May, *Thinking in Time: The Uses of History for Decision Makers* (New York: Free Press, 1986).

12. "The critical element in political maneuver for advantage is the creation of meanings: the construction of beliefs about the significance of events, of problems, of crises, of policy changes, and of leaders." Murray Edelman, "Political Language and Political Reality," *PS: Political Science and Politics* 18, no. 1 (Winter 1985), p. 10.

13. This sketch draws on materials presented in Chapter 7, Parts One and Two. It is meant to be suggestive rather than conclusive, and the reader is invited to consider the more nuanced treatment offered later in the text.

14. As we shall see in Chapter 7, Roosevelt hoped to change a lot more than he was able to achieve.

15. In elaborating Max Weber's principles of social organization, Edward Shils has shown how the residues of charismatic authority continue to operate within legal rational institutions. I have drawn on Shils's notion of the charisma of office formulated in *The Constitution of Society* (Chicago: University of Chicago Press, 1982), pp. 119–142.

16. On this point see also Michael Nelson and Erwin Hargrove, *Presidents, Politics and Policy* (New York: Knopf, 1984), pp. 268–274.

17. Stephen Skowronek, "Presidential Leadership in Political Time," in *The Presidency and the Political System,* ed. Nelson, pp. 119–161.

3. Structure and Action

1. The reelected presidents whom I am counting as opposition leaders are Washington, Jefferson, Jackson, Lincoln, Cleveland, Wilson, Franklin Roosevelt, Eisenhower, Nixon, and Reagan.

2. This typology first appeared in Stephen Skowronek, "Notes on the Presidency in the Political Order," *Studies in American Political Development,* Vol. 1 (New Haven: Yale University Press, 1986), pp. 286–302.

3. William Howard Taft is another obvious candidate for inclusion in this list, and I would certainly not resist such a designation. I would simply point out that the characteristic features of the disjunction type are complicated in Taft's case by the peculiar relationship between Taft and his immediate predecessor, Theodore Roosevelt. These complications, I think, lead directly to difficulties of describing Woodrow Wilson as a reconstructive leader. Just how vulnerable the Republican regime was, apart from the Roosevelt challenge to Taft in 1912 and Taft's refusal to step aside, is debatable. I note the complications of the Wilson case shortly, and I deal with the Roosevelt-Taft relationship at some length in Chapter 6, Part Two.

4. For an especially astute reading of Truman as an orthodox-innovator see David Plotke, *The Democratic Political Order from the 1930's to the 1970's: Change and Order in Modern American Politics* (New York: Cambridge University Press, forthcoming). Also see Alonzo Hamby, *Beyond the New*

Deal: Harry S. Truman and American Liberalism (New York: Columbia University Press, 1973).

5. The discerning reader might still question this selection: Why James Monroe and not James Madison? Why Theodore Roosevelt and not William McKinley? Why Lyndon Johnson and not John Kennedy? Indeed, why not? In fact in an earlier incarnation of this scheme, I did choose Kennedy rather than Johnson to illustrate these dynamics. There are, as I have stated in the text, more presidents in this category than any other: Van Buren, Truman, Grant, Hays, Benjamin Harrison, Harding, and Coolidge might be added to the list. Bush is taken up in Chapter 8. My object has not been to exhaust the examples that might illuminate any of these categories, but to select the examples which seem to me best to highlight the characteristic tensions and dynamics in each and to prompt readers to see similar dynamics at work in kindred cases. One decision rule was to eliminate the immediate successor of the reconstructive leader—Madison, Van Buren, Truman—so as not to confuse the general dilemmas of affiliated leadership with that particular relationship. Beyond that, I chose the affiliated leader who did the most.

6. Lonnie Maness and Richard Chesteen, "The First Attempt at Presidential Impeachment: Partisan Conflict and Intra-Party Conflict at Loose," *Presidential Studies Quarterly*, 10, no. 1 (Winter 1980), pp. 51–73.

7. The example of Richard Nixon, I am arguing, is only one instance of this. See Richard Nathan, *The Plot That Failed: Nixon and the Administrative Presidency* (New York: Wiley, 1975).

8. Fred I. Greenstein, *The Hidden-Hand Presidency: Eisenhower as Leader* (New York: Basic Books, 1982).

9. Stephen E. Ambrose, *Eisenhower: The President* (New York: Simon and Schuster, 1984), pp. 619, 624–625; Elmo Richardson, *The Presidency of Dwight Eisenhower* (Lawrence: University of Kansas Press, 1979), pp. 59–60.

10. Refusing a nomination that was likely to be his for the asking, Coolidge was quoted by Jim Watson of Indiana as saying: "I do not want the nomination. I think I know myself very well. I fitted into the situation that existed right after the war, but I might not fit into the next one." Arthur Schlesinger, Jr., *The Age of Roosevelt: The Crisis of the Old Order, 1919–1933* (Boston: Houghton Mifflin, 1957), p. 88.

11. William Allen White, *A Puritan in Babylon: The Story of Calvin Coolidge* (New York: Macmillan, 1958), esp. pp. 263–264, 295–298; William Leuchtenberg, *The Perils of Prosperity, 1914–1932* (Chicago: University of Chicago Press, 1958), esp. p. 96. On the relationships between Hoover and Coolidge, and Hoover and the Republican party, see Chapter 6, Part Three.

12. A similar argument is made by Jerome M. Clubb, William H. Flanagan, and Nancy H. Zingale in *Partisan Realignments: Voters, Parties, and Government in American History* (Beverly Hills: Sage, 1980), p. 264. On the political debacle of Cleveland's second term more generally see Alan Nevins, *Grover Cleveland: A Study in Courage* (New York: Dodd, Mead, 1962), pp. 523–712; and Richard E. Welch, Jr., *The Presidencies of Grover Cleveland* (Lawrence: University of Kansas Press, 1988), pp. 113–212.

13. For a critique of the electorally driven realignment framework on this ground, see Daniel J. Gans, "Persistence of Party Success in American Presidential Elections," *Journal of Interdisciplinary History*, 16, no. 2 (Winter 1986), pp. 221–237; Richard L. McCormick, *The Party Period and Public Policy: American Politics from the Age of Jackson to the Progressive Era* (New York: Oxford University Press, 1986); Allan Lichtman, "Critical Election Theory and the Reality of American Presidential Politics, 1916–40," *American Historical Review*, 81, no. 2 (April 1986), pp. 317–351; Allan Lichtman, "The End of Realignment Theory? Toward a New Research Program for American Political History," *Historical Methods*, 15, no. 4 (Fall 1982), pp. 170–188; Everett Carl Ladd, Jr., and Charles D. Hadley, *Transformations of the American Party System: Political Coalitions from the New Deal to the 1970s* (New York: Norton, 1975). The turn to the study of elites for refining this perspective is marked in Martin Shefter, "Party, Bureaucracy and Political Change in the United States," in *Political Parties: Development and Decay*, ed. Louis Maisel and Joseph Cooper (Beverly Hills: Sage, 1978), pp. 211–266.

14. The distinctiveness of patrician politics and the transition from a patrician to a partisan presidency has been captured by Ralph Ketcham, *Presidents above Party: The First American Presidency, 1789–1829* (Chapel Hill: University of North Carolina Press, 1984); M. G. Heale, *The Presidential Quest: Candidates and Images in American Political Culture, 1787–1852* (New York: Longman, 1982); Richard P. McCormick, *The Presidential Game: The Origins of American Presidential Politics* (New York: Oxford University Press, 1982); James W. Ceaser, *Presidential Selection: Theory and Development* (Princeton: Princeton University Press, 1979), pp. 41–169; Richard Hofstadter, *The Idea of a Party System: The Rise of Legitimate Opposition in the United States* (Berkeley: University of California Press, 1969); Roy F. Nichols, *The Invention of American Political Parties* (New York: Macmillan, 1967); James Sterling Young, *The Washington Community, 1800–1829* (New York: Harcourt Brace, 1966); Ronald Formisano, *The Transformation of Political Culture: Massachusetts, 1790s–1840s* (New York: Oxford University Press, 1983).

15. On the distinctiveness of party politics and the transition from a partisan to a pluralist presidency see Joel Silbey, *The Partisan Imperative: The Dynamics of American Politics before the Civil War* (New York: Oxford University Press, 1985); Stephen Skowronek, *Building a New American State: The Expansion of National Administrative Capacities, 1877–1920* (New York: Cambridge University Press, 1982); McCormick, *The Party Period*; Peri Arnold, *The Making of the Managerial Presidency: Comprehensive Reorganization Planning, 1905–1980* (Princeton: Princeton University Press, 1986); Sidney Milkis, *The Presidents and the Parties: The Transformation of the American Party System since the New Deal* (New York: Oxford University Press, 1993).

16. The distinctiveness of pluralist politics and the transition from a pluralist to a plebiscitary presidency is captured in Richard Neustadt, *Presidential Power: The Politics of Leadership from FDR to Carter* (New York: Wiley, 1980);

Samuel Kernell, *Going Public: New Strategies of Presidential Leadership* (Washington, D.C.: Congressional Quarterly Press, 1986); Milkis, *New Deal*.

17. On the distinctiveness of plebiscitary politics and the plebiscitary presidency see Kernell, *Going Public*; Milkis, *Presidents and Parties*; Theodore J. Lowi, *The Personal President: Power Invested, Promise Unfulfilled* (Ithaca: Cornell University Press, 1985); Jeffrey Tulis, *The Rhetorical Presidency* (Princeton: Princeton University Press, 1987); Richard Rose, *The Post-Modern President: George Bush Meets the World* (Chatham, N.J.: Chatham House, 1988).

18. See for example, Robert Shogun, "Bush Increasingly Veering Off Course Set by Reagan," *Los Angeles Times*, May 27, 1991, p. 1; Robert Shogun, "GOP Aims May Pose Dilemma for President," *Los Angeles Times*, May 28, 1991, p. 1.

4. Jeffersonian Leadership: Patrician Prototypes

Part One: Thomas Jefferson's Reconstruction

1. "To Theodore Sedgwick," May 10, 1800, *The Works of Alexander Hamilton*, Vol. 10, ed. Henry Cabot Lodge (New York: Putnum, 1904), p. 375. Hamilton continued to support Jefferson when the election was thrown into the House of Representatives and the Federalists turned to Aaron Burr in hopes of preventing Jefferson's election. Noble Cunningham, Jr., *In Pursuit of Reason: The Life of Thomas Jefferson* (Baton Rouge: Louisiana State University Press, 1987), p. 228–234.

2. The younger Federalists did make assiduous efforts to regroup and capitalize on Jefferson's vulnerabilities, but unlike defeated partisans of later periods, they failed to find any issue potent enough to extend their appeal beyond their narrow base of operation in New England. David Hackett Fischer, *The Revolution of American Conservatism: The Federalist Party in the Era of Jeffersonian Democracy* (New York: Harper and Row, 1965), esp. pp. 150–181. Also see Richard Buel, Jr., *Securing the Revolution: Ideology in American Politics, 1789–1815* (New York: Cornell University Press, 1972), pp. 241–291.

3. "Jefferson to Levi Lincoln," October 25, 1802, in *The Works of Thomas Jefferson*, Vol. 9, ed. Paul L. Ford (New York: Putnam, 1955), p. 401.

4. The most frequently cited reference to "revolution" is to be found in a letter to Spencer Roane, September 6, 1819, *The Writings of Thomas Jefferson*, Vol. 15, ed. Andrew A. Lipscomb and Albert E. Bergh (Washington, D.C.: Thomas Jefferson Memorial of the United States, 1903), p. 212.

5. Daniel Sisson mounts an impressive defense of Jefferson's language, arguing that it was entirely appropriate within the political lexicon of the early national period. In attempting to straighten out all the misconceptions that surround the notion of revolution, he reminds us again just how peculiar Jefferson's use of the term "revolution" was. *The American Revolution of 1800* (New York: Knopf, 1974).

6. Consistent with its position as the classic analysis of Jefferson's presidency,

Henry Adams's *History of the United States during the Administrations of Jefferson and Madison,* 9 vols. (New York: Charles Scribner's Sons, 1889–1891), may be read to endorse both points of view. The first view may be traced to its origins in Alexander Hamilton's comment that Jefferson was not "zealot enough to do anything in the pursuance of his principles which will contravene his popularity or his interest. He is as likely as any man I know to temporize—to calculate what will be likely to promote his own reputation and advantage; and the probable result of such a temper is the preservation of systems which, once established, could not be overturned without danger to the person who did it." "Hamilton to Charles Bayard," January 16, 1801, *Works,* Vol. 10, p. 413. In one form or another, this view of the "Revolution of 1800" has tended to dominate the literature. Its central themes entered modern scholarship with a particularly strong restatement by Herbert Agar in his Pulitzer Prize–winning book, *The People's Choice* (Boston: Houghton Mifflin, 1933). More recently, Norman Risjord has observed that "even the most friendly historian is hard put to find anything revolutionary about the changes of 1800." "New Meaning for Jefferson's Democracy," *Reviews in American History,* 1, no. 1 (March 1973), pp. 88–95. See also Gary J. Schmitt, "Jefferson and the Presidency" in *Inventing the Presidency,* ed. Thomas Cronin (Lawrence: University of Kansas Press, 1989), pp. 61–88. The recent rediscovery of the republican political tradition in America, and in particular of the roots of the ideology of the country-party opposition, has given new force to the interpretation of Jefferson as a determined ideologue. Forrest McDonald, a leading authority on Alexander Hamilton, offers a stunning refutation of Hamilton's assessment of Jefferson, and views Jefferson as a true revolutionary in the presidency who failed for the provincial naiveté of his republican vision. *The Presidency of Thomas Jefferson* (Lawrence: University of Kansas Press, 1976). For another view of Jefferson's republican vision see Lance Banning, *The Jeffersonian Persuasion: Evolution of a Party Ideology* (Ithaca: Cornell University Press, 1978).

7. John R. Nelson, Jr., *Liberty and Property: Political Economy and Policy Making in the New Nation, 1789–1812* (Baltimore: Johns Hopkins University Press, 1987), pp. 22–80.

8. Ibid.; John Miller, *The Federalist Era, 1789–1801* (New York: Harper and Row, 1960), pp. 140–182.

9. Joseph Charles, *The Origins of the American Party System: Three Essays* (Williamsburg: Institute of Early American History, 1956), pp. 103–140.

10. Jefferson's parting salvo as Washington's secretary of state was a comprehensive statement of opposition to Hamilton's program and an outline of a counter program for the emergent Republican party. Thomas Jefferson, "Report on the Privileges and Restrictions on the Commerce of the United States in Foreign Countries," December 16, 1793, *Writings,* Vol. 3, pp. 261–283; Merrill Peterson, *Thomas Jefferson: A Biography* (London: Oxford University Press, 1970), pp. 512–515; Nelson, *Liberty and Property,* pp. 73–77.

11. "To James Madison," January 8, 1797, *Works,* Vol. 8, p. 268; for earlier statements along the same lines before this election was settled: "I pray you

and authorize you fully, to solicit on my behalf that mr. Adams may be preferred. He has always been my senior . . . I think [foreign affairs] never wore so gloomy an aspect since the year '83. Let those come to the helm who think they can steer clear of the difficulties." "To James Madison," December 17, 1796, *Works*, Vol. 8, p. 256. Also, "This is certainly not a moment to covet the helm," "To Edward Rutledge," December 27, 1796, *Works*, Vol. 8, p. 258; Stephen G. Kurtz, *The Presidency of John Adams: The Collapse of Federalism* (Philadelphia: University of Pennsylvania Press, 1957), p. 95.

12. Interestingly, Adams had a similar thought about Jefferson. Considering the prospect of Jefferson's election in 1796, Adams asserted that Jefferson would not be able to "stir a step in any other system than that which is begun." *Letters of John Adams to His Wife*, Vol. 2, ed. Charles Francis Adams (Boston: Little, Brown, 1841), p. 201; Manning J. Dauer, *The Adams Federalists* (Baltimore: Johns Hopkins University Press, 1968), p. 94.

13. Quoted in Ralph Adams Brown, *The Presidency of John Adams* (Lawrence: University of Kansas Press, 1975), p. 37.

14. Kurtz, *Presidency of John Adams*, pp. 230–231.

15. It should be noted that the practice of retaining officers in place during good behavior was fully in keeping with the prevailing mores of government at the time. This said, it must be observed further that Adams's position as the first successor was unprecedented and it presented him with a choice. The choice he made was for as near a continuation of the administration of his predecessor as might be imagined. As Brown makes the case, Adams "feared that changes in the cabinet in March 1797 might split the Federalist party wide open." Brown, *Presidency of John Adams*, p. 27; Kurtz, *Presidency of John Adams*, pp. 277–279.

16. April 22, 1812, *The Spur of Fame: Dialogues of John Adams and Benjamin Rush, 1805–1813*, ed. John Schutz and Douglas Adair (San Marino: Huntington Library, 1966), pp. 212–215.

17. Quoted in Richard H. Kohn, *Eagle and Sword: The Beginnings of the Military Establishment in America* (New York: Free Press, 1975), p. 267. The passage is from Adams's later recollection of the events.

18. Dauer, *Adams Federalists*, p. 223; Brown, *Presidency of John Adams*, pp. 114–129.

19. Brown, ibid., pp. 63–76; Kohn, *Eagle and Sword*, pp. 219–238.

20. Cited in Kohn, ibid., pp. 257–258.

21. Brown, *Presidency of John Adams*, pp. 112–113; more generally, Kurtz, *Presidency of John Adams*, pp. 354–408.

22. "To James Lloyd," February 6, 1815, *The Works of John Adams*, Vol. 10, ed. Charles Francis Adams (Boston: Little, Brown, 1856), p. 115; Dauer, *Adams Federalists*, pp. 225–237.

23. Kohn, *Eagle and Sword*, pp. 263–273.

24. The congressional races in 1800 went more strongly against the Federalists than the presidential race. Adams ran ahead of the Federalist candidates for Congress, and Jefferson ran behind Republican candidates. The results, however, were a clean sweep for the Republicans—too clean, in fact, for Jefferson

and Burr, presumed by all to be running for president and vice president respectively, tied in electoral votes. The election was thrown into the House where the Federalists momentarily revived their prospects by hatching a plan to support Burr over Jefferson. On the election of 1800 see, Brown, *Presidency of John Adams,* pp. 175–195; Dauer, *Adams Federalists,* pp. 246–259; also Sisson, *American Revolution of 1800,* passim.

25. On Jefferson's adaptation of the role of the disinterested tribune see Ralph Ketcham, *Presidents above Party: The First American Presidency, 1789–1829* (Chapel Hill: University of North Carolina, 1984), esp. pp. 101–113.

26. Richard Hofstadter, *The Idea of a Party System: The Rise of Legitimate Opposition in the United States, 1780–1840* (Berkeley: University of California Press, 1969), pp. 123–128.

27. "Inaugural Address," March 4, 1801, *A Compilation of the Messages and Papers of the Presidents,* Vol. 1, ed. James D. Richardson (New York: Bureau of National Literature, 1897), pp. 309–312.

28. "To Thomas McKean," July 24, 1801, *Works,* Vol. 9, p. 284. Hofstadter, *Party System,* p. 165. On Roosevelt see Chapter 7, Part One.

29. "To Lincoln Levi," October 25, 1802, *Works,* Vol. 9, pp. 400–402.

30. "To Elias Shipman and Others, Committee of the Merchants of New Haven," July 12, 1801, *Works,* Vol. 9, pp. 270–272.

31. Leonard White, *The Jeffersonians: A Study in Administrative History, 1801–1829* (New York: Free Press, 1951), pp. 352–354; Noble Cunningham, *The Process of Government under Jefferson* (Princeton: Princeton University Press, 1978), pp. 165–187; Robert M. Johnstone, Jr., *Jefferson and the Presidency: Leadership in the Young Republic* (Ithaca: Cornell University Press, 1978), pp. 102–113; Carl Russell Fish, *The Civil Service and the Patronage* (Cambridge: Harvard University Press, 1920), pp. 42–43. Jefferson's calculation excluded "the judiciary and the military because not removable but by established process, nor the officers of the internal revenue because discontinued by law, nor postmasters or others not named by me." To William Duane, July 24, 1803, *Works,* Vol. 10, pp. 20–25.

32. Theodore Crackle, *Mr. Jefferson's Army: Political and Social Reform of the Military, 1801–1809* (New York: New York University Press, 1987), pp. 43–45, 54–73.

33. Carl E. Prince, "The Passing of the Aristocracy: Jefferson's Removal of the Federalists, 1801–1805," *Journal of American History,* Vol. 57, no. 3 (December 1970), pp. 563–575; White, *Jeffersonians,* pp. 347–359. Noble Cunningham, *The Jeffersonian Republicans in Power: Party Operations, 1801–1909* (Chapel Hill: University of North Carolina Press, 1963), pp. 13–70.

34. Quoted in Cunningham, *Pursuit of Reason,* pp. 249–250; see also James Sterling Young and Russell L. Riley, "Party Government and Political Culture," paper from White Burkett Miller Center of Public Affairs, University of Virginia, August 1990.

35. Quoted in Richard Ellis, *The Jeffersonian Crisis: Courts and Politics in the Young Republic* (New York: Norton, 1971), p. 45.

36. Cunningham, *Process of Government,* pp. 188–272; Johnstone, *Jefferson and the Presidency,* pp. 114–161.

37. Dumas Malone, *Jefferson: The President, The First Term* (Boston: Little, Brown, 1970), p. 110.

38. Wilfred Binkley, *President and Congress* (New York: Random House, 1962), pp. 65–66.

39. Schmitt, "Jefferson and the Presidency," p. 329.

40. Marshall quoted in Binkley, *President and Congress,* p. 63.

41. Especially illuminating in this regard is James Sterling Young, *The Washington Community, 1800–1828* (New York: Harcourt Brace, 1966).

42. Jefferson's formal deference to the legislature was, in Timothy Pickering's view, "a screen from all responsibility." Binkley, *President and Congress,* p. 65. Also Cunningham, *The Process of Government,* pp. 188–213, and Johnstone, *Jefferson and the Presidency,* pp. 114–161.

43. When John Randolph proposed an amendment in the wake of his disgrace in the impeachment trial of Justice Samuel Chase, Jefferson let the initiative die. To launch such an effort on the heels of the failure of his own party's radicalism simply would not do. But when Jefferson felt that the Federalist Court had discredited itself, he was more enthusiastic. After the acquittal of Aaron Burr, he wrote, "If his punishment can be commuted now for a useful amendment, I shall rejoice in it." Despite rumblings in a few states, no general movement for an amendment arose. Ellis, *Jeffersonian Crisis,* p. 107; "Jefferson to William Branch Giles," April 20, 1807, *Works,* Vol. 10, pp. 387–388.

44. Cunningham, *Pursuit of Reason,* p. 243.

45. Ellis, *Jeffersonian Crisis,* pp. 36–52, 83–95, 104; Peterson, *Biography,* pp. 796–797, 821; Malone, *First Term,* pp. 467–481; Norman Risjord, *The Old Republicans: Southern Conservatism in the Age of Jefferson* (New York: Columbia University Press, 1965), p. 42; Johnstone, *Jefferson and the Presidency,* pp. 163–209.

46. Peterson, *Biography,* p. 700.

47. Ellis, *Jeffersonian Crisis,* pp. 62–68; Johnstone, *Jefferson and the Presidency,* p. 178; Robert Lowry Clinton, *Marbury v. Madison and Judicial Review* (Lawrence: University of Kansas Press, 1989), pp. 81–103.

48. Peterson, *Biography,* pp. 865–874.

49. Ellis, *Jeffersonian Crisis,* pp. 64–66; Malone, *First Term,* p. 483.

50. On the administration's views of commerce and manufacturing see Nelson, *Liberty and Property.* A picture, different in emphasis but not antithetical, is presented by Drew McCoy, *The Elusive Republic: Political Economy in Jeffersonian America* (Chapel Hill: University of North Carolina Press, 1980), pp. 185–208.

51. McDonald, *Presidency of Thomas Jefferson,* pp. 41–44; Peterson, *Biography,* pp. 687–689; Dumas Malone, *Jefferson the President: The Second Term* (Boston: Little, Brown, 1974), pp. 507–523; Samuel Huntington, *The Soldier and the State: The Theory and Practice of Civil Military Relations* (New York: Vintage Books, 1957), pp. 195–203. Crackle argues that the demobilization of the Army was already so far advanced by the time Jeffersonians reformed it that the retrenchment and savings were more rhetorical than real. *Mr. Jefferson's Army,* pp. 43–45.

52. McDonald, *Presidency of Thomas Jefferson,* pp. 41–44; Burton Spivak, *Jef-*

ferson's English Crisis: Commerce, Embargo, and the Republican Revolution (Charlottesville: University of Virginia Press, 1979), pp. 7–13. Jefferson's second inaugural on the prospect for internal improvements, *Works,* Vol. 10, p. 130; his last annual message echoed this call in the midst of the embargo, November 8, 1808, *Works,* Vol. 11, p. 71.

53. "There is on the globe one single spot, the possessor of which is our natural and habitual enemy. It is New Orleans . . . The day that France takes possession of New Orleans fixes the sentence which is to restrain her forever within her low water mark. It seals the union of two nations who in conjunction can maintain exclusive possession of the ocean. From that moment we must marry ourselves to the British fleet and nation." "Jefferson to Livingston," April 18, 1802, *Works,* Vol. 11, p. 364.

54. *Memoirs of John Quincy Adams,* ed. Charles Francis Adams (Philadelphia: Lippincott, 1875), pp. 364–365.

55. "To Wilson Cary Nicholas," September 7, 1803, *Writings,* Vol. 8, p. 247. Peterson, *Biography,* p. 775; Malone, *First Term,* pp. 311–332.

56. Richard P. McCormick, *The Presidential Game: The Origins of American Presidential Politics* (New York: Oxford University Press, 1982), pp. 80–87.

57. Malone, *First Term,* pp. 450–454. Edward Channing, *The Jeffersonian System, 1801–1811* (New York: Greenwood, 1906/1969), pp. 126–139. Malone, *First Term,* p. 452; Johnstone, *Jefferson and the Presidency,* p. 135.

58. Risjord, *Old Republicans,* pp. 40–96; Cunningham, *Jeffersonians in Power,* pp. 222–235; Johnstone, *Jefferson and the Presidency,* pp. 153–161; Peterson, *Biography,* p. 840.

59. Jefferson's dismissal of the treaty offended his friend and negotiator James Monroe and raised the spectre of Monroe's challenging James Madison for the succession. Jefferson's efforts to head off this division and explain his opposition to the treaty are documented in "To James Monroe," February 18, 1808, *Works,* Vol. 11, pp. 9–11, and March 10, 1808, pp. 11–17.

60. Peterson, *Biography,* p. 885; Jefferson to Gallatin, May 20, 1808, Jefferson Papers, Library of Congress, Series 1, Reel 42, doc. 3150.

61. Spivak, *Jefferson's English Crisis,* pp. 102–155; Peterson, *Biography,* pp. 874–921; Malone, *Second Term,* pp. 469–490.

62. "There can be no question in a mind truly American whether it is best to send our citizens and property into certain captivity, or keep them at home to turn seriously to that policy which plants the manufacturer and the husbandman side by side and establishes at every door that exchange of mutual labors and comforts which we have hitherto sought in distant regions and under perpetual risk of broils." "Jefferson to Tammany Society," February 29, 1808, *The Complete Jefferson,* ed. Saul Padover (New York: Duell, Sloan and Pearce, 1943), pp. 529–530. Also, "To the delgates of the Democratic Republicans in the City of Philadelphia," May 25, 1808: "This measure will, indeed, produce some temporary inconvenience; but promises lasting good by promoting among ourselves the establishment of manufactures hitherto sought abroad." *Complete Jefferson,* p. 530. In the "Eighth Annual Message," November 8, 1808: "The situation . . . has impelled us to apply a

portion of our industry and capital to internal manufactures and improvements. The extent of this conversion is daily increasing and little doubt remains that the establishments formed and forming . . . will become permanent." *Works,* Vol. 11, p. 70. And to Thomas Leiper, January 21, 1809: "I have lately inculcated the encouragement of manufactures to the extent of our own consumption at least, in all articles of which we raise the raw material. On this the federal papers and meetings sound the alarm of Chinese policy and the destruction of commerce . . . this absurd hue and cry has contributed much to federalize New England, their doctrine goes to the sacrificing agriculture and manufacturing to commerce; to the calling all our people from the interior to the sea shore to turn merchants, and to convert this great agricultural country into a city of Amsterdam." *Works,* Vol. 11, pp. 90–91. Spivak, *Jefferson's English Crisis,* p. 204; Peterson, *Biography,* p. 911; McCoy, *Elusive Republic,* pp. 209–233.

63. Cunningham, *Pursuit of Reason,* p. 316; "To Gallatin," August 11, 1808, *Works,* Vol. 11, p. 41.

64. For example, "To the Secretary of War," August 9, 1808, *Works,* Vol. 11, pp. 40–41; "To the Governor of Massachusetts," August 12, 1808, *Works,* Vol. 11, pp. 24–47; "Circular for the Secretary of War to the Governors," January 17, 1809, *Works,* Vol. 11, pp. 87–89.

65. "To James Monroe," January 28, 1809, *Works,* Vol. 11, pp. 93–96; "To Thomas Mann Randolph," February 7, 1809, *Works,* Vol. 11, pp. 96–97; Spivak, *Jefferson's English Crisis,* pp. 156–197; Malone, *Second Term,* pp. 561–657; Peterson, *Biography,* pp. 887–913.

66. Ibid.; Peterson, *Biography,* pp. 913–916.

Part Two: James Monroe's Articulation

1. "Our principle dangers and difficulties have passed, and the character of our deliberations and the course of our government itself, will become more harmonious and happy than it has heretofore been." "To the Republicans of Massachusetts" in 1817, *The Writings of James Monroe,* Vol. 6, ed. Stanislaus Murray Hamilton (New York: Putnam's, 1902), p. 29. George Dangerfield, *The Awakening of American Nationalism, 1815–1828* (New York: Harper and Row, 1965), p. 34.

2. "Inaugural Address," March 4, 1817, *A Compilation of the Messages and Papers of the Presidents,* Vol. 2, ed. James D. Richardson (Washington: Bureau of National Literature and Art, 1907), p. 579.

3. "Jefferson to James Monroe," March 21, 1807, *The Works of Thomas Jefferson,* Vol. 10, ed. Paul L. Ford (New York: Putnam, 1955), pp. 374–378; "Jefferson to James Monroe," February 18, 1808, *Works,* Vol. 11, pp. 9–11; "Jefferson to James Madison," November 30, 1809, *Works,* Vol. 11, pp. 126–129.

4. Ibid.

5. For portraits of the Monroe who passively oversaw the political disintegration around him see James Sterling Young, *The Washington Community, 1800–1828* (New York: Columbia University Press, 1966), and George Dangerfield,

The Era of Good Feelings (New York: Harcourt Brace, 1952). For the activist Monroe see Harry Ammon, *James Monroe: The Quest For National Identity* (New York: McGraw Hill, 1971).

6. Ammon, *James Monroe,* pp. 359–362; Merrill Peterson, *The Great Triumvirate: Webster, Clay, and Calhoun* (New York: Oxford University Press, 1987), pp. 50, 82; Young, *Washington Community,* p. 133.

7. "Second Inaugural Address," March 5, 1821, *Messages and Papers,* Vol. 2, p. 662.

8. Richard Radcliffe, *The President's Tour: A Collection of Addresses* (New-Ipswich: Salmon Wilder, 1822). Also, Dangerfield, *Awakening,* pp. 20, 141–144. *Messages and Papers,* Vol. 2, p. 662.

9. Joel Silbey, "The Incomplete World of American Politics, 1815–1829: Presidents, Parties and the Era of Good Feelings," *Congress and the Presidency,* 11, no. 1 (Spring 1984), pp. 1–17.

10. The proliferation of standing committees appointed by the Speaker was the major development in Congressional organization in this period. In 1822, standing committees were formally given the power to decide for themselves whether or not to report a bill. *Origins and Development of Congress,* ed. Robert A. Diamond (Washington, D.C.: Congressional Quarterly Press, 1976), p. 90; George Galloway, *History of the House of Representatives,* 2nd ed. (New York: Crowell, 1976), p. 86.

11. Joseph Story quoted in Peterson, *Great Triumvirate,* p. 52.

12. Young, *Washington Community,* pp. 187, 202, 245; "To James Madison," May 10, 1922, *Writings,* Vol. 6, p. 286. "I have never known such a state of things nor have I personally ever experienced so much embarrassment and mortification."

13. Richard P. McCormick, *The Presidential Game: The Origins of American Presidential Politics* (New York: Oxford University Press, 1982), pp. 103–120; Richard Hofstadter, *The Idea of A Party System: The Rise of Legitimate Opposition in the United States, 1780–1840* (Berkeley: University of California Press, 1969), pp. 213–271.

14. Charles M. Wiltse, *John C. Calhoun: Nationalist* (Indianapolis: Bobbs Merrill, 1944), p. 160.

15. It is possible that Monroe knew of, or at least suspected, Jackson's intentions from the beginning, and thus implicitly sanctioned them. This at least was Jackson's own position, and it has been forcefully presented recently by Robert V. Remini, in *Andrew Jackson and the Course of American Empire, 1767–1821* (New York: Harper and Row, 1977), pp. 351–377.

16. July 15, 16, 17, 1818, *The Diary of John Quincy Adams,* ed. Allan Nevins (New York: Scribner's, 1951), pp. 54–61.

17. "To General Jackson," July 19, 1818, *Writings,* Vol. 6 (New York: Putnam, 1902), pp. 54–61. On Monroe's rejection of Adams's position in favor of his own see Ammon, *James Monroe,* pp. 422–425.

18. "To Thomas Jefferson," July 22, 1818, *Writings,* Vol. 6, pp. 62–64: "The occurrence at Pensacola has been full of difficulty, but without incurring the charge of committing a breach of the Constitution, or of giving to Spain just

cause of war, we have endeavor'd to turn it to the best account of our country and credit of the Commanding General."

19. Ibid., "To General Jackson," October 20, 1818, *Writings,* Vol. 6, pp. 74–75; "To General Jackson," December 21, 1818, *Writings,* Vol. 6, pp. 85–87.

20. "Second Annual Message," November 16, 1818, *Messages and Papers,* Vol. 2, p. 612.

21. Peterson, *Great Triumvirate,* p. 56.

22. Ibid., pp. 52–57; Dangerfield, *Awakening,* pp. 164–167.

23. "Seventh Annual Message," December 2, 1823, *Messages and Papers,* Vol. 2, pp. 787–788; Dangerfield, *Era,* p. 309; Ernest R. May, *The Making of the Monroe Doctrine* (Cambridge: Harvard University Press, 1975). As May concludes in his analysis of the domestic politics of formulating the doctrine: "The basic policies of the administration . . . were . . . policies tailored to satisfy the widest possible spectrum of the electorate" (p. 253).

24. *Messages and Papers,* Vol. 2, p. 577; Radcliffe, *President's Tour,* p. 58; Joseph Hobson Harrison, Jr., "The Internal Improvement Issue in the Politics of the Union, 1783–1825," unpublished Ph.D. dissertation, University of Virginia, 1954, p. 400.

25. "First Annual Message to Congress," December 17, 1817, *Messages and Papers,* Vol. 2, pp. 580–592.

26. Quoted in Harrison, "Internal Improvements," p. 378.

27. "To James Madison," November 24, 1817, *Writings,* Vol. 6, p. 32.

28. "First Annual Message," December 17, 1817, *Messages and Papers,* Vol. 2, p. 587.

29. Harrison, "Internal Improvements," pp. 380–456; Ammon, *James Monroe,* pp. 388–391.

30. "To James Madison," December 22, 1817, p. 46.

31. *The Writings of James Madison,* Vol. 8, ed. Gaillard Hunt (New York: Putnam's Sons, 1908), pp. 403–406.

32. "Veto Message," May 7, 1822, *Messages and Papers,* Vol. 2, pp. 711–752. Harrison, "Internal Improvements," pp. 474–540.

33. *Diary of John Quincy Adams,* December 3 and 6, 1819, pp. 219–221.

34. Charles Lowery, *James Barbour, A Jeffersonian Republican* (Tuscaloosa: University of Alabama Press, 1984), pp. 103–104, 115–131; Glover Moore, *The Missouri Controversy, 1819–1821* (Lexington: University of Kentucky Press, 1953), pp. 234–238, 252, 339–342.

35. Monroe's argument suffered for the fact that the federal government had taken an active part in the "construction" of the Cumberland road. Monroe declared this involvement a minor and insignificant deviation from the basic principle and dismissed it as adequate ground for future action.

36. *Messages and Papers,* Vol. 2, p. 744 (my emphasis).

37. In his "Seventh Annual Message," December 2, 1823, for example, Monroe recommended congressional support for a canal between the Chesapeake and the Potomac, and he asked for authority to enter into agreements with states along the Cumberland Road under which they would set up and operate toll booths to finance repairs. The most important bill worked out by Congress

in compliance with the President's views appropriated funds for a general survey to be undertaken by the Army Corps of Engineers of such roads and canals that might be of national importance. *Messages and Papers,* Vol. 2, p. 785; Harrison, "Internal Improvements," pp. 540–633.

38. Peterson, *Great Triumvirate,* p. 2; Harrison, "Internal Improvements," pp. 540–633; Risjord, *Old Republicans,* pp. 237–244.
39. "To James Madison," May 10, 1822, *Writings,* Vol. 6, p. 289.
40. Robert V. Remini, *Martin Van Buren and the Making of the Democratic Party* (New York: Columbia University Press, 1951), pp. 12–29. The issue which focused this particular attack was the Monroe-Calhoun peacetime defense program. The Radicals, now promoting the presidential ambitions of Treasury Secretary Crawford, led the assault, with the Old Republicans close behind. Monroe correctly saw this as an effort to "raise up a new party on the presumed basis of economy." Monroe, *Writings,* Vol. 6, p. 247. It should be noted here that the economic downturn of 1819–1821 played into the hands of those who accused Monroe of heresy for it made the moderate nationalism to which he had committed the nation appear all the more extravagent and politically deviant. For more on the "era of good feeling" as a Federalist plot see Michael Wallace, "Changing Concepts of Party in the United States: New York, 1815–1828," *American Historical Review* 74, no. 2 (December 1968), esp. pp. 428–429.
41. "To James Madison," May 10, 1822, pp. 284–291. This, in fact, restates the patronage policy which Monroe had outlined at the beginning of his administration. He promised a spirit of accommodation with all those who would accept the Republican party, but he refused to appoint even moderate Federalists to high office for the very reason that it might be considered an offer of compromise with them. Indeed, if there was anything that Monroe self-consciously set out to eradicate, it was the Federalist party. He explicitly rejected amalgamation in a letter rejecting Andrew Jackson's recommendation that he appoint a moderate Federalist to the cabinet. His goal, he said, was "to bring the whole into the republican fold as quick as possible." *Writings,* Vol. 5, pp. 341–349. See also Monroe's speech to the Republican minority in Boston, in Radcliffe, *President's Tour,* p. 31. And Hofstadter, *Idea of a Party System,* pp. 188–203.

Part Three: John Quincy Adams's Disjunction

1. *A Compilation of the Messages and Papers of the Presidents,* Vol. 2, ed. James D. Richardson (New York: Bureau of National Literature, 1897), pp. 860–864.
2. Dangerfield, *The Era of Good Feelings* (New York: Harcourt Brace, 1952), p. 332.
3. On Adams's alleged ineptitude see Peterson, *The Great Triumvirate: Webster, Clay, Calhoun* (New York: Oxford University Press, 1987), p. 146. Peterson relates the toast of the day to President Adams: "May he strike confusion to his foes, as he has already done to his friends." Also Robert V. Remini, *The Election of Andrew Jackson* (Philadelphia: Lippincott, 1963), p. 16; Samuel

Flagg Bemis, *John Quincy Adams and the Union* (New York: Knopf, 1956), p. 71.

4. For a persuasive defense of Adams as a politician, see Daniel Walker Howe, *The Political Culture of the American Whigs* (Chicago: University of Chicago Press, 1979), pp. 46–50.

5. "To Rufus King," October 8, 1802, *The Writings of John Qunicy Adams,* Vol. 3, ed. Worthington Chauncey Ford (New York: Macmillan, 1913–1917), p. 9.

6. Ernest R. May, *The Making of the Monroe Doctrine* (Cambridge: Harvard University Press, 1975).

7. John Quincy Adams, *Memoirs of John Quincy Adams,* Vol. 6, (Philadelphia: Lippincott, 1875), pp. 246–247.

8. *The Missouri Compromises and Presidential Politics, 1820–1825: From the Letters of William Plumer, Jr.,* ed. Everett Somerville Brown (St. Louis: Missouri Historical Society, 1926), pp. 83–88.

9. Mary Hargreaves, *The Presidency of John Quincy Adams* (Lawrence: University Press of Kansas, 1985), pp. 19–40; Marie B. Hecht, *John Quincy Adams: A Personal History of an Independent Man* (New York: Macmillan, 1972), pp. 370–406.

10. May, *Making of the Monroe Doctrine,* p. 181; Peterson, *Great Triumvirate,* pp. 126–131; William Morgan, "John Quincy Adams Versus Andrew Jackson: Their Biographers and the Corrupt Bargain Charge," *Tennessee Historical Quarterly,* 26 (Spring-Winter 1967), pp. 43–46.

11. Even here there were differences to be overcome. Adams was not a committed protectionist as Clay was, nor was he as zealous in support of national liberation movements elsewhere. On both counts, Adams moved in Clay's direction after the election. Hargreaves, *Presidency,* pp. 25–38.

12. Peterson, *Great Triumvirate,* pp. 126–129.

13. *Memoirs,* Vol. 6, pp. 431–501, *passim.* Dangerfield, *Era,* pp. 339–341.

14. Bemis, *John Quincy Adams,* p. 72; Rufus King was also an antislavery agitator in the Missouri debates, see William Freehling, *The Road to Disunion: Vol. 1, Sessionists at Bay, 1776–1854* (New York: Oxford University Press, 1990), p. 148.

15. *Memoirs,* Vol. 6, pp. 505ff:; Dangerfield, *Era,* p. 346; Hargreaves, *Presidency,* pp. 41–50.

16. *Memoirs,* Vol. 7, pp. 59–63.

17. December 6, 1925, *Messages and Papers* Vol. 2, pp. 881–882.

18. Hargreaves, *Presidency,* pp. 208, 264–265; Remini, *Election of Andrew Jackson* p. 145.

19. Dangerfield, *Era,* pp. 244–266.

20. *Record of Debates in Congress,* Vol. 11 (Washington: Gales and Seaton, 1826), pp. 889–404; George Dangerfield *The Awakening of American Nationalism, 1815–1828* (New York: Harper and Row, 1965), p. 256.

21. Dangerfield, Ibid., pp. 242–266.

22. "To the House of Representatives," March 15, 1826, *Messages and Papers,* Vol. 2, pp. 895–907.

23. Hecht, *John Quincy Adams,* pp. 459–460; Dangerfield, *Era,* p. 350.
24. *Memoirs, John Quincy Adams,* Vol. 6, p. 547.
25. Ibid.; Robert V. Remini, *Andrew Jackson and the Course of American Freedom, 1822–1832* (New York: Harper and Row, 1981), pp. 103ff.
26. Hargreaves, *Presidency,* pp. 242–243; "On Retrenchment," May 15, 1828, *House Reports,* 20th Congress, 1st Session, No. 259, pp. 1–128; "Report of the Minority of the Committee," pp. 129–199.

5. Jacksonian Leadership: Classic Forms

Part One: Andrew Jackson's Reconstruction

1. Quoted in Merrill D. Peterson, *The Great Triumvirate: Webster, Clay and Calhoun* (New York: Oxford University Press, 1987), p. 165.
2. Robert V. Remini, *The Election of Andrew Jackson* (Philadelphia: Lippincott, 1963), pp. 11–120.
3. Quoted in Peterson, *Great Triumvirate,* p. 194.
4. One of the more surprising things about the Jackson literature is how clearly the current controversy about the significance of Jackson's presidency echoes the initial political debate between Democrats and Whigs. Debunking Jackson's democratic pretensions has proven all too easy for political and social historians, especially since Arthur Schlesinger, Jr., in *The Age of Jackson* (Boston: Little, Brown, 1945) attempted to draw a parallel between the social composition of Jacksonian Democracy and the New Deal coalition. See Thomas Abernathy, "Andrew Jackson and the Rise of Southwestern Democracy," *American Historical Review,* 33 (October 1927), pp. 64–77; Charles G. Sellers, "Andrew Jackson vs. the Historians," *Mississippi Valley Historical Review,* 44, no. 4 (March 1958), pp. 615–634; Richard P. McCormick, "New Perspectives on Jacksonian Politics," *American Historical Review,* 65 (January 1960), pp. 288–301; Ronald Formisano, "Toward a Reorientation of Jacksonian Politics: A Review of the Literature, 1959–1975," *Journal of American History,* 63, no. 1 (June 1976), pp. 42–65. In the present study, the parallel between Jackson and Roosevelt, like the parallel between Jackson and Jefferson, is drawn on the ground of the political structure of their leadership projects.
5. James C. Curtis, *Andrew Jackson and the Search for Vindication* (Boston: Little, Brown, 1976).
6. "First Annual Message," December 8, 1829, *A Compilation of the Messages and Papers of the Presidents,* Vol. 3, ed. James D. Richardson (New York: Bureau of National Literature, 1897), pp. 1005–1025. Unless otherwise cited the quotations in the following paragraphs are taken from this message.
7. Richard Longaker, "Andrew Jackson and the Judiciary," *Political Science Quarterly,* 71, no. 3 (September 1956), pp. 341–364.
8. Richard E. Ellis, *The Union at Risk: Jacksonian Democracy, States Rights and the Nullification Crisis* (New York: Oxford University Press, 1987), pp.7–8; William W. Freehling, *The Road to Disunion,* Vol. 1: *Sessionists at Bay, 1776–1854* (New York: Oxford University Press, 1990), pp. 257–270.

9. Joseph Burke, "The Cherokee Cases: A Study in Law, Politics, and Morality," *Stanford Law Review,* 21 (February 1969), pp. 500–531; Longaker, "Andrew Jackson."

10. Peterson, *Great Triumvirate,* pp. 170–172.

11. Robert V. Remini, *Andrew Jackson and the Course of American Freedom, 1822–1832,* Vol. 2 (New York: Harper and Row, 1981), pp. 233–247; Richard Latner, *The Presidency of Andrew Jackson: White House Politics, 1829–1837* (Athens: University of Georgia Press, 1979), pp. 58–79; Marquis James, *The Life of Andrew Jackson* (New York: Bobbs Merrill, 1940), pp. 534–543, 567–582.

12. Quoted in Remini, *Course,* p. 245.

13. The Washington *Globe* quoted in Latner, *Presidency,* p. 81. Also Peterson, *Great Triumvirate,* pp. 183–194; Remini, *Course,* pp. 300–314; James, *Life,* pp. 567–580.

14. Leonard White, *The Jacksonians: A Study in Administrative History* (New York: Macmillan, 1954), pp. 106–107; Erik McKinley Eriksson, "The Federal Civil Service under Jackson," *Mississippi Valley Historical Review,* 13, no. 4 (March 1927), pp. 517–540; Remini, *Course,* p. 232.

15. Remini, *Course,* pp. 263–265; Latner, *Presidency,* pp. 93–97.

16. Remini, *Course,* p. 261.

17. "Veto Message," May 27, 1830, *Messages and Papers,* Vol. 3, pp. 1046–1056.

18. "Second Annual Message," December 6, 1830; *Messages and Papers,* Vol. 3, pp. 1063–1092; Remini, *Course,* pp. 304–305.

19. Latner, *Presidency,* p. 82; Burton W. Folsom II, "Party Formation and Development in Jacksonian America: The Old South," *Journal of American Studies,* 7, no. 3 (December 1973), pp. 217–229.

20. "Third Annual Message," December 6, 1831; *Messages and Papers,* Vol. 3, p. 1119. Merrill D. Peterson, *Olive Branch and Sword: The Compromise of 1833* (Baton Rouge: Louisiana State University Press, 1982), pp. 22–25. Latner, *Presidency,* pp. 145–147.

21. Quoted in Ellis, *Union at Risk,* p. 46.

22. Richard G. Miller, "The Tariff of 1832: The Issue that Failed," *Filson Club History Quarterly,* 49, no. 3 (July 1975), pp. 221–230.

23. Folsom, "Party Formation"; Remini, *Course,* pp. 345–352.

24. Burke, "Cherokee Cases."

25. Robert V. Remini, *Andrew Jackson and the Bank War: A Study in the Growth of Presidential Power* (New York: Norton, 1967), pp. 66–80.

26. "Veto Message," July 10, 1832, *Messages and Papers,* Vol. 3, pp. 1139–1154.

27. Robert V. Remini, "The Election of 1832," in *History of American Presidential Elections,* ed. Arthur Schlesinger, Jr. (New York: McGraw-Hill, 1971), p. 512.

28. "Fourth Annual Messsage," December 4, 1832, *Messages and Papers,* Vol. 3, pp. 1154–1169.

29. Quotations cited in Peterson, *Great Triumvirate,* pp. 216–219.

30. In fact Jackson, had ordered the tariff at Charleston to be collected at sea

before entering the harbor. Failure to pay was to result in the confiscation of the cargo at the island Fort Moultrie. Freehling, *Road to Disunion,* p. 279.

31. "Proclamation," December 10, 1832, in *Messages and Papers,* Vol. 3, pp. 1203–1219.

32. "Special Message," January 16, 1833, in *Messages and Papers,* Vol. 3, pp. 1173–1195.

33. On Webster's debate with Senator Robert Hayne over the nature of the federal compact see Peterson, *Great Triumvirate,* pp. 170–183.

34. Ellis, *Union at Risk,* pp. 74–101.

35. Ibid., pp. 158–177; Peterson, *Olive Branch,* pp. 40–84; Peterson, *Great Triumvirate,* pp. 212–233.

36. Remini, *Bank War,* p. 106; Ellis, *Union at Risk,* pp. 177–187; Freehling, *Road to Disunion,* pp. 282–285.

37. Peterson, *Olive Branch,* p. 91; Peterson, *Great Triumvirate,* p. 238.

38. Frank Otto Gatell, "Spoils of the Bank War: Political Bias in the Selection of the Pet Banks," *American Historical Review,* 70, no. 1 (October 1964), pp. 35–58. Frank Otto Gatell, "Secretary Taney and the Baltimore Pets: A Study in Banking and Politics," *Business History Review,* 39 (Spring 1965), pp. 205–227.

39. Remini, *Bank War,* pp. 109–155; Robert V. Remini, *Andrew Jackson and the Course of American Empire* (New York: Harper and Row, 1984), pp. 84–131; Thomas Paine Govan, *Nicholas Biddle: Nationalist and Public Banker, 1786–1844* (Chicago: University of Chicago Press, 1959).

40. U.S. Congress *Register,* March 1, 1833, 2nd session, 22nd Congress, pp. 1898–1902.

41. "Removal of the Deposits," September 18, 1833, *Messages and Papers,* Vol. 3, pp. 1225–1226.

42. Ibid.; Peterson, *Great Triumvirate,* pp. 234–241; Frank Otto Gatell, "Sober Second Thoughts on Van Buren, the Albany Regency, and the Wall Street Conspiracy," *Journal of American History,* 3, no. 1 (June 1953), pp. 19–40.

43. Charles Sellers, "Who Were the Southern Whigs?" *American Historical Review,* 59, no. 2 (January 1954), pp. 335–346; Richard P. McCormick, *The Second American Party System,* pp. 177–356; Remini, *Empire,* pp. 132–141.

44. Remini, *Empire,* p. 131.

45. Peterson, *Great Triumvirate,* pp. 241–244.

46. Govan, *Nicholas Biddle,* pp. 265–267; Remini, *Bank War,* pp. 165–166.

47. "Protest," April 15, 1834, *Messages and Papers,* Vol. 3, pp. 1288–1313; Remini, *Empire,* pp. 142–178.

48. McCormick, *Second Party System;* Sellers, "Who Were the Southern Whigs."

49. Remini, *Empire,* pp. 375–377; Peterson, *Great Triumvirate,* pp. 251–252. Change in the complexion of Congress between 1833 and 1835 reflects the stiffening of partisan division as well as the consolidation of Democratic control. The 23rd Congress hosted in the House 147 Democrats, 53 Anti-Masonic, and 60 others; in the Senate 20 Democrats, 20 National Republicans, 8 others. The 24th Congress hosted in the House 145 Democrats and 98 Whigs; 27 Democrats and 25 Whigs. *Congressional Quarterly's Guide to*

Congress, 2nd ed. (Washington, D.C.: Congressional Quarterly Press, 1976), pp. 182A–183A.

50. David J. Russo, "The Major Political Issues of the Jackson Period and the Development of Party Loyalty in Congress, 1830–1840," *Transactions of the American Philosophical Society,* new series, Vol. 62, pt. 2 (1972), pp. 3–51.

51. John M. McFaul, *The Politics of Jacksonian Finance* (Ithaca: Cornell University Press, 1972), pp. 82–178; Richard H. Timberlake, Jr., "The Specie Circular and Distribution of the Surplus" *Journal of Political Economy,* 68, no. 2 (April 1960), pp. 109–117; Richard Timberlake, Jr., "The Specie Standard and Central Banking in the United States before 1860," *Journal of Economic History,* 21, no. 3 (September 1961), pp. 318–341.

52. McFaul, *Jacksonian Finance,* pp. 82–178.

Part Two: James Polk's Articulation

1. Leonard White, *The Jacksonians: A Study in Administrative History, 1829–1861* (New York: Macmillan, 1954), pp. 311–312.

2. For an analysis of the Democratic party in the states between 1840 and 1849 with special attention to the surge in the congressional elections of 1842 and defeat in the congressional elections of 1846–47 see Brian J. G. Walton, "James K. Polk and the Democratic Party in the Aftermath of the Wilmot Proviso," unpublished doctoral dissertation, Vanderbilt University, 1968.

3. Take, for example, Polk's decision to dismantle the *Globe,* the chief propaganda organ of the Jackson and Van Buren presidencies, in favor of launching his own organ *(Washington Union).* This action, fully consonant with Jackson's understanding of the president's political role as party leader, raised eyebrows from Tennessee to New York and instantly strained the pretense of taking control in the service of political continuity.

4. Jackson, "To the Senate and House of Representatives," December 21, 1836, in *A Compilation of the Messages and Papers of the Presidents,* Vol. 4, ed. James D. Richardson (New York: Bureau of National Literature, 1897), pp. 1484–1488.

5. William Freehling, *The Road to Disunion,* Vol. 1: *Secessionists at Bay, 1776–1854* (New York: Oxford University Press, 1990), pp. 427–428.

6. Charles Sellers, *James K. Polk: Jacksonian* (Princeton: Princeton University Press, 1957); Charles Sellers, *James K.Polk: Continentalist* (Princeton: Princeton University Press, 1966), pp. 3–107; Freehling, *Road to Disunion,* pp. 429–439.

7. Eugene Irving McCormick, *James K. Polk: A Political Biography* (Berkeley: University of California Press, 1922), pp. 239, 261, 282.

8. "Statement of Acceptance of the nomination," June 12, 1844, Polk Papers, Library of Congress.

9. "Statement of intent to cabinet appointees," January 15, 1845, Polk Papers.

10. Sellers, *Continentalist,* pp. 282–283; "Polk to Silas Wright," July 8, 1845, Polk Papers; "J. K. Walker to E. F. Purdy," July 19, 1845, Polk Papers; Washington *Union,* May 13, 1845.

11. "Polk to Cave Johnson," December 21, 1844, "Polk-Johnson Letters," ed. St.

George L. Sioussat *Tennessee Historical Magazine,* 1, no. 3 (September 1915), p. 254.

12. See Joseph Raybeck, "Martin Van Buren's Break with James K. Polk: The Record," *New York History,* 36, no. 1 (January 1955), pp. 51–62.

13. "Polk to Wright," December 7, 1844, Polk Papers. Changes in the final draft of this letter are noted by Sellers, *Continentalist,* p. 178.

14. "Wright to Polk," December 20, 1844, Polk Papers.

15. "Polk to Wright," January 4, 1845, Polk Papers; "Polk to Van Buren," January 30, 1845, Van Buren Papers, Library of Congress.

16. Sellers, *Continentalist,* p. 184. According to Sellers's analysis, four of the six men on this list could be safely classified as friendly to Van Buren, and only one, Robert Walker of Mississippi in the Attorney General slot, was obviously hostile to the Van Buren wing. The Northwest was the only section not represented on this preliminary list, and it would be the only section not represented in the final cabinet.

17. Paul Bergeron, *The Presidency of James K. Polk* (Lawrence: University of Kansas Press, 1987), pp. 23–50.

18. "Polk to Van Buren," February 22, 1845, Polk Papers.

19. Ibid.

20. Sellers, *Continentalist,* p. 201.

21. "Van Buren to Polk," February 27, 1845, Van Buren Papers; "Van Buren to Polk," March 1, 1845, Polk Papers; Sellers, *Continentalist,* p. 202; John Niven, *Martin Van Buren: The Romantic Age of American Politics* (New York: Oxford University Press, 1983), pp. 560–564.

22. Sellers, *Continentalist,* p. 203.

23. *The Diary of James K. Polk, 1845–1849,* Vol. 1, ed. Milo Milton Quaife (Chicago: A. C. McClurg, 1910), pp. 103–104; Niven, *Van Buren,* pp. 564–565. On the purge of the Free Soilers in 1848 see McCormick, *Polk,* p. 643, and Charles McCoy, *Polk and the Presidency* (Austin: University of Texas Press, 1960), pp. 197–198, 203–204. For a general treatment of Polk's patronage difficulties see Norman A. Graebner, "James K. Polk: A Study in Federal Patronage," *Mississippi Valley Historical Review,* 38, no. 4 (March 1952), pp. 613–632.

24. This program was articulated in Polk's inaugural address and his first annual message; see *Messages and Papers,* Vol. 5, pp. 2223–2232, 2235–2266.

25. Ibid., pp. 2241–2242.

26. The terms "reannexation" and "reoccupation" referred back to agreements made during John Quincy Adams's stewardship as secretary of state under Monroe and as president. One excluded Texas from American claims under the Florida Treaty, and the other permitted a joint occupation of the Oregon Territory by Great Britain and the United States that could be terminated upon one year's notification by either country.

27. See Major Wilson, *Space, Time, and Freedom: The Quest for Nationality and the Irrepressible Conflict, 1815–1861* (Westport: Greenwood Press, 1974), pp. 94–120.

28. The following discussion draws heavily on my essay "Presidential Leadership in Political Time" in *The Presidency and the Political System,* ed. Michael

Nelson (Washington, D.C.: Congressional Quarterly Press, 1988), pp. 105–108. See also, Sellers, *Continentalist*, pp. 213–487; and John H. Schroeder, *Mr. Polk's War: American Opposition and Dissent, 1846–1848* (Madison: University of Wisconsin Press, 1973).

29. Chaplain W. Morrison, *Democratic Politics and Sectionalism: The Wilmot Proviso Controversy* (Chapel Hill: University of North Carolina Press, 1967), pp. 11–13, 25.

30. *Diary*, Vol. 1, esp. pp. 107, 140–141. On November 29, 1845, Polk expressed his belief that his administration risked more by compromise than by belligerence over Oregon. On December 24, however, Polk recorded the following conversation with Senator Turney of Tennessee: "He said many members of Congress were opposed to war and would follow Mr. Calhoun, while some members from the West were almost mad on the subject of Oregon, and that I was between these two fires and whatever I might do I must dissatisfy the one or the other of these sections of the party. He then asked me . . . if I had made up my mind what course I would take if Great Britain should renew the offer of 49$ or some equivalent to it. To this I answered that my opinions . . . were candidly set forth in the message [to Congress], and that I adhered to the opinions there expressed; but that if such a proposition . . . was made, the decision upon it would probably involve the question of peace or War. I told [him] in event of such a proposition being made I would feel inclined to take the advise of the Senate confidentially before I acted upon it."

31. *Messages and Papers*, Vol. 6, pp. 2287–2293. The war message was delivered on May 11, 1846.

32. Ibid., pp. 2299–2300. The call on the Senate to decide the Oregon issue was made on June 10, 1846.

33. The decision to send Col. Kearney West to California was made by the cabinet on June 2; the issue of settling the Oregon boundary was taken up on June 4. See *Diary*, Vol. 1, pp. 443–444, 447–463. For Polk's attempt to deal with the fall-out on the Oregon issue, most especially the resignation of the chairman of the foreign affairs committee, see *Diary*, Vol. 1, pp. 473, 475–476.

34. Thomas Stirton, "Party Disruption and the Rise of the Slavery Extension Controversy, 1840–1846," unpublished doctoral dissertation, University of Chicago, 1957.

35. Stirton distinguishes a pocket of vehement opposition to the Oregon settlement in the central and southern parts of the Northwest, and a pocket of grudging acquiescence around the Great Lakes. See ibid., pp. 284–290. Sellers, *Continentalist*, pp. 445–488; Stirton, ibid., pp. 271–283, 290–314.

36. August 3, 1846, *Messages and Papers*, Vol. 6, pp. 2310–2316; Paul Bergeron, "President Polk and Economic Legislation," *Presidential Studies Quarterly*, 15, no. 4 (Fall 1985), pp. 782–796.

37. August 8, 1846, *Messages and Papers*, Vol. 6, pp. 2309–2310.

38. Eric Foner, "The Wilmot Proviso Revisited," *Journal of American History*, 56 (1969), pp. 262–279.

39. Morrison, *Democratic Politics*, pp. 3–37. Sellers, *Continentalist*, pp. 478–485.

40. *Diary*, Vol. 2, pp. 75, 334–335, 347–348; Vol. 4, pp. 33–34.

41. See Schroeder, *Mr. Polk's War,* p. 42.
42. Morrison, *Democratic Politics,* pp. 21–51, 75–120.
43. This dismay with the established parties was evident not only in the Free Soil campaign but also in the nonpartisan appeal of Zachary Taylor and the effort of the Taylor administration to break down the old party division. Michael Holt, *The Political Crisis of the 1850's* (New York: Norton, 1978), pp. 67–69.
44. Bergeron, "President Polk," pp. 201–215.
45. *Diary,* Vol. 3, pp. 501–502.
46. August 14, 1848, *Messages and Papers,* Vol. 6, pp. 2456–2460.
47. Morrison, *Democratic Politics,* pp. 168–169; McCormick, *Polk,* p. 635.
48. Holt, *Political Crisis* Joel Silbey, *The Partisan Imperative: The Dynamics of American Politics before the Civil War* (New York: Oxford University Press, 1985).
49. Holt himself suggests as much in *Political Crisis,* p. 104.

Part Three: Franklin Pierce's Disjunction

1. Roy Nichols, *The Democratic Machine, 1850–1854* (New York: AMS Press, 1967); Michael Holt, *The Political Crisis of the 1850's* (New York: Norton, 1978), pp. 87–99.
2. Nichols, *Democratic Machine,* p. 144.
3. Roy Nichols, *Franklin Pierce: Young Hickory of the Granite Hills* (Philadelphia: University of Pennsylvania Press, 1931), pp. 63–186.
4. Nichols, *Young Hickory,* p. 202.
5. William Freehling, *The Road to Disunion,* Vol. 1: *Secessionists at Bay, 1776–1854* (New York: Oxford University Press, 1990), p. 554.
6. Holt, *Political Crisis,* pp. 140–143.
7. For this and the following paragraphs see Nichols, *Democratic Machine,* pp. 169–226.
8. Freehling, *Road to Disunion,* p. 536–537.
9. Nichols, *Franklin Pierce,* pp. 287–293.
10. Robert Johannsen, *Stephen A. Douglas* (New York: Oxford University Press, 1973), p. 389.
11. "First Annual Message," December 5, 1853, in *A Compilation of the Messages and Papers of Presidents,* ed. James D. Richardson (New York: Bureau of National Literature, 1897), Vol. 6, pp. 2740–2753; Vol. 7, pp. 2754–2759.
12. "Inaugural Address," March 4, 1853, *Messages and Papers,* Vol. 6, p. 2731.
13. Ibid., p. 2736.
14. Roy Nichols, "The Kansas-Nebraska Act: A Century of Historiography," *Mississippi Valley Historical Review,* 43 (December 1956), pp. 187–212; David M. Potter, *The Impending Crisis, 1848–1861* (New York: Harper and Row, 1963), p. 154; Paul Neff Garber, *The Gadsden Treaty* (Gloucester, Mass.: Peter Smith, 1959), pp. 77–93. Johannsen, *Douglas,* pp. 374–400.
15. Nichols, "Kansas-Nebraska Act"; Potter, *Impending Crisis,* pp. 152–161; Garber, *Gadsden Treaty,* p. 101; Johannsen, *Douglas,* pp. 401–413; Holt, *Political Crisis,* p. 146; Freeling, *Road to Disunion,* pp. 550–565.
16. Nichols, *Franklin Pierce,* pp. 321–322.

17. Ibid., pp. 315–316; Johannsen, *Douglas,* p. 389.
18. Nichols, *Franklin Pierce,* p. 324.
19. *The Congressional Globe,* 33rd Congress, 1st Session, January 30, 1854, pp. 280–282; *Appendix to the Congressional Globe,* 33rd Congress, 1st Session, p. 133. William Gienapp, *The Origins of the Republican Party* (New York: Oxford University Press, 1987), pp. 71–76; Holt, *Political Crisis,* pp. 151–154.
20. Nichols, *Franklin Pierce,* p. 324; on Douglas's role in the Senate see Johannsen, *Douglas,* pp. 401–434; Gienapp, *Origins,* p. 81.
21. Nichols, "The Kansas-Nebraska Act" Nichols, *Franklin Pierce,* pp. 333–338. Gienapp, *Origins,* p. 77.
22. Daniel Walker Howe, *The Political Culture of the American Whigs* (Chicago: University of Chicago Press, 1979), p. 276.
23. Garber, *Gadsden Treaty,* pp. 109–145; Potter, *Impending Crisis,* pp. 182–183.
24. March 15, 1854, *Messages and Papers,* Vol. 7, pp. 2767–2768.
25. Nichols, *Franklin Pierce,* pp. 328–329, 340–344; Potter, *Impending Crisis,* pp. 183–188; *Messages and Papers,* Vol. 7, p. 2779.
26. On this point see Gienapp, *Origins,* esp. pp. 81, 161, 299.
27. Potter, *Impending Crisis,* pp. 189–192; Nichols, *Franklin Pierce,* pp. 366–371; Gienapp, *Origins,* pp. 335, 337.
28. Nichols, *Franklin Pierce,* pp. 400–415, 441–445; Gienapp, *Origins,* pp. 168–172, 295–303.
29. Quoted in Nichols, *Franklin Pierce,* p. 421.
30. "Third Annual Message," December 31, 1855, *Messages and Papers,* Vol. 7, pp. 2873–2883.
31. Nichols, *Franklin Pierce,* pp. 466–469; Gienapp, *Origins,* pp. 305–307.

6. Republican Leadership: Stiffening Crosscurrents

Part One: Abraham Lincoln's Reconstruction

1. William Herndon, *Herndon's Life of Lincoln,* ed. Paul M. Angle (New York: Albert and Charles Boni, 1930), p. 304.
2. "On the Perpetuation of Our Political Institutions: An Address before the Springfield Young Men's Lyceum," January 22, 1838, *The Collected Works of Abraham Lincoln,* Vol. 1, ed. Roy P. Bassler (New Brunswick, N.J.: Rutgers University Press, 1953), pp. 108–115. Also George Forgie, *Patricide in the House Divided: A Psychological Interpretation of Lincoln and His Age* (New York: Norton, 1979), pp. 14–55.
3. Harold S. Schultz, "Lincoln: Partisan or Patriot?" in *The Leadership of Abraham Lincoln,* ed. Don E. Fehrenbacher (New York: Wiley, 1970), p. 19; "To Ichabod Codding," November 27, 1854, *Collected Works,* Vol. 2, p. 288; "To Thomas Henderson," November 27, 1854, ibid., p. 288.
4. Stephen B. Oates, *With Malice toward None: The Life of Abraham Lincoln* (New York: Harper and Row, 1977). Oates opens his sensitive biography with the following observations: "Outside of Illinois, people knew little about him.

Even newspapers were conspicuously reticent about his life and background . . . In the South, Democrats who understood nothing about the candidate as a man, nothing at all, castigated him as a symbol of 'Black Republicanism' . . . Even many Republicans were hard pressed to talk about their candidate, to sell voters on his appeal and his talents." See also, James M. McPherson, *Battle Cry of Freedom: The Civil War Era* (New York: Oxford University Press, 1988), p. 219.

5. Joel H. Silbey, *A Respectable Minority: The Democratic Party in the Civil War Era, 1860–1868* (New York: Norton, 1977).

6. J. G. Randall, *Lincoln, The President: Springfield to Gettysburg,* Vol. 2 (New York: Dodd, Mead, 1945), pp. 232–237.

7. William B. Hesseltine, *Lincoln and the War Governors* (New York: Knopf, 1948), p. 253.

8. Edward S. Corwin, *The President: Office and Powers* (New York: New York University Press, 1957), p. 452.

9. Randall, in *Lincoln,* Vol. 2, devotes an entire chapter to "Politics as Usual," pp. 203–237. T. Harry Williams treats this theme as a point of controversy in Lincoln historiography in "Shall We Keep the Radicals?" in Fehrenbacher, *Leadership,* pp. 99–110.

10. Oates, *Malice,* pp. 202–203; McPherson, *Battle Cry,* p. 228.

11. Randall, *Lincoln,* Vol. 1, pp. 218–220.

12. "Annual Message to Congress," December 6, 1864, in *Collected Works,* Vol. 8, p. 151.

13. "Oneida County Proceedings of the Republican Party Convention," held at Rome, N.Y., September 26, 1892, published in *The Utica Morning Herald,* Utica, N.Y.

14. David Donald, "A. Lincoln, Politician," in *Lincoln Reconsidered: Essays on the Civil War Era* (New York: Random House, 1961), p. 65. See also Eric McKitrick, "Party Politics in the Union and Confederate War Efforts," in *The American Party Systems: Stages of Development,* ed. Walter Dean Burnham and William Nisbet Chambers (New York: Oxford University Press, 1967), pp. 117–151. More generally, see Harry J. Carman and Reinhard H. Luthin, *Lincoln and the Patronage* (New York: Columbia University Press, 1943).

15. "Memorandum on the Charges against Simon Cameron," December 31, 1860, *Collected Works,* Vol. 6, p. 165; "To Simon Cameron," January 3, 1861, *Collected Works,* Vol. 4, pp. 169–170; Randall, *Lincoln,* Vol. 1, pp. 264–267; Randall, *Lincoln,* Vol. 2, pp. 54–61; Oates, *Malice,* pp. 290–300; McPherson, *Battle Cry,* pp. 321–324.

16. This point might be broadened. Those who would root Lincoln's success in his skill in manipulating the patronage point out that the President would often be guided by political rather than military considerations in appointing generals to the Army. There is no denying that Lincoln had good reasons for doing this; patronage was the key to sustaining political power in the party state. These appointments, like the appointment of Cameron, looked toward bolstering Lincoln's position within the Republican party and building national support for the war effort. But the frustrating, often tragic, performance

of these political generals in the field proved a dubious asset. Lincoln may have been constrained to appoint military incompetents, but his leadership was certainly not enhanced by them. Patronage politics was as much a no-win game for him as it was for the other presidents of the party period.

17. Carl Sandburg, *Abraham Lincoln: The Prairie Years and the War Years*, 1-vol. ed. (New York: Harcourt Brace, 1954), pp. vii–viii.

18. Donald, "Abraham Lincoln and the American Pragmatic Tradition," in *Lincoln Reconsidered*, pp. 128–143; also on Lincoln as a "pragmatic revolutionary," see James M. McPherson, *Abraham Lincoln and the Second American Revolution* (New York: Oxford University Press, 1991), p. 41. McPherson's essays offer a compelling blend of realist and romantic themes.

19. Oates, *Malice*, p. 197; McPherson, *Battle Cry*, pp. 217–219.

20. "A House Divided" at Springfield, Illinois, June 16, 1858, *Collected Works*, Vol. 2, pp. 461–468.

21. Ibid., p. 467.

22. Generally, see Harry Jaffa, *The Crisis of the House Divided: An Interpretation of the Lincoln-Douglas Debates* (Seattle: University of Washington Press, 1959).

23. "At Peoria, Illinois," October 16, 1854, *Collected Works*, Vol. 2, p. 276.

24. Competing claims to the legacy of Thomas Jefferson figured prominently in the Lincoln-Douglas debates, *Collected Works*, Vol. 3, passim. Also Daniel Walker Howe, *The Political Culture of the American Whigs* (Chicago: University of Chicago Press, 1979), pp. 290–298; more generally, J. David Greenstone, *The Lincoln Persuasion: Polarity and Synthesis in American Politics* (Princeton: Princeton Universtiy Press, 1993).

25. "To H. L. Pierce and Others," Springfield, Illinois, April 6, 1859, *Collected Works*, Vol. 3, pp. 364–376.

26. Oates, *Malice*, pp. 196–199.

27. "A House Divided," *Collected Works*, Vol. 2, pp. 461–468.

28. "Address at Cooper Institute," February 27, 1860, *Collected Works*, Vol. 3, pp. 374–376.

29. "At Peoria, Illinois," *Collected Works*, Vol. 2, p. 276.

30. Oates, *Malice*, pp. 215–216; Randall, *Lincoln*, Vol. 1, pp. 236–237; McPherson, *Battle Cry*, p. 253; McPherson, *Abraham Lincoln*, p. 118; see also Schultz, "Lincoln: Partisan or Patriot," in Fehrenbacher, *Leadership*, p. 23, and Allan Nevins, "Why Lincoln Said 'No,'" ibid., pp. 26–29; letters to Lyman Trumble, William Kellogg, Elihu Washburne, John Gimer, William Seward, and John Defrees, in *Collected Works*, Vol. 4, pp. 253–283.

31. On the political debate over the Constitution as a constraint or warrant for radical action see Harold M. Hyman, *A More Perfect Union: The Impact of the Civil War and Reconstruction on the Constitution* (New York: Knopf, 1973), pp. 99–125. Also see Otto H. Olsen, "Abraham Lincoln as Revolutionary," *Civil War History*, 24, no. 3 (September 1978), pp. 213–221; Herman Belz, "Lincoln and the Constitution: The 'Dictatorship Question' Reconsidered," *Congress and the Presidency*, 15, no. 2 (Autumn 1988), pp. 147–164; Glen E. Thurow, *Abraham Lincoln and the American Political*

Religion (Albany: State University of New York Press, 1976); Greenstone, *Lincoln Persuasion.*

32. On the relationship between Lincoln and the radicals leading up to this action see T. Harry Williams, *Lincoln and the Radicals* (Madison: University of Wisconsin Press, 1941); Hans Trefousse, *The Radical Republicans: Lincoln's Vanguard for Racial Justice* (Baton Rouge: Louisiana State University Press, 1968); Mark Krug, "The Republican Party and the Emancipation Proclamation," in *Civil War and Reconstruction,* ed. Irwin Unger (New York: Holt, Reinhart and Winston, 1970), pp. 275–286; David Donald, "Devils Facing Zionwards," in *Grant, Lee, Lincoln, and the Radicals* (Evanston: Northwestern University Press, 1964); Williams, "Shall We Keep the Radicals?" The position taken here stands apart from both sides of the argument as presented in these works.

33. On the revolutionary significance of the Emancipation Proclamation, see McPherson, *Abraham Lincoln,* passim.

34. Oates, *Malice,* pp. 333–347.

35. "First Inaugural Address," March 4, 1861, *Collected Works,* Vol. 4, pp. 262–271.

36. "Message to Congress in Special Session," July 4, 1861, *Collected Works,* Vol. 4, pp. 421–441.

37. Michael F. Holt, "Abraham Lincoln and the Politics of Union," in *Abraham Lincoln and the American Political Tradition,* ed. John L. Thomas (Amherst: University of Massachusetts Press, 1986), pp. 110–141; Sandburg, *Lincoln,* pp. 514–521.

38. *Collected Works,* Vol. 4, p. 263.

39. Randall, *Lincoln,* Vol. 2, pp. 126–150; Oates, *Malice,* pp. 333–335; McPherson, *Battle Cry,* pp. 494–503; "Appeal to Border State Representatives in Favor of Compensated Emancipation," July 12, 1862, *Collected Works,* Vol. 5, pp. 317–319.

40. "Preliminary Emancipation Proclamation," September 22, 1862, *Collected Works,* Vol. 5, pp. 433–436; Oates, *Malice,* pp. 345–354; McPherson, *Battle Cry,* pp. 503–505, 557–562.

41. "Emancipation Proclamation," January 1, 1863, *Collected Works,* Vol. 6, pp. 28–30; "To Andrew Johnson," March 26, 1863, *Collected Works,* Vol. 6, p. 149. Oates, *Malice,* pp. 355–373; McPherson, *Battle Cry,* p. 565.

42. The Republican/Union party convention met on June 7; the House failed to pass the amendment on June 15. Oates, *Malice,* pp. 421–423; Herman Belz, *Reconstructing the Union: Theory and Policy during the Civil War* (Ithaca: Cornell University Press, 1969), pp. 213–216.

43. Quoted in Oates, *Malice,* pp. 439–440.

44. Ibid., p. 441.

45. Belz, "Lincoln and the Constitution."

46. "To Albert Hodges," April 4, 1864, *Collected Works,* Vol. 7, p. 282.

47. David Donald, "Abraham Lincoln: Whig in the White House," *Lincoln Reconsidered,* pp. 187–208.

48. Phillip Shaw Paludan, *"A People's Contest": The Union and Civil War, 1861–*

1865 (New York: Harper and Row, 1988), pp. 105–169; Leonard P. Curry, *Blueprint for Modern America: Nonmilitary Legislation of the First Civil War Congress* (Nashville: Vanderbilt University Press, 1968); also G. S. Boritt, *Lincoln and the Economics of the American Dream* (Memphis: Memphis State University Press, 1978); G. S. Boritt, "Old Wine into New Bottles: Abraham Lincoln and the Tariff Reconsidered," *Historian,* 28 (1966), pp. 289–317; Reinhard H. Luthin, "Abraham Lincoln and the Tariff," *American Historical Review,* 49, no. 4 (July 1944), pp. 609–629; McPherson, *Abraham Lincoln,* pp. 37–40.

49. Randall, *Lincoln,* Vol. 2, pp. 1–125; Oates, *Malice,* pp. 249–303; McPherson, *Battle Cry,* pp. 352–362.

50. Holt, "Abraham Lincoln and the Politics of Union," p. 117.

51. Ibid., pp. 117–141.

52. "Proclamation of Amnesty and Reconstruction," December 8, 1863, *Collected Works,* Vol. 7, pp. 53–56; Belz, *Reconstructing the Union,* pp. 100–167.

53. This analysis of the Louisiana situation and the development of the Wade-Davis bill draws most directly on the following sources: Belz, *Reconstructing the Union,* pp. 100–243; La Wanda Cox, *Lincoln and Black Freedom: A Study in Presidential Leadership* (Urbana: University of Illinois Press, 1985); Peyton McCrary, *Abraham Lincoln and Reconstruction: The Louisiana Experiment* (Princeton: Princeton University Press, 1978); more generally see Eric Foner, *Reconstruction: America's Unfinished Revolution, 1863–1877* (New York: Harper and Row, 1987), pp. 35–76.

54. Cox, *Lincoln and Black Freedom,* pp. 81, 166–167.

55. Oates, *Malice,* pp. 426–427.

56. "Proclamation Concerning Reconstruction," July 8, 1864, *Collected Works,* Vol. 7, pp. 433–434.

57. Wade-Davis Manifesto, "To the Supporters of the Government," *New York Tribune,* August 5, 1864, p. 5.

58. Oates, *Malice,* p. 427; Belz, *Reconstructing the Union,* pp. 230–231.

59. Oates, *Malice,* pp. 431–433; McPherson, *Battle Cry,* p. 776.

60. Foner, *Reconstruction,* pp. 176–227.

61. For an especially well-balanced treatment of the prospects, see Cox, *Lincoln and Black Freedom,* pp. 144–184.

Part Two: Theodore Roosevelt's Articulation

1. *Theodore Roosevelt: An Autobiography* (New York: Scribners, 1913), p. 379.

2. Speech at Cambridge, May 26, 1910, cited in John M. Cooper, *The Warrior and the Priest: Woodrow Wilson and Theodore Roosevelt* (Cambridge: Harvard University Press, 1983), p. 118; or as he put it in the early years of his presidency: "If during the lifetime of a generation no crisis occurs sufficient to call out in marked manner the energies of the strongest leader, then of course the world does not and cannot know of the existence of such a leader." "Speech at Canton," Ohio, January 27, 1903, *The Works of Theodore*

Roosevelt: Presidential Addresses and State Papers, Vol. 1, ed. Albert Shaw (New York: Review of Reviews, 1904), pp. 231–232.

3. "Introduction," *The Letters of Theodore Roosevelt,* Vol. 5, ed. Elting Morison (Cambridge: Harvard University Press, 1953), pp. xiii–xiv. See also Matthew Josephson, *The President Makers: The Culture and Politics of Leadership in an Age of Enlightenment* (New York: Harcourt Brace, 1940); Richard Hoftstadter, *The American Political Tradition and the Men Who Made It* (New York: Knopf, 1948), pp. 206–237. Ambivalent judgments about Roosevelt's presidency may be traced back before the New Deal to Henry F. Pringle, *Theodore Roosevelt: A Biography* (New York: Harcourt Brace, 1931).

4. Dewey W. Grantham, Jr., "Theodore Roosevelt in American Historical Writing," *Mid-America,* 43, no. 1 (January 1961), pp. 3–35.

5. Benchmarks of the Roosevelt revival include John Morton Blum, *The Republican Roosevelt* (Cambridge: Harvard University Press, 1954); George Mowry, *The Era of Theodore Roosevelt and the Birth of Modern America, 1900–1912* (New York: Harper and Row, 1958); Howard K. Beale, *Theodore Roosevelt and the Rise of America to World Power* (Baltimore: Johns Hopkins University Press, 1956); William Harbaugh, *Power and Responsibility* (New York: Farrar, Straus and Cudahy, 1961); Grantham, "Theodore Roosevelt in American Historical Writing."

6. "Evasions and compromises," see Henry F. Pringle, *The Life and Times of William Howard Taft,* Vol. 1, (New York: Farrar and Reinhart, 1939), p. 382.

7. Pringle, *Roosevelt,* p. 223.

8. Ibid., pp. 151–164.

9. "To Paul Dana," May 7, 1900, *Letters,* Vol. 2, p. 1290; "To Arthur Hamilton Lee," July 25, 1900, *Letters,* Vol. 2, pp. 1362–1363; "To Winthrop Chanler," July 26, 1900, *Letters,* Vol. 2, p. 1364; "To William Howard Taft," August 6, 1900, *Letters,* Vol. 2, p. 1377.

10. This summary is gleaned from *Addresses and State Papers,* Vols. 1 and 2.

11. At Boston, August 25, 1902, *Addresses and State Papers,* Vol. 1, p. 112. On this point see Richard Hofstadter, *American Political Tradition,* pp. 206–237.

12. *Autobiography,* pp. 364–367.

13. Roosevelt cited Robert La Follette approvingly when the progressive Senator from Wisconsin commended him for "making reform respectable in a commercialized world," *Autobiography,* p. 406.

14. "To Sydney Brooks," November 20, 1908, *Letters,* Vol. 6, p. 1369.

15. *Autobiography,* p. 283; Harbaugh, *Power,* pp. 252–253.

16. Roosevelt quoted from Burke often. This passage is taken from a speech he made at the opening of the Jamestown exposition, April 26, 1907, *Works,* Vol. 6, pp. 1213–1228.

17. For a sampling of these usages in just one six-week period consider: "Speech at the Charleston Exposition," April 9, 1902, *Addresses and State Papers,* Vol. 1, p. 24; "At the Exercises of the Society of the Army of the Cumberland," May 17, 1902, *Addresses,* Vol. 1, p. 40; "At the Centennial Meeting of the Presbyterian Home Missions," May 20, 1902, *Addresses,* Vol. 1, p. 51.

18. James Anthony Rosmond, "Nelson Aldrich, Theodore Roosevelt and the Tariff," Ph.D. dissertation, University of North Carolina, Chapel Hill, 1974.
19. "To Nicholas Murray Butler," September, 24, 1907, *Letters,* Vol. 5, p. 805.
20. Rosmond, "Nelson Aldrich," passim. Also see Mowry, *Era,* pp. 127–129; Lewis Gould, *The Presidency of Theodore Roosevelt* (Lawrence: University of Kansas Press, 1991), pp. 47–72, 101–126, 147–172.
21. "To William Howard Taft," March 19, 1903, *Letters,* Vol. 3, p. 450.
22. "To Elihu Root," June 2, 1904, *Letters,* Vol. 4, p. 813.
23. Rosmond, "Nelson Aldrich," pp. 150–165; Gould, *Presidency,* pp. 64–65.
24. "At Logansport Indiana," September 23, 1903, *Addresses and State Papers,* Vol. 1, pp. 192–194. Or as he said in Minneapolis, *Addresses,* Vol. 1, pp. 299–302:

    It is almost as necessary that our policy should be stable as that it should be wise. A nation like ours could not stand the ruinous policy of readjusting its business to radical changes in the tariff at short intervals . . . Sweeping and violent changes in such a tariff, touching so vitally the interests of all of us, embracing agriculture, labor manufactures, and commence, would be disasterous in any event, and they would be fatal to our present well being if approached on the theory that the principle of the protective tariff should be abandoned . . .

    Our aim should be to preserve the policy of the protective tariff, in which the Nation as a whole has acquiesced, and yet wherever and whenever necessary to change the duties in particular paragraphs or schedules as matters of legislative detail, if such change is demanded by the interests of the Nation as a whole . . .

    We can not afford to become fossilized or to fail to recognize the fact that as the needs of the country change it may be necessary to meet these needs by changing certain features of our tariff laws. Still less can we afford to fail to recognize the further fact that these changes must not be made until the need for them outweighs the disadvantages which may result; and when it becomes necessary to make them they should be made with full recognition of the need of stability in our economic system and of keeping unchanged the principle of that system which has now become settled policy in our national life. We have prospered marvelously at home. As a nation we stand in the very forefront in the giant international industrial competition of the day. We can not afford by any freak or folly to forfeit the position to which we have thus triumphantly attained.

25. "To Nicholas Murray Butler," August 22, 1904, *Letters,* Vol. 4, pp. 899–900.
26. "Accepting the Presidential Nomination of the Republican National Convention," *Addresses and State Papers,* Vol. 3, pp. 72–73.
27. "To James Ford Rhodes," November 29, 1904, *Letters,* Vol. 4, p. 1050. Also "To Lyman Abbott," January 11, 1905: "On the tariff, which I regard as a matter of expediency, I shall endeavor to get the best results I can, but I shall not break with my party." *Letters,* Vol. 4, p. 1100.
28. "To Nicholas Murray Butler," December 2, 1904, *Letters,* Vol. 4, pp. 1055–1056.

29. "To Joseph Gurney Cannon," November 30, 1904, *Letters,* Vol. 4, p. 1052. See Morrison's explanatory note to Roosevelt's letter to James Tawney, November 10, 1904, *Letters,* Vol. 4, pp. 1028–1029.
30. "To Nicholas Murray Butler," September 20, 1907, *Letters,* Vol. 5, p. 798.
31. "To Nicholas Murray Butler," September 24, 1907, *Letters,* Vol. 5, p. 806.
32. "To William Howard Taft," November 10, 1908, *Letters,* Vol. 6, p. 1340; Pringle, *William Howard Taft,* pp. 402–407. George Mowry, *Theodore Roosevelt and the Progressive Movement* (Madison: University of Wisconsin Press, 1947), p. 42.
33. For a while after Roosevelt's intervention, Taft continued to resist the counsel of reconciliation and took some concrete steps to encourage the progressive insurgency before backing down. Mowry, *Era,* pp. 238–241.
34. Mowry, *Progressive Movement,* pp. 42–65.
35. "To George Otto Trevelyan," June 19, 1908, *Letters,* Vol. 6, pp. 1085–1087; *Autobiography,* pp. 278–280; "The Presidency," *Addresses and State Papers,* Vol. 1, pp. 1–3.
36. "Orderly progress," see "To James E. Watson," *Letters,* August 18, 1906, Vol. 5, p. 373.
37. "To George Otto Trevelyan," Washington, D.C., March 9, 1905, *Letters,* Vol. 4, p. 1133.
38. "Speech at Wheeling West Virginia," September 6, 1902, *Addresses and State Papers,* Vol. 1, p. 147.
39. See for example, "Speech to the G.A.R.," February 19, 1902, *Addresses and State Papers,* Vol. 1, p. 17; "Speech at Topeka Kansas," May 1, 1903, *Addresses,* p. 354; "To Maria Longworth Storer," December 8, 1902, *Letters,* Vol. 3, pp. 391–392; "To George Otto Trevelyan," November 6, 1908, *Letters,* Vol. 6, p. 1329. Also Cooper, *Warrior and Priest,* p. 111.
40. "At Providence Rhode Island," August 23, 1902, *Addresses and State Papers,* Vol. 1, p. 106.
41. "To Maria Longworth Storer," December 8, 1902, *Letters,* Vol. 3, p. 392: "Of course political life in a position such as this is one long strain on the temper, one long acceptance of the second best, one long experiment in checking one's impulses with an iron hand and learning to subordinate one's own desires to what some hundreds of associates can be forced or cajoled or led into desiring."
42. Beale, *Theodore Roosevelt,* pp. 71–73; Gould, *Presidency,* p. 73.
43. Gould, ibid., pp. 173–179.
44. "To Congress," December 3, 1901, *Addresses and State Papers,* Vol. 2, pp. 273–284; Mowry, *Era,* pp. 144–163; Beale, *Theodore Roosevelt,* passim; Gould, *Presidency,* pp. 91–99, 264–268.
45. For example, "To George Bruce Cortelyou," July 18, 1904, *Letters,* Vol. 4, p. 861.
46. Albert Shaw, "The Progress of the World," *American Monthly Review of Reviews,* 25 (April 1902), p. 398; Gould, *Presidency,* p. 52.
47. Stephen Skowronek, *Building a New American State: The Expansion of Na-*

tional Administrative Capacities, 1887–1920 (New York: Cambridge University Press, 1982).

48. Jeffrey Tulis, *The Rhetorical Presidency* (Princeton: Princeton University Press, 1987), pp. 97–110.

49. On the coal strike see Robert Wiebe, "The Anthracite Coal Strike of 1902: A Record of Confusion," *Mississippi Valley Historical Review,* 48, no. 2, (September 1961), pp. 229–249.

50. Arthur M. Johnson, "Theodore Roosevelt and the Bureau of Corporations," *Mississippi Valley Historical Review,* 46, no. 4 (March 1959), pp. 571–590. Also, more generally, Martin Sklar, *The Corporate Reconstruction of American Capitalism, 1890–1916: The Market, The Law and Politics* (New York: Cambridge University Press, 1988), pp. 179–332; Gould, *Presidency,* pp. 105–108.

51. "At Cincinnatti," September 20, 1902, *Addresses and State Papers,* Vol. 1, pp. 176–177; "At Milwaulkee," April 3, 1903, *Addresses,* Vol. 1, p. 285.

52. "At Jamestown, North Dakota," April 7, 1903, *Addresses and State Papers,* Vol. 1, p. 322.

53. "At Milwaukee," April 13, 1903, *Addresses and State Papers,* Vol. 1, pp. 273–277. Roosevelt also called attention to the creation of an Industrial Commission, to his Northern Securites suit under the Sherman Act, and to his efforts to strengthen the Interstate Commerce Commission with power to regulate railroad practices more effectly.

54. "To Lymon Abbott," January 11, 1905, *Letters,* Vol. 4, p. 1100.

55. John M. Blum, "Theodore Roosevelt and the Hepburn Act: Toward an Orderly System of Control," Appendix II, *Letters,* Vol. 6; Blum, *Republican Roosevelt,* pp. 73–105; Morrison's explanatory note at *Letters,* Vol. 4, pp. 1028–1029; Gould, *Presidency,* pp. 147–165.

56. Samuel P. Hays, *Conservation and the Gospel of Efficiency: The Progressive Conservation Movement, 1890–1920* (Cambridge: Harvard University Press, 1959).

57. Carl E. Hatch, *The Big Stick and the Congressional Gavel: A Study of Theodore Roosevelt's Relations with His Last Congress, 1907–1909* (New York: Pageant, 1967); Skowronek, *Building a New American State,* pp. 182–186; Gould, *Presidency,* pp. 199–206.

58. Hatch, *Big Stick,* passim.

59. "To Ansley Wilcox," November 8, 1907, *Letters,* Vol. 5, p. 833.

60. Hatch, *Big Stick;* "Seventh Annual Message," December 3, 1907, in *A Compilation of the Messages and Papers of Presidents,* Vol. 16, ed. James D. Richardson (New York: Bureau of National Literature, 1897), pp. 7070–7126; "Special Message," January 31, 1908, *Messages and Papers,* Vol. 16, pp. 7126–7133.

61. For example, "To Hamlin Garland," November 23, 1907, *Letters,* Vol. 5, p. 855; also "To David Scull," August 16, 1907, *Letters,* Vol. 5, pp. 754–755; "To Alexander Lambert," November 1, 1907, *Letters,* Vol. 5, p. 826; "To Ansley Wilcox," November 8, 1907, *Letters,* Vol. 5, pp. 833–834.

62. Hatch, *Big Stick,* p. 20; Johnson, "Bureau," pp. 588–589; Robert Wiebe, "The House of Morgan and the Executive, 1905–13," *American Historical Review,* 65, no. 1 (October 1959), pp. 49–60; Gould, *Presidency,* pp. 277–281.

63. "To Cecil Arthur Spring Rice," December 27, 1904, *Letters,* Vol. 4, p. 1083.

64. Hatch, *Big Stick,* p. 54.

65. Gould, *Presidency,* p. 144. For an especially sensitive treatment see Cooper, *Warrior and Priest,* p. 110.

66. "To George Otto Trevelyan," November 24, 1904, *Letters,* Vol. 4, pp. 1043–1044.

67. There is something of this preference for a man safe on the issues in a later letter "To Nicholas Murray Butler," September 24, 1907, *Letters,* Vol. 5, p. 807: "The business of this nation is complicated . . . Nobody can learn about the Navy and the Panama Canal, and the Philippines, and our foreign policy, and what it is possible to do about the trusts, save by experience; that is by being prominently identified with officeholding . . . A man like Root or Taft does not have to learn any of [the issues] and can do his best work from the beginning." Again, after the election in a letter "To Theodore Roosevelt," Jr., November 20, 1908, *Letters,* Vol. 6, p. 1372. "Here in this country I do not at present see any symptoms of our going too far. The overwhelming defeat of Bryan by Taft shows how completely unable as yet the agitators are to do any damage, even when those conditions favor them, provided that we can oppose them with men whose honesty is above suspicion and who are known to be sincerely opposed to wrongdoing by men of property as to wrongdoing by men of no property."

68. Cooper, *Warrior and Priest,* p. 114, and generally pp. 114–118, 143–163.

69. "To Henry Beach Needham," July 19, 1905, *Letters,* Vol. 4, pp. 1281–1282.

70. "To Henry Cabot Lodge," April 10, 1910, *Letters,* Vol. 7, p. 73.

71. "To Nicholas Longworth," July 11, 1910, *Letters,* Vol. 7, p. 99.

72. "To Arthur Hamilton Lee," August 14, 1912, *Letters,* Vol. 7, p. 597.

73. Mowry, *Progressive Movement,* pp. 247–249; John Allen Cable, "The Bull Moose Years: Theodore Roosevelt and the Progressive Party, 1912–1916," Ph.D. dissertation, Brown University, 1962.

74. "To Joseph Cannon," September 17, 1906, *Letters,* Vol. 5, p. 414.

75. "To Horace Plunkett," August 3, 1912, *Letters,* Vol. 7, p. 593.

76. "To Peter Ewert," July 5, 1912, *Letters,* Vol. 7, p. 572.

77. Mowry, *Progressive Movement,* pp. 189–191.

78. Ibid., pp. 213–219.

79. Ibid., pp. 150–151, 257, 269–272.

80. Ibid., p. 266.

81. Norman M. Wilensky, *Conservatives in the Progressive Era: The Taft Republicans of 1912,* University of Florida Monographs, Social Sciences, No. 25 (Gainsville: University of Florida Press, Winter 1965), p. 13.

82. "To Gifford Pinchot," November 13, 1912, *Letters,* Vol. 7, p. 641.

Part Three: Herbert Hoover's Disjunction

1. *The Memoirs of Herbert Hoover, 1920–1933*, Vol. 1, (New York: Macmillan, 1931), p. vi.

2. See for example Carl Degler, "The Ordeal of Herbert Hoover," *Yale Review*, 52 (1963), pp. 563–583; Joan Hoff Wilson, *Herbert Hoover, Forgotten Progressive* (Boston: Little, Brown, 1975), and David Burner, *Herbert Hoover: A Public Life* (New York: Knopf, 1979). Suggestive of the scope of the new interest in Hoover are a number of recent historiographic essays: *Herbert Hoover and the Historians*, ed. Mark M. Dodge (West Branch, Iowa: Herbert Hoover Presidential Library, 1989), and *The Hoover Presidency: A Reappraisal*, ed. M. Fausold and G. Mazuzan (Albany: State University of New York Press, 1974); Lee Nash, *Understanding Herbert Hoover: Ten Perspectives* (Stanford: Hoover Institute Press, 1987).

3. "Address at the Fifty Sixth Annual Convention of the American Bankers' Association," October 2, 1930, *The State Papers and Other Public Writings of Herbert Hoover*, Vol. 1, ed. William Starr Myers, Jr. (New York: Doubleday, 1934), p. 379. More generally, Guy Alchon, *The Invisible Hand of Planning: Capitalism, Social Science, and the State in the 1920's* (Princeton: Princeton University Press, 1985), and William J. Barber, *From New Era to New Deal: Herbert Hoover, the Economists, and American Economic Policy, 1921–1933* (New York: Cambridge University Press, 1985); *Herbert Hoover as Secretary of Commerce, 1921–1928: Studies in New Era Thought and Practice*, ed. Ellis W. Hawley (Iowa City: University of Iowa Press, 1981).

4. Albert U. Romasco, "Hoover-Roosevelt and the Great Depression: A Historiographic Inquiry into a Perrenial Comparison," in *The New Deal: The National Level*, ed. John Braeman, Robert Bremmer, and David Brody (Columbus: Ohio State University Press, 1975), pp. 3–26; also Murray Rothbard, *America's Great Depression* (Princeton: Van Nostrand, 1963).

5. A further implication of this is that Hoover's failure was not in any meaningful sense an indictment of his personal skills and talents. For a contrary view that also dismisses the ideological explanation for Hoover's failure, see Gerald Nash's essay in *Herbert Hoover and the Crisis of American Capitalism*, Ellis Hawley, Murray Rothbard, Robert Himmelberg, and Gerald Nash, contributors (Cambridge, Mass.: Schenkman, 1973).

6. "Campaign Speech at Madison Square Garden," October 31, 1932, *State Papers*, Vol. 2, p. 408.

7. Burner, *Herbert Hoover*, pp. 150–153; Wilson, *Herbert Hoover*, pp. 31–78, 125; Martin L. Fausold, *The Presidency of Herbert Hoover* (Lawrence: University of Kansas Press, 1985), pp. 7–14.

8. Ellis Hawley, "Herbert Hoover, the Commerce Secretariate and the Vision of an 'Associative State', 1921–1928," *Journal of American History*, 61 (1974), pp. 116–140. Also see note 2, above.

9. Herbert Hoover, *American Individualism* (Garden City, New York: Doubleday Page, 1922); Peri Arnold, "Ambivalent Leviathan: Herbert Hoover and the Positive State," in *Public Values and Private Power in American Politics*, ed. David Greenstone (Chicago: University of Chicago Press, 1982), pp. 109–

138. The work of Ellis Hawley is also sensitive to the ambivalences of Hoover's break with past practice. See in addition to his other works cited Hawley's essay in *Herbert Hoover and the Crisis of American Capitalism.*

10. Quoted in Harris Gaylord Warren, *Herbert Hoover and the Great Depression* (New York: Norton, 1967), p. 36.

11. "Inaugural Address," March 4, 1929, *State Papers,* Vol. 1, p. 8.

12. In addition to the other works already cited on these themes see for example Peri Arnold, "The 'Great Engineer' as Administrator: Herbert Hoover and Modern Bureaucracy," *Review of Politics,* 42, no. 3 (July 1980), pp. 329–348.

13. Craig Lloyd, *Aggressive Introvert: A Study of Herbert Hoover and Public Relations Management, 1921–32* (Columbus: Ohio State University Press, 1972).

14. Donald R. McCoy, "To the White House: Herbert Hoover, August 1927–March 1929," in *Hoover Presidency: A Reappraisal,* p. 31; also *The New Day: Campaign Speeches of Herbert Hoover,* ed. Ray Lyman Wilbur (Stanford: Stanford University Press, 1928).

15. Hoover, *New Day,* pp. 17–20, 53.

16. Albert U. Romasco, *The Poverty of Abundance: Hoover, the Nation and the Depression* (New York: Oxford University Press, 1965), pp. 97–104.

17. "Message to the Special Session," April 16, 1929, *State Papers,* Vol. 1, pp. 31–37.

18. Fausold, *Presidency,* p. 49.

19. Ibid., p. 33

20. This review draws on the following sources: Jordan Schwarz, *The Interregnum of Despair: Hoover, Congress and the Depression* (Urbana: University of Illinois Press, 1970), pp. 5–9; Fausold, *Presidency,* pp. 49–54, 93–96; Warren, *Herbert Hoover,* pp. 85–97, 169–177; David Horowitz, "The Perils of Western Farm Politics: Herbert Hoover, Gerald Nye, and Agricultural Reform, 1926–32," in *Herbert Hoover and the Republican Era: A Reconsideration,* ed. Carl E. Krog and William R. Tanner (New York: University Press of America, 1984), pp. 220–243.

21. J. Richard Snyder, "Hoover and the Hawley-Smoot Tariff: A View of Executive Leadership," *Annals of Iowa,* 41, no. 7 (Winter 1973), pp. 1173–1189.

22. Fausold, *Presidency,* pp. 51, 54; Schwarz, *Interregnum,* p. 9.

23. John D. Hicks, *The Republican Ascendancy, 1921–1933* (New York: Harper and Row, 1960), pp. 222–224; Warren, *Herbert Hoover,* pp. 95–97.

24. See, for example, "Announcement of Conferences of Business and Government Agencies on Maintaining Business Progress," November 21, 1929, *State Papers,* Vol. 1, pp. 133–134; "Appeal to the Governors," November 23, 1929, p. 137; "To the United States Chamber of Commerce on Responsibility and Opportunity for Stabilization of the Economy," December 5, 1929, pp. 181–184.

25. "First Annual Message to Congress," December 3, 1929, *State Papers,* Vol. 1, pp. 138–180.

26. Quoted in Warren, *Herbert Hoover,* p. 117.

27. Albert U. Romasco, *Poverty of Abundance,* pp. 24–65.

28. Romasco, *Poverty of Abundance*, pp. 66–96; James Stewart Olson, *Herbert Hoover and the Reconstruction Finance Corporation, 1931–33* (Ames: Iowa State University Press, 1977), pp. 3–24.
29. Warren, *Herbert Hoover*, p. 173; Romasco, *Poverty of Abundance*, pp. 97–124.
30. "Second Annual Address to Congress," December 2, 1930, *State Papers*, Vol. 1, p. 428.
31. Quoted in Schwarz, *Interregnum*, p. 79; Fausold, *Presidency*, p. 145.
32. *Memoirs*, Vol. 1: *Cabinet and Presidency*, pp. 226–230.
33. "Message to the Senate: Veto of the Muscle Shoals Joint Resolution," March 3, 1931, *State Papers*, Vol. 1, pp. 521–529; Fausold, *Presidency*, pp. 134–136; Warren, *Herbert Hoover*, pp. 72–83.
34. "Press Statement: Reasons for the Pocket Veto of the Wagner Bill for the Improvement of Public Employment Agencies," March 7, 1931, *State Papers*, Vol. 1, p. 530; Fausold, *Presidency*, pp. 122, 134–137; Schwarz, *Interregnum*, pp. 23–44.
35. On Hoover's relations with the last session of the old Congress, see Arthur W. MacMahon, "Third Session of the Fifty-First Congress," *American Political Science Review*, 25, no. 4 (November 1931), pp. 932–955.
36. On this point generally see Elliot A. Rosen, *Hoover, Roosevelt and the Brains Trust: From Depression to New Deal* (New York: Columbia University Press, 1977) esp. pp. 66–95.
37. Schwarz, *Interregnum*, pp. 79–86.
38. Ibid.
39. "Press Conference Statement: No Extra Session of Congress To Be Called," May 22, 1931, *State Papers*, Vol. 1, p. 565.
40. "The Importance of the Preservation of Self-Help," Press Statement, February, 3, 1931, *State Papers*, Vol. 1, pp. 496–499.
41. James S. Olson, "The End of Voluntarism: Herbert Hoover and the National Credit Corporation," *Annals of Iowa*, 41, no. 6 (Fall 1972), pp. 1104–1113; Gerald D. Nash, "Herbert Hoover and the Origins of the Reconstruction Finance Corporation," *The Mississippi Valley Historical Review*, 44, no. 3 (December 1959), pp. 455–468. Olson, *RFC*, pp. 24–32.
42. "Campaign Speech at Des Moines, Iowa," October 4, 1932, *State Papers*, Vol. 2, p. 317.
43. "Radio Address: Expression of Confidence in Our Popular Ability To Overcome Difficulty," February 12, 1932, *State Papers*, 2, p. 112.
44. Schwarz, *Interregnum*, pp. 25–105; "Statement Signing the Federal Home Loan Bank Act, July 22, 1932," *Public Papers of the Presidents: Herbert Hoover* (Washington, D.C.: Government Printing Office, 1977), pp. 331–335; "Presidential News Conference," July 22, 1932, *Public Papers*, pp. 329–331.
45. "Third Annual Message to Congress," *State Papers*, Vol. 2, p. 36; Nash, "Origins"; Olson, *RFC*, pp. 43, 72–73; "Signing Emergency Relief and Reconstruction Act," July 17, 1932, *Public Papers*, pp. 322–323.
46. Franklin Roosevelt, "Campaign Address on the Federal Budget at Pittsburgh, Pa.," October 19, 1932, *The Public Papers and Addresses of Franklin D.*

Roosevelt, Vol. 1, ed. Samuel I. Rosenman (New York: Random House, 1938), pp. 795–812.

47. On this point, Olson, *RFC,* is especially persuasive. The Emergency Relief Act was passed just before the opening of the Republican National Convention.

48. Hoover repeatedly voiced his objections to the Garner bill, hoping to head off the embarrassment of having to veto a relief bill after he had asked for one. In a news conference on May 22, 1932, he declared: "This is not unemployment relief. It is the most gigantic pork barrel ever proposed to the American Congress. It is an exampled raid on the Public Treasury . . . Our Nation was not founded on the pork barrel, and it has not become great by logrolling." *Public Papers,* pp. 238–239. Also "Statement on Emergency Relief Legislation," July 6, 1932, *Public Papers,* pp. 295–301; "Veto of the Emergency Relief and Construction Bill," July 11, 1932, *Public Papers,* pp. 305–311.

49. Olson, *RFC,* pp. 33–75; Pinchot, quoted in Olson, *RFC,* p. 84; Schwarz, *Interregnum,* pp. 142–178.

50. "Address Accepting the Republican Nomination for President," August 11, 1932, *State Papers,* Vol. 2, p. 252.

51. "Campaign Speech at Salt Lake City," November 7, 1932, *State Papers,* Vol. 2, p. 467.

52. "Campaign Speech at Madison Square Garden," October 31, 1932, *State Papers,* Vol. 2, pp. 412–413.

53. On this point see the Hoover-Roosevelt comparison by Frank Freidel, *FDR: Launching the New Deal* (Boston: Little, Brown, 1973), p. 72.

54. Especially good on this point is Rosen, *Hoover, Roosevelt and the Brains Trust.*

55. "At Madison Square Garden," *State Papers,* Vol. 2, p. 408.

7. Liberal Leadership: Fraying Boundaries

Part One: Franklin Roosevelt's Reconstruction

1. "The party to offer [a workable program of reconstruction] is the party with clean hands." "Acceptance Speech before the Democratic National Convention," Chicago, July 2, 1932, *The Public Papers and Addresses of Franklin D. Roosevelt,* 13 vols., ed. Samuel I. Rosenman (New York: Random House, 1938–1950), Vol. 1, p. 649.

2. "Note well that in this campaign I shall not use the words 'Republican Party', but I shall use, day in and day out, the words 'Republican leadership.'" Ibid., pp. 648–649.

3. Ibid., p. 650. "The people of this country want a genuine choice this year, not a choice between two names for the same reactionary doctrine."

4. Ibid., pp. 648, 649.

5. Sidney Milkis, *The President and the Parties: The Transformation of the American Party System since the New Deal* (New York: Oxford University Press, forthcoming 1993), pp. 52–75. Also, Arthur Schlesinger, Jr., *The Age*

of Roosevelt: Crisis of the Old Order (Boston: Houghton Mifflin, 1957), esp. p. 377.

6. Cordell Hull quoted in Frank Freidel, *Roosevelt and the South* (Baton Rouge: Louisiana State University Press, 1965), p. 42.

7. See note 1, above.

8. "Campaign Address on Progressive Government at the Commonwealth Club of San Francisco," September 23, 1932, *Public Papers and Addresses,* Vol. 1, pp. 752–763.

9. Franklin Roosevelt, "The Election: An Interpretation," in *Liberty,* 9, no. 50 (December 10, 1932), p. 9.

10. "Second Fireside Chat," May 7, 1933, *Public Papers and Addresses,* Vol. 2, p. 165.

11. "Introduction," November 1, 1937, *Public Papers and Addresses,* Vol. 1, p. 5.

12. Quoted in James MacGregor Burns, *Roosevelt: The Lion and the Fox* (New York: Harcourt Brace and World, 1956), p. 208.

13. George Wolfskill, *The Revolt of the Conservatives: A History of the American Liberty League, 1934–1940* (Boston: Houghton Mifflin, 1962), esp. pp. 21–36.

14. "Address at the Jackson Day Dinner," January 8, 1936, *Public Papers and Addresses,* Vol. 5, p. 40.

15. Roosevelt's preoccupation with Jackson as well as the other presidents who had engaged in a politics of reconstruction before him is sensitively elaborated in Philip Abbott, *The Exemplary President: Franklin Roosevelt and the American Political Tradition* (Amherst: University of Massachusetts Press, 1990).

16. See, for example, Milkis, *Presidents and the Parties;* Theodore Lowi, *The Personal President: Power Invested, Promise Unfulfilled* (Ithaca: Cornell University Press, 1985), pp. 44–66; Richard Neustadt, *Presidential Power: The Politics of Leadership* (New York: Wiley, 1960).

17. "As a politician per se, Roosevelt has been overrated." Arthur Schlesinger, Jr., *The Age of Roosevelt: The Coming of the New Deal* (Boston: Houghton Mifflin, 1958), p. 573.

18. "Inaugural Address," March 4, 1933, *Public Papers and Addresses,* Vol. 2, pp. 14–15.

19. Hoover's opinion of the TVA is found in his rejection of Senator Norris's proposal for the development of Muscle Shoals, *State Papers and Other Public Writings,* Vol. pp. 526–527; on the TVA as a "piece of socialism" see *Memoirs* of Herbert Hoover, Vol. 2, p. 232. For his opinion of the NRA idea see *Memoirs,* Vol. 3, pp. 334–335, 430.

20. On the prominence of these themes during the New Deal see George Wolfskill and John Hudson, *All but the People: Franklin D. Roosevelt and His Critics* (London: Collier-Macmillan, 1969); also Wolfskill, *Revolt of the Conservatives.*

21. Frances Perkins, *The Roosevelt I Knew* (New York: Viking, 1946), pp. 328–333.

22. Ibid. On pragmatism as Roosevelt's discipline see Arthur Schlesinger, Jr., *The Age of Roosevelt: The Politics of Upheaval* (Boston: Houghton Mifflin, 1960), pp. 649–651.

23. As Thomas McGraw has recently restated the standard view: "In the overall sense . . . the New Deal was a melange of inconsistent and conflicting principles" Thomas McGraw, "The New Deal and the Mixed Economy" in *Fifty Years Later: The Deal Evaluated,* ed. Harvard Sitkoff (Philadelphia: Temple University Press, 1985), p. 62. For an important demur, see Robert Eden, "On the Origins of the Regime of Pragmatic Liberalism: John Dewey, Adolf Berle, and FDR's Commonwealth Club Address of 1932," *Studies in American Political Development,* 7, no. 1 (Spring 1993), pp. 71–147.

24. The diverse set of interpreters who find a hollow core at the center of Roosevelt's reconstruction include Burns, *Roosevelt,* pp. 472–475; Richard Hofstadter, *The American Political Tradition and the Men Who Made It* (New York: Vintage, 1948), pp. 315–352; Rexford Tugwell, "The Experimental Roosevelt," in *Franklin D. Roosevelt: A Profile,* ed. William E. Leuchtenburg (New York: Hill and Wang, 1967), esp. pp. 71–72; Paul Conkin, *The New Deal* (Arlington Heights, Ill.: Harlan Davidson, 1975); Louis Hartz, *The Liberal Tradition in America* (New York: Harcourt, Brace, Jovanovich, 1955).

25. "Inaugural Address," *Public Papers,* Vol. 2, pp. 11–16.

26. On this as the theme of Roosevelt's 1932 campaign address at the Commonwealth Club in San Fransciso see Eden, "Origins."

27. "Inaugural Address," *Public Papers,* Vol. 2, pp. 11–16.

28. See Joseph Alsop, *FDR: A Centenary Remembrance* (New York: Viking, 1982), pp. 11–13.

29. "Forgotten Man" speech, Radio Address, Albany, New York, April 7, 1932, *Public Papers and Addresses,* Vol. 1, p. 625. Also Schlesinger, *Crisis,* pp. 289–290.

30. "The Election: An Interpretation," pp. 7–8.

31. William E. Leuchtenburg, *Franklin Roosevelt and the New Deal, 1932–1940* (New York: Harper and Row, 1963), p. 63.

32. Leuchtenburg, *Franklin Roosevelt,* p. 90. Especially good on Roosevelt's maneuvering around the economic orthodoxy of the bankers in particular is Albert Romasco, *The Politics of Recovery: Roosevelt's New Deal* (New York: Oxford University Press, 1983).

33. See Wolfskill and Hudson, *"All but the People . . ."* For a celebratory reading of Roosevelt's appeal to traditional values that tends to wash out the radical thrust of his proposals see Morton Frisch, "Franklin Delano Roosevelt," in *American Political Thought: The Philosophic Dimension of American Statesmanship,* ed. Morton Frisch and Richard Stevens (New York: Scribners', 1971), pp. 219–236. On Frisch's argument see note 77, below.

34. "Annual Message to Congress," January 3, 1936, *Public Papers and Addresses,* Vol. 5, p. 16.

35. Ibid., pp. 230–236, emphasis added.

36. "Campaign Address at Madison Square Garden," October 31, 1936, *Public*

Papers and Addresses, Vol. 5, p. 568; compare Jefferson, "Letter to Thomas McKean," July 24, 1801, cited in Chapter 4, Part One, note 28.

37. Burns, *Roosevelt,* pp. 280–297; Michael Nelson, "The President and the Court: Reinterpreting the Court-Packing Episode of 1937," *Political Science Quarterly,* 103, no. 2 (November 2, 1988), esp. p. 288.

38. "The Goal of the National Industrial Recovery Act," June 16, 1933, *Public Papers and Addresses,* vol. 2, p. 246.

39. As Donald Brand has written of Roosevelt's ambitions for the NRA, "The first new deal is the radical new deal." Donald Brand, *Corporatism and the Rule of Law: A Study of the National Recovery Administration* (Ithaca: Cornell University Press, 1988), p. 288.

40. Robert F. Himmelberg, *The Origins of the National Recovery Administration: Business, Government and the Trade Association Issue, 1921–1933* (New York: Fordham University Press, 1976), pp. 196–207; Brand, *Corporatism,* pp. 82–95; Ellis Hawley, *The New Deal and the Problem of Monopoly* (Princeton: Princeton University Press, 1966), pp. 19–52.

41. "On the basis of this principle of everybody doing things together, we are starting out on this nationwide attack on unemployment. It will succeed if our people understand it—in the big industries, in the little shops, in the great cities, and in the small villages." "Third Fireside Chat," July 24, 1933, *Public Papers and Addresses,* Vol. 2, p. 299.

42. Frank Freidel, *The Launching of the New Deal* (Boston: Little, Brown, 1973), p. 418; Burns, *Roosevelt,* p. 180. Leuchtenburg, *Franklin Roosevelt,* pp. 55–56; Brand, *Corporatism,* p. 85.

43. Steven Fraser, *Labor Will Rule: Sidney Hillman and the Rise of American Labor* (New York: Free Press, 1991), pp. 282–293.

44. Brand is especially good in identifying the transformative implications of the NRA with its public purposes, rather than in the push and pull of the interests. See *Corporatism,* esp. pp. 261–290.

45. Schlesinger, *Coming of the New Deal,* p. 162; Wolfskill and Hudson, "*All but the People . . . ,*" p. 213.

46. On government "partnership" and government "rights" see "Second Fireside Chat," May 7, 1933, *Public Papers and Addresses,* Vol. 2, p. 164.

47. Quoted in Schlesinger, *Coming of the New Deal,* p. 98.

48. *Schechter Poultry Corp. v. United States,* 295 U.S. 495 (1935).

49. On the problem of state capacity in industrial regulation see Theda Skocpol and Kenneth Finegold, "State Capacity and Economic Intervention in the Early New Deal," *Political Science Quarterly,* 97, no. 2 (Summer 1982), pp. 255–278.

50. Schlesinger, *Coming of the New Deal,* pp. 103–110; Leuchtenburg, *Franklin Roosevelt,* p. 70.

51. Ibid., pp. 110–135, 152–160; Hawley, *New Deal,* pp. 53–129, esp. p. 100; Brand, *Corporatism,* pp. 99–149.

52. Schlesinger, *Coming of the New Deal,* pp. 136–151; Brand, *Corporatism,* pp. 229–260. On the relationship between worker insurgency and political

reform in the New Deal see David Plotke, "The Wagner Act Again: Politics and Labor, 1935–37," *Studies in American Political Development,* (1989), pp. 105–156; Kenneth Finegold and Theda Skocpol, "State Party and Industry: From Business Recovery to the Wagner Act in America's New Deal," in *State Making and Social Movements: Essays in History and Theory,* ed. Charles Bright and Susan Harding (Ann Arbor: University of Michigan Press, 1984), pp. 159–192. Michael Goldfield, "Worker Insurgency, Radical Organization, and New Deal Labor Legislation," *American Political Science Review,* 83, no. 4 (December 1989), pp. 1257–1282. Kenneth Finegold, Theda Skocpol, and Michael Goldfield, "Explaining New Deal Labor Policy," *American Political Science Review,* 84, no. 4 (December 1990), pp. 1297–1315.

53. Hawley, *New Deal,* p. 71; Schlesinger, *Coming of the New Deal,* p. 121.

54. Leuchtenburg, *Franklin Roosevelt,* p. 146; Frank Freidel, *Franklin D. Roosevelt: A Rendezvous with Destiny* (Boston: Little, Brown, 1990), pp. 154–155.

55. "Gains under the NRA and Recommendation for a Two Year Extension," February 20, 1935, *Public Papers and Addresses,* Vol. 4, p. 82.

56. Ibid.

57. Arthur Schlesinger, Jr., *The Age of Roosevelt: The Politics of Upheaval* (Boston: Houghton Mifflin, 1960), pp. 271–272; also William Wilson, "How the Chamber of Commerce Viewed the NRA: A Reconsideration," *Mid America* 44 (1962), pp. 95–108.

58. Joseph Alsop and Turner Catledge, *The 168 Days* (Garden City: Doubleday, 1938), p. 7.

59. "The Two Hundred and Ninth Press Conference," May 31, 1935, *Public Papers and Addresses,* Vol. 4, pp. 200–222.

60. Schlesinger, *Politics of Upheaval,* pp. 468–496; Peter Irons, *The New Deal Lawyers* (Princeton: Princeton University Press, 1982), pp. 17–199.

61. Brand, *Corporatism,* p. 286; Burns, *Roosevelt,* p. 219; Schlesinger, *Coming of the New Deal,* pp. 405–406.

62. Leuchtenburg, *Franklin Roosevelt,* pp. 143–167; Schlesinger, *Politics of Upheaval,* pp. 385–442; Burns, *Roosevelt,* pp. 220–226. A different though not inconsistent analysis of this shift is provided by Thomas Ferguson, "Industrial Conflict and the Coming of the New Deal: The Triumph of Multinational Liberalism in America," in *The Rise and Decline of the New Deal Order, 1930–1980,* ed. Steve Fraser and Gary Gerstle (Princeton: Princeton University Press, 1989), pp. 3–31. Ferguson's thesis that the shift in the second New Deal was away from industrial capital toward finance capital, and more particularly away from the industry-connected House of Morgan toward insurgent banking establishments, would fit the broad pattern of the politics of reconstruction. The Jacksonian and Republican reconstructions can also be read as the empowerment of newly emergent interests in banking and finance.

63. James T. Patterson, *Congressional Conservatism and the New Deal: The Growth of the Conservative Coalition in Congress* (Lexington: University of Kentucky Press, 1967), pp. 251–287; J. B. Shannon, "Presidential Politics in

the South—1938, II," *Journal of Politics,* 1, no. 3 (August 1939), pp. 278–300.

64. Alsop and Catledge, *168 Days,* pp. 138–145; Bruce Ackerman, *We The People: Foundations* (Cambridge: Harvard University Press, 1991), pp. 266–294.

65. Patterson, *Congressional Conservatism,* pp. 278–300; Frank Freidel, *Roosevelt and the South;* Freidel, *Rendezvous,* p. 287.

66. Richard Polenberg, *Reorganizing Roosevelt's Government, 1936–1939: The Controversy over Executive Reorganization* (Cambridge: Harvard University Press, 1966); Peri E. Arnold, *Making the Managerial Presidency: Comprehensive Reorganization Planning* (Princeton: Princeton University Press, 1986), pp. 93–117.

67. Patterson, *Congressional Conservatism,* p. 287.

68. Leuchtenburg, *Franklin Roosevelt,* pp. 188–189; Schlesinger, *Politics of Upheaval,* p. 594.

69. Louise Overacker, "Labor's Political Contributions," *Political Science Quarterly,* 54, no. 1 (1939), pp. 56–68.

70. Alsop and Catledge, *168 Days,* pp. 163–176.

71. Polenberg, *Reorganizing,* pp. 79–122.

72. "White House Statement on the Appointment of a Committee to Formulate a Plan for the Reorganization of the Executive Branch," March 22, 1936, *Public Papers and Addresses,* Vol. 5, p. 144; Milkis, *President and the Parties,* Chapter 5.

73. "A Recommendation for Legislation to Reorganize the Executive Branch," January 12, 1937, *Public Papers and Addresses,* Vol. 5, pp. 668–681, also p. 144.

74. Patterson, *Congressional Conservatism,* pp. 215–229. Milkis, *President and the Parties,* Chapter 5.

75. On the contrast between the initial proposal and the final enactment see Polenberg, *Reorganizing,* pp. 184–185; Patterson, *Congressional Conservatism,* pp. 300–302; Milkis, *The President and the Parties,* pp. 125–145; Arnold, *Managerial Presidency.*

76. On the broader implications of this dynamic for the evolution of the modern presidency see Terry Moe, "The Politicized Presidency," in *The New Direction in American Politics,* ed. John E. Clubb and Paul E. Peterson (Washington, D.C.: Brookings Institution, 1985), pp. 235–272.

77. It might be worth pausing here to consider the contrary position outlined by Morton Frisch which downplays the radicalism of Roosevelt's actual proposals by emphasizing the compatibility of what the New Deal actually accomplished with older American traditions. This argument is elusive. It downplays the implications of the quest for mastery that Roosevelt openly avowed in 1936 as well as the concrete proposals he ventured in 1937 to realize that objective. The matter is complicated by the abrupt change in presidential rhetoric in 1937 when Roosevelt offered familiar progressive nostrums to justify Court-packing and government reorganization. Moving from that rhetoric to an assessment of what Roosevelt actually got eases the way to the

conclusions that the Court and Congress gave Roosevelt what he really wanted and that what he really wanted was quite compatible with the Constitution's design. But why should we dismiss the rhetoric of 1936 in favor of the rhetoric of 1937, and why should we read Roosevelt's intentions from the results rather than from his initial proposals and his actions on their behalf? It seems to me that what Roosevelt said he was going to do in 1936 is just what he tried to do in 1937, and that while his proposals would have gained him the mastery he sought, they flew in the face of the basic constitutional design. Thus, the rhetoric of 1937 belies the radicalism of the proposals themselves. Roosevelt's tenacity in pressing judicial reform after the Court had capitulated to New Deal policies tells us more about what he was really after than the Court's capitulation itself. The compatibility of the progressive rhetoric of 1937 with the actual result (and the result with the basic consitutional frame) misses the real historic significance of the rejection of the President's designs. Finally, the fact that Roosevelt failed to mount a constitutional argument in defense of those proposals, and instead resorted to washed out progressive nostrums, indicates a historical weakening of the reconstructive stance in the modern period as well as a weakening of the reconstructive posture Roosevelt himself had adopted in 1936. See Frisch, "Franklin Delano Roosevelt."

78. "Recommendation for Legislation to Reorganize," *Public Papers,* Vol. 5, p. 672.

79. Polenberg, *Reorganizing,* pp. 28–29.

80. On the ideology of the President's Committee on Administrative Management and its relationship to the President's political aims, see Barry Karl, *Executive Reorganization and Reform in the New Deal* (Chicago: University of Chicago, 1963). Roosevelt's political aims in reorganization are detailed by Milkis in *President and the Parties,* pp. 125–145, and Peri Arnold, *Managerial Presidency,* pp. 81–117. On the search for a way to package an assault on judicial intransigence see Alsop and Catledge, *168 Days,* pp. 13–65.

81. "Speech at Democratic Victory Dinner," March 4, 1937, *Public Papers and Addresses,* Vol. 6, pp. 120, 123.

82. Alsop and Catledge, *168 Days,* p. 74. On the court-packing controversy see also Nelson, "President and the Court;" Leonard Baker, *Back to Back: The Dual between FDR and the Supreme Court* (New York: Macmillan, 1967); William E. Leuchtenburg, "The Origins of Franklin Roosevelt's Court Packing Plan," in *The Supreme Court Review,* ed. Philip Kurland (Chicago: University of Chicago Press, 1966), pp. 347–400; William E. Leuchtenburg, "Roosevelt's Supreme Court 'Packing' Plan," in *Essays on the New Deal,* ed. Harold Hollingsworth and William Holmes (Austin: University of Texas Press, 1969); William Leutenberg, "FDR's Court-Packing Plan: A Second Life, A Second Death," *Duke Law Journal,* 3, no. 4 (June–December 1985), pp. 673–689.

83. "Recommendation for Legislation to Reorganize," *Public Papers,* Vol. 5, p. 669.

84. Alsop and Catledge, *168 Days,* p. 127.

85. Ibid., p. 229–233.

86. "President Refutes Dictatorship Charge," March 31, 1938, *Public Papers and Addresses,* Vol. 7, pp. 179–181. Polenberg, *Reorganizing,* pp. 147–161; Leuchtenburg, *Franklin Roosevelt,* pp. 275–283.

87. Arnold, *Managerial Presidency,* pp. 111–113.

88. That Roosevelt did in fact continue unprecedented if still oblique challenges to the constitutional separation of powers is documented by Edward Corwin, *The President: Office and Powers* (New York: New York University Press, 1957), pp. 250–252.

89. On the tension structured into the relationship between the modern plebiscitary presidency and the original constitutional presidency see Jeffrey Tulis, "The Two Constitutional Presidencies" in *The Presidency and the Political System,* ed. Michael Nelson (Washington, D.C.: Congressional Quarterly Press, 1988), pp. 85–114.

Part Two: Lyndon Johnson's Articulation

1. "Address before a Joint Session of Congress," November 27, 1963, *Public Papers of the Presidents: Lyndon Baines Johnson* (Washington, D.C.: Government Printing Office, 1966), p. 8.

2. Doris Kearns, *Lyndon Johnson and the American Dream* (New York: Mentor, 1976), p. 229. Rowland Evans and Robert Novak, *Lyndon Johnson: The Exercise of Power* (New York: New American Library, 1966), p. 489. As Johnson told Jack Valenti, he "knew all the tremors and soft spots and the unknowns that infested every cranny of the political jungle." Valenti, *A Very Human President* (New York: Norton, 1975), p. 11.

3. Quoted in Kearns, *Johnson,* p. 223.

4. "The Tyranny of Benevolence" was the original subtitle proposed for Kearns's study.

5. Eric F. Goldman, *The Tragedy of Lyndon Johnson* (New York: Dell, 1974), p. 395; William E. Leuchtenburg, *In the Shadow of FDR: From Harry Truman to Ronald Reagan* (Ithaca: Cornell University Press, 1983), esp. pp. 142–147; Kearns, *Johnson,* p. 299.

6. Johnson's words quoted in Vaughn Bornet, *The Presidency of Lyndon Johnson* (Lawrence: University of Kansas Press, 1983), pp. 13, 57.

7. "The President's Inaugural Address," January 20, 1965, *Public Papers,* p. 74.

8. Leuchtenburg, *Shadow,* pp. 121, 130; Valenti, *Very Human President,* pp. 308–309.

9. Robert Caro, *The Years of Lyndon Johnson: The Path to Power* (New York: Vintage, 1983), p. 395; Robert Dallek, *Lone Star Rising: Lyndon Johnson and His Times* (New York: Oxford University Press, 1991), pp. 148–150.

10. Leuchtenburg, *Shadow,* p. 130; Caro, *Years,* pp. 765–767; Dallek, *Lone Star Rising,* pp. 159–224.

11. Leuchtenburg, *Shadow,* p. 148; Evans and Novak, *Johnson,* p. 490.

12. Leuchtenburg, *Shadow,* p. 147.

13. Especially useful in elaborating the regime shift in the postwar era are essays in *The Rise and Fall of the New Deal Political Order,* ed. Steve Fraser and Gary Gerstle (Princeton: Princeton University Press, 1989), esp. the introduc-

tion by the editors, pp. xv–xvii. Also Alan Wolfe, *America's Impasse: The Rise and Fall of the Politics of Growth* (New York: Pantheon, 1981); David Plotke, *The New Deal Political Order* (Cambridge: Cambridge University Press, forthcoming).

14. Caro, *Years,* p. 126; Ronald Dugger, *The Politician: The Life and Times of Lyndon Johnson, The Drive for Power from the Frontier to Master of the Senate* (New York: Norton, 1982), pp. 52–321. Dallek, *Lone Star Rising,* p. 277–278.

15. Dallek is especially helpful in uncovering continuities of commitment during this period. Also Joe Frantz, "Opening a Curtain: The Metamorphosis of Lyndon B. Johnson," *Journal of Southern History,* 45, no. 1 (February 1979), pp. 3–26; T. Harry Williams, "Huey, Lyndon, and Southern Radicalism," *Journal of Southern History,* 60 (September 1973), pp. 267–293.

16. Quoted from the *Congressional Record,* January 16, 1956, in Kearns, *Johnson,* p. 162.

17. Dallek, *Lone Star Rising,* pp. 517–528; Kearns, *Johnson,* pp. 153–155. Hugh Graham, *The Civil Rights Era: Origins and Development of National Policy* (New York: Oxford University Press, 1990), p. 23; Paul K. Conkin, *Big Daddy from the Pedernales: Lyndon Baines Johnson* (Boston: Twayne, 1986), pp. 139–143.

18. Carl M. Bauer, *John F. Kennedy and the Second Reconstruction* (New York: Columbia University Press, 1977), pp. 30–38; Arthur M. Schlesinger, Jr., *A Thousand Days: John F. Kennedy in the White House* (Boston: Houghton Mifflin, 1965), pp. 47–52; Dallek, *Lone Star Rising,* pp. 574–582.

19. Quoted in Bornet, *Presidency,* p. 9.

20. Lyndon Johnson, *The Vantage Point: Perspectives of the Presidency, 1963–1969* (New York: Popular Library, 1971), p. 324.

21. "Remarks at the University of Michigan, Ann Arbor," May 22, 1964, *Public Papers,* p. 704.

22. "Special Message to Congress: The American Promise," March 15, 1965, *Public Papers,* p. 284; more generally see John Frederick Martin, *Civil Rights and the Crisis of Liberalism: The Democratic Party, 1945–1976* (Boulder: Westview, 1979).

23. Quoted in Leuchtenburg, *Shadow,* p. 147.

24. Goldman, *Tragedy,* p. 307; Jack Bell, *The Johnson Treatment: How Lyndon B. Johnson Took Over the Presidency and Made It His Own* (New York: Harper and Row, 1965), pp. 282–285.

25. "Remarks on the City Hall Steps, Dayton Ohio," October 16, 1964, *Public Papers,* p. 1373; Allen J. Matusow, *The Unravelling of America: A History of Liberalism in the 1960s* (New York: Harper and Row, 1984), pp. 131–152; Theodore White, *The Making of the President, 1964* (New York: Atheneum, 1965).

26. Goldman, *Tragedy,* pp. 300–302.

27. "Television Address to the American People," October 7, 1964, *Public Papers,* p. 1241.

28. Goldman, *Tragedy,* p. 395.

29. Leuchtenburg, *Shadow,* p. 149; Kearns, *Johnson,* p. 226.

30. Quoted in Herbert Y. Shandler, *Lyndon Johnson and Vietnam: The Unmaking of a President* (Princeton: Princeton University Press, 1977), p. 300.
31. Bornet, *Presidency,* p. 283.
32. "Remarks at the University of Michigan, Ann Arbor," *Public Papers,* p. 704.
33. Johnson, *Vantage Point,* p. 160
34. Quoted in Kearns, *Johnson,* p. 263.
35. Quoted in Hugh Sidey, *A Very Personal Presidency: Lyndon Johnson in the White House* (New York: Atheneum, 1968), p. 260.
36. Wilson Carey McWilliams, "Lyndon Johnson and the Politics of Mass Society," in *Leadership in America: Consensus, Corruption, and Charisma,* ed. Peter Bathory (New York: Longman, 1978), p. 189.
37. The August debate on the Gulf of Tonkin resolution came not only in the midst of the campaign against Goldwater but also in the midst of debate over the Economic Opportunity Act, the centerpiece of Johnson's War on Poverty. Meeting the political threat on the right, Johnson refused to let weary legislators go home for the campaign and insisted instead on letting him complete Kennedy's domestic agenda. He subsequently campaigned as the peace candidate. "So if you don't want to enlarge it and you seek no larger war, and you don't want to pull out and run home, the only thing you can do is what we are doing. We let them know that when they shoot at us as they did in Tonkin Gulf, we will make a prompt, adequate and sufficient response." "Remarks in Louisville, Kentucky," October 9, 1964, *Public Papers,* p. 1267; Goldman, *Tragedy,* pp. 203–224; Kearns, *Johnson,* p. 207; Matusow, *Unravelling,* pp. 150–151; Conkin, *Big Daddy,* p. 257.
38. Quoted in Larry Berman, *Planning a Tragedy: The Americanization of the War in Vietnam* (New York: Norton, 1982), p. 92.
39. "Address at Johns Hopkins: Peace without Conquest," April 7, 1965, *Public Papers,* p. 395.
40. "The American Promise," *Public Papers,* pp. 286–287.
41. "Address at Johns Hopkins," *Public Papers,* p. 398.
42. Cited phrases from General Maxwell Taylor to Dean Rusk on how to handle the press's response to the onset of combat operations. Quoted in Berman, *Planning a Tragedy,* pp. 57–58.
43. "Remarks in Louisville," *Public Papers,* p. 1267.
44. Leslie H. Gelb and Richard K. Betts, *The Irony of Vietnam: The System Worked* (Washington, D.C.: Brookings Institution, 1979).
45. Goldman, *Tragedy,* p. 450.
46. Carl Solberg, *Hubert Humphrey: A Biography* (New York: Norton, 1984), pp. 272–273; Berman, *Planning a Tragedy,* p. 146; Clark Clifford, *Counsel to the President: A Memoir* (New York: Random House, 1991), pp. 406–422.
47. "Address before a Joint Session," November 27, 1963, *Public Papers,* p. 9; Graham, *Civil Rights Era,* pp. 74–152.
48. "Remarks with President Truman at the Signing in Independence of the Medicare Bill," July 30, 1965, *Public Papers,* pp. 811–821; Goldman, *Tragedy,* p. 336–350.
49. "Address before a Joint Session," *Public Papers,* p. 9.
50. Evans and Novak, *Johnson,* pp. 451–469; Milkis, *The President and the*

Parties: The Transformation of the American Party System since the New Deal (New York: Oxford University Press, forthcoming 1993), pp. 184–218; Goldman, *Tragedy*, p. 206.

51. Quoted in Kearns, *Johnson*, p. 199.
52. Graham, *Civil Rights Era*, pp. 153–227.
53. See generally the essays and speeches collected in the political profile *To Heal and to Build: The Programs of Lyndon Johnson*, ed. James McGregor Burns (New York: McGraw Hill, 1968).
54. David Zarefsky, *Lyndon Johnson's War on Poverty: Rhetoric and History* (University, Alabama: University of Alabama Press, 1986), p. 35.
55. Ibid., pp. 1–56; Mark Gelfand, "The War on Poverty," *The Johnson Years*, Vol. 1 (Lawrence: University of Kansas Press, 1987), pp. 126–154; Matusow, *Unravelling*, pp. 217–221; Conkin, *Big Daddy*, pp. 219–226; Kearns, *Johnson*, p. 226.
56. "Annual Message to Congress on the State of the Union," January 12, 1966, *Public Papers*, pp. 3, 4.
57. John Quincy Adams, *Memoirs*, Vol. 7, ed. Charles Francis Adams (Philadelphia: Lippincott, 1875), p. 81.
58. Leonard White, *The Jeffersonians: A Study in Administrative History, 1801–1829* (New York: Free Press, 1951), p. 66.
59. "Remarks before the National Convention upon Acceptance of the Nomination," August 27, 1964, *Public Papers*, p. 1010.
60. Solberg, *Humphrey*, p. 256.
61. Ibid., pp. 239–256; Evans and Novak, *Johnson*, pp. 451–456; Milkis, Chapter 7.
62. Solberg, *Humphrey*, pp. 264–284; James Harvey, *Black Civil Rights during the Johnson Administration* (Jackson: University Press of Mississippi, 1973), pp. 59–63; Graham, *Civil Rights Era*, pp. 175, 180–183; Emmette S. Redford and Marlan Blissett, *Organizing the Executive Branch: The Johnson Presidency* (Chicago: University of Chicago Press, 1981), pp. 122–123.
63. Theodore White, *The Making of the President, 1968* (New York: Atheneum, 1969), p. 129; Kearns, *Johnson*, p. 256; David Broder, *The Party's Over: The Failure of Politics in America* (New York: Harper and Row, 1972).
64. Evans and Novak, "Inside Report," *Washington Post*, December 21, 1966; Larry Berman, "Johnson and the White House Staff," in *The Johnson Years*, Vol. 1, ed. Robert Devine (Lawrence: University of Kansas Press, 1987), p. 200.
65. Berman, *Planning a Tragedy*, pp. 145–153.
66. Donald Kettl, "The Economic Education of Lyndon Johnson: Guns, Butter, and Taxes," in *Johnson Years*, Vol. 2, pp. 54–78. "Annual Budget Message to Congress, Fiscal Year 1967," January 24, 1966, *Public Papers*, p. 48.
67. Ibid.; Shandler, *Johnson and Vietnam*, pp. 218–228; Kearns, *Johnson*, p. 310; Conkin, *Big Daddy*, pp. 204–205; Matusow, *Unravelling*, pp. 160, 170–173.
68. One of the more widely circulated press reports of the time was from an army major who observed: "It became necessary to destroy the town to save it." One wonders what the impact of the mass media might have been on the similar sentiments expressed during our own civil war.

69. Johnson also reaped benefits from television, especially in the early civil rights struggles when southern racists indicted themselves before the cameras and cleared the way for Johnson's initiatives. Generally see David Culbert, "Johnson and the Media," *Johnson Years*, Vol. 1, pp. 214–248.

70. Bruce Miroff, "Presidential Leverage over Social Movements: The Johnson White House and Civil Rights," *Journal of Politics*, 43, no. 1 (February 1981), pp. 2–23; Steven Lawson, "Civil Rights," *Johnson Years*, Vol. 1, pp. 93–125.

71. Goldman, *Tragedy*, p. 505; Conkin, *Big Daddy*, p. 188.

72. *New York Review of Books*, October 12, 1967; Matusow, *Unravelling*, p. 378.

73. *New York Times*, March 26, 1967, p. 44; *New York Times*, April 2, 1967, p. 1.

74. Matusow, *Unravelling*, pp. 162–169.

75. Kathleen J. Turner, *Lyndon Johnson's Dual War: Vietnam and the Press* (Chicago: University of Chicago Press, 1985), pp. 42, 177; Culbert, "Johnson and the Media."

76. Kearns, *Johnson*, p. 329.

77. Turner, *Dual War*, pp. 231–232; Culbert, "Johnson and the Media," pp. 223–224.

78. Kearns, *Johnson*, p. 329.

79. Quoted in Kearns, ibid., p. 359.

80. Johnson had toyed with the idea of withdrawal from the 1964 race. After he was elected, he told several intimates that he would not run again, but no one seems to have believed him. Of the many recountings of Johnson's ambivalence about continuing in power, Bornet's is the most detailed, though the credence he gives to Johnson's health reasons seems to diminish the hard-pressed realities of his political situation. Bornet, *Presidency*, pp. 283–305.

81. Turner, *Dual War*, p. 248.

82. Shandler, *Johnson and Vietnam*, pp. 77–78; Bornet, *Presidency*, pp. 272–273.

83. Ibid.; Larry Berman, *Lyndon Johnson's War: The Road to Stalemate in Vietnam* (New York: Norton, 1989), pp. 114–175. Turner, *Dual War*, p. 219; George Herring, "The War in Vietnam," *Johnson Years*, Vol. 1, pp. 50–51;

84. Berman, *Lyndon Johnson's War*, p. 186.

85. "The President's Address to the Nation Announcing Steps to Limit the War in Vietnam and Reporting His Decision Not to Seek Reelection," March 31, 1968, *Public Papers*, pp. 469–476.

86. "The President's News Conference," March 31, 1968, pp. 478–479.

87. Shandler, *Johnson and Vietnam*, p. 310; Johnson, *Vantage Point*, pp. 422–423.

88. White, *Making of the President, 1968*, pp. 352–386.

89. Matusow, *Unravelling*, p. 431.

90. Ibid., p. 394; Don Oberdorfer, *Tet!* (Garden City: Doubleday, 1971), p. 99.

Part Three: Jimmy Carter's Disjunction

1. Theodore Lowi, *The End of Liberalism: Ideology, Policy and the Crisis of Public Authority* (New York: Norton 1969).

2. James L. Sundquist, *The Decline and Resurgence of Congress* (Washington,

D.C.: Brookings Institution, 1981); Morris Fiorina, *Congress: Keystone of the Washington Establishment* (New Haven: Yale University Press, 1977); Eric Davis, "Legislative Reform and the Decline of Presidential Influence on Capitol Hill," *British Journal of Political Science*, 9 (October 1979), pp. 465–479.

3. David Mayhew, *Divided We Govern: Party Control, Lawmaking and Investigations, 1946–1990* (New Haven: Yale University Press, 1991), esp. pp. 82–87.

4. On Carter as a problem-solving president, see Erwin Hargrove, *Jimmy Carter as President: Leadership and Politics of the Public Good* (Baton Rouge: Louisiana State University Press, 1988), esp. p. 164, and a closely related formulation by Charles O. Jones, *The Trusteeship Presidency: Jimmy Carter and the United States Congress* (Baton Rouge: Louisiana State University Press, 1988).

5. James Fallows, "The Passionless Presidency I," *Atlantic Monthly*, 243, no. 5 (May 1979), pp. 33–48; James Fallows, "The Passionless Presidency II," *Atlantic Monthly*, 243, no. 6 (June 1979), pp. 55–76; Aaron Wildavsky and Jack Knott, "Jimmy Carter's Theory of Governing," in *American Politics and Public Policy*, ed. Walter Dean Burnham (Cambridge: MIT Press, 1978), pp. 55–76; Aaron Wildavsky, "Skepticism and Dogma in the White House: Jimmy Carter's Theory of Governing," in Aaron Wildavsky, *Speaking Truth to Power* (Boston: Little, Brown, 1979), pp. 238–251.

6. *The Presidential Campaign 1976*, Vol. 1, Part 1: *Jimmy Carter* (Washington, D.C.: United States Government Printing Office, 1978), p. 90.

7. Jimmy Carter, *Why Not the Best?* (Nashville: Broadway Press, 1975); also *Presidential Campaign*, Vol. 1, passim.

8. *Presidential Campaign*, Vol. 1, p. 582.

9. Ibid., p. 244.

10. Laurence H. Shoup, *The Carter Presidency and Beyond: Power and Politics in the 1980's* (Palo Alto: Ramparts Press, 1980), pp. 39–64; Carter said: "Those Trilateral Commission meetings for me were like classes in foreign policy—reading papers produced on every conceivable subject, hearing experienced leaders debate international issues and problems, and meeting the big names like Cy Vance, Harold Brown and Zbig," quoted in Hamilton Jordan, *Crisis: The Last Year of the Carter Presidency* (New York: Putnam, 1982), p. 45.

11. *Presidential Campaign*, Vol. 1, p. 45.

12. Ibid., p. 60; Betty Glad, *Jimmy Carter: In Search of the Great White House* (New York: Norton, 1980), p. 350.

13. William E. Leuchtenburg, *In the Shadow of FDR: From Harry Truman to Ronald Reagan* (Ithaca: Cornell University Press, 1983), pp. 200–201.

14. Emmet John Hughes, "The Presidency vs. Jimmy Carter," *Fortune*, 98, no. 11 (December 4, 1978), p. 52; also Sidney Weintraub, "Nothing New on Inflation: Carter's Hoover Syndrome," *New Leader*, March 24, 1980, pp. 5–6; also Tom Wicker, "Carter at the Precipice," *New York Times*, July 10, 1979, p. 15.

15. Hendrick Smith, "Carter and the 100 Days," *New York Times*, April 29,

1977, p. 16; Dan Hahn, "The Rhetoric of Jimmy Carter, 1976–1980," *Presidential Studies Quarterly*, 14, no. 2 (Spring 1984), pp. 265–288. James L. Sundquist, "The Crisis of Competence in Our National Government," *Political Science Quarterly*, 95, no. 2 (Summer 1980), pp. 183–208.

16. Weintraub, "Nothing New," p. 5.

17. See for example Sundquist, "Crisis of Competence"; Nelson Polsby, "Opening Carter's Cabinet," *The Alternative: An American Spectator*, October 1977, pp. 11–13; Michael Genovese, "Jimmy Carter and the Age of Limits: Presidential Power in a Time of Decline and Diffusion," paper prepared for Hofstra University presidential conference, November 1990.

18. Dilys M. Hill and Phil Williams, "Introduction" to *The Carter Years: The President and Policy Making*, ed. M. Glen Abernathy, Dilys M. Hill, and Phil Williams (London: Frances Pinter, 1984), p. 10.

19. Gary W. Reichard, "Early Returns: Assessing Jimmy Carter," *Presidential Studies Quarterly*, 20, no. 3 (Summer 1990), pp. 603–620; Hahn, "Rhetoric of Jimmy Carter."

20. Fallows, "Passionless Presidency, I," esp. p. 38.

21. *Presidential Campaign*, Vol. 1, March 15, 1975, p. 61.

22. William Schneider, "The November 4 Vote for President: What Does It Mean?" in *The American Elections of 1980*, ed. Austin Ranney (Washington, D.C.: American Enterprise Institute, 1980), pp. 241–247.

23. Robert Sheer, "Playboy Interview: Jimmy Carter," *Playboy Magazine*, 23, no. 11 (November 1976), p. 64.

24. Glad, *Carter*, p. 472.

25. William Lee Miller, *Jimmy Carter: Yankee from Georgia* (New York: Times Books, 1978), p. 69; more generally, see also Theodore Lowi, *The Personal President: Power Invested, Promise Unfulfilled* (Ithaca: Cornell University Press, 1985).

26. On this last point about the prospects for party government, see for example *Presidential Campaign*, Vol. 1, pp. 349, 548–549.

27. *Presidential Campaign*, Vol. 1, pp. 330, 207.

28. Ibid., pp. 348–352.

29. Quotes are from Carter campaign ads cited in Glad, *Carter*, p. 317.

30. John Aldrich, *Before the Convention: Strategies and Choices in Presidential Nominating Conventions* (Chicago: University of Chicago Press, 1980), pp. 157–159; Kandy Stroud, *How Jimmy Won: The Victory Campaign from Plains to the White House* (New York: William Morrow, 1977), pp. 261–270; Jules Witcover, *Marathon: The Pursuit of the Presidency, 1972–1976* (New York: Viking, 1977), pp. 253–288.

31. For example, *Presidential Campaign*, Vol.1, p. 292; *The Presidential Campaign*, Vol. 1, Part 2, p. 766.

32. Witcover, *Marathon*, pp. 306, 335, 349–350.

33. Quoted in Robert Shogan, *Promises to Keep: Carter's First Hundred Days* (New York: Thomas Crowell, 1977), p. 50.

34. Witcover, *Marathon*, p. 645.

35. Martin Schram, *Running for President, 1976: The Carter Campaign* (New York: Stein and Day, 1977), pp. 158–159.

36. "Carter Assails Opponents Who Seek to Block Drive," *New York Times*, May 28, 1978, p. 12.

37. Sheer, "Playboy Interview," p. 86.

38. Schram, *Running*, pp. 300–313; Shogan, *Promises*, p. 53; Witcover, *Marathon*, pp. 580–581; Glad, *Carter*, p. 386.

39. *Presidential Campaign*, Vol. 1, p. 348.

40. Sheer, "Playboy Interview," p. 64; *Presidential Campaign*, Vol. 1, p. 292; Glad, *Carter*, p. 321.

41. For a sampling from the summer of 1980 see *Public Papers of the Presidents: Jimmy Carter* (Washington, D.C.: Government Printing Office, 1977–1981): June 6, 1980, p. 1045; June 6, 1980, p. 1047; June 10, 1980, p. 1078; July 15, 1980, p. 1238; July 16, 1980, p. 1241; July 31, 1980, p. 1341; and his acceptance speech at the nominating convention, August 14, 1980, p. 1533.

42. *Presidential Campaign*, Vol. 1, p. 174.

43. Ibid., pp. 298, 203; also Jimmy Carter, *Keeping Faith: Memoirs of a President* (New York: Bantam, 1982), p. 73–77.

44. The campaign memos of Patrick Caddell, Carter's chief pollster, on the "softness" and volatility of the Carter vote are reviewed throughout Schram's *Running*.

45. George Edwards, *At the Margins: Presidential Leadership in Congress* (New Haven: Yale University Press, 1989), p. 214.

46. Carter, *Keeping Faith*, p. 73.

47. Ibid., p. 108.

48. "To Democratic Congressional Campaign Committee," *Public Papers*, August 14, 1980, p. 1530.

49. Objective measures of the legislative performance of modern presidents suggest that he actually did a bit less well overall than the Democratic administrations of the sixties in gaining support for his measures in Congress but that he did a bit better than the Republican presidents of the 1970s. Jones, *Trusteeship Presidency*, p. 206; Edwards, *Margins*, p. 18 and passim; also Richard Fleisher and Jon R. Bond, "Assessing Presidential Support in the House: Lessons for Reagan and Carter," *Journal of Politics*, 45, no. 3 (August 1983), pp. 745–758.

50. For another view of the limits of the explanation of skill to account for Carter's failings see Edwards, *Margins*, esp. pp. 210.

51. Quoted in Shogan, *Promises*, p. 243.

52. Quoted in Shogan, ibid., p. 111; also Glad, *Carter*, p. 413.

53. See note 10, above.

54. Hugh Sidey, "Grafting Job: Old Body, New Head," *Time Magazine*, January 17, 1977, p. 13.

55. Quoted in Shogan, *Promises*, p. 84.

56. "Carter Chooses the Painful Past," *Washington Post*, December 26, 1976, pp. C1–C2.

57. Quoted in Shogan, *Promises*, p. 129.

58. Shogan, ibid., pp. 96–164.

59. Carter, *Keeping Faith*, pp. 76–77.

60. Quoted in Laurence E. Lynn, Jr., and David deF. Whitman, *The President as Policy Maker: Jimmy Carter and Welfare Reform* (Philadelphia: Temple University Press, 1981), p. 103.

61. Ibid.; Joseph A. Califano, Jr., *Governing America: An Insiders Report from the White House and the Cabinet* (New York: Simon and Schuster, 1981), pp. 320–364; Hargrove, *Jimmy Carter as President*, pp. 54–60; Dilys M. Hill, "Domestic Policy," in *Carter Years*, pp. 19–23.

62. "Water Resource Projects," Message to Congress, February 21, 1977, *Public Papers*, p. 207.

63. Carter, *Keeping Faith*, pp. 78–79.

64. "Interview with the President," March 5, 1977, *Public Papers*, pp. 287–288; "Remarks in Charleston, West Virginia, March 17, 1977," *Public Papers*, p. 435; "Letter to Members of Congress," March 16, 1977, *Public Papers*, pp. 453–455; "Statement Announcing Administration Decisions," April 18, 1977, *Public Papers*, pp. 651–655.

65. Carter, *Keeping Faith*, p. 102. On this point see also Bond and Fleisher, "Assessing Presidential Support," pp. 752–753.

66. Jones, *Trusteeship Presidency*, pp. 143–150; Shogan, *Promises*, pp. 212–215; Haynes Johnson, *In the Absence of Power: Governing America* (New York: Viking, 1980), pp. 158–161.

67. August 8, 1977, *Public Papers*, pp. 1461–1462.

68. Carter, *Keeping Faith*, p. 79.

69. "Presidential News Conference of September 21, 1977," *Public Papers*, p. 1636.

70. Quoted in Jones, *Trusteeship Presidency*, p. 151.

71. Carter, *Keeping Faith*, p. 127.

72. "The office of management and budget is one of the crucial assignments that will determine the success or failure of my administration . . . My choice, without any competition, I might say, was Bert Lance." August 23, 1977, *Public Papers*, p. 1492.

73. Glad, *Carter*, p. 439 50n.

74. "Remarks at a News Conference," August 18, 1977, *Public Papers*, pp. 1480–1481.

75. See press questions in *Public Papers* August 18, 1977, pp. 1480–1481; August 23, 1977, pp. 1489–1494; September 17, 1977, pp. 1616–1620; September 21, 1977, pp. 1635–1643.

76. *The Gallop Opinion Index: Carter's First Year*, March 1978, pp. 1, 8, 10.

77. Jones, *Trusteeship Presidency*, pp. 135–143.

78. Carter, *Keeping Faith*, p. 111.

79. "The Energy Plan," Address to the Nation, April 18, 1977, *Public Papers*, p. 656.

80. "National Energy Plan," Address to a Joint Session of Congress, April 19, 1977, *Public Papers*, pp. 663–688.

81. "National Energy Plan," Address to the Nation, November 8, 1977, *Public Papers*, pp. 1981–1987.

82. Ibid.

83. "Many Factors Led to Energy Stalemate," *Congressional Quarterly Weekly Report,* 35, no. 52 (December 24, 1977), pp. 2631–2635; "Conversation with the President," December 28, 1977, *Public Papers,* pp. 2187, 2196.

84. "Chronology of Action on Carter's Energy Plan Reflects Slow Progress in Congress," *Congressional Quarterly Weekly Report,* 36, no. 21 (May 27, 1978), pp. 1292–1293; "Energy Bill," ibid., 36, no. 41 (October 14, 1978), p. 2920; "Energy Bill: The End of an Odyssey," ibid., 36, no. 42 (October 21, 1978), pp. 3039–3042; Hargrove, *Jimmy Carter as President,* pp. 47–54; Jones, *Trusteeship Presidency,* pp. 135–143; Hill and Williams, *President and Policy Making,* pp. 14–19.

85. "Signing the Energy Security Act," June 30, 1980, *Public Papers,* pp. 1252–1253; "Remarks to the NAACP," July 4, 1980, ibid., pp. 1326–1327.

86. Leuchtenburg, *Shadow,* p. 195; Hargrove, *Jimmy Carter as President,* p. 36.

87. *The Presidential Campaign,* Vol. 1, p. 473; "Consumer Agency Legislation," June 1, 1977, *Public Papers,* p. 1048; "Consumer Protection Legislation," August 1, 1977, *Public Papers,* p. 1396.

88. Michael Pertschuk, *Revolt against Regulation: The Rise and Pause of the Consumer Movement* (Berkeley: University of California Press, 1982); "Consumer Agency: Is This Finally the Year," *Congressional Quarterly Weekly Reports,* 35, no. 6 (February 5, 1977), pp. 205–206; "Anti Consumer Agency Effort Underscores Difficulties in Tightening Lobby Law," ibid., 35, no. 21 (May 21, 1977), pp. 993–994; "Consumer Agency Bill Stalled in Congress," ibid., 35, no. 24 (June 11, 1977), pp. 1147–1150; "Why the Consumer Agency Is Stalled," *Wall Street Journal,* July 12, 1977, p. 22; "House Vote Set on New Consumer Agency," *Congressional Quarterly Weekly Report,* 35, no. 44 (October 29, 1977), pp. 2341–2342; "Carter Dealt Major Defeat on Consumer Bill," ibid., 36, no. 6 (February 11, 1978), pp. 323–325; "A Rude Awakening for Activists in Government," *U.S. News and World Report,* March 6, 1978, p. 54; "Ralph Nader Takes on Congress as Well as Business," *National Journal,* 10, no. 10 (March 11, 1978), pp. 388–390; George Schwartz, "The Successful Fight against a Consumer Protection Agency," *MSU Business Topics,* 27, no. 3 (Summer 1979), pp. 45–57.

89. As one reporter put it to the President in December 1977: "Labor is unhappy because you are dragging your feet on medical insurance and full employment. Business says it is unhappy; they just don't have confidence in you. Blacks are unhappy again because of full employment and the lack of it. Vernon Jordon is still unhappy with you . . . Many women are unhappy because of your stand on federal aid for abortion and because there aren't enough women appointed to administrative posts. Striking farmers are rolling up their tractors in Plains. Who is your constituency?" "Conversation with the President," December 28, 1977, *Public Papers,* p. 2199.

90. Carter advisor quoted in Leuchtenburg, *Shadow,* p. 195.

91. Jack W. Germond and Jules Witcover, *Blue Smoke and Mirrors: How Reagan Won and Why Carter Lost the Election of 1980* (New York: Viking, 1981), p. 305.

92. "The Rebirth of the 'Real Jimmy Carter': Interview with Hamilton Jordan," *U.S. News and World Report*, May 22, 1978, pp. 22–24.
93. Califano, *Governing America*, pp. 88–135; Carter, *Keeping Faith*, pp. 84–87.
94. "Kennedy, Meany Assail Carter," *Washington Post*, July 29, 1978, p. 1; "Kennedy Assails Carter on Health," *New York Times*, July 29, 1978, p. 20; "Dilemma over National Health Insurance Delays Promised Carter Plan: Kennedy and Labor Pushing," *Congressional Quarterly Weekly Report*, 36, no. 28 (July 15, 1978), pp. 1770–1773; "Carter Lists Principles of National Health Plan: Reactions Mixed," ibid., 36, no. 31 (August 5, 1978), p. 2058; "Kennedy, Labor Launch Drive for National Health Insurance," ibid., 36, no. 41 (October 14, 1978), pp. 2955–2957; "Administration May Link Hospital Cost Bill, Catastrophic Insurance," ibid., 36, no. 51 (December 23, 1978), pp. 3477–3478.
95. Genovese, "Jimmy Carter and the Age of Limits."
96. "Kennedy Warns of a Party Split by Arms Outlays," *Washington Post*, December 10, 1978, p. 1; "Kennedy Assails Carter on Budget at Midterm Meeting of Democrats," *New York Times*, December 10, 1978, p. 1.
97. Califano, *Governing America*, pp. 123–125.
98. Carter, *Keeping Faith*, p. 464.
99. Press conference, June 10, 1980, *Public Papers*, p. 1085
100. Johnson, *Absence of Power*, pp. 302–313.
101. "Energy and National Goals," July 15, 1979, *Public Papers*, pp. 1235–1239.
102. William Greider, *Secrets of the Temple: How the Federal Reserve Runs the Country* (New York: Simon and Schuster, 1987), pp. 11–180.
103. "Remarks at Lansdown, Pennsylvania," October 2, 1980, *Public Papers*, p. 2040; Greider, *Secrets*, pp. 216–217. Carter expressed more sympathy for the Board and its goals after the election. See "Economic Report of the President," January 17, 1981, *Public Papers*, pp. 3012–3013.
104. Johnson, *Absence of Power*, pp. 314–315.
105. Nelson Polsby, "The Democratic Nomination," in *American Elections of 1980* p. 47; Glad, *Carter*, pp. 437–450.
106. Jordan, *Crisis*, p. 55.
107. Ibid., p. 53.
108. Ibid., pp. 252–254, 270–275; Carter, *Keeping Faith*, pp. 450–520.
109. "American Federation of Labor and Congress of Industrial Organization: Remarks," November 15, 1979, *Public Papers*, pp. 2122–2126.
110. "Interview with the President," January 15, 1980, *Public Papers*, p. 87.
111. Ibid., p. 88.
112. For example, "Iranian Situation and United States Energy Conservation: Remarks at the White House Briefing for State Governors," November 16, 1979, *Public Papers*, pp. 2132–2135.
113. Genovese, "Jimmy Carter and the Age of Limits"; Michael Howard, "Return of the Cold War?" *Foreign Affairs*, 59, no. 3 (1980), pp. 459–473.
114. The Gallup Poll, *Public Opinion 1979*, pp. 187–188, 217–218, 280, 285–286. The Gallup Poll, *Public Opinion 1980*, pp. 5, 71, 79.

115. Quoted in Germond and Witcover, *Blue Smoke,* p. 295.
116. Jordan, *Crisis,* pp. 359–366; Republican polling showed a fairly consistent Reagan lead throughout the final week. Albert Hunt, "The Campaign and the Issues," in *American Elections of 1980,* p. 173.
117. "New York, New York: Remarks Accepting the Presidential Nomination," August 14, 1980, *Public Papers,* p. 1532.
118. Jordan, *Crisis,* pp. 324–339; Jody Powell, *The Other Side of the Story* (New York: William Morrow, 1984), p. 248: "Time and again we accepted platform provisions that we did not like, because we knew they would be political liabilities in the campaign against the GOP . . . Looking back I cannot help but wish we had told [Kennedy] to kiss off . . . We certainly would have lost a number of floor fights over platform planks. But we probably would have been better off repudiating the document anyway."
119. "Text of Reagan's Speech Accepting the Republican's Nomination," *New York Times,* July 18, 1980, p. 8.

8. Reagan, Bush, and Beyond

1. Richard Rose, *The Postmodern President: George Bush Meets the World* (Chatham, N.J.: Chatham House, 1991); Ryan J. Barilleaux, *The Post-Modern Presidency: The Office after Reagan* (New York: Praeger, 1988); Theodore Lowi, *The Personal President: Power Invested, Promise Unfulfilled* (Ithaca: Cornell University Press, 1985); Samuel Kernell, *Going Public: New Strategies of Presidential Leadership* (Washington, D.C.: Congressional Quarterly Press, 1986).
2. Lowi poses the question directly, asking what kind of exception Reagan presents. His answer is: not much. Writing in 1985, with the President riding high, Lowi offered a bold prediction that before Reagan was finished he would be judged as harshly as the other presidents of the contemporary period. Why? "Because that is the way the presidency is now built." Looking back today, it is readily apparent that this projection of the logic of recent developments in government and politics onto the likely outcome of Reagan's second term was not entirely off the mark. *The Personal President,* pp. 12–21. In 1989 Lowi confirmed his position: "Despite a tremendous effort to rewrite the theory of the presidency, Reagan leaves no major institutional legacy." Cited in "Reagan Added Luster but Little Clout to Office," *Congressional Quarterly Weekly Report,* January 7, 1989, p. 3.
3. "The Presidency," *We the People: An American Celebration, Pictoral History of the 50th American Presidential Inaugural and Events Leading Up to It* (Washington, D.C.: Presidential Inaugural Committee, 1985), p. 3.
4. Richard Reeves, *The Reagan Detour* (New York: Simon and Schuster, 1985), p. 94.
5. *Washington Post,* January 20, 1989, Section F, p. 4.
6. "Reagan Added Luster," p. 10.
7. Larry Berman, "Looking Back on the Reagan Presidency," in *Looking Back*

on the Reagan Presidency, ed. Larry Berman (Baltimore: Johns Hopkins University Press, 1990), p. 3.

8. Paul E. Peterson and Mark Rom, "Lower Taxes, More Spending, and Budget Deficits," in *The Reagan Legacy: Promise and Performance,* ed. Charles O. Jones (Chatham, N.J.: Chatham House, 1988), p. 236.

9. For a more penetrating view of the election of 1980 see Stanley Kelly, *Interpreting Elections* (Princeton: Princeton University Press, 1983).

10. For Reagan's life-long preparation to deliver this message see Kurt Ritter and David Henry, *Ronald Reagan: The Great Communicator* (New York: Greenwood, 1992).

11. "Inaugural Address," January 20, 1981, *Public Papers of the Presidents of the United States: Ronald Reagan* (Washington, D.C.: United States Government Printing Office, 1982), p. 1.

12. Organized labor, the cornerstone of the liberal political order, was a chief target. For a regime perspective see Terry Moe, "Interests, Institutions and Positive Theory: The Politics of the NLRB," *Studies in American Political Development,* 2 (1987), pp. 266–270. More generally see Robert Kuttner, "Reaganism, Liberalism and the Democrats" in *The Reagan Legacy,* ed. Sidney Blumenthal and Thomas Byne Edsall (New York: Pantheon, 1988).

13. "Remarks Accepting the Presidential Nomination of the Republican Party at the Republican National Convention in Dallas," August 23, 1984, *Public Papers,* p. 1180.

14. "Address to the Nation on the Program for Economic Recovery," September 24, 1981, *Public Papers,* p. 834.

15. Charles R. Hulten and Isabel V. Sawhill, "The Legacy of Reaganomics: An Overview," in *The Legacy of Reaganomics: Prospects for Long Term Growth,* ed. Charles R. Hulten and Isabel Sawhill (Washington, D.C.: The Urban Institute, 1984), p. 1. "It's Morning in America" was the theme of Reagan's 1984 reelection campaign and figured prominently in the campaign's television adds.

16. David Stockman, *The Triumph of Politics: How the Reagan Revolution Failed* (New York: Harper and Row, 1986) p. 79. The Reagan-Roosevelt comparison was commonplace at the time, especially with regard to the question of whether Reagan would repeat Roosevelt's performance and do to the politics of the 1980s what Roosevelt did to the politics of the 1930s. William Leuchtenburg takes offense at Reagan's constant invocation of Roosevelt and Rooseveltian rhetoric, pointing out that the two men held diametrically opposed beliefs. Those who insisted on the comparison were more impressed with the structural similarities than the ideological differences. See William Leuchtenburg, *In the Shadow of FDR: From Harry Truman to Ronald Reagan* (Ithaca: Cornell University Press, 1983), pp. 209–235.

17. Kuttner, "Reganism, Liberalism." On the use of the unspeakable "L" word in the 1988 campaign, see Charles O. Jones, "Meeting Low Expectations: Strategy and Prospects of the Bush Presidency," in *The Bush Presidency: First Appraisals,* ed. Colin Campbell, S.J., and Bert A. Rockman (Chatham, N.J.: Chatham House, 1991), p. 45.

18. As Reagan himself said in his televised farewell address: "I wasn't a great communicator, but I communicated great things." "Farewell Address to the Nation," January 11, 1989, *Public Papers*, p. 1720; also Ritter and Henry, *Ronald Reagan*, p. 118.

19. See Michael Rogin, *Ronald Reagan the Movie and other Episodes in Political Demonology* (Berkeley: University of California Press, 1987).

20. See Kernell, *Going Public*.

21. For a substantive elaboration of this point in the area of regulatory reform see Susan Rose-Ackerman, *Rethinking the Progressive Agenda: The Reform of the American Regulatory State* (New York: Free Press, 1992). As Rose-Ackerman sums it up: "Conscientious and thoughtful reform was sacrificed to rhetoric and to a singleminded preoccupation with reducing the size of the federal government's domestic programs," p. 147.

22. For example, "Message to Congress Transmitting the Proposed Package on the Program for Economic Recovery," February 18, 1981, *Public Papers*, p. 115; "White House Report on the Program for Economic Recovery," February 18, 1981, *Public Papers*, pp. 116–132. In his "Address to the Nation on Federal Tax Reduction Legislation," Reagan said again: "Each part of this package is vital. It cannot be considered piecemeal. It was proposed as a package, and it has been supported as such by the American people." July 27, 1981, *Public Papers*, p. 665.

23. Stockman, *Triumph of Politics*, p. 97–98.

24. As Matthew McCubbins confirms: "Throughout the decade, the Democrats in the House and the Republicans in the Senate forged a union that enacted policies *contrary* to the basic tenets of Reagan's budget policy." "Party Government and U.S. Budget Deficits: Divided Government and Fiscal Stalemate," in *Politics and Economics in the Eighties*, p. 100 and passim pp. 83–111.

25. Ibid., p. 159.

26. Ibid., p. 200.

27. Leuchtenburg, *Shadow*, pp. 210–211, 228.

28. As Hulton and Sawhill put it, "The second basic assumption of Reaganomics was that all the program's goals could be achieved simultaneously, and according to some members of the administration, all at once," p. 1.

29. Stockman, *Triumph of Politics*, p. 83.

30. Ibid., p. 199.

31. Paul Light identifies two temporal cycles at work in modern administrations, including Reagan's: a cycle of decreasing influence and a cycle of increasing competence. *The President's Agenda: Domestic Policy Choice from Kennedy to Carter, with Notes on Ronald Reagan* (Baltimore: Johns Hopkins University Press, 1982), esp. pp. viii–ix.

32. William Greider, "The Education of David Stockman," *Atlantic*, 248, no. 6 (December 1981), p. 54.

33. "Remarks and Question and Answer Session on the Program for Economic Recovery," February 19, 1981, *Public Papers*, p. 132. As Treasury Secretary Donald Regan put it in his remarks, "This program is really bold. Its inno-

vative; its new; it breaks with the past, and its different. From the point of view of why we're breaking with the past, it is that we can no longer go on with what we have been doing."

34. Stockman, *Triumph of Politics,* pp. 124–126.

35. "Senate Opposes Social Security Cuts," *Congressional Quarterly Weekly Reports,* May 23, 1981, pp. 895–896; Greider, "Education," pp. 43–46.

36. Stockman, *Triumph of Politics,* pp. 125, 163, 180–181, 193, 222–228.

37. As David Stockman put it: "The whole thing is premised on faith. On a belief about how the world works." Greider, "Education," p. 29.

38. "Address before a Joint Session of the Congress on the Program for Economic Recovery," April 28, 1981, *Public Papers,* p. 392.

39. Ibid., p. 394.

40. "Address to the Nation on Federal Tax Reduction Legislation," July 27, 1981, *Public Papers,* p. 688.

41. Stephen Skowronek, *Building a New American State: The Expansion of National Administrative Capacities, 1877–1920* (New York: Cambridge University Press, 1982), pp. 204–209.

42. See Harvey Zeidenstein, "The Reassertion of Congressional Power," *Political Science Quarterly,* 93, no. 3 (Fall 1978), pp. 393–409. Note that by centralizing its own procedures, Congress unwittingly made it easier for a reconstructive leader to subvert them.

43. Stockman, *Triumph of Politics,* p. 198.

44. On these standards see Allen Schick, *Congress and Money* (Washington D.C.: Urban Institute, 1980).

45. "Reconciliation's Long Term Consequences in Question as Reagan Signs Massive Bill," *Congressional Quarterly Weekly Reports,* August 15, 1981, p. 1465. Quotation is from Democrat Dan Rostenkowski, Chairman of the House Ways and Means Committee.

46. Jane Mayer and Doyle McManus, *Landslide: The Unmaking of a President* (Boston: Houghton Mifflin, 1988); Michael A. Ledeen, *Perilous Statecraft: An Insider's Account of the Iran-Contra Affair* (New York: Scribner's, 1988).

47. David Johnston, "Meese Testifies that Impeachment was a Worry," *New York Times,* March 29, 1989, p. 17; George Lardner, Jr., "Meese Details White House Crisis: Fear of Impeachment Gripped Staff in Late '86," *Washington Post,* March 29, 1989, p. 5.

48. On intimidation of Congress in the face of Reagan's potential culpability see Seymour M. Hersh, "The Iran Contra Committees: Did They Protect Reagan?" *New York Times Magazine,* April 29, 1990, pp. 47ff.

49. See, for example, Arnold Beichman, "The Secret of the Teflon Presidency," *Wall Street Journal,* August 8, 1985, p. 22; also Sarah Cagle, "AA to Rep. Pat Schroeder Unearths Skeletons of What May Be Butch Cassidy, Sundance Kid," *Roll Call,* April 16, 1992, p. 3.

50. "The politics of high exposure" is a phrase drawn from an analysis of George Bush by Anthony King and Giles Alston, "Good Government and the Politics of High Exposure," in *Bush Presidency,* pp. 249–285.

51. On the Tower Commission theory of unfortunate mistakes see Haynes Johnson, *Sleepwalking through History: America in the Reagan Years* (New York: Doubleday, 1991), p. 350.

52. William Greider, *Secrets of the Temple: How the Federal Reserve Board Runs the Country* (New York: Simon and Schuster, 1987), p. 516; Joseph A. Peckman and Barry Bosworth, "The Budget and the Economy," in *Setting National Priorities: The 1983 Budget,* ed. Joseph A. Peckman (Washington, D.C.: Brookings Institution, 1982). pp. 43–44.

53. Greider, *Secrets,* pp. 472–478.

54. Greider, *Secrets,* pp. 495–506; also Joseph A. Pechman, "The Budget and the Economy," in ed. Joseph A. Pechman, *Setting National Priorities* (Washington, D.C.: Brookings Institution, 1983), p. 35, and James Alt, "Leaning into the Wind or Ducking Out of the Storm: U.S. Monetary Policy in the 1980's," in *Politics and Economics in the Eighties,* ed. Alberto Alesina and Geoffrey Carliner (Chicago: University of Chicago Press, 1991), pp. 41–77.

55. Greider, *Secrets,* pp. 516, 541, 576–577.

56. Ibid., p. 561.

57. With the stock market crash of 1987, the Fed's reversal became complete. It loosened its grip on credit, flooded the market with dollars, and guaranteed liquidity in the financial system. See Johnson, *Sleepwalking,* p. 381.

58. As the economist William Nordhaus summed it up in 1984, "The Reagan administration's dismantling of the welfare state is a shot in the dark whose only casualties thus far are the economy and the poor." "Reaganomics and Economic Growth: A Summing Up," *The Legacy of Reaganomics,* p. 261.

59. James Ceaser, "The Reagan Presidency and American Public Opinion," in *Reagan Legacy,* pp. 171–210.

60. Joseph J. Minarik and Rudolph G. Penner, "Fiscal Choices," in *Challenge to Leadership: Economic and Social Issues for the Next Decade,* ed. Isabel V. Sawhill (Washington, D.C.: Urban Institute, 1988).

61. Eric Pianin, "Bush Vetoes $77 Billion Tax Relief Bill: War of Words between White House and Hill Democrats Escalates" *Washington Post,* March 21, 1992, p. A8.

62. Robert Shogun tells of the early usages of the Truman model, "GOP Aims May Pose Dilemma for the President," *Los Angeles Times,* May 28, 1991, p. 21. "To find a likely model for such a campaign by an incumbent President, Republican strategists go back to 1948 and Democrat Harry Truman waging war against the 'do-nothing' Republican Congresses and warning that Republicans were ready to take away the benefits the New Deal brought to average citizens."

63. Bert Rockman, "The Leadership Style of George Bush," in *Bush Presidency,* pp. 3–7. Also instructive on these themes is Walter Dean Burnham, "The Politics of Repudiation 1992: Edging toward Upheaval," *American Prospect,* 12 (Winter 1993), pp. 22–33.

64. Michael Duffy and Dan Goodgame, *Marching in Place: The Status Quo Presidency of George Bush* (New York: Simon and Schuster, 1992), p. 22.

65. "Speech to Employees of the Republican National Committee," January 18,

1989, *Federal News Service*, "Candidate and Election: Related Interviews and Debates."

66. "Bush: Our Work's Not Done, Our Force Is Not Spent," Acceptance Speech before Republican National Convention, transcript printed in *Washington Post*, August 19, 1988, p. A28.

67. Bush television campaign quoted by David Hiffman, "Bush Becomes Pragmatic Champion of the Reagan Revolution," *Washington Post*, March 5, 1988, p. 12.

68. "Campaign Report: Bush Challenges Reagan on 'Free Lunch' Economy," *New York Times*, April 17, 1980, p. D17; John F. Stacks, *Watershed: Campaign for the Presidency, 1980* (New York: Times Books, 1981), p. 155.

69. Bill Peterson and Kathy Sawyer, "Reagan-Bush Show Opens in Motown," *Washington Post*, July 19, 1980, p. 11.

70. Jimmy Carter made the point in attacking the Reagan-Bush team at the Democratic convention of 1980. "He called it 'voodoo economics.' He suddenly changed his mind toward the end of the Republican convention, but he was right the first time." "Remarks Accepting the Presidential Nomination of the Democratic Party," August 14, 1980, *Public Papers of the Presidents of the United States: Jimmy Carter* (Washington, D.C.: United States Government Printing Office, 1981), p. 1538.

71. "Campaign Notes," *Washington Post*, September 23, 1980, p. A3. Also Duffy and Goodgame, *Marching in Place*, p. 68.

72. David Hoffman, "How Bush Has Altered Views: One-Time Moderate Claims Reagan Mantle," *Washington Post*, August 17, 1988, p. A1.

73. For example, "Bush is known as a man who hates the very idea of being handled, who thinks campaigning has nothing to do with governing and thus can't always be counted on to read his stage directions." Lloyd Grove, "Robert Teeter on the Brink," *Washington Post*, October 29, 1992, p. C1.

74. Duffy and Goodgame, *Marching in Place*, p. 24.

75. Ibid., pp. 28–33; Paul Quirk, "Domestic Policy: Divided Government and Cooperative Presidential Leadership," in *Bush Presidency*, pp. 82–87.

76. Quirk, "Domestic Policy"; Charles O. Jones, "Strategy and Prospects of the Bush Presidency," in *Bush Presidency*, pp. 52–58; "Bush Hopes for a Little Help for Hill Friends," *Congressional Quarterly Weekly Reports*, December 31, 1988, pp. 3599–3603; "Will Bush-Hill Honeymoon Bring Bipartisanship?" ibid., February 18, 1989, pp. 332–337; "Rules of Political Navigation Altered by Bush Centrism," Ibid., May 6, 1989, pp. 1017–1019.

77. Robert Shogan, "Bush Increasingly Veering Off Course Set by Reagan," *Los Angeles Times*, May 27, 1991, p. 24; also Robert Shogan, "GOP Aims May Pose Dilemma for President," *Los Angeles Times*, May 28, 1991, p. 1.

78. Duffy and Goodgame, *Marching in Place*, pp. 94, 101.

79. On Bush's long struggle with this dilemma see William Safire, "Bush's Gamble," *New York Times Magazine*, October 18, 1992, pp. 31ff.

80. Bob Woodward, "Origin of the Tax Pledge: In '88 Bush Camp Was Split on 'Read My Lips' Vow," *Washington Post*, October 4, 1992, pp. 1ff.

81. Ibid.

82. Woodward, "Origins"; also Bob Woodward, "No-Tax Vow Scuttled Anti-Deficit Mission," *Washington Post,* October 5, 1992, pp. 1ff.

83. "Read My Lips: No Conditions, Bush Tells Democrats," *Congressional Quarterly Weekly Reports,* May 12, 1990, pp. 1457–1463; Andrew Rosenthal, "Three Little Words: How Bush Dropped His Tax Pledge," *New York Times,* June 29, 1990; "Bush's Sudden Shift on Taxes Gets Budget Talks Moving," *Congressional Quarterly Weekly Reports,* June 30, 1990, pp. 2029–2032.

84. Louis Uchitelle, "A Gamble against Keynes's Theory," *New York Times,* June 28, 1990, p. 20.

85. Duffy and Goodgame, *Marching in Place,* p. 221; for an alternative view of this compromise see Barbara Sinclair, "Governing Unheroically (and Sometimes Unappetizingly): Bush and the 101st Congress," in *Bush Presidency,* pp. 178–181.

86. Edward Rollins, the head of the Republican Congressional Campaign Committee, protested the idea of giving up the tax pledge with this outburst: "You can't give it up . . . You're going to get killed . . . Its the last line between us and the Democrats that anybody can differentiate." Quoted in Woodward, "Origins," p. 22.

87. Richard Berke, "G.O.P., in Revolt on Taxes, Steps Up Criticism of Bush," *New York Times,* June 28, 1990, p. 20; "President's Hill Troops Have Mutinied," *Congressional Quarterly Weekly Reports,* September 29, 1990, p. 3096.

88. If a contrast is to be made here that distinguishes the current state of the nation in world affairs it lies in the relatively reactive and defensive course Bush set in foreign policy. He was, in fact, more apt to defend the existing order of things than to seize the initiative to forge a new one. From his reluctance to renounce the attempted Soviet coup in 1990, his reluctance to chastise the Chinese for their crackdown on student demonstrators, to his defense of the Emir of Kuwait, to his salesmanship on behalf of American manufactures in Japan, Bush showed a pronounced preference for working within established relationships over forging new ones.

89. "The President's News Conference," June 29, 1990, *Public Papers of the Presidents of the United States: George Bush* (Washington, D.C.: United States Government Printing Office, 1991), p. 885.

90. Bob Woodward, "Primary Heat Turned Deal into a 'Mistake,'" *Washington Post,* October, 6, 1992, pp. 1ff.

91. The point was made by A. M. Rosenthal, "Mr. Bush Steps Aside," *New York Times,* October 13, 1992, p. 23.

92. Russell Baker, "The '92 Follies," *New York Times Magazine,* November 1, 1992, p. 58.

93. "George Bush in TV Interview with David Frost," January 3, 1992, Federal News Service Transcript; Mary McGrory, "Traveling in Poor Company," *Washington Post,* January 14, 1992, p. A2.

94. Maureen Dowd, "Bush: As the Loss Sinks In, Some Begin Pointing Fingers," *New York Times,* November 5, 1992, p. 1.

95. "Perot: Our Objective Is to Improve Our Country," *Washington Post,* July 17, 1992, p. A17.
96. "President's Address to a Joint Session of Congress," cited in *New York Times,* February 18, 1993, p. 20.

Afterword

An earlier version of this Afterword appeared in "A Presidency at Risk," *Extensions,* Spring 1996, pp. 10–15, and is reprinted by permission of *Extensions,* a copyrighted publication of the Carl Albert Congressional Research and Studies Center, University of Oklahoma. I would also like to thank Bruce Miroff, Karen Orren, and Susan Jacobs for reading and commenting on all the new material contained in this edition. I am especially indebted in this Afterword to Sidney Milkis, John Skrentny, Terri Bimes, and Larry Barrios for sharing with me ideas and materials from their own research. Of course, I bear sole responsibility for the errors and omissions that remain in these pages.

1. On Clinton protesting that he was still relevant in the aftermath of the Republican sweep see *New York Times,* April 19, 1995, p. 1
2. As Democratic congressional leader and liberal representative Richard Gephardt has repeatedly said, "We are all 'New' Democrats now." See, for example, *The Washington Post,* September 16, 1996.
3. Nor is the 40 percent victory fully determinative of a preemptive stance. Abraham Lincoln, a 40 percent victor in 1860, was decidedly reconstructive in his leadership. The most obvious difference is that Lincoln came to power with a new party, one that boasted a core commitment with revolutionary implications. A more important difference, perhaps, is that much of Lincoln's opposition seceded. It is interesting to speculate about how the Lincoln presidency might have unfolded had the South not seceded, for the impediments to a reconstructive stance would have been considerably greater and the preemptive alternative far more compelling.
4. Quoted in Mathew Josephson, *The Politicos* (New York: Harcourt, Brace and World), p. 362.
5. Since the establishment of national two-party competition in the 1830s, only two affiliated leaders (Grant and McKinley) have been elected to second terms, and Grant won with much of his likely opposition under force of arms. Grover Cleveland, the leading vote getter through three presidential elections, was defeated in the electoral college vote in 1888 but reelected to the presidency in 1892. Zachary Taylor, a preemptive leader elected to the presidency in the first instance, died during his second year in office.
6. Joan Hoff, *Nixon Reconsidered* (New York: Basic Books, 1994), pp. 129–137; Michael A. Genovese, *The Nixon Presidency: Power and Politics in Turbulent Times* (Westport, Conn.: Greenwood Press, 1990), pp. 76–80. Also A. James Reichley, *Conservatives in an Age of Change: The Nixon and Ford Administrations* (Washington, D.C.: Brookings, 1981) pp. 138–153.
7. Genovese, pp. 61–76, 100–110.

8. On this theme see John Skrentny, *The Ironies of Affirmative Action: Constructing Justice in American Politics and Culture* (Chicago: University of Chicago Press, 1996).

9. "George Fred Williams Quotes from Professor's History: Assails Governor Wilson's Contempt for the Poor," *San Francisco Examiner,* February 11, 1912, pp. 1, 30; also "Mr. Hearst Exposes Prof. Wilson as Dodging, Crafty Federalist: Ideas Suddenly Change When His Ambition Leads Him to Covet High Office of the President," *San Francisco Examiner,* March 14, 1912. I am indebted to Sidney Milkis and his current study of the 1912 election for this material.

10. Herbert Croly, *Progressive Democracy* (New York: MacMillan, 1914), p. 20. For an analysis of what the Wilson hybrid represented intellectually in the range of Progressive thought and of Progressives' skepticism about it see Eldon Eisenach, *The Lost Promise of Progressivism* (Lawrence: University of Kansas Press, 1994), pp. 122–129.

11. *New Republic,* June 24, 1916, p. 185. "In no region has Mr. Wilson been more successfully opportunistic than in his selection and adaptation of political parties. He began with a philosophical interpretation of the progressive movement and transformed it into a revival of Jeffersonianism."

12. See "Presidential Complacency," *New Republic,* November 21, 1914. These sentiments were expressed at later dates as well. See "Unregenerate Democracy," *New Republic,* February 5, 1916; and "The Future of the Democratic Party," *New Republic, July 7,* 1920, p. 164. Consider Arthur Link's judgment that "Croly's analysis of the superficial character of Wilson's progressivism is essentially correct." *Woodrow Wilson and the Progressive Era, 1910–1917* (New York: Harper, 1954), p. 80. Also, Terri Bimes and Stephen Skowronek, "Woodrow Wilson's Critique of Popular Leadership," *Polity,* xxix, 1 (Fall 1996), pp. 27–63.

13. Peter MacFarlane, "The President in Practice," *Collier's Weekly,* 53, 5 (April 18, 1914), pp. 5–7.

14. Oswald Valliard, "The Shifting Administration: Mr Wilson Changes on Preparedness, the Tariff Commission, and Other Policies," *The Nation,* 102, 2642 (February 17, 1916), pp. 189–191; "The President's SOP to Tammany," *The Nation,* 102, 2652 (April 27, 1916), pp. 450–451; "The Week," *The Nation,* 102, 2654 (May 11, 1916), p. 506; "Wilson and the Presidency," *The Nation,* 102, 2660 (June 22, 1916), p. 661; "Mr. Wilson's Acceptance," *The Nation,* 103, 2671 (September 7, 1916), pp. 213–214.

15. "Shall We Vote for Wilson," *Outlook,* August 23, 1916, pp. 941–942; "The President's Opportunity," *Outlook,* December 13, 1916, pp. 792–793.

16. Mr. Washburn of Massachusetts quoted in John Dinan, "Keeping the People's Liberties: Republican, Populist, and Judicialist Regimes of Rights Protection in the American State," unpublished doctoral dissertation, University of Virginia, 1996.

17. Bob Woodward, *The Agenda: Inside the Clinton White House* (New York: Simon and Schuster, 1994), p. 165.

18. "Prepared Text for the President's State of the Union Message," *New York Times,* January 24, 1996, p. 14; "Second Inaugural Address," *New York Times,* January 21, 1997, p. 14.

19. Grover Cleveland, "Third Annual Message," December 6, 1887, in James Richardson, ed., *A Compilation of the Messages and Papers of Presidents* (New York: Bureau of National Literature, 1897), p. 5175.

20. Theda Skocpol, *Boomerang: Clinton's Health Security Effort and the Turn against Big Government* (New York: Norton, 1996); Haynes Johnson and David Broder, *The System: The American Way of Politics at the Breaking Point* (Boston: Little Brown, 1996).

21. MacFarlane, *Collier's Weekly,* April 18, 1914, pp. 5–7.

22. *Outlook,* December 10, 1916, p. 793.

23. "Wilson, the Country and the War," *The Nation,* 103, 2678 (October 26, 1916), p. 389.

24. *The Letters of Theodore Roosevelt,* vol. 8, Elting Morison, ed. (Cambridge: Harvard University Press, 1954), pp. 1031, 1199.

25. Henry Cabot Lodge, *The Senate and the League of Nations* (New York: Scribners, 1925), pp. 79–80, 212–213, 216–226.

26. Vernon Van Dyke, *Ideology and Political Choice: The Search for Freedom, Justice, and Virtue* (Chatham, New Jersey: Chatham House, 1995), pp. 274–283.

27. Geoffrey Blodgett, "The Political Leadership of Grover Cleveland," *South Atlantic Quarterly,* 82, 2 (Summer 1983), pp. 290–291; Pearl Louise Robertson, *Grover Cleveland as a Political Leader* (Chicago: University of Chicago Libraries, 1939).

28. It remains to be seen whether Clinton will, at the opening of his second term, repair to the Cleveland model and take up the issue of campaign reform. Given the questions raised about his own reelection campaign, this might be his ultimate preemption.

29. On the party-building strategies of preemptive leaders as they relate particularly to the Wilson and Cleveland presidencies, see Scott James, *Parties, Presidents and the State: The Construction of America's Regulatory Institutions* (New York: Cambridge University Press, forthcoming).

30. Bob Dole went so far as to identify Clinton's reelection campaign with Nixon's in 1972 and to link Clinton's fate in the presidency to Nixon's in 1974. Dan Balz and Blaine Harden, "Dole Raises Spectre of Watergate," *Washington Post Service,* November 1, 1996.

Index